Clashing Views on Controversial

Issues in American History, Volume I, The Colonial Period to Reconstruction

ELEVENTH EDITION

TAKING SIDES

Clashing Views on Controversial

Issues in American History, Volume I, The Colonial Period to Reconstruction

ELEVENTH EDITION

Selected, Edited, and with Introductions by

Larry Madaras
Howard Community College

and

James M. SoRelle
Baylor University

McGraw-Hill/Dushkin
A Division of The McGraw-Hill Companies

To Maggie and Cindy

Photo Acknowledgment
Cover image: photos.com

Cover Acknowledgment
Maggie Nickles

Manufactured in the United States of America

Eleventh Edition

123456789DOCDOC987654

Library of Congress Cataloging-in-Publication Data
Main entry under title:
Taking sides: clashing views on controversial issues in American history, volume i, the colonial
period to reconstruction/selected, edited, and with introductions by Larry Madaras and James M.
SoRelle.—11th ed.
Includes bibliographical references and index.
1. United States—History. I. Madaras, Larry, *comp.* II. SoRelle, James M., *comp.*
973
0-07-310216-4
ISSN: 1091-8833

Printed on Recycled Paper

Preface

The success of the past ten editions of *Taking Sides: Clashing Views on Controversial Issues in American History* has encouraged us to remain faithful to its original objectives, methods, and format. Our aim has been to create an effective instrument to enhance classroom learning and to foster critical thinking. Historical facts presented in a vacuum are of little value to the educational process. For students, whose search for historical truth often concentrates on *when* something happened rather than on *why*, and on specific events rather than on the *significance* of those events, *Taking Sides* is designed to offer an interesting and rewarding departure. The understanding that the reader arrives at based on the evidence that emerges from the clash of views encourages the reader to view history as an *interpretive* discipline, not one of rote memorization.

As in previous editions, the eighteen issues and thirty-six essays that follow are arranged in chronological order and can be incorporated easily into any American history survey course. Each issue has an *introduction*, which sets the stage for the debate that follows in the pro and con selections and provides historical and methodological background to the problem that the issue examines. Each issue concludes with a *postscript*, which ties the readings together, briefly mentions alternative interpretations, and supplies detailed *suggestions for further reading* for the student who wishes to pursue the topics raised in the issue. Also, Internet site addresses (URLs), which should prove useful as starting points for further research, have been provided on the *On the Internet* page that accompanies each part opener. At the back of the book is a listing of all the *contributors to this volume* with a brief biographical sketch of each of the authors whose views are debated here.

While we have selected a pair of essays to offer differing points of view in response to each issue question, readers should understand that there are likely many more ways in which these questions can be addressed. Further, the authors of each pair of essays may agree with one another on many historical points and yet still reach opposing conclusions. Readers, therefore, are expected to examine the essays with a critical eye, recognize the strengths and weaknesses of particular arguments, determine which pieces of evidence are most useful in reaching an objective, reasoned conclusion, and consider alternative answers to the questions asked.

Changes to this edition In this edition we have continued our efforts to maintain a balance between the traditional political, diplomatic, and cultural issues and the new social history, which depicts a society that benefited from the presence of Native Americans, African Americans, women, and workers of various racial and ethnic backgrounds. With this in mind, we present nine new issues: "Is History True?" (Issue 1); "Were the First Colonists in the Chesapeake Region Ignorant, Lazy, and Ambitious?" (Issue 3); "Did Colonial New England Women Enjoy Significant Economic Autonomy?" (Issue 4); "Was There a Great

Awakening in Mid-Eighteenth-Century America?" (Issue 5); "Was the American Revolution a Conservative Movement?" (Issue 6); "Was President Thomas Jefferson a Political Compromiser?" (Issue 8); "Was the Monroe Doctrine of 1823 a Well-Designed Policy to Protect the Latin American Countries from European Intervention?" (Issue 9); "Were the Abolitionists "Unrestrained Fanatics"?" (Issue 13); and "Have Historians Overemphasized the Slavery Issue as a Cause of the Civil War?" (Issue 14). In all, there are twenty new selections.

A word to the instructor   An *Instructor's Manual With Test Questions* (multiple-choice and essay) is available through the publisher for the instructor using *Taking Sides* in the classroom. A general guidebook, *Using Taking Sides in the Classroom*, which discusses methods and techniques for integrating the pro-con approach into any classroom setting, is also available. An online version of *Using Taking Sides in the Classroom* and a correspondence service for *Taking Sides* adopters can be found at http://www.dushkin.com/usingts/.

Acknowledgments   Many individuals have contributed to the successful completion of this edition. We appreciate the evaluations submitted to McGraw-Hill/Dushkin by those who have used *Taking Sides* in the classroom. Special thanks to those who responded with specific suggestions for the ninth and tenth editions:

Gary Best
University of Hawaii–Hilo

James D. Bolton
Coastline Community College

Mary Borg
University of Northern Colorado

John Whitney
Evans College of St. Scholastica

Mark Hickerson
Chaffey College

Maryann Irwin
Diablo Valley College

Gordon Lam
Sierra College

Jon Nielson
Columbia College

Andrew O'Shaugnessy
University of Wisconsin–Oshkosh

Manian Padma
DeAnza College

Elliot Pasternack
Middlesex County College (N.J.)

Robert M. Paterson
Armstrong State College

Charles Piehl
Mankato State University

Ethan S. Rafuse
University of Missouri–Kansas City

John Reid
Ohio State University–Lima

Murray Rubinstein
CUNY Baruch College

Neil Sapper
Amarillo College

Preston She
Plymouth State College

Tim Koerner
Oakland Community College

Jack Traylor
William Jennings Bryan College

We are particularly indebted to Maggie Cullen, Cindy SoRelle, the late Barry A. Crouch, Virginia Kirk, Joseph and Helen Mitchell, and Jean Soto, who shared their ideas for changes, pointed us toward potentially useful historical works, and provided significant editorial assistance. Megan Arnold performed indispensable typing duties connected with this project. Susan E. Myers, Ela Ciborowski, and Karen Higgins in the library at Howard Community College provided essential help in acquiring books and articles on interlibrary loan. Finally, we are sincerely grateful for the commitment, encouragement, and patience provided over the years by David Dean, former list manager for the Taking Sides series; David Brackley, former senior developmental editor; and the entire staff of McGraw-Hill/Dushkin. Indispensable to this project are Ted Knight, the former list manager, and Jill Peter, the current editor-in-charge of the Taking Sides series.

Larry Madaras
Howard Community College

James M. SoRelle
Baylor University

Contents In Brief

Contents

hardworking, energetic, and young individuals who went through two stages of history: From 1640 to 1660 servants provided large planters with an inexpensive labor force, but they also achieved greater wealth and mobility in the Chesapeake than if they remained in England; after 1660 opportunities for servants to achieve land, wealth, and status drastically declined.

Prize-winning historian Gordon S. Wood argues that the American Revolution was a far-reaching, radical event that produced a unique democratic society in which ordinary people could make money, pursue happiness, and be self-governing.

Political scientist John P. Roche asserts that the Founding Fathers were not only revolutionaries but also superb democratic politicians who created a Constitution that supported the needs of the nation and at the same time was acceptable to the people. Historian Alfred F. Young argues that the Founding Fathers were an elite group of college-educated lawyers, merchants, slave-holding planters, and "monied men" who strengthened the power of the central government yet, at the same time, were forced to make some democratic accommodations in writing the Constitution in order to ensure its acceptance in the democratically controlled ratifying conventions.

Professor Morton Borden argues that President Thomas Jefferson was a moderate and pragmatic politician who placed the nation's best interests above those of the states. History professor Forrest McDonald believes that President Jefferson attempted to replace Hamiltonian Federalist Principles with a Republican ideology in order to restore America's agrarian heritage.

According to Professor Dexter Perkins, President James Monroe issued his famous declaration of December 2, 1823 to protest Russian expansionism in the Pacific Northwest and to prevent European intervention in South America from restoring to Spain her former colonies. According to Professor Ernest R. May, domestic political considerations brought about the Monroe Doctrine when the major presidential candidates attempted to gain a political advantage over their rivals during the presidential campaign of 1824.

Historical biographer Robert V. Remini argues that Andrew Jackson did not seek to destroy Native American life and culture. He portrays Jackson as a national leader who sincerely believed that the Indian Removal Act of 1830 was the only way to protect Native Americans from annihilation at the hands of white settlers. Historian and anthropologist Anthony F. C. Wallace contends that Andrew Jackson oversaw a harsh policy with regard to Native Americans. This policy resulted in the usurpation of land, attempts to destroy tribal culture, and the forcible removal of Native Americans from the southeastern United States to a designated territory west of the Mississippi River.

PART 3   ANTEBELLUM AMERICA   231

Professor Wilma A. Dunaway believes that modern historians have exaggerated the amount of control slaves exercised over their lives and underplayed the cruelty of the slave experience—family separations, nutritional deficiencies, sexual exploitation and physical abuse—that occurred on the majority of small plantations. Professor Genovese argues that slaves developed their own system of family and cultural values within the southern paternalistic and pre-capitalistic slave society.

Professor of history Rodolfo Acuña argues that Euroamericans took advantage of the young, independent, and unstable government of Mexico and waged unjust and aggressive wars against the Mexican government in the 1830s and 1840s in order to take away half of Mexico's original soil. Professor of diplomatic history Norman A. Graebner argues that President James Polk pursued an aggressive policy that he believed would force Mexico to sell New Mexico and California to the United States and to recognize the annexation of Texas without starting a war.

C. Vann Woodward depicts John Brown as a fanatic who committed whole-sale murder in Kansas in 1856 and whose ill-fated assault on Harpers Ferry, Virginia, in 1859, while admired by his fellow abolitionists and many northern intellectuals, was an irrational act of treason against the United States. Donald G. Mathews describes abolitionists as uncompromising agitators, not unprincipled fanatics, who employed flamboyant rhetoric but who crafted a balanced and thoughtful critique of the institution of slavery as a social evil that violated the nation's basic values.

PART 4   CONFLICT AND RESOLUTION   305

Professor of history Joel H. Silbey argues that historians have overempha-sized the sectional conflict over slavery and have neglected to analyze local ethnocultural issues among the events leading to the Civil War. Professor of history Michael F. Holt maintains that both Northern Republicans and Southern Democrats seized the slavery issue to sharply distinguish party differences and thus reinvigorate the loyalty of party voters.

Attorney Alan T. Nolan argues that General Robert E. Lee was a flawed grand strategist whose offensive operations produced heavy casualties in an unnecessarily prolonged war that the South could not win. According to professor of American history Gary W. Gallagher, General Lee was the most revered and unifying figure in the Confederacy, and he "formulated a national strategy predicated on the probability of success in Virginia and the value of battlefield victories."

Allen Guelzo insists that Abraham Lincoln was committed to freeing the nation's slaves from the day of his inauguration and that, by laying the founda-tion for liberating some four million African Americans held in bondage, the

Emancipation Proclamation represents the most epochal of Lincoln's writings. Vincent Harding credits slaves themselves for engaging in a dramatic movement of self-liberation while Abraham Lincoln initially refused to declare the destruction of slavery as a war aim and then issued the Emancipation Proclamation, which failed to free any slaves in areas over which he had any authority.

Issue 17.   Did William M. Tweed Corrupt Post–Civil War New York?   371

YES: **Alexander B. Callow, Jr.,** from *The Tweed Ring* (Oxford University Press, 1966)   *373*

NO: **Leo Hershkowitz,** from *Tweed's New York: Another Look* (Anchor Press, 1977)   *382*

Professor emeritus of history Alexander B. Callow, Jr., asserts that by exercising a corrupting influence over the city and state governments as well as over key elements within the business community, William M. "Boss" Tweed and his infamous "ring" extracted enormous sums of ill-gotten money for their own benefit in post–Civil War New York. Professor of history Leo Hershkowitz portrays Tweed as a devoted public servant who championed New York City's interests during his 20-year career and whose reputation as the symbol for urban political corruption is grossly undeserved.

Issue 18.   Was Reconstruction a "Splendid Failure"?   391

YES: **Eric Foner,** from "The New View of Reconstruction," *American Heritage* (October/November 1983)   *393*

NO: **LaWanda Cox,** from *Lincoln and Black Freedom: A Study in Presidential Leadership* (University of South Carolina Press, 1981)   *403*

Eric Foner asserts that although Reconstruction did not achieve radical goals, it was a "splendid failure" because it offered African Americans in the South a temporary vision of a free society. LaWanda Cox explores the hypothetical question of whether Reconstruction would have succeeded had Lincoln lived and concludes that, despite his many talents, not even Lincoln could have guaranteed the success of the full range of reform, including land redistribution and political empowerment for African Americans, envisioned by the proponents of radical rule.

Introduction

The Study of History

Larry Madaras

James M. SoRelle

In a pluralistic society such as ours, the study of history is bound to be a complex process. How an event is interpreted depends not only on the existing evidence but also on the perspective of the interpreter. Consequently, understanding history presupposes the evaluation of information, a task that often leads to conflicting conclusions. An understanding of history, then, requires the acceptance of the idea of historical relativism. Relativism means that redefinition of our past is always possible and desirable. History shifts, changes, and grows with new and different evidence and interpretations. As is the case with the law and even with medicine, beliefs that were unquestioned 100 or 200 years ago have been discredited or discarded since.

Relativism, then, encourages revisionism. There is a maxim that "the past must remain useful to the present." Historian Carl Becker argued that every generation should examine history for itself, thus ensuring constant scrutiny of our collective experience through new perspectives. History, consequently, does not remain static, in part because historians cannot avoid being influenced by the times in which they live. Almost all historians commit themselves to revising the views of other historians, synthesizing theories into macro-interpretations, or revising the revisionists.

Schools of Thought

Three predominant schools of thought have emerged in American history since the first graduate seminars in history were given at The Johns Hopkins University in Baltimore in the 1870s. The *progressive* school dominated the professional field in the first half of the twentieth century. Influenced by the reform currents of Populism, progressivism, and the New Deal, these historians explored the social and economic forces that energized America. The progressive scholars tended to view the past in terms of conflicts between groups, and they sympathized with the underdog.

The post–World War II period witnessed the emergence of a new group of historians who viewed the conflict thesis as overly simplistic. Writing against the backdrop of the Cold War, these *neoconservative,* or *consensus,* historians argued that Americans possess a shared set of values and that the areas of agreement within our nation's basic democratic and capitalistic framework are more important than the areas of disagreement.

In the 1960s, however, the civil rights movement, women's liberation, and the student rebellion (with its condemnation of the war in Vietnam) fragmented the consensus of values upon which historians and social scientists of the 1950s had centered their interpretations. This turmoil set the stage for the emergence of another group of scholars. *New Left* historians began to reinterpret the past once again. They emphasized the significance of conflict in American history, and they resurrected interest in those groups ignored by the consensus school. In addition, New Left historians critiqued the expansionist policies of the United States and emphasized the difficulties confronted by Native Americans, African Americans, women, and urban workers in gaining full citizenship status.

Progressive, consensus, and New Left history is still being written. The most recent generation of scholars, however, focuses upon social history. Their primary concern is to discover what the lives of "ordinary Americans" were really like. These new social historians employ previously overlooked court and church documents, house deeds and tax records, letters and diaries, photographs, and census data to reconstruct the everyday lives of average Americans. Some employ new methodologies, such as quantification (enhanced by advancing computer technology) and oral history, while others borrow from the disciplines of political science, economics, sociology, anthropology, and psychology for their historical investigations.

The proliferation of historical approaches, which are reflected in the issues debated in this book, has had mixed results. On the one hand, historians have become so specialized in their respective time periods and methodological styles that it is difficult to synthesize the recent scholarship into a comprehensive text for the general reader. On the other hand, historians know more about the American past than at any other time in history. They dare to ask new questions or ones that previously were considered to be germane only to scholars in other social sciences. Although there is little agreement about the answers to these questions, the methods employed and issues explored make the "new history" a very exciting field to study.

Issue 1 discusses the key element of historical truth and the extent to which historians, applying the technique of empirical research, can determine exactly what happened in the past. Oscar Handlin insists that the truth of past events is absolute and knowable if pursued by historians employing the scientific method of research. William McNeill, however, argues that the absolute truth about human behavior is unattainable because historians do not have all the facts at their disposal and because they tend to organize their evidence and make intellectual choices based on subjective judgments. Consequently, historians' interpretations may be challenged by others who approach the evidence from a different point of view.

The topics that follow represent a variety of perspectives and approaches. Each of these controversial issues can be studied for its individual importance to our nation's history. Taken as a group, they interact with one another to illustrate larger historical themes. When grouped thematically, the issues reveal continuing motifs in the development of American history.

Comparative History: America in a Global Perspective

The role of American history within the larger framework of world history is central to the discussion presented in Issue 2. Kirkpatrick Sale places the "discovery" of America by Christopher Columbus within the context of European imperialism of the late fifteenth century. Robert Royal takes Sale and other Columbus denigrators to task for failing to recognize Columbus's courage and the many benefits derived from his and other European explorer's voyages to the New World.

Issue 9 addresses the intent of the Monroe Doctrine, which served as the foundation of United States foreign policy through most of the nineteenth century. Dexter Perkins, in one of the earliest scholarly analyses of this policy, argues that President James Monroe hoped to use this doctrine to prevent Spain from restoring control over her former colonies in South America. Ernest May, however, concludes that the Monroe Doctrine was more a consequence of domestic political considerations as presidential hopefuls jockeyed for position in advance of the presidential election of 1824.

A discussion of early nineteenth-century foreign policy in Issue 12 concerns both U.S. diplomatic relations with the rest of the world and America's self-perception within the world of nations. Did the U.S. government conceive of its power as continental, hemispheric, or worldwide? And what were the consequences of these attitudes? Rodolfo Acuña argues that the United States waged a racist and imperialistic war against Mexico for the purpose of conquering what became the American Southwest. Norman A. Graebner contends that President James K. Polk pursued an aggressive (but not imperialistic) policy that would force Mexico to recognize U.S. annexation of Texas and to sell New Mexico and California to its northern neighbor without starting a war.

The New Social History

Some of the most innovative historical research over the last thirty years reflects the interests of the new social historians. The work of several representatives of this group who treat the issues of class, gender, and race appears in this volume.

Issue 3 debates the work habits of the early settlers in the Chesapeake colonies. Describing the difficulties of Virginia's first European residents, Edmund Morgan blames the colonists themselves for their misfortunes. According to Morgan, these settlers suffered because they placed the goal of getting rich quick above the basic need of supplying food and shelter for themselves. Russell Menard's essay examines the status of indentured servants in seventeenth-century Maryland. Menard characterizes the members of this labor force as ambitious, energetic, and hardworking.

The economic status of women in colonial New England is debated in Issue 4. Gloria Main supports the view that white women in colonial America were better off than their European counterparts. In the seventeenth century, women's work was highly valued and not restricted by a clearly defined division of labor; after 1760, more women entered the paid labor force, and their wages rose. Lyle Koehler, on the other hand, emphasizes the subordinate economic status occupied by colonial New England women and concludes that the only way for these women to experience upward mobility was to marry well.

The impact of the institution of slavery on the African American family is explored in Issue 11. Focusing on the harsh realities of the antebellum plantation system in the South, Wilma Dunaway criticizes those historians who have insisted that slaves succeeded in exercising a significant amount of control over their own lives, including the realm of family relations. John Blassingame, one of Dunaway's targets, recognizes that slave families were unstable and frequently broken by sale, but he nevertheless believes that African American slaves took their family obligations seriously and that the slave family was a significant survival mechanism for them.

Religion, Revolution, Reform, and Reconstruction

Beyond suggesting that much of the colonizing experiment in British North America was motivated by a search for religious freedom, many textbooks avoid extended discussions of religion as a force in history. In the last half-century, however, professional historians have assumed that the religious revivals of the mid-eighteenth century, known as the "Great Awakening," represented a major social and cultural event in the lives of the American people. In Issue 5, Patricia U. Bonomi offers a traditional view of the Great Awakening as a series of revivals occurring throughout the American colonies from 1739 to 1745, which generated a divisiveness that affected a number of religious, social, and political institutions. Jon Butler's essay represents a significant departure from this line of thought as he denies that any great, unified revival movement existed in the eighteenth century at all. In fact, Butler suggests that historians should abandon altogether the label "Great Awakening."

The nature of the American Revolution is considered in Issue 6. Carl N. Degler depicts the Revolution as a conservative movement that produced few political or economic changes. Gordon S. Wood, in contrast, views the American Revolution as a truly radical event that led to the adoption of a republican form of government in the newly established nation.

During the 1830s and 1840s, a wave of reformism swept across the United States. Various individuals and groups sought to strengthen the democratic experiment in the nation by ridding the society of its imperfections. Issue 10 is framed within the context of the role of humanitarianism in the formulation of public policy with regard to Native Americans. Robert V. Remini argues that President Andrew Jackson's support for the Indian Removal Act of 1830 was predicated on Jackson's desire to protect Native Americans from almost certain annihilation at the hands of white settlers in the southeastern United States. Anthony F. C. Wallace depicts Jackson as a key initiator of the brutal program of forced removal of several tribes from their longtime homeland.

The major and most controversial reform effort in the pre–Civil War period was the movement to abolish slavery. Issue 13 deals with the motivations of those who became abolitionists. In his profile of John Brown, C. Vann Woodward lends support to the view that abolitionists like Brown were "unrestrained fanatics." Brown, says Woodward, was passionately and fanatically dedicated to his war against slavery, and his actions in Kansas and at Harpers Ferry indicated his willingness to go to any lengths, including murder and treason, to emancipate southern slaves. Donald Mathews, however, believes that the abolitionists' flamboyant rhetoric and uncompromising agitation should not be mistaken as evidence of irrational fanaticism. Instead, he portrays the abolitionists as dedicated reformers who crafted a balanced, reasoned critique that defined slavery as a violation of the nation's basic values.

The Civil War is one of the most frequently studied episodes in American history. The military leadership of Confederate General Robert E. Lee is the focus of the essays in Issue 15. Alan T. Nolan argues that Lee was a flawed strategist whose offensive operations produced heavy casualties in a war the South could not win. Gary W. Gallagher, however, seeks to restore Lee's reputation as the most revered and unifying figure in the Confederacy.

Perhaps no other period of American history has been subjected to more myths than the era of Reconstruction. Only within the past twenty-five years has the traditional, pro-southern interpretation been revised in high school and college texts. In Issue 18, Eric Foner concedes that Reconstruction was not very radical, much less revolutionary. It was, nevertheless, a "splendid failure" because it offered the former slaves a vision of what a free society should look like. LaWanda Cox explores the possibility for success of the Reconstruction program from the hypothetical query of whether Abraham Lincoln could have avoided the failures of his successors had he lived. She concludes that, despite Lincoln's unquestionable leadership skills, there is no guarantee that he could have persuaded white southerners to adopt peacefully a program of land reform and political empowered for their former slaves.

Politics in America

The American people gave legitimacy to their revolution through the establishment of a republican form of government. The United States has operated under two constitutions: the first established the short-lived confederation from 1781 to 1789; the second was written in 1787 and remains in effect over 200 years later. In Issue 7, John P. Roche contends that the drafters of the Constitution of the United States were democratic reformers. Alfred F. Young argues that the Founding Fathers were an elitist group who made some democratic accommodations in framing the Constitution to make sure it was acceptable to the democratically controlled ratifying conventions.

Issue 8 addresses the presidential leadership of Thomas Jefferson. Although Jefferson was a leader of the Democratic-Republican Party that defeated the Federalists in 1800, Morton Borden does not view Jefferson as a political ideologue. Instead, according to Borden, as president, Jefferson was a pragmatic, moderate politician who placed the nation's best interests above ideological considerations. Forrest McDonald, by contrast, presents Jefferson as a rigid ideologue whose foremost concern was to restore the agrarian heritage idealized by his Republican supporters.

Most historians have argued that Abraham Lincoln became president in 1860 because sectional conflicts over the slavery issue in the late 1850s divided the nation and destroyed the second political party system, which was comprised of Whigs and Democrats. Political historians, employing a statistical analysis of election issues, voter behavior, and legislative patterns on the local, state, and national levels, however, have rejected or significantly modified the traditional emphasis on sectionalism in the 1850s. In Issue 14, Joel H. Silbey argues that historians have paid too much attention to the sectional conflict over slavery and have neglected to analyze local ethnocultural issues as keys to the Civil War. Michael F. Holt maintains that both northern Republicans and southern Democrats seized the slavery issue to highlight the sharp differences existing between them and thus to reinvigorate the loyalty of their traditional partisans.

Abraham Lincoln's image as "the Great Emancipator" is the focus of the essays in Issue 16. Allen Guelzo insists that the Emancipation Proclamation represented a culmination of Lincoln's long-standing commitment to end slavery in the United States. Vincent Harding, however, defends the position that slaves were the agents of their own freedom, while Lincoln was reluctant to make emancipation a war issue.

In Issue 17, post–Civil War political corruption is discussed with a focus on William M. "Boss" Tweed and his activities at Tammany Hall, the Democratic machine's headquarters in New York City. Alexander B. Callow, Jr., asserts that Tweed exercised a corrupting influence over the city and state governments and the business community. Leo Hershkowitz emphasizes the services that Tweed provided to benefit New York City.

Conclusion

The process of historical study should rely more on thinking than on memorizing data. Once the basics of who, what, when, and where are determined, historical thinking shifts to a higher gear. Analysis, comparison and contrast, evaluation, and explanation take command. These skills not only increase our knowledge of the past but also provide general tools for the comprehension of all the topics about which human beings think.

The diversity of a pluralistic society, however, creates some obstacles to comprehending the past. The spectrum of differing opinions on any particular subject eliminates the possibility of quick and easy answers. In the final analysis, conclusions are often built through a synthesis of several different interpretations, but, even then, they may be partial and tentative.

The study of history in a pluralistic society allows each citizen the opportunity to reach independent conclusions about the past. Since most, if not all, historical issues affect the present and future, understanding the past becomes essential to social progress. Many of today's problems have a direct connection with the past. Additionally, other contemporary issues may lack obvious direct antecedents, but historical investigation can provide illuminating analogies. At first, it may appear confusing to read and to think about opposing historical views, but the survival of our democratic society depends on such critical thinking by acute and discerning minds.

On the Internet . . .

Institute for the Study of Civic Values

The Institute for the Study of Civic Values is a nonprofit organization established in Philadelphia in 1973 to promote the fulfillment of America's historic civic ideals. At a time when millions of Americans are struggling to identify the values that we share, the institute believes that it is our civic values—the principles embodied in the Declaration of Independence, the Constitution, and the Bill of Rights—that bring us together as a people.

http://www.iscv.org

The Columbus Navigation Homepage

This noted site by Keith A. Pickering examines the history, navigation, and landfall of Christopher Columbus. Click on "Links to other sites about Columbus and his times" to find dozens of sites on Columbus, including scholarly papers on Columbus's treatment of the American Indians.

http://www1.minn.net/~keithp/

13 Originals: Founding the American Colonies

This Web site concerning the 13 original colonies provides a history of the foundation of each colony. On this site, you will find maps of colonial America as well as the text of colonial charters, grants, and related documents. This is a comprehensive site with many links to detailed historical information.

http://www.timepage.org/spl/13colony.html

Religion and the Founding of the American Republic

This segment of the Library of Congress site summarizes religious developments in the American colonies in the eighteenth century, including denominational history and the rise of evangelicalism. Numerous images include examples of church architecture and portraits of leading ministers of the 1700s.

http://www.loc.gov/exhibits/religion/rel02.html

PART 1

Colonial Society

*C*olonial settlement took place in the context of conditions that were unique to time and place. These European settlers migrated to the North American colonies for a variety of reasons, and their ethnic identity affected relations with Native Americans and Africans, as well as with each other. Over the course of the seventeenth and eighteenth centuries, they established permanent residences that varied from region to region and gradually developed political, economic, social, and cultural institutions that served the early settlers well.

- Is History True?

- Was Columbus an Imperialist?

- Were the First Colonists in the Chesapeake Region Ignorant, Lazy, and Unambitious?

- Did Colonial New England Women Enjoy Significant Economic Autonomy?

- Was There a Great Awakening in Mid-Eighteenth-Century America?

ISSUE 1

Is History True?

YES: Oscar Handlin, from *Truth in History* (The Belknap Press of Harvard University Press, 1979)

NO: William H. McNeill, from "Mythistory, or Truth, Myth, History, and Historians," *The American Historical Review* (February 1986)

ISSUE SUMMARY

YES: Oscar Handlin insists that historical truth is absolute and knowable by historians who adopt the scientific method of research to discover factual evidence that provides both a chronology and context for their findings.

NO: William McNeill argues that historical truth is general and evolutionary and is discerned by different groups at different times and in different places in a subjective manner that has little to do with a scientifically absolute methodology.

The basic premise of this volume of readings is that the study of history is a complex process that combines historical facts and the historian's interpretation of those facts. Underlying this premise is the assumption that the historian is committed to employing evidence that advances an accurate, truthful picture of the past. Unfortunately, the historical profession in the last several years has been held up to close public scrutiny as a result of charges that a few scholars, some quite prominent, have been careless in their research methods, cited sources that do not exist, and reached conclusions that were not borne out by the facts. The result has been soiled or ruined reputations and the revocation of degrees, book awards, and tenure. Certainly, this is not the end to which most historians aspire, and the failures of a few should not cast a net of suspicion on the manner in which the vast majority of historians practice their craft.

In reflecting upon her role as a historian, the late Barbara Tuchman commented, "To write history so as to enthrall the reader and make the subject as captivating and exciting to him as it is to me has been my goal. . . . A prerequisite . . . is to be enthralled one's self and to feel a compulsion to communicate the magic." For Tuchman, it was the historian's responsibility to the reader to conduct thorough research on a particular topic, sort through the mass of facts to determine what was essential and what was not, and to formulate what remained into a dramatic narrative. Tuchman and most practicing historians also agree with the nineteenth-century German historian Leopold von Ranke that the task of the historian is to discover what really happened. In most instances, however, historians write about events at which they were not present. According to Tuchman, "We can never be certain that we have recaptured [the past] as it really was. But the least we can do is to stay within the evidence."

David Hackett Fischer has written about the difficulties confronting historians as they attempt to report a truthful past, and he is particularly critical of what he terms the "absurd and pernicious doctrine" of historical relativism as it developed in the United States in the 1930s under the direction of Charles Beard and Carl Becker. Becker's suggestion that each historian will write a history based upon his or her own values or the climate of opinion in a particular generation strikes Fischer as a slippery slope leading to the loss of historical accuracy. In conclusion, Fischer writes, "The factual errors which academic historians make today are rarely deliberate. The real danger is not that a scholar will delude his readers, but that he will delude himself."

The selections that follow explore the topic of historical truth. In the late 1970s, Oscar Handlin, like Fischer, became extremely concerned about the impact of the historical and cultural relativism of postmodern and deconstructionist approaches to the study of history. For Handlin, historical truth is absolute and knowable if pursued by the historian adopting the scientific method of research. The value of history, he believes, lies in the capacity to advance toward the truth by locating discrete events, phenomena, and expressions in the historical record.

In contrast, William McNeill recognizes a very thin line between fact and fiction. He claims that historians distinguish between the truth of their conclusions and the myth of those conclusions they reject. The result is what he terms "mythistory." Moreover, the arrangement of historical facts involves subjective judgments and intellectual choices that have little to do with the scientific method. Historical truth, McNeill proposes, is evolutionary, not absolute.

Oscar Handlin

 **YES**

The Uses of History

Why resist the temptation to be relevant? The question nags historians in 1978 as it does other scholars. The world is turning; it needs knowledge; and possession of learning carries an obligation to attempt to shape events. Every crisis lends weight to the plea: transform the library from an ivory tower into a fortress armed to make peace (or war), to end (or extend) social inequality, to alter (or preserve) the existing economic system. The thought boosts the ego, as it has ever since Francis Bacon's suggestion that knowledge is power. Perhaps authority really does lie in command of the contents of books!

In the 1960s the plea became an order, sometimes earnest, sometimes surly, always insistent. Tell us what we need to know—straight answers. Thus, students to teachers, readers to authors. The penalties for refusal ranged from mere unpopularity to organized boycotts and angry confrontations—in a few cases even to burning manuscripts and research notes. Fear added to the inducements for pleasing the audience, whether in the classroom or on the printed page.

To aim to please is a blunder, however. Sincere as the supplicants generally are, it is not knowledge they wish. Having already reached their conclusions, they seek only reassuring confirmation as they prepare to act. They already know that a unilateral act of will could stop wars, that the United States is racist, and that capitalism condemns the masses to poverty. The history of American foreign policy, of the failure of post-Civil War Reconstruction, and of industrial development would only clutter the mind with disturbing ambiguities and complexities.

At best, the usable past demanded of history consists of the data to flesh out a formula. We must do something about the war, the cities, pollution, poverty, and population. Our moral sense, group interest, and political affiliation define the goals; let the historian join the other social scientists in telling us how to reach them. At worst, the demand made of the past is for a credible myth that will identify the forces of good and evil and inspire those who fight with slogans or fire on one side of the barricades or the other.

The effort to meet either demand will frustrate the historian true to his or her craft. Those nimble enough to catch the swings of the market in the classroom or in print necessarily leave behind interior standards of what is important and drop by the wayside the burden of scrupulous investigation and rigorous judgment. Demands for relevance distort the story of ethnicity as they corrupt the historical novel.

Whoever yields, forgoes the opportunity to do what scholars are best qualified to do. Those who chase from one disaster to another lose sight of the long-term trend; busy with the bandaids, they have no time to treat the patient's illness. The family did not originate yesterday, or the city, or addiction to narcotics; a student might well pick up some thoughts on those subjects by shifting his sights from the 1970s to Hellenistic society.

Above all, obsession with the events of the moment prevents the historian from exercising the faculty of empathy, the faculty of describing how people, like us, but different, felt and behaved as they did in times and places similar to, but different, from our own. The writer or teacher interested only in passing judgment on the good guys and the bad will never know what it meant to be an Irish peasant during a famine, or the landlord; an Alabama slave in the 1850s, or the master; a soldier at Antietam, or a general.

❧◉❧

The uses of history arise neither from its relevance nor from its help in preparing for careers—nor from its availability as a subject which teachers pass on to students who become teachers and in turn teach others to teach.

Nevertheless, again and again former pupils who come back for reunions after twenty-five years or more spontaneously testify to the utility of what they had learned at college in the various pursuits to which life's journey had taken them. Probing usually reveals not bits of information, not a general interpretation, but a vague sense that those old transactions of classroom and library had somehow expanded their knowledge of self. The discipline of history had located them in time and space and had thereby helped them know themselves, not as physicians or attorneys or bureaucrats or executives, but as persons.

These reassuring comments leave in suspense the question of why study of the past should thus help the individuals understand himself or herself. How do those who learn this subject catch a glimpse of the process of which they are part, discover places in it?

Not by relevance, in the competition for which the other, more pliable, social sciences can always outbid history. Nor by the power of myth, in the peddling of which the advantage lies with novelists. To turn accurate knowledge to those ends is, as C. S. Peirce noted, "like running a steam engine by burning diamonds."

The use of history lies in its capacity for advancing the approach to truth.

The historian's vocation depends on this minimal operational article of faith: Truth is absolute; it is as absolute as the world is real. It does not exist because individuals wish it to anymore than the world exists for their convenience. Although observers have more or less partial views of the truth, its actuality is unrelated to the desires or the particular angles of vision of the viewers. Truth is knowable and will out if earnestly pursued; and science is the procedure or set of procedures for approximating it.

❧◉❧

What is truth? Mighty above all things, it resides in the small pieces which together form the record.

History is not the past, any more than biology is life, or physics, matter. History is the distillation of evidence surviving from the past. Where there is no evidence, there is no history. Much of the past is not knowable in this way, and about those areas the historian must learn to confess ignorance.

No one can relive the past; but everyone can seek truth in the record. Simple, durable discoveries await the explorer. So chronology—the sequential order of events reaching back beyond time's horizon—informs the viewer of the long distance traversed and of the immutable course of occurrences: no reversal of a step taken; no after ever before. The historian cannot soar with the anthropologists, who swoop across all time and space. Give or take a thousand years, it is all one to them in pronouncements about whether irrigation systems succeeded or followed despotisms, or in linking technology, population, food, and climatic changes. In the end they pick what they need to prop up theory. The discipline of dates rails off the historian and guards against such perilous plunges. No abstraction, no general interpretation, no wish or preference can challenge chronology's dominion, unless among those peoples who, lacking a sense of time, lack also a sense of history. And whoever learns to know the tyranny of the passing hours, the irrecoverable nature of days passed, learns also the vanity of all aspirations to halt the clock or slow its speed, of all irridentisms, all efforts to recapture, turn back, redeem the moments gone by.

Another use of history is in teaching about vocabulary, the basic component of human communication. Words, singularly elusive, sometimes flutter out of reach, hide in mists of ambiguity, or lodge themselves among inaccessible logical structures, yet form the very stuff of evidence. The historian captures the little syllabic clusters only by knowing who inscribed or spoke them—a feat made possible by understanding the minds and hearts and hands of the men and women for whom they once had meaning. Words released by comprehension wing their messages across the centuries. A use of history is to instruct in the reading of a word, in the comprehension of speakers, writers different from the listener, viewer.

And context. Every survival bespeaks a context. Who graved or wrote or built did so for the eyes of others. Each line or shape denotes a relation to people, things, or concepts—knowable. The identities of sender and recipient explain the content of the letter; the mode of transmission explains the developing idea, the passions of employers and laborers, the organization of the factory. A use of history is its aid in locating discrete events, phenomena, and expressions in their universes.

The limits of those universes were often subjects of dispute. Early in the nineteenth century Henry Thomas Buckle complained, in terms still applicable decades thereafter, of "the singular spectacle of one historian being ignorant of political economy; another knowing nothing of law; another nothing of ecclesiastical affairs and changes of opinion; another neglecting the philosophy of statistics, another physical science," so that those important pursuits, being cultivated, "some by one man, and some by another, have been isolated rather than united," with no disposition to concentrate them upon history. He thus echoed Gibbon's earlier injunction to value all facts. A Montesquieu, "from the meanest of them, will draw conclusions unknown to ordinary men" and arrive at "philosophical history."

On the other hand, a distinguished scholar fifty years later pooh-poohed the very idea that there might be a relation among the Gothic style, feudalism, and scholasticism, or a link between the Baroque and Jesuitism. Nevertheless, the dominant thrust of twentieth-century historians has been toward recognition of the broader contexts; in a variety of fashions they have searched for a totality denominated civilization, culture, or spirit of an epoch, and which they have hoped would permit examination of enlightening linkages and reciprocal relations. Even those who deny that history is a single discipline and assert that it is only "congeries of related disciplines" would, no doubt, expect each branch to look beyond its own borders.

In the final analysis, all the uses of history depend upon the integrity of the record, without which there could be no counting of time, no reading of words, no perception of the context, no utility of the subject. No concern could be deeper than assaults upon the record, upon the very idea of a record.

∘✦∘

Although history is an ancient discipline, it rests upon foundations laid in the seventeenth century, when a century of blood shed in religious and dynastic warfare persuaded those who wrote and read history to accept a vital difference in tolerance between facts and interpretation. The text of a charter or statute was subject to proof of authenticity and validity, whatever the meanings lawyers or theologians imparted to its terms. The correct date, the precise phrasing, the seal were facts which might present difficulties of verification, but which, nevertheless, admitted of answers that were right or wrong. On the other hand, discussion of opinions and meanings often called for tolerance among diverse points of view, tolerance possible so long as disputants distinguished interpretation from the fact, from the thing in itself. Scholars could disagree on large matters of interpretation; they had a common interest in agreeing on the small ones of fact which provided them grounds of peaceful discourse.

From that seminal insight developed the scientific mechanisms that enabled historians to separate fact from opinion. From that basis came the Enlightenment achievements which recognized the worth of objectivity and asserted the possibility of reconstructing the whole record of the human past.

True, historians as well as philosophers often thereafter worried about the problems of bias and perspective; and some despaired of attaining the ideal of ultimate objectivity. None were ever totally free of bias, not even those like Ranke who most specifically insisted on the integrity of the fact which he struggled to make the foundation of a truly universal body of knowledge. But, however fallible the individual scholar, the historian's, task, Wilhelm von Humboldt explained, was "to present what actually happened." It may have been a dream to imagine that history would become a science meaningful to all people, everywhere. If so, it was a noble dream.

By contrast, historians in the 1970s and increasingly other scientists regarded the fact itself as malleable. As the distinction between fact and interpretation faded, all became faction—a combination of fact and fiction. The passive acceptance of that illegitimate genre—whatever mixes with fiction ceases to be fact—revealed the erosion of scholarly commitment. More and more often, the factual elements in an account were instrumental to the purpose the author-manipulator wished them to serve. It followed that different writers addressing different readers for different purposes could arrange matters as convenient. In the end, the primacy of the fact vanished and only the authority of the author, the receptivity of the audience, and the purpose intended remained.

Whence came this desertion, this rejection of allegiance to the fact?

Chroniclers of the past always suffered from external pressure to make their findings relevant, that is, to demonstrate or deny the wisdom, correctness, or appropriateness of current policies. They resisted out of dedication to maintaining the integrity of the record; and long succeeded in doing so. In the 1970s, however, the pressures toward falsification became more compelling than ever before.

Although the full fruits of the change appeared only in that decade, its origins reached back a half-century. It was one of Stalin's most impressive achievements to have converted Marxism from its nineteenth-century scientific base to an instrument of state purpose, and it was not by coincidence that history was the first discipline to suffer in the process. The Soviet Union did more than impose an official party line on interpretations of Trotsky's role in the revolution of 1917; it actually expunged the name Trotsky from the record, so that the fact of the commissar's existence disappeared. What started in the domain of history led in time to Lysenko's invasion of the natural sciences. The Nazis, once in power, burned the nonconforming books; and after 1945 the assault spread to all countries subject to totalitarian control. Those developments were neither surprising nor difficult to comprehend; they followed from the nature of the regimes which fostered them.

More surprising, more difficult to comprehend, was the acquiescence by the scholars of free societies in the attack on history, first, insofar as it affected colleagues less fortunately situated, then as it insinuated itself in their own ranks. External and internal circumstances were responsible.

In a sensate society the commercial standards of the media governed the dissemination of information. Since whatever sold was news, the salient consideration was one of attracting attention; factual accuracy receded to the remote background. An affluent and indulgent society also mistook flaccid permissiveness for tolerance. Everything went because nothing was worth defending, and the legitimate right to err became the disastrous obliteration of the difference between error and truth.

Difficult critical issues tempted the weak-minded to tailor fact to convenience. In the United States, but also in other parts of the world, the spread of a kind of tribalism demanded a history unique to and written for the specifications of particular groups. Since knowledge was relative to the knowers, it was subject to manipulation to suit their convenience. The process by which blacks, white ethnics, and women alone were conceded the capability of understanding and writing their own histories wiped out the line between truth and myth.

That much was comprehensible; these forces operated outside the academy walls and were not subject to very much control. More important, more susceptible to control, and less explicable was the betrayal by the intellectuals of their own group interests and the subsequent loss of the will to resist. A variety of elements contributed to this most recent *trahison des clercs*. Exaggerated concern with the problems of bias and objectivity drove some earnest scholars to despair. Perhaps they reacted against the excessive claims of the nineteenth century, perhaps against the inability of historians, any more than other scholars, to withstand the pressures of nationalism in the early decades of the twentieth century. In any case, not a few followed the deceptive path from acknowledgment that no person was entirely free of prejudice or capable of attaining a totally objective view of the past to the conclusion that all efforts to do so were vain and that, in the end, the past was entirely a recreation emanating from the mind of the historian. Support from this point of view came from the philosophers Benedetto Croce in Italy and, later, R. G. Collingwood in England. Support also came from a misreading of anthropological relativism, which drew from the undeniable circumstances that different cultures evolved differently, the erroneous conclusion that judgments among them were impossible.

Perhaps playfully, perhaps seriously, Carl L. Becker suggested that the historical fact was in someone's mind or it was nowhere, because it was "not the past event," only a symbol which enabled later writers to recreate it imaginatively. His charmingly put illustrations deceived many a reader unaware that serious thinkers since Bayle and Hume had wrestled with the problem. "No one could ever object to the factual truth that Caesar defeated Pompey; and whatever the principles one wishes to use in dispute, one will find nothing less questionable than this proposition—Caesar and Pompey existed and were not just simple modification of the minds of those who wrote their lives"—thus Bayle.

The starting point in Becker's wandering toward relativism, as for others among his contemporaries, was the desire to be useful in solving "the everlasting riddle of human experience." Less subtle successors attacked neutrality "toward the main issues of life" and demanded that society organize all its forces in support of its ideals. "Total war, whether it be hot or cold, enlists everyone and calls upon everyone to assume his part. The historian is no freer from this obligation than the physicists." Those too timid to go the whole way suggested that there might be two kinds of history, variously defined: one, for instance, to treat the positive side of slavery to nurture black pride; another, the negative, to support claims for compensation.

Historians who caved in to pressure and ordered the past to please the present neglected the future, the needs of which would certainly change and in unpredictable ways. Scholarship could no more provide the future than the present with faith, justification, self-confidence, or sense of purpose unless it first preserved the record, intact and inviolable.

History does not recreate the past. The historian does not recapture the bygone event. No amount of imagination will enable the scholar to describe exactly what happened to Caesar in the Senate or to decide whether

Mrs. Williams actually lost two hundred pounds by an act of faith. History deals only with evidence from the past, with the residues of bygone events. But it can pass judgment upon documentation and upon observers' reports of what they thought they saw.

Disregarding these constraints, Becker concluded that, since objectivity was a dream, everyman could be his own historian and contrive his own view of the past, valid for himself, if for no one else. He thus breached the line between interpretation, which was subjective and pliable, and fact, which was not.

Internal specialization allowed historians to slip farther in the same direction. The knowledge explosion after 1900 made specialization an essential, unavoidable circumstance of every form of scholarly endeavor. No individual could presume to competence in more than a sector of the whole field; and the scope of the manageable sector steadily shrank. One result was the dissolution of common standards; each area created its own criteria and claimed immunity from the criticism of outsiders. The occupants of each little island fortress sustained the illusion that the dangers to one would not apply to others. Lines of communication, even within a single faculty or department, broke down so that, increasingly, specialists in one area depended upon the common mass media for knowledge about what transpired in another.

The dangers inherent in these trends became critical as scholarship lost its autonomy. Increasingly reliance on support from external sources—whether governments or foundations—circumscribed the freedom of researchers and writers to choose their own subjects and to arrive at their own conclusions. More generally, the loss of autonomy involved a state of mind which regarded the fruits of scholarship as dependent and instrumental—that is, not as worthy of pursuit for their own sake, not for the extent to which they brought the inquirer closer to the truth, but for other, extrinsic reasons. Ever more often, scholars justified their activity by its external results—peace, training for citizenship, economic development, cure of illness, and the like—in other words, by its usefulness. The choice of topics revealed the extent to which emphasis had shifted from the subject and its relation to the truth to its instrumental utility measured by reference to some external standard.

The plea from utility was dangerous. In the 1930s it blinded well-intentioned social scientists and historians to the excesses of totalitarianism. It was inevitable in creating the omelette of a great social experiment that the shells of a few eggs of truth would be broken, so the argument ran. So, too, in the avid desire for peace, in the praiseworthy wish to avoid a second world war, Charles A. Beard abandoned all effort at factual accuracy. Yet the errors to which the plea for utility led in the past have not prevented others from proceeding along the same treacherous path in pursuit of no less worthy, but equally deceptive utilitarian goals.

Finally, the reluctance to insist upon the worth of truth for its own sake stemmed from a decline of faith by intellectuals in their own role as intellectuals. Not many have, in any conscious or deliberate sense, foresworn their allegiance to the pursuit of truth and the life of the spirit. But power tempted them as it tempts other men and women. The twentieth-century intellectual had unparalleled access to those who actually wielded political or military influence. And few could resist the temptation of being listened to by presidents and ministers, of seeing ideas translated into action. Moreover, a more subtle, more insidious temptation nested in the possibility that possession of knowledge may itself become a significant source of power. The idea that a name on the letterhead of an activist organization or in the endorsement of a political advertisement might advance some worthy cause gives a heady feeling of sudden consequence to the no-longer-humble professor. Most important of all is the consciousness that knowledge can indeed do good, that it is a usable commodity, not only capable of bringing fame to its possessor but actually capable of causing beneficent changes in the external world.

All too few scholars are conscious that in reducing truth to an instrument, even an instrument for doing good, they necessarily blunt its edge and expose themselves to the danger of its misuse. For, when truth ceases to be an end in itself and becomes but a means toward an end, it also becomes malleable and manageable and is in danger of losing its character—not necessarily, not inevitably, but seriously. There may be ways of avoiding the extreme choices of the ivory tower and the marketplace, but they are far from easy and call for extreme caution.

⁂

In 1679 Jacques Bossuet wrote for his pupil the Dauphin, heir apparent to the throne of France, a discourse on universal history. Here certainly was an opportunity to influence the mind of the future monarch of Europe's most powerful kingdom. Bossuet understood that the greatest service he could render was to tell, not what would be pleasant to hear, but the truth about the past, detached and whole, so that in later years his pupil could make what use he wished of it.

Therein Bossuet reverted to an ancient tradition. The first law for the historian, Cicero had written, "is never to dare utter an untruth and the second, never to suppress anything true." And, earlier still, Polybius had noted that no one was exempt from mistakes made out of ignorance. But "deliberate misstatements in the interest of country or of friends or for favour" reduced the scholar to the level of those who gained "their living by their pens" and weighed "everything by the standard of profit."

In sum, the use of history is to learn from the study of it and not to carry preconceived notions or external objectives into it.

⁂

The times, it may be, will remain hostile to the enterprise of truth. There have been such periods in the past. Historians would do well to regard the example of those clerks in the Dark Ages who knew the worth of the task. By retiring from an alien world to a hidden monastic refuge, now and again one of them at least was able to maintain a true record, a chronicle that survived the destructive passage of armies and the erosion of doctrinal disputes and informed the future of what had transpired in their day. That task is ever worthy. Scholars should ponder its significance.

Mythistory, or Truth, Myth, History, and Historians

Myth and history are close kin inasmuch as both explain how things got to be the way they are by telling some sort of story. But our common parlance reckons myth to be false while history is, or aspires to be, true. Accordingly, a historian who rejects someone else's conclusions calls them mythical, while claiming that his own views are true. But what seems true to one historian will seem false to another, so one historian's truth becomes another's myth, even at the moment of utterance.

A century and more ago, when history was first established as an academic discipline, our predecessors recognized this dilemma and believed they had a remedy. Scientific source criticism would get the facts straight, whereupon a conscientious and careful historian needed only to arrange the facts into a readable narrative to produce genuinely scientific history. And science, of course, like the stars above, was true and eternal, as Newton and Laplace had demonstrated to the satisfaction of all reasonable persons everywhere.

Yet, in practice, revisionism continued to prevail within the newly constituted historical profession, as it had since the time of Herodotus. For a generation or two, this continued volatility could be attributed to scholarly success in discovering new facts by diligent work in the archives; but early in this century thoughtful historians began to realize that the arrangement of facts to make a history involved subjective judgments and intellectual choices that had little or nothing to do with source criticism, scientific or otherwise.

In reacting against an almost mechanical vision of scientific method, it is easy to underestimate actual achievements. For the ideal of scientific history did allow our predecessors to put some forms of bias behind them. In particular, academic historians of the nineteenth century came close to transcending older religious controversies. Protestant and Catholic histories of post-Reformation Europe ceased to be separate and distinct traditions of learning—a transformation nicely illustrated in the Anglo-American world by the career of Lord Acton, a Roman Catholic who became Regius Professor of History at Cambridge and editor of the first *Cambridge Modern History*. This was a great accomplishment. So was the accumulation of an enormous fund of exact and reliable data through painstaking source criticism that allowed the writing of

history in the western world to assume a new depth, scope, range, and precision as compared to anything possible in earlier times. No heir of that scholarly
tradition should scoff at the faith of our predecessors, which inspired so much
toiling in archives.

Yet the limits of scientific history were far more constricting than its
devotees believed. Facts that could be established beyond all reasonable doubt
remained trivial in the sense that they did not, in and of themselves, give
meaning or intelligibility to the record of the past. A catalogue of undoubted
and indubitable information, even if arranged chronologically, remains a
catalogue. To become a history, facts have to be put together into a pattern that
is understandable and credible; and when that has been achieved, the resulting
portrait of the past may become useful as well—a font of practical wisdom
upon which people may draw when making decisions and taking action.

Pattern recognition of the sort historians engage in is the chef d'oeuvre of
human intelligence. It is achieved by paying selective attention to the total input
of stimuli that perpetually swarm in upon our consciousness. Only by leaving
things out, that is, relegating them to the status of background noise deserving
only to be disregarded, can what matters most in a given situation become recog-
nizable. Suitable action follows. Here is the great secret of human power over
nature and over ourselves as well. Pattern recognition is what natural scientists
are up to; it is what historians have always done, whether they knew it or not.

Only some facts matter for any given pattern. Otherwise, useless clutter
will obscure what we are after: perceptible relationships among important facts.
That and that alone constitutes an intelligible pattern, giving meaning to the
world, whether it be the world of physics and chemistry or the world of inter-
acting human groups through time, which historians take as their special
domain. Natural scientists are ruthless in selecting aspects of available sensory
inputs to pay attention to, disregarding all else. They call their patterns theories
and inherit most of them from predecessors. But, as we now know, even
Newton's truths needed adjustment. Natural science is neither eternal nor
universal; it is instead historical and evolutionary, because scientists accept a
new theory only when the new embraces a wider range of phenomena or
achieves a more elegant explanation of (selectively observed) facts than its
predecessor was able to do.

No comparably firm consensus prevails among historians. Yet we need
not despair. The great and obvious difference between natural scientists and historians is the greater complexity of the behavior historians seek to understand.
The principal source of historical complexity lies in the fact that human beings
react both to the natural world and to one another chiefly through the media-
tion of symbols. This means, among other things, that any theory about
human life, if widely believed, will alter actual behavior, usually by inducing
people to act as if the theory were true. Ideas and ideals thus become self-
validating within remarkably elastic limits. An extraordinary behavioral motility
results. Resort to symbols, in effect, loosened up the connection between external reality and human responses, freeing us from instinct by setting us adrift on
a sea of uncertainty. Human beings thereby acquired a new capacity to err, but
also to change, adapt, and learn new ways of doing things. Innumerable errors,

corrected by experience, eventually made us lords of creation as no other species on earth has ever been before.

The price of this achievement is the elastic, inexact character of truth, and especially of truths about human conduct. What a particular group of persons understands, believes, and acts upon, even if quite absurd to outsiders, may nonetheless cement social relations and allow the members of the group to act together and accomplish feats otherwise impossible. Moreover, membership in such a group and participation in its sufferings and triumphs give meaning and value to individual human lives. Any other sort of life is not worth living, for we are social creatures. As such we need to share truths with one another, and not just truths about atoms, stars, and molecules but about human relations and the people around us.

Shared truths that provide a sanction for common effort have obvious survival value. Without such social cement no group can long preserve itself. Yet to outsiders, truths of this kind are likely to seem myths, save in those (relatively rare) cases when the outsider is susceptible to conversion and finds a welcome within the particular group in question.

The historic record available to us consists of an unending appearance and dissolution of human groups, each united by its own beliefs, ideals, and traditions. Sects, religions, tribes, and states, from ancient Sumer and Pharaonic Egypt to modern times, have based their cohesion upon shared truths—truths that differed from time to time and place to place with a rich and reckless variety. Today the human community remains divided among an enormous number of different groups, each espousing its own version of truth about itself and about those excluded from its fellowship. Everything suggests that this sort of social and ideological fragmentation will continue indefinitely.

Where, in such a maelstrom of conflicting opinions, can we hope to locate historical truth? Where indeed?

Before modern communications thrust familiarity with the variety of human idea-systems upon our consciousness, this question was not particularly acute. Individuals nearly always grew up in relatively isolated communities to a more or less homogeneous world view. Important questions had been settled long ago by prophets and sages, so there was little reason to challenge or modify traditional wisdom. Indeed there were strong positive restraints upon any would-be innovator who threatened to upset the inherited consensus.

To be sure, climates of opinion fluctuated, but changes came surreptitiously, usually disguised as commentary upon old texts and purporting merely to explicate the original meanings. Flexibility was considerable, as the modern practice of the U.S. Supreme Court should convince us; but in this traditional ordering of intellect, all the same, outsiders who did not share the prevailing orthodoxy were shunned and disregarded when they could not be converted. Our predecessors' faith in a scientific method that would make written history absolutely and universally true was no more than a recent example of such a belief system. Those who embraced it felt no need to pay attention to ignoramuses who had not accepted the truths of "modern science." Like other true believers, they were therefore spared the task of taking others' viewpoints seriously or wondering about the limits of their own vision of historical truth.

But we are denied the luxury of such parochialism. We must reckon with multiplex, competing faiths—secular as well as transcendental, revolutionary as well as traditional—that resound amongst us. In addition, partially autonomous professional idea-systems have proliferated in the past century or so. Those most important to historians are the so-called social sciences—anthropology, sociology, political science, psychology, and economics—together with the newer disciplines of ecology and semeiology. But law, theology, and philosophy also pervade the field of knowledge with which historians may be expected to deal. On top of all this, innumerable individual authors, each with his own assortment of ideas and assumptions, compete for attention. Choice is everywhere; dissent turns into cacaphonous confusion; my truth dissolves into your myth even before I can put words on paper.

The liberal faith, of course, holds that in a free marketplace of ideas, Truth will eventually prevail. I am not ready to abandon that faith, however dismaying our present confusion may be. The liberal experiment, after all, is only about two hundred and fifty years old, and on the appropriate world-historical time scale that is too soon to be sure. Still, confusion is undoubted. Whether the resulting uncertainty will be bearable for large numbers of people in difficult times ahead is a question worth asking. Iranian Muslims, Russian communists, and American sectarians (religious and otherwise) all exhibit symptoms of acute distress in face of moral uncertainties, generated by exposure to competing truths. Clearly, the will to believe is as strong today as at any time in the past; and true believers nearly always wish to create a community of the faithful, so as to be able to live more comfortably, insulated from troublesome dissent.

The prevailing response to an increasingly cosmopolitan confusion has been intensified personal attachment, first to national and then to subnational groups, each with its own distinct ideals and practices. As one would expect, the historical profession faithfully reflected and helped to forward these shifts of sentiment. Thus, the founding fathers of the American Historical Association and their immediate successors were intent on facilitating the consolidation of a new American nation by writing national history in a WASPish mold, while also claiming affiliation with a tradition of Western civilization that ran back through modern and medieval Europe to the ancient Greeks and Hebrews. This version of our past was very widely repudiated in the 1960s, but iconoclastic revisionists felt no need to replace what they attacked with any architectonic vision of their own. Instead, scholarly energy concentrated on discovering the history of various segments of the population that had been left out or ill-treated by older historians: most notably women, blacks, and other ethnic minorities within the United States and the ex-colonial peoples of the world beyond the national borders.

Such activity conformed to our traditional professional role of helping to define collective identities in ambiguous situations. Consciousness of a common past, after all, is a powerful supplement to other ways of defining who "we" are. An oral tradition, sometimes almost undifferentiated from the practical wisdom embodied in language itself, is all people need in a stable social universe where in-group boundaries are self-evident. But with civilization, ambiguities multipled, and formal written history became useful in defining "us" versus "them." At first, the central ambiguity ran between rulers and ruled. Alien conquerors who lived on taxes collected from their subjects were at best a necessary evil when looked at from the bottom of civilized society. Yet in some situations, especially when confronting natural disaster or external attack, a case could be made for commonality, even between taxpayers and tax consumers. At any rate, histories began as king lists, royal genealogies, and boasts of divine favor—obvious ways of consolidating rulers' morale and asserting their legitimacy vis-à-vis their subjects. . . .

All human groups like to be flattered. Historians are therefore under perpetual temptation to conform to expectation by portraying the people they write about as they wish to be. A mingling of truth and falsehood, blending history with ideology, results. Historians are likely to select facts to show that we—whoever "we" may be—conform to our cherished principles: that we are free with Herodotus, or saved with Augustine, or oppressed with Marx, as the case may be. Grubby details indicating that the group fell short of its ideals can be skated over or omitted entirely. The result is mythical: the past as we want it to be, safely simplified into a contest between good guys and bad guys, "us" and "them." Most national history and most group history is of this kind, though the intensity of chiaroscuro varies greatly, and sometimes an historian turns traitor to the group he studies by setting out to unmask its pretensions. Groups struggling toward self-consciousness and groups whose accustomed status seems threatened are likely to demand (and get) vivid, simplified portraits of their admirable virtues and undeserved sufferings. Groups accustomed to power and surer of their internal cohesion can afford to accept more subtly modulated portraits of their successes and failures in bringing practice into conformity with principles.

Historians respond to this sort of market by expressing varying degrees of commitment to, and detachment from, the causes they chronicle and by infusing varying degrees of emotional intensity into their pages through particular choices of words. Truth, persuasiveness, intelligibility rest far more on this level of the historians' art than on source criticism. But, as I said at the beginning, one person's truth is another's myth, and the fact that a group of people accepts a given version of the past does not make that version any truer for outsiders.

Yet we cannot afford to reject collective self-flattery as silly, contemptible error. Myths are, after all, often self-validating. A nation or any other human group that knows how to behave in crisis situations because it has inherited a heroic historiographical tradition that tells how ancestors resisted their enemies successfully is more likely to act together effectively than a group lacking such a tradition. Great Britain's conduct in 1940 shows how world politics can be redirected by such a heritage. Flattering historiography does more than assist a given group to survive by affecting the balance of power among warring peoples, for an appropriately idealized version of the past may also allow a group of human beings to come closer to living up to its noblest ideals. What is can move toward what ought to be, given collective commitment to a flattering self-image. The American civil rights movement of the fifties and sixties illustrates this phenomenon amongst us.

These collective manifestations are of very great importance. Belief in the virtue and righteousness of one's cause is a necessary sort of self-delusion for human beings, singly and collectively. A corrosive version of history that emphasizes all the recurrent discrepancies between ideal and reality in a given group's behavior makes it harder for members of the group in question to act cohesively and in good conscience. That sort of history is very costly indeed. No group can afford it for long.

On the other hand, myths may mislead disastrously. A portrait of the past that denigrates others and praises the ideals and practice of a given group naively and without restraint can distort a people's image of outsiders so that foreign relations begin to consist of nothing but nasty surprises. Confidence in one's own high principles and good intentions may simply provoke others to resist duly accredited missionaries of the true faith, whatever that faith may be. Both the United States and the Soviet Union have encountered their share of this sort of surprise and disappointment ever since 1917, when Wilson and Lenin proclaimed their respective recipes for curing the world's ills. In more extreme cases, mythical, self-flattering versions of the past may push a people toward suicidal behavior, as Hitler's last days may remind us.

More generally, it is obvious that mythical, self-flattering versions of rival groups' pasts simply serve to intensify their capacity for conflict. With the recent quantum jump in the destructive power of weaponry, hardening of group cohesion at the sovereign state level clearly threatens the survival of humanity; while, within national borders, the civic order experiences new strains when subnational groups acquire a historiography replete with oppressors living next door and, perchance, still enjoying the fruits of past injustices.

The great historians have always responded to these difficulties by expanding their sympathies beyond narrow in-group boundaries. Herodotus set out to award a due meed of glory both to Hellenes and to the barbarians; Ranke inquired into what really happened to Protestant and Catholic, Latin and German nations alike. And other pioneers of our profession have likewise expanded the range of their sympathies and sensibilities beyond previously recognized limits without ever entirely escaping, or even wishing to escape, from the sort of partisanship involved in accepting the general assumptions and beliefs of a particular time and place.

Where to fix one's loyalties is the supreme question of human life and is especially acute in a cosmopolitan age like ours when choices abound. Belonging to a tightly knit group makes life worth living by giving individuals something beyond the self to serve and to rely on for personal guidance, companionship, and aid. But the stronger such bonds, the sharper the break with the rest of humanity. Group solidarity is always maintained, at least partly, by exporting psychic frictions across the frontiers, projecting animosities onto an outside foe in order to enhance collective cohesion within the group itself. Indeed, something to fear, hate, and attack is probably necessary for the full expression of human emotions; and ever since animal predators ceased to threaten, human beings have feared, hated, and fought one another.

Historians, by helping to define "us" and "them," play a considerable part in focusing love and hate, the two principal cements of collective behavior known to humanity. But myth making for rival groups has become a dangerous game in the atomic age, and we may well ask whether there is any alternative open to us.

In principle the answer is obvious. Humanity entire possesses a commonality which historians may hope to understand just as firmly as they can comprehend what unites any lesser group. Instead of enhancing conflicts, as parochial historiography inevitably does, an intelligible world history might be expected to diminish the lethality of group encounters by cultivating a sense of individual identification with the triumphs and tribulations of humanity as a whole. This, indeed, strikes me as the moral duty of the historical profession in our time. We need to develop an ecumenical history, with plenty of room for human diversity in all its complexity.

Yet a wise historian will not denigrate intense attachment to small groups. That is essential to personal happiness. In all civilized societies, a tangle of overlapping social groupings lays claim to human loyalties. Any one person may therefore be expected to have multiple commitments and plural public identities, up to and including membership in the human race and the wider DNA community of life on planet Earth. What we need to do as historians and as human beings is to recognize this complexity and balance our loyalties so that no one group will be able to command total commitment. Only so can we hope to make the world safer for all the different human groups that now exist and may come into existence.

The historical profession has, however, shied away from an ecumenical view of the human adventure. Professional career patterns reward specialization; and in all the well-trodden fields, where pervasive consensus on important matters has already been achieved, research and innovation necessarily concentrate upon minutiae. Residual faith that truth somehow resides in original documents confirms this direction of our energies. An easy and commonly unexamined corollary is the assumption that world history is too vague and too general to be true, that is, accurate to the sources. Truth, according to this view, is only attainable on a tiny scale when the diligent historian succeeds in exhausting the relevant documents before they exhaust the historian. But as my previous remarks have made clear, this does not strike me as a valid view of historical method. On the contrary, I call it naive and erroneous.

All truths are general. All truths abstract from the available assortment of data simply by using words, which in their very nature generalize so as to bring order to the incessantly fluctuating flow of messages in and messages out that constitutes human consciousness. Total reproduction of experience is impossible and undesirable. It would merely perpetuate the confusion we seek to escape. Historiography that aspires to get closer and closer to the documents—all the documents and nothing but the documents—is merely moving closer and closer to incoherence, chaos, and meaninglessness. That is a dead end for sure. No society will long support a profession that produces arcane trivia and calls it truth.

Fortunately for the profession, historians' practice has been better than their epistemology. Instead of replicating confusion by paraphrasing the totality of relevant and available documents, we have used our sources to discern, support, and reinforce group identities at national, transnational, and subnational levels and, once in a while, to attack or pick apart a group identity to which a school of revisionists has taken a scunner.

If we can now realize that our practice already shows how truths may be discerned at different levels of generality with equal precision simply because different patterns emerge on different time-space scales, then, perhaps, repugnance for world history might diminish and a juster proportion between parochial and ecumenical historiography might begin to emerge. It is our professional duty to move toward ecumenicity, however real the risks may seem to timid and unenterprising minds.

With a more rigorous and reflective epistemology, we might also attain a better historiographical balance between Truth, truths, and myth. Eternal and universal Truth about human behavior is an unattainable goal, however delectable as an ideal. Truths are what historians achieve when they bend their minds as critically and carefully as they can to the task of making their account of public affairs credible as well as intelligible to an audience that shares enough of their particular outlook and assumptions to accept what they say. The result might best be called mythistory perhaps (though I do not expect the term to catch on in professional circles), for the same words that constitute truth for some are, and always will be, myth for others, who inherit or embrace different assumptions and organizing concepts about the world.

This does not mean that there is no difference between one mythistory and another. Some clearly are more adequate to the facts than others. Some embrace more time and space and make sense of a wider variety of human behavior than others. And some, undoubtedly, offer a less treacherous basis for collective action than others. I actually believe that historians' truths, like those of scientists, evolve across the generations, so that versions of the past acceptable today are superior in scope, range, and accuracy to versions available in earlier times. But such evolution is slow, and observable only on an extended time scale, owing to the self-validating character of myth. Effective common action can rest on quite fantastic beliefs. *Credo quia absurdum* may even become a criterion for group membership, requiring initiates to surrender their critical faculties as a sign of full commitment to the common cause. Many sects have prospered on this principle and have served their members well for many generations while doing so.

But faiths, absurd or not, also face a long-run test of survival in a world where not everyone accepts any one set of beliefs and where human beings must interact with external objects and nonhuman forms of life, as well as with one another. Such "foreign relations" impose limits on what any group of people can safely believe and act on, since actions that fail to secure expected and desired results are always costly and often disastrous. Beliefs that mislead action are likely to be amended; too stubborn an adherence to a faith that encourages or demands hurtful behavior is likely to lead to the disintegration and disappearance of any group that refuses to learn from experience.

Thus one may, as an act of faith, believe that our historiographical myth making and myth breaking is bound to cumulate across time, propagating mythistories that fit experience better and allow human survival more often, sustaining in-groups in ways that are less destructive to themselves and to their neighbors than was once the case or is the case today. If so, ever-evolving mythistories will indeed become truer and more adequate to public life, emphasizing the really important aspects of human encounters and omitting irrelevant background noise more efficiently so that men and women will know how to act more wisely than is possible for us today.

This is not a groundless hope. Future historians are unlikely to leave out blacks and women from any future mythistory of the United States, and we are unlikely to exclude Asians, Africans, and Amerindians from any future mythistory of the world. One hundred years ago this was not so. The scope and range of historiography has widened, and that change looks as irreversible to me as the widening of physics that occurred when Einstein's equations proved capable of explaining phenomena that Newton's could not.

It is far less clear whether in widening the range of our sensibilities and taking a broader range of phenomena into account we also see deeper into the reality we seek to understand. But we may. Anyone who reads historians of the sixteenth and seventeenth centuries and those of our own time will notice a new awareness of social process that we have attained. As one who shares that awareness, I find it impossible not to believe that it represents an advance on older notions that focused attention exclusively, or almost exclusively, on human intentions and individual actions, subject only to God or to a no less inscrutable Fortune, while leaving out the social and material context within which individual actions took place simply because that context was assumed to be uniform and unchanging.

Still, what seems wise and true to me seems irrelevant obfuscation to others. Only time can settle the issue, presumably by outmoding my ideas and my critics' as well. Unalterable and eternal Truth remains like the Kingdom of Heaven, an eschatological hope. Mythistory is what we actually have—a useful instrument for piloting human groups in their encounters with one another and with the natural environment.

To be a truth-seeking mythographer is therefore a high and serious calling, for what a group of people knows and believes about the past channels expectations and affects the decisions on which their lives, their fortunes, and their sacred honor all depend. Formal written histories are not the only shapers of a people's notions about the past; but they are sporadically powerful, since even the most abstract and academic historiographical ideas do trickle down to the level of the commonplace, if they fit both what a people want to hear and what a people need to know well enough to be useful.

As members of society and sharers in the historical process, historians can only expect to be heard if they say what the people around them want to hear—in some degree. They can only be useful if they also tell the people some things they are reluctant to hear—in some degree. Piloting between this Scylla and Charybdis is the art of the serious historian, helping the group he or she addresses and celebrates to survive and prosper in a treacherous and changing world by knowing more about itself and others.

Academic historians have pursued that art with extraordinary energy and considerable success during the past century. May our heirs and successors persevere and do even better!

POSTSCRIPT

Is History True?

Closely associated to the question of historical truth is the matter of historical objectivity. Frequently, we hear people begin statements with the phrase "History tells us . . ." or "History shows that . . . ," followed by a conclusion that reflects the speaker or writer's point of view. In fact, history does not directly tell or show us anything. That is the job of historians, and as William McNeill argues, much of what historians tell us, despite their best intentions, often represents a blending of historical evidence and myth.

Is there such a thing as a truly objective history? Historian Paul Conkin agrees with McNeill that objectivity is possible only if the meaning of that term is sharply restricted and is not used as a synonym for certain truth. History, Conkin writes, "is a story about the past; it is not the past itself. . . . Whether one draws a history from the guidance of memory or of monuments, it cannot exactly mirror some directly experienced past nor the feelings and perceptions of people in the past." He concludes, "In this sense, much of history is a stab into partial darkness, a matter of informed but inconclusive conjecture. . . . Obviously, in such areas of interpretation, there is no one demonstrably correct 'explanation,' but very often competing, equally unfalsifiable, theories. Here, on issues that endlessly fascinate the historian, the controversies rage, and no one expects, short of a great wealth of unexpected evidence, to find a conclusive answer. An undesired, abstractive precision of the subject might so narrow it as to permit more conclusive evidence. But this would spoil all the fun." For more discussion on this and other topics related to the study of history, see Paul K. Conkin and Roland N. Stromberg, *The Heritage and Challenge of History* (Dodd, Mead & Company, 1971).

The most thorough discussion of historical objectivity in the United States is Peter Novick, *That Noble Dream: The 'Objectivity Question' and the American Historical Profession* (Cambridge University Press, 1988), which draws its title from Charles A. Beard's article in the *American Historical Review* (October 1935) in which Beard reinforced the views expressed in his 1933 presidential address to the American Historical Association. [See "Written History as an Act of Faith," *American Historical Review* (January 1934).] Novick's thorough analysis generated a great deal of attention, the results of which can be followed in James T. Kloppenberg, "Objectivity and Historicism: A Century of American Historical Writing," *American Historical Review* (October 1989), Thomas L. Haskell, "Objectivity Is Not Neutrality: Rhetoric vs. Practice in Peter Novick's *That Noble Dream*," *History & Theory* (1990), and the scholarly forum "Peter Novick's *That Noble Dream*: The Objectivity Question and the Future of the Historical Profession," *American Historical Review* (June 1991). A critique of recent historical writing that closely follows the concerns expressed by Handlin can be found in Keith Windschuttle, *The Killing of History: How Literary Critics and Social Theorists Are Murdering Our Past* (The Free Press, 1996).

Readers interested in this subject will also find the analyses in Barbara W. Tuchman, *Practicing History: Selected Essays* (Alfred A. Knopf, 1981) and David Hackett Fischer, *Historians' Fallacies: Toward a Logic of Historical Thought* (Harper & Row, 1970) to be quite stimulating. Earlier, though equally rewarding, volumes include Harvey Wish, *The American Historian: A Social-Intellectual History of the Writing of the American Past* (Oxford University Press, 1960), John Higham, with Leonard Krieger and Felix Gilbert, *History: The Development of Historical Studies in the United States* (Prentice-Hall, 1965), and Marcus Cunliffe and Robin Winks, eds., *Pastmasters: Some Essays on American Historians* (Harper & Row, 1969).

ISSUE 2

Was Columbus an Imperialist?

YES: Kirkpatrick Sale, from *The Conquest of Paradise: Christopher Columbus and the Columbian Legacy* (Alfred A. Knopf, 1990)

NO: Robert Royal, from *1492 and All That: Political Manipulations of History* (Ethics and Public Policy Center, 1992)

ISSUE SUMMARY

YES: Kirkpatrick Sale, a contributing editor of *The Nation*, characterizes Christopher Columbus as an imperialist who was determined to conquer both the land and the people he encountered during his first voyage to the Americas in 1492.

NO: Robert Royal, vice president for research at the Ethics and Public Policy Center, objects to Columbus's modern-day critics and insists that Columbus should be admired for his courage, his willingness to take a risk, and his success in advancing knowledge about other parts of the world.

On October 12, 1492, Christopher Columbus, a Genoese mariner sailing under the flag and patronage of the Spanish monarchy, made landfall on a tropical Caribbean island, which he subsequently named San Salvador. This action established for Columbus the fame of having discovered the New World and, by extension, America. Of course, this "discovery" was ironic since Columbus and his crew members were not looking for a new world but, instead, a very old one—the much-fabled Orient. By sailing westward instead of eastward, Columbus was certain that he would find a shorter route to China. He did not anticipate that the land mass of the Americas would prevent him from reaching this goal or that his "failure" would guarantee his fame for centuries thereafter.

Columbus's encounter with indigenous peoples, whom he named "Indians" (*los indios*), presented further proof that Europeans had not discovered America. These "Indians" were descendants of the first people who migrated from Asia at least 30,000 years earlier and fanned out in a southeasterly direction until they populated much of North and South America. By the time Columbus arrived, Native Americans numbered approximately 40 million, 3 million of whom resided in the continental region north of Mexico.

None of this, however, should dilute the significance of Columbus's explorations, which were representative of a wave of Atlantic voyages emanating from Europe in the fifteenth, sixteenth, and seventeenth centuries. Spawned by the intellectual ferment of the Renaissance in combination with the rise of the European nation-state, these voyages of exploration were made possible by advances in shipbuilding, improved navigational instruments and cartography, the desirability of long-distance commerce, support from ruling monarchs, and the courage and ambition of the explorers themselves.

Columbus's arrival (and return on three separate occasions between 1494 and 1502) possessed enormous implications not only for the future development of the United States but for the Western Hemisphere as a whole, as well as for Europe and Africa. These consequences attracted a significant amount of scholarly and media attention in 1992 in connection with the quincentennial celebration of Columbus's first arrival on American shores and sparked often acrimonious debate over the true meaning of Columbus's legacy. Many wished to use the occasion to emphasize the positive accomplishments of Europe's contact with the New World. Others sought to clarify some of the negative results of Columbus's voyages, particularly as they related to European confrontations with Native Americans.

This debate provides the context for the selections that follow. To what extent should we applaud Columbus's exploits? Are there reasons that we should question the purity of Columbus's motivations? Did the European "discovery" of America do more harm than good?

In the first selection, Kirkpatrick Sale treats Columbus's arrival as an invasion of the land and the indigenous peoples that he encountered. By assigning European names to virtually everything he observed, Columbus, according to Sale, was taking possession on behalf of the Spanish monarchy. Similarly, one of Columbus's major goals was to build and arm a fortress by which he could carry out the subjugation and enslavement of the native population. Columbus's policies of conquest, religious conversion, settlement, and exploitation of natural resources were an example of European imperialism.

In the second selection, Robert Royal rejects the argument that Columbus was motivated by European arrogance and avarice. He also disputes the notion that Columbus was driven by a desire for gold or by racist assumptions of Native American inferiority. Royal asserts that Columbus exhibited genuine concern for justice in his contacts with the Native Americans and concludes that Columbus, though not without his faults, merits the admiration traditionally accorded his accomplishments.

1492–93

Admiral [Cristóbal] Colón [Christopher Columbus] spent a total of ninety-six days exploring the lands he encountered on the far side of the Ocean Sea—four rather small coralline islands in the Bahamian chain and two substantial coastlines of what he finally acknowledged were larger islands—every one of which he "took possession of" in the name of his Sovereigns.

The first he named San Salvador, no doubt as much in thanksgiving for its welcome presence after more than a month at sea as for the Son of God whom it honored; the second he called Santa María de la Concepcíon, after the Virgin whose name his flagship bore; and the third and fourth he called Fernandina and Isabela, for his patrons, honoring Aragon before Castile for reasons never explained (possibly protocol, possibly in recognition of the chief sources of backing for the voyage). The first of the two large and very fertile islands he called Juana, which Fernando says was done in honor of Prince Juan, heir to the Castilian throne, but just as plausibly might have been done in recognition of Princess Juana, the unstable child who eventually carried on the line; the second he named la Ysla Española, the "Spanish Island," because it resembled (though he felt it surpassed in beauty) the lands of Castile.

It was not that the islands were in need of names, mind you, nor indeed that Colón was ignorant of the names the native peoples had already given them, for he frequently used those original names before endowing them with his own. Rather, the process of bestowing new names went along with "taking possession of" those parts of the world he deemed suitable for Spanish ownership, showing the royal banners, erecting various crosses and pronouncing certain oaths and pledges. If this was presumption, it had an honored heritage: it was Adam who was charged by his Creator with the task of naming "every living creature," including the product of his own rib, in the course of establishing "dominion over" them.

Colón went on to assign no fewer than sixty-two other names on the geography of the islands—capes, points, mountains, ports—with a blithe assurance suggesting that in his (and Europe's) perception the act of name-giving was in some sense a talisman of conquest, a rite that changed raw neutral stretches of far-off earth into extensions of Europe. The process began slowly, even haltingly—he forgot to record, for example, until four days afterward that he named the landfall island San Salvador—but by the time he came to

From Kirkpatrick Sale, *The Conquest of Paradise: Christopher Columbus and the Columbian Legacy* (Alfred A. Knopf, 1990). Copyright © 1990 by Kirkpatrick Sale. Reprinted by permission of Alfred A. Knopf, a division of Random House, Inc. Notes omitted.

Española at the end he went on a naming spree, using more than two-thirds of all the titles he concocted on that one coastline. On certain days it became almost a frenzy: on December 6 he named six places, on the nineteenth six more, and on January 11 no fewer than ten—eight capes, a point, and a mountain. It is almost as if, as he sailed along the last of the islands, he was determined to leave his mark on it the only way he knew how, and thus to establish his authority—and by extension Spain's—even, as with baptism, to make it thus sanctified, and real, and official. (One should note that it was only his *own* naming that conveyed legitimacy: when Colón thought Martín Alonso Pinzón had named a river after himself, he immediately renamed it Río de Gracia instead.)

This business of naming and "possessing" foreign islands was by no means casual. The Admiral took it very seriously, pointing out that "it was my wish to bypass no island without taking possession" (October 15) and that "in all regions [I] always left a cross standing" (November 16) as a mark of Christian dominance. There even seem to have been certain prescriptions for it (the instructions from the Sovereigns speak of "the administering of the oath and the performing of the rites prescribed in such cases"), and Rodrigo de Escobedo was sent along as secretary of the fleet explicitly to witness and record these events in detail.

But consider the implications of this act and the questions it raises again about what was in the Sovereigns' minds, what in Colón's. Why would the Admiral assume that these territories were in some way *un*possessed—even by those clearly inhabiting them—and thus available for Spain to claim? Why would he not think twice about the possibility that some considerable potentate—the Grand Khan of China, for example, whom he later acknowledged (November 6) "must be" the ruler of Española—might descend upon him at any moment with a greater military force than his three vessels commanded and punish him for his territorial presumption? Why would he make the ceremony of possession his very first act on shore, even before meeting the inhabitants or exploring the environs, or finding out if anybody there objected to being thus possessed—particularly if they actually owned the great treasures he hoped would be there? No European would have imagined that anyone—three small boatloads of Indians, say—could come up to a European shore or island and "take possession" of it, nor would a European imagine marching up to some part of North Africa or the Middle East and claiming sovereignty there with impunity. Why were these lands thought to be different?

Could there be any reason for the Admiral to assume he had reached "unclaimed" shores, new lands that lay far from the domains of any of the potentates of the East? Can that really have been in his mind—or can it all be explained as simple Eurocentrism, or Eurosuperiority, mixed with cupidity and naiveté?

In any case, it is quite curious how casually and calmly the Admiral took to this task of possession, so much so that he gave only the most meager description of the initial ceremony on San Salvador, despite its having been a signal event in his career. He recorded merely that he went ashore in his longboat, armed, followed by the captains of the two caravels, accompanied by royal standards and banners and two representatives of the court to "witness how he before them all was taking, as in fact he took, possession of the said island for the King and Queen." He added that he made "the declarations that are required, as is contained at greater length in the testimonies which were there taken down in writing," but he unfortunately didn't specify what these were and no such documents survive; we are left only with the image of a party of fully dressed and armored Europeans standing there on the white sand in the blazing morning heat while Escobedo, with his parchment and inkpot and quill, painstakingly writes down the Admiral's oaths.

Fernando Colón did enlarge on this scene, presumably on the authority of his imagination alone, describing how the little party then "rendered thanks to Our Lord, kneeling on the ground and kissing it with tears of joy for His great favor to them," after which the crew members "swore obedience" to the Admiral "with such a show of pleasure and joy" and "begged his pardon for the injuries that through fear and little faith they had done him." He added that these goings-on were performed in the presence of the "many natives assembled there," whose reactions are not described and whose opinions are not recorded. . . .

Once safely "possessed," San Salvador was open for inspection. Now the Admiral turned his attention for the first time to the "naked people" staring at him on the beach—he did not automatically give them a name, interestingly enough, and it would be another six days before he decided what he might call them—and tried to win their favor with his trinkets.

> They all go around as naked as their mothers bore them; and also the women, although I didn't see more than one really young girl. All that I saw were young people [*mancebos*], none of them more than 30 years old. They are very well built, with very handsome bodies and very good faces; their hair [is] coarse, almost like the silk of a horse's tail, and short. They wear their hair over their eyebrows, except for a little in the back that they wear long and never cut. Some of them paint themselves black (and they are of the color of the Canary Islanders, neither black nor white), and some paint themselves white, and some red, and some with what they find. And some paint their faces, and some of them the whole body, and some the eyes only, and some of them only the nose.

It may fairly be called the birth of American anthropology.

A crude anthropology, of course, as superficial as Colón's descriptions always were when his interest was limited, but simple and straightforward enough, with none of the fable and fantasy that characterized many earlier (and even some later) accounts of new-found peoples. There was no pretense to objectivity, or any sense that these people might be representatives of a culture equal to, or in any way a model for, Europe's. Colón immediately presumed the inferiority of the natives, not merely because (a sure enough sign) they were naked, but because (his society could have no surer measure) they seemed so technologically backward. "It appeared to me that these people were very poor in everything," he wrote on that first day, and, worse still, "they have no iron." And they went on to prove their inferiority to the Admiral by being ignorant of even such a basic artifact of European life as a sword: "They bear no arms, nor are they acquainted with them," he wrote, "for I showed them swords and they grasped them by the blade and cut themselves through ignorance." Thus did European arms spill the first drops of native blood on the sands of the New World, accompanied not with a gasp of compassion but with a smirk of superiority.

Then, just six sentences further on, Colón clarified what this inferiority meant in his eyes:

> They ought to be good servants and of good intelligence [*ingenio*]. . . . I believe that they would easily be made Christians, because it seemed to me that they had no religion. Our Lord pleasing, I will carry off six of them at my departure to Your Highnesses, in order that they may learn to speak.

No clothes, no arms, no possessions, no iron, and now no religion—not even speech: hence they were fit to be servants, and captives. It may fairly be called the birth of American slavery.

Whether or not the idea of slavery was in Colón's mind all along is uncertain, although he did suggest he had had experience as a slave trader in Africa (November 12) and he certainly knew of Portuguese plantation slavery in the Madeiras and Spanish slavery of Guanches in the Canaries. But it seems to have taken shape early and grown ever firmer as the weeks went on and as he captured more and more of the helpless natives. At one point he even sent his crew ashore to kidnap "seven head of women, young ones and adults, and three small children"; the expression of such callousness led the Spanish historian Salvador de Madariaga to remark, "It would be difficult to find a starker utterance of utilitarian subjection of man by man than this passage [whose] form is no less devoid of human feeling than its substance."

To be sure, Colón knew nothing about these people he encountered and considered enslaving, and he was hardly trained to find out very much, even if he was moved to care. But they were in fact members of an extensive, populous, and successful people whom Europe, using its own peculiar taxonomy, subsequently called "Taino" (or "Taíno"), their own word for "good" or "noble," and their response when asked who they were. They were related distantly by both language and culture to the Arawak people of the South American mainland, but it is misleading (and needlessly imprecise) to call them Arawaks, as historians are wont to do, when the term "Taino" better establishes their ethnic and historical distinctiveness. They had migrated to the islands from the mainland at about the time of the birth of Christ, occupying the three large islands we now call the Greater Antilles and arriving at Guanahani (Colón's San Salvador) and the end of the Bahamian chain probably sometime around A.D. 900. There they displaced an earlier people, the Guanahacabibes (sometimes called Guanahatabeys), who by the time of the European discovery occupied only the western third of Cuba and possibly remote corners of Española; and there, probably in the early fifteenth century, they eventually confronted another people moving up the islands from the mainland, the Caribs, whose culture eventually occupied a dozen small islands of what are called the Lesser Antilles.

The Tainos were not nearly so backward as Colón assumed from their lack of dress. (It might be said that it was the Europeans, who generally kept clothed head to foot during the day despite temperatures regularly in the eighties, who were the more unsophisticated in garmenture—especially since the Tainos, as Colón later noted, also used their body paint to prevent sunburn.) Indeed, they had achieved a means of living in a balanced and fruitful harmony with their natural surroundings that any society might well have envied. They had, to begin with, a not unsophisticated technology that made exact use of their available resources, two parts of which were so impressive that they were picked up and adopted by the European invaders: *canoa* (canoes) that were carved and fire-burned from large silk-cotton trees, "all in one piece, and wonderfully made" (October 13), some of which were capable of carrying up to 150 passengers; and *hamaca* (hammocks) that were "like nets of cotton" (October 17) and may have been a staple item of trade with Indian tribes as far away as the Florida mainland. Their houses were not only spacious and clean— as the Europeans noted with surprise and appreciation, used as they were to the generally crowded and slovenly hovels and huts of south European peasantry—but more apropos, remarkably resistant to hurricanes; the circular walls were made of strong cane poles set deep and close together ("as close as the fingers of a hand," Colón noted), the conical roofs of branches and vines tightly interwoven on a frame of smaller poles and covered with heavy palm leaves. Their artifacts and jewelry, with the exception of a few gold trinkets and ornaments, were based largely on renewable materials, including bracelets and necklaces of coral, shells, bone, and stone, embroidered cotton belts, woven baskets, carved statues and chairs, wooden and shell utensils, and pottery of variously intricate decoration depending on period and place.

Perhaps the most sophisticated, and most carefully integrated, part of their technology was their agricultural system, extraordinarily productive and perfectly adapted to the conditions of the island environment. It was based primarily on fields of knee-high mounds, called *conucos,* planted with *yuca* (sometimes called manioc), *batata* (sweet potato), and various squashes and beans grown all together in multicrop harmony: the root crops were excellent in resisting erosion and producing minerals and potash, the leaf crops effective in providing shade and moisture, and the mound configurations largely resistant to erosion and flooding and adaptable to almost all topographic conditions including steep hillsides. Not only was the *conuco* system environmentally appropriate—"conuco agriculture seems to have provided an exceptionally ecologically well-balanced and protective form of land use," according to David Watts's recent and authoritative *West Indies*—but it was also highly productive, surpassing in yields anything known in Europe at the time, with labor that amounted to hardly more than two or three hours a week, and in continuous yearlong harvest. The pioneering American geographical scholar Carl Sauer calls Taino agriculture "productive as few parts of the world," giving the "highest returns of food in continuous supply by the simplest methods and modest labor," and adds, with a touch of regret, "The white man never fully appreciated the excellent combination of plants that were grown in conucos."

In their arts of government the Tainos seem to have achieved a parallel sort of harmony. Most villages were small (ten to fifteen families) and autonomous, although many apparently recognized loose allegiances with neighboring villages, and they were governed by a hereditary official called a *kaseke* (*cacique*, in the Spanish form), something of a cross between an arbiter and a prolocutor, supported by advisers and elders. So little a part did violence play in their system that they seem, remarkably, to have been a society without war (at least we know of no war music or signals or artifacts, and no evidence of intertribal combats) and even without overt conflict (Las Casas reports that no Spaniard ever saw two Tainos fighting). And here we come to what was obviously the Tainos' outstanding cultural achievement, a proficiency in the social arts that led those who first met them to comment unfailingly on their friendliness, their warmth, their openness, and above all—so striking to those of an acquisitive culture—their generosity.

"They are the best people in the world and above all the gentlest," Colón recorded in his *Journal* (December 16), and from first to last he was astonished at their kindness:

> They became so much our friends that it was a marvel. . . . They traded and gave everything they had, with good will [October 12].
>
> I sent the ship's boat ashore for water, and they very willingly showed my people where the water was, and they themselves carried the full barrels to the boat, and took great delight in pleasing us [October 16].
>
> They are very gentle and without knowledge of what is evil; nor do they murder or steal [November 12].
>
> Your Highnesses may believe that in all the world there can be no better or gentler people . . . for neither better people nor land can there be. . . . All the people show the most singular loving behavior and they speak pleasantly [December 24].
>
> I assure Your Highnesses that I believe that in all the world there is no better people nor better country. They love their neighbors as themselves, and they have the sweetest talk in the world, and are gentle and always laughing [December 25].

Even if one allows for some exaggeration—Colón was clearly trying to convince Ferdinand and Isabella that his Indians could be easily conquered and converted, should that be the Sovereigns' wish—it is obvious that the Tainos exhibited a manner of social discourse that quite impressed the rough Europeans. But that was not high among the traits of "civilized" nations, as Colón and Europe understood it, and it counted for little in the Admiral's assessment of these people. However struck he was with such behavior, he would not have thought that it was the mark of a benign and harmonious society, or that from it another culture might learn. For him it was something like the wondrous behavior of children, the naive guilelessness of prelapsarian creatures who knew no better how to bargain and chaffer and cheat than they did to dress themselves: "For a lace-point they gave good pieces of gold the size of two fingers" (January 6), and "They even took pieces of the broken hoops of the wine casks and, like beasts [*como besti*], gave what they had" (Santangel Letter). Like beasts; such innocence was not human.

It is to be regretted that the Admiral, unable to see past their nakedness, as it were, knew not the real virtues of the people he confronted. For the Tainos' lives were in many ways as idyllic as their surroundings, into which they fit with such skill and comfort. They were well fed and well housed, without poverty or serious disease. They enjoyed considerable leisure, given over to dancing, singing, ballgames, and sex, and expressed themselves artistically in basketry, woodworking, pottery, and jewelry. They lived in general harmony and peace, without greed or covetousness or theft. In short, as Sauer says, "the tropical idyll of the accounts of Columbus and Peter Martyr was largely true." . . .

One of the alternative possibilities for future Spanish glory in these none too promising islands suggested itself to Colón almost from the first. On his third day of exploration—a Sunday at that—he had set out to see "where there might be a fortress [built]" and in no time at all found a spit of land on which "there might be a fortress"—and from which "with fifty men they [the Tainos] could all be subjected and made to do all that one might wish" (October 14). Now, during the second leg of exploration along the north coast of Cuba, this grew into a full-blown fantasy of a colonial outpost, complete with a rich trade and merchants. And so Colón went on, rather like a young boy playing soldiers, turning various pieces of landscape into military sites: Puerto de Mares on November 5, a harbor for "a store and a fortress" on November 12, another harbor where "a fortress could be erected" on November 16, a placed where "a town or city and fortress" could be built on November 27—until finally, as we shall see, misfortune enabled him to translate his fancy into reality.

Now there was no particular reason to go about constructing fortresses— "I don't see that it would be necessary, because these people are very unskilled in arms" (October 14)—but that was the way his architectural imagination, suffused with his vision of colonial destiny, seemed to work: a spit of land, a promontory, a protected harbor, and right away he saw a fort. Such was the deeply ingrained militarism of fifteenth-century Europe, in which fortresses represent edifices more essential to civilization even than churches or castles.

It may have been that Colón began his explorations with nothing more than an idea of establishing some sort of entrepôt in these islands, a fortress protected trading post rather like the one the Portuguese had established, and Colón had perhaps visited, on the Gold Coast of Africa, at El Mina. But as he sailed along the coast of Cuba he seems to have contrived something even grander, not just a trading port but an outright colonial settlement, an outpost of empire where Spaniards would settle and prosper, living off the labor of the natives ("Command them to do what you will," December 16) and the trade of the Europeans.

On November 27, toward the end of his sojourn along Cuba, Colón put into a large "very singular harbor" which he named Puerto Santo (today known as Puerto Baracoa, about a hundred miles from the eastern tip of the island) and was nearly speechless at its tropical splendor: "Truly, I was so astounded at the sight of so much beauty that I know not how to express myself." The vision of conquest, however, loosened his tongue, and at great length, too:

> And Your Highnesses will command a city and fortress to be built in these parts, and these lands converted; and I assure Your Highnesses that it seems to me that there could never be under the sun [lands] superior in fertility, in mildness of cold and heat, in abundance of good and healthy water. . . . So may it please God that Your Highnesses will send here, or that there will come, learned men and they will see the truth of all. And although before I have spoken of the site of a town and fortress on the Rio de Mares . . . yet there is no comparing that place with this here or with the Mar de Nuestra Señora; for inland here must be great settlements and innumerable people and things of great profit; for here, and in all else that I have discovered and have hopes of discovering before I return to Castile, I say that all Christendom will do business [*dad negociaçion*] with them, but most of all Spain, to which all this should be subject. And I say that Your Highnesses ought not to consent that any foreigner trade or set foot here except Catholic Christians, since this was the end and the beginning of the enterprise [*proposito*], that it was for the enhancement and glory of the Christian religion, nor should anyone who is not a good Christian come to these parts.

It may fairly be called the birth of European colonialism.

Here, for the first time that we know, are the outlines of the policy that not only Spain but other European countries would indeed adopt in the years to come, complete with conquest, religious conversion, city settlements, fortresses, exploitation, international trade, and exclusive domain. And that colonial policy would be very largely responsible for endowing those countries with the pelf, power, patronage, and prestige that allowed them to become the nation-states they did.

Again, one is at a loss to explain quite why Colón would so casually assume a right to the conquest and colonialization, even the displacement and enslavement, of these peaceful and inoffensive people 3,000 miles across the ocean. Except, of course, insofar as might, in European eyes, made that right, and after all "they bear no arms, and are all naked and of no skill in arms, and so very cowardly that a thousand would not stand against [*aguardariá*] three" (December 16). But assume it he did, and even Morison suggests that "every man in the fleet from servant boy to Admiral was convinced that no Christian need do a hand's turn of work in the Indies; and before them opened the delightful vision of growing rich by exploiting the labor of docile natives." The Admiral at least had no difficulty in seeing the Tainos in this light: "They are fit to be ordered about and made to work, to sow and do everything else that may be needed" (December 16); "nothing was lacking but to know the language and to give them orders, because all that they are ordered to do they will do without opposition" (December 21).

Missed in the dynamics of the assumed right of colonialism was an extraordinary opportunity, had it only been possible for the Christian intruders to know it, an opportunity for a dispirited and melancholy Europe to have learned something about fecundity and regeneration, about social comeliness and amity, about harmony with the natural world. The appropriate architecture for Colón to have envisioned along these shores might have been a forum, or an amphitheater, or an academy, perhaps an auditorium or a tabernacle; instead, a fortress. . . .

Originally, so he tells us (October 19), Colón had planned to return to Castile sometime in April, when, he presumably knew from his earlier travels, the North Atlantic would be past its winter storm season. But now, after the wreck of the *Santa María* and with news that the *Pinta* was not far away, he apparently decided to sail back immediately. It was a risky decision and most unseamanlike—as he would soon discover, when he was blown off course and almost capsized by two fierce storms in February and March—that leads one to assume that the Admiral's need was dire. Yet all he ever said, a few days later, was that he intended to head back home "without detaining himself further," because "he had found that which he was seeking" (January 9) and intended "to come at full speed to carry the news" (January 8). . . .

Whatever the reasons for his haste, the Admiral certainly made his way along the remainder of the island's coast with great alacrity, and little more than a week after he met up with Pinzón, the two caravels were off on the homeward leg. Only one notable stop was made, at a narrow bay some 200 miles east of La Navidad, where a party Colón sent ashore discovered, for the first time, some Indians with bows and arrows.

The Admiral having given standing orders that his men should buy or barter away the weaponry of the Indians—they had done so on at least two previous occasions, presumably without causing enmity—these men in the longboat began to dicker with the bowmen with the plumes. After just two bows were sold, the Indians turned and ran back to the cover of the trees where they kept their remaining weapons and, so the sailors assumed, "prepared . . . to attack the Christians and capture them." When they came toward the Spaniards again brandishing ropes—almost certainly meaning to trade these rather than give up their precious bows—the sailors panicked and, "being prepared as always the Admiral advised them to be," attacked the Indians with swords and halberds, gave one "a great slash on the buttocks" and shot another in the breast with a crossbow. The Tainos grabbed their fallen comrades and fled in fright, and the sailors would have chased them and "killed many of them" but for the pilot in charge of the party, who somehow "prevented it." It may fairly be called the first pitched battle between Europeans and Indians in the New World—the first display of the armed power, and the will to use it, of the white invaders.

And did the Admiral object to this, transgressing as it did his previous idea of trying to maintain good relations with the natives so as to make them willing trading partners, if not docile servants? Hardly at all: now, he said, "they would have fear of the Christians," and he celebrated the skirmish by naming the cape and the harbor de las Flechas—of the Arrows.

It was not the first time (or the last) that Colón was able to delude himself—it may indeed have been a European assumption—that violence can buy obedience. Twice before, he had used a display of European arms to frighten the Tainos, to no purpose other than instilling more fear and awe than they already felt: once on December 26, when he had a Turkish longbow, a gun [*espingarda*], and a lombard demonstrated, at which occasion the people "all fell to earth" in terror and the *kaseke* "was astonished"; then again on the eve of his departure from La Navidad, when he ordered a lombard fired from the new fortress out at the remains of the *Santa María* so that Guacanagarí, when he saw "how it pierced the side of the ship and how the ball went far out to sea," would then "hold the Christians whom [Colón] left behind as friends" and be so scared "that he might fear them." Strange behavior at any time; toward this softhearted *kaseke* and his kindly people, almost inexplicable.

NO

Robert Royal

El Almirante

Let us hear what their comments are now those who are so ready with accusations and quick to find fault, saying from their safe berths there in Spain, Why didn t you do this or that when you were over there." I d like to see their sort on this adventure. Verily I believe, there s another journey, of quite a different order, for them to make, or all our faith is vain.

— Columbus
Lettera Rarissima

After centuries of controversies, the life of Columbus lies beneath mountains of interpretation and misinterpretation. Sharp criticism of *El Almirante* (the admiral)—and sharp reaction to it—go back to the very beginnings of his explorations, as the passage cited above, written at a particularly threatening moment during Columbus's fourth and final voyage to the New World, graphically shows. Then, as now, it was easy for people who had never dared comparable feats to suggest how the whole business might have been done better. And in truth, Columbus's manifest errors and downright incapacities as a leader of men, anywhere but on the sea, played into the hands of his critics and properly made him the target of protests. His failures in leadership provoked atrocities against the Caribbean natives and harsh punishment, including executions, of Spaniards as well. Stubbornness, obsessiveness, and paranoia often dominated his psyche. Even many of his closest allies in the initial ventures clashed with him over one thing or another. In the wake of the titanic passions his epochal voyages unleashed, it is no wonder that almost every individual and event connected with his story has been praised or damned by someone during the past five hundred years. . . .

Fact and Imagination

The temptation to project modern categories back upon earlier historical periods is always strong. Reviewing these first late-fifteenth-century contacts now, with knowledge of what befell indigenous peoples later, we are particularly inclined to read large-scale portents into small events. If Columbus mentions how easy it would be to subdue the natives, or expresses impatience with his failure to find the high and rich civilization of Asia, many historians readily fall into the error of seeing his attitudes as a combination of careless imperialism and greed, or even as a symbol of all that was to follow. We would do well to recall, however, that the Spanish record after Columbus is complex and not wholly bad, particularly in its gradual elaboration of native rights.

In Columbus the man, several conflicting currents existed side by side. [Bartolomé de] Las Casas is an important witness here because of both his passionate commitment to justice for Indians and his personal association with Columbus for several years. In a telling remark, Las Casas notes that while Christopher's brother, Bartolomé, was a resolute leader, he lacked the "sweetness and benignity" of the admiral. Columbus's noble bearing and gentle manners are confirmed in many other sources. Nevertheless, Las Casas can be harsh in his criticism. Chapter 119 of *History of the Indies* concludes with the judgment that both brothers mistakenly began to occupy land and exact tribute owing to "the most culpable ignorance, which has no excuse, of natural and divine law."

After five hundred years it may seem impossible to reconcile the contradictory traits Las Casas mentions. He attempted an explanation of his own:

> Truly, I would not dare blame the admiral's intentions, for I knew him well and I know his intentions were good. But . . . the road he paved and the things he did of his own free will, as well as sometimes under constraint, stemmed from his ignorance of the law. There is much to ponder here and one can see the guiding principle of this whole Indian enterprise, namely, as is clear from the previous chapters, that the admiral and his Christians, as well as all those who followed after him in this land, worked on the assumption that the way to achieve their desires was first and foremost to instill fear in these people, to the extent of making the name Christian synonymous with terror. And to do this, they performed outstanding feats never before invented or dreamed of, as, God willing, I will show later. And this is contrary and inimical to the way that those who profess Christian benignity, gentleness and peace ought to negotiate the conversion of infidels.

As this excerpt shows, Las Casas's style of writing and mode of reasoning do not always yield great clarity, and his assessment here begs several questions. Columbus's policies, and official Spanish policy generally, were much more given to gentleness and kindness in the beginning than Las Casas, who only witnessed later troubled times, allows to appear. There is no question that conflicts with natives and factional infighting among Spaniards drove the admiral to more onerous measures, including enslavement of Indians captured in military actions.

While Las Casas's condemnation is cast in terms of absolute justice and as such has permanent relevance to evaluating Columbus's role in the New World, we should remember that Columbus was placed in unprecedented circumstances and should not be judged in the same way as we would a modern trained anthropologist. Paolo Emilio Taviani, an admiring but not uncritical recent biographer of Columbus, demonstrates the difficulty attending every particular of the first contact:

> The European scale of values was different from that of the natives. "They give everything for a trifle"; obviously what was a trifle on the European scale was not so for the natives. For them "a potsherd or a broken glass cup" was worth "sixteen skeins of cotton." Columbus warned that would never do, because from unrestricted trade between the two mentalities, the two conceptions of value, grave injustices would result, and so he immediately prohibited the cotton trade, allowing no one to take any and reserving the acquisition entirely for the king of Spain. A just prohibition, not easy to impose on ninety men—what strength could it have when nine hundred, nine thousand, or ninety thousand Europeans would arrive? Such were the first troubles in an encounter between two worlds that did not understand one another.

If we wish to task Columbus for all the asymmetries that ensued, we should credit him as well for this initial attempt, later repeated by many Spanish governors and theologians, to find some just route through the thicket of massive cultural difference. He failed and permitted far more wicked practices than unequal trade, but we should not let subsequent events blind us to his authentic concern for justice in the first contacts.

Some Brighter Moments

In spite of the cultural gulf, mutual affections and understanding did, at times, appear. After over two months of exploration in the Caribbean, Columbus's ship, the *Santa Maria,* went aground on Christmas 1492 in what is now Haiti. There Columbus encountered a people and a chief so helpful that his log entries for the following days view the entire episode as providential. He would never have chosen, as he admits, to come ashore or build the settlement of La Navidad (Christmas) there. He did not like the harbor at all. Yet he concluded that his relations with the Taínos and their chief Guacanagarí must be part of a divine plan in light of the friendship that sprung up between the two peoples.

Some Columbus scholars, perhaps a bit jaded from staring overlong at the historical lacunae and inconsistencies of the man, see in these log entries only an attempt to cover up the disastrous loss of the ship or a propaganda ploy to make the Spanish monarchs think well of the discoveries. Robert H. Fuson, a modern translator of the log, is a marine historian rather than a Columbus specialist. He is sometimes rightly criticized for his rather naive historical interpretations. But it is precisely because he is not predisposed to suspicion that he notices something overlooked by scholars occupied with weighing too many contradictory theories about the Haiti episode:

> Affection for the young chief in Haiti, and vice versa, is one of the most touching stories of love, trust, and understanding between men of different races and cultures to come out of this period in history. His [Columbus's] instructions to the men he left behind at La Navidad, for January 2, clearly illustrate his sincere fondness and respect for the Indians.

The January 2 entry, as we shall see below, indicates that Columbus had some ulterior motives in placating the natives. But that does not negate his genuine good feeling toward them or his gratitude for their generosity. Even if we assume that Columbus is putting the best interpretation on events for Ferdinand and Isabella, some sort of fellow feeling undeniably had arisen, at least temporarily, across the vast cultural divide separating the Taínos and the Europeans. Despite the great evils that would come later, this altruism was not without its own modest legacies.

An extreme but common form of the over-simple charges often leveled against the Europeans in general and Columbus in particular has come from the pen of the novelist Hans Koning. Writing in the *Washington Post* to influence public sentiments about the quincentenary, Koning insisted that from 1492 to 1500,

> there is not one recorded moment of awe, of joy, of love, of a smile. There is only anger, cruelty, greed, terror, and death. That is the record. Nothing else, I hold, is relevant when we discuss our commemoration of its 500th anniversary.

Riding the wave of revisionism about American history now sweeping over education, Koning made these claims under the title "Teach the Truth About Columbus."

The only problem with his assessment is that every particular in his catalog of what constitutes the truth is false. To take them in order: Columbus certainly records awe at his discoveries throughout his four voyages. His praise of the land's beauty was partly meant, of course, to convince the king and queen of the value of the properties Columbus had discovered for them. But some of it is simply awe; Columbus's enthusiasm for many of the new lands reaches a climax when he describes the sheer loveliness of the Venezuelan coast, which he believed to be the site of the original Garden of Eden, the earthly paradise. If that is not a record of awe, it is difficult to imagine what would be.

The relations between natives and Spaniards before 1500 are not, *pace* Koning, unrelieved darkness either. If anything, they are a frustrating reminder of a road not taken. Smiles there were—recorded smiles—at least on the native Taíno side: "They love their neighbors as themselves, and they have the softest and gentlest voices in the world and are always smiling" (*Log*, Tuesday, 25 December 1492). Columbus had reason to appreciate these people since they had just helped him salvage what was salvageable from the wreck of the *Santa Maria*. In the feast natives and Spaniards held after the rescue, the cacique Guacanagarí placed a crown on Columbus's head. The admiral reciprocated by giving him a scarlet cloak and a pair of colored boots, "and I placed upon his finger a large silver ring. I had been told that he had seen a silver ring on one of my sailors and desired it very much. The King was joyful and overwhelmed." Guacanagarí grew so close to Columbus that he asked if he and his brother might return with him to Castile.

When it came time to leave for Spain, Columbus placed thirty-nine men "under the command of three officers, all of whom are very friendly to King

Guacanagarí," and furthermore ordered that "they should avoid *as they would death* annoying or tormenting the Indians, bearing in mind how much they owe these people." The emphasis added to this last quotation has a double purpose. Clearly, Columbus recognized the temptations his men would have; just as clearly he was determined, to the best of his ability, to anticipate and block those temptations. This is the entry of January 2 that Fuson reads as expressing sincere kindness and affection. That reading may be a little too simple, but it is not entirely mistaken.

What this incident and the founding of the settlement definitely are *not*, however, are instances of simple European arrogance and imperialism, or what John Noble Wilford, a recent biographer of Columbus, has called "a personal transition from discoverer to imperialist." Even when full-scale war between some Indians and Spaniards broke out during Columbus's second voyage, Guacanagarí remained loyal to Columbus in spite of—or perhaps in opposition to—commands from another local chief, Caonabó, for a cacique alliance. No source denies this loyalty between the Taíno and the admiral, even under trying cultural tensions and warfare. Though we are right to abhor many far-less-happy subsequent events between the inhabitants of the two worlds, the record of the early interaction is richer and more diverse than most people, blinded by contemporary polemics, think. Hans Koning might do well to calm down and read some of these passages.

The List of Charges

The principal moral questions about Columbus arise essentially from three of his actions:

1. He immediately kidnapped some Taínos during his first voyage for questioning and use as interpreters. In that act he showed not only his contempt for Indian life but his belief that Spanish language, culture, and religion were superior and rightly to be imposed on native peoples.
2. After the destruction of La Navidad and the turmoil that ensued during the second voyage, Columbus foolishly ordered exploratory missions without adequate safeguards to restrain outrageously violent men like Mosen Pedro Margarit and Alonso de Ojeda. He then punished the natives who objected to Spaniards living off the land or who resisted their commands. In addition to setting this evil precedent, he shipped home some natives to become slaves with a very poor excuse:

Since of all the islands those of the cannibals are much the largest and much more fully populated, it is thought here that to take some of the men and women and to send them home to Castile would not be anything but well, for they may one day be led to abandon that inhuman custom that they have of eating men, and there in Castile, learning the language, they will much more readily receive baptism and secure the welfare of their souls.

3. Columbus instituted a system of gold tribute from the natives that was heavy—nearly impossible, in fact, given the small quantity of gold on the island of Hispaniola—and that was harshly enforced.

Each of these charges is true and no amount of admiration for Christopher Columbus can excuse what is simply inexcusable. Even the argument by Felipe Fernández-Armesto, one of the fairest Columbus historians, that "Columbus and his successors were guilty only of applying the best standards of their time" makes two false assumptions. First, that such behavior represents the best contemporary standards. . . . Second, that individuals should not be criticized for acting like the majority of their contemporaries because they are bound by culture and history. The latter argument draws strength from current philosophical schools that hold there are no privileged or absolute positions outside of historically conditioned views. But if we think we should condemn Aztec human sacrifice as wrong—not simply a different cultural form, but wrong—then we must admit there are universal principles that also allow us to criticize improper European use of force, enslavement, and exploitation.

Yet just as we try to understand the reasons behind Aztec human sacrifice or Carib cannibalism, and both tribes' imperialism toward other native peoples, we should also try to see what led to Columbus's behavior. Columbus, as Las Casas testified above, was not by nature a brutal man like Ojeda or Cortés. The first sign of harshness by him, in fact, seems to have been his acquiescence, during the second voyage, in a death sentence against some Indians on Hispaniola who had been caught stealing. Significantly, the pleading of another Indian moved him to remit the sentence in that case (the wavering too is characteristic of the uncertainty in handling questions of governance). Though he apparently regarded the Indians as inferior and always approached them with much the same assumption of superiority that Spaniards approached the Guanches of the Canary Islands and African tribes, he seemed at least partly—and when circumstances allowed—aware that good treatment was both morally called for and favorable to Spanish interests.

A fairer reading of the record reveals some mitigating factors, though these by no means add up to an exoneration.

1. Though Columbus did kidnap some Indians, two interpreters among them, he set one of them free immediately upon returning to Hispaniola during the second voyage. He hoped that the Indian set at liberty would tell others of Spain's wonders and of Columbus's good intentions. This was naive, crude, and manipulative on his part, but shows some perspicacity and good will.
2. Slavery was always a bone of contention between Columbus and the Spanish monarchs—they vehemently opposed this way of "civilizing" their subjects in the Indies. Columbus was not clear in his own mind about the issue. As late as the third voyage, the last in which he would be permitted to visit the growing colony on Hispaniola, Columbus ordered that slaves could only be taken during just war. His thinking was muddled, as was the thinking of the world for at least another half century until several crucial questions about Indian rights and just claims were sorted out.
3. The imposition of gold tribute for Spanish services stemmed from the belief that much gold existed on Hispaniola. And Indian failures to meet what seemed to the Spaniards modest levies were mistakenly

attributed to laziness. Indians loved the tiny hawk's bells that the Spaniards brought as trinkets; asking them to fill a bell with gold every two months seemed a reasonable request.

Since all governments tax in some fashion, Spain was doing only what caciques and Carib conquerors had been doing for time immemorial. The Spanish system did not "introduce" a new evil to an idyllic people without politics, but it proved peculiarly burdensome because it was imposed from the outside and in ignorance of the realities on Hispaniola. Furthermore, contrary to many wild charges, the Spaniards never intended to commit "genocide." A ready supply of native workers served Spanish self-interest. European and African diseases, however, soon laid waste whole tribes.

Fernández-Armesto argues that Columbus's recourse to violence on Hispaniola resulted mostly from his basic inability to rule well, from "misjudgment rather than wickedness." Gonzalo Fernandez de Oviedo, who became the official Spanish historian of the New World, said that to govern the Hispaniola colony correctly a person would have to be "angelic indeed superhuman." Columbus was far from either; in fact, he was far from possessing even normal political acumen. During his second and third voyages he clearly tried to avoid facing political difficulties on Hispaniola by exploring further. The problem was not merely lack of political skill. As a foreigner, he felt that he could trust only family members and close personal friends. (In fact, recent research has revealed that the Columbus family belonged to an anti-Spanish faction in Genoa, a political embarrassment that may help account for some of Columbus's reticence about his early life.) The resentments arising from difficult conditions, moreover, served to reinforce his tendencies toward paranoia. His rule of both Indians and Spanish oscillated between being too indecisive and too harsh.

We should also understand the kinds of Indians and colonists he had to govern. Columbus had trouble enough with the natives and complained:

> At home they judge me as a governor sent to Sicily or to a city or two under settled government and where the laws can be fully maintained, without fear of all being lost. . . . I ought to be judged as a captain who went from Spain to the Indies to conquer a people, warlike and numerous, and with customs and beliefs very different from ours.

Even the Taínos were probably far less gentle than Columbus earlier reported and "not so innocent as Las Casas tried to show." The Caribs, their fierce, cannibalistic enemies, seem to have been as terrified of the supposedly pacific Taínos as vice versa. And recent archeological investigations suggest that the Taínos, contrary to Columbus's impression of them as being without religion, had a complex system of belief and ritual akin to those in Central America and Mexico. They appear to have played a ritual ball game re-enacting the cosmic struggle between light and darkness and ending with the religious sacrifice of one or more human victims. An early Spanish conquistador estimated that twenty thousand people were sacrificed yearly on Hispaniola alone, though that figure may be wildly exaggerated. In any event, native tribes were profoundly *other* to the unsophisticated sailors and explorers in Columbus's day—and remain profoundly other to us today.

The Spaniards with whom Columbus had to deal were not much better. After the second voyage he asked the monarchs to think carefully about whom they were sending on the voyages and to choose "such persons that there be no suspicion of them and that they consider the purpose for which they have been sent rather than their personal interests." Not only were some of the colonists unusually violent, but many Spanish gentlemen who had come expecting easy wealth resented Columbus, the need to work, and the unhealthy conditions on the island. In dealing with these settlers, as Las Casas observed, "The Admiral had to use violence, threats, and constraint to have the work done at all." . . .

Bad in Any Case

. . . In Kirkpatrick Sale [*The Conquest of Paradise: Christopher Columbus and the Columbian Legacy*], Columbus is uniquely and doubly condemned for being medieval *and* for being of the Renaissance. His medieval side reflects superstitions, and his Renaissance side shows the destructive force of naked instrumental and mathematical reason, which Sale largely identifies with Renaissance Europe. Nevertheless, Sale also feels free to castigate Columbus for his lack of interest in numbers, that is, for not giving us the exact mathematical coordinates of the island where he made first landfall. Poor Columbus is merely the product of various opposing evil traditions that define Europe and Europeans—of which we are all the heirs, save, of course, the Kirkpatrick Sales who transcend cultural determinism.

All these attempts at neat categorizations assume that we can define a man, as well as a historical period, with far sharper boundaries than is ever the case. The mixture of human weakness and human greatness in even a key figure is never easy to calculate. The novelist Anthony Burgess has recently created a Mozart who says, "My desire and my hope is to gain honor, fame, and money." That sentence plausibly formulates a great deal of truth about Mozart's life. Yet few music lovers would deduce from this that Mozart's work is, therefore, solely the product of ambition and cupidity, or try to explain the man and his music by sociological analysis of the late eighteenth century. Columbus similarly spoke of "God, gold, and glory," and many of the Europeans who followed him were driven by multiple motives, not all of which were, by any means, merely self-serving.

Kirkpatrick Sale, as usual, well formulates the ultimate issue behind much of the public controversy over 1992:

> In the final analysis, it is not so important whether Columbus was a good man. What matters is that he brought over a culture centered on its own superiority. The failings of the man were and remain the failures of the culture.

This is a strained argument. It certainly does matter, if only for the sake of historical justice, that we try to discern the mix of good and evil in Columbus *per se.* Furthermore, no one can simply be identified with a whole culture. Every individual both draws on and opposes elements in his surroundings. If the preceding pages show anything, they show that Columbus, like the rest of us, was not simply good or bad. As a great human spirit, both his virtues and faults appear larger and more vivid than they do in most people. And his historical influence reflects the dimensions of what he was. The argument about the European sense of superiority, however, can be engaged quite well without dragging in Columbus, as if he were a mere conduit for European culture.

One reason that freedom arose in the West is the traditional Western separation of the City of Man from the City of God. . . . [M]any of the early missionaries and theologians showed, in the very face of state power and financial interests, that Christian principles pointed toward other paths than those most often taken by settlers in the New World. Columbus and Las Casas were sometimes at odds over specifics, but were not fundamentally opposed on these matters. Las Casas is the greater figure for his moral passion and courage, but Columbus, in spite of his faults, deserves no little admiration. Emblematic, perhaps, of their relationship is the suggestion of Simón Bolívar in 1819 that a newly liberated area of South America be named Colombia and its capital Las Casas: "Thus will we prove to the world that we not only have the right to be free, but we will demonstrate that we know how to honor the friends and benefactors of mankind."

POSTSCRIPT

Was Columbus an Imperialist?

Whether or not Christopher Columbus's actions in the Americas are viewed as the work of an imperialist, there is no doubt that the impact of his arrival in the Western Hemisphere carried with it enormous consequences, not the least of which was the so-called "Columbian Exchange," which involved a reciprocal trade in plants and animals, human beings, diseases, and ideas. For example, the introduction of destructive microorganisms produced epidemic outbreaks of smallpox, tuberculosis, measles, typhoid, and syphilis that decimated human populations on both sides of the Atlantic. On a more positive note, Europeans brought food items such as wheat and potatoes to the New World and brought home maize, beans, and manioc. Native Americans benefited from horses and other farm animals introduced from Europe, but these benefits were offset by the efforts of the Europeans to enslave and kill the indigenous peoples whom they encountered. The best study of these various by-products of European exploration is Alfred W. Crosby, *The Columbian Exchange: Biological and Cultural Consequences of 1492* (Greenwood Press, 1973).

The effects of the encounters between Europeans and Native Americans is explored in Gary B. Nash, *Red, White and Black: The Peoples of Early North America,* 3rd ed. (Prentice Hall, 1992) and in two works by James Axtell: *The European and the Indian: Essays in the Ethnohistory of Colonial North America* (Oxford University Press, 1981) and *The Invasion Within: The Contest of Cultures in Colonial North America* (Oxford University Press, 1985). Alvin M. Josephy, Jr., examines the pre-Columbian Native Americans in *1492: The World of the Indian Peoples Before the Arrival of Columbus* (Alfred A. Knopf, 1992).

Samuel Eliot Morison, *The European Discovery of America: The Northern Voyages* (Oxford University Press, 1971); David Beers Quinn, *England and the Discovery of America, 1481–1620* (Harper & Row, 1974); Wallace Notestein, *The English People on the Eve of Colonization, 1603–1630* (Harper & Brothers, 1954); Charles Gibson, *Spain in America* (Harper & Row, 1966); and W. J. Eccles, *France in America* (Harper & Row, 1972) all discuss European contacts in North America.

Perhaps the best biographical treatment of Columbus is Samuel Eliot Morison's generally sympathetic *Admiral of the Ocean Sea: A Life of Christopher Columbus,* 2 vols. (Little, Brown, 1942). For a more recent objective and scholarly study, see Felipe Fernandez-Armesto, *Columbus* (Oxford University Press, 1991).

ISSUE 3

Were the First Colonists in the Chesapeake Region Ignorant, Lazy, and Unambitious?

YES: Edmund S. Morgan, from *American Slavery, American Freedom: The Ordeal of Colonial Virginia* (W. W. Norton, 1975)

NO: Russell R. Menard, from "From Servant to Freeholder: Status Mobility and Property Accumulation in Seventeenth-Century Maryland," *William and Mary Quarterly* (January 1973)

ISSUE SUMMARY

YES: Professor Edmund S. Morgan argues that Virginia's first decade as a colony was a complete "fiasco" because the settlers were too lazy to engage in the subsistence farming necessary for their survival and failed to abandon their own and the Virginia's company's expectations of establishing extractive industries such as mining, timber, and fishing.

NO: According to Professor Russell R. Menard, the indentured servants of seventeenth-century Maryland were hardworking, energetic, and young individuals who went through two stages of history: From 1640 to 1660 servants provided large planters with an inexpensive labor force, but they also achieved greater wealth and mobility in the Chesapeake than if they remained in England; after 1660 opportunities for servants to achieve land, wealth, and status drastically declined.

Until the 1970s American history textbooks ignored the seventeenth century once the colonies were founded. The new social history that has incorporated ordinary people—not just elite white males, but common white males, females, African-Americans, women, and Indians—has added a whole new dimension to the colonial period. Racial, class, gender, and sectional differences emerge, and for the first time historians clearly distinguished the seventeenth and eighteenth centuries.

The English were latecomers in colonizing the new world. Earlier voyages by John Cabot in 1497 and 1498 around Canada were not followed up in the same way the Spaniards established colonies in Latin America. Before Jamestown there were notable failures at colonization.

The first permanent English settlements were established in the Chesapeake Bay region—Virginia in 1607 and Maryland in 1634. There were many similarities between the two colonies. Both colonies started out with charters granted by the British monarchy. Both experienced economic hardships in the beginning. Relations with the Indians were strained. Mortality rates were higher in New England because of the hot climates and concomitant rampant diseases so few lived past the age of 45. Combined with late marriages, the population growth was low. Only sustained immigration from England prevented the two colonies from collapsing in their first two decades.

One major difference between Virginia and Maryland was the fact that Virginia was the first "successful" English colony. It became the model for the mistakes that other colonies tried to avoid. The Jamestown settlement, which the 105 colonists (39 died at sea) had established in May 1607, bartered with the Indians for corn, but even Captain John Smith could not trade for enough food or force the settlers to stop arguing among themselves and plant crops. Only 38 of the original settlers survived until January 1608 when a fresh supply of food and 120 new settlers arrived from England. Still the experiences of the first year did not prevent the "starving time" of the winter of 1609–1610 when several of the inhabitants resorted to eating their deceased family members.

In the first selection, Professor Edmund Morgan is highly critical of the first settlers of Virginia. Others have pointed out that the earliest immigrants came from the "gentlemen" class and lacked the farming skills necessary for survival. But Morgan puts as much of the blame on the policies of the Virginia company and the London government as he does on the settlers. Even after the "starving time," the survivors and the new immigrants continued to pursue extraction industries such as gold, silver, iron mining, fishing, and lumber and silk binding at the expense of subsistence agriculture.

In the second selection, Professor Russell R. Menard describes the indentured servants who came to Maryland in the years from 1640 to 1690 to make up for the shortage of labor in the Chesapeake Bay until slave labor filled this void in the eighteenth century. Because land and jobs were scarce, many English migrants indentured their services to a ships' captain for passage to the New World. The captain in turn sold the contract to a craftsman or farmer, which bound over the servant for a term that lasted around five years. Upon completion of the contract, these servants would receive their "freedom dues"—usually three barrels of corn, a suit of clothes, and access to 50 acres of land if they could fulfill the requirements.

How well did the servants fare after they were freed? According to Professor Menard, there were two periods for Maryland's indentured servants. In the years from 1640 to 1660, servants were treated well and upon completion of their indentures moved from renters to landowners and often attained positions of wealth and power. After 1660 the dramatic rise in the population accompanied by increasing land prices and falling tobacco prices made it harder for the newly freed indentured servants to achieve land ownerships, power, and status. In the eighteenth century, the Chesapeake became a less egalitarian and more stratified society.

YES

Edmund S. Morgan

The Jamestown Fiasco

The first wave of Englishmen reached Virginia at Cape Henry, the southern headland at the opening of Chesapeake Bay, on April 26, 1607. The same day their troubles began. The Indians of the Cape Henry region (the Chesapeakes), when they found a party of twenty or thirty strangers walking about on their territory, drove them back to the ships they came on. It was not the last Indian victory, but it was no more effective than later ones. In spite of troubles, the English were there to stay. They spent until May 14 exploring Virginia's broad waters and then chose a site that fitted the formula Hakluyt had prescribed. The place which they named Jamestown, on the James (formerly Powhatan) River, was inland from the capes about sixty miles, ample distance for warning of a Spanish invasion by sea. It was situated on a peninsula, making it easily defensible by land; and the river was navigable by oceangoing ships for another seventy-five miles into the interior, thus giving access to other tribes in case the local Indians should prove as unfriendly as the Chesapeakes.

Captain Christopher Newport had landed the settlers in time to plant something for a harvest that year if they put their minds to it. After a week, in which they built a fort for protection, Newport and twenty-one others took a small boat and headed up the river on a diplomatic and reconnoitering mission, while the settlers behind set about the crucial business of planting corn. Newport paused at various Indian villages along the way and assured the people, as best he could, of the friendship of the English and of his readiness to assist them against their enemies. Newport gathered correctly from his attempted conversations that one man, Powhatan, ruled the whole area above Jamestown, as far as the falls at the present site of Richmond. His enemies, the Monacans, lived above the falls (where they might be difficult to reach if Powhatan proved unfriendly). Newport also surmised, incorrectly, that the Chesapeake Indians who had attacked him at Cape Henry were not under Powhatan's dominion. He accordingly tried to make an alliance against the Chesapeakes and Monacans with a local chief whom he mistook for Powhatan. At the same time, he planted a cross with the name of King James on it (to establish English dominion) and tried to explain to the somewhat bewildered and justifiably suspicious owners of the country that one arm of the cross was Powhatan, the other himself, and that the fastening of them together signified the league between them.

FROM AMERICAN SLAVERY, AMERICAN FREEDOM by Edmund S. Morgan, pp. 71–73, 75, 81–91.

If the Indians understood, they were apparently unimpressed, for three days later, returning to Jamestown, Newport found that two hundred of Powhatan's warriors had attacked the fort the day before and had only been prevented from destroying it by fire from the ships. The settlers had been engaged in planting and had not yet unpacked their guns from the cases in which they were shipped. That was a mistake they were not likely to repeat. But for the next ten years they seem to have made nearly every possible mistake and some that seem almost impossible. It would take a book longer than this to recount them all, and the story has already been told many times. But if we are to understand the heritage of these ten disastrous years for later Virginia history, we should look at a few of the more puzzling episodes and then try to fathom the forces behind them.

Skip over the first couple of years, when it was easy for Englishmen to make mistakes in the strange new world to which they had come, and look at Jamestown in the winter of 1609–10. It is three planting seasons since the colony began. The settlers have fallen into an uneasy truce with the Indians, punctuated by guerrilla raids on both sides, but they have had plenty of time in which they could have grown crops. They have obtained corn from the Indians and supplies from England. They have firearms. Game abounds in the woods; and Virginia's rivers are filled with sturgeon in the summer and covered with geese and ducks in the winter. There are five hundred people in the colony now. And they are starving. They scour the woods listlessly for nuts, roots, and berries. And they offer the only authentic examples of cannibalism witnessed in Virginia. One provident man chops up his wife and salts down the pieces. Others dig up graves to eat the corpses. By spring only sixty are left alive.

Another scene, a year later, in the spring of 1611. The settlers have been reinforced with more men and supplies from England. The preceding winter has not been as gruesome as the one before, thanks in part to corn obtained from the Indians. But the colony still is not growing its own corn. The governor, Lord De la Warr, weakened by the winter, has returned to England for his health. His replacement, Sir Thomas Dale, reaches Jamestown in May, a time when all hands could have been used in planting. Dale finds nothing planted except "some few seeds put into a private garden or two." And the people he finds at "their daily and usuall workes, bowling in the streetes."

It is evident that the settlers, failing to plant for themselves, depend heavily on the Indians for food. The Indians can finish then off at any time simply by leaving the area. And the Indians know it One of them tells the English flatly that "we can plant any where . . . and we know that you cannot live if you want [i.e., lack] our harvest, and that reliefe we bring you." If the English drive out the Indians, they will starve. . . .

It is not easy to make sense out of the behavior displayed in these episodes. How to explain the suicidal impulse that led the hungry English to destroy the corn that might have fed them and to commit atrocities upon the people who grew it? And how to account for the seeming unwillingness or incapacity of the English to feed themselves? Although they had invaded Indian territory and quarreled with the owners, the difficulty of obtaining land was not great. The Indians were no match for English weapons. More-over, since the Indians could afford to give up the land around Jamestown as well as Henrico without seriously endangering their own economy, they made no concerted effort to drive the English out. Although Indian attacks may have prevented the English from getting a crop into the ground in time for a harvest in the fall of 1607, the occasional Indian raids thereafter cannot explain the English failure to grow food in succeeding years. How, then, can we account for it?

The answer that comes first to mind is the poor organization and direction of the colony. The government prescribed by the charter placed full powers in a council appointed by the king, with a president elected by the other members. The president had virtually no authority of his own; and while the council lasted, the members spent most of their time bickering and intriguing against one another and especially against the one man who had the experience and the assurance to take command. The names of the councillors had been kept secret (even from themselves) in a locked box, until the ships carrying the first settlers arrived in Virginia. By that time a bumptious young man named John Smith had made himself unpopular with Captain Christopher Newport (in command until their arrival) and with most of the other gentlemen of conse-quence aboard. When they opened the box, they were appalled to find Smith's name on the list of councillors. But during the next two years Smith's confi-dence in himself and his willingness to act while others talked overcame most of the handicaps imposed by the feeble frame of government. It was Smith who kept the colony going during those years. But in doing so he dealt more decisively with the Indians than with his own quarreling countrymen, and he gave an initial turn to the colony's Indian relations that was not quite what the company had intended. . . .

In their relations to the Indians, as in their rule of the settlers, the new governing officers of the colony were ruthless. The guerrilla raids that the two races conducted against each other became increasingly hideous, especially on the part of the English. Indians coming to Jamestown with food were treated as spies. Gates had them seized and killed "for a Terrour to the Reste to cawse them to desiste from their subtell practyses." Gates showed his own subtle practices by enticing the Indians at Kecoughtan (Point Comfort) to watch a display of dancing and drumming by one of his men and then "espyeinge a fitteinge oportunety fell in upon them putt fyve to the sworde wownded many others some of them beinge after fownde in the woods with Sutche extrordinary Lardge and mortall wownds that itt seemed strange they Cold flye so far." It is possible that the rank and file of settlers aggravated the bad relations with the Indians by unauthorized attacks, but unauthorized frat-ernization seems to have bothered the governors more. The atrocities com-mitted against the queen of the Paspaheghs, though apparently demanded by the men, were the work of the governing officers, as were the atrocities committed against the Englishmen who fled to live with the Indians.

John Smith had not had his way in wishing to reduce the Indians to sla-very, or something like it, on the Spanish model. But the policy of his successors, though perhaps not with company approval made Virginia look far more like the Hispaniola of Las Casas that it did when Smith was in charge. And the company and the colony had few benefits to show for all the rigor. At the end of ten years, in spite of the military discipline of work gangs, the colonists were still not growing enough to feed themselves and were still begging, bullying, and buying corn from the Indians whose lands they scorched so deliberately. We cannot, it seems, blame the colony's failures on lax discipline and diffusion of authority. Failures continued and atrocities multiplied after authority was made absolute and concentrated in one man.

Another explanation, often advanced, for Virginia's early troubles, and especially for its failure to feed itself, is the collective organization of labor in the colony. All the settlers were expected to work together in a single community effort, to produce both the food and the exports that would make the company rich. Those who held shares would ultimately get part of the profits, but meanwhile the incentives of private enterprise were lacking. The work a man did bore no direct relation to his reward. The laggard would receive as large a share in the end as the man who worked hard.

The communal production of food seems to have been somewhat modified after the reorganization of 1609 by the assignment of small amounts of land to individuals for private gardens. It is not clear who received such allotments, perhaps only those who came at their own expense. Men who came at company expense may have been expected to continue working exclusively for the common stock until their seven-year terms expired. At any rate, in 1614, the year when the first shipment of company men concluded their service, Governor Dale apparently assigned private allotments to them and to other independent "farmers." Each man got three acres, or twelve acres if he had a family. He was responsible for growing his own food plus two and a half barrels of corn annually for the company as a supply for newcomers to tide them over the first year. And henceforth each "farmer" would work for the company only one month a year.

By this time Gates and Dale had succeeded in planting settlements at several points along the James as high up as Henrico, just below the falls. The many close-spaced tributary rivers and creeks made it possible to throw up a palisade between two of them to make a small fortified peninsula. Within the space thus enclosed by water on three sides and palisaded on the fourth, the settlers could build their houses, dig their gardens, and pasture their cattle. It was within these enclaves that Dale parceled out private allotments. Dignified by hopeful names like "Rochdale Hundred" or "Bermuda City," they were affirmations of an expectation that would linger for a century, that Virginia was about to become the site of thriving cities and towns. In point of fact, the new "cities" scarcely matched in size the tiny villages from which Powhatan's people threatened them. And the "farmers" who huddled together on the allotments assigned to them proved incapable of supporting themselves or the colony with adequate supplies of food.

At first it seemed to sympathetic observers that they would. Ralph Hamor, in an account of the colony published in 1615, wrote, "When our people were fedde out of the common store and laboured jointly in the manuring of the ground and planting corne, glad was that man that could slippe from his labour, nay the most honest of them in a generall businesse, would not take so much faithfull and true paines in a weeke, as now he will doe in a day, neither cared they for the increase, presuming that howsoever their harvest prospered, the generall store must maintain them, by which meanes we reaped not so much corne from the labours of 30 men, as three men have done for themselves."

According to John Rolfe, a settler who had married John Smith's fair Pocahontas, the switch to private enterprise transformed the colony's food deficit instantly to a surplus: instead of the settlers seeking corn from the Indians, the Indians sought it from them. If so, the situation did not last long. Governor Samuel Argall, who took charge at the end of May, 1617, bought 600 bushels from the Indians that fall, "which did greatly relieve the whole Colonie." And when Governor George Yeardley relieved Argall in April, 1619, he found the colony "in a great scarcity for want of corn" and made immediate preparations to seek it from the Indians, If, then, the colony's failure to grow food arose from its communal organization of production, the failure was not overcome by the switch to private enterprise.

Still another explanation for the improvidence of Virginia's pioneers is one that John Smith often emphasized, namely, the character of the immigrants. They were certainly an odd assortment, for the most conspicuous group among them was an extraordinary number of gentlemen. Virginia, as a patriotic enterprise, had excited the imagination of England's nobility and gentry. The shareholders included 32 present or future earls, 4 countesses, and 3 viscounts (all members of the nobility) as well as hundreds of lesser gentlemen, some of them perhaps retainers of the larger men. Not all were content to risk only their money. Of the 105 settlers who started the colony, 36 could be classified as gentlemen. In the first "supply" of 120 additional settlers, 28 were gentlemen, and in the second supply of 70, again 28 were gentlemen. These numbers gave Virginia's population about six times as large a proportion of gentlemen as England had.

Gentlemen, by definition, had no manual skill, nor could they be expected to work at ordinary labor. They were supposed to be useful for "the force of knowledge, the exercise of counsell"; but to have ninety-odd wise men offering advice while a couple of hundred did the work was inauspicious, especially when the wise men included "many unruly gallants packed thether by their friends to escape il destinies" at home.

What was worse, the gentlemen were apparently accompanied by the personal attendants that gentlemen thought necessary to make life bearable even in England. The colony's laborers "were for most part footmen, and such as they that were Adventurers brought to attend them, or such as they could perswade to goe with them, that never did know what a dayes worke was." Smith complained that he could never get any real work from more than thirty out of two hundred, and he later argued that of all the people sent to Virginia, a hundred good laborers "would have done more than a thousand of those that went." Samuel Argall and John Rolfe also argued that while a few gentlemen would have been useful to serve as military leaders, "to have more to wait and play than worke, or more commanders and officers than industrious labourers was not so necessarie."

The company may actually have had little choice in allowing gentlemen and their servants to make so large a number of their settlers. The gentlemen were paying their own way, and the company perhaps could not afford to deny them. But even if unencumbered by these volunteers, the colony might have foundered on the kind of settlers that the company itself did want to send. What the company wanted for Virginia was a variety of craftsmen. Richard Hakluyt had made up a list for Walter Raleigh that suggests the degree of specialization contemplated in an infant settlement: Hakluyt wanted both carpenters and joiners, tallow chandlers and wax chandlers, bowstave preparers and bowyers, fletchers and arrowhead makers, men to rough-hew pikestaffs and other men to finish them. In 1610 and again in 1611 the Virginia Company published lists of the kind of workers it wanted. Some were for building, making tools, and other jobs needed to keep the settlers alive, but the purpose of staying alive would be to see just what Virginia was good for and then start sending the goods back to England. Everybody hoped for gold and silver and jewels, so the colony needed refiners and mineral men. But they might have to settle for iron, so send men with all the skills needed to smelt it. The silk grass that Hariot described might produce something like silk, and there were native mulberry trees for growing worms, so send silk dressers. Sturgeon swam in the rivers, so send men who knew how to make caviar. And so on. Since not all the needed skills for Virginia's potential products were to be found in England, the company sought them abroad: glassmakers from Italy, millwrights from Holland, pitch boilers from Poland, vine dressers and saltmakers from France. The settlers of Virginia were expected to create a more complex, more varied economy than England itself possessed. As an extension of England, the colony would impart its variety and health to the mother country.

If the company had succeeded in filling the early ships for Virginia with as great a variety of specialized craftsmen as it wanted, the results might conceivably have been worse than they were. We have already noticed the effect of specialization in England itself, where the division of labor had become a source not of efficiency but of idleness. In Virginia the effect was magnified. Among the skilled men who started the settlement in 1607 were four carpenters, two bricklayers, one mason (apparently a higher skill than bricklaying), a blacksmith, a tailor, and a barber. The first "supply" in 1608 had six tailors, two goldsmiths, two refiners, two apothecaries, a blacksmith, a gunner (i.e., gunsmith?), a cooper, a tobacco pipe maker, a jeweler, and a perfumer. There were doubtless others, and being skilled they expected to be paid and fed for doing the kind of work for which they had been hired. Some were obviously useful. But others may have found themselves without means to use their special talents. If they were conscientious, the jeweler may have spent some time looking for jewels, the goldsmiths for gold, the perfumer for something to make perfume with. But when the search proved futile, it did not follow that they should or would exercise their skilled hands at any other tasks. It was not suitable for a perfumer or a jeweler or a goldsmith to put his hand to the hoe. Rather, they could join the gentlemen in genteel loafing while a handful of ordinary laborers worked at the ordinary labor of growing and gathering food.

The laborers could be required to work at whatever they were told to; but they were, by all accounts, too few and too feeble. The company may have rounded them up as it did in 1609 when it appealed to the mayor of London to rid the city of its "swarme of unnecessary inmates" by sending to Virginia any who were destitute and lying in the streets.

The company, then, partly by choice, partly by necessity, sent to the colony an oversupply of men who were not prepared to tackle the work essential to settling in a wilderness. In choosing prospective Virginians, the company did not look for men who would be particularly qualified to keep themselves alive in a new land. The company never considered the problem of staying alive in Virginia to be a serious one. And why should they have? England's swarming population had had ample experience in moving to new areas and staying alive. The people who drifted north and west into the pasture-farming areas got along, and the lands there were marginal, far poorer than those that awaited the settlers of tidewater Virginia. Though there may have been some farmers among the early settlers, no one for whom an occupation is given was listed as a husbandman or yeoman. And though thirty husbandmen were included in the 1611 list of men wanted, few came. As late as 1620 the colony reported "a great scarcity, or none at all" of "husbandmen truely bred," by which was meant farmers from the arable regions. In spite of the experience at Roanoke and in spite of the repeated starving times at Jamestown, the company simply did not envisage the provision of food as a serious problem. They sent some food supplies with every ship but never enough to last more than a few months. After that people should be able to do for themselves.

The colonists were apparently expected to live from the land like England's woodland and pasture people, who gave only small amounts of time to their small garden plots, cattle, and sheep and spent the rest in spinning, weaving, mining, handicrafts, and loafing. Virginians would spend their time on the more varied commodities of the New World. To enable them to live in this manner, the company sent cattle, swine, and sheep: and when Dale assigned them private plots of land, the plots were small, in keeping with the expectation that they would not spend much time at farming. The company never intended the colony to supply England with grain and did not even expect that agricultural products might be its principal exports. They did want to give sugar, silk, and wine a try, but most of the skills they sought showed an expectation of setting up extractive industries such as iron mining, smelting, salt-making, pitch making, and glassmaking. The major part of the colonists' work time was supposed to be devoted to processing the promised riches of the land for export; and with the establishment of martial law the company had the means of seeing that they put their shoulders to the task.

Unfortunately, the persons charged with directing the motley work force had a problem, quite apart from the overload of gentlemen and specialized craftsmen they had to contend with. During the early years of the colony they could find no riches to extract. They sent back some cedar wood, but lumber was too bulky a product to bear the cost of such long transportation to market. Sassafras was available in such quantities that the market for it quickly collapsed. The refiners found no gold or silver or even enough iron to be worth mining. Silk grass and silk proved to be a will-o'-the-wisp.

The result was a situation that taxed the patience both of the leaders and of the men they supervised. They had all come to Virginia with high expectations. Those who came as servants of the company had seven years in which to make their employers rich. After that they would be free to make themselves rich. But with no prospect of riches in sight for anybody, it was difficult to keep them even at the simple tasks required for staying alive or to find anything else for them to do.

The predicament of those in charge is reflected in the hours of work they prescribed for the colonists, which contrast sharply with those specified in the English Statute of Artificers. There was no point in demanding dawn-to-dusk toil unless there was work worth doing. When John Smith demanded that men work or starve, how much work did he demand? By his own account, "4 hours each day was spent in worke, the rest in pastimes and merry exercise." The governors who took charge after the reorganization of 1609 were equally modest in their demands. William Strachey, who was present, described the work program under Gates and De la Warr in the summer of 1610:

> It is to be understood that such as labor are not yet so taxed but that easily they perform the same and ever by ten of the clock they have done their morning's work: at what time they have their allowances [of food] set out ready for them, and until it be three of the clock again they take their own pleasure, and afterward, with the sunset, their day's labor is finished.

The Virginia Company offered much the same account of this period. According to a tract issued late in 1610, "the setled times of working (to effect all themselves, or the Adventurers neede desire) [require] no more pains then from sixe of clocke in the morning untill ten and from two of the clocke in the afternoone till foure." The long lunch period described here was spelled out in the *Lawes Divine, Morall and Martiall*. If we calculate the total hours demanded of the work gangs between the various beatings of the drum, they come to roughly five to eight hours a day in summer and three to six hours in winter. And it is not to be supposed that these hours refer only to work done in the fields and that the men were expected to work at other tasks like building houses during the remainder of the day. The *Laws* indicate that at the appointed hours every laborer was to repair to his work "and every crafts man to his occupation, Smiths, Joyners, Carpenters, Brick makers, etc." Nor did military training occupy the time not spent in working. The *Laws* provided for different groups to train at different times and to be exempt from work during the training days. Although colonists and historians alike have condemned the *Laws* as harsh, and with reason, the working hours that the code prescribed sound astonishingly short to modern ears. They certainly fell way below those demanded at the time in English law; and they seem utterly irrational in a chronically starving community.

To have grown enough corn to feed the colony would have required only a fraction of the brief working time specified, yet it was not grown. Even in their free time men shunned the simple planting tasks that sufficed for the Indians.

And the very fact that the Indians did grow corn may be one more reason why the colonists did not. For the Indians presented a challenge that Englishmen were not prepared to meet, a challenge to their image of themselves, to their self-esteem, to their conviction of their own superiority over foreigners, and especially over barbarous foreigners like the Irish and the Indians.

If you were a colonist, you knew that your technology was superior to the Indians'. You knew that you were civilized, and they were savages. It was evident in your firearms, your clothing, your housing, your government, your religion. The Indians were supposed to be overcome with admiration and to join you in extracting riches from the country. But your superior technology had proved insufficient to extract anything. The Indians, keeping to themselves, laughed at your superior methods and lived from the land more abundantly and with less labor than you did. They even furnished you with the food that you somehow did not get around to growing enough of yourselves. To be thus condescended to by heathen savages was intolerable. And when your own people started deserting in order to live with them, it was too much. If it came to that, the whole enterprise of Virginia would be over. So you killed the Indians, tortured them, burned their villages, burned their cornfields. It proved your superiority in spite of your failures. And you gave similar treatment to any of your own people who succumbed to the savage way of life. But you still did not grow much corn. That was not what you had come to Virginia for.

By the time the colony was ten years old and an almost total loss to the men who had invested their lives and fortunes in it, only one ray of hope had appeared. It had been known, from the Roanoke experience, that the Indians grew and smoked a kind of tobacco; and tobacco grown in the Spanish West Indies was already being imported into England, where it sold at eighteen shillings a pound. Virginia tobacco had proved, like everything else, a disappointment; but one of the settlers, John Rolfe, tried some seeds of the West Indian variety, and the result was much better. The colonists stopped bowling in the streets and planted tobacco in them—and everywhere else that they could find open land. In 1617, ten years after the first landing at Jamestown, they shipped their first cargo to England. It was not up to Spanish tobacco, but it sold at three shillings a pound.

To the members of the company it was proof that they had been right in their estimate of the colony's potential. But the proof was bitter. Tobacco had at first been accepted as a medicine, good for a great variety of ailments. But what gave it its high price was the fact that people had started smoking it for fun. Used this way it was considered harmful and faintly immoral. People smoked it in taverns and brothels. Was Virginia to supplement England's economy and redeem her rogues by pandering to a new vice? The answer, of course, was yes. But the men who ran the Virginia Company, still aiming at ends of a higher nature, were not yet ready to take yes for an answer.

Russell R. Menard

 **NO**

From Servant to Freeholder: Status Mobility and Property Accumulation in Seventeenth-Century Maryland

. . . Miles Gibson, Stephen Sealus, and William Scot all arrived in Maryland as indentured servants in the 1660s. They completed their terms and soon accumulated enough capital to purchase land. Thereafter, their careers diverged sharply. Gibson, aided by two good marriages, gained a place among the local gentry and served his country as justice of the peace, burgess, and sheriff. At his death in 1692, he owned more than two thousand acres of land and a personal estate appraised at over six hundred pounds sterling, including nine slaves. Sealus's career offers a sharp contrast to that of his highly successful contemporary. He lost a costly court case in the mid-1670s and apparently was forced to sell his plantation to cover the expenses. He spent the rest of his days working other men's land. By 1691, Sealus was reduced to petitioning the county court for relief. He was "both weake and lame," he pleaded, "and not able to worke whereby to maintaine himselfe nor his wife." His petition was granted, but the Sealus family remained poor. Stephen died in 1696, leaving an estate appraised at £18 6s. William Scot did not approach Gibson's success, but he did manage to avoid the dismal failure of Sealus. He lived on his small plantation for nearly forty years, served his community in minor offices, and slowly accumulated property. In his will, Scot gave all seven of his sons land of their own and provided his three daughters with small dowries. Although interesting in themselves, these brief case histories do not reveal very much about the life chances of servants in the seventeenth century. They do suggest a range of accomplishment, but how are we to tell whether Scot, Sealus, or Gibson is most typical, or even if any one of them represents the position that most servants attained? Did servitude offer any hard-working Englishman without capital a good chance of becoming, like Miles Gibson, a man of means and position in a new community? Or did servitude only offer, as it finally offered Stephen Sealus, a chance to live in poverty in another place? Perhaps Scot was more typical. Did servitude promise poor men a chance to obtain moderate prosperity and respectability for themselves and their families? How much property and status mobility did most servants manage to achieve in the seventeenth century? This essay examines the careers of a group of men who immigrated to Maryland in the seventeenth century in order to provide some of the data needed for answers to such questions.

The study of mobility requires an assessment of a man's position in society for at least two points in his career, a task that the general absence of census materials, tax lists, and assessment records makes difficult. Nevertheless, a study of mobility among servants is possible because we know their place in the social structure at the beginning of their careers in the New World. Servants started at the bottom of white society: they entered the colonies with neither freedom nor capital. Since we can define their position on arrival, measuring the degree of success they achieved is a fairly simple task. We can, as the capsule biographies of Gibson, Sealus, and Scot demonstrate, describe their progress in the New World. A study of the fortunes of indentured servants and the way those fortunes changed over time provides a sensitive indicator of the opportunities available within colonial society.

The broadest group under study in this essay consists of 275 men who entered Maryland as servants before the end of 1642, although the main concern is with 158 for whom proof exists that they survived to be freemen. Not all the men who came into Maryland as servants by 1642 are included in the 275. No doubt a few servants escape any recorded mention, while others appear who are not positively identified as servants. One large group falling into this latter category included 66 men, not specifically called servants, who were listed in the proofs of headrights as having been transported into the colony at the expense of someone else to whom they were not related. It is probable that all of these men emigrated under indentures, but since proof was lacking they have been excluded from the study.

The mortality rate among these servants was probably high. One hundred and seventeen of the 275—more than 40 percent—did not appear in the records as freemen. The deaths of 14 of the missing are mentioned, but we can only speculate on the fate of most of the servants who disappeared. Some may have been sold out of the province before their terms were completed, and some may have run away, while others may have left Maryland immediately after becoming freemen. A majority probably died while still servants, victims of the unusual climate, poor food, ill housing, hard work, or an occasional cruel master, before they had a chance to discover for themselves if America was a land of opportunity.

For the 158 who definitely survived the rigors of servitude, opportunity was abundant. Seventy-nine to 81 (identification is uncertain in two cases) of the survivors, about 50 percent, eventually acquired land in Maryland. To be properly interpreted, however, this figure must be understood within the context of the careers of those who failed to acquire land. Fourteen of those who survived servitude but did not acquire land in Maryland died within a decade of completing their terms. Another 25 left before they had lived in the colony for ten years as freemen. These figures are conservative, for they include only those for whom death or migration can be proven. Twenty-five of the 158 survivors appear only briefly in the records and then vanish without a trace, presumably among the early casualties or emigrants. Furthermore, there is no reason to believe that those who left were any less successful than those who remained. At least 11 of the 25 known emigrants became landowners in Virginia. Only 13 to 15 of the 158 servants who appeared in the records as freemen (less than 10 percent) lived for more than a decade in Maryland as freemen without becoming landowners.

Those who acquired land did so rapidly. The interval between achieving freedom and acquiring land, which was discovered in forty-six cases, ranged from two years for Richard Nevill and Phillip West to twelve for John Norman and Walter Walterlin. Francis Pope, for whom the interval was seven years, and John Maunsell, who took eight, came closer to the median of seven and one-half years.

The holdings of the vast majority of those who acquired land were small. Most lived as small planters on tracts ranging in size from fifty acres to four hundred acres, although fourteen former servants managed to become large landowners, possessing at least one thousand acres at one time in their lives. Zachary Wade, who owned over four thousand acres at his death in 1678 and about five thousand acres in the early 1670s, ranked with the largest landowners in Maryland.

Inventories of personal estates, taken at death, have survived for 31 of the 158 former servants. Analysis of the inventories reinforces the conclusion that most of these men became small planters. About 60 percent of the inventories show personal property appraised at less than one hundred pounds sterling. Men whose estates fell into this range led very simple lives. In most cases, livestock accounted for more than half the total value of their personal possessions. At best their clothing and household furnishings were meager. They either worked their plantations themselves or with the help of their wives and children, for few of these small planters owned servants and even fewer owned slaves. In Aubrey Land's apt phrase, they led lives of "rude sufficiency." But they fared no better than if they had remained in England.

Not all former servants remained small planters. Twelve of the thirty-one left estates appraised at more than one hundred pounds. Men such as John Halfhead, Francis Pope, and James Walker could be described as substantial planters. Their life style was not luxurious, but their economic position was secure and their assets usually included a servant or two and perhaps even a slave. Two men, Zachary Wade and Henry Adams, gained entry into the group of planter-merchants who dominated the local economy in the seventeenth century. Wade, whose estate was appraised at just over four hundred pounds, was wealthier than 95 percent of his contemporaries, while Adams left an estate valued at £569 15s. 1d. when he died in 1686.

There are still other measures of mobility which confirm the picture of abundant opportunity for ex-servants that the study of property accumulation has indicated. Abbot E. Smith has estimated that only two of every ten servants brought to America in the seventeenth century became stable and useful members of colonial society, but if we take participation in government as indicative of stability and usefulness, the careers of the 158 men who survived servitude demonstrate that Smith's estimates are much too low, at least for the earlier part of the century.

Former servants participated in the government of Maryland as jurors, minor office holders, justices of the peace, sheriffs, burgesses, and officers in the militia. Many also attended the Assembly as freemen at those sessions at which they were permitted. The frequency with which responsible positions were given to ex-servants testifies to the impressive status mobility they achieved in the mid-seventeenth century. Seventy-five or seventy-six of the survivors—just under 50 percent—sat on a jury, attended an Assembly session, or filled an office in Maryland. As was the case with landholding, this figure must be understood in light of the careers of those who failed to participate. Fourteen of the nonparticipants died within a decade of becoming freemen; another twenty-seven left the province within ten years of completing their terms. There is no reason to assume that those who left did not participate in their new homes—two of the twenty-seven, John Tue and Mathew Rhodan, became justices of the peace in Virginia, while two others, Thomas Yewell and Robert Sedgrave, served as militia officer and clerk of a county court respectively. If we eliminate the twenty-five who appeared but fleetingly in the records, only sixteen or seventeen (slightly more than 10 percent) lived for more than a decade in the province as freemen without leaving any record of contribution to the community's government.

For most former servants participation was limited to occasional service as a juror, an appointment as constable, or service as a sergeant in the militia. Some compiled remarkable records in these minor positions. William Edwin, who was brought into the province in 1634 by Richard Gerard and served his time with the Jesuits, sat on nine provincial court juries and served a term as constable. Richard Nevill, who also entered Maryland in 1634, served on six provincial court juries and was a sergeant in the militia. A former servant of Gov. Leonard Calvert, John Halfhead, served on eleven juries and attended two sessions of the Assembly. John Robinson managed, in five years before his death in 1643, to attend two Assemblies, sit on three provincial court juries, and serve as constable and coroner of St. Clement's Hundred.

A high percentage of the 158 survivors went beyond service in these minor posts to positions of authority in the community. Twenty-two of them served the province as justice of the peace, burgess, sheriff, councillor, or officer in the militia. They accounted for four of Maryland's militia officers, twelve burgesses, sixteen justices, seven sheriffs, and two members of the Council.

For nine of the twenty-two former servants who came to hold major office in Maryland, tenure was brief. They served for a few years as an officer in the militia or as a county justice, or sat as burgess in a single session of the Assembly. . . .

Although the personal history of each of these 158 men is unique, common patterns may be discerned. We can construct a career model for indentured servants in Maryland in the middle of the seventeenth century which should reveal something about the way opportunity was structured and what options were open to men at various stages in their lives. We can also identify some of the components necessary for constructing a successful career in Maryland.

As a group, the indentured servants were young when they emigrated. While they ranged in age from mere boys such as Ralph Hasleton to the "old and decripit" Original Browne, the great majority were in their late teens and early twenties. Age on arrival was determined in thirty-six cases with a median of nineteen. Probably most were from English families of the "middling sort," yeomen, husbandmen, and artisans, men whose expectations might well include the acquisition of a freehold or participation in local government.

The careers of these men suggest that a few had formal education. Robert Vaughan and Robert Sedgrave both served as clerks in county court, a position requiring record-keeping skills. Cuthbert Fenwick was attorney to Thomas Cornwallis, who was probably the wealthiest man in Maryland in the 1630s and 1640s. It seems unlikely that Cornwallis would have allowed a man without education to manage his estate during his frequent absences from the province. These men were, however, not at all typical, for most of the 158 survivors were without education. Total illiterates outnumbered those who could write their names by about three to two, and it is probable that many who could sign their names could do little more.

A servant's life was not easy, even by seventeenth-century standards. Probably they worked the ten to fourteen hours a day, six days a week, specified in the famous Elizabethan Statute of Artificers. Servants could be sold, and there were severe penalties for running away. They were subject to the discipline of their masters, including corporal punishment within reason. On the other hand, servants had rights to adequate food, clothing, shelter, and a Sunday free from hard labor. Servants could not sue at common law, but they could protest ill-treatment and receive a hearing in the courts. Cases in this period are few, but the provincial court seems to have taken seriously its obligation to enforce the terms of indentures and protect servants' rights. No instances of serious mistreatment of servants appear in the records in the late 1630s and early 1640s. Servants were worked long and hard, but they were seldom abused. Moreover, the servant who escaped premature death soon found himself a free man in a society that offered great opportunities for advancement.

None of the indentures signed by these servants has survived, but it is possible to offer some reasonable conjecture concerning the terms of their service. John Lewger and Jerome Hawley, in their *Relation of Maryland,* offered some advice to men thinking of transporting servants into the province and they also printed a model indenture. A servant was to work at whatever his master "shall there imploy him, according to the custome of the Countrey." In return, the master was to pay his passage and provide food, lodging, clothing, and other "necessaries" during the servant's term "and at the end of the said term, to give him one whole yeeres provision of Corne, and fifty acres of Land, according to the order of the countrey." The order or custom of the country was specified in an act passed by the October 1640 session of the Assembly. Upon completion of his term the servant was to receive "one good Cloth Suite of Keirsey or Broadcloth a Shift of white linen one new pair of Stockins and Shoes two hoes one axe 3 barrels of Corne and fifty acres of land five whereof at least to be plantable." The land records make it clear that the requirement that masters give their former servants fifty acres of land cannot be taken literally. In practice, custom demanded only that a master provide a servant with the rights for fifty acres, an obligation assumed by the proprietor in 1648. If a servant wished to take advantage of this right and actually acquire a tract, he had to locate some vacant land and pay surveyor's and clerk's fees himself.

The usual term of service, according to Lewger and Hawley, was five years. However, they suggested, "for any artificer, or one that shall deserve more than ordinary, the Adventurer shall doe well to shorten that time . . . rather then to want such usefull men." A bill considered but not passed by the 1639 Assembly would have required servants arriving in Maryland without indentures to serve for four years if they were eighteen years old or over and until the age of twenty-four if they were under eighteen. The gap between time of arrival and first appearance in the records as freemen for the men under study suggests that the terms specified in this rejected bill were often followed in practice.

Servants were occasionally able to work out arrangements with their masters which allowed them to become freemen before their terms were completed. John Courts and Francis Pope purchased their remaining time from Fulke Brent, probably arranging to pay him out of whatever money they could earn by working as freemen. Thomas Todd, a glover, was released from servitude early by his master, John Lewger. In return, Todd was to dress a specified number of skins and also to make breeches and gloves to Lewger. George Evelin released three of his servants, Philip West, William Williamson, and John Hopson, for one year, during which they were to provide food, clothing, and lodging for themselves and also pay Evelin one thousand pounds of tobacco each. Such opportunities were not available to all servants, however, and most probably served full terms.

On achieving freedom there were three options open to the former servant: he could either hire out for wages, lease land and raise tobacco on his own, or work on another man's plantation as a sharecropper. Although custom demanded that servants be granted the rights to fifty acres of land on completing their terms, actual acquisition of a tract during the first year of freedom was simply impracticable, and all former servants who eventually became freeholders were free for at least two years before they did so. To acquire land, one had to either pay surveyor's and clerk's fees for a patent or pay a purchase price to a landholder. The land then had to be cleared and housing erected. Provisions had to be obtained in some way until the crop was harvested, for a man could not survive a growing season on a mere three barrels of corn. Tools, seed, and livestock were also necessary. All this required capital, and capital was precisely what servants did not have. Wage labor, sharecropping, and leaseholding all offered men a chance to accumulate enough capital to get started on their own plantations and to sustain themselves in the meantime.

Wages were high in mid-seventeenth-century Maryland, usually fifteen to twenty pounds of tobacco per day for unskilled agricultural labor and even higher for those with much needed skills. These were remarkable rates given the fact that a man working alone could harvest, on the average, no more than fifteen hundred to two thousand pounds of tobacco a year. Thirty-two of the 158 survivors were designated artisans in the records: 11 carpenters,

4 blacksmiths, 5 tailors, 4 sawyers, 2 millwrights, a brickmason, mariner, cooper, glover, and barber-surgeon. These men probably had little trouble marketing their skills. At a time when labor was scarce, even men who had nothing but a strong back and willing hands must have found all the work they wanted. However, few of the 158 men devoted themselves to full time wage labor for extended periods. Instead, most worked their own crop and only hired out occasionally to supplement their planting income.

Nevertheless, some men did sign contracts or enter into verbal agreements for long-term wage labor. There were some differences between their status and that of indentured servants. They probably could not be sold, they could sue at common law for breach of covenant, and they may have possessed some political privileges. There were severe restrictions on their personal freedom, however, and their daily life must have been similar to a servant's. Wages ranged from eleven hundred to fifteen hundred pounds of tobacco a year plus shelter, food, and clothing. Ex-servants occasionally hired out for long terms, perhaps because of heavy indebtedness or lack of alternative opportunities, or perhaps because of the security such contracts afforded. Recently freed servants may have found long-term wage contracts an attractive means of making the transition from indentured laborer to free colonist. While long-term wage labor was, in a sense, a prolongation of servitude, it could also serve as a means of capital accumulation and an avenue of mobility.

The records reveal little of the extent or conditions of sharecropping in the 1640s, but it is clear that several of the 158 former servants did work on another man's plantation for a share of the crop. By the 1660s—and there seems no reason to assume that this was not also the case in the earlier period—working for a "share" meant that a man joined other workers on a plantation in making a crop, the size of his share to be determined by dividing the total crop by the number of laborers. Contracts often required the plantation owner to pay the cropper's taxes and provide diet, lodging, and washing, while obliging the cropper to work at other tasks around the plantation. The status of such sharecroppers seems indistinguishable from that of wage laborers on long-term contracts.

Most of the 158 former servants established themselves as small planters on leased land immediately after they had completed their terms. There were two types of leases available to ex-servants, leaseholds for life or for a long term of years and short-term leaseholds or tenancies at will. Although these forms of leaseholding differed in several important respects, both allowed the tenant to become the head of a household. As householders, former bondsmen achieved a degree of independence and a measure of responsibility denied to servants, wage laborers, and sharecroppers. Heads of households were masters in their own families, responsible for the discipline, education, and maintenance of their subordinates. They formed the backbone of the political community, serving on juries, sitting in Assembly, and filling the minor offices. The favorable man/land ratio in early Maryland made the formation of new households a fairly easy task and servants usually became householders soon after completing their terms.

In many ways there was little difference between land held in fee simple and a lease for life or for a long term of years. Such leases were inheritable and could be sold; they were usually purchased for a lump sum and yearly rents were often nominal. Terms varied considerably, but all long-term leaseholds provided the tenant a secure tenure and a chance to build up equity in his property. Such leases were not common in seventeenth-century Maryland, although a few appear on the private manors in St. Mary's County in the 1640s. Probably men were reluctant to purchase a lease when they could acquire land in fee simple for little additional outlay.

Tenancies at will or short-term leaseholds, usually running for no more than six or seven years, were undoubtedly the most common form of tenure for recently freed servants. In contrast to long-term leases, short-term leaseholds offered little security, could not be sold or inherited, and terminated at the death of either party to the contract. Their great advantage was the absence of an entry fee, a feature particularly attractive to men without capital. Since land was plentiful and labor scarce, rents must have been low, certainly no higher than five hundred pounds of tobacco a year for a plantation and perhaps as low as two hundred pounds. Rent for the first year, furthermore, was probably not demanded until after the crop was in. No contracts for the 1640s have survived, but later in the century tenants were often required to make extensive improvements on the plantation. Although tenure was insecure, short-term leaseholding afforded ample opportunity for mobility as long as tobacco prices remained high. In the 1640s and 1650s, leaseholding benefited both landlord and tenant. Landlords had their land cleared, housing erected, and orchards planted and fenced while receiving a small rental income. Tenants were able to accumulate the capital necessary to acquire a tract of their own.

Prior to 1660, small planters, whether leaseholders or landowners, frequently worked in partnership with another man when attempting to carve new plantations out of the wilderness. Much hard work was involved in clearing land, building shelter, and getting in a crop; men who could not afford to buy servants or pay wages often joined with a mate. Partners Joseph Edlow and Christopher Martin, John Courts and Francis Pope, John Shirtcliffe and Henry Spinke, and William Brown and John Thimbelly were all former servants who arrived in Maryland before the end of 1642. They must have found their "mateships" mutually beneficial, since, except for Martin who died in 1641, all eventually became landowners.

Some men—about 10 percent of those former servants who lived in Maryland for more than a decade as freemen—did not manage to escape tenancy. Rowland Mace, for example, was still a leaseholder on St. Clement's Manor in 1659, after which he disappeared from the records. The inventory of the estate of Charles Steward, who lived on Kent Island as a freeman for more than forty years and was frequently called planter, indicates that he was operating a plantation when he died in 1685, but Steward failed to acquire freehold title to a tract of his own. A few others acquired land, held it briefly, and then returned to leaseholding arrangements. John Maunsell had some prosperous years in Maryland. He arrived in the province in 1638 as a servant to William Bretton and served about four years. He patented one hundred acres in 1649 and added five hundred more in 1651, but he could not hold the land and in 1653 sold it all to William Whittle. He then moved to St. Clement's

Manor, where he took up a leasehold, and was still a tenant on the manor when he died in 1660. John Shanks, although he too suffered fluctuations in prosperity, ended his career on a more positive note. Entering Maryland in 1640 as a servant to Thomas Gerard, he must have been quite young when he arrived, for he did not gain his freedom until 1648. In 1652 he patented two hundred acres and also purchased the freedom of one Abigail, a servant to Robert Brooke, whom he soon married. He sold his land in 1654, and, following Maunsell's path, took up a leasehold on St. Clement's Manor. Shanks, however, managed to attain the status of a freeholder again, owning three hundred acres in St. Mary's County when he died in 1684. His inventory—the estate was appraised at just under one hundred pounds—indicates that Shanks ended life in Maryland as a fairly prosperous small planter.

Most of the 158 former servants, if they lived in Maryland for more than ten years as freemen, acquired land and held it for as long as they remained in the province. Almost any healthy man in Maryland in the 1640s and 1650s, if he worked hard, practiced thrift, avoided expensive lawsuits, and did not suffer from plain bad luck, could become a landowner in a short time. Tobacco prices were relatively high, and, while living costs may also have been high, land was not expensive. Even at the highest rates a one hundred-acre tract could be patented for less than five hundred pounds of tobacco, and even the lowest estimates indicate that a man could harvest twelve hundred pounds in a year. Again barring ill-health and misfortune, retaining land once acquired must not have been too difficult a task, at least before tobacco prices fell after the Restoration.

Hard work and thrift were, of course, not the only paths to landownership. For some the fruits of office cleared the way. William Empson, for example, was still a tenant to Thomas Baker in 1658, after ten years of freedom. In 1659, Nicholas Gwyther employed him as deputy sheriff, and in the next year Empson was able to purchase a plantation from his former landlord. Others charmed their way to the status of freeholder. Henry Adams married Mary Cockshott, daughter of John Cockshott and stepdaughter of Nicholas Causine, both of whom were substantial Maryland planters. To the historian, though perhaps not to Adams, Miss Cockshott's most obvious asset was twelve hundred acres of land which her mother had taken up for her and her sister Jane in 1649.

For most former servants progress stopped with the acquisition of a small plantation. Others managed to go beyond small planter status to become men of wealth and power. What was it that distinguished the 13 former servants who became men of importance in Maryland politics from the other 145 who survived servitude?

Education was one factor. We have already seen that a few of the 158 probably possessed some formal training. Early colonial Maryland did not have enough educated men to serve as justices or sheriffs, perform clerical and surveying functions, or work as attorneys in the courts. Under such conditions, a man proficient with the pen could do quite well for himself. Men such as Cuthbert Fenwick, Robert Vaughan, and Robert Sedgrave found their education valuable in making the transition from servant to man of consequence.

While approximately 60 percent of the 158 who survived servitude were totally illiterate, only 2 of the 13 who came to exercise real power in Maryland and only 7 of the 22 who held major office were unable to write their names.

Marriage played a role in some of the most impressive success stories. Henry Adams's marriage has already been mentioned. Zachary Wade married a niece of Thomas Hatton, principal secretary of Maryland in the 1650s. James Langsworth married a Gardiner thereby allying himself with a very prominent southern Maryland family. Cuthbert Fenwick married at least twice. We know nothing of his first wife, but Fenwick found fame and fortune by marrying in 1649 Jane Moryson, widow of a prominent Virginian, a niece of Edward Eltonhead, one of the masters of chancery, and a sister of William Eltonhead, who sat on the Maryland Council in the 1650s.

It would be a mistake, however, to overestimate the significance of education and marriage in the building of a successful career. Certainly they helped, but they were not essential ingredients. Nicholas Gwyther became a man of consequence in Maryland, but married a former servant. John Warren served as justice of St. Mary's County for nine years, but could not write his name. Daniel Clocker and John Maunsell both held major office in Maryland. Both were illiterate and both married former servants. Clearly, Maryland in the middle of the seventeenth century was open enough to allow a man who started at the bottom without special advantages to acquire a substantial estate and a responsible position.

It seems probable that Maryland continued to offer ambitious immigrants without capital a good prospect of advancement throughout the 1640s and 1650s. But there is evidence to suggest that opportunities declined sharply after 1660. True, the society did not become completely closed and some men who started life among the servants were still able to end life among the masters. Miles Gibson is a case in point, and there were others. Philip Lynes emigrated as a servant in the late 1660s and later became a member of the Council and a man of considerable wealth. Christopher Goodhand, who also entered Maryland as a servant in the late 1660s, later served as justice of Kent County and left an estate appraised at nearly six hundred pounds. However, in the latter part of the century men such as Gibson, Goodhand, and Lynes were unusual; at mid-century they were not. . . .

This reduction in the proportion of former servants among Maryland's rulers is directly related to basic demographic processes that worked fundamental changes in the colony's political structure. The rapid growth in the population of the province during the seventeenth century affected the life chances of former servants in at least two ways. First, there was a reduction in the number of offices available in proportion to the number of freemen, resulting in increased competition for positions of power and profit. Secondly, there was an increase in the number of men of wealth and status available to fill positions of authority. In the decades immediately following the founding of the province there were simply not enough men who conformed to the standards people expected their rulers to meet. As a consequence, many uneducated small planters of humble origins were called upon to rule. Among the immigrants to Maryland after the Restoration were a number of younger sons of English gentry families and an even larger number of merchants, many of whom were attracted to the Chesapeake as a result of their engagement in the tobacco trade. By the late seventeenth century, these new arrivals, together with a steadily growing number of native gentlemen, had created a ruling group with more wealth, higher status, and better education than the men who had ruled earlier in the century. As this group grew in size, poor illiterate planters were gradually excluded from office. . . .

Former servants also found that their chances of acquiring land and of serving as jurors and minor office holders were decreasing. Probably the movement of prices for tobacco and land was the most important factor responsible for this decline of opportunity. During the 1640s and 1650s, the available evidence—which, it must be admitted, is not entirely satisfactory—indicates that farm prices for Chesapeake tobacco fluctuated between one and one-half and three pence per pound. After 1660, prices declined due to overproduction, mercantilist restrictions, and a poorly developed marketing system that allowed farm prices to sink far below those justified by European price levels. . . .

One consequence of these price changes was a change in the nature and dimensions of short-term leaseholding. In the 1640s and 1650s, tenancy was a typical step taken by a man without capital on the road to land acquisition. However, falling tobacco prices and rising land prices made it increasingly difficult to accumulate the capital necessary to purchase a freehold. In the 1660s fragmentary results suggest that only 10 percent of the householders in Maryland were established on land they did not own. By the end of the century the proportion of tenants had nearly tripled. Tenancy was no longer a transitory status; for many it had become a permanent fate.

A gradual constriction of the political community paralleled the rise *in* tenancy. In years immediately following settlement, all freemen, whether or not they owned land, regularly participated in government as voters, jurors and minor office holders. At the beginning of the eighteenth century a very different situation prevailed. In a proclamation of 1670, Lord Baltimore disfranchised all freemen who possessed neither fifty acres of land nor a visible estate worth forty pounds sterling. This meant, in effect, that short-term leaseholders could no longer vote, since few could meet the forty pounds requirement. Furthermore, by the early eighteenth century landowners virtually monopolized jury duty and the minor offices. In the middle of the seventeenth century, most freemen in Maryland had an ample opportunity to acquire land and participate in community government; by the end of the century a substantial portion of the free male heads of households were excluded from the political process and unable to become landowners. . . .

From 1662 to 1672, 179 servants were brought into the Charles County Court to have their ages judged. Only 58 of the 179 definitely appeared in the records as freemen, a fact which in itself suggests declining opportunities, since there does seem to be a relationship between a man's importance in the community and the frequency of his appearance in the public records. Of the 58 of whom something could be learned, only 13 to 17—22 to 29 percent—eventually became landowners. Furthermore, none acquired great wealth. Mark Lampton, who owned 649 acres in the early 1690s, was the largest landowner in the group and the only one who owned more than 500 acres. Robert Benson, whose estate was appraised at just over two hundred pounds, left the largest inventory. Lampton was the only other one of the 58 whose estate was valued at more than one hundred pounds.

A study of the participation of these men in local government indicates that opportunities in this field were also declining. Only twenty-three to twenty-five of the fifty-eight sat on a jury or filled an office, and the level at which they participated was low. Only one, Henry Hardy, who was appointed to the Charles County bench in 1696, held major office. A few others compiled impressive records as minor office holders. Mathew Dike, for example, sat on eight juries and served as overseer of the highways and constable, while Robert Benson was twice a constable and fourteen times a juryman. For most of these men, however, occasional service as a juror was the limit of their participation. Five of the twenty-three known participants served only once as a juror, while another six only sat twice.

The contrast between the careers of these 58 men and the 158 who entered Maryland before 1642 is stark. At least 46 of the 58 lived in the province as freemen for over a decade. In other words, 50 to 57 percent lived in Maryland as freemen for more than ten years and did not acquire land, while 36 to 40 percent did not participate in government. Only about 10 percent of the 158 who arrived in the earlier period and lived in the colony for a decade as freemen failed to become landowners and participants.

How successful, then, in the light of these data, was the institution of servitude in seventeenth-century Maryland? The answer depends on perspective and chronology. Servitude had two primary functions. From the master's viewpoint its function was to supply labor. From the point of view of the prospective immigrant without capital, servitude was a means of mobility, both geographic and social; that is, it was a way of getting to the New World and, once there, of building a life with more prosperity and standing than one could reasonably expect to attain at home. Its success in performing these two quite different functions varied inversely as the century progressed. Prior to 1660, servitude served both purposes well. It provided large planters with an inexpensive and capable work force and allowed poor men entry into a society offering great opportunities for advancement. This situation in which the two purposes complemented each other did not last, and the institution gradually became more successful at supplying labor as it became less so at providing new opportunities. Some men were always able to use servitude as an avenue of mobility, but, over the course of the century, more and more found that providing labor for larger planters, first as servants and later as tenants, was their permanent fate.

POSTSCRIPT

Were the First Colonists in the Chesapeake Region Lazy, Ignorant, and Unambitious?

Professor Edmund S. Morgan is the preeminent colonial American historian who has trained three generations of scholars at Yale University. Now in his eighties, Morgan is still a productive scholar writing books and review essays for the *New York Review of Books* on the latest output of scholarship in the field. For a convenient compilation of Morgan's essays, see *The Genuine Article: A Historian Looks at Early America* (Norton, 2004).

Morgan's chapter on the "Jamestown Fiasco" is important for several reasons. First of all, he rejects the New England model of colonization as being typical. Earlier generations of colonial historians wrote a lot about the Puritans because they kept extensive written legal and church records as well as diaries—all of which provided historians with an abundance of traditional historical sources. Morgan anticipated the framework of Jack P. Greene, *Pursuits of Happiness: The Social Development of Early Modern British Colonies and the Formation of American Culture* (University of North Carolina Press, 1988) and others who see the Chesapeake settlements (and not New England) as typical of the expansionist policies of the British empire in Ireland and the West Indies. He also implies that the original colonists were trying to imitate the Spaniards to the extent that they hoped to extract mineral wealth from the colonists for export such as iron ore, salt making, glass making, silk making, and pitch. Unfortunately these resources were not available in the original Virginia settlements.

Professor Morgan also dispatches the romantic view that many historians attributed to the colonists. He discusses in other parts of his book the "guerilla warfare" that existed between the first European settlers and the Indians. Though earlier historians have focused on the hardships of the first Virginians and the starving time of the winter of 1609–1610 that led to cannibalism. Morgan blames the colonists themselves for their plight. The colonists did not take advantage of the abundance of fish and game in Virginia nor did they plant enough grain and corn to feed themselves. Why this occurred was partly due to the social backround of the earliest settlers—too many "gentlemen" and not enough farmers. But Morgan extends his argument even further. The colonists modeled themselves after their English kin and hoped to set up small industries producing exports with agriculture as only a minor part of the economy. As previously mentioned the mineral resources did not exist. Ironically Virginia became a productive colony in later decades when tobacco became the export of salvation.

Professor Russell R. Menard is part of the group of Chesapeake scholars who have mined the records of the Maryland archives, which contain county records of land deeds, land sales, slave transactions, indentured servant contracts, marriages, probation of wills, and contested court cases. Because the population of seventeenth century Maryland was relatively small, increasing from 4,018 in 1660 to 34,172 in 1700, quantitative historians can study large aggregates of the seventeenth century population and get answers to questions about average family sizes, mortality rates, trade patterns, consumption habits, economic wealth, and mobility patterns.

Menard's study of the social mobility in seventeenth century Maryland employs modern sociological concepts in studying the records of the indentured servants found in the Maryland archives. By studying the land records and indentured contracts for the various southern and eastern shore Maryland counties found in the Maryland archives, Menard argues that the first generation of the newly freed indentured servants were upwardly mobile, and achieved land ownership, and sizeable amounts of wealth and political offices.

But Menard argues that the second generations of servants freed in the 1660s and thereafter achieved limited success due to the lack of good cheap land, fluctuating and often downward tobacco prices, and the inability to achieve political offices.

Professors Morgan and Menard disagree on the quality and backgrounds of the earliest settlers to Virginia and Maryland, respectively. Perhaps Maryland's indentured servants were better because the founders of Maryland profited from the mistakes of England's first successful colony. Perhaps the traditional sources used by Morgan and the quantitative by Menard lend themselves to differing interpretations. But both historians agree that by 1700 both Virginia and Maryland created a more stratified society with a wealthy planter class tied into tobacco growing where slave labor replaced the indentured servants as the major workforce.

The starting point for the modern study of *Seventeenth Century America: Essays in Colonial History,* ed. by James Norton Smith (University of North Carolina Press, 1959), are the essays by Bernard Bailyn, "Politics and Social Structure in Virginia" and Mildred Campbell's "Social Origins of Some Early Americans," the latter's middle-class origins challenged by David Galenson's books and articles. See for example "'Middling People' or 'Common Sort'? The Social Origins of Some Early Americans Reexamined . . . " with Campbell's rebuttal in the *William and Mary Quarterly* xxxv/3 (July 1978), pp. 499–540. Both views are challenged by Lorena S. Walsh's study of servants. See "Servitude and Opportunity in Charles County, Maryland, 1658–1705."

Walsh's essay and those of many seventeenth century "cliometricians" can be found in Aubrey C. Land, Lois Green Carr, and Edward C. Papenfuse, *Law, Society and Politics in Early Maryland* (John Hopkins University Press, 1977). See the introductions and the essays in two other important collections: Thad W. Tate and David L. Ammerman, eds., *The Chesapeake in the Seventeenth Century: Essays on Anglo-American Society* (University of North Carolina Press, 1979) and Lois Green Carr, Philip D. Morgan and Jean B. Russo, eds., *Colonial Chesapeake Society* (University of North Carolina Press, 1988).

ISSUE 4

Did Colonial New England Women Enjoy Significant Economic Autonomy?

YES: Gloria L. Main, from "Gender, Work, and Wages in Colonial New England," *The William and Mary Quarterly*, 3d series, 51 (January 1994)

NO: Lyle Koehler, from *A Search for Power: The "Weaker Sex" in Seventeenth-Century New England* (University of Illinois Press, 1980)

ISSUE SUMMARY

YES: Gloria Main notes that New England women were highly valued for their labor and relative scarcity in the early colonial period and that their economic autonomy increased in the years during and following the Seven Years War as more women entered the paid labor force and received higher wages for their work.

NO: Lyle Koehler contends that Puritan attitudes toward rights of inheritance, as well as the division of labor that separated work into male and female spheres, discouraged productive, independent activity on the part of New England women.

Students in American history classes have for generations read of the founding of the colonies in British North America, their political and economic development, and the colonists' struggles for independence, without ever being confronted by a female protagonist in this magnificent historical drama. The terms "sons of liberty" and "founding fathers" reflect the end result of a long tradition of gender-specific myopia. In fact, only in the last generation have discussions of the role of women in the development of American society made their appearance in standard textbooks. Consequently, it is useful to explore the status of women in colonial America.

The topic, of course, is quite complex. The status of colonial women was determined by cultural attitudes that were exported to the New World from Europe, by the specific conditions confronting successive waves of settlers—male and female—in terms of labor requirements, and by changes produced by colonial maturation over time. It would be impossible to pinpoint a single, static condition in which *all* colonial women existed.

What was the status of women in the British North American colonies? To what degree did the legal status of women differ from their *de facto* status? A half-century of scholarship has produced the notion that colonial women enjoyed a more privileged status than either their European contemporaries or their nineteenth-century descendants. In the 1970s John Demos and Roger Thompson reinforced this view developed earlier in the writings of Richard B. Morris, Elizabeth Dexter, and Mary Beard. For example, Demos contends that despite the fact that Plymouth Colony was based on a patriarchal model in which women were expected to subordinate themselves to men, women still shared certain responsibilities with their husbands in some business activities and in matters relating to their children. They not only performed all the household duties but also assisted the men with agricultural duties outside the home when the necessity arose.

Women were closed off from any formal public power in the colony even when they performed essential economic functions within the community. In colonial America and during the American Revolution, they practiced law, pounded iron as blacksmiths, trapped for furs and tanned leather, made guns, built ships, and edited and printed newspapers. At the same time, however, colonial society viewed women as subordinate beings. They held no political power within the individual colonies and still were suspect as the transmitters of evil, simply because they were women. Nor was it a coincidence that most suspected witches were female. Many of those accused of witchcraft in late-seventeenth-century New England were older women who had inherited land that traditionally would have gone to males. Such patterns of inheritance disrupted the normative male-dominated social order. Witchcraft hysteria in colonial America, then, was a by-product of economic pressures *and* gender exploitation.

The following essays explore the economic status of women in colonial New England. Gloria Main compares types of work, pay scales, and trends in wages in the seventeenth and eighteenth centuries and discovers that the division of labor between men and women was less clearly defined than traditionally assumed. Because they were relatively scarce, she concludes, women were valued for their labor and, as time passed, New England women developed a significant degree of economic autonomy.

Lyle Koehler insists that economic and social factors discouraged productive, independent activity on the part of New England women. Given limited opportunities for occupational training and denied access to public schools, most women were resigned to poorly paid jobs. Rarely did they inherit enough to start their own businesses. The only way for most women to experience upward economic mobility, Koehler claims, was to marry well.

Gloria L. Main

 **YES**

Gender, Work, and Wages in Colonial New England

. . . Historians of colonial women . . . tend to ignore economic issues when debating trends in women's status and condition. Most believe that white women were more highly regarded in the colonies than at home, because of the higher value of their labor and their relative scarcity, at least in the seventeenth century in regions such as the Chesapeake. Others posit that economic opportunities for women narrowed as colonial society developed beyond primitive conditions in which women shouldered burdens customarily borne by men. Data presented below lend support to the first proposition but dispute the second.

This article examines the types of work women in early New England did compared to men, weighs relative pay scales, and explores trends in the wages of both sexes. Evidence comes from two types of sources: wage ceilings discussed or imposed by governments in 1670 and 1777 and pay rates found in account books, diaries, and probate records. These sources also supply the basis for estimating women's rates of participation in the paid labor force and for tabulating the types of work women performed for pay. All of this material can be conveniently summarized by dividing the colonial period into four phases: initial growth (1620–1674), crisis and recovery (1675–1714), stability (1715–1754), and expansion (1755–1774). The sequence, however, defies simple linear interpretations of progression, either from good conditions to bad, declension, or from bad conditions to good, progress. Both the status of women and the region's economy experienced cycles of good and bad times, but the closing decades of the period saw real improvement for both. Perhaps the most important lesson of this investigation is that even relatively modest economic changes can, by their cumulative actions, significantly alter family relations and living standards. . . .

Settlers in a new land must find ways to acquire the goods they want and cannot make for themselves. For New Englanders, this proved a major challenge. Probably the most notable characteristic of the economy that is evident in probate inventories was the economy's dependence on England for manufactures of all sorts, including textiles. In the first generation after settlement, few women could have engaged in spinning, weaving, or dyeing simply because unprocessed

From *William & Mary Quarterly* by Gloria Main, pp. 41–42, 52–66. Copyright © 1994 by Omohundro Institute of Early American History & Culture. Reprinted by permission.

textile fibers were in short supply. "Farmers deem it better for their profit to put away [sell] their cattel and corn for cloathing, then to set upon making of cloth." Flax production was labor intensive, and sheep did not thrive under pioneering conditions: wolves found them easy prey, and the woodland underbrush tore away their wool. By the 1670s these conditions had changed. An aggressive bounty system and the spread of settlements into the interior gradually exterminated the wolves and cleared enough pastureland so that sheep became a more familiar sight on mainland farms. Spinning wheels, mentioned in Plymouth Colony inventories as early as 1644, gradually became common, and most mid-century householders' inventories in Plymouth and neighboring colonies listed wool and flax, and some mention sheep, cotton, and even homemade cloth. Still, textile production must have continued to fall short of potential demand, because few people chose to invest their time in weaving. Of roughly 1,500 inventories dating from before 1675, only thirty, all for men, list looms. Similarly, when Carl Bridenbaugh recorded the occupations of men in the early volumes of Rhode Island land evidences, he identified only one weaver and one cloth worker out of forty-two artisans before 1670.

Nor did many early households possess the tools for such women's tasks as brewing, baking, or dairying. Only a few women appear anywhere in John Pynchon's Connecticut Valley accounts. Of the four women he mentioned in the 1640s, one received pay for chickens and eggs, one for weeding, one for making hay, and the fourth for domestic service. There is no mention of brewing, baking, or butter making, although in 1648 Pynchon paid Henry Burt for making malt, probably from the barley mowed by Richard Excell that year, and Pynchon paid another man for milking his cows in 1666–1667. The first reference to spinning appears in 1663, to knitting in 1668, and to sewing in 1669.

Most of New England's people were farmers. Women who were not tied down by young children probably spent their time outdoors working in gardens or with their men in the fields. Although English women did not customarily do heavy field work, they did garden with hoes, and in the colonies the hoe played a major role wherever families could use existing Indian fields. In early Saybrook Alice Apsley marketed medicinal herbs and onions from her garden. Goody Macksfield supplied a Boston shopkeeper with apples, squashes, beans, cucumbers, carrots, and cabbages, as well as honey, butter, cheese, and eggs. C. Dallett Hemphill examined the work activities of Salem women recorded in testimony before the Essex County court between 1636 and 1683 and found them engaged in men's work or working with men: servant Ann Knight winnowed corn, another woman carried grain to the mill, and others milked cows and branded steers in the company of men; a witness in one case remembered seeing the wife of Joseph Dalaber working alongside her husband planting and covering corn.

. . . [T]he ratio of women's pay to men's pay was at its highest point in this early period when the division of labor between men and women was less clearly defined than in contemporary England or as it later came to be in New England. Women could hoe in already-cleared Indian fields, and meadows and salt marshes supplied their small herds of animals with forage. When these sites filled up and the numbers of livestock expanded, newcomers had to break new ground and create meadows planted with English grasses. Inventories record the gradual advent of a more English farming style using heavy plows drawn by teams of oxen, while tax lists and town genealogies trace the growing supply of sturdy young sons. Similarly, the appearance of spinning wheels, firkins, brewing vats, and dye pots attests to the kinds of activities that came to employ women. The division of labor between the sexes widened and, as it did so, separated them physically.

The use of ox teams, restricted to older men, effectively segregated family members into field and home workers. Men and older boys also did the sowing and harrowing at the beginning of the farm year and the reaping and mowing at harvest. In early spring they planted and pruned orchards and carted and spread dung. In June they washed and sheared sheep. In fall they pressed cider and slaughtered hogs. In the slack seasons men cut and dragged timber, built and maintained fences, cleared underbrush, ditched bogs, and dug out stones. In most of these activities, handling draft animals was essential and was work for males only. The men used oxen to remove stumps and boulders, drag timber, cart dung, and haul hay and horses to drive cider presses. Only men and older boys paddled canoes, steered scows, piloted "gundalows" (gondolas), or rowed boats.

Women participated in none of these activities except at harvest time, when their help was welcomed. Even then, they did not mow grass or grain, because most did not have the height or upper body strength to handle scythes. Diaries after 1750 show them helping with the reaping, probably binding sheaves and sickling wheat and rye. Young Jabez Fitch of Norwich, Connecticut, reported enthusiastically in his diary on July 24, 1759, "there was a great Reeping[;] we Liv'd very well[;] we had Women anough & Some more." A story related in a town history about one woman's feat is no doubt apocryphal but interesting for its celebration of women's physical achievements in a less genteel age: a Mrs. Brown of Chester, New Hampshire, around the year 1800 or earlier, with others had sowed rye for its seed. At harvest time she prepared breakfast, nursed her child, walked five or six miles to the field, reaped her rye (finishing before any of the men), and walked back home.

Men's diaries also describe both sexes and all ages gathering corn by day and husking together at night, making the work an occasion for a frolic. Both sexes and all ages went berrying and nutting together. Young people often turned such occasions to their own devices, especially when gathering strawberries on long June evenings. The excitement these occasions could create is recorded in the diary of a Harvard undergraduate, who, with other young men, succeeded in transforming a quilting party into a late night gala.

Many farm tasks fell more or less exclusively to the female members of the household. Girls and women tended the fowl and small animals. They milked the cows at dawn and dusk, separated the cream, churned the butter, and made the cheese. They planted and hoed kitchen gardens in plots men had prepared by plowing and harrowing. Women boiled the offal for such by-products as sausage casings, head cheese, calf's foot jelly, and rennet after men killed, cleaned, and butchered animals. Gender-based assignment of many farm chores centered on objective differences in body height and strength rather than on what was deemed culturally appropriate to one sex or the other. Females carried out some of the same tasks as younger boys—they helped hay, hoe, weed, harvest crops, and husk corn.

Yet gender ordered male and female spheres in ways that went beyond obvious physical distinctions. For instance, men and older boys not only cut timber but operated sawmills, erected buildings, dug wells and cellars, laid stone, pointed chimneys, and shaved shingles and staves. Men tanned and curried hides, made saddles or gloves, and bound shoes. Older boys got the bark for tanning, shaved it, ground it, and laid the leather away. . . . [S]killed craftsmen in these trades earned substantially more than farm laborers. Females never participated in these activities. Nor did girls drive cattle or carry grain on horseback to the mill, as boys did. Women did not thresh grain, even though boys of thirteen or fourteen did so. Although men and boys traveled abroad freely in their duties, women's work more often kept them inside or near their own home or those of kinsmen or employers. In and around the home they earned income from tasks that males assiduously avoided: cleaning, cooking, sewing, spinning, washing clothes, nursing, and caring for children.

Thus, people allocated work among themselves based on physical capacity but also on gender. The advent of English-style agriculture, involving large draft animals and deep plowing, helped fix many boundaries between the sexes. The case of John Graves II of East Guilford is illustrative. Five daughters and four sons survived infancy; all of them appear in his accounts at one time or another credited for a day's or a week's work. Of the eighty-nine work occasions he recorded between 1703 and 1726 (the year he died), he identified daughters on twenty-one occasions and sons on sixty-eight. Thus, sons appeared more than three times as often. Graves hired occasional male help in addition to his sons and kept a young servant named Thome for two years when his younger boys were too small to hoe, make fences, or mow hay. Meanwhile, his girls did chores—but never farm work—for his neighbors. They sewed, spun, nursed, and kept house.

An account book of great interest because of the economic activities of women that it records is that of merchant Elisha Williams of Wethersfield, Connecticut, a commercial farm town situated on the Connecticut River just south of Hartford. Williams's ledger begins in 1738, and its pages are filled with references to women credited for onions. A bunch of roped onions weighed about three or four pounds, and Williams bought them for 5d. per bunch in 1738. Women earned a penny per bunch for tying them in the early 1740s. They generally took their pay in the form of store merchandise, mostly luxury imports such as sugar, chocolate, pepper, rum, cotton lace, and silk romall, a silken handkerchief used as a head covering. Other goods paid for by women's onions included medicine, a pair of spectacles, and a copy of Homer's *Iliad*.

So far, the evidence from account books and diaries has helped locate the boundaries demarcating women's work from men's work. Those boundaries, however, were permeable. Men could and did cross into women's domain when the size of the market justified a larger scale of operations than the home could provide. For example, baking and brewing were normally women's work, but men in port towns also made their living by these activities. Men in

New England did not lose self-respect if they milked cows, but they did not normally make cheese or churn cream into butter.

If, however, the family began to specialize in dairying for sale, the men might take part. Matthew Patten of New Hampshire mentioned husbands as well as wives buying and selling butter. Thus, when nominally feminine tasks became important to household income, men undertook a share of the responsibility, even if only to keep track of the profits. Male account keepers commonly listed payments due from boarders and lodgers but never credited the work by their wives that made the hospitality possible. On the other hand, some male-dominated occupations were always open to women. Retail trade was perhaps the most common, although before 1740 such opportunities arose in only a few commercial areas. Most women in retailing were widows who had taken over a deceased husband's shop, although one Mary Johnson of Boston, who was not identified as a widow, owned shop goods worth over two hundred pounds, according to the 1669 inventory of her estate. Helen Hobart ran a shop in Hingham in 1682 with her husband's approval. By the late colonial period, such opportunities had spread deeper into the interior. In Worcester County in 1760, for instance, twelve out of 267 licensed dispensers of spirituous liquors (4.5 percent) were women.

Though women had always acted as midwives, nursed the sick, and disbursed homemade remedies, a few also "doctored." The administrator of the estate of David Clark of Wrentham listed payment to Mary Johnson, "Doctoress" for "Physick and Tendance." William Corbin, minister of the Anglican church in Boston, willed his medical books to Jane Allen of Newbury, spinster and daughter of the Honorable Samuel Allen, Esquire. In 1758 the Reverend Ebenezer Parkman went to see the widow Ruhamah Newton, who had broken her leg in a fall. Friends had called a Mrs. Parker to set the leg, and the time it took her to get her apparatus in order and carry out the operation delayed the diarist's return home "till night."

Women taught school, as did men. Generally speaking, women taught young pupils of both sexes to read and spell, and men instructed more advanced classes in writing and arithmetic. Seventeenth-century records occasionally identify "school dames" who took students for fees, but they do not seem to have been common outside the largest settlements.

In the eighteenth century, women usually taught the younger children and girls during the summer, often for only half the wages of the young male college graduates who took the older children the rest of the year. The town of Amesbury, Massachusetts, voted in 1707 that the selectmen "hire four or five school Dames for the town to teach children to read" and allowed five pounds to two men "to keep a school to teach young parsons to write and sifer two months this year." Most towns seem to have found the two-tier system a cheap and efficient way to comply with the provincial school laws. The town meeting of Hingham instructed its selectmen to "hire a schoolmaster as cheap as they can get one, provided they shall hire a single man and not a man that have a family."

There was also a two-tier system in making apparel. Men normally tailored coats and breeches, and women sewed shirts and gowns; however, women in the eighteenth century also engaged in tailoring to a limited extent. In 1708, the estate of Simon Gross, deceased mariner of Hingham, paid for forty weeks of training as a tailor for his daughter Allis. John Ballantine, minister at Westfield, Massachusetts, mentioned two occasions in 1768 when Ruth Weller came for a week to make garments; in 1773 he noted that "Sally Noble, Tailer" was working at his house.

Gender distinctions were very clear in the processing of textiles. Females did not comb worsted or hackle flax, which was men's work, although women, along with boys, pulled flax, carded wool, and picked seeds out of cotton. Girls and women spun, dyed, and knitted yarn, but few engaged in weaving, traditionally a male occupation in England. Women did take up the craft in the eighteenth century, doing simple weaves while men concentrated on more complex patterns.

Few inventoried estates mention looms in the seventeenth century, and only 6 percent in Essex County, Massachusetts, list them around 1700. By 1774, the proportion of inventories with looms in Alice Hanson Jones's New England sample ranged from a low of 17 percent in Essex County to a high of 37.5 percent in Plymouth County. The spread of looms did not mean that the region's textile industry was in the throes of protoindustrialization. Rather, households in less commercial areas were producing more cloth for home use in order to spend their cash and vendible products on new consumer goods like tea and sugar. The newer weavers included women who took up weaving as a nearly full-time activity in the years before marriage or during widowhood. Growing numbers of married women also wove part time to conserve or expand family income.

Weaving may be the only occupation in the colonial period for which there is sufficient documentation to compare men's and women's pay for the same type of work. Women weavers appear in account books as early as 1704 in Norwich, Connecticut, and in 1728, when Mary Stodder purchased a loom from John Marsh of Litchfield. Altogether, eighteen women weavers appear in the diaries, probate records, and account books consulted for this study, of whom just four are identified as "widow." Of those for whom pay rates are available, comparisons with contemporary male weavers show that the sexes earned similar rates per yard for common kinds of cloth. We can conclude that, in this instance, women did earn equal pay for equal work. However, only two women weavers in the sample, Mary Parker and Hannah Smith of Hingham, received credit for weaving more than the common fabrics—"plain," drugget, shirting, linen, tow, and "blanketing." Men produced a much wider variety, including relatively fancy weaves. Judging from these examples, an expanding demand for domestic cloth created opportunities for women to do simple weaving. They could do so without driving down piece rates, which rose by a third between the 1750s and the 1770s; from 4.1d. to 5.4d. and then to 5.5d. in the early 1770s. Although the sources do not reveal great numbers of women working at looms, women's growing presence in the late colonial period signals a trend that accelerated during the Revolution.

The history of weaving and tailoring in New England illustrates the flexibility inherent in the region's gender-based work roles. The further removed the activity was from hard-core masculine tasks associated with oxen, plows, and heavy equipment, the more likely that respectable women did it. The history of work and gender in New England during the colonial years divides readily into four periods of unequal duration. In the earliest period, before the 1670s, the economy simplified compared to England's economy, and the variety of occupations open to either sex contracted sharply. Women spent more time outdoors and working alongside men. The second period came with the proliferation of activities by which men habitually and strictly segregated themselves from women, and women undertook domestic manufacturing tasks with which historians have so often associated them: brewing beer, baking bread, churning butter, making cheese, spinning yarn, and knitting stockings and mittens. Not every housewife practiced all these arts, and specialization encouraged exchange between them.

The third period, beginning about 1715, constituted the farm maintenance stage in older settlements during which demand for unskilled labor declined relative to skilled labor. Increasing population densities created exchange opportunities that encouraged both men and women to specialize and invest more time in nonfarm occupations. This stage might have continued indefinitely, with population growth putting continuous downward pressure on wages, but outside forces intervened, creating the fourth and final phase of New England's colonial development. Beginning in 1739, wars and their aftermaths administered a succession of shocks to the system, creating sudden demands for men and provisions and putting large amounts of money into circulation. The conclusion to the Seven Years' War opened up northern New England and Nova Scotia to British settlement, and the treaty that ended the War for Independence swung open the gates to Iroquoia in New York, as did the Battle of Fallen Timbers (1794) for the Ohio Valley. Much of the labor supply that might have depressed wage rates emigrated instead; in New England, it was not replaced by immigrants.

Despite New England's limited resources and the absence of technological change, demand generated by war and export markets drove the region's economy at a faster rate than its population grew. Evidence for economic expansion appears in both account books and probate inventories. First, stores with new consumer wares appeared. Storekeepers began moving into the rural interior during the 1740s, and their numbers grew dramatically in the ensuing decades. Proportionately, there were nearly as many retailers in Massachusetts in 1771 as there were in the United States in 1929. Many hopeful young businessmen were assisted by merchants in port cities who had advanced their wares on credit to the neophytes.

The lure was the money jingling in farmers' pockets from increasing prices for their products, beginning with the preparations against Louisbourg in 1744–1745. Prices for livestock began to soar faster than inflation, offering strong inducements to farmers to expand their herds. The sterling equivalent of Connecticut inventory values of oxen, for instance, jumped 19 percent in the 1740s, continued to rise in the 1750s, and by the early 1760s reached 80 percent above levels of the 1730s. During the height of the Seven Years' War, Connecticut prices for cows and barreled pork climbed 50 percent, while prices for sheep doubled. After dropping modestly in the late 1760s, prices for oxen and cows rose sharply in the early 1770s, attaining levels not seen since the 1640s. Livestock values in Massachusetts did not keep up with this torrid pace, but the cost of oxen ballooned by more than 70 percent in 1758–1763 and grew again in the early 1770s. Connecticut wheat prices ascended a bit more demurely: 43 percent in the 1750s and 48 percent in 1772–1774. Farmers in newer settlements sent off, besides barreled meat and draft animals, loads of lumber products, such as staves and shingles, potash, tar, turpentine, and maple syrup. New Englanders also shipped thousands of pounds of well-preserved butter and cheese every year.

For men with resources, the rational reaction to such prices would have been to devote more of their own and their sons' time to farming and less time to crafts such as weaving. To raise and feed more livestock, farmers had to create more pasture and mowing lands, plant more timothy and clover, maintain longer fence lines, and store many more tons of hay in their newly erected barns. Winter chores expanded, cutting the time available for craft activities.

When farmers endeavored to raise more livestock and the grass to feed them, and when farm wives found themselves milking more cows, churning more butter, and making more cheese, men and women were putting pressure on a labor force that in the short run could expand only by crossing the gender division of labor. Every attempt by the colonial governments during the Seven Years' War to recruit soldiers for the summer campaigns further reduced the available pool of young men, and farmers found themselves engaged in a bidding war that raised wages and bounties. According to Fred Anderson, men in military service during these years could earn far more than a fully employed farm laborer. With an eight-month enlistment, plus bounty, minimum income for soldiers in Massachusetts rose from £10.1 sterling in 1755 to £13.9 in 1757, and bounced between a high of £21.75 and a low of £15.75 thereafter. When bounties for reenlistment are figured in, estimated maximum incomes reached £32.3 in 1760 and £29.2 in 1762. Anywhere from one-fourth to one-third of men aged sixteen to twenty-nine served with Massachusetts forces at some point during the war.

The rise in wages beginning in the 1740s at first touched only men but in the long term affected everyone by loosening the bonds between parents and their grown children as daughters found work outside the home and sons joined the military or emigrated. The account books show that men abruptly began employing greater numbers of women in the final two decades of the colonial period. Women had already begun moving into tailoring and weaving, but the labor shortages of the Seven Years' War boosted demand for their services, and the migration out of southern New England in the 1760s apparently worked to cushion the postwar depression in farm wages and prices.

Rising wages and expanding employment meant higher incomes for those who did not emigrate. The probate inventories of the late colonial period show that most New England families were prospering. The estimated sterling value per capita of consumer goods in 1774 was 10 percent higher than in the middle colonies, for instance, and an index of amenities in probate inventories from rural New England registered substantial gains in the decades before 1774, catching up and then keeping pace with Chesapeake households that had long been engaged in a commercial economy.

The New England economy took time to recover from the crises of war and destruction in 1675–1694; it grew only slowly for a long period before heating up during the Seven Years' War. That war accelerated economic change, bringing more women into the paid labor force and expanding the penetration of the market into the rural interior. The growing proportion of young women working outside the home in the final decades of the colonial period accompanied a rise in their wages, which no doubt helped attract them. When combined with evidence that increasing numbers of country girls were attending school and learning how to write, the growing ability of women to earn money and conduct business at the local store can be viewed as a positive good, giving them greater control over their own lives. Furthermore, the addition of tea, sugar, and spices to their diets, painted earthenware to their tables, featherbeds to sleep on, and greater privacy, all surely added pleasures to generally hard lives. Although marriage still meant coverture, more women chose to remain single and access to divorce became easier. There is also a demographic indicator that women's lot was improving: life expectancy of married women rose. Mean age at death increased from sixty-two to sixty-six for women marrying between 1760 and 1774 and to sixty-eight for those marrying between 1775 and 1800. On balance, these changes appear beneficial. Women would not gain politically or legally from American Independence, and equality was never even a prospect, but in the decades before 1776 they had won a little liberty, and comfort is no mean thing.

NO

Lyle Koehler

Women in Work and Poverty: The Difficulties of Earning a Living

For some time now, many scholars of early American history have asserted that the absence of sufficient manpower resulted in extensive economic freedom for the "weaker sex." As Page Smith puts it, "There were, in the early years, very few negative definitions—that this or that activity was unsuitable or inappropriate for a woman to engage in. In consequence colonial women moved freely into most occupations in response to particular needs and opportunities rather than abstract theories of what was proper." Eleanor Flexner has more emphatically concluded, "In a struggling society in which there was a continuous labor shortage, no social taboos could keep a hungry woman idle." Barbara Mayer Wertheimer enthusiastically catalogues many of the jobs held by colonial women, and asserts that the earliest female settlers possessed "power and responsibility such as they had never known in seventeenth-century England or on the European continent . . . [They labored at] many kinds of work outside the home from which they were later barred."

Despite such assertions, there has been no systematic effort to determine the exact occupations available to women, and the extent to which these utilized skills *not* focused strictly around the domesticity and nurturance of the conventional female role. Moreover, we do not know how many women worked at some occupation other than that of housewife and mother, or how much they earned. Because the characterization of woman as the weaker sex affected Puritan views of sexual behavior, intelligence, and social privilege, we might suspect that it also deterred women from supporting themselves. In fact, as we shall see, economic factors discouraged productive, independent activity on the part of women.

Limitations on Searching Out a Calling

Puritans certainly believed in the efficacy of work. Detesting those who lived "idle like swine," they felt that labor brought "strength to the body, and vigour to the mynde," thereby providing an outlet for energies which could otherwise lead one to sin. The authorities encouraged each person to search out a suitable calling through apprenticeship, self-training, or hiring out. Boys had considerably more options than girls; apprenticeship contracts specified that the latter be taught only housewifely duties like cooking and sewing, while boys could learn the "secrets" of any number of trades, including blacksmithing, husbandry, shop management, milling, carpentry, and seamanship. It is unlikely that those daughters who never served as apprentices learned any of the male occupational "secrets," because limited opportunities for occupational training, as well as denial of access to public schools, put at a disadvantage any "strong-minded" woman who wished to advance in the world of work. Even if she could overcome the limits of her socialization for domesticity, or use that training to hire herself out in a female vocation, a young woman still could not readily accrue the funds necessary to set herself up in a business or trade; besides, she was unable to earn very much at women's jobs.

Moreover, fathers neglected to give their daughters a portion of the family estate as a nest egg, while they did sometimes convey realty to sons. . . . The daughter who inherited very much from her father's estate was quite a rarity in seventeenth-century Connecticut; only the daughter of a very wealthy man could actually have taken steps to become economically self-sufficient after her father's demise. Furthermore, daughters tended to receive their share in personalty, not in realty which could be converted into a permanent productive income, whereas for sons the reverse was true. In fact, daughters inherited proportionally smaller legacies than had been customary in late medieval England.

The mean and median (£22) values of daughters' inheritances yielded some immediate purchasing power, but did little to increase their occupational possibilities. The average inheritance did not allow a daughter money enough to purchase a home lot near the town's center, which sold for £80 or £100. Nor could she rent a shop and stock it with goods. While the young man could work at a trade and save a tidy sum by his late twenties, the young woman possessed no similar option. Hartford County records indicate that seventeenth-century inheritance patterns made it virtually impossible for a maiden, whose access to employment was already limited by her training and lack of education, to become part of the property-holding group which ran New England affairs.

The Single Woman as Servant

While her parents were still alive, or after she inherited too little to buy her own financial independence, a single woman could strive to earn money at only one occupation before 1685. Domestic servitude did little more than insure that the young woman would continue to exist as a member of the submissive, inferior, financially dependent class. Female servants assisted with household duties, child care, and garden maintenance—but always under the supervision of a "mistress" or "master," whose orders had to be obeyed unless they violated criminal law. Servants received meals, clothing, and a place to sleep, but generally earned no financial remuneration in return for their valuable work. The few women who hired themselves out (unlike those invariably single ones who served as apprentices, redemptioners, indentured domestics, and even slaves) enjoyed a small measure of economic reward. Their typical annual salary was just £3 or £4, only 50 to 60 percent of the male hired servant's wage. Even with the addition of a sum for the room and board furnished by the master, the female domestic drew one of the lowest annual incomes of any working person.

Since before 1650 domestic servitude was considered an honorable occupation for a woman, some newly arrived single women sought employment in that capacity. These females, whose mean age was 20.7 years, often lived briefly in Puritan households under conditions of relative equality, and then married into the best families. Still, their actual numbers were few; in addition, male domestic migrating to New England outnumbered females three to one. . . .

In the first three decades of settlement, then, a handful of women used servitude as a vehicle for marital advancement, although not as a means to accumulate money for future investment. Since such women labored as indentured servants or redemptioners (usually for seven years, in return for the cost of their passage), before 1650 there is no instance of a female hiring out her own time. After that date, however, the image of the servant deteriorated so remarkably that only a severely impoverished single woman would want to become a domestic. Scottish, Irish, Indian, black, and poor English servants soon replaced the earlier "most honourable" English. . . .

The deterioration of servant status after 1650 made domestic work no longer a realistic option for the "middling" and "better sorts." Because women of those classes no longer became servants, opportunities for them to leave home and hire out their labor decreased. Nor did the poor English, Scottish, Irish, black, and Indian women who became servants and slaves gain even a small measure of control over their own lives. For sustenance, every woman had to rely on a father, master, or husband; marriage became literally basic to survival for many New England women.

As a result, housewifery served as the chief "occupation" for almost all New England women, and it no more facilitated financial independence than had other forms of domestic servitude. Women certainly contributed to the productivity of the family farm. Although they did not often work outdoors planting and harvesting crops, as English farm wives did, many spent a good deal of time cleaning house, spinning flax, dipping candles, canning preserves, roasting meat, caring for children, and performing untold other tasks. Some spun and made stockings, shirts, or breeches, which they sold to neighbors for an occasional shilling. Goodwives also sold poultry, butter, cheese, and garden produce, or bartered such items for desired commodities in the informal village trade networks. However, woman's work in the home was assumed to be less dangerous and time-consuming than men's—a conclusion which may have rankled Puritan women as much as it has irritated housewives in more modern times. Above all else, the wife was not to use her presumed "free time" to exceed her ordained station by taking an interest in commercial activities or any other "outward matters." She could contract for rents and wages, sell goods, and collect debts only when her husband had so authorized. The records from seventeenth-century civil cases reveal that New England husbands granted their wives such privileges in only 6 or 7 percent of all families. The wife's access to experience in "outward matters" which could have provided her with some income in either marriage or widowhood was, therefore, much circumscribed.

The Nurturant Callings of Wet Nurse, Teacher, Doctor, and Midwife

Of course, Puritans did allow married women to labor at activities other than housewifery; but those activities also centered around the female's assumed nurturance, and were unremunerative and part-time. Serving as a wet nurse was one such activity, even though its short-term and low-demand character- istics made it a very insubstantial "occupation." Wet nurses enjoyed some popularity because, despite the strong cultural ideal affirming maternal breast- feeding, Puritan mothers sometimes found it impossible to perform that "duty." Puerperal fever or other serious illnesses incapacitated mothers and, it was believed, could be transmitted through the milk. Sore or inverted nipples, breast inflammations, and scanty milk also necessitated the occasional use of a wet nurse. Fear of the presumed toxic effects of colostrum caused mothers to observe a taboo on suckling infants for three or four days after delivery, which increased possibilities for wet nursing. Still, wet nurses rarely received more than temporary employment, and the payment for that service was probably never very great. In fact, such short-term help may have been freely given, much the way neighboring wives helped out during measles or other epidem- ics. There is no record of New Englanders "farming out" babies to wet nurses for anywhere from ten to nineteen months, as was common in England. Indeed, Puritan women who wet nursed infants probably did not even think of themselves as being employed at an occupation.

Like wet nurses, teachers maternally provided for the needs of the young. At dame schools, where a wife or "poor patient widow sits/And awes some twenty infants as she knits," the female teacher instructed her neighbor's younger offspring for 10s to £2 per year, 1/10th to 1/120th of the salary for male teachers in the public schools. As early as 1639 Mistress Jupe taught pupils at the Ipswich dame school; before the century's end, twenty-three or twenty-four other women assisted young scholars in reading, writing, and reli- gion at fourteen different New England locales. These schoolmarms were expected to rely upon their husbands' or ex-husbands' estates for sustenance, not upon any salary for their own work. Moreover, they were barred from working with the upper grades (over age nine or ten), lest the difficulty of the material studied at those levels overtax a woman's "weak" intellectual ability. They constituted only 12.6 percent (25 of 199) of all school-teachers this researcher could locate in the seventeenth-century Puritan records.

The practice of medicine was another nurturant occupational activity open to married women. Many English housewives and their American counterparts learned "chirurgery"—the use of herbs, potions, and poultices to cure any number of maladies. Knowledge of the medicinal properties of wild herbs passed through the female line in some families for generations. Alice Apsley, Lady Fenwick, one of the first women to settle at Ft. Saybrook,

Connecticut, distributed homegrown herbs to sick callers at her residence from 1639 until her departure from the colony in 1645. Mistress Field of Salem prepared a green "sympathetic oynment" which purportedly healed sprains, aches, cramps, scaldings, cuts, mange in cattle, stench blood, tumors, the bites of "Venomous Beasts," and "old Rotten Sores." Doctor Margaret Jones of Charlestown, Massachusetts, secured some reputation as a witch because the aniseed, liquors, and small doses of herbs she administered produced "extraordinary violent effects." Hannah Bradford of Windsor, Connecticut, was such a capable physician that she reputedly "taught the first male doctor much of his medical lore." At least three women proved to be able surgeons. Henry Winthrop's widow reportedly "hath very good successe" in her "Surgerye"; Mistress Allyn patched up wounded soldiers as an army surgeon during King Philip's War; and, on Martha's Vineyard, Mistress Blande dispensed "Phisicke and Surgery" to many sick Indians.

Altogether, women comprised 24 percent (N = 42 of 175) of New England's medical practitioners. These female doctors, nurses, and midwives earned the respect of their neighbors, but evidence suggests that they received little income from their services. Medicine in the seventeenth century lacked the financial advantages of ministry, governorship, or commerce; not until the 1690s did physicians begin to achieve some recognition as highly paid, self-conscious professionals. Before that, almost all doctors practiced medicine as a second profession, spending the bulk of their working hours in the ministry, the magistracy, husbandry, or housewifery. . . .

In the 1690s, the professionalization of medicine had severe consequences for female physicians. Men trained through apprenticeship to male doctors began displacing local female chirurgeons. One can search the colonial records in vain for some mention of female physicians during that decade. For the first time, particularly in urban areas, Puritans began distinguishing between male "doctors" and female "nurses," even though such "nurses" assisted Boston wives in recovering from childbirth, cared for infants' ailments, and treated cases of smallpox. Sam Sewall mentions seven different male physicians in his diary for the years 1674 to 1699, but all women who treat illnesses are referred to either as midwives or as nurses.

Throughout the seventeenth century both sexes dispensed medical advice, but one realm of expertise, midwifery, remained the exclusive province of women. (In fact, the York County authorities fined one man fifty shillings "for presumeing to Act the Part of a Midwife.") Women learned midwifery from personal experience, from other midwives, or from standard obstetrical texts like Nicholas Culpeper's *Directory for Midwives* (1651). There were no medical examinations to pass in New England, nor did a prospective midwife take out a license to practice, as was required in England and in nearby New Amsterdam.

Midwives occupied a position of some influence. They were given the important function of examining women accused of premarital pregnancy, infanticide, or witchcraft; often the guilt or innocence of the accused rested on the findings of these female juries. In return for this necessary service, the town selectmen sometimes issued grants of land to widowed midwives. However, that happened only in a few instances, and it is significant that this researcher has found no account book or other record which mentions a midwife receiving any reward for her services. . . .

Women in Business

Limitations on daughters' inheritances and the lack of remunerative work for single women meant that few could join the property-holding group which controlled capital investment in land. So, too, did the paltry wages of midwives, physicians, teachers, and wet nurses, along with husbandly control over their incomes, prevent working wives from acquiring the economic security which would have enabled them to become property owners. As urbanization increased, especially late in the century, working women were generally unable to accumulate the capital necessary to participate in the Commercial Revolution enveloping New England.

Of course, some women who possessed both money and prestige also maintained small-scale businesses. As early as 1640 Philippa Hammond operated a shop at Boston. So did Widow Howdin (1645), Alice Thomas (before 1672), Ann Carter (1663), Jane Bernard (1672–76), Abigail Johnson (1672–73), Mistress Gutteridge (1690), Elizabeth Connigrave (1672–74), Rebecca Windsor (1672–74), and Mary Castle (1690). Almost all of these women ran coffee or cook shops, thereby utilizing their domestic training. Mary Avery and Susanna Jacob kept shop between 1685 and 1691, but whether they were owners or merely employees is unknown. Esther Palmer, a merchant, located in the metropolis in 1683, and Florence Mackarta, in partnership with two men, constructed a slaughterhouse on Peck's Wharf in 1693. A 1687 Boston tax list gives the names of forty-eight different women who derived some income from a trade or their estates—11.4 percent of all such persons rated. But businesswomen were rarer than the initial impression suggests. For example, it is not actually specified how many of the women on the 1687 list owned businesses and how many merely drew income from the estates of their deceased husbands. What *is* clear is that fully 85.4 percent of these women were widows.

Businesswomen, whether married or widowed, were few throughout New England. The paucity of early businesswomen can be readily demonstrated by searching through transcriptions of courtroom proceedings, town records, and other sources. . . . In all of New England outside Boston there are records of only nine women who worked at a trade or who ran a business other than innkeeping. By late century Margaret Barton of Salem, a chair frame maker, had accrued a fortune in "ventures at sea." In Hartford County, Elizabeth Gardner, Mary Phelps, and Mary Stanly owned interests in (respectively) an iron mill, a grist mill, and a shop. Jane Stolion appeared in court in 1645–46, accused of charging excessive prices at her New Haven dress and cloth shop. Mistress Jenny came before the Plymouth General Court in 1644 for not keeping the mortars at her mill clean, nor the bags of corn there from spoiling. Elizabeth Cadwell operated her husband's ferry across the Connecticut River at Hartford after his death in 1695. One Maine widow, Elizabeth Rowdan, maintained a blacksmith shop and mill. Other women may have worked in their husbands' bakery, cook, or apparel shops, or may have tailored clothing for sale; but the records observe a rigorous silence on that score, mentioning only one female baker at Salem (1639). Altogether, only 2.3 percent (N = 23 of 988) of all tradespeople-merchants (again excluding innkeepers) were members of the "weaker sex."

An examination of those licensed to keep inns or sell alcoholic beverages indicates that few women supported themselves in this occupation, at least before the 1690s. Since all innkeepers had to secure licenses from the authorities, the records are quite complete. The first female innkeeper does not appear until 1643. Between 1643 and 1689 at least fifty-seven other women operated inns; however, they constituted but 18.9 percent of Boston's innkeepers and only 5 percent of those in the remainder of New England. On Ebenezer Peirce's *Civil, Military, and Professional Lists of Plymouth and Rhode Island Colonies* just three of seventy Plymouth innkeepers are female. In the 1690s, with large numbers of men away fighting in the Maine Indian wars, the New England total increased sharply, to eighty-four women—eight in Maine, twenty-four in New Hampshire, and fifty-two in the Bay Colony. Women then comprised over half of the tavernkeepers in Boston and approximately 20 percent of those in other locales. . . .

Although innkeeping or some other business may have given the individual woman some measure of personal satisfaction and self-sufficiency, the Boston tax list of 1687 suggests that businesswomen fared less well than businessmen. An occasional woman like the Widow Kellond might derive an annual income as high as £80 from her trade and estates, but she was much the exception. Only nineteen members of the "weaker sex"—39.6 percent of all tradeswomen—earned £10 or more from their trades and estates, while 74 percent of all tradesmen earned that much. The forty-eight female traders made £580 over the previous year, an average of £12, whereas the 373 male traders made £7,383, or £20 each.

There were several reasons why tradeswomen, when they managed to open shops, earned only 60 percent as much as tradesmen. Since the women possessed little training, their businesses tended to accent service in a way that was compatible with female sex-role stereotyping. Distributing beer, maintaining a cook shop, keeping an inn, and operating a millinery shop utilized talents common to housewives, but ones which returned little profit. Women in such businesses could not easily attract customers on the open market, for they lacked the mobility of carpenters, bricklayers, blacksmiths, and coopers. They could not advertise in newspapers, for none existed. They could not reap the benefits of an international trade, since they lacked ties to the great English trading houses and familiarity with foreign markets. Even credit was a problem. As milliner Hannah Crowell complained in 1696, "being a Woman [I] was not able to ride up and down to get in debts."

Women also lacked the capital necessary to establish large scale businesses. Only after her husband died did the typical woman strike out on her own, with the help of her widow's portion. Of all women who were licensed to sell spirituous liquors, some 71.1 percent were widows. Innkeeping was a ready source of sustenance for any widow whose husband left her their house and little else. Working at a trade became an acceptable means of support for widows of artisans, but even they could only rarely increase the net value of their estates over the amounts they inherited. Age, decreased mobility, and a lack of appropriate training or education each took a toll. Moreover, husbands were often reluctant to provide for their wives by leaving them a full or part interest in their trade tools or their shops. Only two of fifty-seven Hartford County artisans, merchants, and shopkeepers bequeathed their widows interest in their businesses. Another man left a shop at Hartford to his sister.

Even those few widows who enjoyed some occupational independence were expected to restrict their activities to nurturant, housewifely, and comparatively low-status occupations. Highstatus positions such as public grammar-school teaching, the ministry, and major public offices were limited to men. Elizabeth Jones, appointed the Boston poundkeeper in 1670, 1676, and 1689, was the only woman to serve as a public official on even a minor level.

The woman who wished to work "by her own hand," whether widowed, married, or single, faced still other disadvantages. Before 1647 the Maine General Court forbade any woman from inhabiting the Isles of Shoales, thereby making it impossible for females to help out with the fishing or to operate stores at which the fishermen might buy provisions. Perhaps deterred by the sentiment expressed in Maine law, no woman of record ever fished at sea for a profit. Nor could women become sailors—when one dressed as a man and left Massachusetts on a vessel, her fellow seamen, upon discovering her sex, tarred and feathered her in a nearly fatal maltreatment. The presence of working women on the Atlantic was so inconceivable to Puritans that when a mysterious "Shallop at Sea man'd with women" was reported, men attributed the phenomenon to witchcraft.

Wealth and Poverty

The limited, poorly paid, comparatively low status employment opportunities available to early New England women meant that they could not really participate in the expanding possibilities opened by the Commercial Revolution. Despite such disabilities, some observers might argue that dependent wives were rewarded in the end, by inheriting sizable properties (although not businesses) from their deceased husbands. Such widows could enjoy some independence in their later years. The tax lists seem to provide some evidence for this view; women appear as heads of families approximately 6 percent of the time, and fare well when their estates are compared to those of male family heads. . . .

It would be incorrect to assume, however, that as a group widows in Puritan New England were comparatively well-to-do, for most never appeared on a tax list. . . . Many husbands, well aware that their wives might have difficulty maintaining an estate, specified that their widows live with one or more sons in the family dwelling unit. Such men usually reserved one room, a garden, a cow, and some household goods for their widow's use. In one-tenth of all wills (N = 30 of 282) fathers directed children to maintain their mother with annual supplies or a monetary allotment. The annual maintenance payment rarely amounted to much, however, averaging £9 13s.; most widows received less than £7. . . .

Although one-sixth or one-fifth of all widows (those of the middling and better sorts) enjoyed limited affluence, many more suffered poverty. . . . The appointment of "keepers" for the indigent, or lodging them in the almshouse under a male attendant's supervision, blatantly reinforced female dependence. Such control angered some poor women, and at least two of them entirely rejected the dependence entailed in any form of relief. Mary Webster, a "wretched woman" of Hadley, Massachusetts, protested the efforts of church deacon Philip Smith to mitigate her indigence, expressing herself so sharply "that he declared himself apprehensive of receiving mischief at her hands" (ca. 1684). Jane Bourne of Cambridge refused to accept an allotment from the town for her food and lodging, instead moving out of town to secure employment elsewhere as a servant (1663). A third woman, Abigail Day, was "full of Discontent" and "Impatience under her Afflictions" while at the Boston almshouse. She would "thank neither God nor man" for the objectionable diet there, and she complained that her keeper "had several times made attempts upon her chastity" (1697).

The dissatisfaction of poor women like Abigail Day, Jane Bourne, and Mary Webster is readily understandable, for the paternalism of the Puritan system of poor relief too easily reflected women's difficulties in searching for gainful employment or starting businesses. Wherever they turned, women encountered the fruits of Puritan sexism—in low pay, lack of education and job training, decreased opportunities to secure the funds needed to open a business, and limitations on the kinds of employment available. . . . The great majority of women in early New England worked under a condition of dependence, whether as servants under the control of masters, poor women under the control of almshouse attendants or other keepers, widows under the relative control of their children, or (in the most common occupation of all) housewives under the control of their husbands.

The circumstances of life in seventeenth-century Puritan New England hardly had an emancipating effect. New England wives sometimes maintained family businesses in their husband's absence, or occasionally ran shops of their own; but so did English women. In fact, Alice Clark's research indicates that English women, as members of a more urbanized society, labored at many more occupations than did their New England counterparts. . . . While all of the information is not yet in, it is striking that 40 percent of New England's adult population comprised just 25 percent of all servants, 24 percent of all medical practitioners (if nurses and midwives are subtracted, the percentage drops to 9.6), 12.6 percent of all schoolteachers, 18 percent of all innkeepers, and 2.3 percent of all tradespeople-merchants. Moreover, these women received much less remuneration than their male counterparts. Although labor shortages were frequent in the first few decades of settlement, such times did not lead to more women on the job market, or to women doing men's work. Inheritance patterns in agrarian locales made it virtually impossible for daughters and wives to exercise much control over capital investment in land. All but a few urban women were similarly unable to acquire real estate or capital which would have enabled them to expand their incomes. The only way for women to experience any upward mobility was to marry well. Seventeenth-century New England was a "Garden of Eden" only for the woman who pursued economic opportunity dependently, as the rib of a (hopefully) prospering and generous Adam.

POSTSCRIPT

Did Colonial New England Women Enjoy Significant Economic Autonomy?

Students wishing to explore further the status of women in colonial British North America should read the classic essay by Lois Green Carr and Lorena S. Walsh, "The Planter's Wife: The Experience of White Women in Seventeenth-Century Maryland," *The William and Mary Quarterly* (October 1977) and Mary Beth Norton's "The Evolution of White Women's Experience in Early America," *American Historical Review* (June 1984). Norton's research on this topic is extended further in her *Founding Mothers & Fathers: Gendered Power and the Forming of American Society* (Knopf, 1996).

Surveys of American women's history that address the colonial period include June Sochen, *Herstory: A Woman's View of American History* (Alfred, 1974); Mary P. Ryan, *Womanhood in America: From Colonial Times to the Present* (New Viewpoints, 1974); and Nancy Woloch, *Women and the American Experience* (Knopf, 1984). Support for the view that women experienced significant upward mobility by migrating to the American colonies can be found in Richard B. Morris, *Studies in the History of American Law*, 2d ed. (Octagon Books, 1964); Elizabeth Anthony Dexter, *Colonial Women of Affairs*, 2d ed. (Houghton Mifflin, 1931); Mary Ritter Beard, *Woman as Force in History* (Macmillan, 1946); Eleanor Flexner, *Century of Struggle* (Belknap Press, 1959); Roger Thompson, *Women in Stuart England and America: A Comparative Study* (Routledge and Kegan, 1974); and Page Smith, *Daughters of the Promised Land: Women in American History* (Little, Brown, 1977).

Many of the scholarly monographs that include discussions of colonial women focus disproportionately on New England. For example, Edmund S. Morgan, *The Puritan Family: Religion and Domestic Relations in Seventeenth-Century New England* (Boston Public Library, 1944) and John Demos, *A Little Commonwealth: Family Life in Plymouth Colony* (Oxford, 1970) both discuss the status of women within the context of the New England family. N. E. H. Hull's *Female Felons: Women and Serious Crime in Colonial Massachusetts* (Illinois, 1987) and Cornelia Hughes Dayton's *Women Before the Bar: Gender, Law, and Society in Connecticut, 1639–1789* (University of North Carolina Press, 1995) treat the legal status of female New Englanders. For the relationship between women and witchcraft, see John Putnam Demos, *Entertaining Satan: Witchcraft and the Culture of Early New England* (Oxford, 1982) and Carol F. Karlsen, *The Devil in the Shape of a Woman: Witchcraft in Colonial New England* (Random House, 1987). Also of interest is Laurel Thatcher Ulrich, *Good Wives: Image and Reality in the Lives of Women in Northern New England, 1650–1750* (Knopf, 1980).

Women in colonial Virginia are treated in Darrett B. Rutman and Anita H. Rutman, *A Place in Time: Middlesex County, Virginia, 1650–1750* (W. W. Norton, 1984) and Kathleen M. Brown, *Good Wives, Nasty Wenches, and Anxious Patriarchs: Gender, Race, and Power in Colonial Virginia* (University of North Carolina Press, 1996).

Women in the age of the American Revolution are the focus of Carol Ruth Berkin, *Within the Conjurer's Circle: Women in Colonial America* (General Learning Press, 1974), Linda Grant DePauw and Conover Hunt, *"Remember the Ladies": Women in America, 1750–1815* (Viking Press, 1976), Mary Beth Norton, *Liberty's Daughters: The Revolutionary Experience of American Women, 1750–1800* (Little, Brown, 1980), Linda Kerber, *Women of the Republic: Intellect and Ideology in Revolutionary America* (North Carolina, 1980), Charles W. Akers, *Abigail Adams: An American Woman* (Little, Brown, 1980), and Joy Day Buel and Richard Buel, Jr., *The Way of Duty: A Woman and Her Family in Revolutionary America* (W. W. Norton, 1984). For the conclusion that the American Revolution failed to advance women's status, see Joan Hoff Wilson's "The Illusion of Change: Women and the American Revolution" in Alfred F. Young, ed., *The American Revolution: Explorations in the History of American Radicalism* (Northern Illinois University Press, 1976).

ISSUE 5

Was There a Great Awakening in Mid-Eighteenth-Century America?

YES: Patricia U. Bonomi, from *Under the Cope of Heaven: Religion, Society, and Politics in Colonial America* (Oxford University Press, 1986)

NO: Jon Butler, from "Enthusiasm Described and Decried: The Great Awakening as Interpretative Fiction," *Journal of American History* (September 1982)

ISSUE SUMMARY

YES: Patricia Bonomi defines the Great Awakening as a period of intense revivalistic fervor from 1739 to 1745 that laid the foundation for socio-religious and political reform by spawning an age of contentiousness in the British mainland colonies.

NO: Jon Butler claims that to describe the religious revival activities of the eighteenth century as the "Great Awakening" is to seriously exaggerate their extent, nature, and impact on pre-revolutionary American society and politics.

Although generations of American schoolchildren have been taught that the British colonies in North America were founded by persons fleeing religious persecution in England, the truth is that many of those early settlers were motivated by other factors, some of which had little to do with theological preferences. To be sure, the Pilgrims and Puritans of New England sought to escape the proscriptions established by the Church of England. Many New Englanders, however, did not adhere to the precepts of Calvinism and, therefore, were viewed as outsiders. The Quakers who populated Pennsylvania were mostly fugitives from New England, where they had been victims of religious persecution. But to apply religious motivations to the earliest settlers of Virginia, South Carolina, or Georgia is to engage in a serious misreading of the historical record. Even in New England the religious mission of Massachusetts Bay Colony Governor John Winthrop's "city upon a hill" began to erode as the colonial settlements matured and stabilized.

Although religion was a central element in the lives of the seventeenth- and eighteenth-century Europeans who migrated to the New World, proliferation of religious sects and denominations, emphasis upon material gain in all parts of the colonies, and the predominance of reason over emotion that is associated with the Deists of the enlightenment period all contributed to a gradual but obvious movement of the colonists away from the church and clerical authority. William Bradford of Plymouth Colony, for example, expressed grave concern that many Plymouth residents were following a path of perfidy, and Pennsylvania founder William Penn was certain that the "holy experiment" of the Quakers had failed. Colonial clergy, fearful that a fall from grace was in progress, issued calls for a revival of religious fervor. The spirit of revivalism that spread through the colonies in the 1730s and 1740s, therefore, was an answer to these clerical prayers.

The episode known as the First Great Awakening coincided with the Pietistic movement in Europe and England and was carried forward by dynamic preachers such as Gilbert Tennant, Theodore Frelinghuysen, and George Whitefield. They promoted a religion of the heart, not of the head, in order to produce a spiritual rebirth. These revivals, most historians agree, reinvigorated American Protestantism. Many new congregations were organized as a result of irremediable schisms between "Old Lights" and "New Lights." Skepticism about the desirability of an educated clergy sparked a strong strain of anti-intellectualism. Also, the emphasis on conversion was a message to which virtually everyone could respond, regardless of age, sex, or social status. For some historians, the implications of the Great Awakening extended beyond the religious sphere into the realm of politics and were incorporated into the American Revolution.

In the following selections, Patricia U. Bonomi writes from the traditional assumption that a powerful revivalistic force known as the "Great Awakening" occurred in the American colonies in the mid-eighteenth century. Following a survey of the converging forces that served as precursors to this revivalistic movement, she explains that the Great Awakening grew out of clerical disputes among Presbyterians and quickly spread to other denominations throughout the colonies, abetted by dynamic itinerant preachers such as Whitefield. Before the enthusiasm subsided, she concludes, the Awakening had instilled a tradition of divisiveness that would affect a number of American social and political, as well as religious, structures.

Jon Butler claims that historians, by accepting without much question the existence of the Great Awakening, have become accomplices in Napoleon's insistence that "history is fable agreed upon." Closer scrutiny of this event, says Butler, reveals that the revivals were regional episodes that did not affect all of the colonies equally and, hence, had only a modest impact on American colonial religion. Because the mid-eighteenth-century revivals did not produce the kinds of dramatic changes—religious or political—frequently ascribed to them, Butler suggests that historians should abandon the concept of the "Great Awakening" altogether.

YES

Patricia U. Bonomi

"The Hosannas of the Multitude": The Great Awakening in America

The Great Awakening—that intense period of revivalist tumult from about 1739 to 1745—is one of the most arresting subjects of American history. The eighteenth century, and the latter part of the seventeenth, were of course punctuated with religious episodes that seemed to erupt without warning and draw entire communities into a vortex of religious conversions and agitations of soul. Yet those episodes tended not to spread beyond the individual churches or towns in which they originated. By the third decade of the eighteenth century, however, a number of currents were converging to prepare the way for an unprecedented burst of religious fervor and controversy.

The two major streams of thought shaping western religious belief in the eighteenth century—Enlightenment rationalism and Continental pietism—were by the 1720s reaching increasing numbers of Americans through the world of print, transatlantic learned societies, and such recently arrived spokesmen as the Anglican moderate George Berkeley, on the one side, and the Dutch Reformed pietist Theodore Frelinghuysen, on the other. By the 1730s, American clergymen influenced by the spiritual intensity and emotional warmth of Reformed pietism were vigorously asserting that religion was being corrupted by secular forces; in their view a conversion experience that touched the heart was the only road to salvation. The rationalists demurred, preferring a faith tempered by "an enlightened Mind . . . not raised Affections." This contest between reason and innate grace was in one sense as old as Christianity itself. In New England, where it was often cast as a competition between Arminians and Antinomians, only the Calvinists' ability to hold the two elements in exquisite balance had averted a schism. Rationalist attitudes, as noted earlier, were sufficiently prevalent in the eighteenth-century South to obstruct the development of heart religion there until the later colonial years. In the Middle Colonies, every point of view was heard, though by the 1730s tension was rising between the entrenched ministers of more orthodox opinion and incoming clergymen who insisted on conversion as the *sine qua non* of vital religion.

Adding to currents of religious unease in the early eighteenth century were a number of other developments: an accelerating pace of commercial growth; land shortages as well as land opportunities; the unprecedented diversity of eighteenth-century immigration; and a rapid climb in total population. Population growth now created dense settlements in some rural as well as urban areas, facilitating mass public gatherings. Moreover, the proliferation of churches and sects, intensifying denominational rivalries, and smallpox and earthquake alarms that filled meeting-houses to overflowing all contributed to a sense of quickening in church life.

Into this volatile and expectant environment came some of the most charismatic and combative personalities of the age. And as the electricity of a Tennent crackled, and the thunder of a Whitefield rolled, a storm broke that, in the opinion of many, would forever alter American society. The Great Awakening created conditions uniquely favorable to social and political, as well as religious, reform by piercing the facade of civility and deference that governed provincial life to usher in a new age of contentiousness. By promoting church separations and urging their followers to make choices that had political as well as religious implications, the Awakeners wrought permanent changes in public practices and attitudes. Before it subsided, the revival had unsettled the lives of more Americans and disrupted more institutions than any other single event in colonial experience to that time. To see how a religious movement could overspill its boundaries to reshape cultural understanding and political expectations, we must take a closer look at some of the churches and people caught up in the revival.

Presbyterian Beginnings

The Great Awakening began not as a popular uprising but as a contest between clerical factions. Thus only those churches with a "professional" clergy and organized governing structure—the Presbyterian, Congregational, Dutch Reformed, and eventually the Anglican—were split apart by the revival. The newer German churches and the sects, having little structure to overturn, remained largely outside the conflict. These events have usually been viewed from the perspective of New England Congregationalism, though the first denomination to be involved in the Awakening was the Presbyterian Church in the Middle Colonies. All of the strains and adjustments experienced by other colonial denominations over a longer time span were compressed, in the Presbyterian case, into the fifty years from the beginning of Ulster immigration around 1725 to the Revolution. Thus the Presbyterian example serves as a kind of paradigm of the experience of all churches from their initial formation through the Great Awakening and its aftermath. It reveals too how a dispute between ministers rapidly widened into a controversy that tested the limits of order and introduced new forms of popular leadership that challenged deferential traditions.

Presbyterians looked to the future with reasonably high hopes by the third decade of the eighteenth century. To all appearances they possessed a more stable and orderly church structure than any of their middle-colony competitors. Unlike the Anglicans, they required no bishop to perform the essential rites of ordination and confirmation; nor did they suffer quite the same shortage of ministers as the German churches. The supply of Presbyterian clergy, if never adequate, had at least been sufficient to support the formation of a rudimentary governing structure. Three presbyteries and the Synod of Philadelphia were in place before the first wave of immigration from Ulster reached the Delaware basin, enabling the twenty-five to thirty ministers active in the Middle Colonies to direct growth and protect professional standards in the period of expansion after 1725. Congregations were under the care of laymen ordained to the office of "elder" and, when available, ministers. Supervising presbyteries in each region maintained oversight of local congregations and ordained and disciplined the clergy. At the top was the synod, which provided a forum where clerical disputes over church doctrine and governing authority could be resolved *in camera*.

Yet the controls imposed by the Presbyterian hierarchy were hardly all that they appeared to be. Beneath orderly processes were tensions which had been expanding steadily before finally bursting forth in fratricidal strife and schism after 1739. Any reading of eighteenth-century Presbyterian records discloses at least three kinds of strains beneath the surface: between parishioners, between people and minister, and within the professional clergy itself.

The Presbyterian Church was the focal point and mediator of Scotch-Irish community life from the late 1720s on, when thousands of Ulster Scots began entering the colonies annually. As the westward-migrating settlers moved beyond the reach of government and law, the Presbyterian Church was the only institution that kept pace with settlement. By stretching resources to the limit, the synod, and especially the presbyteries, kept in touch with their scattered brethren through itinerant preachers and presbyterial visitations. Ministers, invariably the best educated persons on the early frontier, were looked to for leadership in both religious and community affairs, and they often took up multiple roles as doctors, teachers, and even lawyers. So closely did the Scotch-Irish identify with the Kirk that it was often said they "could not live without it."

But if the church was a vital center it was also an agency of control. Presbyterian ministers—whom some regarded as a "stiffnecked . . . [and] pedantick crew"—expected to guide their parishioners' spiritual growth and moral safety in America as they had done in the Old Country, and at first, by and large, they succeeded. Congregations gathered spontaneously in Scotch-Irish settlements, much as they did in immigrant German communities. A major difference between the two societies was that from an early stage lay Presbyterians submitted themselves to clerical authority. As soon as a Presbyterian congregation was formed, it requested recognition and the supply of a minister from the local presbytery. Often the presbytery could provide only a probationer or itinerant preacher for the Sabbath, and many settlements were fortunate to hear a sermon one or two Sundays a month. The congregations nonetheless proceeded to elect elders, deacons to care for the poor and sick, and trustees to oversee the collection of tithes for the minister's salary. The governing "session," comprised of elders and minister, functioned as a kind of court, hearing charges and ruling on a variety of matters, including disputes between parishioners over land or debt, domestic difficulties, and church doctrine. The main responsibility of the session was to enforce moral discipline. Its rulings could be appealed to the supervising presbytery. The presbytery minutes consequently have much to tell us about the quality of clerical authority. But they also disclose the growing undercurrent of resistance that such authority aroused among the freer spirits in the Scotch-Irish settlements. . . .

New Sides vs. Old Sides

The Great Awakening split the Presbyterian Church apart, and through the cracks long-suppressed steam hissed forth in clouds of acrimony and vituperation that would change the face of authority in Pennsylvania and elsewhere. As the passions of the Awakening reached their height in the early 1740s, evangelical "New Side" Presbyterians turned on the more orthodox "Old Sides" with the ferocity peculiar to zealots, charging them with extravagant doctrinal and moral enormities. The internecine spectacle that ensued, the loss of proportion and professional decorum, contributed to the demystification of the clergy, forced parishioners to choose between competing factions, and overset traditional attitudes about deference and leadership in colonial America.

The division that surfaced in 1740–1741 had been developing for more than a decade. Presbyterian ministers had no sooner organized their central association, the Synod of Philadelphia, in 1715 than the first lines of stress appeared, though it was not until a cohesive evangelical faction emerged in the 1730s that an open split was threatened. Most members of the synod hoped to model American Presbyterianism along orderly lines, and in 1729 an act requiring all ministers and ministerial candidates to subscribe publicly to the Westminster Confession had been approved. In 1738 the synod had further ruled that no minister would be licensed unless he could display a degree from a British or European university, or from one of the New England colleges (Harvard or Yale). New candidates were to submit to an examination by a commission of the synod on the soundness of their theological training and spiritual condition. The emergent evangelical faction rightly saw these restrictions as an effort to control their own activities. They had reluctantly accepted subscription to the Westminster Confession, but synodical screening of new candidates struck them as an intolerable invasion of the local presbyteries' right of ordination.

The insurgents were led by the Scotsman William Tennent, Sr., and his sons, William, Jr., Charles, John, and Gilbert. William, Sr. had been educated at the University of Edinburgh, receiving a bachelor's degree in 1693 and an M.A. in 1695. He may have been exposed to European pietism at Edinburgh, where new ideas of every sort were brewing in the last quarter of the seventeenth century. Though ordained a minister of the Anglican church in 1706, Tennent did not gain a parish of his own, and in 1718 he departed the Old World for the New. When he applied for a license from the Synod of Philadelphia in 1718, Tennent was asked his reasons for leaving the Church of England. He responded that he had come to view government by bishops as anti-scriptural, that he opposed ecclesiastical courts and plural benefices, that the church was leaning toward Arminianism, and that he disapproved of "their ceremonial way of worship." All this seemed sound enough to the Presbyterians, and Tennent was licensed forthwith. Having a strong interest in scholarship and pedagogy, Tennent built a one-room schoolhouse in about 1730 in Neshaminy, Bucks County—the Log College, as it was later derisively called—where he set about training young men for the ministry. Exactly when Tennent began to pull away from the regular synod leadership is unclear, but by 1736 his church at Neshaminy was split down the middle and the anti-evangelical members were attempting to expel him as minister.

In 1739 the synod was confronted with a question on professional standards that brought the two factions closer to a complete break. When the previous year's synod had erected commissions to examine the education of all ministerial candidates not holding degrees from approved universities, Gilbert Tennent had charged that the qualification was designed "to prevent his father's school from training gracious men for the Ministry." Overriding the synod's rule in 1739, the radical New Brunswick Presbytery licensed one John Rowland without reference to any committee, though Rowland had received "a private education"—the synod's euphemism for the Log College. Sharply criticizing the presbytery for its disorderly and divisive action, the synod refused to approve Rowland until he agreed to submit himself for examination, which he in turn refused to do.

Since education was central to the dispute, it is unfortunate that no Log College records have survived to describe the training given the remarkable group of men that came under William Tennent, Sr.'s tutelage. We do know that they emerged to become leaders of the revivalist movement, and would in turn prepare other religious and educational leaders of the middle and southern colonies. The little existing evidence casts doubt on the synod's charge that Tennent and his followers were "destroyers of good learning" who persisted in foisting unlettered Log College students upon an undiscriminating public. As Gilbert Tennent insisted, the insurgents "desired and designed a well-qualified Ministry as much as our Brethren." To be sure, their theological emphasis was at variance with that of the Old Side clergy, and there may have been parts of the traditional curriculum they did not value as highly, as had been true with the innovative dissenting academies in Britain. But as competition between the two factions intensified, restrained criticism gave way to enmity. Thus when the synod charged that Gilbert Tennent had called "Physicks, Ethicks, Metophysicks and Pnuematicks [the rubric under which Aristotelian philosophy was taught in medieval universities] meer Criticks, and consequently useless," its members could not resist adding that he did so "because his Father cannot or doth not teach them."

Yet there is much that attests to both William Tennent, Sr.'s learning and his pedagogical talents. That he was a polished scholar of the classics, spoke Latin and English with equal fluency, and was a master of Greek was confirmed by many who knew him. He also "had some acquaintance with the . . . Sciences." A hint of the training Tennent offered comes from the licensing examination given his youngest son Charles in 1736 by the Philadelphia Presbytery, among whose members were several who would later emerge as chief critics of the Tennents. Young Charles was tested on his "ability in prayer [and] in the Languages," in the delivery of a sermon and exegesis, and on his answers to "various suitable questions on the arts and sciences, especially

Theology and out of Scripture." He was also examined on the state of his soul. Charles Tennent was apparently approved without question.

The strongest evidence of the quality of a Log College education comes, however, from the subsequent careers and accomplishments of its eighteen to twenty-one "alumni." Their deep commitment to formal education is demonstrated by the number of academies they themselves founded, including Samuel Blair's "classical school" at Faggs Manor in Pennsylvania, Samuel Finley's academy at Nottingham, and several others. Two early presidents of the College of New Jersey (Princeton) were Samuel Finley and Samuel Davies (the latter having been educated by Blair at Faggs Manor). Moreover, the published sermons and essays of Samuel Finley, Samuel Blair, and Gilbert Tennent not only pulse with evangelical passion but also display wide learning. In the opinion of a leading Presbyterian historian the intellectual accomplishments of the Log College revivalists far outshone those of the Old Side opposers, among whom only the scholarly Francis Alison produced significant writings. As George Whitefield observed when he visited Neshaminy in 1739 and saw the rough structure of logs that housed the school: "All that we can say of most universities is, that they are glorious without."

But the distinction that the Log College men would achieve was still unknown in 1739, when the New Brunswick Presbytery defied the synod by licensing John Rowland. It was at this juncture, moreover, that the twenty-six-year-old English evangelist, George Whitefield, made his sensational appearance. Whitefield's visits to New Jersey and Pennsylvania in the winter of 1739–1740 provided tremendous support for the Presbyterian insurgents, as thousands of provincials flocked to hear him and realized, perhaps for the first time, something of what the American evangelists had been up to. The public support that now flowed to Tennent and the New Side exhilarated its members, inciting them to ever bolder assaults on the synod.

The revivalists had to this point preached only in their own churches or in temporarily vacant pulpits, but that winter they began to invade the territory of the regular clergy. This action raised the issue of itinerant preaching, perhaps the thorniest of the entire conflict, for it brought the parties face to face on the question of who was better qualified to interpret the word of God. It was in this setting that Gilbert Tennent was moved on March 8, 1740 to deliver his celebrated sermon, *The Danger of an Unconverted Ministry,* to a Nottingham congregation engaged in choosing a new preacher. It was an audacious, not to say reckless, attack on the Old Side clergy, and Tennent would later qualify some of his strongest language. But the sermon starkly reveals the gulf that separated the two factions by 1740. It also demonstrates the revivalists' supreme disregard for the traditional limits on public discussion of what amounted to professional questions. . . .

In this influential and widely disseminated sermon Tennent set forth the three principal issues over which Presbyterians would divide: the conversion experience, education of the clergy, and itinerant preaching. While his tone may have owed something to Whitefield's recent influence—humility was never a strong point with the evangelists—it also reflected the growing self-confidence of the insurgents, as a wave of public support lifted them to popular heights.

During the synod of 1740 the anti-revivalist clergy, in a demonstration of their reasonableness, agreed to certain compromises on the issues of itinerancy and licensing, but when the revivalists continued to denounce them publicly as carnal and unconverted, their patience came to an end.

The break between Old Side and New Side Presbyterians came during the synod of 1741 when a protest signed by twelve ministers and eight elders demanded that the revivalists be expelled from the synod. In a preemptive move, the New Side clergy voluntarily withdrew from the Philadelphia Synod to their presbyteries, where their work continued with great zeal and met with success that would outshine that of their rivals. In 1745 the evangelical party, joined by other friends of the revival from the Middle Colonies, formed the Synod of New York, which would sustain a lively existence until 1758 when the Presbyterian schism was finally repaired.

Disagreements over theological emphasis, professional standards, and centralized authority were the most immediate causes of the Presbyterian schism, but other differences between Old and New Sides had the effect of making the conflict sharper. Disparities in education, age (and therefore career expectations), and cultural bias are of special interest.

The twelve Old Sides who moved to expel the revivalist radicals in 1741 have sometimes been labeled the "Scotch-Irish" party for good reason. Nine were born in Northern Ireland, and two in Scotland (the birthplace of the twelfth is unknown). All were educated abroad, mainly in Scotland, and especially at the University of Glasgow. Most came to the colonies between the ages of twenty-eight and thirty-two, after having completed their education. The typical Old Side clergyman was about forty-two at the time of the schism. The New Side ministers who formed the Synod of New York in 1745 numbered twenty-two. Of the twenty-one whose places of birth can be ascertained, ten were born in New England or on eastern Long Island, one in Newark, New Jersey, eight in Northern Ireland (including Gilbert, William, Jr., and Charles Tennent), one in Scotland, and one in England. Most of those born abroad emigrated to the colonies during their middle teens; Charles Tennent was but seven, and the oldest was William Robinson, the son of an English Quaker doctor, who emigrated at about twenty-eight after an ill-spent youth. The educational profile of the New Side preachers is in striking contrast to that of the Old. Of the twenty-two, nine received degrees from Yale College, two were Harvard men, and ten were educated at the Log College. One had probably gone to a Scottish university. The typical New Side minister was about thirty-two at the time of the schism, or a decade younger than his Old Side counterpart.

Several tendencies suggest themselves. The Old Sides, more mature than their adversaries, were also more settled in their professional careers; further, their Scottish education and early professional experiences in Ulster may have instilled a respect for discipline and ecclesiastical order that could not easily be cast aside. They knew it was difficult to keep up standards in provincial societies, especially the heterodox Middle Colonies where competition in religion, as in everything else, was a constant challenge to good order. Still, it was irritating to be treated as intruders by the resident notables, or by such as the Anglicans, who pretended to look down on the Presbyterians as "men of small talents and mean education." There was security in knowing that the first generation of Presbyterian leaders had been educated and licensed in accordance with the most exacting Old World criteria. But the tradition must be continued, for succeeding generations would gain respect only if the ministry were settled on a firm professional base. Though Harvard and Yale were not Edinburgh and Glasgow, they did pattern their curricula after the British universities and to that extent could serve until the Presbyterian Church was able to establish a college of its own. And only if Presbyterian leaders could control the education and admission of candidates to the ministry might they hold their heads high among rival religious groups. A professional ministry was thus crucial to the "Scotch-Irish" party's pride and sense of place.

The New Side party, on the other hand, cared less about professional niceties than about converting sinners. Its members were at the beginning of their careers, and most, being native-born or coming to the colonies in their youth, were not so likely to be imbued with an Old World sense of prerogative and order. They never doubted that an educated clergy was essential, but education had to be of the right sort. By the 1730s Harvard and Yale were being guided, in their view, by men of rationalist leanings who simply did not provide the type of training wanted by the revivalists. Thus the New Sides chafed against the controls favored by their more conservative elders, controls that restricted their freedom of action, slowed their careers, and were in their opinion out of touch with New World ways.

The anti-institutionalism of the revivalists caused some critics to portray them as social levellers, though there were no significant distinctions in social outlook or family background between Old and New Sides. But as with any insurgent group that relies in part on public support for its momentum, the New Sides tended to clothe their appeals in popular dress. At every opportunity they pictured the opposers as "the Noble & Mighty" elders of the church, and identified themselves with the poor and "common People"—images reinforced by the Old Sides' references to the evangelists' followers as an ignorant and "wild Rabble."

The revivalists may not have been deliberate social levellers, but their words and actions had the effect of emphasizing individual values over hierarchical ones. Everything they did, from disrupting orderly processes and encouraging greater lay participation in church government, to promoting mass assemblies and the physical closeness that went with them, raised popular emotions. Most important, they insisted that there were choices, and that the individual himself was free to make them.

The people, it might be suspected, had been waiting for this. The long years of imposed consensus and oversight by the Kirk had taken their toll, and undercurrents of restlessness had strengthened as communities stabilized and Old World values receded. Still, the habit of deferring to the clergy was deeply rooted in Presbyterian culture, making inertia an accomplice of church authority. By 1740, however, with the clergy themselves, or a part of them, openly promoting rebellion, many Presbyterians "in imitation of their example," as it was said, joined the fray. The result was turbulence, shattered and divided congregations, and a rash of slanderous reports against Old Side clergymen. Most such charges were either proved false or are deeply suspect, owing to their connection with the factional conflict. But aspersions against the ministerial character had now become a subject of public debate, suggesting that the schisms of the Awakening were effectively challenging the old structures of authority. . . .

So volatile had the revival become that it could no longer be contained within a single region. Thus when George Whitefield carried the crusade northward, the tumults and divisions that had seized the Presbyterian Church spread to the Congregational meetinghouses of New England.

The "divine fire" Kindled in New England

Whitefield's initial visit to Boston in September 1740 was greeted with tremendous interest, for the "Grand Itinerant" was the first figure of international renown to tour the colonies. During an eleven-day period he preached at least nineteen times at a number of different churches and outdoor sites, including New South Church where the huge crowd was thrown into such a panic that five were killed and many more injured. Fifteen thousand persons supposedly heard Whitefield preach on Boston Common. Even allowing for an inflated count, these were surely the largest crowds ever assembled in Boston or any other colonial city. As Samuel Johnson once said, Whitefield would have been adored if he wore a nightcap and preached from a tree. Whitefield's tours outside of Boston, and then into western Massachusetts and Connecticut, were attended by similar public outpourings. No one, it seems, wanted to miss the show. In December Gilbert Tennent arrived in Boston, having been urged by Whitefield to add more fuel to the divine fires he had kindled there. Tennent's preaching, which lacked Whitefield's sweetness but none of his power, aroused a popular fervor that matched or exceeded that inspired by the Englishman.

Most Congregational ministers, including those at Boston, had welcomed Whitefield's tour as an opportunity to stimulate religious piety. Tennent's torrid preaching may have discomfited some, but it was not until 1742 that three events led to a polarization of the clergy into "New Light" supporters and "Old Light" opposers of the Great Awakening. First came the publication in Boston of Tennent's sermon, *The Danger of an Unconverted Ministry,* which one Old Light would later blame for having "sown the Seeds of all that Discord, Intrusion, Confusion, Separation, Hatred, Variance, Emulations, Wrath, Strife, Seditions, Heresies, &c. that have been springing up in so many of the Towns and Churches thro' the Province. . . ." Another was the publication of Whitefield's 1740 *Journal,* in which he criticized "most" New England preachers for insufficient piety and observed of Harvard and Yale that "their Light is become Darkness." The final provocation was the arrival in Boston on June 25, 1742 of the Reverend James Davenport, a newly fledged evangelist who already had Connecticut in an uproar and would soon have all Boston by the ears.

Davenport had been expelled from Connecticut on June 3 after being adjudged "disturbed in the rational Faculties of his Mind." Now the twenty-six-year-old evangelist was determined to share his special insights with the people of Boston. Forewarned about Davenport's odd behavior, the ministers of Boston and Charlestown (the majority of whom favored the Awakening) requested that the intruder restrain his "assuming Behavior . . . especially in judging the spiritual State of Pastors and People," and decided not to offer him their pulpits. Davenport was undeterred. He preached on the Common and in the rain on Copp's Hill; he proclaimed first three and then nine more of Boston's ministers "by name" to be unconverted; and he announced that he was "ready to drop down dead for the salvation of but one soul." Davenport was followed, according to one critic, by a "giddy Audience . . . chiefly made up of idle or ignorant Persons" of low rank. To some of Boston's soberer citizens the crowd appeared "menacing," and one newspaper essayist found Davenport's followers "so red hot, that I verily believe they would make nothing to kill Opposers." Such was the anarchy threatened by religious enthusiasm. . . .

In the months that followed, New Englanders, like middle-colony Presbyterians before them, would witness and then be drawn into a fierce struggle between the two factions, as their once-decorous ministers impugned the intelligence and integrity of their rivals in public sermons and essays. The Old Light writers were especially bellicose, losing no opportunity to rebuke the "enthusiastic, factious, censorious Spirit" of the revivalists. Schisms were threatened everywhere, and as early as 1742 some congregations had "divided into Parties, and openly and scandalously separated from one another." As the Connecticut Old Light, Isaac Stiles, warned, the subversion of all order was threatened when "Contempt is cast upon Authority both Civil and Ecclesiastical." Most distressing to those who believed that "Good Order is the Strength and Beauty of the World," was the Awakening's tendency to splinter New England society. "Formerly the People could bear with each other in Charity when they differ'd in Opinion," recalled one writer, "but they now break Fellowship and Communion with one another on that Account."

Indeed, awakened parishioners were repeatedly urged to withdraw from a "corrupt ministry." "O that the precious Seed might be preserved and *separated* from all gross Mixtures!" prayed the Connecticut New Light Jonathan Parsons. And spurred on by Parsons and other New Lights, withdraw they did. In Plymouth and Ipswich, from Maine to the Connecticut River Valley, the New England separatist movement gained momentum from 1743 onward. . . .

The Great Awakening, as Richard Hofstadter put it, was "the first major intercolonial crisis of the mind and spirit" in eighteenth-century America. No previous occurrence in colonial history compared with it in scale or consequences. True, the floodtide of evangelical fervor soon subsided, but nothing could quite restore the old cultural landscape. The unitary ideal of the seventeenth century continued to be eroded in the post-Awakening years by further church separations. Moreover, as the Reverend William Shurtleff noted in 1745, the "dividing Spirit is not confin'd to those that are Friends" of the revival. Nor was it confined to the religious sphere. That "dividing Spirit" would be manifested everywhere after mid-century in the proliferation of religious and political factions.

NO

Jon Butler

Enthusiasm Described and Decried: The Great Awakening as Interpretative Fiction

In the last half century, the Great Awakening has assumed a major role in explaining the political and social evolution of prerevolutionary American society. Historians have argued, variously, that the Awakening severed intellectual and philosophical connections between America and Europe (Perry Miller), that it was a major vehicle of early lower-class protest (John C. Miller, Rhys Isaac, and Gary B. Nash), that it was a means by which New England Puritans became Yankees (Richard L. Bushman), that it was the first "intercolonial movement" to stir "the people of several colonies on a matter of common emotional concern" (Richard Hofstadter following William Warren Sweet), or that it involved "a rebirth of the localistic impulse" (Kenneth Lockridge).

American historians also have increasingly linked the Awakening directly to the Revolution. Alan Heimert has tagged it as the source of a Calvinist political ideology that irretrievably shaped eighteenth-century American society and the Revolution it produced. Harry S. Stout has argued that the Awakening stimulated a new system of mass communications that increased the colonists' political awareness and reduced their deference to elite groups prior to the Revolution. Isaac and Nash have described the Awakening as the source of a simpler, non-Calvinist protest rhetoric that reinforced revolutionary ideology in disparate places, among them Virginia and the northern port cities. William G. McLoughlin has even claimed that the Great Awakening was nothing less than "the Key to the American Revolution."

These claims for the significance of the Great Awakening come from more than specialists in the colonial period. They are a ubiquitous feature of American history survey texts, where the increased emphasis on social history has made these claims especially useful in interpreting early American society to twentieth-century students. Virtually all texts treat the Great Awakening as a major watershed in the maturation of prerevolutionary American society. *The Great Republic* terms the Awakening "the greatest event in the history of religion in eighteenth-century America." *The National Experience* argues that the Awakening brought "religious experiences to thousands of people in every

From *Journal of American History* by Jon Butler, vol. 69, no. 2, September 1982, pp. 305–314, 316–317, 322–325. Copyright © 1982 by the Organization of American Historians. Reprinted by permission.

rank of society" and in every region. *The Essentials of American History* stresses how the Awakening "aroused a spirit of humanitarianism," "encouraged the notion of equal rights," and "stimulated feelings of democracy" even if its gains in church membership proved episodic. These texts and others describe the weakened position of the clergy produced by the Awakening as symptomatic of growing disrespect for all forms of authority in the colonies and as an important catalyst, even cause, of the American Revolution. The effect of these claims is astonishing. Buttressed by the standard lecture on the Awakening tucked into most survey courses, American undergraduates have been well trained to remember the Great Awakening because their instructors and texts have invested it with such significance.

Does the Great Awakening warrant such enthusiasm? Its puzzling historiography suggests one caution. The Awakening has received surprisingly little systematic study and lacks even one comprehensive general history. The two studies, by Heimert and Cedric B. Cowing, that might qualify as general histories actually are deeply centered in New England. They venture into the middle and southern colonies only occasionally and concentrate on intellectual themes to the exclusion of social history. The remaining studies are thoroughly regional, as in the case of books by Bushman, Edwin Scott Gaustad, Charles Hartshorn Maxson, Dietmar Rothermund, and Wesley M. Gewehr, or are local, as with the spate of articles on New England towns and Jonathan Edwards or Isaac's articles and book on Virginia. The result is that the general character of the Great Awakening lacks sustained, comprehensive study even while it benefits from thorough local examinations. The relationship between the Revolution and the Awakening is described in an equally peculiar manner. Heimert's seminal 1966 study, despite fair and unfair criticism, has become that kind of influential work whose awesome reputation apparently discourages further pursuit of its subject. Instead, historians frequently allude to the positive relationship between the Awakening and the Revolution without probing the matter in a fresh, systematic way.

The gap between the enthusiasm of historians for the social and political significance of the Great Awakening and its slim, peculiar historiography raises two important issues. First, contemporaries never homogenized the eighteenth-century colonial religious revivals by labeling them "the Great Awakening." Although such words appear in Edwards's *Faithful Narrative of the Surprising Work of God,* Edwards used them alternately with other phrases, such as "general awakening," "great alteration," and "flourishing of religion," only to describe the Northampton revivals of 1734–1735. He never capitalized them or gave them other special emphasis and never used the phrase "the Great Awakening" to evaluate all the prerevolutionary revivals. Rather, the first person to do so was the nineteenth-century historian and antiquarian Joseph Tracy, who used Edwards's otherwise unexceptional words as the title of his famous 1842 book, *The Great Awakening.* Tellingly, however, Tracy's creation did not find immediate favor among American historians. Charles Hodge discussed the Presbyterian revivals in his *Constitutional History of the Presbyterian Church* without describing them as part of a "Great Awakening," while the influential Robert Baird refused even to treat the eighteenth-century revivals as discrete and important events, much less label them "the Great Awakening." Baird all but ignored these revivals in the chronological segments of his *Religion in America* and mentioned them elsewhere only by way of explaining the intellectual origins of the Unitarian movement, whose early leaders opposed revivals. Thus, not until the last half of the nineteenth century did "the Great Awakening" become a familiar feature of the American historical landscape.

Second, this particular label ought to be viewed with suspicion, not because a historian created it—historians legitimately make sense of the minutiae of the past by utilizing such devices—but because the label itself does serious injustice to the minutiae it orders. The label "the Great Awakening" distorts the extent, nature, and cohesion of the revivals that did exist in the eighteenth-century colonies, encourages unwarranted claims for their effects on colonial society, and exaggerates their influence on the coming and character of the American Revolution. If "the Great Awakening" is not quite an American Donation of Constantine, its appeal to historians seeking to explain the shaping and character of prerevolutionary American society gives it a political and intellectual power whose very subtlety requires a close inspection of its claims to truth.

How do historians describe "the Great Awakening"? Three points seem especially common. First, all but a few describe it as a Calvinist religious revival in which converts acknowledged their sinfulness without expecting salvation. These colonial converts thereby distinguished themselves from Englishmen caught up in contemporary Methodist revivals and from Americans involved in the so-called Second Great Awakening of the early national period, both of which imbibed Arminian principles that allowed humans to believe they might effect their own salvation in ways that John Calvin discounted. Second, historians emphasize the breadth and suddenness of the Awakening and frequently employ hurricane metaphors to reinforce the point. Thus, many of them describe how in the 1740s the Awakening "swept" across the mainland colonies, leaving only England's Caribbean colonies untouched. Third, most historians argue that this spiritual hurricane affected all facets of prerevolutionary society. Here they adopt Edwards's description of the 1736 Northampton revival as one that touched "all sorts, sober and vicious, high and low, rich and poor, wise and unwise," but apply it to all the colonies. Indeed, some historians go farther and view the Great Awakening as a veritable social and political revolution itself. Writing in the late 1960s, Bushman could only wonder at its power: "We inevitably will underestimate the effect of the Awakening on eighteenth-century society if we compare it to revivals today. The Awakening was more like the civil rights demonstrations, the campus disturbances, and the urban riots of the 1960s combined. All together these may approach, though certainly not surpass, the Awakening in their impact on national life."

No one would seriously question the existence of "the Great Awakening" if historians only described it as a short-lived Calvinist revival in New England during the early 1740s. Whether stimulated by Edwards, James Davenport, or the British itinerant George Whitefield, the New England revivals between 1740 and 1745 obviously were Calvinist ones. Their sponsors vigorously criticized the soft-core Arminianism that had reputedly overtaken New England Congregationalism, and they stimulated the ritual renewal of a century-old society by reintroducing colonists to the theology of distinguished seventeenth-century Puritan clergymen, especially Thomas Shepard and Solomon Stoddard.

Yet, Calvinism never dominated the eighteenth-century religious revivals homogenized under the label "the Great Awakening." The revivals in the middle colonies flowed from especially disparate and international sources. John B. Frantz's recent traversal of the German revivals there demonstrates that they took root in Lutheranism, German Reformed Calvinism (different from the New England variety), and Pietism (however one wants to define it). Maxson stressed the mysticism, Pietism, Rosicrucianism, and Freemasonry rampant in these colonies among both German and English settlers. In an often overlooked observation, Maxson noted that the Tennents' backing for revivals was deeply linked to a mystical experience surrounding the near death of John Tennent and that both John Tennent and William Tennent, Jr., were mystics as well as Calvinists. The revivals among English colonists in Virginia also reveal eclectic roots. Presbyterians brought Calvinism into the colony for the first time since the 1650s, but Arminianism underwrote the powerful Methodist awakening in the colony and soon crept into the ranks of the colony's Baptists as well.

"The Great Awakening" also is difficult to date. Seldom has an "event" of such magnitude had such amorphous beginnings and endings. In New England, historians agree, the revivals flourished principally between 1740 and 1743 and had largely ended by 1745, although a few scattered outbreaks of revivalism occurred there in the next decades. Establishing the beginning of the revivals has proved more difficult, however. Most historians settle for the year 1740 because it marks Whitefield's first appearance in New England. But everyone acknowledges that earlier revivals underwrote Whitefield's enthusiastic reception there and involved remarkable numbers of colonists. Edwards counted thirty-two towns caught up in revivals in 1734–1735 and noted that his own grandfather, Stoddard, had conducted no less than five "harvests" in Northampton before that, the earliest in the 1690s. Yet revivals in Virginia, the site of the most sustained such events in the southern colonies, did not emerge in significant numbers until the 1750s and did not peak until the 1760s. At the same time, they also continued into the revolutionary and early national periods in ways that make them difficult to separate from their predecessors.

Yet even if one were to argue that "the Great Awakening" persisted through most of the eighteenth century, it is obvious that revivals "swept" only some of the mainland colonies. They occurred in Massachusetts, Connecticut, Rhode Island, Pennsylvania, New Jersey, and Virginia with some frequency at least at some points between 1740 and 1770. But New Hampshire, Maryland, and Georgia witnessed few revivals in the same years, and revivals were only occasionally important in New York, Delaware, North Carolina, and South Carolina. The revivals also touched only certain segments of the population in the colonies where they occurred. The best example of the phenomenon is Pennsylvania. The revivals there had a sustained effect among English settlers only in Presbyterian churches where many of the laity and clergy also opposed them. The Baptists, who were so important to the New England revivals, paid little attention to them until the 1760s, and the colony's taciturn Quakers watched them in perplexed silence. Not even Germans imbibed them universally.

At the same time that Benjamin Franklin was emptying his pockets in response to the preaching of Whitefield in Philadelphia—or at least claiming to do so—the residents of Germantown were steadily leaving their churches, and Stephanie Grauman Wolf reports that they remained steadfast in their indifference to Christianity at least until the 1780s.

Whitefield's revivals also exchanged notoriety for substance. Colonists responded to him as a charismatic performer, and he actually fell victim to the Billy Graham syndrome of modern times: his visits, however exciting, produced few permanent changes in local religious patterns. For example, his appearances in Charleston led to his well-known confrontation with Anglican Commissary Alexander Garden and to the suicide two years later of a distraught follower named Anne LeBrasseur. Yet they produced no new congregations in Charleston and had no documented effect on the general patterns of religious adherence elsewhere in the colony. The same was true in Philadelphia and New York City despite the fact that Whitefield preached to enormous crowds in both places. Only Bostonians responded differently. Supporters organized in the late 1740s a new "awakened" congregation that reputedly met with considerable initial success, and opponents adopted a defensive posture exemplified in the writings of Charles Chauncy that profoundly affected New England intellectual life for two decades.

Historians also exaggerate the cohesion of leadership in the revivals. They have accomplished this, in part, by overstressing the importance of Whitefield and Edwards. Whitefield's early charismatic influence later faded so that his appearances in the 1750s and 1760s had less impact even among evangelicals than they had in the 1740s. In addition, Whitefield's "leadership" was ethereal, at best, even before 1750. His principal early importance was to serve as a personal model of evangelical enterprise for ministers wishing to promote their own revivals of religion. Because he did little to organize and coordinate integrated colonial revivals, he also failed to exercise significant authority over the ministers he inspired.

The case against Edwards's leadership of the revivals is even clearer. Edwards defended the New England revivals from attack. But, like Whitefield, he never organized and coordinated revivals throughout the colonies or even throughout New England. Since most of his major works were not printed in his lifetime, even his intellectual leadership in American theology occurred in the century after his death. Whitefield's lack of knowledge about Edwards on his first tour of America in 1739–1740 is especially telling on this point. Edwards's name does not appear in Whitefield's journal prior to the latter's visit to Northampton in 1740, and Whitefield did not make the visit until Edwards had invited him to do so. Whitefield certainly knew of Edwards and the 1734–1735 Northampton revival but associated the town mainly with the pastorate of Edwards's grandfather Stoddard. As Whitefield described the visit in his journal: "After a little refreshment, we crossed the ferry to Northampton, where no less than three hundred souls were saved about five years ago. Their pastor's name is Edwards, successor and grandson to the great Stoddard, whose memory will be always precious to my soul, and whose books entitled 'A Guide to Christ,' and 'Safety of Appearing in Christ's Righteousness,' I would recommend to all."

What were the effects of the prerevolutionary revivals of religion? The claims for their religious and secular impact need pruning too. One area of concern involves the relationship between the revivals and the rise of the Dissenting denominations in the colonies. Denomination building was intimately linked to the revivals in New England. There, as C. C. Goen has demonstrated, the revivals of the 1740s stimulated formation of over two hundred new congregations and several new denominations. This was accomplished mainly through a negative process called "Separatism," which split existing Congregationalist and Baptist churches along prorevival and antirevival lines. But Separatism was of no special consequence in increasing the number of Dissenters farther south. Presbyterians, Baptists, and, later, Methodists gained strength from former Anglicans who left their state-supported churches, but they won far more recruits among colonists who claimed no previous congregational membership.

Still, two points are important in assessing the importance of revivals to the expansion of the Dissenting denominations in the colonies. First, revivalism never was the key to the expansion of the colonial churches. Presbyterianism expanded as rapidly in the middle colonies between 1710 and 1740 as between 1740 and 1770. Revivalism scarcely produced the remarkable growth that the Church of England experienced in the eighteenth century unless, of course, it won the favor of colonists who opposed revivals as fiercely as did its leaders. Gaustad estimates that between 1700 and 1780 Anglican congregations expanded from about one hundred to four hundred, and Bruce E. Steiner has outlined extraordinary Anglican growth in the Dissenting colony of Connecticut although most historians describe the colony as being thoroughly absorbed by the revivals and "Separatism."

Second, the expansion of the leading evangelical denominations, Presbyterians and Baptists, can be traced to many causes, not just revivalism or "the Great Awakening." The growth of the colonial population from fewer than three hundred thousand in 1700 to over two million in 1770 made the expansion of even the most modestly active denominations highly likely. This was especially true because so many new colonists did not settle in established communities but in new communities that lacked religious institutions. As Timothy L. Smith has written of seventeenth-century settlements, the new eighteenth-century settlements welcomed congregations as much for the social functions they performed as for their religious functions. Some of the denominations reaped the legacy of Old World religious ties among new colonists, and others benefited from local anti-Anglican sentiment, especially in the Virginia and Carolina backcountry. As a result, evangelical organizers formed many congregations in the middle and southern colonies without resorting to revivals at all. The first Presbyterian congregation in Hanover County, Virginia, organized by Samuel Blair and William Tennent, Jr., in 1746, rested on an indigenous lay critique of Anglican theology that had turned residents to the works of Martin Luther, and after the campaign by Blair and Tennent, the congregation allied itself with the Presbyterian denomination rather than with simple revivalism.

The revivals democratized relations between ministers and the laity only in minimal ways. A significant number of New England ministers changed their preaching styles as a result of the 1740 revivals. Heimert quotes Isaac Backus on the willingness of evangelicals to use sermons to "'insinuate themselves into the affections' of the people" and notes how opponents of the revivals like Chauncy nonetheless struggled to incorporate emotion and "sentiment" into their sermons after 1740. Yet revivalists and evangelicals continued to draw sharp distinctions between the rights of ministers and the duties of the laity. Edwards did so in a careful, sophisticated way in *Some Thoughts concerning the Present Revival of Religion in New England.* Although he noted that "disputing, jangling, and contention" surrounded "lay exhorting," he agreed that "some exhorting is a Christian duty." But he quickly moved to a strong defense of ministerial prerogatives, which he introduced with the proposition that "the Common people in exhorting one another ought not to clothe themselves with the like authority, with that which is proper for ministers." Gilbert Tennent was less cautious. In his 1740 sermon *The Danger of an Unconverted Ministry,* he bitterly attacked "Pharisee-shepherds" and "Pharisee-teachers" whose preaching was frequently as "unedifying" as their personal lives. But Gilbert Tennent never attacked the ministry itself. Rather, he argued for the necessity of a *converted* ministry precisely because he believed that only preaching brought men and women to Christ and that only ordained ministers could preach. Thus, in both 1742 and 1757, he thundered against lay preachers. They were "of dreadful consequence to the Church's peace and soundness in principle. . . . . [F]or Ignorant Young Converts to take upon them authoritatively to Instruct and Exhort publickly tends to introduce the greatest Errors and the greatest anarchy and confusion."

The 1740 revival among Presbyterians in New Londonderry, Pennsylvania, demonstrates well how ministers shepherded the laity into a revival and how the laity followed rather than led. It was Blair, the congregation's minister, who first criticized "dead Formality in Religion" and brought the congregation's members under "deep convictions" of their "natural unregenerate state." Blair stimulated "soul exercises" in the laity that included crying and shaking, but he also set limits for these exercises. He exhorted them to "moderate and bound their passions" so that the revival would not be destroyed by its own methods. Above this din, Blair remained a commanding, judgmental figure who stimulated the laity's hopes for salvation but remained "very cautious of expressing to People my Judgment of the Goodness of their States, excepting where I had pretty clear Evidences from them, of their being savingly changed." . . .

Nor did the revivals change the structure of authority within the denominations. New England Congregationalists retained the right of individual congregations to fire ministers, as when Northampton dismissed Edwards in 1750. But in both the seventeenth and eighteenth centuries, these congregations seldom acted alone. Instead, they nearly always consulted extensively with committees of ordained ministers when firing as well as when hiring ministers. In the middle colonies, however, neither the prorevival Synod of New York nor the antirevival Synod of Philadelphia tolerated such independence in congregations whether in theory or in practice. In both synods, unhappy congregations had to convince special committees appointed by the synods and composed exclusively of ministers that the performance of a fellow cleric was sufficiently dismal to warrant his dismissal. Congregations that acted independently in such matters quickly found themselves censured, and they usually lost the aid of both synods in finding and installing new ministers.

Did the revivals stir lower-class discontent, increase participation in politics, and promote democracy in society generally if not in the congregations? Even in New England the answer is, at best, equivocal. Historians have laid to rest John C. Miller's powerfully stated argument of the 1930s that the revivals were, in good part, lower-class protests against dominant town elites. The revivals indeed complicated local politics because they introduced new sources of potential and real conflict into the towns. New England towns accustomed to containing tensions inside a single congregation before 1730 sometimes had to deal with tensions within and between as many as three or four congregations after 1730. Of course, not all of these religious groups were produced by the revivals, and, as Michael Zuckerman has pointed out, some towns never tolerated the new dissidents and used the "warning out" system to eject them. Still, even where it existed, tumult should not be confused with democracy. Social class, education, and wealth remained as important after 1730 in choosing town and church officers as they had been before 1730, and Edward M. Cook, Jr., notes that after 1730 most new revival congregations blended into the old order: "dissenters [took] their place in town affairs once they stopped threatening the community and symbolically became loyal members of it." . . .

What, then, ought we to say about the revivals of religion in prerevolutionary America? The most important suggestion is the most drastic. Historians should abandon the term "the Great Awakening" because it distorts the character of eighteenth-century American religious life and misinterprets its relationship to prerevolutionary American society and politics. In religion it is a deus ex machina that falsely homogenizes the heterogeneous; in politics it falsely unites the colonies in slick preparation for the Revolution. Instead, a four-part model of the eighteenth-century colonial revivals will highlight their common features, underscore important differences, and help us assess their real significance.

First, with one exception, the prerevolutionary revivals should be understood primarily as regional events that occurred in only half the colonies. Revivals occurred intermittently in New England between 1690 and 1745 but became especially common between 1735 and 1745. They were uniformly Calvinist and produced more significant local political ramifications—even if they did not democratize New England—than other colonial revivals except those in Virginia. Revivals in the middle colonies occurred primarily between 1740 and 1760. They had remarkably eclectic theological origins, bypassed large numbers of settlers, were especially weak in New York, and produced few demonstrable political and social changes. Revivals in the southern colonies did not occur in significant numbers until the 1750s, when they were limited largely to Virginia, missed Maryland almost entirely, and did not occur with any regularity in the Carolinas until well after 1760. Virginia's Baptist revivalists stimulated major political and social changes in the colony, but the secular importance of the other revivals has been exaggerated. A fourth set of revivals, and the exception to the regional pattern outlined here, accompanied the preaching tours of the Anglican itinerant Whitefield. These tours frequently intersected with the regional revivals in progress at different times in New England, the middle colonies, and some parts of the southern colonies, but even then the fit was imperfect. Whitefield's tours produced some changes in ministerial speaking styles but few permanent alterations in institutional patterns of religion, although his personal charisma supported no less than seven tours of the colonies between 1740 and his death in Newburyport, Massachusetts, in 1770.

Second, the prerevolutionary revivals occurred in the colonial backwaters of Western society where they were part of a long-term pattern of erratic movements for spiritual renewal and revival that had long characterized Western Christianity and Protestantism since its birth two centuries earlier. Thus, their theological origins were international and diverse rather than narrowly Calvinist and uniquely American. Calvinism was important in some revivals, but Arminianism and Pietism supported others. This theological heterogeneity also makes it impossible to isolate a single overwhelmingly important cause of the revivals. Instead, they appear to have arisen when three circumstances were present—internal demands for renewal in different international Christian communities, charismatic preachers, and special, often unique, local circumstances that made communities receptive to elevated religious rhetoric.

Third, the revivals had modest effects on colonial religion. This is not to say that they were "conservative" because they did not always uphold the traditional religious order. But they were never radical, whatever their critics claimed. For example, the revivals reinforced ministerial rather than lay authority even as they altered some clergymen's perceptions of their tasks and methods. They also stimulated the demand for organization, order, and authority in the evangelical denominations. Presbyterian "New Lights" repudiated the conservative Synod of Philadelphia because its discipline was too weak, not too strong, and demanded tougher standards for ordination and subsequent service. After 1760, when Presbyterians and Baptists utilized revivalism as part of their campaigns for denominational expansion, they only increased their stress on central denominational organization and authority.

Indeed, the best test of the benign character of the revivals is to take up the challenge of contemporaries who linked them to outbreaks of "enthusiasm" in Europe. In making these charges, the two leading antirevivalists in the colonies, Garden of Charleston and Chauncy of Boston, specifically compared the colonial revivals with those of the infamous "French Prophets" of London, exiled Huguenots who were active in the city between 1706 and about 1730. The French Prophets predicted the downfall of English politicians, raised followers from the dead, and used women extensively as leaders to prophesy and preach. By comparison, the American revivalists were indeed "conservative." They prophesied only about the millennium, not about local politicans, and described only the necessity, not the certainty, of salvation. What is most important is that they eschewed radical change in the position of women in the churches. True, women experienced dramatic conversions, some of the earliest being described vividly by Edwards. But, they preached only irregularly, rarely prophesied, and certainly never led congregations, denominations, or sects in a way that could remotely approach their status among the French Prophets.

Fourth, the link between the revivals and the American Revolution is virtually nonexistent. The relationship between prerevolutionary political change and the revivals is weak everywhere except in Virginia, where the Baptist revivals indeed shattered the exclusive, century-old Anglican hold on organized religious activity and politics in the colony. But, their importance to the Revolution is weakened by the fact that so many members of Virginia's Anglican aristocracy also led the Revolution. In other colonies the revivals furnished little revolutionary rhetoric, including even millennialist thought, that was not available from other sources and provided no unique organizational mechanisms for anti-British protest activity. They may have been of some importance in helping colonists make moral judgments about eighteenth-century English politics, though colonists unconnected to the revivals made these judgments as well.

In the main, then, the revivals of religion in eighteenth-century America emerge as nearly perfect mirrors of a regionalized, provincial society. They arose erratically in different times and places across a century from the 1690s down to the time of the Revolution. Calvinism underlay some of them, Pietism and Arminianism others. Their leadership was local and, at best, regional, and they helped reinforce—but were not the key to—the proliferation and expansion of still-regional Protestant denominations in the colonies. As such, they created no intercolonial religious institutions and fostered no significant experiential unity in the colonies. Their social and political effects were minimal and usually local, although they could traumatize communities in which they upset, if only temporarily, familiar patterns of worship and social behavior. But the congregations they occasionally produced usually blended into the traditional social system, and the revivals abated without shattering its structure. Thus, the revivals of religion in prerevolutionary America seldom became proto-revolutionary, and they failed to change the timing, causes, or effects of the Revolution in any significant way.

Of course, it is awkward to write about the eighteenth-century revivals of religion in America as erratic, heterogeneous, and politically benign. All of us have walked too long in the company of Tracy's "Great Awakening" to make our journey into the colonial past without it anything but frightening. But as Chauncy wrote of the Whitefield revivals, perhaps now it is time for historians "to see that Things have been carried too far, and that the Hazard is great . . . lest we should be over-run with *Enthusiasm.*"

POSTSCRIPT

Was There a Great Awakening in Mid-Eighteenth-Century America?

Few scholars are likely to be persuaded by Butler's insistence upon abandoning the label "Great Awakening" when referring to the colonial revivals of the mid-eighteenth century, but some do find merit in certain aspects of his interpretation. In particular, Butler's critique of efforts to link the Awakening with the American Revolution is part of a longstanding historical debate. Even if William McLoughlin's thesis that the revivals were a "key" that opened the door to the War for Independence is invalid, there is room to argue that the Revolution was not without its religious elements. In his book *Religion in America: Past and Present* (Prentice-Hall, 1961), Clifton E. Olmstead argues for a broader application of religious causes to the origins of the American Revolution. First, and consistent with McLoughlin, Bonomi, and others, Olmstead contends that the Great Awakening did foster a sense of community among American colonists, thus providing the unity required for an organized assault on English control. Moreover, the Awakening further weakened existing ties between colonies and Mother Country by drawing adherents of the Church of England into the evangelical denominations that expanded as a result of revivalistic Protestantism. Second, tensions were generated by the demand that an Anglican bishop be established in the colonies. Many evangelicals found in this plan evidence that the British government wanted further control over the colonies. Third, the Quebec Act, enacted by Parliament in 1774, not only angered American colonists by nullifying their claims to western lands, but also heightened religious prejudice in the colonies by granting tolerance to Roman Catholics. Fourth, ministers played a significant role in encouraging their parishioners to support the independence movement. Olmstead claims that Congregationalist, Presbyterian, Dutch Reformed, and Baptist ministers overwhelmingly defended this revolutionary movement in the colonies. Finally, many of the revolutionaries, imbued with the American sense of mission, believed that God was ordaining their revolutionary activities.

Further support for these views can be found in Alan Heimert, *Religion and the American Mind from the Great Awakening to the Revolution* (Cambridge University Press, 1966), Cedric B. Cowing, *The Great Awakening and the American Revolution: Colonial Thought in the Eighteenth Century* (University of Chicago, 1971), Richard Hofstadter, *America at 1750: A Social Portrait* (Knopf, 1973), Rhys Isaac, *The Transformation of Virginia, 1740–1790* (University of North Carolina Press, 1982), Ruth H. Bloch, *Visionary Republic* (Cambridge University Press, 1985), and Harry S. Stout, *The New England Soul: Preaching and Religious Culture in Colonial New England* (Oxford University Press, 1986). Jon Butler has expanded his views on the colonial religious experience in *Awash in a Sea of Faith: Christianizing the American People* (Harvard University Press, 1990).

Students interested in further analyses of the Great Awakening should consult Edwin Scott Gaustad, *The Great Awakening in New England* (Harper & Brothers, 1957), David S. Lovejoy, *Religious Enthusiasm and the Great Awakening* (Prentice-Hall, 1969), and Marilyn J. Westerkamp, *Triumph of the Laity: Scots-Irish Piety and the Great Awakening, 1625–1760* (Oxford University Press, 1987). Richard Bushman, ed., *The Great Awakening: Documents on the Revival of Religion, 1740–1745* (University of North Carolina Press, 1989) offers an excellent introduction to this topic through collected sermons and first-person accounts. Biographies of two of the leading figures of eighteenth-century revivalism can be found in Frank Lambert, *"Pedlar of Divinity": George Whitefield and the Transatlantic Revivals* (Princeton University Press, 1994), Harry S. Stout, *The Divine Dramatist: George Whitefield and the Rise of Modern Evangelicalism* (Eerdmans, 1991), and Patricia Tracy, *Jonathan Edwards, Pastor: Religion and Society in Eighteenth-Century Northampton* (Hill & Wang, 1980).

Virtual Marching Tour of the American Revolution

Sponsored by the Independence Hall Association in Philadelphia, this site is a promising work in progress. Its goal is to provide information about Revolutionary times through text and images.

```
http://www.ushistory.org/march/
```

The Constitution of the United States

Sponsored by the National Archives and Records Administration, this site presents a wealth of information on the U.S. Constitution. From here you can link to the biographies of the 55 delegates to the Constitutional Convention, take an in-depth look at the convention and the ratification process, read a transcription of the complete text of the Constitution, and view high-resolution images of each page of the Constitution.

```
http://www.nara.gov/exhall/charters/
constitution/conmain.html
```

Thomas Jefferson Papers: Home Page

The Thomas Jefferson Papers: Home Page site consists of the complete Thomas Jefferson Papers from the Manuscript Division at the Library of Congress. This collection of 27,000 documents is the largest collection of original Jefferson documents in the world. Organized into nine series, this collection includes correspondence, manuscripts, and miscellaneous bound volumes. Also provided on this site are selected quotations of Thomas Jefferson and essays written about him.

```
http://memeory.loc.gov/ammem/mtjhtml/
mtjhome.html
```

Andrew Jackson Speaks: Indian Removal

A segment of the Tracking Westward Expansion & the Trail of Tears, this site developed with text and images by Patrick Jennings is an excellent source for Jackson's own words pertaining to Indian removal in the years from 1830 to 1836.

```
http://www.synaptic.bc.ca/ejournal/jackson.htm
```

PART 2

Revolution and the New Nation

*T*he American Revolution led to independence from England and to the establishment of a new nation. As the United States matured, its people and leaders struggled to implement fully the ideals that had sparked the revolution. What had been abstractions before the formation of the new government had to be applied and refined in day-to-day practice. The nature of post–Revolutionary America, government stability, the transition of power against the backdrop of political factionalism, the nation's role in world affairs, and the extension of democracy had to be worked out.

- Was the American Revolution a Conservative Movement?

- Were the Founding Fathers Democratic Reformers?

- Was President Thomas Jefferson a Political Compromiser?

- Was the Monroe Doctrine of 1823 Designed to Protect the Latin American Countries from European Intervention?

- Was Andrew Jackson's Indian Removal Policy Motivated by Humanitarian Impulses?

ISSUE 6

Was the American Revolution a Conservative Movement?

YES: Carl N. Degler, from *Out of Our Past: The Forces That Shaped Modern America,* rev. ed. (Harper & Row, 1970)

NO: Gordon S. Wood, from *The Radicalism of the American Revolution* (Alfred A. Knopf, 1991)

ISSUE SUMMARY

YES: Pulitzer Prize-winning author Carl N. Degler argues that upper-middle-class colonists led a conservative American Revolution that left untouched the prewar economic and social class structure of an upwardly mobile people.

NO: Prize-winning historian Gordon S. Wood argues that the American Revolution was a far-reaching, radical event that produced a unique democratic society in which ordinary people could make money, pursue happiness, and be self-governing.

Was the American Revolution a true revolution? The answer may depend on how the term *revolution* is defined. *Strict constructionists,* for example, perceive revolution as producing significant and deep societal change, while *loose constructionists* define the term as "any resort to violence within a political order to change its constitution, rulers, or policies." Historians agree that American Revolutionaries fulfilled the second definition because they successfully fought a war that resulted in the overthrow of their British rulers and established a government run by themselves. However, historians disagree over the amount of social and economic changes that took place in America.

Early historians did not concern themselves with the social and economic aspects of the American Revolution. They instead argued over the causes of the Revolution and refought the political arguments advanced by the rebelling colonists and the British government. George Bancroft was the first historian to advance the *Whig,* or *pro-American,* interpretation of the war. America won, he said, because God was on our side.

Bancroft's view remained unchallenged until the beginning of the twentieth century, when a group of *imperialist* historians analyzed the Revolution from

120

the perspective of the British empire. These historians tended to be sympathetic to the economic and political difficulties that Great Britain faced in running an empire in the late eighteenth century.

Both the Whig and the imperialist historians assumed that the Revolution was an *external* event whose primary cause was the political differences between the colonists and their British rulers. In 1909, however, historian Carl Becker paved the way for a different interpretation of the Revolution when he concluded in his study of colonial New York that an *internal* revolution had taken place. The American Revolution, said Becker, created a struggle not only for home rule but also one for who should rule at home. This *progressive*, or *conflict*, interpretation dominated most of the writings on the American Revolution from 1910 through 1945. During this time progressive historians searched for the social and economic conflicts among groups struggling for political power.

Since World War II, most professional historians have rejected what they considered to be an oversimplified conflict interpretation of the Revolution by the previous generation of progressive historians. Robert E. Brown, in his studies on colonial Massachusetts and Virginia, argued that America had become a middle-class democracy before the American Revolution. Consequently, Brown maintained, there was no need for a social revolution. Most influential have been the works of Harvard University professor Bernard Bailyn, who used a neoconservative approach in analyzing the Revolution. In his *Ideological Origins of the American Revolution* (Harvard University Press, 1968), Bailyn took ideas seriously once again and saw the colonists implementing the views of radical British thinkers in their struggle for independence. The most recent statement on the American Revolution from the neoconservative perspective is *Becoming America: The Revolution Before 1776* by Jon Butler (Howard University Press, 2000). In it, Butler argues that American colonial society—politically, socially, and economically—was dramatically transformed between 1680 and 1770.

In the first of the following selections, Carl N. Degler argues the neoconservative view of the American Revolution, maintaining that the upper-middle-class colonists led a conservative Revolution that left untouched the prewar economic and social class structure of an upwardly mobile people. This essay is an excellent example of the loose constructionist definition of revolution.

Since the late 1960s, historians have written a great deal about blacks, women, Native Americans, and "ordinary" people. This neoprogressive interpretation of America's past has also made views on the events surrounding the Revolution more complicated. See the collection of articles in *The American Revolution: Explorations in the History of American Radicalism* edited by Alfred F. Young (Northern Illinois University Press, 1976).

Gordon S. Wood has given a new dimension to the neoprogressive studies of the Revolutionary era. In his book *The Radicalism of the American Revolution*, he argues the strict constructionist view that the Revolution produced major social changes. In the second selection, taken from this book, Wood maintains that the American Revolution was a radical event because America was the first nation to hold democratic values, allowing ordinary people to make money, pursue happiness, and rule themselves.

 **YES**

A New Kind of Revolution

Conservatives Can Be Innovators

Like fabled genii grown too big to be imprisoned in their bottles, wars and revolutions frequently take on a life of their own irrespective of their first purposes. The overarching considerations of survival or victory distort or enlarge the narrow and limited aims for which the conflict was begun. The American War for Independence was such an event. Begun for only limited political and constitutional purposes, the war released social forces which few of the leaders ever anticipated, but which have helped to mold the American tradition.

One such unforeseen result was the rapid and final disestablishment of the Anglican Church, heretofore the state-supported religion in all of the colonies south of Mason and Dixon's Line and in parts of New York and New Jersey as well.[1] In knocking out the props of the State from beneath the Anglican Church, the states provided the occasion for wider and more fundamental innovations. Virginia in 1786, in disestablishing the Anglican Church, put no other church in its place and instead passed a law guaranteeing religious freedom. This law, with which Madison and Jefferson had so much to do, prepared the ground for the ultimate triumph of the American doctrine of separation of Church and State.

The ratification of the federal Constitution in 1788 constituted the first step in the acceptance of the principle that a man's religion was irrelevant to government, for the Constitution forbade all religious tests for officeholding.[2] Then in 1791, when the first ten amendments were added, Congress was enjoined from legislating in any manner "respecting an establishment of religion or prohibiting the free exercise thereof." These legalistic and now commonplace phrases had centuries of man's religious history packed within them; upon their implementation western Christendom reached a milestone in its long quest for a viable accommodation between man's religious conscience and *raison d'état*.

For millennia a man's religion had been either a passport or a barrier to his freedom and the opportunity to serve his State; it had always mattered how a man worshiped God. Since Emperor Theodosius in the fourth century of the Christian era, religious orthodoxy had been considered necessary for good citizenship and for service to the state. All this weighty precedence was boldly overthrown by Americans in 1789–91 when they erected a government wherein "a man's religious tenets will not forfeit the protection of the Laws nor deprive him of the right of attaining and holding the highest offices that are known in the United States," as George Washington said.

In the course of the early nineteenth century, the federal example of a strict divorce of State and Church was emulated by the individual states. At the time of the Revolution many states had demanded Christian and often Protestant affiliations for officeholding, and some had even retained a state-supported Church. Gradually, however, and voluntarily—Massachusetts was last in 1833—all the states abandoned whatever connections they might have had with the churches. The doctrine of separation has been more deeply implanted in our tradition in the twentieth century by the Supreme Court, which has declared that separation is a freedom guaranteed by the Fourteenth Amendment to the Constitution and therefore obligatory upon the states as well as the federal government. Thus the two extremes of the American political spectrum—the popular state governments and the august Supreme Court—have joined in sanctioning this doctrine born out of the Revolution by the liberalism of the Enlightenment.

It was a remarkably novel and even unique approach to the question of the relation between the State and religion. Although the doctrine repudiates any connection between the State and the Church, the American version has little in common with the practice in countries like revolutionary France and Mexico and atheistic Soviet Russia, where separation has been so hostile to religion as to interfere, at times, with freedom of worship. The American conception is not antireligious at all. Our Presidents invoke the Deity and offer Thanksgiving prayers, our armies and legislatures maintain chaplains, and the state and federal governments encourage religion through the remission of taxes. In America the State was declared to be secular, but it continued to reflect the people's concern with religion. The popular interest in religion was still evident in 1962 and 1963 when the Supreme Court invoked the principle of separation of church and state to ban prayers and Bible-reading from the public schools. In both Congress and the public press there was a loud protest against such a close and allegedly antireligious interpretation of the principle. But efforts to amend the Constitution in order to circumvent the Supreme Court's interpretation failed.

In the eighteenth century the American principle of separation of Church and State was indeed an audacious experiment. Never before had a national state been prepared to dispense with an official religion as a prop to its authority and never before had a church been set adrift without the support of the state. Throughout most of American history the doctrine has provided freedom for religious development while keeping politics free of religion. And that, apparently, had been the intention of the Founding Fathers.

As the principle of the separation of Church and State was a kind of social side effect of the Revolution, so also was the assertion in the Declaration of Independence that "all men are created equal." These five words have been sneered at as idealistic, refuted as manifestly inaccurate, and denied as preposterous, but they have, nonetheless, always been capable of calling forth deep emotional response from Americans. Even in the Revolutionary era, their power was evident. In 1781 the Supreme Judicial Court of Massachusetts declared slavery at an end in that state because it "is inconsistent with our own conduct and Constitution" which "set out with declaring that all men are born free and equal. . . ." The Reverend Samuel Hopkins told the Continental Congress that it was illogical to "be holding so many hundreds of blacks in slavery . . . while we are maintaining this struggle for our own and our Children's liberty." In 1782 William Binford of Henrico County, Virginia, set free twelve slaves because he was "fully persuaded that freedom is the natural right of all mankind." Another Virginian, a few years later, freed all his slaves which had been "born after the Declaration of Independence." Such efforts to reconcile the theory of the Declaration with the practices of life represent only the beginnings of the disquieting echoes of the celebrated phrase.

It is wrong to assume, however, that the mere inclusion of that phrase in the Declaration worked the mighty influence implied in the foregoing examples; social values are not created so deliberately or so easily. Like so much else in the Declaration, this sentence was actually the distillation of a cherished popular sentiment into a ringing phrase, allegiance to which stemmed from its prior acceptance rather than from its eloquence. The passionate belief in social equality which commentators and travelers in Jacksonian America would later find so powerful was already emergent in this earlier period. Indeed, we have already seen its lineaments during the colonial period. After 1776 the conviction was reinforced by the success of the Revolution and by the words of the great Declaration itself.

It was also supported by the facts of American social life. Despite the lowly position accorded the Negro, wrote the French traveler [Jacques-Pierre] Brissot in 1788, it still must be admitted "that the Americans more than any other people are convinced that all men are born free and equal." Moreover, he added, "we must acknowledge, that they direct themselves generally by this principle of equality." German traveler Johann Schoepf noticed that in Philadelphia "rank of birth is not recognized, is resisted with a total force. . . . People think, act, and speak here precisely as it prompts them. . . ."[3] And in the privacy of the Federal Convention of 1787, Charles Pinckney of South Carolina urged his fellow delegates to recognize the uniqueness of their country. "There is more equality of rank and fortune in America than in any other country under the sun," he told them.

There were other signs of what an earlier generation would have stigmatized as "leveling tendencies" in the new post-Revolutionary society. The attacks made by the Democratic-Republican societies upon the privileged Order of the Cincinnati, because it was secret and confined to Revolutionary officers and their descendants, were obviously inspired by a growing egalitarian sentiment. French traveler Moreau de Saint-Méry recalled with disgust how Americans proudly told him that the hotel custom of putting strange travelers together in the same bed was "a proof of liberty." By the end of the century old social distinctions like rank-seating in churches and the differentiating title of esquire were fast passing out of vogue. On an economic level, this abiding American faith was translated as equality of opportunity, and here dour

Federalist Fisher Ames could lock arms with his Republican opponents when he averred that "all cannot be rich, but all have a right to make the attempt."

Though economic grievances seem to have played a negligible role in bringing on the Revolution, this is not to say that there were no economic consequences. The economic stimulus afforded by the war demands and the freedom from English mercantilistic restrictions which victory made permanent provided adventuresome American merchants and entrepreneurs with wide opportunities for gaining new markets and new sources of profit. The expansion of the American economy, which was to be characteristic all through the nineteenth century, was thus begun.

But even when one has added together the new constitutions, the enlightened religious innovations, and the stimulus to equality, it is quickly apparent that the social consequences of the Revolution were meager indeed. In both purpose and implementation they were not to be equated with the massive social changes which shook France and Russia in later years. For the most part, the society of post-Revolutionary America was but the working out of social forces which were already evident in the colonial period.

It is significant, for example, that no new social class came to power through the door of the American Revolution. The men who engineered the revolt were largely members of the colonial ruling class. Peyton Randolph and Patrick Henry were well-to-do members of the Virginia Assembly; Washington, reputed to be the richest man in America, was an officer in the Virginia militia. The New York leaders John Morin Scott and Robert Livingston were judges on the Supreme Court of the colony, while William Drayton, a fire-eating radical of South Carolina, was a nephew of the lieutenant governor of the province, and himself a member of the Governor's Council until his anti-British activities forced his removal. Certainly Benjamin Franklin, citizen of the Empire, celebrated scientist, and long retired, well-to-do printer, was no submerged member of Philadelphia's society—or London's for that matter. Moreover, Franklin's natural son, William, was a Royal Governor at the outbreak of the Revolution. Hancock of Boston and Christopher Gadsden of Charleston were only two of the many respected and wealthy merchants who lent their support to the patriot cause. In fact, speaking of wealth, the Revolution in Virginia was made and led by the great landed class, and its members remained to reap the benefits. Farther down the social scale, in the backwoods of Massachusetts, it has been shown that the chief revolutionists in the western counties were the old leaders, so that no major shift in leadership took place there either, as a result of the Revolution.

This emphasis on position and wealth among the Revolutionary leaders should not be taken as a denial that many men of wealth and brains left the colonies in the exodus of the Loyalists. Certainly few patriots were the peers of Jared Ingersoll in the law, Jonathan Boucher in the Church, and Thomas Hutchinson and James Galloway in government. But the Loyalist departure did not decapitate the colonial social structure, as some have suggested—it only removed those most attached to the mother country.[4] A large part of the governing class remained to guide the Revolution and reap its favors. It is true, that in the states of Georgia and Pennsylvania, where the radical democrats held sway in the early years of the Revolution, new men seemed to occupy positions of power. But these men were still unknowns on the periphery of government and business, and generally remained there; they cannot be compared with the Robespierres and the Dantons, the Lenins and the Trotskys, of the great continental eruptions.

A convenient gauge of the essential continuity of the governing class in America before and after the Revolution is to be found in an examination of the careers of the signers of the Declaration of Independence. Surely these fifty-five men are important patriot leaders and presumably among the chief beneficiaries of the Revolution they advocated. Yet they were by no means a disadvantaged lot. Fully 40 percent of them attended college or one of the Inns of Court in England at a time when such a privilege was a rarity. An additional 21 percent of them came from important families of their respective colonies, or, like Robert Morris and Joseph Hewes, were men of acquired wealth. Over 69 percent of them held office under the colonial regimes, 29 percent alone holding some office within the executive branch; truly these were not men held at arm's length from the plums of office.

Most striking about the careers of these men is the fact that so many of them held office before and after the dividing line of the Revolution. Of those who held an office under the state governments after the Revolution, 75 percent had occupied offices before 1774, proving, if need be, that service in the colonial governments before the Revolution was no obstacle to political preferment for a patriot afterward. If those who held no office before 1774 are not counted—and several might be considered too young to be expected to have held office—then the continuity shows up even more clearly. Eighty-nine percent of those who filled an office before the Revolution also occupied an office under one of the new state governments. And if federal office after 1789 is included, then the proportion rises to 95 percent. Add to this the fact that other leaders, not included in the group of signers, had similarly good social backgrounds—men like Washington, Robert Livingston, Gouverneur Morris, Philip Schuyler, and a dozen more—and the conclusion that the Revolution was a thoroughly upper-middle-class affair in leadership and aim is inescapable.

A further and perhaps more important conclusion should be drawn from this analysis of the political careers of the signers after the Revolution. These conservative, upper-class leaders who proclaimed the Revolution suffered no repudiation in the course of the struggle; no mass from the bottom rose and seized control of the Revolutionary situation to direct the struggle into new channels. Rather these men merely shifted, as it were, from their favored status under the colonial regimes to comparable, if not improved, positions after the Revolution.

As a colonial revolt against an alien power, such a development is not surprising. But certainly—for better or for worse—the continuity brought a degree of social and political stability to the new nation rarely associated with the word "revolution" and serves, once again, to illustrate the truly conservative nature of the American revolt.

Similarly, in the redistribution of land, which played such a crucial role in France and Russia, the American Revolution set no example of social motivation or consequence. The Crown's lands, it is true were confiscated, and—of greater import—so were the lands of the proprietors and those of the literally thousands of Tories. But the disposition of these lands hardly constitutes a social revolution of major proportions. One can collect, of course, examples of the breakup of great estates, like the De Lancey manor in New York, which was sold to 275 individuals, or the 40,000-acre estate in North Carolina which was carved into scores of plots averaging 200 acres apiece, or the vast 21,000,000-acre proprietary lands of the Penns. But the more significant question to be answered is who got the land. And, from the studies which have been made, it would appear that most often the land went to speculators or men already possessing substantial acreage, not to the landless or even to the small holder. To be sure, much Tory land which first fell under the auctioneer's hammer to a speculator ultimately found its way into the hands of a yeoman, but such a procedure is a rather slow and orderly process of social revolution.

Furthermore, it is obvious from the Confiscation Acts in the several states and the commissioners who operated pursuant to them that the motive behind the acquisition of Tory lands was enhancement of the state revenues—as, indeed, the original resolution from Congress had suggested. Under such circumstances, pecuniary motives, not democratic theories of society, determined the configuration distribution would take. And it is here that we begin to touch upon the fundamental reason why the confiscation of the royal, proprietary, and Loyalist lands never assumed crucial social importance. Land was just too plentiful in America for these acres to matter. Speculators were loaded down with it; most men who wanted it already possessed it, or were on the way toward possession. One recent investigator of the confiscations in New York, for example, has pointed out that land there could be bought cheaper from speculators than from a former Tory estate.

Even the abolition of primogeniture in all the southern states by 1791 cannot be taken as a significant example of the Revolution's economic influence. The fact of the matter is that primogeniture had never appreciably affected land distribution, since it came into play only when the owner died intestate. Considering the notorious litigiousness of eighteenth-century Americans, it is hardly to be doubted that partible inheritance was the practice, if not the theory, long before primogeniture was wiped from the statute books. Furthermore, in almost half of the country—New Jersey, Pennsylvania, and all of the New England states—primogeniture never prevailed anyway.

As for the abolition of entail, it was frequently welcomed by owners of entailed estates, as was the case in Jefferson's Virginia, since it would permit the sale of otherwise frozen assets. These laws had not created a landed aristocracy in America and their repeal made no significant alteration in the social landscape.

Instead of being an abrupt break, the Revolution was a natural and even expected event in the history of a colonial people who had come of age. It is true that social and political changes accompanied the Revolution, some of which were destined to work great influence upon American institutions in the future, but these had been implicit in the pre-Revolutionary society. Moreover, important social institutions were left untouched by the Revolution: the class structure, the distribution of property, the capitalistic economy, the ideas of the people concerning government.

This lack of profound and widespread social and economic change is not surprising. These Americans, for all their talk, had been a contented and prosperous people under the British Crown and they were, therefore, contented revolutionaries who wanted nothing more than to be undisturbed in their accustomed ways. They are in no wise to be compared with the disgruntled lawyers, the frustrated bourgeois, the tyrannized workers, and the land-hungry peasants of the *anciens régimes* of France and Russia.

Yet, in conclusion, it is perhaps fitting to recall that America was born in revolution, for this fact has become embedded in our folk and sophisticated traditions alike. It was apparent in the self-conscious, often naïve enthusiasm displayed by American statesmen and people in support of the colonial rebellions in South America and in Greece in the first two decades of the nineteenth century. Revolutionaries of the middle of the century, like Louis Kossuth [Hungary] and [Giuseppe] Garibaldi [Italy], garnered moral and material benefits from this continuing American friendship for rebellion. European exiles and revolutionaries of 1848 were entertained at the London residence of United States Minister James Buchanan. And it is still apparent today. The declarations of independence of Ho Chi Minh's Democratic Republic of (North) Vietnam in 1945 and Ian Smith's Rhodesia in 1965 both begin with quotations from the United States Declaration of Independence! And [President Gamal Abdel] Nasser of Egypt, at the time of the United States intervention in Lebanon in July, 1958, taunted Americans with their revolutionary tradition. "How can the United States, which pushed off British colonialism many years ago, forget its history?" he shouted to a crowd in Damascus.

An anticolonial tradition of such weight could not fail to leave its stamp upon American attitudes. . . . It was invoked again and again in debates over American foreign policy, and its continuing influence is evident in the movement of former colonies like Hawaii and Alaska into statehood and the Philippines into independence. Long before, in the era of the Revolution, American leaders, profiting from the lessons of Britain's imperial problems, agreed in the Ordinance of 1787 and the Constitution that newly acquired territories could attain, in the natural course of events, equal constitutional status with the original thirteen states. Thus, in a single stroke, Americans sidestepped the tensions and divisions attendant upon a colonial empire and laid the enduring foundations for an expanding and united country.

Constitutional devices, however, no matter how clever or farsighted, cannot of themselves create a new people. The forces of economics and geography can wreak havoc with the best laid plans of Founding Fathers. Whether Americans would retain their independence and become a truly united people was to be determined only by time and the people themselves.

Notes

1. This is not to say, however, that disestablishment of all churches was brought about by the Revolution. All of the New England states, with the exception of Rhode Island—still loyal to Roger Williams in this respect—continued to support the Congregational Church.

2. Just because the so-called conservatives dominated the Constitutional Convention, such religious indifference was possible. Generally the radials during the Revolutionary era were in favor of state support or recognition of some religion. Thus in the states where the radicals dominated, religious tests were part of the Constitution: Georgia (all members of the legislature had to be Protestants); North Carolina (no one could hold office who denied "God or the truth of the Protestant religion"); and Pennsylvania (the test oath demanded a belief in one God and his rewarding and punishing, and the acknowledgment that the Old and New Testaments were "given by Divine Inspiration"). The contrast with the Constitutional Convention of 1787 is striking. The Continental Congress, which had been dominated by the radicals, always opened its deliberations with chaplain-led prayers; the Convention of 1787, however, failed to have either a chaplain or prayers, though Franklin made an eloquent plea for both. He wrote later that "the Convention except three or four persons thought Prayers unnecessary." Whereas the Declaration of Independence refers to "God" and "Divine Providence," such words are completely absent from the "conservative" Constitution—much to the mystification of modern conservatives.

3. Schoepf, interestingly enough, discovered in the economic opportunities available in America the source of the social equality. "Riches make no positive material difference," he wrote concerning Philadelphia society, "because in this regard every man expects at one time or another to be on a footing with his rich neighbor, and in this expectation shows him no knavish reverence, but treats him with an open, but seemly familiarity."

4. William Nelson, *American Tory* (Oxford, 1961), suggests in his last chapter that America lost an organic or conservative view of society with the departure of the Loyalists. Insofar as that is true, it would reinforce the liberal bias that has been so characteristic of American political and social thought.

Gordon S. Wood  NO

The Radicalism of the American Revolution

We Americans like to think of our revolution as not being radical; indeed, most of the time we consider it downright conservative. It certainly does not appear to resemble the revolutions of other nations in which people were killed, property was destroyed, and everything was turned upside down. The American revolutionary leaders do not fit our conventional image of revolutionaries—angry, passionate, reckless, maybe even bloodthirsty for the sake of a cause. We can think of Robespierre, Lenin, and Mao Zedong as revolutionaries, but not George Washington, Thomas Jefferson, and John Adams. They seem too stuffy, too solemn, too cautious, too much the gentlemen. We cannot quite conceive of revolutionaries in powdered hair and knee breeches. The American revolutionaries seem to belong in drawing rooms or legislative halls, not in cellars or in the streets. They made speeches, not bombs; they wrote learned pamphlets, not manifestos. They were not abstract theorists and they were not social levelers. They did not kill one another; they did not devour themselves. There was no reign of terror in the American Revolution and no resultant dictator—no Cromwell, no Bonaparte. The American Revolution does not seem to have the same kinds of causes—the social wrongs, the class conflict, the impoverishment, the grossly inequitable distributions of wealth—that presumably lie behind other revolutions. There were no peasant uprisings, no jacqueries, no burning of châteaux, no storming of prisons.

Of course, there have been many historians—Progressive or neo-Progressive historians, as they have been called—who have sought, as Hannah Arendt put it, "to interpret the American Revolution in the light of the French Revolution," and to look for the same kinds of internal violence, class conflict, and social deprivation that presumably lay behind the French Revolution and other modern revolutions. Since the beginning of the twentieth century these Progressive historians have formulated various social interpretations of the American Revolution essentially designed to show that the Revolution, in Carl Becker's famous words, was not only about "home rule" but also about "who was to rule at home." They have tried to describe the Revolution essentially as a social struggle by deprived and underprivileged groups against entrenched elites. But, it has been correctly pointed out, despite an extraordinary amount of research

From Gordon S. Wood, *The Radicalism of the American Revolution* (Alfred A. Knopf, 1991). Copyright © 1991 by Gordon S. Wood. Reprinted by permission of Alfred A. Knopf, a division of Random House, Inc. Notes omitted.

and writing during a good part of this century, the purposes of these Progressive and neo-Progressive historians—"to portray the origins and goals of the Revolution as in some significant measure expressions of a peculiar economic malaise or of the social protests and aspirations of an impoverished or threatened mass population—have not been fulfilled." They have not been fulfilled because the social conditions that generically are supposed to lie behind all revolutions—poverty and economic deprivation—were not present in colonial America. There should no longer be any doubt about it: the white American colonists were not an oppressed people; they had no crushing imperial chains to throw off. In fact, the colonists knew they were freer, more equal, more prosperous, and less burdened with cumbersome feudal and monarchical restraints than any other part of mankind in the eighteenth century. Such a situation, however, does not mean that colonial society was not susceptible to revolution.

Precisely because the impulses to revolution in eighteenth-century America bear little or no resemblance to the impulses that presumably account for modern social protests and revolutions, we have tended to think of the American Revolution as having no social character, as having virtually nothing to do with the society, as having no social causes and no social consequences. It has therefore often been considered to be essentially an intellectual event, a constitutional defense of American rights against British encroachments ("no taxation without representation"), undertaken not to change the existing structure of society but to preserve it. For some historians the Revolution seems to be little more than a colonial rebellion or a war for independence. Even when we have recognized the radicalism of the Revolution, we admit only a political, not a social radicalism. The revolutionary leaders, it is said, were peculiar "eighteenth-century radicals concerned, like the eighteenth-century British radicals, not with the need to recast the social order nor with the problems of the economic inequality and the injustices of stratified societies but with the need to purify a corrupt constitution and fight off the apparent growth of prerogative power." Consequently, we have generally described the Revolution as an unusually conservative affair, concerned almost exclusively with politics and constitutional rights, and, in comparison with the social radicalism of the other great revolutions of history, hardly a revolution at all.

If we measure the radicalism of revolutions by the degree of social misery or economic deprivation suffered, or by the number of people killed or manor houses burned, then this conventional emphasis on the conservatism of the American Revolution becomes true enough. But if we measure the radicalism by the amount of social change that actually took place—by transformations in the relationships that bound people to each other—then the American Revolution was not conservative at all; on the contrary: it was as radical and as revolutionary as any in history. Of course, the American Revolution was very different from other revolutions. But it was no less radical and no less social for being different. In fact, it was one of the greatest revolutions the world has known, a momentous upheaval that not only fundamentally altered the character of American society but decisively affected the course of subsequent history.

It was as radical and social as any revolution in history, but it was radical and social in a very special eighteenth-century sense. No doubt many of the concerns and much of the language of that premodern, pre-Marxian eighteenth century were almost entirely political. That was because most people in that very different distant world could not as yet conceive of society apart from government. The social distinctions and economic deprivations that we today think of as the consequence of class divisions, business exploitation, or various isms—capitalism, racism, etc.—were in the eighteenth century usually thought to be caused by the abuses of government. Social honors, social distinctions, perquisites of office, business contracts, privileges and monopolies, even excessive property and wealth of various sorts—all social evils and social deprivations—in fact seemed to flow from connections to government, in the end from connections to monarchical authority. So that when Anglo-American radicals talked in what seems to be only political terms—purifying a corrupt constitution, eliminating courtiers, fighting off crown power, and, most important, becoming republicans—they nevertheless had a decidedly social message. In our eyes the American revolutionaries appear to be absorbed in changing only their governments, not their society. But in destroying monarchy and establishing republics they were changing their society as well as their governments, and they knew it. Only they did not know—they could scarcely have imagined—how much of their society they would change. J. Franklin Jameson, who more than two generations ago described the Revolution as a social movement only to be roundly criticized by a succeeding generation of historians, was at least right about one thing: "the stream of revolution, once started, could not be confined within narrow banks, but spread abroad upon the land."

By the time the Revolution had run its course in the early nineteenth century, American society had been radically and thoroughly transformed. One class did not overthrow another; the poor did not supplant the rich. But social relationships—the way people were connected one to another—were changed, and decisively so. By the early years of the nineteenth century the Revolution had created a society fundamentally different from the colonial society of the eighteenth century. It was in fact a new society unlike any that had ever existed anywhere in the world.

That revolution did more than legally create the United States; it transformed American society. Because the story of America has turned out the way it has, because the United States in the twentieth century has become the great power that it is, it is difficult, if not impossible, to appreciate and recover fully the insignificant and puny origins of the country. In 1760 America was only a collection of disparate colonies huddled along a narrow strip of the Atlantic coast—economically underdeveloped outposts existing on the very edges of the civilized world. The less than two million monarchical subjects who lived in these colonies still took for granted that society was and ought to be a hierarchy of ranks and degrees of dependency and that most people were bound together by personal ties of one sort or another. Yet scarcely fifty years later these insignificant borderland provinces had become a giant, almost continentwide republic of nearly ten million egalitarian-minded bustling citizens who not only had thrust themselves into the vanguard of history but had fundamentally altered their society and their social relationships. Far from remaining monarchical, hierarchy-ridden subjects on the margin of civilization, Americans had become almost overnight, the most liberal, the most democratic, the most commercially minded, and the most modern people in the world.

And this astonishing transformation took place without industrialization, without urbanization, without railroads, without the aid of any of the great forces we usually invoke to explain "modernization." It was the Revolution that was crucial to this transformation. It was the Revolution, more than any other single event, that made America into the most liberal, democratic, and modern nation in the world.

Of course, some nations of Western Europe likewise experienced great social transformations and "democratic revolutions" in these same years. The American Revolution was not unique; it was only different. Because of this shared Western-wide experience in democratization, it has been argued by more than one historian that the broader social transformation that carried Americans from one century and one kind of society to another was "inevitable" and "would have been completed with or without the American Revolution." Therefore this broader social revolution should not be confused with the American Revolution. America, it is said, would have emerged into the modern world as a liberal, democratic, and capitalistic society even without the Revolution. One could, of course, say the same thing about the relationship between the French Revolution and the emergence of France in the nineteenth century as a liberal, democratic, and capitalistic society; and indeed, much of the current revisionist historical writing on the French Revolution is based on just such a distinction. But in America, no more than in France, that was not the way it happened: the American Revolution and the social transformation of America between 1760 and the early years of the nineteenth century were inextricably bound together. Perhaps the social transformation would have happened "in any case," but we will never know. It was in fact linked to the Revolution; they occurred together. The American Revolution was integral to the changes occurring in American society, politics, and culture at the end of the eighteenth century.

These changes were radical, and they were extensive. To focus, as we are today apt to do, on what the Revolution did not accomplish—highlighting and lamenting its failure to abolish slavery and change fundamentally the lot of women—is to miss the great significance of what it did accomplish; indeed, the Revolution made possible the anti-slavery and women's rights movements of the nineteenth century and in fact all our current egalitarian thinking. The Revolution not only radically changed the personal and social relationships of people, including the position of women, but also destroyed aristocracy as it had been understood in the Western world for at least two millennia. The Revolution brought respectability and even dominance to ordinary people long held in contempt and gave dignity to their menial labor in a manner unprecedented in history and to a degree not equaled elsewhere in the world. The Revolution did not just eliminate monarchy and create republics; it actually reconstituted what Americans meant by public or state power and brought about an entirely new kind of popular politics and a new kind of democratic officeholder. The Revolution not only changed the culture of Americans—making over their art, architecture, and iconography—but even altered their understanding of history, knowledge, and truth. Most important, it made the interests and prosperity of ordinary people—their pursuits of happiness—the goal of society and government. The Revolution did not merely create a political and legal environment conducive to economic expansion; it also released powerful popular entrepreneurial and commercial energies that few realized existed and transformed the economic landscape of the country. In short, the Revolution was the most radical and most far-reaching event in American history. . . .

•◦◉◦•

By the late 1760s and early 1770s a potentially revolutionary situation existed in many of the colonies. There was little evidence of those social conditions we often associate with revolution (and some historians have desperately sought to find): no mass poverty, no seething social discontent, no grinding oppression. For most white Americans there was greater prosperity than anywhere else in the world; in fact, the experience of that growing prosperity contributed to the unprecedented eighteenth-century sense that people here and now were capable of ordering their own reality. Consequently, there was a great deal of jealousy and touchiness everywhere, for what could be made could be unmade; the people were acutely nervous about their prosperity and the liberty that seemed to make it possible. With the erosion of much of what remained of traditional social relationships, more and more individuals had broken away from their families, communities, and patrons and were experiencing the anxiety of freedom and independence. Social changes, particularly since the 1740s, multiplied rapidly, and many Americans struggled to make sense of what was happening. These social changes were complicated, and they are easily misinterpreted. Luxury and conspicuous consumption by very ordinary people were increasing. So, too, was religious dissent of all sorts. The rich became richer, and aristocratic gentry everywhere became more conspicuous and self-conscious; and the numbers of poor in some cities and the numbers of landless in some areas increased. But social classes based on occupation or wealth did not set themselves against one another, for no classes in this modern sense yet existed. The society was becoming more unequal, but its inequalities were not the source of the instability and anxiety. Indeed, it was the pervasive equality of American society that was causing the problems. . . .

This extraordinary touchiness, this tendency of the colonists in their political disputes to argue "with such vehemence as if all had been at Stake," flowed from the precariousness of American society, from its incomplete and relatively flattened character, and from the often "rapid ascendency" of its aristocracy, particularly in the Deep South, where families "in less than ten years have risen from the lowest rank, have acquired upward of £100,000 and have, moreover, gained this wealth in a simple and easy manner." Men who had quickly risen to the top were confident and aggressive but also vulnerable to challenge, especially sensitive over their liberty and independence, and unwilling to brook any interference with their status or their prospects.

For other, more ordinary colonists the promises and uncertainties of American life were equally strong. Take, for example, the lifelong struggle of farmer and sawmill owner Moses Cooper of Glocester, Rhode Island, to rise from virtual insignificance to become the richest man in the town. In 1767–68, at the age of sixty, Cooper was finally able to hire sufficient slaves and workers to do all his manual labor; he became a gentleman and justice of the peace and appended "Esq." to his name. Certainly by this date he could respond to the rhetoric of his fellow Rhode Islanders talking about their colony as "the promised land . . . a land of milk and honey and wherein we eat bread to the full . . . a land whose stones are iron . . . and . . . other choice mines and minerals; and a land whose rivers and adjacent seas are stored with the best of fish." And Cooper might well have added, "whose forests were rich with timber," for he had made his money from lumber. Yet at the same time Cooper knew only too well the precariousness of his wealth and position and naturally feared what Britain's mercantile restrictions might mean for his lumber sales to the West Indies. What had risen so high could as readily fall: not surprisingly, he became an enthusiastic patriot leader of his tiny town of Glocester. Multiply Cooper's experience of uneasy prosperity many thousandfold and we have the stuff of a popular revolutionary movement.

. . . The great social antagonists of the American Revolution were not poor vs. rich, workers vs. employers, or even democrats vs. aristocrats. They were patriots vs. courtiers—categories appropriate to the monarchical world in which the colonists had been reared. Courtiers were persons whose position or rank came artificially from above—from hereditary or personal connections that ultimately flowed from the crown or court. Courtiers, said John Adams, were those who applied themselves "to the Passions and Prejudices, the Follies and Vices of Great Men in order to obtain their Smiles, Esteem, and Patronage and consequently their favors and Preferments. Patriots, on the other hand, were those who not only loved their country but were free of dependent connections and influence; their position or rank came naturally from their talent and from below, from recognition by the people. "A real patriot," declared one American in 1776, was "the most illustrious character in human life. Is not the interest and happiness of his fellow creatures his care?" . . .

It is in this context that we can best understand the revolutionaries' appeal to independence, not just the independence of the country from Great Britain, but, more important, the independence of individuals from personal influence and "warm and private friendship." The purpose of the Virginia constitution of 1776, one Virginian recalled, was "to prevent the undue and overwhelming influence of great landholders in elections." This was to be done by disfranchising the landless "tenants and retainers" who depended "on the breath and varying will" of these great men and by ensuring that only men who owned their own land could vote.

A republic presumed, as the Virginia declaration of rights put it, that men in the new republic would be "equally free and independent," and property would make them so. Property in a republic was still conceived of traditionally—in proprietary terms—not as a means of personal profit or aggrandizement but rather as a source of personal authority or independence. It was regarded not merely as a material possession but also as an attribute of a man's personality that defined him and protected him from outside pressure. A carpenter's skill, for example, was his property. Jefferson feared the rabble of the cities precisely because they were without property and were thus dependent.

All dependents without property, such as women and young men, could be denied the vote because, as a convention of Essex County, Massachusetts, declared in 1778, they were so situated as to have no wills of their own." Jefferson was so keen on this equation of property with citizenship that he proposed in 1776 that the new state of Virginia grant fifty acres of land to every man that did not have that many. Without having property and a will of his own—without having independence—a man could have no public spirit; and there could be no republic. For, as Jefferson put it, "dependence begets subservience and venality, suffocates the germ of virtue, and prepares fit tools for the designs of ambition."

In a monarchical world of numerous patron-client relations and multiple degrees of dependency, nothing could be more radical than this attempt to make every man independent. What was an ideal in the English-speaking world now became for Americans an ideological imperative. Suddenly, in the eyes of the revolutionaries, all the fine calibrations of rank and degrees of unfreedom of the traditional monarchical society became absurd and degrading. The Revolution became a full-scale assault on dependency.

At the beginning of the eighteenth century the English radical whig and deist John Toland had divided all society into those who were free and those who were dependent. "By *Freeman,*" wrote Toland, "I understand men of property, or persons that are able to live of themselves; and those who cannot subsist in this independence, I call *Servants.*" In such a simple division everyone who was not free was presumed to be a servant. Anyone tied to someone else, who was someone's client or dependent, was servile. The American revolutionary movement now brought to the surface this latent logic in eighteenth-century radical whig thinking.

Dependency was now equated with slavery, and slavery in the American world had a conspicuous significance. "What is a slave," asked a New Jersey writer in 1765, "but one who depends upon the will of another for the enjoyment of his life and property?" "Liberty," said Stephen Hopkins of Rhode Island, quoting Algernon Sidney, "solely consists in an independency upon the will of another; and by the name of slave we understand a man who can neither dispose of his person or goods, but enjoys all at the will of his master." It was left to John Adams in 1775 to draw the ultimate conclusion and to destroy in a single sentence the entire conception of society as a hierarchy of graded ranks and degrees. "There are," said Adams simply, "but two *sorts* of men in the world, freemen and slaves." Such a stark dichotomy collapsed all the delicate distinctions and dependencies of a monarchical society and created radical and momentous implications for Americans.

Independence, declared David Ramsay in a memorable Fourth of July oration in 1778, would free Americans from that monarchical world where "favor is the source of preferment," and where "he that can best please his superiors, by the low arts of fawning and adulation, is most likely to obtain favor." The revolutionaries wanted to create a new republican world in which "all offices lie open to men of merit, of whatever rank or condition." They believed that "even the reins of state may be held by the son of the poorest men, if possessed of abilities equal to the important station." They were "no more to look up for the blessings of government to hungry courtiers, or the needy dependents of British nobility"; but they had now to educate their "own children for these exalted purposes." Like Stephen Burroughs, the author of an extraordinary memoir of these years, the revolutionaries believed they were "so far republican" that they considered "a man's merit to rest entirely with himself, without any regard to family, blood, or connection." We can never fully appreciate the emotional meaning these commonplace statements had for the revolutionaries until we take seriously their passionate antagonism to the prevalence of patronage and family influence in the *ancien régime*.

Of course, the revolutionary leaders did not expect poor, humble men—farmers, artisans, or tradesmen—themselves to gain high political office. Rather, they expected that the sons of such humble or ungenteel men, if they had abilities, would, as they had, acquire liberal and genteel republican attributes, perhaps by attending Harvard or the College of New Jersey at Princeton, and would thereby rise into the ranks of gentlemen and become eligible for high political office. The sparks of genius that they hoped republicanism would fan and kindle into flame belonged to men like themselves—men "drawn from obscurity" by the new opportunities of republican competition and emulation into becoming "illustrious characters, which will dazzle the world with the splendor of their names." Honor, interest, and patriotism together called them to qualify themselves and posterity "for the 'bench, the army, the navy, the learned professions, and all the departments of civil government." They would become what Jefferson called the "natural aristocracy"—liberally educated, enlightened gentlemen of character. For many of the revolutionary leaders this was the emotional significance of republicanism—a vindication of frustrated talent at the expense of birth and blood. For too long, they felt, merit had been denied. In a monarchical world only the arts and sciences had recognized talent as the sole criterion of leadership. Which is why even the eighteenth-century *ancien régime* called the world of the arts and sciences "the republic of letters." Who, it was asked, remembered the fathers or sons of Homer and Euclid? Such a question was a republican dagger driven into the heart of the old hereditary order. "Virtue," said Thomas Paine simply, "is not hereditary." . . .

In their revolutionary state constitutions and laws the revolutionaries struck out at the power of family and hereditary privilege. In the decades following the Revolution all the new states abolished the legal devices of primogeniture and entail where they existed, either by statute or by writing the abolition into their constitutions. These legal devices, as the North Carolina statute of 1784 stated, had tended "only to raise the wealth and importance of particular families and individuals, giving them an unequal and undue influence in a republic, and prove in manifold instances the source of great contention and injustice." Their abolition would therefore "tend to promote that equality of property which is of the spirit and principle of a genuine republic." . . .

Women and children no doubt remained largely dependent on their husbands and fathers, but the revolutionary attack on patriarchal monarchy made all other dependencies in the society suspect. Indeed, once the revolutionaries collapsed all the different distinctions and dependencies of a monarchical society into either freemen or slaves, white males found it increasingly impossible to accept any dependent status whatsoever. Servitude of any sort suddenly became anomalous and anachronistic. In 1784 in New York, a group believing that indentured servitude was "contrary to . . . the idea of liberty this country has so happily established" released a shipload of immigrant servants and arranged for public subscriptions to pay for their passage. As early as 1775 in Philadelphia the proportion of the work force that was unfree—composed of servants and slaves—had already declined to 13 percent from the 40 to 50 percent that it had been at mid-century. By 1800 less than 2 percent of the city's labor force remained unfree. Before long indentured servitude virtually disappeared. . . .

One obvious dependency the revolutionaries did not completely abolish was that of nearly a half million Afro-American slaves, and their failure to do so, amidst all their high-blown talk of liberty, makes them seem inconsistent and hypocritical in our eyes. Yet it is important to realize that the Revolution suddenly and effectively ended the cultural climate that had allowed black slavery, as well as other forms of bondage and unfreedom, to exist throughout the colonial period without serious challenge. With the revolutionary movement, black slavery became excruciatingly conspicuous in a way that it had not been in the older monarchical society with its many calibrations and degrees of unfreedom; and Americans in 1775–76 began attacking it with a vehemence that was inconceivable earlier.

For a century or more the colonists had taken slavery more or less for granted as the most base and dependent status in a hierarchy of dependencies and a world of laborers. Rarely had they felt the need either to criticize black slavery or to defend it. Now, however, the republican attack on dependency compelled Americans to see the deviant character of slavery and to confront the institution as they never had to before. It was no accident that Americans in Philadelphia in 1775 formed the first anti-slavery society in the world. As long as most people had to work merely out of poverty and the need to provide for a living, slavery and other forms of enforced labor did not seem all that different from free labor. But the growing recognition that labor was not simply a common necessity of the poor but was in fact a source of increased wealth and prosperity for ordinary workers made slavery seem more and more anomalous. Americans now recognized that slavery in a republic of workers was an aberration, "a peculiar institution," and that if any Americans were to retain it, as southern Americans eventually did, they would have to explain and justify it in new racial and anthropological ways that their former monarchical society had never needed. The Revolution in effect set in motion ideological and social forces that doomed the institution of slavery in the North and led inexorably to the Civil War.

With all men now considered to be equally free citizens, the way was prepared as well for a radical change in the conception of state power. Almost at a stroke the Revolution destroyed all the earlier talk of paternal or maternal government, filial allegiance, and mutual contractual obligations between rulers and ruled. The familial image of government now lost all its previous relevance, and the state in America emerged as something very different from what it had been.

POSTSCRIPT

Was the American Revolution a Conservative Movement?

In arguing that the American Revolution was a conservative affair, Degler compares the American colonial leadership classes of lawyers, merchants, and planters with those who led similar revolutions later in France, Russia, and China. The American leadership was different, maintains Degler, because most held positions in government both before and after the Revolution. The goals of the American leaders also appear tame compared to revolutionaries in other countries. The Americans got rid of mercantilism but preserved capitalism. Also, loyalists were dispatched to Canada and England, but an upper middle class of pre-Revolutionary leaders remained in power.

Degler challenges the views of the earlier progressive historian J. Franklin Jameson, who argues in *The American Revolution Considered as a Social Movement* (Princeton University Press, 1926, 1967) that a radical transformation had taken place in the postwar distribution of land. Jameson also argues that the abolition of the slave trade and the separation of church and state were radical results of the American Revolution. And if the abolition of slavery and the attainment of equal rights for women were to come later, its roots were in the Revolutionary period.

Wood concedes that the American Revolution was not radical in the strict constructionist definition of the term. There were no major land reforms or political upheavals. Tories such as Massachusetts governor Thomas Hutchinson were given a one-way ticket to England—not a trip to the guillotine. Nevertheless, Wood argues that the Revolution was radical and social in a special eighteenth-century, premodern, pre-Marxian sense. Prior to the Industrial Revolution, class divisions and economic exploration of the people resulted from abuses by corrupt, tyrannical governments run by various kings and queens. Once the monarchy was overthrown, says Wood, the American Revolution created "a society fundamentally different from the colonial society of the eighteenth century."

Although Degler and Wood disagree on whether the American Revolution was radical or conservative, their arguments converge in several areas. Degler sees the disestablishment of the Anglican Church and the acceptance of the separation of the church from the state as an unintended result of the Revolution. Both Degler and Wood concede that deference to authority was weakened and that small farmers entered state legislatures, a number of state capitals were moved west, and legislative sessions were opened to the public. Obviously, the new social history caused both historians to think about the long-range effects of the Revolution on the rights of women and the eventual abolition of slavery. For a contrary view, see Linda De Pauw, "Land of the Unfree: Legal Limitations on Liberty in Pre-Revolutionary America," *Maryland Historical Magazine* (Winter 1973).

Neo-Left historians such as Alfred F. Young, Gary B. Nash, and Edward Countryman have written books and articles that stress racial, ethnic, and especially class conflicts that took place in the colonies in the 1760s and 1770s. In *The Urban Crucible: Social Change, Political Consciousness, and the Origins of the American Revolution* (Harvard University Press, 1979), for example, Nash interprets colonial life and the origins of the American Revolution in a comparative history of the three largest seaport cities in the colonies—Boston, New York, and Philadelphia.

Students who wish to explore Degler's suggestion that the American Revolution established "a new model for mankind" and influenced other revolutions by fighting the first successful anticolonial war of national liberation should read Richard B. Morris, *The Emerging Nations and the American Revolution* (Harper & Row, 1970) and the appropriate sections of Robert R. Palmer, *The Age of the Democratic Revolution* (Princeton University Press, 1959, 1964). A contrary view is advanced by Sung Bok Kim in "The American Revolution and the Modern World," in Larry R. Gerlach, James A. Dolph, and Michael L. Nicholls, eds., *Legacies of the American Revolution* (Utah State University Press, 1978). Kim concludes that the French Revolution had a greater impact on world history because the American Revolution established a society that values civil liberties and private ownership of property.

There are numerous anthologies that offer a diverse range of interpretations about the American Revolution. Two of the best-edited collections are George Athan Billias, *The American Revolution: How Revolutionary Was It?* (Holt, Rinehart & Winston, 1980) and Richard M. Fulton, *The Revolution That Wasn't: A Contemporary Assessment of 1776* (Kennikat Press, 1981), which discusses numerous theories of revolution. Among the most recent edited collections is Kirk D. Werner, ed., *The American Revolution* (Greenhaven Press, 2000). William Dudley has edited some of the most useful primary sources to a reasonable length in *The American Revolution: Opposing Viewpoints* (Greenhaven Press, 1992). Finally, Alfred F. Young provides a massive annotated and interpretative bibliography of works on the American Revolution in Ronald Hoffman and Peter J. Albert, eds., *The Transforming Hand of Revolution: Reconsidering the American Revolution as a Social Movement* (University Press of Virginia, 1995).

ISSUE 7

Were the Founding Fathers Democratic Reformers?

YES: John P. Roche, from "The Founding Fathers: A Reform Caucus in Action," *American Political Science Review* (December 1961)

NO: Alfred F. Young, from "The Framers of the Constitution and the 'Genius' of the People," *Radical History Review* (vol. 42, 1988)

ISSUE SUMMARY

YES: Political scientist John P. Roche asserts that the Founding Fathers were not only revolutionaries but also superb democratic politicians who created a Constitution that supported the needs of the nation and at the same time was acceptable to the people.

NO: Historian Alfred F. Young argues that the Founding Fathers were an elite group of college-educated lawyers, merchants, slaveholding planters, and "monied men" who strengthened the power of the central government yet, at the same time, were forced to make some democratic accommodations in writing the Constitution in order to ensure its acceptance in the democratically controlled ratifying conventions.

The United States possesses the oldest written constitution of any major power. The 55 men who attended the Philadelphia Convention of 1787 could scarcely have dreamed that 200 years later the nation would venerate them as the most "enlightened statesmen" of their time. James Madison, the principal architect of the document, may have argued that the Founding Fathers had created a system that might "decide forever the fate of Republican Government which we wish to last for ages," but Madison also told Thomas Jefferson in October 1787 that he did not think the document would be adopted, and if it was, it would not work.

The enlightened statesmen view of the Founding Fathers, presented by nineteenth-century historians like John Fiske, became the accepted interpretation among the general public until the Progressive Era. In 1913 Columbia University professor Charles A. Beard's *An Economic Interpretation of the Constitution of the United States* (Free Press, 1913, 1986) caused a storm of controversy because it questioned the motivations of the Founding Fathers. The Founding Fathers supported the creation of a stronger central government, argued Beard, not for patriotic reasons but because they wanted to protect their own economic interests.

Beard's research method was fairly simple. Drawing upon a collection of old, previously unexamined treasury records in the National Archives, he discovered that a number of delegates to the Philadelphia Convention and, later, the state ratifying conventions, held substantial amounts of continental securities that would sharply increase in value if a strong national government were established. In addition to attributing economic motives to the Founding Fathers, Beard included a Marxist class conflict interpretation in his book. Those who supported the Constitution, he said, represented "personalty interests which had been adversely affected under the Articles of Confederation: money, public securities, manufactures, and trade and shipping." Those who opposed ratification of the Constitution were the small farmers and debtors.

Beard's socioeconomic conflict interpretation of the supporters and opponents of the Constitution raised another issue: How was the Constitution ratified if the majority of Americans opposed it? Beard's answer was that most Americans could not vote because they did not own property. Therefore, the entire process, from the calling of the Philadelphia Convention to the state ratifying conventions, was nonrepresentative and nondemocratic.

An Economic Interpretation was a product of its times. Economists, sociologists, and political scientists had been analyzing the conflicts that resulted from the Industrial Revolution, which America had been experiencing at the turn of the twentieth century. Beard joined a group of progressive historians who were interested in reforming the society in which they lived and who also shared his discontent with the old-fashioned institutional approach. The role of the new historians was to rewrite history and discover the real reason why things happened. For the progressive historians, reality consisted of uncovering the hidden social and economic conflicts within society.

In the years between the world wars, the general public held steadfastly to the enlightened statesmen view of the Founding Fathers, but Beard's thesis on the Constitution became the new orthodoxy in most college texts on American history and government. The post–World War II period witnessed the emergence of the neoconservative historians, who viewed the Beardian approach to the Constitution as overly simplistic.

In the first of the following selections, which is a good example of consensus history, John P. Roche contends that although the Founding Fathers may have been revolutionaries, they were also superb democratic politicians who framed a Constitution that supported the needs of the nation and at the same time was acceptable to the people. A good example of Beard's lasting influence can be found in the second selection, in which Alfred F. Young argues that although the Constitution may have strengthened the powers of the central government, the Founding Fathers were forced to make concessions to the people in the final document. Otherwise, the delegates to the state ratifying conventions would have rejected the new Constitution.

YES

John P. Roche

The Founding Fathers:
A Reform Caucus in Action

The work of the Constitutional Convention and the motives of the Founding Fathers have been analyzed under a number of different ideological auspices. To one generation of historians, the hand of God was moving in the assembly; under a later dispensation, the dialectic (at various levels of philosophical sophistication) replaced the Deity: "relationships of production" moved into the niche previously reserved for Love of Country. . . . The Framers have undergone miraculous metamorphoses: at one time acclaimed as liberals and bold social engineers, today they appear in the guise of sound Burkean conservatives, men who in our time would subscribe to *Fortune*. . . .

The "Fathers" have thus been admitted to our best circles; the revolutionary ferocity which confiscated all Tory property in reach . . . has been converted . . . into a benign dedication to "consensus" and "prescriptive rights." . . . It is not my purpose here to argue that the "Fathers" were, in fact, radical revolutionaries; that proposition has been brilliantly demonstrated. . . . My concern is with the further position that not only were they revolutionaries, but also they were democrats. Indeed, in my view, there is one fundamental truth about the Founding Fathers . . . : They were first and foremost superb democratic politicians. . . . As recent research into the nature of American politics in the 1780s confirms, they were committed (perhaps willy-nilly) to working within the democratic framework, within a universe of public approval. . . . The Philadelphia Convention was not a College of Cardinals or a council of Platonic guardians working within a manipulative, pre-democratic framework; it was a nationalist reform caucus which had to operate with great delicacy and skill in a political cosmos full of enemies to achieve the one definitive goal— popular approbation. . . .

What they did was to hammer out a pragmatic compromise which would both bolster the "national interest" and be acceptable to the people. What inspiration they got came from their collective experience as professional politicians in a democratic society. As John Dickinson put it to his fellow delegates on August 13, "Experience must be our guide. Reason may mislead us."

In this context, let us examine the problems they confronted and the solutions they evolved. The Convention has been described picturesquely as a

From John P. Roche, "The Founding Fathers: A Reform Caucus in Action," *American Political Science Review*, vol. 55, no. 4 (December 1961). Copyright © 1961 by The American Political Science Association. Reprinted by permission of Cambridge University Press.

counter-revolutionary junta and the Constitution as a coup d'état, but this has been accomplished by withdrawing the whole history of the movement for constitutional reform from its true context. No doubt the goals of the constitutional elite were "subversive" to the existing political order, but it is overlooked that their subversion could only have succeeded if the people of the United States endorsed it by regularized procedures. . . .

I

When the Constitutionalists went forth to subvert the Confederation, they utilized the mechanisms of political legitimacy. And the roadblocks which confronted them were formidable. At the same time, they were endowed with certain potent political assets. The history of the United States from 1786 to 1790 was largely one of a masterful employment of political expertise by the Constitutionalists as against bumbling, erratic behavior by the opponents of reform. Effectively, the Constitutionalists had to induce the states, by democratic techniques of coercion, to emasculate themselves. . . . And at the risk of becoming boring, it must be reiterated that the only weapon in the Constitutionalist arsenal was an effective mobilization of public opinion.

The group which undertook this struggle was an interesting amalgam of a few dedicated nationalists with the self-interested spokesmen of various parochial bailiwicks. The Georgians, for example, wanted a strong central authority to provide military protection for their huge, underpopulated state against the Creek Confederacy; Jerseymen and Connecticuters wanted to escape from economic bondage to New York; the Virginians hoped to establish a system which would give that great state its rightful place in the councils of the republic. The dominant figures in the politics of these states therefore cooperated in the call for the Convention. In other states, the thrust towards national reform was taken up by opposition groups who added the "national interest" to their weapons system; in Pennsylvania, for instance, the group fighting to revise the Constitution of 1776 came out four-square behind the Constitutionalists, and in New York, [Alexander] Hamilton and the Schuyler [family] ambiance took the same tack against George Clinton. There was, of course, a large element of personality in the affair: there is reason to suspect that Patrick Henry's opposition to the Convention and the Constitution was founded on his conviction that Jefferson was behind both, and a close study of local politics elsewhere would surely reveal that others supported the Constitution for the simple (and politically quite sufficient) reason that the "wrong" people were against it. . . .

What distinguished the leaders of the Constitutionalist caucus from their enemies was a "Continental" approach to political, economic and military issues. To the extent that they shared an institutional base of operations, it was the Continental Congress (thirty-nine of the delegates to the Federal Convention had served in Congress), and this was hardly a locale which inspired respect for the state governments. . . . Membership in the Congress under the Articles of Confederation worked to establish a continental frame of reference, that a Congressman from Pennsylvania and one from North Carolina would share. . . . This was particularly true with respect to external affairs: the average state legislator was probably about as concerned with foreign policy than as he is today, but Congressmen were constantly forced to take the broad view of American prestige, were compelled to listen to the reports of Secretary John Jay and to the dispatches and pleas from their frustrated envoys in Britain, France and Spain. From considerations such as these, a "Continental" ideology developed which seems to have demanded a revision of our domestic institutions primarily on the ground that only by invigorating our general government could we assume our rightful place in the international arena. . . .

Note that I am not endorsing the "Critical Period" thesis; on the contrary, Merrill Jensen seems to me quite sound in his view that for most Americans, engaged as they were in self-sustaining agriculture, the "Critical Period" was not particularly critical. In fact, the great achievement of the Constitutionalists was their ultimate success in convincing the elected representatives of a majority of the white male population that change was imperative. A small group of political leaders with a Continental vision and essentially a consciousness of the United States' international impotence, provided the matrix of the movement. To their standard other leaders rallied with their own parallel ambitions. Their great assets were (1) the presence in their caucus of the one authentic American "father figure," George Washington, whose prestige was enormous; (2) the energy and talent of their leadership (in which one must include the towering intellectuals of the time, John Adams and Thomas Jefferson, despite their absence abroad), and their communications "network," which was far superior to anything on the opposition side; (3) the preemptive skill which made "their" issue The Issue and kept the locally oriented opposition permanently on the defensive; and (4) the subjective consideration that these men were spokesmen of a new and compelling credo: American nationalism, that ill-defined but nonetheless potent sense of collective purpose that emerged from the American Revolution. . . .

The Constitutionalists got the jump on the "opposition" (a collective noun: oppositions would be more correct) at the outset with the demand for a Convention. Their opponents were caught in an old political trap: they were not being asked to approve any specific program of reform, but only to endorse a meeting to discuss and recommend needed reforms. If they took a hard line at the first stage, they were put in the position of glorifying the status quo and of denying the need for any changes. Moreover, the Constitutionalists could go to the people with a persuasive argument for "fair play"—"How can you condemn reform before you know precisely what is involved?" Since the state legislatures obviously would have the final say on any proposals that might emerge from the Convention, the Constitutionalists were merely reasonable men asking for a chance. Besides, since they did not make any concrete proposals at that stage, they were in a position to capitalize on every sort of generalized discontent with the Confederation.

Perhaps because of their poor intelligence system, perhaps because of over-confidence generated by the failure of all previous efforts to alter the Articles, the opposition awoke too late to the dangers that confronted them in 1787. Not only did the Constitutionalists manage to get every state but Rhode Island . . . to appoint delegates to Philadelphia, but when the results were in, it appeared that they dominated the delegations. Given the apathy of the opposition, this was a natural phenomenon: in an ideologically nonpolarized political atmosphere those who get appointed to a special committee are likely to be the men who supported the movement for its creation. . . . Much has been made of the fact that the delegates to Philadelphia were not elected by the people; some have adduced this fact as evidence of the "undemocratic" character of the gathering. But put in the context of the time, this argument is wholly specious: the central government under the Articles was considered a creature of the component states and in all the states but Rhode Island, Connecticut and New Hampshire, members of the national Congress were chosen by the state legislatures. This was not a consequence of elitism or fear of the mob; it was a logical extension of states'-rights doctrine to guarantee that the national institution did not end-run the state legislatures and make direct contact with the people.

II

With delegations safely named, the focus shifted to Philadelphia. While waiting for a quorum to assemble, James Madison got busy and drafted the so-called Randolph or Virginia Plan with the aid of the Virginia delegation. This was a political master-stroke. Its consequence was that once business got under way, the framework of discussion was established on Madison's terms. There was no interminable argument over agenda; instead the delegates took the Virginia Resolutions—"just for purposes of discussion"—as their point of departure. And along with Madison's proposals, many of which were buried in the course of the summer, went his major premise: a new start on a Constitution rather than piecemeal amendment. . . .

Standard treatments of the Convention divide the delegates into "nationalists" and "states'-righters" with various improvised shadings ("moderate nationalists," etc.), but these are a posteriori categories which obfuscate more than they clarify. What is striking to one who analyzes the Convention as a case-study in democratic politics is the lack of clear-cut ideological divisions in the Convention. Indeed, I submit that the evidence—Madison's Notes, the correspondence of the delegates, and debates on ratification—indicates that this was a remarkably homogeneous body on the ideological level. [Robert] Yates and [John] Lansing [of New York], who favored the New Jersey Plan] . . . left in disgust on July 10. . . . Luther Martin, Maryland's bibulous narcissist, left on September 4 in a huff when he discovered that others did not share his self-esteem; others went home for personal reasons. But the hard core of delegates accepted a grinding regimen throughout the attrition of a Philadelphia summer precisely because they shared the Constitutionalist goal.

Basic differences of opinion emerged, of course, but these were not ideological; they were structural. If the so-called "states'-rights" group had not accepted the fundamental purposes of the Convention, they could simply have pulled out and by doing so have aborted the whole enterprise. Instead of bolting, they returned day after day to argue and to compromise. An interesting symbol of this basic homogeneity was the initial agreement on secrecy: these professional politicians did not want to become prisoners of publicity;

they wanted to retain that freedom of maneuver which is only possible when men are not forced to take public stands in the preliminary stages of negotiation. There was no legal means of binding the tongues of the delegates: at any stage in the game a delegate with basic principled objections to the emerging project could have taken the stump (as Luther Martin did after his exit) and denounced the convention to the skies. Yet . . . the delegates generally observed the injunction. Secrecy is certainly uncharacteristic of any assembly marked by strong ideological polarization. . . .

Commentators on the Constitution who have read *The Federalist* in lieu of reading the actual debates have credited the Fathers with the invention of a sublime concept called "Federalism." . . . Federalism, as the theory is generally defined, was an improvisation which was later promoted into a political theory. Experts on "federalism" should take to heart the advice of David Hume, who warned . . . "there is no subject in which we must proceed with more caution than in [history], lest we assign causes which never existed and reduce what is merely contingent to stable and universal principles." In any event, the final balance in the Constitution between the states and the nation must have come as a great disappointment to Madison. . . .

It is indeed astonishing how those who have glibly designated James Madison the "father" of Federalism have overlooked the solid body of fact which indicates that he shared Hamilton's quest for a unitary central government. To be specific, they have avoided examining the clear import of the Madison-Virginia Plan, and have disregarded Madison's dogged inch-by-inch retreat from the bastions of centralization. The Virginia Plan envisioned a unitary national government effectively freed from and dominant over the states. The lower house of the national legislature was to be elected directly by the people of the states with membership proportional to population. The upper house was to be selected by the lower and the two chambers would elect the executive and choose the judges. The national legislature was to be empowered to disallow the acts of state legislatures, and the central government was vested, in addition to the powers of the nation under which the Articles of Confederation, with plenary authority wherever ". . . the separate States are incompetent or in which the harmony of the United States may be interrupted by the exercise of individual legislation." Finally, just to lock the door against state intrusion, the national Congress was to be given the power to use military force on recalcitrant states. This was Madison's "model" of an ideal national government, though it later received little publicity in *The Federalist.*

The interesting thing was the reaction of the Convention to this militant program for a strong autonomous central government. Some delegates were startled, some obviously leery of so comprehensive a project of reform, but nobody set off any fireworks and nobody walked out. Moreover, in the two weeks that followed, the Virginia Plan received substantial endorsement *en principe;* the initial temper of the gathering can be deduced from the approval "without debate or dissent," on May 31, of the Sixth Resolution which granted Congress the authority to disallow state legislation ". . . contravening in its opinion the Articles of Union." Indeed, an amendment was included to bar states from contravening national treaties.

The Virginia Plan may therefore be considered, in ideological terms, as the delegates' Utopia, but as the discussions continued and became more specific, many of those present began to have second thoughts. . . . They were practical politicians in a democratic society, and no matter what their private dreams might be, they had to take home an acceptable package and defend it—and their own political futures—against predictable attack. On June 14 the breaking point between dream and reality took place. Apparently realizing that under the Virginia Plan, Massachusetts, Virginia and Pennsylvania could virtually dominate the national government—and probably appreciating that to sell this program to "the folks back home" would be impossible—the delegates from the small states dug in their heels and demanded time for a consideration of alternatives. . . .

Now the process of accommodation was put into action smoothly—and wisely, given the character and strength of the doubters. Madison had the votes, but this was one of those situations where the enforcement of mechanical majoritarianism could easily have destroyed the objectives of the majority: the Constitutionalists were in quest of a qualitative as well as a quantitative consensus; . . . it was a political imperative if they were to attain ratification.

III

According to the standard script, at this point the "states'-rights" group intervened in force behind the New Jersey Plan, which has been characteristically portrayed as a revision to the status quo under the Articles of Confederation with but minor modifications. A careful examination of the evidence indicates that only in a marginal sense is this an accurate description. It is true that the New Jersey Plan put the states back into the institutional picture, but one could argue that to do so was a recognition of political reality rather than an affirmation of states'-rights. A serious case can be made that the advocates of the New Jersey Plan, far from being ideological addicts of states'-rights, intended to substitute for the Virginia Plan a system which would both retain strong national power and have a chance of adoption in the states. The leading spokesman for the project asserted quite clearly that his views were based more on counsels of expediency than on principle. . . . In his preliminary speech on June 9, Paterson had stated ". . . to the public mind we must accommodate ourselves," and in his notes for this and his later effort as well, the emphasis is the same. The structure of government under the Articles should be retained:

> 2. Because it accords with the Sentiments of the People
>
>> [Proof:] 1. Coms. [Commissions from state legislatures defining the jurisdiction of the delegates]
>> 2. News-papers—Political Barometer. Jersey never would have sent Delegates under the first [Virginia] Plan—
>
> Not here to sport Opinions of my own. Wt. [What] can be done. A little practicable Virtue preferrable to Theory.

This was a defense of political acumen, not of states'-rights. . . .

In other words, the advocates of the New Jersey Plan concentrated their fire on what they held to be the political liabilities of the Virginia Plan—which were matters of institutional structure—rather than on the proposed scope of national authority. Indeed, the Supremacy Clause of the Constitution first saw the light of day in Paterson's Sixth Resolution; the New Jersey Plan contemplated the use of military force to secure compliance with national law; and finally Paterson made clear his view that under either the Virginia or the New Jersey systems, the general government would ". . . act on individuals and not on states." From the states'-rights viewpoint, this was heresy: the fundament of that doctrine was the proposition that any central government had as its constituents the states, not the people, and could only reach the people through the agency of the state government.

Paterson then reopened the agenda of the Convention, but he did so within a distinctly naturalist framework. Paterson's position was one of favoring a strong central government in principle, but opposing one which in fact put the big states in the saddle.

How attached would the Virginians have been to their reform principles if Virginia were to disappear as a component geographical unit (the largest) for representational purposes? Up to this point, the Virginians had been in the happy position of supporting high ideals with that inner confidence born of knowledge that the "public interest" they endorsed would nourish their private interest. Worse, they had shown little willingness to compromise. Now the delegates from the small states announced that they were unprepared to be offered up as sacrificial victims to a "national interest" which reflected Virginia's parochial ambition. Caustic Charles Pinckney was not far off when he remarked sardonically that ". . . the whole [conflict] comes to this: Give N. Jersey an equal vote, and she will dismiss her scruples, and concur in the Natil. system." What he rather unfairly did not add was that the Jersey delegates were not free agents who could adhere to their private convictions; they had to take back, sponsor and risk their reputations on the reforms approved by the Convention—and in New Jersey, not in Virginia. . . .

IV

On Tuesday morning, June 19, . . . James Madison led off with a long, carefully reasoned speech analyzing the New Jersey Plan which, while intellectually vigorous in its criticisms, was quite conciliatory in mood. "The great difficulty," he observed, "lies in the affair of Representation; and if this could be adjusted, all others would be surmountable." (As events were to demonstrate, this diagnosis was correct.) When he finished, a vote was taken on whether to continue with the Virginia Plan as the nucleus for a new constitution: seven states voted "Yes"; New York, New Jersey, and Delaware voted "No"; and Maryland, whose position often depended on which delegates happened to be on the floor, divided. Paterson, it seems, lost decisively; yet in a fundamental sense he and his allies had achieved their purpose: from that day onward, it could never be forgotten that the state governments loomed ominously in the background. . . . Moreover, nobody bolted the convention: Paterson and his colleagues took their defeat in stride and set to work to modify the Virginia Plan, particularly with respect to its provisions on representation in the national legislature. Indeed, they won an immediate rhetorical bonus; when Oliver Ellsworth of Connecticut rose to move that the word "national" be expunged from the Third Virginia Resolution ("Resolved that a national Government ought to be established consisting of a supreme Legislative, Executive and Judiciary"), Randolph agreed and the motion passed unanimously. The process of compromise had begun.

For the next two weeks, the delegates circled around the problem of legislative representation. The Connecticut delegation appears to have evolved a possible compromise quite early in the debates, but the Virginians and particularly Madison (unaware that he would later be acclaimed as the prophet of "federalism") fought obdurately against providing for equal representation of states in the second chamber. . . . On July 2, the ice began to break when through a number of fortuitous events—and one that seems deliberate—the majority against equality of representation was converted into a dead tie. The Convention had reached the stage where it was "ripe" for a solution (presumably all the therapeutic speeches had been made), and the South Carolinians proposed a committee. Madison and James Wilson wanted none of it, but with only Pennsylvania dissenting, the body voted to establish a working party on the problem of representation.

The members of this committee, one from each state, were elected by the delegates—and a very interesting committee it was. Despite the fact that the Virginia Plan had held majority support up to that date, neither Madison nor Randolph was selected (Mason was the Virginian) and Baldwin of Georgia, whose shift in position had resulted in the tie, was chosen. From the composition, it was clear that this was not to be a "fighting" committee: the emphasis in membership was on what might be described as "second-level political entrepreneurs." On the basis of the discussions up to that time, only Luther Martin of Maryland could be described as a "bitter-ender." Admittedly, some divination enters into this sort of analysis, but one does get a sense of the mood of the delegates from these choices—including the interesting selection of Benjamin Franklin, despite his age and intellectual wobbliness, over the brilliant and incisive Wilson or the sharp, polemical Gouverneur Morris, to represent Pennsylvania. His passion for conciliation was more valuable at this juncture than Wilson's logical genius, or Morris' acerbic wit. . . .

It would be tedious to continue a blow-by-blow analysis of the work of the delegates; the critical fight was over representation of the states and once the Connecticut Compromise was adopted on July 17, the Convention was over the hump. Madison, James Wilson, and Gouverneur Morris of New York (who was there representing Pennsylvania!) fought the compromise all the way in a last-ditch effort to get a unitary state with parliamentary supremacy. But their allies deserted them. . . . Moreover, once the compromise had carried (by five states to four, with one state divided), its advocates threw themselves vigorously into the job of strengthening the general government's substantive powers—as might have been predicted, indeed, from Paterson's early statements. It nourishes an increased respect for Madison's devotion to the art of politics, to realize that this dogged fighter could sit down six months later and prepare essays for *The Federalist* in contradiction to his basic convictions about the true course the Convention should have taken.

V

Two tricky issues will serve to illustrate the later process of accommodation. The first was the institutional position of the Executive. Madison argued for an executive chosen by the National Legislature and on May 29 this had been adopted with a provision that after his seven-year term was concluded, the chief magistrate should not be eligible for reelection. In late July this was reopened and for a week the matter was argued from several different points of view. . . . One group felt that the states should have a hand in the process; another small but influential circle urged direct election by the people. There were a number of proposals: election by the people, election by state governors, by electors chosen by state legislatures, by the National legislature, . . . and there was some resemblance to three-dimensional chess in the dispute because of the presence of two other variables, length of tenure and reeligibility. Finally, after opening, reopening, and re-reopening the debate, the thorny problem was consigned to a committee for resolution.

The Brearley Committee on Postponed Matters was a superb aggregation of talent and its compromise on the Executive was a masterpiece of political improvisation. (The Electoral College, its creation, however, had little in its favor as an institution—as the delegates well appreciated.) The point of departure for all discussion about the presidency in the Convention was that in immediate terms, the problem was non-existent; in other words, everybody present knew that under any system devised, George Washington would be President. Thus they were dealing in the future tense and to a body of working politicians the merits of the Brearley proposal were obvious: everybody got a piece of cake. (Or to put it more academically, each viewpoint could leave the Convention and argue to its constituents that it had really won the day.) First, the state legislatures had the right to determine the mode of selection of the electors; second, the small states received a bonus in the Electoral College in the form of a guaranteed minimum of three votes while the big states got acceptance of the principle of proportional power; third, if the state legislatures agreed (as six did in the first presidential election), the people could be involved directly in the choice of electors; and finally, if no candidate received a majority in the College, the right of decision passed to the National Legislature with each state exercising equal strength. (In the Brearley recommendation, the election went to the Senate, but a motion from the floor substituted the House; this was accepted on the ground that the Senate already had enough authority over the executive in its treaty and appointment powers.)

This compromise was almost too good to be true, and the Framers snapped it up with little debate or controversy. No one seemed to think well of the College as an institution; indeed, what evidence there is suggests that there was an assumption that once Washington had finished his tenure as President, the electors would cease to produce majorities and the chief executive would usually be chosen in the House. George Mason observed casually that the selection would be made in the House nineteen times in twenty and no one seriously disputed this point. The vital aspect of the Electoral College was that it got the Convention over the hurdle and protected everybody's interests. . . .

In short, the Framers did not in their wisdom endow the United States with a College of Cardinals—the Electoral College was neither an exercise in applied Platonism nor an experiment in indirect government based on elitist distrust of the masses. It was merely a jerry-rigged improvisation which has subsequently been endowed with a high theoretical content. . . .

The second issue on which some substantial practical bargaining took place was slavery. The morality of slavery was, by design, not at issue; but in its other concrete aspects, slavery colored the arguments over taxation, commerce, and representation. The "Three-Fifths Compromise," that three-fifths of the slaves would be counted both for representation and for purposes of direct taxation (which was drawn from the past—it was a formula of Madison's utilized by Congress in 1783 to establish the basis of state contributions to the Confederation treasury) had allayed some Northern fears about Southern over-representation. . . . The Southerners, on the other hand, were afraid that Congressional control over commerce would lead to the exclusion of slaves or to their excessive taxation as imports. Moreover, the Southerners were disturbed over "navigation acts," i.e., tariffs or special legislation providing, for example, that exports be carried only in American ships; as a section depending upon exports, they wanted protection from the potential voracity of their commercial brethren of the Eastern states. To achieve this end, Mason and others urged that the Constitution include a proviso that navigation and commercial laws should require a two-thirds vote in Congress.

These problems came to a head in late August and, as usual were handed to a committee in the hope that, in Gouverneur Morris' words, ". . . these things may form a bargain among the Northern and Southern states." The Committee reported its measures of reconciliation on August 25, and on August 29 the package was wrapped up and delivered. What occurred can best be described in George Mason's dour version (he anticipated Calhoun in his conviction that permitting navigation acts to pass by majority vote would put the South in economic bondage to the North—it was mainly on this ground that he refused to sign the Constitution):

> The Constitution as agreed to till a fortnight before the Convention rose was such a one as he would have set his hand and heart to. . . . [Until that time] The 3 New England States were constantly with us in all questions . . . so that it was these three States with the 5 Southern ones against Pennsylvania, Jersey and Delaware. With respect to the importation of slaves, [decision-making] was left to Congress. This disturbed the two Southernmost States who knew that Congress would immediately suppress the importation of slaves. Those two States therefore struck up a bargain with the three New England States. If they would join to admit slaves for some years, the two Southern-most States would join in changing the clause which required the 2/3 of the Legislature in any vote [on navigation acts]. It was done.

On the floor of the Convention there was a virtual love-feast on this happy occasion. Charles Pinckney of South Carolina attempted to overturn the committee's decision, when the compromise was reported to the Convention, by insisting that the South needed protection from the imperialism of the Northern states. But his Southern colleagues were not prepared to rock the boat and General C. C. Pinckney arose to spread oil on the suddenly ruffled waters; he admitted that:

> It was in the true interest of the S[outhern] States to have no regulation of commerce; but considering the loss brought on the commerce of the Eastern States by the Revolution, their liberal conduct towards the views of South Carolina [on the regulation of the slave trade] and the interests the weak Southn. States had in being united with the strong Eastern states, he thought it proper that no fetters should be imposed on the power of making commercial regulations; and that his constituents, though prejudiced against the Eastern States, would be reconciled to this liberality. He had himself prejudices against the Eastern States before he came here, but would acknowledge that he had found them as liberal and candid as any men whatever.

Pierce Butler took the same tack, essentially arguing that he was not too happy about the possible consequences, but that a deal was a deal. . . .

VI

Drawing on their vast collective political experience, utilizing every weapon in the politician's arsenal, looking constantly over their shoulders at their constituents, the delegates put together a Constitution. It was a makeshift affair; some sticky issues (for example, the qualification of voters) they ducked entirely; others they mastered with that ancient instrument of political sagacity, studied ambiguity (for example, citizenship), and some they just overlooked. In this last category, I suspect, fell the matter of the power of the federal courts to determine the constitutionality of acts of Congress. When the judicial article was formulated (Article III of the Constitution), deliberations were still in the stage where the legislature was endowed with broad power under the Randolph formulation, authority which by its own terms was scarcely amenable to judicial review. In essence, courts could hardly determine when ". . . the separate States are incompetent or . . . the harmony of the United States may be interrupted"; the National Legislature, as critics pointed out, was free to define its own jurisdiction. Later the definition of legislative authority was changed into the form we know, a series of stipulated powers, but the delegates never seriously reexamined the jurisdiction of the judiciary under this new limited formulation. All arguments on the intention of the Framers in this matter are thus deductive and a posteriori, though some obviously make more sense than others.

The Framers were busy and distinguished men, anxious to get back to their families, their positions, and their constituents. . . . They were trying to do an important job, and do it in such a fashion that their handiwork would be acceptable to very diverse constituencies. No one was rhapsodic about the final document, but it was a beginning, a move in the right direction, and one they had reason to believe the people would endorse. In addition, since they had modified the impossible amendment provisions of the Articles . . . to one demanding approval by only three-quarters of the states, they seemed confident that gaps in the fabric which experience would reveal could be rewoven without undue difficulty.

So with a neat phrase introduced by Benjamin Franklin (but devised by Gouverneur Morris) which made their decision sound unanimous, and an inspired benediction by the Old Doctor urging doubters to doubt their own infallibility, the Constitution was accepted and signed. Curiously, Edmund Randolph, who had played so vital a role throughout, refused to sign, as did his fellow Virginian George Mason and Elbridge Gerry of Massachusetts. Randolph's behavior was eccentric; . . . the best explanation seems to be that he was afraid that the Constitution would prove to be a liability in Virginia politics, where Patrick Henry was burning up the countryside with impassioned denunciations. Presumably, Randolph wanted to check the temper of the populace before he risked his reputation, and perhaps his job, in a fight with both Henry and Richard Henry Lee. Events lend some justification to this speculation: after much temporizing . . . Randolph endorsed ratification in Virginia and ended up getting the best of both worlds. . . .

The Constitution, then, was an apotheosis of "constitutionalism," a triumph of architectonic genius; it was a patchwork sewn together under the pressure of both time and events by a group of extremely talented democratic politicians. They refused to attempt the establishment of a strong, centralized sovereignty on the principle of legislative supremacy for the excellent reason that the people would not accept it. They risked their political fortunes by opposing the established doctrines of state sovereignty because they were convinced that the existing system was leading to national impotence and probably foreign domination. For two years, they worked to get a convention established. For over three months, in what must have seemed to the faithful participants an endless process of give-and-take, they reasoned, cajoled, threatened, and bargained amongst themselves. The result was a Constitution which the people, in fact, by democratic processes, did accept, and a new and far better national government was established. . . .

To conclude, the Constitution was neither a victory for abstract theory nor a great practical success. Well over half a million men had to die on the battlefields of the Civil War before certain constitutional principles could be defined—a baleful consideration which is somehow overlooked in our customary tributes to the farsighted genius of the Framers and to the supposed American talent for "constitutionalism." The Constitution was, however, a vivid demonstration of effective democratic political action, and of the forging of a national elite which literally persuaded its countrymen to hoist themselves by their own boot straps.

Alfred F. Young

The Framers of the Constitution and the "Genius" of the People

On June 18, 1787, about three weeks into the Constitutional Convention at Philadelphia, Alexander Hamilton delivered a six-hour address that was easily the longest and most conservative the Convention would hear. Gouverneur Morris, a delegate from Pennsylvania, thought it was "the most able and impressive he had ever heard."

Beginning with the premise that "all communities divide themselves into the few and the many," "the wealthy well born" and "the people," Hamilton added the corollary that the "people are turbulent and changing; they seldom judge or determine right." Moving through history, the delegate from New York developed his ideal for a national government that would protect the few from "the imprudence of democracy" and guarantee "stability and permanence": a president and senate indirectly elected for life ("to serve during good behavior") to balance a house directly elected by a popular vote every three years. This "elective monarch" would have an absolute veto over laws passed by Congress. And the national government would appoint the governors of the states, who in turn would have the power to veto any laws by the state legislatures.

If others quickly saw a resemblance in all of this to the King, House of Lords and House of Commons of Great Britain, with the states reduced to colonies ruled by royal governors, they were not mistaken. The British constitution, in Hamilton's view, remained "the best model the world has ever produced."

Three days later a delegate reported that Hamilton's proposals "had been praised by everybody," but "he has been supported by none." Acknowledging that his plan "went beyond the ideas of most members," Hamilton said he had brought it forward not "as a thing attainable by us, but as a model which we ought to approach as near as possible." When he signed the Constitution the framers finally agreed to on September 17, 1787, Hamilton could accurately say, "no plan was more remote from his own."

Why did the framers reject a plan so many admired? To ask this question is to go down a dark path into the heart of the Constitution few of its celebrants care to take. We have heard so much in our elementary and high school civics books about the "great compromises" within the Convention—between the large states and the small states, between the slaveholders and nonslaveholders, between North and South—that we have missed the much larger accommodation

From Alfred F. Young, "The Framers of the Constitution and the 'Genius' of the People," *Radical History Review*, vol. 42 (1988). Copyright © 1988 by MARHO: The Radical Historians Organization, Inc. Reprinted by permission of Duke University Press.

that was taking place between the delegates as a whole at the Convention and what they called "the people out of doors."

The Convention was unmistakably an elite body. [In 1987] the official exhibit for the bicentennial, "Miracle at Philadelphia," [opened] appropriately enough with a large oil portrait of Robert Morris, a delegate from Philadelphia, one of the richest merchants in America, and points out elsewhere that 11 out of 55 delegates were business associates of Morris'. The 55 were weighted with merchants, slaveholding planters and "monied men" who loaned money at interest. Among them were numerous lawyers and college graduates in a country where most men and only a few women had the rudiments of a formal education. They were far from a cross section of the four million or so Americans of that day, most of whom were farmers or artisans, fishermen or seamen, indentured servants or laborers, half of whom were women and about 600,000 of whom were African-American slaves.

The First Accommodation

Why did this elite reject Hamilton's plan that many of them praised? James Madison, the Constitution's chief architect, had the nub of the matter. The Constitution was "intended for the ages." To last it had to conform to the "genius" of the American people. "Genius" was a word eighteenth-century political thinkers used to mean spirit: we might say character or underlying values.

James Wilson, second only to Madison in his influence at Philadelphia, elaborated on the idea. "The British government cannot be our model. We have no materials for a similar one. Our manners, our law, the abolition of entail and primogeniture," which made for a more equal distribution of property among sons, "the whole genius of the people, are opposed to it."

This was long-range political philosophy. There was a short-range political problem that moved other realistic delegates in the same direction. Called together to revise the old Articles of Confederation, the delegates instead decided to scrap it and frame an entirely new constitution. It would have to be submitted to the people for ratification, most likely to conventions elected especially for the purpose. Repeatedly, conservatives recoiled from extreme proposals for which they knew they could not win popular support.

In response to a proposal to extend the federal judiciary into the states, Pierce Butler, a South Carolina planter, argued, "the people will not bear such innovations. The states will revolt at such encroachments." His assumption was "we must follow the example of Solomon, who gave the Athenians not the best government he could devise but the best they would receive."

The suffrage debate epitomized this line of thinking. Gouverneur Morris, Hamilton's admirer, proposed that the national government limit voting for the House to men who owned a freehold, i.e. a substantial farm, or its equivalent. "Give the vote to people who have no property and they will sell them to the rich who will be able to buy them," he said with some prescience. George Mason, author of Virginia's Bill of Rights, was aghast. "Eight or nine states have extended the right of suffrage beyond the freeholders. What will people there say if they should be disfranchised?"

Benjamin Franklin, the patriarch, speaking for one of the few times in the convention, paid tribute to "the lower class of freemen" who should not be disfranchised. James Wilson explained, "it would be very hard and disagreeable for the same person" who could vote for representatives for the state legislatures "to be excluded from a vote for this in the national legislature." Nathaniel Gorham, a Boston merchant, returned to the guiding principle: "the people will never allow" existing rights to suffrage to be abridged. "We must consult their rooted prejudices if we expect their concurrence in our propositions."

The result? Morris' proposal was defeated and the convention decided that whoever each state allowed to vote for its own assembly could vote for the House. It was a compromise that left the door open and in a matter of decades allowed states to introduce universal white male suffrage.

Ghosts of Years Past

Clearly there was a process of accommodation at work here. The popular movements of the Revolutionary Era were a presence at the Philadelphia Convention even if they were not present. The delegates, one might say, were haunted by ghosts, symbols of the broadly based movements elites had confronted in the making of the Revolution from 1765 to 1775, in waging the war from 1775 to 1781 and in the years since 1781 within their own states.

The first was the ghost of Thomas Paine, the most influential radical democrat of the Revolutionary Era. In 1776 Paine's pamphlet *Common Sense* (which sold at least 150,000 copies), in arguing for independence, rejected not only King George III but the principle of monarchy and the so-called checks and balances of the unwritten English constitution. In its place he offered a vision of a democratic government in which a single legislature would be supreme, the executive minimal, and representatives would be elected from small districts by a broad electorate for short terms so they could "return and mix again with the voters." John Adams considered *Common Sense* too "democratical," without even an attempt at "mixed government" that would balance "democracy" with "aristocracy."

The second ghost was that of Abraham Yates, a member of the state senate of New York typical of the new men who had risen to power in the 1780s in the state legislatures. We have forgotten him; Hamilton, who was very conscious of him, called him "an old Booby." He had begun as a shoemaker and was a self-taught lawyer and warm foe of the landlord aristocracy of the Hudson Valley which Hamilton had married into. As James Madison identified the "vices of the political system of the United States" in a memorandum in 1787, the Abraham Yateses were the number-one problem. The state legislatures had "an itch for paper money" laws, laws that prevented foreclosure on farm mortgages, and tax laws that soaked the rich. As Madison saw it, this meant that "debtors defrauded their creditors" and "the landed interest has borne hard on the mercantile interest." This, too, is what Hamilton had in mind when he spoke of the "depredations which the democratic spirit is apt to make on property" and what others meant by the "excess of democracy" in the states.

The third ghost was a very fresh one—Daniel Shays. In 1786 Shays, a captain in the Revolution, led a rebellion of debtor farmers in western Massachusetts which the state quelled with its own somewhat unreliable militia. There were "combustibles in every state," as George Washington put it, raising the specter of "Shaysism." This Madison enumerated among the "vices" of the system as "a want of guaranty to the states against internal violence." Worse still, Shaysites in many states were turning to the political system to elect their own kind. If they succeeded they would produce legal Shaysism, a danger for which the elites had no remedy.

The fourth ghost we can name was the ghost of Thomas Peters, although he had a thousand other names. In 1775, Peters, a Virginia slave, responded to a plea by the British to fight in their army and win their freedom. He served in an "Ethiopian Regiment," some of whose members bore the emblem "Liberty to Slaves" on their uniforms. After the war the British transported Peters and several thousand escaped slaves to Nova Scotia from whence Peters eventually led a group to return to Africa and the colony of Sierra Leone, a long odyssey to freedom. Eighteenth-century slaveholders, with no illusions about happy or contented slaves, were haunted by the specter of slaves in arms.

Elite Divisions

During the Revolutionary Era elites divided in response to these varied threats from below. One group, out of fear of "the mob" and then "the rabble in arms," embraced the British and became active Loyalists. After the war most of them went into exile. Another group who became patriots never lost their obsession with coercing popular movements. . . .

Far more important, however, were those patriot leaders who adopted a strategy of "swimming with a stream which it is impossible to stem." This was the metaphor of Robert R. Livingston, Jr., . . . a gentleman with a large tenanted estate in New York. Men of his class had to learn to "yield to the torrent if they hoped to direct its course."

Livingston and his group were able to shape New York's constitution, which some called a perfect blend of "aristocracy" and "democracy." John Hancock, the richest merchant in New England, had mastered this kind of politics and emerged as the most popular politician in Massachusetts. In Maryland Charles Carroll, a wealthy planter, instructed his anxious father about the need to "submit to partial losses" because "no great revolution can happen in a state without revolutions or mutations of private property. If we can save a third of our personal estate and all of our lands and Negroes, I shall think ourselves well off."

The major leaders at the Constitutional Convention in 1787 were heirs to both traditions: coercion and accommodation—Hamilton and Gouverneur Morris to the former, James Madison and James Wilson much more to the latter.

They all agreed on coercion to slay the ghosts of Daniel Shays and Thomas Peters. The Constitution gave the national government the power to "suppress insurrections" and protect the states from "domestic violence." There would be a national army under the command of the president, and authority to nationalize the state militias and suspend the right of habeas corpus in "cases of rebellion or invasion." In 1794 Hamilton, as secretary of the treasury, would exercise such powers fully (and needlessly) to suppress the Whiskey Rebellion in western Pennsylvania.

Southern slaveholders correctly interpreted the same powers as available to shackle the ghost of Thomas Peters. As it turned out, Virginia would not need a federal army to deal with Gabriel Prosser's insurrection in 1800 or Nat Turner's rebellion in 1830, but a federal army would capture John Brown after his raid at Harpers Ferry in 1859.

But how to deal with the ghosts of Thomas Paine and Abraham Yates? Here Madison and Wilson blended coercion with accommodation. They had three solutions to the threat of democratic majorities in the states.

Their first was clearly coercive. Like Hamilton, Madison wanted some kind of national veto over the state legislatures. He got several very specific curbs on the states written into fundamental law: no state could "emit" paper money or pass "laws impairing the obligation of contracts." Wilson was so overjoyed with these two clauses that he argued that if they alone "were inserted in the Constitution I think they would be worth our adoption."

But Madison considered the overall mechanism adopted to curb the states "short of the mark." The Constitution, laws and treaties were the "supreme law of the land" and ultimately a federal court could declare state laws unconstitutional. But this, Madison lamented, would only catch "mischiefs" after the fact. Thus they had clipped the wings of Abraham Yates but he could still fly.

The second solution to the problem of the states was decidedly democratic. They wanted to do an end-run around the state legislatures. The Articles of Confederation, said Madison, rested on "the pillars" of the state legislatures who elected delegates to Congress. The "great fabric to be raised would be more stable and durable if it should rest on the solid grounds of the people themselves"; hence, there would be popular elections to the House.

Wilson altered only the metaphor. He was for "raising the federal pyramid to a considerable altitude and for that reason wanted to give it as broad a base as possible." They would slay the ghost of Abraham Yates with the ghost of Thomas Paine.

This was risky business. They would reduce the risk by keeping the House of Representatives small. Under a ratio of one representative for every 30,000 people, the first house would have only 65 members; in 1776 Thomas Paine had suggested 390. But still, the House would be elected every two years, and with each state allowed to determine its own qualifications for voting, there was no telling who might end up in Congress.

There was also a risk in Madison's third solution to the problem of protecting propertied interests from democratic majorities: "extending the sphere" of government. Prevailing wisdom held that a republic could only succeed in a small geographic area; to rule an "extensive" country, some kind of despotism was considered inevitable.

Madison turned this idea on its head in his since famous *Federalist* essay No. 10. In a small republic, he argued, it was relatively easy for a majority to gang up on a particular "interest." "Extend the sphere," he wrote, and "you take in a greater variety of parties and interests." Then it would be more difficult for a majority "to discover their own strength and to act in unison with each other."

This was a prescription for a non-colonial empire that would expand across the continent, taking in new states as it dispossessed the Indians. The risk was there was no telling how far the "democratic" or "leveling" spirit might go in such likely would-be states as frontier Vermont, Kentucky and Tennessee.

Democratic Divisions

In the spectrum of state constitutions adopted in the Revolutionary era, the federal Constitution of 1787 was, like New York's, somewhere between "aristocracy" and "democracy." It therefore should not surprise us—although it has eluded many modern critics of the Constitution—that in the contest over ratification in 1787–1788, the democratic minded were divided.

Among agrarian democrats there was a gut feeling that the Constitution was the work of an old class enemy. "These lawyers and men of learning and monied men," argued Amos Singletary, a working farmer at the Massachusetts ratifying convention, "expect to be managers of this Constitution and get all the power and all the money into their own hands and then will swallow up all of us little folks . . . just as the whale swallowed up Jonah."

Democratic leaders like Melancton Smith of New York focused on the small size of the proposed House. Arguing from Paine's premise that the members of the legislature should "resemble those they represent," Smith feared that "a substantial yeoman of sense and discernment will hardly ever be chosen" and the government "will fall into the hands of the few and the great." Urban democrats, on the other hand, including a majority of the mechanics and tradesmen of the major cities who in the Revolution had been a bulwark of Paineite radicalism, were generally enthusiastic about the Constitution. They were impelled by their urgent stake in a stronger national government that would advance ocean-going commerce and protect American manufacturers from competition. But they would not have been as ardent about the new frame of government without its saving graces. It clearly preserved their rights to suffrage. And the process of ratification, like the Constitution itself, guaranteed them a voice. As early as 1776 the New York Committee of Mechanics held it as "a right which God has given them in common with all men to judge whether it be consistent with their interest to accept or reject a constitution."

Mechanics turned out en masse in the parades celebrating ratification, marching trade by trade. The slogans and symbols they carried expressed their political ideals. In New York the upholsterers had a float with an elegant "Federal Chair of State" flanked by the symbols of Liberty and Justice that they identified with the Constitution. In Philadelphia the bricklayers put on their banner "Both buildings and rulers are the work of our hands."

Democrats who were skeptical found it easier to come over because of the Constitution's redeeming features. Thomas Paine, off in Paris, considered the Constitution "a copy, though not quite as base as the original, of the form of the British government." He had always opposed a single executive and he objected to the "long duration of the Senate." But he was so convinced of "the absolute necessity" of a stronger federal government that "I would have voted for it myself had I been in America or even for a worse, rather than have none." It was crucial to Paine that there was an amending process, the means of "remedying its defects by the same appeal to the people by which it was to be established."

The Second Accommodation

In drafting the Constitution in 1787 the framers, self-styled Federalists, made their first accommodation with the "genius" of the people. In campaigning for its ratification in 1788 they made their second. At the outset, the conventions in the key states—Massachusetts, New York and Virginia—either had an anti-Federalist majority or were closely divided. To swing over a small group of "antis" in each state, Federalists had to promise that they would consider amendments. This was enough to secure ratification by narrow margins in Massachusetts, 187 to 168; in New York, 30 to 27; and in Virginia, 89 to 79.

What the anti-Federalists wanted were dozens of changes in the structure of the government that would cut back national power over the states, curb the powers of the presidency as well as protect individual liberties. What they got was far less. But in the first Congress in 1789, James Madison, true to his pledge, considered all the amendments and shepherded 12 amendments through both houses. The first two of these failed in the states; one would have enlarged the House. The 10 that were ratified by December 1791 were what we have since called the Bill of Rights, protecting freedom of expression and the rights of the accused before the law. Abraham Yates considered them "trivial and unimportant." But other democrats looked on them much more favorably. In time the limited meaning of freedom of speech in the First Amendment was broadened far beyond the framers' original intent. Later popular movements thought of the Bill of Rights as an essential part of the "constitutional" and "republican" rights that belonged to the people.

The "Loser's" Role

There is a cautionary tale here that surely goes beyond the process of framing and adopting the Constitution and Bill of Rights from 1787 to 1791. The Constitution was as democratic as it was because of the influence of popular movements that were a presence, even if not present. The losers helped shape the results. We owe the Bill of Rights to the opponents of the Constitution, as we do many other features in the Constitution put in to anticipate opposition.

In American history popular movements often shaped elites, especially in times of crisis when elites were concerned with the "system." Elites have often divided in response to such threats and according to their perception of the "genius" of the people. Some have turned to coercion, others to accommodation. We run serious risk if we ignore this distinction. Would that we had fewer Gouverneur Morrises and Alexander Hamiltons and more James Madisons and James Wilsons to respond to the "genius" of the people.

POSTSCRIPT

Were the Founding Fathers Democratic Reformers?

Roche stresses the political reasons for writing a new Constitution. In a spirited essay that reflects great admiration for the Founding Fathers as enlightened politicians, Roche describes the Constitution as "a triumph of architectonic genius; it was a patch-work sewn together under the pressure of both time and events by a group of extremely talented democratic politicians."

Roche narrates the events of the convention of 1787 with a clarity rarely seen in the writings on this period. He makes the telling point that once the dissenters left Philadelphia, the delegates were able to hammer out a new Constitution. All the Founding Fathers agreed to create a stronger national government, but differences centered around the shape the new government would take. The delegates' major concern was to create as strong a national government as possible that would be acceptable to all states. Had the ratifying conventions rejected the new Constitution, the United States might have disintegrated into 13 separate countries.

Young asserts that the Constitution was written by an elite group of people to strengthen the powers of the national government against those of the people. He believes that four ghosts that made their presence felt at the Philadelphia Convention caused the Founding Fathers to react in a paradoxical manner. On the one hand, the shadows of the radical Democrat Thomas Paine and arch Anti-Federalist Abraham Yates of the New York State senate forced the Founding Fathers to support universal white male suffrage, a House of Representatives directly elected by the people every two years, and a bill of rights to protect the individual liberties of people from a tyrannical government. On the other hand, the national government was able to quell the ghosts of Daniel Shays and ex-slave Thomas Peters with its power to "suppress insurrections" and protect the states from "domestic violence."

Historian Gordon S. Wood tries to recapture the eighteenth-century world in *The Creation of the American Republic, 1776–1787* (University of North Carolina Press, 1969), a seminal work that has replaced Beard as the starting point for scholarship on this topic. A devastating critique of the methodolo gical fallacies of Wood and other intellectual writers on this period can be found in Ralph Lerner's "The Constitution of the Thinking Revolutionary," in Richard Beeman et al., eds., *Beyond Confederation: Origins of the Constitution and American National Identity* (University of North Carolina Press, 1987). Also see Richard B. Morris, *The Forging of the Union, 1781–1789* (Harper & Row, 1987) and Michael Kammen, *A Machine That Would Go of Itself: The Constitution in American Culture* (Alfred A. Knopf, 1986).

ISSUE 8

Was President Thomas Jefferson a Political Compromiser?

YES: Morton Borden, from "Thomas Jefferson," in Morton Borden, ed., *America's Eleven Greatest Presidents,* 2nd ed. (Rand McNally, 1971)

NO: Forrest McDonald, from *The Presidency of Thomas Jefferson* (The University Press of Kansas, 1976)

ISSUE SUMMARY

YES: Professor Morton Borden argues that President Thomas Jefferson was a moderate and pragmatic politician who placed the nation's best interests above those of the states.

NO: History professor Forrest McDonald believes that President Jefferson attempted to replace Hamiltonian Federalist Principles with a Republican ideology in order to restore America's agrarian heritage.

J efferson still lives, stated John Adams on July 4, 1826, the 50th anniversary of Independence Day. Unknown to Adams, Jefferson had indeed passed away a few hours earlier the same day. But Jefferson never really died. He was one of the few heroes of history to become a living legend. According to recent biography Joseph J. Ellis, Jefferson is the *American Sphinx* (Random House, 1997).

There are many Jeffersons. One was the true Renaissance man who knew a little about everything. "Not a sprig of grass shoots uninteresting to me," he once wrote to his daughter. As a philosopher who spoke to posterity, he waxed eloquent in his letters about civil liberties, the rights of man, states' rights, strict construction of the Constitution, and the virtues of the agrarian way of life. A practical man, he was an architect of the nation's capital, the University of Virginia, and his own home. Visitors to his Monticello plantation are amazed by the elaborate pulley and drainage systems that he devised. A respected member of the Virginia aristocracy who owned about 10,000 acres and from 100 to 200 slaves, Jefferson ran his farm in a self-sufficient manner and carefully studied the efficiency of employing slave labor. When he traveled, he recorded everything he observed in detailed journals. The newest inventions— steam engines, thermometers, elevators—fascinated him.

Another Jefferson was the man who has been ranked among the top half-dozen U.S. presidents in every major poll taken by historians in the last 35 years. Does Jefferson deserve such an honor? It depends on how the functions of the presidency are perceived. One role that Jefferson disdained more than any other president in our history was the function of chief of state. So important to the modern presidency, the ceremonial role could have been played by the tall, dignified Virginia aristocrat as well as it was by George Washington, had he so desired. But Jefferson hated formalities. He walked to his inauguration and refused to wear a hat. Because he was a widower, he abandoned the practice of holding large, formal parties. He also felt they smacked too much of monarchy. He preferred small, intimate dinners with his intellectual friends and political cronies. A shy, soft-spoken individual with a slight speech impediment, the author of the Declaration of Independence did not campaign for office. He also refused to deliver an annual address to Congress, preferring to send them a written message. In short, if one uses modern terminology, Jefferson was not "mediagenic." In 2004, Jefferson might not have even been nominated by his party, much less elected to the presidency. Considering the vitriolic fights over Hamilton's economic policies, Washington's foreign policy of neutrality as well as the fiasco in the 1800 election that resulted in an electoral college tie, Jefferson's presidency was remarkable for the smooth transition in which the opposition party took power. As Professor Richard Hofstadter points out in *The Idea of a Party System: The Rise of Legitimate Opposition in the United States, 1780–1840* (University of California Press, 1969), Jefferson's pragmatic "disposition dictated an initial strategy of conciliation toward the Federalist which led to a basic acceptance of the Hamiltonian fiscal system, including even the bank, to a patronage policy which Jefferson considered to be fair and compromising and hoped would appease moderate Federalists, and to an early attempt to pursue neutrality and to eschew aggravating signs of that Francophia and Anglophobia with which the Federalists so obsessively and hyperbolically charged him." His first term was more successful than his second. He waged a winning war against the Barbary pirates in the Mediterranean and took advantage of Napoleon's offer to purchase the Louisiana territory, thereby nearly doubling the size of the United States. His second term, however, was consumed with a failed embargo.

In the first of the following selections, Professor Morton Borden substantiates the views of moderate Federalists who believed that Jefferson was a practical politician and, above all, a nationalist who incorporated Federalist policies with traditional Republican views in running his presidency. Forrest McDonald, in the second selection, sees Jefferson as a backward-looking agrarian ideologue staunchly opposed to Alexander Hamilton's Federalist programs and his philosophy of government. In the author's view, Jefferson wanted to take government away from the mercantile classes and return it to the masses.

YES

Morton Borden

Thomas Jefferson

For twelve years the Constitution worked, after a fashion. From its inception the new document had been subjected to severe trials and divisive strains. A rebellion in Pennsylvania, a naval war with France, a demand for states' rights from Virginia and Kentucky, and various Western schemes of disunion—all had been surmounted. Had it not been for the great prestige of George Washington and the practical moderation of John Adams, America's second attempt at a federal union might have failed like the first. Partisan passions had run high in the 1790's, and any single factor on which men disagreed—Hamilton's financial plans or the French Revolution or the Sedition Act—might easily have caused a stoppage of the nation's political machinery.

The two-party system emerged during this decade, and on each important issue public opinion seemed to oscillate between Federalist and Democratic-Republican. Perhaps this was to be expected of a young nation politically adolescent. Year by year Americans were becoming more politically alert and active; if there was little room for middle ground between these two factions, yet opinions were hardly fixed and irrevocable. The culmination of partisan controversy and the test of respective strengths took place in the monumental election of 1800.

Jefferson was feared, honestly feared, by almost all Federalists. Were he to win the election, so they predicted, all the hard constructive gains of those twelve years would be dissipated. Power would be returned to the individual states; commerce would suffer; judicial power would be lessened; and the wonderful financial system of Hamilton would be dismantled and destroyed. Jefferson was an atheist, and he would attack the churches. Jefferson was a hypocrite, an aristocrat posing as democrat, appealing to the baser motives of human beings in order to obtain votes. Jefferson was a revolutionary, a Francophile and, after ruining the army and navy under the guise of economy measures, might very well involve the nation in a war with England. In short, it was doubtful if the Constitution could continue its successful course under such a president.

In like manner the Republicans feared another Federalist victory. To be sure, John Adams had split with Hamilton and had earned the enmity of the Essex Junto. But would he not continue Hamilton's "moneyed system"? Did not Adams share the guilt of every Federalist for the despicable Alien and Sedition

Acts? Was it not true that "His Rotundity" so admired the British system that he was really a monarchist at heart? Republicans were not engaging in idle chatter, nor were they speaking solely for effect, when they predicted many dire consequences if Adams were elected. A typical rumor had Adams uniting "his house to that of his majesty of Britain" and "the bridegroom was to be king of America."

Throughout the country popular interest in the election was intense, an intensity sustained over months of balloting. When the Republicans carried New York City, Alexander Hamilton seriously suggested that the results be voided. And when the breach between Adams and Hamilton became public knowledge, Republicans nodded knowingly and quoted the maxim: "When thieves fall out, honest men come by their own."

The Federalists were narrowly defeated. But the decision was complicated by a result which many had predicted: a tied electoral vote between the two Republican candidates, Aaron Burr and Thomas Jefferson. (Indeed, the Twelfth Amendment was adopted in 1804 to avoid any such recurrence.) A choice between the two would be made by the House of Representatives. At this moment, February, 1801, the Constitution seemed on the verge of collapse. Federalist members of the lower house united in support of Burr; Republicans were just as adamant for Jefferson. After thirty-five ballots, neither side had yet obtained the necessary majority. The issue seemed hopelessly deadlocked. What would happen on March 4, inauguration day?

One representative from Maryland sick with a high fever, was literally carried into Congress on a stretcher to maintain the tied vote of his state. The Republican governor of Pennsylvania, Thomas McKean, threatened to march on Washington with troops if the Federalists persisted in thwarting the will of the people. Hamilton was powerless; his advice that Jefferson was the lesser evil went unheeded. So great was their hatred of the Virginian that most Federalists in Congress would have opposed him regardless of the consequences. After all, they reasoned, Jefferson would dismantle the federal government anyway. In the end, however, patriotism and common sense prevailed. For the choice was no longer Jefferson or Burr, but Jefferson or no president at all. A few Federalists, led by James A. Bayard of Delaware, could not accept the logic of their party, and threw the election to Jefferson.

What a shock it was, then, to read Jefferson's carefully chosen words in his inaugural address:

> But every difference of opinion is not a difference of principle. We have called by different names brethren of the same principle. We are all republicans— we are all federalists. If there be any among us who would wish to dissolve this Union or to change its republican form, let them stand undisturbed as monuments of the safety with which error of opinion may be tolerated where reason is left free to combat it. I know, indeed, that some honest men fear that a republican government cannot be strong; that this government is not strong enough. But would the honest patriot, in the full tide of successful experiment, abandon a government which has so far kept us free and firm, on the theoretic and visionary fear that this government, the world's best hope, may by possibility want energy to preserve itself? I trust not. I believe this, on the contrary, the strongest government on earth. I believe it

is the only one where every man, at the call of the laws, would fly to the standard of the law, and would meet invasions of the public order as his own personal concern. Sometimes it is said that man cannot be trusted with the government of himself. Can he, then, be trusted with the government of others? Or have we found angels in the form of kings to govern him? Let history answer this question.

The words were greeted with applause—and confusion. It was obvious that Jefferson wanted to salve the wounds of bitter factionalism. While many Federalists remained distrustful and some even regarded it as hypocritical, most men approved the tone of their new president's message.

But what did Jefferson mean? Were there no economic principles at stake in his conflicts with Hamilton? Were there no political and constitutional principles implicit in the polar views of the respective parties? And, in the last analysis, did not these differences reflect a fundamental philosophical quarrel over the nature of human beings? Was not the election of 1800 indeed a revolution? If not, then what is the meaning of Jeffersonianism?

For two terms Jefferson tried, as best he could, to apply the standards of his inaugural address. Naturally, the Alien and Sedition Acts were allowed to lapse. The new secretary of the treasury, Albert Gallatin, was instructed to devise an easily understood program to erase the public debt gradually. Internal taxes were either abolished or reduced. Frugality and economy were emphasized to an extreme. Elegant and costly social functions were replaced by simple and informal receptions. The expense of maintaining ambassadors at the courts of Portugal, Holland, and Prussia was erased by withdrawing these missions. The army and navy were pared down to skeleton size. To be sure, Jefferson had to reverse himself on the matter of patronage for subordinate government posts. Originally he planned to keep these replacements to a minimum, certainly not to permit an individual's partisan opinions to be a basis for dismissal unless the man manifestly used his office for partisan purposes. This position was politically untenable, according to Jefferson's lieutenants, and they pressed him to accept a moderate number of removals. Indeed, Jefferson's handling of patronage is symbolic of what Hamilton once called his "ineradicable duplicity."

The Federalist leaders cried out in anguish at every one of these policy changes. The lowering of the nation's military strength would increase the danger of invasion. It was a rather risky gamble to assume that peace could be maintained while European war was an almost constant factor, and the United States was the major neutral carrier. The abolition of the excises, especially on distilled spirits, would force the government to rely on tariffs, on unpredictable source of revenue depending on the wind and waves. It was charged that several foreign ambassadors were offended by Jefferson's rather affected and ultrademocratic social simplicity. Most important, the ultimate payment of the public debt would reduce national power.

This time, however, the people did not respond to the Federalist lament of impending anarchy. After all, commerce prospered throughout most of Jefferson's administration. Somehow the churches remained standing. No bloodbaths took place. The Bank of the United States still operated. Peace was maintained. Certainly, some Federalist judges were under attack, but the judicial power passed through this ordeal to emerge unscathed and even enhanced. Every economic indicator—urban growth, westward expansion, agricultural production, the construction of canals, turnpikes and bridges—continued to rise, undisturbed by the political bickering in Washington.

At first the Federalists were confident that they would regain power. Alexander Hamilton's elaborate scheme for an organization to espouse Christianity and the Constitution, as the "principal engine" to restore Federalist power, was rejected out of hand. He was told that "our adversaries will soon demonstrate to the world the soundness of our doctrines and the imbecility and folly of their own." But hope changed to despair as the people no longer responded; no "vibration of opinion" took place as in the 1790's. Federalism was the party of the past, an antiquated and dying philosophy. "I will fatten my pigs, and prune my trees; nor will I any longer . . . trouble to govern this country," wrote Fisher Ames: "You federalists are only lookers-on." Jefferson swept the election of 1804, capturing every state except Connecticut and Delaware from the Federalist candidate, Charles C. Pinckney. "Federalism is dead," wrote Jefferson a few years later, "without even the hope of a day of resurrection. The quondam leaders indeed retain their rancour and principles; but their followers are amalgamated with us in sentiment, if not in name."

꘎ꗈ꘎

It is the fashion of some historians to explain the Federalist demise and Republican ascendancy in terms of a great change in Jefferson. A radical natural law philosopher when he fought as minority leader, he became a first-rate utilitarian politician as president. The Virginian became an American. Revolutionary theory was cast aside when Jefferson faced the prosaic problem of having to run the country. He began to adopt some of the techniques and policies of the Federalists. Indeed, it is often observed that Jefferson "outfederalized the Federalists."

There is much to be said for this view. After all, less than three months after he assumed the presidency, Jefferson dispatched a naval squadron to the Mediterranean on a warlike mission, without asking the permission of Congress. Two members of his Cabinet, Levi Lincoln and Albert Gallatin, thought the action unconstitutional, and so advised the President. Almost from the moment of its birth the young nation had paid tribute, as did every European power, rather than risk a war with the Barbary pirates. But Jefferson could not abide such bribery. No constitutional scruples could delay for a moment his determination to force the issue. Later, Congress declared war, and in four years Barbary power was shattered. The United States under Jefferson accomplished an object that England, France, Spain, Portugal, and Holland had desired for more than a century— unfettered commerce in the Mediterranean. Here, then, in this episode, is a totally different Jefferson—not an exponent of states' rights and strict interpretation of the Constitution, but an American nationalist of the first order.

Perhaps the most frequently cited example of Jefferson's chameleon quality, however, was on the question of whether the United States should or should not purchase the Louisiana Territory from France. On this question the fundamental issue was squarely before Jefferson, and a choice could not be avoided. The purchase would more than double the size of the United States. Yet the Constitution did not specifically provide for such acquisition of foreign territory. Further, the treaty provided that this area would eventually be formed into states, full partners in the Union. Again, the Constitution did not specifically cover such incorporation. A broad interpretation of Article IV, Section III, however, might permit United States' ratification of the treaty. Should theory be sacrificed and an empire gained? Or were the means as important as the ends?

Broad or loose construction of the Constitution was the key to the growth of federal power. Federalists had argued in this vein to justify most of their legislation in the 1790's. To Jefferson, individual liberty and governmental power were on opposite ends of a seesaw, which the Federalists had thrown off balance. He believed that government, especially the central government, must be restricted within rather narrow and essential limits. Only by continually and rigidly applying strict construction to the Constitution could this tendency to overweening power be controlled and individual liberty be safeguarded. As early as 1777, Jefferson, then governor of Virginia, had warned that constitutions must be explicit, "so as to exclude all possible doubt; . . . [lest] at some future day . . . power[s] should be assumed."

On the other hand, the purchase of Louisiana would fulfill a dream and solve a host of problems. Jefferson envisioned an American empire covering "the whole northern, if not the southern continent, with a people speaking the same language, governed in similar forms, and by similar laws." The purchase would be a giant step in the direction of democracy's inevitable growth. "Is it not better," asked Jefferson, "that the opposite bank of the Mississippi should be settled by our own brethren and children, than by strangers of another family?"

Of more immediate interest, westerners would be able to ship their goods down the Mississippi without fear that New Orleans might be closed. Indian attacks undoubtedly would taper off without the Spanish to instigate them. Uppermost in Jefferson's mind, however, was the freedom from England that the purchase would assure. He did not fear Spanish ownership. A feeble; second-rate nation like Spain on the frontier offered little threat to America's future security. The continued possession of Louisiana by an imperialistic France led by the formidable Napoleon, however, might force the United States into an alliance with England. At first Jefferson thought a constitutional amendment specifically permitting the purchase might solve the dilemma. But Napoleon showed signs of wavering. The treaty had to be confirmed immediately, with no indication of constitutional doubt. Jefferson asked the Republican leaders in the Senate to ratify it "with as little debate as possible, and particularly so far as respects the constitutional difficulty."

In still other ways Jefferson's presidency was marked by Federalist policies which encouraged the growth of central power. Internal improvements loomed large in Jefferson's mind. While many turnpikes and canals were financed by private and state capital, he realized that federal support would be necessary, especially in the western part of the nation. With the use of federal money obtained from the sale of public lands, and (later) aided by direct congressional appropriations, the groundwork for the famous Cumberland road was established during Jefferson's administration. He enthusiastically supported Gallatin's plan to spend twenty million dollars of federal funds on a network of national roads and canals. Other more pressing problems intervened, however, and it was left to later administrations to finance these local and interstate programs. If Hamilton had pressed for internal improvements in the 1790's (he suggested them in the *Report on Manufactures*), Jefferson probably would have raised constitutional objections.

Finally, is not Jefferson's change of tack further reflected in the political history of that era? Over the span of a few years it seemed as if each party had somehow reversed directions. In 1798–99 Jefferson and Madison penned the Virginia and Kentucky Resolutions as an answer to the Federalists' infamous Alien and Sedition Acts. In 1808–9 more radical but comparable rumblings of dissatisfaction emanated from some New England Federalists over Jefferson's Embargo Act. For the embargo, says one of Jefferson's biographers, was "the most arbitrary, inquisitorial, and confiscatory measure formulated in American legislation up to the period of the Civil War." Further, both parties splintered during Jefferson's administration. Many moderate Federalists, like John Quincy Adams, found themselves in closer harmony with administration policy than with Essex Junto beliefs. And Jefferson's actions alienated old comrades, like John Randolph, Jr., whose supporters were called the Tertium Quids. It is interesting to note that there is no historical consensus of why, when, how, or what precipitated the break between Randolph and Jefferson. Randolph is always referred to as brilliant but erratic; and whatever immediate reason is alleged, the cause somehow has to do with Randolph's personality and Jefferson's betrayal of the true doctrines.

◦◦◉◦◦

It is part of Jefferson's greatness that he could inspire a myth and project an image. But one must not confuse myth and reality, shadow and substance. Thomas Jefferson as he was, and Thomas Jefferson as people perceived him, are quite different. While both concepts of course, are of equal value in understanding our past, it is always the historian's task to make the distinction. Too often, in Jefferson's case, this has not been done. Too often the biographers have described the myth—have taken at face value the popular view of Jefferson and his enemies, contained in the vitriolic newspaper articles and pamphlets, the passionate debates and fiery speeches of that period—and missed or misconstrued the reality.

This is understandable. Even the principals inevitably became involved and helped to propagate the exaggerated images of the 1790's and thus misunderstood one another's aims and motives. Jefferson, according to his grandson, never considered Federalist fulminations "as abusing him; they had never known him. They had created an imaginary being clothed with odious attributes, to whom they gave his name; and it was against that creature of their imaginations they had levelled their anathemas." John Adams, reminiscing in a letter to Jefferson, wrote: "Both parties have excited artificial terrors and if I were summoned as a witness to say upon oath, which party had excited . . . the most terror, and which had really felt the most, I could not give a more sincere answer, than in the vulgar style 'Put them in a bag and shake them, and then see which comes out first.'"

On March 4, 1801, following a decade of verbal violence, many Americans were surprised to hear that "We are all republicans—we are all federalists." Some historians act as if they, too, are surprised. These historians then describe Jefferson's administration as if some great change took place in his thinking, and conclude that he "outfederalized the Federalists." This is a specious view, predicated on an ultraradical Jefferson of the 1790's in constant debate with an ultraconservative Hamilton. Certainly Jefferson as president had to change. Certainly at times he had to modify, compromise, and amend his previous views. To conclude, however, that he outfederalized the Federalists is to miss the enormous consistency of Jefferson's beliefs and practices.

Jefferson was ever a national patriot second to none, not even to Hamilton. He always conceived of the United States as a unique experiment, destined for greatness so long as a sharp line isolated American civilization from European infection. Thus he strongly advised our youth to receive their education at home rather than in European schools, lest they absorb ideas and traits he considered "alarming to me as an American." From "Notes on Virginia" to his advice at the time of Monroe's doctrine, Jefferson thought of America first. It matters not that Hamilton was the better prophet; Jefferson was the better American. The French minister Adet once reported: "Although Jefferson is the friend of liberty . . . although he is an admirer of the efforts we have made to cast off our shackles . . . Jefferson, I say, is an American, and as such, he cannot sincerely be our friend. An American is the born enemy of all the peoples of Europe."

Jefferson's nature was always more practical than theoretical, more common-sensical than philosophical. Certainly the essence of his Declaration of Independence is a Lockean justification of revolution; but, said Jefferson, "It was . . . an expression of the American mind," meant "to place before mankind the common sense of the subject." Jefferson always preferred precision to "metaphysical subtleties." The Kentucky and Virginia Resolutions can be understood only as a specific rebuttal of the Sedition Act. "I can never fear that things will go far wrong," wrote Jefferson, "where common sense has fair play."

One must also remember that Hamilton's power lessened considerably in the last four years of Federalist rule. He had a strong coterie of admirers, but the vast body of Federalists sided with John Adams. Despite all Hamilton did to insure Adams' defeat, and despite the split in Federalist ranks, the fact that Jefferson's victory in 1801 was won by a narrow margin indicated Federalist approval of Adams' actions. Certainly the people at that time—Jefferson and Adams included—regarded 1801 as the year of revolution. But if historians must have a revolution, perhaps Adams' split with the Hamiltonians is a better date. "The mid-position which Adams desired to achieve," writes Manning Dauer, "was adopted, in the main, by Jefferson and his successors."

To be sure, the two men disagreed on many matters of basic importance. Jefferson placed his faith in the free election of a virtuous and talented natural aristocracy; Adams did not. Within the constitutional balance, Jefferson emphasized the power of the lower house; Adams would give greater weight to the executive and judiciary. Jefferson, as a general rule, favored a strict interpretation of the Constitution; Adams did not fear broad construction. Both believed that human beings enjoyed inalienable rights, but only Jefferson had faith in man's perfectability. Jefferson could say, "I like a little rebellion now and then. It is like a storm in the atmosphere"; Adams had grown more conservative since 1776. Jefferson always defended and befriended Thomas Paine; Adams found Edmund Burke's position on the French Revolution more palatable.

Yet, the sages of Quincy and Monticello were both moderate and practical men. Despite the obvious and basic contrasts, both Adams and Jefferson stood side by side on certain essentials: to avoid war, to quiet factionalism, to preserve republican government. Their warm friendship, renewed from 1812 to 1826 in a remarkable and masterful correspondence, was based on frankness, honesty, and respect. "About facts," Jefferson wrote, "you and I cannot differ, because truth is our mutual guide; And if any opinions you may express should be different from mine, I shall receive them with the liberality and indulgence which I ask for my own." Jefferson and Adams represent, respectively, the quintessence of the very best in American liberalism and conservatism. Their indestructible link, then, was "a keen sense of national consciousness," a realization that America's destiny was unique. This is the meaning of Jefferson's words: "We are all republicans—we are all federalists."

The Faithful and The Crisis of Faith

By most objective criteria, the Americans of 1800 had abundant cause to be proud, confident, even smug. . . .

And yet a sense of decadence had plagued the land for five years and, more. From the pulpit rang cries of despair and doom; dishonesty as well as panic had invaded the marketplace; liars and libelers made a travesty of freedom of the press; violence, hysteria, and paranoia infested the public councils. Those Americans who called themselves Federalists felt betrayed by an ungrateful people for whom they had labored long and well, and feared that the horrors of Jacobinism and anarchy were hourly imminent. Those who called themselves Republicans felt betrayed by the twin evils of money and monarchy, and feared that liberty was about to breathe its last. Many who embraced neither political sect, whether from apathy or disgust, nonetheless shared the general feeling that the nation was in an advanced state of moral rot.

What the Federalists thought was actually of little consequence, for they were soon to expire, in what Thomas Jefferson called the Revolution of 1800. Almost miraculously, with their demise—though not because of it—despair suddenly gave way to euphoria. The new optimism, like the pervasive gloom and the defeat of Federalism that preceded it, stemmed from an interplay of social, religious, ideological, and economic forces and institutions, and from certain ingrained American characteristics. If one would understand the Jeffersonian revolution—how it happened and how it affected the nation's destiny—one must seek first to understand those forces, institutions, and characteristics.

One of the tenets of Republicanism in America was that, contrary to the teachings of Montesquieu and other theorists, republican government was best adapted to large territories, since in an area as vast as the United States the very diversity of the people would prevent an accumulation of power inimical to liberty. If the principle, was sound, the Americans were truly blessed, for their culture was nothing if not plural. At first blush that generalization might appear strong, or indeed entirely unfounded. Overwhelmingly, Americans were farmers or traders of British extraction and the Protestant faith; and even in politics, as Jefferson said in his inaugural address, "we are all republicans, we are all federalists." But the mother country itself was scarcely homogeneous, despite the amalgamation that financial and governmental power had brought to Great Britain in the eighteenth century; it comprised a host of different Celtic peoples—the Irish, the Welsh, the Cornish, and three distinct varieties of Scots—as well as Englishmen who differed from one another from north to south and east to west. Americans had proved slow to cast off the cultural baggage that they or their ancestors had brought with them; and a generation of independence, though building some sense of nationhood, had erased neither their original ethnic traits nor the intense localism that complemented and nourished those traits. As to differences in political principles, Jefferson was right in regarding them as largely superficial; yet they were substantive enough to lead many men to fight, and some to kill, one another. . . .

It should not be surprising that those who were saved through revivalism were also supporters of Jeffersonian Republicanism, for the theology of the one was psychologically akin to the ideology of the other. In part, to be sure, religious dissenters supported Jefferson because of his well-known championship of the cause of religious liberty. New England Baptists, for instance, having fought long and vainly for disestablishment, virtually idolized Jefferson. South and west of New England, however, establishment had long since ceased to be a live issue, and in much of that area Jefferson's religious views, to the extent that they were fully known, were if anything a political handicap. Rather, it was the compatibility of outlooks that made it possible for southern and western revivalists simultaneously to embrace evangelical Arminianism in religion and Republican ideology in politics.

Anglo-Americans, like the English themselves, were by and large non-ideological people, but in 1800 the country was divided into two fiercely antagonistic ideological camps. In a loose, general sort of way, and with allowance for a number of exceptions, it can be said that the revival ideologies derived from contrasting views of the nature of man. The first view, that associated with the Hamiltonian Federalists, was premised upon the belief that man, while capable of noble and even altruistic behavior, could never entirely escape the influence of his inborn baser passions—especially ambition and avarice, the love of power and the love of money. The second, that espoused by the Jeffersonian Republicans, held that man was born with a tabula rasa, with virtually boundless capacity for becoming good or evil, depending upon the wholesomeness of the environment in which he grew. From the premise of the first it followed that government should recognize the evil drives of men as individuals, but check them and even harness them in such a way that they would work for the general good of society as a whole. From the premise of the second it followed that government should work to rid society of as many evils as possible—including, to a very large extent, the worst of evils, government itself. The one was positive, the other negative; the one sought to do good, the other to eradicate evil.

But the ideological division was more specifically focused than that. The High Federalists believed in and had fashioned a governmental system modeled upon the one that began to emerge in England after the Glorious Revolution of 1688 and was brought to maturity under the leadership of Sir Robert Walpole during the 1720s and 1730s. In part the system worked on the basis of what has often, simple-mindedly, been regarded as the essence of Hamiltonianism: tying the interests of the wealthy to those of the national government, or more accurately, inducing people of all ranks to act in the general interest by making it profitable for them to do so. But the genius of Hamilton's system ran much deeper. He erected a complex set of interrelated institutions, based upon the monetization of the public debt, which made it virtually impossible for anyone to pursue power and wealth successfully except through the framework of those institutions, and which simultaneously delimited and dictated the possible courses of government activity, so that government had no choice but to function in the public interest as Hamilton saw it. For instance, servicing the public debt, on which the whole superstructure rested, required a regular source of revenue that was necessarily derived largely from duties on imports from Great Britain. For that reason the United States could not go to war with Britain except at the risk of national bankruptcy, but could fight Revolutionary France or France's ally Spain, which were owners of territories that the United States avidly desired. Hamilton regarded this as the proper American foreign policy, at least for a time; and should circumstances change, he was perfectly capable of redefining the rules and rerigging the institutions so as to dictate another policy. In domestic affairs, a wide range of implications of his system was equally inescapable.

The Jeffersonian Republicans regarded this scheme of things as utterly wicked, even as the English opposition had regarded Walpole's system. Indeed, though the Jeffersonians borrowed some of their ideas from James Harrington and other seventeenth-century writers and some from John Locke, their ideology was borrowed *in toto* from such Oppositionists as Charles Davenant, John Trenchard, Thomas Gordon, James Burgh, and most especially Henry St. John, First Viscount Bolingbroke. As a well-rounded system, it is all to be found in the pages of the *Craftsman,* an Oppositionist journal that Bolingbroke published from 1726 to 1737. The Republicans adjusted the ideology to fit the circumstances, to fit the United States Constitution and the "ministry" of Alexander Hamilton rather than the British constitution and the ministry of Robert Walpole; but that was all, and astonishingly little adjustment was necessary.

The Bolingbroke-Oppositionist *cum* Jeffersonian Republican ideology ran as follows. Corruption was everywhere, it was true; but given a proper environment, that need not be the way of things. Mankind could be rejuvenated through education and self-discipline, but that was possible only in the context of a life style that exalted living on, owning, and working the land. Only the land could give people the independence and unhurried existence that were prerequisite to self-improvement.

In some Edenic past, "the people"—which both Bolingbroke and Jefferson understood to mean the gentry and the solid yeomanry, and not to include aristocrats, money jobbers, priests, or the scum in the cities—had enjoyed the proper atmosphere, and therefore had been happy. Relationships were based upon agriculture and its "handmaiden" commerce, upon ownership of land, honest labor in the earth, craftsmanship in the cities, and free trade between individuals. All men revered God, respected their fellows, deferred to their betters, and knew their place. Because they were secure in their sense of place, they were also secure in their identities and their sense of values; and manly virtue, honor, and public spirit governed their conduct.

Then a serpent invaded the garden. To Bolingbroke, the evil started with the Glorious Revolution, which begat two bastard offspring: the Financial Revolution and the system of government by ministry, rather than the system of separation of powers that had been embodied in the ancient English constitution. To Jefferson, things were slightly more complex. America had been spared the corruption that had poisoned England until the accession of George III, and when it began to infest America, the spirit of 1776 had saved the day. Yet the American Revolution, because of the Hamiltonians, was ultimately undermined in just the way the English revolution had been: both were waged to check executive power, and both ended in the worst form of executive tyranny, ministerial government. The instrument of corruption in both instances was money—not "real" money, gold and silver, but artificial money in the form of public debt, bank notes, stocks, and other kinds of paper—the acquisition of which had nothing to do with either land or labor. Government ministers assiduously encouraged people to traffic in such paper, and with that stimulus the pursuit of easy wealth proved irresistible. A frenzy for gambling, stock-jobbing, and paper shuffling permeated the highest councils of state and spread among the people themselves. Manly virtue gave way to effeminacy and vice; public spirit succumbed to extravagance, venality, and corruption.

Jefferson never tired of telling a story which, to him, epitomized what had gone wrong. Early in Washington's first administration, Jefferson recalled, he had been engaged in a friendly discussion of political principles with Hamilton and Vice-President Adams. Jefferson had maintained that an agrarian republic was most conducive to human happiness. Adams disagreed and, to Jefferson's horror, said that monarchy was better, that if the British government were purged of corruption it would be the best system ever devised. Hamilton, to the astonishment of both his listeners, declared that if the British system were urged of corruption it would not work: it was, he said, the most perfect system of government as it stood, for corruption was the most suitable engine of effective government.

In the matter of foreign relations, Republicans opposed the corrupt new order on two interrelated sets of grounds, with the same logic and often the same language that the Oppositionists had used earlier. One was that it entangled the nation with foreign powers, making independent, self-determined action impossible. Not only had Hamilton's system prevented the United States from siding with Revolutionary France against Britain in the early 1790s—which the Republicans believed to be the moral course, as well as the one most advantageous to the country—but it continually subjected America to alien influences because foreigners owned a large percentage of the public debt and the stock of the Bank of the United States. This involvement, in turn, gave rise to the second set of grounds for objection: foreign entanglements necessitated standing armies and navies, the support of which added to an already oppressive tax burden. The gentry and yeomanry, the Republicans believed, had been carrying more than their share of the tax load, even when taxes had been mainly in the form of import duties; and when excise taxes were levied specifically to support the military during the quasi war with France in 1798, the new burden fell almost exclusively on the landed. Taxes to support standing armies and navies were doubly galling because a professional military corps, as a class distinct from the people, was a threat to liberty in its own right, and it could also be unleashed to collect taxes by force, thus making the people pay for their own oppression. (English Oppositionists had been afraid of standing armies, but not of navies, for they had regarded a strong naval establishment as necessary for the protection of British commerce. The American Republicans' fear of standing armies was largely abstract, since they believed that the traditional American reliance on militias would prevent the rise of dangerous armies; but their hostility to navies was immediate and strong, for navies seemed most likely to involve the United States in fighting, and besides, navies cost a lot of money for upkeep even when they were not actively employed.)

Given all that, a revolution in the form of a return to first principles was called for. The several branches of government must be put back into constitutional balance, the moneychangers must be ousted from the temples, the gentry and yeomanry must be restored to supremacy, commerce must be returned to its subordinate role as agriculture's handmaiden, and the values of the agrarian way of life must be cherished anew. In the undertaking, the Republicans had reason for hope—as, in reality, Bolingbroke and his circle had not—for it could all be done within the framework of the Constitution. The Constitution made it possible for the Republicans to gain control of the national government, and should they prove able to do so, only two major tasks needed to be done. The first was to purge government of extreme, irreconcilable monarchists. Jefferson believed that this could be done quickly and easily, for he thought that all but a handful of the people in government were men of sound and honorable principles. The second was to pay off the public debt as rapidly as possible, since that was the wellspring of the whole system of corruption. This would not be easy; but with good management, honest administration, and rigid economy, Jefferson believed that it could be accomplished within sixteen years.

That was the Republicans' ideology and the essence of their program: restore the separation of powers through the voluntary restraint of virtuous officials, cast out the monarchists and the money men, repeal the most oppressive of taxes, slash expenses, pay off the public debt, and thus restore America to the pristine simplicity of an Arcadian past.

It is to be observed that nothing has been said of strict construction of the Constitution and the extreme states'-rights doctrine of interposition, with which Jefferson was associated in his argument against the constitutionality of the Bank in 1791 and in his authorship of the Kentucky Resolutions against the Alien and Sedition Acts in 1798 and 1799. The fact is that only a handful of people knew of those documents or knew that Jefferson had written them; they were not a part of his public identity. Moreover, they were arguments that had been coined in the first instance as matters of political expediency— as means of heading off what Jefferson regarded as dangerous activity by the Federalists—and he never thought of them as sacred principles of constitutional government.

It is also to be observed that nothing has been said of the federal judiciary or of territorial expansion, two matters that consumed much of the energy and attention of the Jeffersonians when they came to power. The judiciary was of merely tangential consequence in the Jeffersonians' thinking; it became important to them only when it loomed as an unexpected stumbling block. Territorial expansion was an integral part of their program, but only implicitly: it went without saying that the nation should expand as the opportunity arose, to make room for generations of farmers yet unborn.

The Republicans gained control of the national government, after twelve years of Federalist domination, in a bitterly contested election that began in April of 1800 and was not completed until February of 1801. Their triumph was not a popular mandate for the implementation of the Republican ideology, nor was it a popular mandate for anything else. The presidential electors were, for the most part, chosen by the state legislatures, who also chose all the members of the United States Senate. The decision was in the hands of no more than a thousand men, and for practical purposes it turned on the activities of two or three dozen factional leaders. The supporters of Thomas Jefferson proved to be more skillful as political manipulators and masters of intrigue than were the supporters of President John Adams—they had already proved, in capturing majorities in most legislatures, that they were better organized and more artful in arousing the voters—and that was the key to their success.

Nonetheless, their program had a broad basis of popular support, for it was peculiarly suited to the genius of the American people, and it appealed to their prejudices and interests as well. Moreover, there was no doubt that the Republicans had the talent, the energy, and the determination to carry the program into execution. But there was a question, a very large one. Republican theory was wondrous potent as an ideology of opposition. It remained to be seen whether it was a sound basis for administration.

Jeffersonian Republicanism was an ideology and an idea, a system of values and a way of looking at things; and as the aphorism goes, ideas and ideals have consequences. But it was also a program of action, carefully crafted and methodically executed; and as we are sometimes wont to forget, actions have consequences, too. To appraise Jefferson's presidency, it is therefore necessary to take both sets of criteria into account.

In the realm of ideas and ideology, Jeffersonian Republicanism was a body of thought that had been taken largely from the Oppositionist tradition of eighteenth-century England, principally as incorporated in the writings of Charles Davenant, John Trenchard, Thomas Gordon, James Burgh, and most particularly Henry St. John, Viscount Bolingbroke. This system of thought is explicated rather fully in the text, and it would be pointless to reiterate the effort here. It is useful, however, to remember that we are speaking of *oppositionist* thought: Bolingbroke and his predecessors and followers (whether calling themselves Tories or Commonwealthmen or Real Whigs) were condemning and seeking to undo the Financial Revolution and its attendant political corruption, as epitomized by the ministry of Sir Robert Walpole, In its stead, they proposed to restore a pristine and largely imaginary past in which life was rural, relationships were personal, the gentry ruled as a natural aristocracy, the main corpus of the citizenry was an honest yeomanry, commerce and craft-manufacturing existed only as handmaidens to agriculture, standing armies and privileged monopolies and fictitious paper wealth were all unknown, and government was limited—limited to an essentially passive function as impartial arbiter and defender of the existing social order, and limited by the unwritten but inviolable Constitution, dividing power among three separate, distinct, and coequal branches. In other words, the Jeffersonians' ideological forebears were reactionaries, swimming against the tide of history, for the world aborning was the depersonalized world of money, machines, cities, and big government.

The Jeffersonians, though castigated by their enemies as dangerous innovators and radicals, were likewise resisting the emergence of the modern world. They had seen the Hamiltonian Federalists attempting to transform and corrupt America, even as the Oppositionists had seen Walpole and the new monied classes transform and corrupt England, and they swallowed the Oppositionists' ideas and ideology whole. The Jeffersonians republicanized Bolingbroke, to be sure, developing the doctrine that absolute separation of powers, with a strictly limited presidency, was guaranteed by the written Constitution. In their hearts, however, they did not trust paper constitutions, and their view of Jefferson's mission as president did not differ substantively and significantly from Bolingbroke's idea of a Patriot King: a head of state who would rally the entire nation to his banner, and then, in an act of supreme wisdom and virtue, voluntarily restrain himself and thus give vitality and meaning to the constitutional system. The Republicans also added the doctrine of states' rights, but that was mainly a tactical position which most of them abandoned—except rhetorically—once they came into control of the national government. The only genuine changes they brought to the ideology were two. One was to relocate its social base, from that of an Anglican gentry to that of southern slaveholders, Celtic-American back-country men, and evangelical Protestants. The other was to put the ideology into practice.

If who they were and what they were seeking are thus understood, it is evident that they remained remarkably true to their principles throughout Jefferson's presidency—despite charges to the contrary by a host of critics, ranging from Alexander Hamilton to Henry Adams to Leonard Levy. Moreover, they were remarkably successful in accomplishing what they set out to do. They set out to destroy the complex financial mechanism that Hamilton had built around the public debt, and they went a long way toward that goal—so close that if war could have been avoided for another eight years, their success might have been total. They also set out to secure the frontiers of the United States by expanding the country's territorial domain into the vast wilderness, and they succeeded so well that it became possible to dream that the United States could remain a nation of uncorrupted farmers for a thousand years to come.

And yet on the broader scale they failed, and failed calamitously–not because of their own shortcomings, but because their system was incompatible with the immediate current of events, with the broad sweep of history, and with the nature of man and society. As an abstract idea, Bolingbrokism *cum* Jeffersonian Republicanism may have been flawless, and it was certainly appealing. In the real world, it contradicted and destroyed itself.

At the core of the Republicans' thinking lay the assumption, almost Marxian in its naïveté, that only two things must be done to remake America as an ideal society and a beacon unto mankind. First, the public debt must be extinguished, for with it would die stock-jobbing, paper-shuffling, "monopoly" banking, excisemen, placemen, and all the other instrumentalities of corruption that the Walpole/Hamilton system "artificially" created. Second, governmental power must be confined to its constitutional limits, which implied reduction of the functions of government but also, and more importantly, meant adherence to the rules of the separation of powers—that being the only legitimate method, in their view, whereby a free government could exercise its authority. If ancient ways were thus restored, the Jeffersonians believed, liberty and independence would inevitably follow. In turn, liberty and independence—by which they meant the absence of governmental restraint or favor and the absence of effective interference from foreign powers—would make it possible for every man, equal in rights but not in talents, to pursue happiness in his own way and to find his own "natural" level in the natural order.

Things did not work out that way, especially in regard to relations with foreign powers: far from freeing the country from foreign interference, Republican policy sorely impaired the nation's ability to determine its own destiny. In their eagerness to retire the public debt, the Jeffersonians tried diligently to economize. Toward that end they slashed military and naval appropriations so much as to render the United States incapable of defending itself at a time when the entire Western world was at war. Simultaneously, in their haste to destroy all vestiges of the Hamiltonian system, the Jeffersonians abolished virtually all internal taxes. This relieved the farmers and planters of an onerous tax burden and arrested the proliferation of hated excisemen, but it also made national revenues almost totally dependent upon duties on imports—which meant dependent upon the uninterrupted flow of international commerce, which in turn depended upon the will of Napoleon Bonaparte and the ministers of King George III.

For two or three years the Jeffersonians were extremely lucky. That is to say, during that period the kaleidoscope of events in Europe turned briefly and flukishly in their favor. They obtained Louisiana as a result of a concatenation of circumstances that was wildly improbable and was never to be repeated. They were able to pay off much of the public debt and to accumulate sizable treasury surpluses because Great Britain, out of consideration for its own interests, allowed the Americans to engage in a trade of debatable legality, thus swelling the volume of American imports and, concomitantly, the revenues flowing into the United States Treasury.

From 1803 onward, however, each turn of the international wheel was less favorable to the United States. By 1805 it was apparent that West Florida—for which the Jeffersonians hungered almost obsessively, since its strategic and economic value was considerably greater than that of all Louisiana excepting New Orleans—would not become American in the way that Louisiana had. In the same year it began to be clear that the British would not long continue to allow the United States to grow wealthy by trading with Britain's mortal enemies.

But for their ideology, the Jeffersonians could have reversed their earlier policy stance, embraced Britain, and become hostile toward France and Spain, thus enabling the nation to continue to prosper and expand. Given their ideological commitment, they could not do so. Moreover, given the consequences of their actions so far, they lacked the strength to make even a token show of force against Great Britain. Thus in 1807, when both Britain and France forbade the United States to engage in international commerce except as tributaries to themselves, the embargo—a policy of pusillanimity and bungling, billed as a noble experiment in peaceful coercion—was the only course open to them.

At home, as they became ever more deeply impaled upon the horns of their self-created international dilemma, the Jeffersonians became progressively less tolerant of opposition or criticism. From the beginning they had shown considerable disdain for the federal courts; as Jefferson's second term wore on, this disdain degenerated into contempt for due process of law and for law itself. Thus the embargo became a program of domestic tyranny in inverse ratio to its ineffectiveness as an instrument of international policy: the more the policy was found wanting, the more rigorously was it enforced.

The embargo, then, both as a bankrupt foreign policy and as a reign of domestic oppression, was not a sudden aberration but the logical and virtually certain outcome of the Jeffersonian ideology put into practice: the ideology's yield was dependence rather than independence, oppression rather than liberty.

One other aspect of the Jeffersonian experience wants notice, and that concerns the Republicans' conception of the presidency as a limited branch of government, absolutely separate from the legislative branch. In practice, adherence to that ideal was impossible because of the very nature of the presidential office. For one thing, though some presidential powers are relatively independent, others are intermeshed with those of Congress. For another, the American executive branch is "republicanized," or kept from being monarchical, by being made elective for a fixed term of years. To be sure, the Republicans' political machinery was so effective that Jefferson could doubtless have been elected to a third and even a fourth term, had he chosen. But Washington's two-term precedent was strong, and, what was more telling, the psychic cost of the presidential office was and is frightful; by the seventh or eighth year Jefferson, like Washington before him and like most two-term presidents who followed him, was physically, emotionally, and spiritually exhausted. The second term was therefore a lame-duck term, and that fact subtly but significantly altered the relationship between the president and Congress. Pure though Jefferson's motives and the motives of many Republican congressmen were, it was important to them that his popularity would cease to be of use to them in seeking reelection, and it was important to him that he would not need their political support in 1808. In the circumstances, Jefferson did what lame-duck presidents normally do—that is, he gravitated toward the arena in which he had less to do with Congress, the area of foreign relations; and Congress, and especially the Senate, also followed the norm by rising at the end to regain powers that it believed had been more or less usurped from it.

Still another crucial aspect of the American presidency, one with which the Republicans were not at all prepared to cope, is that the Constitution vests in one office and one person two distinct and nearly incompatible roles which under the British system had come to be divided between the king and his ministers. One is the truly monarchical function, that of serving as the ritualistic symbol of the nation. The other is the purely executive function, that of fashioning policy and directing its implementation. Success in the one hinges upon the president's charisma, his leadership, and his abstract appeal to the whole people; success in the other hinges upon the president's skill in tangible dealings with small groups and individual human beings. The Republicans' conception of the presidency was, in these terms, entirely unrealistic: they disavowed the first role and wanted the president to fill the second by standing as aloof from Congress as a proper king stands from his subjects.

Jefferson was superbly gifted at playing both roles, and he was able to play them without offending Republican sensibilities or prejudices. He ostentatiously disdained the pomp and pageantry that had marked the presidencies of Washington and Adams, but all the while he assiduously and effectively courted popularity. Foreign ministers and Federalist critics alike commented upon his inordinate love of popularity, and marked it as a weakness of character; perhaps it was, but it was also true wisdom, for reverence toward the Crown was a deep-rooted habit in the English-speaking world, and love of the president as king-surrogate was a crucial social adhesive for the diffuse and pluralistic infant United States. Indeed, in this respect Jefferson made a profound contribution toward the perdurance of the republic. Washington had been a veritable demigod and a symbol of the nation, and thus provided a sort of half-way house between monarchy and republicanism; Jefferson humanized the presidency and served as a symbol, not of the nation, but of the people, and thus made the transition complete.

In the role of policy-maker and administrator, Jefferson was even more skilled. After his inaugural he abandoned the monarchical practice of appearing in person before Congress; he never held court or levees, but invited congressmen in small groups for dinner, where he word homespun and hosted them in the manner of a country squire; he never openly initiated legislation, and only deferentially suggested that Congress might look into one subject or another; he never vetoed a bill on policy grounds and would not have dreamed of doing so. In sum, he allowed Congress to function with no overt presidential direction and with only the gentlest of presidential guidance. As to cabinet meetings, he conducted them as a democracy of equals. And yet, almost until the end, he ran Congress more successfully and more thoroughly than did any preceding president and precious few succeeding presidents, and the cabinet always reflected his will except when he had no firm opinions on a matter. Moreover, he did so without the use of bribery, patronage, corruption or coercion: it all flowed from the force of his intellect, his character, and his personality.

But, perversely, that too was a weakness of the Jeffersonian scheme of things: the system could be made to work only with a Thomas Jefferson at the helm. When Jefferson himself faltered, as he did on several occasions during his presidency, the government almost stopped functioning except in the routine operations of Galatin's Treasury machinery. When Jefferson left the office, all the shortcomings of his method of administration became manifest. The cabinet became a center of petty bickering and continuous cabalizing, and Congress split into irreconcilable factions and repeatedly asserted its will against the president.

For all these reasons, Jefferson's legacy to his successor was a can of serpents. Jefferson's second term was merely a calamity; Madison's first would be a disaster.

There is more to a presidency than the tangible events that happen during and in consequence of it: there are also the myths it inspires. For a time, of course, memories were too fresh, feelings were too strong, and events were too unpleasant to admit of the kind of romanticization that is a necessary prelude to myth-making. By 1826, however—when Jefferson along with John Adams died on the fiftieth anniversary of the Declaration of Independence—memories had mellowed, new rivalries had replaced the old, and artful and designing men were looking to the past for heroes whose lives could be used or misused to justify their own doings. Jefferson was admirably suited for such use and misuse, for he had written and acted in a greater variety of ways on a greater variety of subjects than any of the other Founding Fathers, and he was more quotable than any of them save possibly Adams alone.

But the Jefferson legend developed along curiously divided lines. In the realm of formal historical writing, he fared poorly until well into the twentieth century. . . .

Meanwhile, in the realm of folklore and political rhetoric, which ordinary Americans heard and heeded more frequently and more trustingly than they did the staid pronouncements of historians, Jefferson was exalted as the patron saint of all good things. The range of causes for which his name was invoked is staggering: democracy and partisanship, states' rights and nationalism, slavery and abolitionism, egalitarianism and racism, imperialism and isolationism, populism and laissez-faire capitalism, the planned and the decentralized society. In the nineteenth century, so long as rural values continued to prevail in America despite the relentless march of industrialization, Jefferson continued to be identified with the agrarian tradition; in the twentieth, when the center of American life and values became the city, his connection with that ideal was all but forgotten, and instead he came to be regarded as the champion of the "have-nots" against the "haves," of the "common man" (or the "forgotten man" or the "little fellow") against aristocrats and plutocrats.

In the 1920s and 1930s the two strands of the legend began to come together. The Democratic politician-historian Claude G. Bowers and the more scholarly Gilbert Chinard began the process of beatification through the written word, and though the Jefferson they described was one he would scarcely have recognized, the process has continued. Franklin Roosevelt's New Deal depicted itself as thoroughly Jeffersonian, though given to the use of "Hamiltonian means to accomplish Jeffersonian ends"—and while building a federal bureaucracy almost as large as the population of the entire country had been during Jefferson's time and while extending its regulatory power apace, it built Jefferson a monument which declared his true mission to have been as a libertarian. In time, and in our own time, "Jefferson" and "Jeffersonian" came to mean merely "good," or "that which the nation aspires to be."

The real Jefferson—the one who once lived in Virginia and once worked in the President's House—was lost in the shuffle. So, too, was the America he wanted his country to become; and in a nation of crime-ridden cities and poisoned air, of credit cards and gigantic corporations, of welfare rolls and massive bureaucracies, of staggering military budgets and astronomical public debts, of corruption and alienation, that loss is the more poignant. He and his followers set out to deflect the course of History, and History ended up devouring them and turning even their memory to its own purposes. History has a way of doing that.

POSTSCRIPT

Was President Jefferson a Political Compromiser?

Professor Borden seems to approve of Jefferson's pragmatic, commonsense and moderate approach to politics. Rejecting many of the differences between Federalists and Republicans as mere political rhetoric, Borden maintains that "Jefferson was ever a national patriot . . . [who] always conceived of the United States as a unique experiment, destined for greatness so long as sharp line isolated American civilization from European infection." Jefferson became a proponent of strong executive power, he argues, because he believed such measures as the Louisiana Purchase and the embargo furthered the nation's best interests.

Professor Forrest McDonald rejects the consensus view of American politics held by Professor Borden that there are little ideological differences between the opposition political parties. He believes there were philosophical differences between Hamilton and Jefferson that effected public policies. Hamilton believed that men were motivated by ambition, avarice, and a lust for power. Jefferson believed human beings were born with a blank slate and were capable of becoming good or evil, "depending upon the wholesomeness of the environment." Drawing upon the political theories of the British Opportunists of the early eighteenth century, the Republican ideology consisted in getting rid of extreme, irreconcilable monarchists and paying off the debt as quickly as possible and "thus restore America to the pristine simplicity of an Arcadian past." Unfortunately, the policies didn't always work. Reduction in land taxes meant the government became excessively dependent upon tariffs for their revenue. The failed embargo against England and France in Jefferson's second term not only created a nationwide economic depression, "the embargo also became a program of domestic tyranny in inverse ratio to its effectiveness as an instrument of international policy: the more the policy was found wanting, the more rigorously it was enforced."

It is not surprising that Jefferson's two major biographers, both professors at the University of Virginia for many years, have written sympathetic portraits. Dumas Malone's magisterial *Jefferson and His Times*, 6 volumes (Little, Brown, 1948–1981) and Merrill Peterson's 900-page opus *Thomas Jefferson and the New Nation: A Bibliography* (Oxford, 1970) contain detailed accounts of most facets of his life and are very useful as reference works. Peterson's *The Jeffersonian Images in the American Mind* (Oxford, 1960) is a wonderful account of the use and misuse of Jefferson's image in American politics since his death up to 1960.

Recent writings on Jefferson reflect a more critical tone. One reason is Jefferson's views on slavery and race. William Cohen in "Thomas Jefferson and the Problem of Slavery," *The Journal of American History* (December, 1969) believes Jefferson was a typical Virginia planter committed to protecting his chattel property. Fawn M. Brodie's psychobiography *Thomas Jefferson: An Intimate History* (Norton, 1974) was one of the first to accept as true the liaison between Jefferson and Sally Hemings that led to five unacknowledged sons and daughters. A shorter version can be found in Brodie's "The Great Taboo," *American Heritage* (June 1972). More recently, DNA tests have confirmed that Jefferson fathered the youngest of Sally's children. See the article by Eric S. Lander and Joseph J. Ellis et. al., "DNA Analysis: Founding Father," *Nature* (November 5, 1998, pp. 13–14, 27–28). A layperson's explanation of the DNA article is "Jefferson's Secret Life" by Barbara Murray and Brian Duffy in *U.S. News and World Report* (November 9, 1998). The controversy is fully examined with a complete bibliography and a critical discussion of Jefferson's earlier biographers who refused to consider the possibility of a Jefferson–Hemings liaison in Annette Gordon-Reed, *Thomas Jefferson and Sally Hemings: An American Controversy* (The University Press of Virginia, 1997).

The most recent analysis of *Jeffersonian America* (Blackwell Publishers, 2002) with the most complete bibliography is by Peter S. Onuf and Leonard Sadorsky. Two collections of essays in the 1990s reflect a more critical tone than the very sympathetic works of Malone and Peterson. See Peter S. Onuf, eds., *Jeffersonian Legacies* (The University of Virginia Press, 1993) and James Horn and Peter S. Onuf, eds., *The Revolution of 1800: Democracy, Race and the New Republic* (The University of Press of Virginia, 2002).

ISSUE 9

Was the Monroe Doctrine of 1823 Designed to Protect the Latin American Countries from European Intervention?

YES: Dexter Perkins, from *The Monroe Doctrine: 1823–1826* (Harvard University Press, 1927)

NO: Ernest R. May, from *The Making of the Monroe Doctrine* (The Belknap Press of the Harvard University Press, 1975)

ISSUE SUMMARY

YES: According to Professor Dexter Perkins, President James Monroe issued his famous declaration of December 2, 1823 to protest Russian expansionism in the Pacific Northwest and to prevent European intervention in South America from restoring to Spain her former colonies.

NO: According to Professor Ernest R. May, domestic political considerations brought about the Monroe Doctrine when the major presidential candidates attempted to gain a political advantage over their rivals during the presidential campaign of 1824.

T he American government in the early 1800s greatly benefitted from the fact that European nations generally considered what was going on in North America of secondary importance to what was happening in their own countries. In 1801 President Thomas Jefferson became alarmed when he learned that France had acquired the Louisiana territory from Spain. He realized that western states might revolt if the government did not control the city of New Orleans as a seaport for shipping their goods. Jefferson pulled off the real estate coup of the nineteenth century when his diplomats caught Napoleon in a moment of despair. With a stroke of the pen and $15 million, the Louisiana Purchase of 1803 nearly doubled the size of the country. The exact northern, western, and southeastern boundaries were not clearly defined. "But," as diplomatic historian Thomas Bailey has pointed out, "the American negotiators knew that they had bought the western half of perhaps the most valuable river valley on the face of the globe . . ."

187

After England fought an indecisive war with the United States from 1812 to 1815, she realized that it was to her advantage to maintain peaceful relations with her former colony. In 1817 the Great Lakes, which border on the United States and Canada, were mutually disarmed. Over the next half-century, the principle of demilitarization was extended to the land, resulting in an undefended frontier line that stretched for more than 3,000 miles. The Convention of 1818 clarified the northern boundary of the Louisiana Purchase and ran a line along the 49th parallel from Lake of the Woods in Minnesota to the Rocky Mountains. Beyond that point there was to be a 10-year joint occupancy in the Oregon Territory. In 1819 Spain sold Florida to the United States after Secretary of State John Quincy Adams sent a note telling the Spanish government to keep the Indians on their side of the border or else to get out of Florida. A few years later, the Spanish Empire crumbled in the New World, and a series of Latin American republics emerged.

Afraid the European powers might attack the newly independent Latin American republics and that Russia might expand south into the Oregon Territory, Adams convinced President James Monroe to reject a British suggestion for a joint declaration and to issue instead a unilateral policy statement. The Monroe Doctrine, as it was called by a later generation, had three parts. First, it closed the Western Hemisphere to any further colonization. Second, it forbade, "any interposition" by the European monarchs that would "extend their system to any portion of this hemisphere as dangerous to our peace and safety." And third, the United States pledged to abstain from any involvement in the political affairs of Europe. Viewed in the context of 1823, it is clear that Monroe was merely restating the principles of unilateralism and nonintervention. Both of these were at the heart of American isolationism.

While Monroe renounced the possibility of American intervention in European affairs, he made no such disclaimer toward Latin America, as was originally suggested by Great Britain. It would be difficult to colonize in South America, but the transportation revolution, the hunger for land, which created political turmoil in Texas, and the need for ports on the Pacific to increase American trade in Asia encouraged the acquisition of new lands contiguous to the southwestern boundaries. In the 1840s, journalists and politicians furnished an ideological rationale for this expansion and said it was the Manifest Destiny of Americans to spread democracy, freedom, and white American settlers across the entire North American continent, excluding Canada because it was a possession of Great Britain. Blacks and Indians were not a part of this expansion.

Was the original Monroe Doctrine of 1823 an attempt to establish a coherent long-term policy towards Latin America? In the first selection Professor Dexter Perkins answers yes. President James Monroe, with a push from his Secretary of State John Quincy Adams, issued his statements to protest Russian expansion in the Pacific Northwest and to prevent the European nations from intervening in South America for the purpose of restoring to Spain her former colonies. But Professor Ernest May disagrees. Domestic political considerations, he argues, brought about the Monroe Doctrine, as the major presidential candidates attempted to gain a political advantage over their rivals during the presidential campaign of 1824.

YES

Dexter Perkins

The Northwest Boundary Controversy and the Non-Colonization Principle. 1823–1824

The famous declaration of December 2, 1823, which has come to be known as the Monroe Doctrine, had a dual origin and a dual purpose. On the one hand, it was the result of the advance of Russia on the northwest coast of America, and was designed to serve as a protest against this advance and to establish a general principle against Russian expansion. Referring to this question of the northwest, President Monroe laid down the principle in his message to Congress that "the American continents, by the free and independent condition which they have assumed and maintain, are henceforth not to be considered as subjects for future colonization by any European powers." On the other hand, the message was provoked by the fear of European intervention in South America to restore to Spain her revolted colonies, and was intended to give warning of the hostility of the United States to any such intervention. "With the governments [that is, of the Spanish-American republics] who have declared their independence, and maintained it," wrote the President, "and whose independence we have, on great consideration and just principles, acknowledged, we could not view any interposition for the purpose of oppressing them, or controlling in any other manner their destiny, by any European power, in any other light than as the manifestation of an unfriendly disposition toward the United States." . . .

Russian interest in the northwest coast of America goes back to the second quarter of the eighteenth century, to the days of the renowned navigator Vitus Behring, who discovered in 1727 the Straits that now bear his name, and fourteen years later the Alaskan coast in the neighborhood of latitude 58. Behring's explorations were followed by the voyages of fur traders and by the establishment of trading posts on the islands off the American mainland. After years of demoralizing competition on the part of private individuals, the Tsar determined to create a commercial monopoly for the exploitation of the rich fisheries to be found in that part of the world. By the ukase of July 8, 1799, the Russian-American Company was constituted, and to this company were

Reprint by permission of the publisher from THE MONROE DOCTRINE, 1823–1826 by Dexter Perkins, pp. 3–5, 7–8, 16–19, 40–43, 80–81, 85, Cambridge, Mass.: Harvard University Press, Copyright © 1927 by the President and Fellows of Harvard College.

granted exclusive trading rights and jurisdiction along the coast as far south as latitude 55, and the right to make settlements on either side of that line in territory not occupied by other powers.

From an early date the operations of this Russian corporation were impeded by interlopers, very largely American. American vessels sold arms and ammunition to the natives, and secured a considerable part of the fur trade. As early as 1808 and 1810 complaints on the part of the Russian government began to be made to the government at Washington. There was, obviously enough, a situation that might lead to serious friction. . . .

On September 4/16, 1821, the Tsar Alexander I, acting at the instigation of the Russian monopoly, promulgated an imperial decree which renewed its privileges and confirmed its exclusive trading rights. This time the southern limit of these rights on the American coast was set, not at 55, but at 51 degrees. And in addition, all foreign vessels were forbidden, between Behring Straits and 51 degrees, to come within 100 Italian miles of the shore, on pain of confiscation. A Russian warship was dispatched to the northwest coast to enforce this remarkable decree, and every intention was manifested of barring all other nations from any participation whatever in the trade or fisheries of the region. Such a course of action very naturally provoked a protest, not only on the part of the United States, but also on the part of Great Britain. At this time the two Anglo-Saxon powers had joint ownership, under the convention of 1818, of the territory north from 42 degrees to a line yet to be determined, and the Russian claims of exclusive jurisdiction as far south as 51 degrees could hardly fail to be disquieting. Both from London and from Washington, therefore, came strong diplomatic remonstrance, and thus began a controversy which was to have the closest relationship to the famous pronouncement of 1823.

It is neither necessary nor desirable, in connection with this narrative, to trace the negotiations on the northwest question in all their details. What is of special interest here is the evolution of the non-colonization principle in the course of the discussions, the reception which it met at the hands of the interested powers, and the effect which it produced upon the diplomatic interchanges themselves. . . .

These discussions, begun in 1822, assumed little importance till the late spring of 1823. By that time it had been agreed that the question should be threshed out at St. Petersburg. In June the cabinet discussed the instructions which were to be sent to Mr. Middleton, American minister at the court of the Tsar. The Secretary of State declared it to be his conviction that the United States ought to contest the right of the Russian government to any territorial establishment on the American continents. Apparently this point of view did not pass unchallenged. It was pointed out that Russia would have little reason to accept such drastic doctrine. The United States, in maintaining it, would be asking everything, and conceding virtually nothing. A compromise was suggested and agreed upon by which this country would recognize the territorial claims of the Tsar north of 55 degrees. On this basis, the negotiations were actually to be conducted.

But Adams, with a curious inconsistency, did not on this account surrender the principle which was taking shape in his mind. At the very moment when he was perfecting the instructions to Middleton along the lines agreed upon in the cabinet, he declared himself to Tuyll, the Russian minister at Washington, in language very much more sweeping.

> I told him specially [he writes in his diary, alluding to an interview of July 17, 1823], that we should contest the right of Russia to *any* territorial establishment on this continent, and that we should assume distinctly the principle that the American continents are no longer subjects for *any* new European colonial establishments.

In this statement, almost five months before the appearance of the President's message, we have the non-colonization principle full-fledged, no longer merely a subject of cabinet debate, but explicitly put forward to the minister of another power, to the minister of the power perhaps most concerned in denying it. One might expect that such a declaration would have been most distasteful to Tuyll. But such evidence as we have leads to a contrary conclusion. There are no indications that the Russian minister challenged or controverted Adams. In his dispatch to St. Petersburg reporting the conversation of July 17, he contented himself with the following allusion to the matter: "The American government will avail itself of the present occasion to ask the acceptance of a general principle by which foreign powers will definitely and finally renounce the right of establishing new colonies in either of the Americas." This is underlined in the text itself, but the Russian minister goes on to say that he sees no great difficulty in the way of a settlement of the northwest question. He clearly did not regard the language of Adams as a serious obstacle to understanding. There was nothing in his attitude which might lead the Secretary of State to modify his position.

We have another statement of the non-colonization dogma almost contemporaneous with the interview with Tuyll. This is found in the instructions to Richard Rush, American minister at the Court of Saint James's. As England had an interest in the northwest controversy, it was obviously desirable that the diplomatic representative of the United States at London should be informed of the views of his government on the subject. Accordingly, on July 22, Adams sent forward a long and careful dispatch, in which he set forth his new theory in greater detail than at any other time. That dispatch will claim our special attention later. . . .

Adams secured Monroe's assent to his new principle in July, at the time of sending the dispatches just alluded to. Whether that assent was cordial and positive, or whether it was given as a mere matter of routine, we have no way of knowing. The President may have warmly approved the non-colonization doctrine; he may, on the other hand, have been little aware of its significance or its implications. On this point his writings provide us with no illumination. But at any rate, he *did* accept it. When, therefore, the Secretary of State drew up in November, the customary sketch of the topics of foreign policy which might interest the President in connection with the preparation of the forthcoming message, he naturally included in the paragraph on the Russian negotiations a reference to the new dogma. That paragraph was taken over almost without verbal change by Monroe, and thus it appeared in his communication to the

Congress. These facts are clear, for we have the actual manuscript of Adams's outline of the diplomatic matters which he wished to draw to the attention of the President, and the language of that outline, so far as the non-colonization principle is concerned, corresponds almost exactly with the language of the message itself.

There was, apparently, no consideration of the principle in the cabinet discussion preceding the publication of the President's declaration. On this point Calhoun, then Secretary of War, was to testify many years later, and the silence of Adams's diary at the time confirms this testimony. There is, after all, nothing strange in such a circumstance. For the question of the hour, in November, 1823, was not the dispute with Russia, but the menace offered by the Holy Alliance to the independence of the States of South America. It was on these problems that all the debates turned; so, very naturally, the other problem was crowded out. . . .

Having thus examined the origins of the non-colonization clause in the message of 1823, we must now turn back to discuss the viewpoint and the reasoning which lay behind it. What was the motive in promulgating such a sweeping theory? What was the logic by which it might be supported?

In later interpretations of this part of the President's declaration, the emphasis has frequently been laid on the dangers involved in bringing the intrigues and conflicting territorial ambitions of Europe across the seas and into the New World. The United States, the argument has run, would thus be swept into the vortex of European politics, and exposed to the wicked influences for which those politics are notorious. Or it has been maintained that new European territorial establishments would endanger American security, and ought to be opposed on these grounds.

These were not the bases, however, on which John Quincy Adams, in 1823, rested his opposition to colonization. The territorial aspects of colonization were not uppermost in his mind. He was thinking (and the point has been all too little emphasized) primarily of the commercial interests of the United States. In the history of American diplomacy, the principle of non-colonization has a certain affinity with the principle of the open door, asserted three quarters of a century later. It was based on immediate economic factors, not on vague fears of the future. It was because the colonial system meant commercial exclusion that the Secretary of State proclaimed its banishment from the American continents.

A close examination of Adams's point of view makes this clear. The principle of equality of commercial opportunity was one for which he contended with the utmost vigor, not only in the northwest controversy, but in other fields. He fought vigorously against the narrow policy of Great Britain in the British West Indies. He instructed the ministers to the South American states, when they set out in 1823, to contend for the principle that the new republics should treat all nations on the same footing, and that they should give no preferences, not even to their former mother country. The right to which he held most tenaciously in the dispute with Russia was not the right to full possession of the territory on the northwest (on this, as we have seen, it had been agreed to compromise on the line of 55 degrees); the right which he deemed of most importance was the right to trade, and this Middleton was instructed stoutly to maintain. In Adams's opinion the notion of European colonization was flatly opposed to the maintenance of these economic interests. The colonizing methods of the Old World, he told Stratford Canning in November, 1822, had always involved a more or less complete commercial monopoly. "Spain had set the example. She had forbidden foreigners from setting a foot in her Colonies, upon pain of death, and the other colonizing states of Europe had imitated the exclusion, though not the rigor of the penalty." From the very beginning, therefore, the Adams doctrine was knit up with the commercial interests of the United States. And so it remained throughout this early period of its development. Nothing shows this more clearly than the important dispatch of July 22, 1823, to Richard Rush, in which the whole theory of the doctrine found most careful expression. After declaring that the American continents will henceforth no longer be subjects for colonization, the American Secretary of State goes on to say:

> Occupied by civilized independent nations, they will be accessible to Europeans and to each other on that footing alone, and the Pacific Ocean in every part of it will remain open to the navigation of all nations, in like manner with the Atlantic. . . . The application of colonial principles of exclusion, therefore, cannot be admitted by the United States as lawful upon any part of the northwest coast of America, or as belonging to any European nation.

In these clear-cut and precise phrases, the innermost connection of the new dogma with American trading rights stands revealed.

It need not be contended, of course, that there was no more to it than this. It would be a clear exaggeration to say that Adams was contending for trading rights alone. He was thinking also of territorial settlement, as the very dispatch just quoted helps to make clear.

> It is not imaginable [he declared] that, in the present condition of the world, *any* European nation should entertain the project of settling a *colony* on the northwest coast of America. That the United States should form establishments there, with views of absolute territorial right and inland communication, is not only to be expected, but is pointed out by the finger of nature.

But these comments were made with an eye to the future. What was interesting in the immediate sense, "the only useful purpose to which the northwest coast of America" had been or could be made "subservient to the settlement of civilized men," was that of trade and of the fishery. The rights of the United States in this regard it was vital to maintain. On the territorial question there might be compromise; this we have already seen. But on the commercial question there ought to be none. "The right of carrying on trade with the natives throughout the northwest coast they [the United States] cannot renounce." Clearly, it was antagonism to commercial restriction that lay at the basis of the Secretary of State's famous dictum. . . .

The Spanish-American Phase of the Message—The Prelude

The revolt of the Spanish-American colonies followed hard upon the Napoleonic conquest of Spain. From the very beginning, the sympathies of the United States appear to have been engaged upon the side of the revolutionists. American sentiment was distinctly favorable to a movement for independence which had at least a superficial resemblance to that of 1776, and which could easily be regarded as an effort to throw off an odious tyranny and establish throughout the greater part of the New World the blessings of republican government. Fellow feeling in a struggle for liberty and independence was an essential element in forming the policy of the United States with regard to South America.

It was indeed, to all appearances, a far more important element than any hope of material gain. In the formative period of this country's relations with the new states of South America, certainly down to 1822, there is little evidence of the working of economic interest. In the absence of exact statistics for much of the period, and in view of the paucity of references to trade with the Spanish colonies, it is difficult to speak with precision. But certain general observations may safely be made. In the first place, the trade with Cuba and with Spain itself was far more important than the trade with the new republics of the South. A diplomatic policy favorable to the South-American states might jeopardize or even sacrifice commercial interests superior to those which it would promote. If economic reasons were to be regarded as shaping political developments, there were more reasons for a cautious than for an active line of policy. In the second place, there was not, as in the case of Great Britain, any powerful pressure from the commercial classes in favor of colonial independence. The evidence on this point is partly negative, it is true, but it is negative evidence of the strongest kind. One can hardly imagine that the existence of such pressure would pass unnoticed in the debates in Congress, and in such contemporary records as the diary and writings of Adams, and the correspondence of Monroe. But it is not necessary to depend upon this fact alone. Statistics indicate that as late as 1821 only 2.3 percent of American exports and 1.6 percent of American imports were South American in destination or origin. In March of the same year Adams could tell Henry Clay that he had little expectation of any commercial advantages from the recognition of the new states. And even later, in 1823, the Secretary of State speaks of commercial development as a matter of hope for the future rather than a present accomplishment. That hope may, of course, have counted for something from the beginning. But, all things considered, it seems highly probable that political sympathy, not economic self-interest, lay at the root of American policy so far as it revealed itself as favorable to the new states of South America.

From the very beginnings of the South American struggle this sympathy asserts itself. As early as 1810, the American government, then headed by Madison, sent agents to South America—Joel R. Poinsett to La Plata and Chile, and Robert Lowry to Venezuela. At the end of 1811, James Monroe, then Secretary of State, thought seriously of raising the question of the recognition of the new states, and of exerting American influence in Europe to secure like action from the principal European powers. He also entered into informal relations with agents from at least one of the revolted provinces. And in Congress, at the same time, in response to the sympathetic language of the President's message, a resolution was passed, expressing a friendly solicitude in the welfare of these communities, and a readiness, when they should become nations by a just exercise of their rights, to unite with the Executive in establishing such relations with them as might be necessary. Thus, very early in the course of the colonial struggle, the general bent of American policy was made plain.

But it was some time before the South-American question became a matter of really first-rate importance. In the years 1810 to 1815, the prime concern of the administration at Washington lay in the preservation of American neutral rights, and, from 1812 to 1814, in the prosecution of the war with Great Britain. Moreover, the course of events in the overseas dominions of Spain was for some time hardly favorable to the revolutionists. In 1814 and 1815, indeed, it seemed entirely possible that the revolutionary movements might be snuffed out. In the north, in Venezuela and Colombia, the army of the Spanish general, Morillo, won victory on victory, and drove the leader of the revolutionists, Bolívar, into exile. In the south, in Chile, Osorio reëstablished the power of the mother country, and in Buenos Aires the struggles of contending factions weakened the new government that had been set up. Under such circumstances, prudence would have dictated a policy of reserve on the part of the United States, even if its government had not been preoccupied with other and more pressing matters.

With the year 1817, however, a change takes place in the status of the colonial question. In the case of one, at any rate, of the new states, the struggle was virtually over. The republic of La Plata had declared its independence and successfully maintained it, so that not a Spanish soldier remained upon its territory; even more, it had dispatched its great general, San Martín, across the Andes, and, with the victory of Chacabuco, taken a great step toward the final liberation of Chile. Perhaps as a result of these developments, interest in favor of the recognition of the new state began to develop in the United States; there were numerous newspaper articles in the summer of 1817, notably the discussions of Lautaro in the Richmond *Enquirer;* and the affairs of South America became a matter of debate both in the councils of the administration and in the halls of Congress.

It is interesting, in the light of later events, to examine these developments. So far as the administration was concerned, the point especially to be emphasized is the warm sympathy of the President himself with the South American cause. There has been a tendency in some quarters, in connection with the evolution of the Monroe Doctrine, to ascribe a very slight importance to the views of the very man who promulgated it. Mr. Monroe has been pictured as "slow-moving and lethargic," as prodded forward only by the more vigorous mind and more determined will of John Quincy Adams, his Secretary of State. But as a matter of fact, Monroe was at all times quite as much interested in the colonial cause, and in as full sympathy with it, as Adams. From the very beginning of his presidency, he showed his concern with regard to it. As early as May, 1817, some months before Adams took office, the President had determined upon a mission of inquiry to the provinces of La Plata, and as early as October he questioned his cabinet on the expediency of recognizing the government of that region. He raised the problem again in the succeeding May, even suggesting the possibility of sending an armed force to the coast of South America, to protect American commerce, "and to countenance the patriots." His views, it is true, were to be overruled or modified by his advisers. But his interest in positive action was very real, and is quite consistent with the character of the man whose flaming sympathy with French republicanism had been so obvious in his earlier career. . . .

In the summer and fall of 1821, however, there occurred events of high importance. Henry Clay, still ardent for the colonial cause, brought up a new resolution in the House of Representatives. It declared that "the House join with the people of the United States in their sympathy with the South Americans; and that it was ready to support the President whenever he should think it expedient to recognize their governments." The first part of this resolution passed by a vote of 134 to 12; and the second, by a vote of 86 to 68. The trend of opinion in Congress was clearly for action, and the hands of the administration were strengthened by this expression of opinion. Meanwhile, events of the greatest importance occurred in South America. In June, Bolívar inflicted a severe defeat upon the army of Morillo at Carabobo. In July, his great rival and associate, San Martín, had entered Lima, bringing the revolution to Peru, the last and most faithful of Spain's American provinces. In August, the Spanish acting viceroy in Mexico, General O'Donoju, signed a treaty with the revolutionary forces in that province on the basis of independence. The facts of the situation pointed toward the complete success of the revolutionists. In March, 1822, the President finally sent to Congress a message recommending that the independence of the new states be acknowledged, and that provision for the sending of ministers be made.

In a sense, the policy of the American government had been prudence itself. Yet in another sense, the recognition of colonial independence was a bold and decisive act, when considered in relation to the past policy of the United States, and to the political situation in 1822. In the earlier period of the discussion of the South American question there was a distinct desire to conciliate European opinion, and even to strengthen the position of the government by active coöperation with European powers. This attitude was never carried to the point of subserviency. The American government never concealed its sympathy with the colonial cause, or its conviction that the only solution of the colonial question lay in the recognition of colonial independence. The language of Adams on this point is unequivocal. "We can neither accede to nor approve of any interference to restore any part of the Spanish supremacy in any of the Spanish American provinces," he wrote to Gallatin, the minister of the United States at Paris, in his instructions of May, 1818, with the pending Congress of Aix-la-Chapelle in mind. "We cannot approve any interposition of other powers, unless it be to promote the total independence, political and commercial, of the colonies," he declared to Campbell, American minister at St. Petersburg, at about the same time. There is nothing of the tone of undue deference in such declarations. But, although the United States thus clearly avowed its views, there was, none the less, great reluctance on the part of the administration to act alone, and in opposition to Europe. In May, 1818, Monroe suggested to his cabinet the possibility of a concert of action with Great Britain to promote the independence of the new states, and he renewed the proposal to Adams two months later. His point of view in regard to the matter had the ardent support of Calhoun. As for Adams himself, his first instincts were to oppose such a policy. The American Secretary of State was not by instinct a coöperator. And yet, despite his temperamental preference for independent action, his policy in 1818 was not based on that preference. His instructions to Gallatin and Campbell professed a desire to act in harmony with the allied powers. In December, 1818, he directly suggested to Bagot, the British minister, concerted action for the recognition of La Plata; at about the same time he told Hyde de Neuville that he hoped France would be prepared to move with the United States; and considerably later, toward the end of 1819, he assured the Russian minister, Poletica, that his desire in these earlier overtures had been to lay the foundations of a general understanding on the colonial question.

When these facts are considered in their entirety, the recognition of the colonies in 1822 assumes a new significance. It required a considerable alteration of American policy to ignore the attitude of the powers of the Old World, and base American action on American interests and sympathies, and nothing else.

This is particularly true when the general European situation is considered. The tendencies of European politics at the close of the Napoleonic wars are too well known to require more than the briefest summary here. They were characterized by the efforts of the Tsar Alexander to found a world alliance for the maintenance of European order. They were characterized by the effort to transact European business in congresses dominated by the great powers. They were characterized by a strong attachment to order, and a strong aversion to revolution. From the time of the Congress of Vienna, the tide of events in the Old World flowed strongly toward reaction. But the events of 1820 and 1821 accentuated that tendency. It needed the actual outbreak of revolution in Spain and in Naples and in Piedmont to develop the new gospel of order to its full. In the Troppau protocol of October, 1820, the three Eastern courts, Russia, Prussia, and Austria, committed themselves to the doctrine that it was the sacred duty of the great states of Europe, in case of danger, to put down pernicious uprisings by force of arms. In the course of the next year, the constitutional movements in Naples and Piedmont were snuffed out summarily, and there was already talk of similar action in Spain. At a time when, in the Old World, the detestation of revolution was finding deeper and deeper expression, it was an act of no equivocal character on the part of the United States to proclaim to the world its recognition of the republics of South America, and to set the seal of its approval on governments which in Continental Europe were regarded by the constituted authorities as fit subjects of moral odium.

Moreover, the administration, when it acted, acted with the most striking independence. It consulted with no European power; it gave no warning to any European chancellery of what was coming; and it paid no attention whatsoever to the situation which existed in Spain. It reckoned not at all with the fact that Ferdinand was in the power of his revolutionary subjects, and that recognition under such circumstances would be particularly distasteful to the legitimists of the Old World; it reckoned no more with the fact that the Spanish constitutionalists were making, or at least professing to make, new efforts at the reconciliation of the colonies with the mother country. Its action was taken on a purely American basis, and from a purely American point of view. It is thus inevitably a fact of profound significance; and its whole character makes it a fitting presage for the still more striking declaration of 1823. . . .

In the discussions upon the northwest controversy, as has been seen, trading influences contributed very materially to the stand which was taken by the administration. But it would be difficult to prove anything of the kind with regard to the warning given to Europe against intervention in South America. This is not to say that such influences necessarily played no rôle at all. John Quincy Adams, of course, came from the great shipping section of the Union. In his instructions to the American ministers sent out to Colombia and La Plata in the spring of 1823, he had laid a very considerable emphasis upon freedom of commercial opportunity, though he was by no means exuberantly optimistic as to the possibilities of the South American trade. In the cabinet discussions of November, he had, on one occasion, brought forward as a reason for action the fact that if the United States stood aside and Great Britain alone vetoed the designs of the Continental powers, the latter country would gain great commercial advantages. It is worth noting, too, that our commerce with the Spanish-American states was considerably more important in 1823 than it had been two or three years before. But these facts would be a slender foundation on which to base an "economic interpretation" of the Monroe Doctrine. And they are offset by many others. Whoever reads the pages of Adams's diary will find it hard to believe that trading considerations played a very considerable rôle in his mind. The distaste produced by the homilies of the Tsar, a genuine and robust disapproval of the trend of European politics, a desire to set forth the political doctrines of the United States in opposition to those of the Alliance, these are the factors that bulked largest in his thought. Economic considerations there may have been in the background. But it was a profound political antagonism that gave force to the action which he advocated in the councils of President Monroe.

With the President himself, this antagonism was even more keenly felt. The letter to Jefferson, written early in June, seems to express his point of view pretty accurately. He was anxious to strike a blow for liberty, and the situation in the fall of 1823 offered him an excellent opportunity. To this must be added the fact that Monroe, like Calhoun, feared that an assault upon the liberties of the Spanish Americans would be dangerous to the safety of the United States itself. It was these considerations, beyond a doubt, that sharpened his pen as he wrote the declaration of December 2. . . .

Monroe's belief in the superiority of American institutions, his conviction that the extension of European dominion would be dangerous to our peace and safety—these are propositions that are hardly capable of rigorous demonstration. Perhaps their strength lies in just that fact. Yet there is, I think, one thing more to be said for them. In resting his opposition to European inter-meddling in Spanish America on the "peace and safety" of the United States, the President was taking up a strong position from the legal and moral point of view. For he was basing American policy on the right of self-preservation, a right that is and always has been recognized as fundamental in international law. If in very truth the interposition of the Holy Alliance in South America imperilled the peace and safety of the United States, then the President's right to protest against it was obvious. Nor was it to be expected that as to the reality of the peril he would accept the conclusions of European statesmen. He stood secure in his own conviction and on his own ground. . . .

Ernest R. May

 **NO**

The Making of the Monroe Doctrine

. . . Books on the [Monroe] doctrine analyzed the principles which had been announced: European powers should not help Spain regain her former colonies; European monarchies should not impose their ideology on nations in the New World; and there should be no future European colonization in the Americas. Dexter Perkins made a convincing case that the dangers envisioned had been unreal. To the extent that statesmen on the continent contemplated aiding Spain, overturning American republics, or establishing new colonies in the Western Hemisphere, they were deterred by fear of Britain, not by concern about the United States.

It was clear from the record, however, that the American doctrine had been developed in large part because Monroe and his advisers faced issues which seemed to require decisions. They had an invitation to join Britain in resisting the alleged European threat to Latin America. Everyone recognized that acceptance would mean abandonment of the posture previously held and, as Monroe put it, entanglement "in European politicks, & wars." On the other hand, Monroe, and most of those whom he consulted, saw the offer as so advantageous that it should not be turned down. Except for the maxim that there should be no future colonization, the Monroe Doctrine expressed general agreement with British positions.

Coincidentally, the administration faced the question of whether to recognize or aid Greeks who were fighting for independence from the Ottoman Empire. There was loud public demand to do so. The argument for resisting this demand was again to avoid entanglement in European politics. Daniel Webster summarized a popular view, however, when he asked how the United States could defend liberty in Latin America and ignore the same cause in Europe.

In the upshot, the British alliance did not materialize, and the United States did not lead in recognizing Greece. These decisions, even more than the rhetoric that accompanied them, reaffirmed a policy of nonentanglement. But why?

The literature on the Monroe Doctrine did not answer this question—at least not to my satisfaction. Among those who knew of the British alliance overture, everyone except Secretary of State Adams favored acceptance. Adams was the only member of the administration consistently to oppose recognition of Greece. Explaining why the outcomes were victories for Adams, Bemis says simply that his "views by the force of their reason had prevailed over everybody." (p. 390)

The same explanation appears in other accounts. In fact, however, there is no evidence that Adams changed anyone's opinion. His own diary records that his colleagues held much the same views at the end as at the beginning. Yet Adams got what he wanted.

When puzzling about what besides Adams's persuasive powers might have produced this outcome, I remembered what had struck me when poring through his manuscripts—the quantity of diary entries and especially correspondence that had to do with the approaching presidential election. It was a preoccupation in his household. His wife characterized the coming contest as "a mighty struggle which arouses alike all the passions and most ardent feelings of mankind." And, as it happened, most of his rivals were in one way or another participants in the foreign debate. William H. Crawford and John C. Calhoun were fellow members of Monroe's cabinet. Henry Clay was the speaker of the house. Andrew Jackson, who had just begun to be talked of as a candidate, was a newly elected member of the Senate. None of the existing accounts of the Monroe Doctrine makes more than passing reference to the "mighty struggle" which filled the mind of Mrs. Adams. Yet the more I thought about it, the more I became convinced that the struggle for the presidency might provide a key to understanding why the foreign policy debates came out as they did.

. . . I explore three hypotheses. The first is that the positions of the various policymakers were largely determined by their ideas of national interest and their personal interplay—in other words, that Adams's convictions were more definite and firm and he more stubborn and forceful than the others. The second is that the outcomes are best understood as products of international politics. The hypothesis is that, in view of what other governments were doing, the range of options open to Americans was very narrow, and the choices actually made were those which would have been made in the same circumstances by almost any reasonable men. The third hypothesis is that the whole process was governed by domestic politics. The positions of the policymakers were determined less by conviction than by ambition. They had different stakes riding on the outcomes, and Adams had a greater stake than the others.

No one of these hypotheses seems to me inherently the more plausible. In a study of American foreign policy during and after World War II, I concluded that convictions about "lessons" of history were a controlling force. Examining in more detail the China policy of that period, I found the strength of character of Secretary of State Marshall a critical determinant. In analyzing American policy during World War I, I was most impressed by the extent to which international politics constrained decision-makers in Washington. In the case of the Monroe Doctrine, however, my conclusion is that the outcomes are best explained in terms of domestic politics. . . .

⋯⊙⋯

Domestic Politics

. . . The men who constructed the Monroe Doctrine were all deeply interested in the approaching presidential election. Indeed, it is not too much to say that this subject preoccupied most of them. Mrs. Adams's diary and letters testify that this was the case for her husband, and his own diary suggests the same. Calhoun's nonofficial correspondence for the period dealt with little else. The same is true of Crawford and Clay. We should therefore examine the stakes for which these men were competing and the strategies which they had adopted, for it seems likely that expectations and fears related to the election could well have influenced their reasoning about the pressing issues of foreign policy. . . .

Throughout, Clay's chief target was Adams. In the summer of 1822, probably with Clay's knowledge if not connivance, a document was issued that accused Adams of having truckled to the British during the peace negotiations at Ghent and having shown a willingness to sacrifice the interests of westerners to those of New England fishermen. The author was Jonathan Russell of Rhode Island who, along with Clay and Adams, had been a member of the delegation at Ghent. All the while, newspapers supporting Clay emphasized Adams's Federalist past, his possible pro-British inclinations, and the likelihood that he represented narrow sectional interests.

The logic of this campaign was self-evident. If Clay could make it appear that he alone was the nationalist candidate, he might rally to himself western and northern Republicans whose concern was to prevent the election of Crawford, the triumph of the Radicals, and the preservation of a southern dynasty.

Adams's strategy was partly dictated by these attacks from Clay, some of which were echoed by supporters of Crawford and Calhoun. He had the advantage of being the only prominent candidate who was not a slaveholder. He thus had some chance of capitalizing on the antislavery sentiment that had manifested itself in the North, parts of the West, and even parts of the South during the controversy of 1819–1820 over the admission of Missouri as a state. He had the disadvantages of being his father's son, a former Federalist, and a citizen of a state that was viewed as having interests adverse to those of many other states. Adams needed to establish his credentials as a Republican, a patriot, and a man with a national and not just sectional perspective. . . .

Like Clay, Adams set forth a foreign policy platform. He did so in 1821 in a Fourth of July speech delivered in Washington and subsequently published not only in pro-Adams newspapers but as a pamphlet. Much of his speech simply attacked Britain. Poletica, then the Russian minister to the United States, characterized it as "from one end to the other nothing but a violent diatribe against England, intermingled with republican exaggerations." Also, however, the speech included a prophecy that colonialism would not survive anywhere. Giving more than an intimation of the forthcoming administration decision to recognize some of the Latin American republics, these passages answered Clay's implied accusation that Adams lacked sympathy for people struggling for independence. Also, Adams's speech countered Clay's appeal for a counterpoise to the Holy Alliance by calling in strident language for America to avoid involvement in European politics and to guard above all her own security and peace. "Wherever the standard of freedom or independence has been or shall be unfurled, there will her heart, her benedictions, and her prayers be," said Adams in the lines best to be remembered later. "But she goes not abroad in search of monsters to destroy. She is the well-wisher to the freedom and independence of all. She is the champion and vindicator only of her own."

Characterizing his speech variously as a direct reply to Clay's Lexington speech and as an address "to and for *man,* as well as to and for my country," Adams emphasized to various correspondents how plainly it demonstrated his hostility to the British. To a friendly Philadelphia editor, he wrote that he had meant to warn the British against yielding to their "malignant passions." To another prominent Philadelphian, he explained, "I thought it was high time that we should be asking ourselves, where we were in our relations with that country." Adams manifestly hoped that his Fourth of July oration would put to rest any suspicion that he was an Anglophile.

In the following year, when there appeared Jonathan Russell's indictment of his conduct at Ghent, Adams set aside all but the most imperative business and employed the better part of his summer composing a book-length answer. Being diligent enough and lucky enough to find the originals of some documents that Russell had misquoted and misused, Adams succeeded in demolishing Russell's case. The episode, had, however, demonstrated that the charge of partiality to Britain was a hydra he would have to fight as long as he remained a candidate, and thereafter he continually hacked at it. The *National Journal,* a newspaper started in Washington in November 1823 as a personal organ for Adams, asserted that independence of Britain and the rest of the Old World would remain the chord of its editorial policy.

In campaigning for the presidency, Adams faced problems that did not face Clay, for he was responsible for what happened as well as for what was said. Apparently, he felt that mere rhetoric would have little practical effect on the policies of other governments toward the United States. Otherwise he would not have drafted the notes and dispatches which Crawford criticized and Monroe fretfully modified nor would he have assailed Great Britain in a public speech. On the other hand, he showed keen concern lest the Monroe administration *do* something that would provoke anger or reprisals abroad. After recognition of the Latin American republics, he counseled Monroe to postpone actually sending envoys until reactions had been reported from London and the continental capitals. He fought in the cabinet against any encouragement of an independence movement in Cuba. The prospect that independence might be followed by American annexation, he argued, could lead the British to take preemptive action and seize the island. Similarly, though publicly declaring himself sympathetic with the Greeks, Adams was emphatic in cabinet in opposing any official encouragement. He protested even the proposal that a fact-finding commission be dispatched, as had been done early on for some of the Latin American states. Both the British and the Holy Allies, he warned, could take offense.

The contrast between the boldness of Adams's language and the cautiousness of his actions was due in part, of course, to differences between his role as candidate and his role as responsible statesman. But Adams's efforts to avoid actual trouble with England or the continental powers also served his interests as a candidate. In the first place, he had to be aware that any real trouble with a foreign nation would be blamed on him. If the trouble were with England, the result could be fatally to weaken Adams's base of support in the sea-dependent New England states and among Anglophiles and former Federalists who, while they were sure to deplore his campaign oratory, might nevertheless vote for him as a lesser evil. In the second place, Adams could not ignore the fact that, if war began to seem imminent, public attention would shift away from the accomplishments for which he could claim credit, such as the annexation of Florida, and focus instead on the probable demands of the conflict to come. Notice, publicity, and interest would go to Calhoun, the secretary of war, who had been a clamorous advocate of preparedness, or perhaps to the military hero, Jackson. Reasons of politics as well as reasons of state could have led Adams to the positions he took within the cabinet.

Adams's optimum strategy thus involved preserving relative tranquility in the nation's international relations while at the same time persuading the doubtful that he was as patriotic and anti-British as any dyed-in-the-wool Jeffersonian and as much a nationalist and as much a partisan of the frontiersmen as was Clay. It was not a strategy easily pursued, especially by a man who felt compelled to explain to a diary the highmindedness of his every action.

Calhoun's task was simpler despite the fact that he, too, held a responsible office. The basis for his campaign was an assumption that none of the other candidates could win. He discounted Clay on the ground that no westerner could receive the votes of the North and South. Crawford would fail, he believed, because his Georgia base and Virginian support would arouse hostility in northern states where electors were chosen by popular ballot and because his advocacy of states rights would alienate people who wanted federal aid for canals, roads, and manufacturing establishments. Adams's disabilities were his identification with New England, his Federalist past, and his lack of experience on domestic issues. Calhoun thought that his own championing of internal improvements, a protective tariff, and frontier defense would capture some of Clay's constituents; his South Carolina background would bring him support in the South; and his nationalistic policies plus his Connecticut ties would allow him to win over some of Adams's partisans.

Calhoun's strategy thus involved out-Claying Clay on internal issues while seeking to chop away at Adams's credibility as a candidate. Through his Federalist allies, the newspapers established by his friends, and Pennsylvania organs controlled by the "Family Party," Calhoun advertised his positions and sounded the refrain that, if neither Clay nor Adams could win, then all opponents of Crawford and the Radicals should rally in his camp. At first, this campaign avoided direct attacks on either Clay or Adams. By 1823, however, Calhoun had become more confident. Late that summer, he directed a change in policy, writing confidentially to his lieutenants that they and the pro-Calhoun press should begin to emphasize policy differences with Adams and to call attention to the fact that Adams's onetime Federalism so compromised him that he would never win the votes of true Republicans outside New England and might even fail to win their votes there. Calhoun's strategy was thus in part complementary to Clay's. It aimed at discrediting Adams and driving him out of the race.

Crawford, too, had a simpler problem that Adams. He had to take blame or credit for what he did as secretary of the treasury, and he and his friends had continually to fight unfounded charges of misuse of funds or patronage. At least by 1823, however, he had less answerability for other activities of the administration, for it has become notorious that he opposed not only Adams and Calhoun but also Monroe on almost every domestic issue.

Crawford campaigned as, in effect, the leader of an old Jeffersonian party whose principles had been deserted by the Monroe administration. His managers branded all other candidates as actual or potential tools of the Federalists. They contended that the whole Missouri question had been gotten up by Federalists as a device for disrupting Republican unity, and they labeled the domestic programs espoused by Clay and Calhoun as Hamilton's programs in new disguise. They said and for the most part believed that, in any case, these two renegade Republicans would eventually drop out. The ultimate contest would be between Crawford and Adams. Hence they persistently voiced the theme that Adams, the ex-Federalist, was in fact the Federalist candidate.

Until late in 1823, there was no Jackson strategy, for Jackson himself was not yet committed to running, and the men urging him to do so took no action except to disparage other candidates and stimulate signs of the general's personal popularity.

As of the autumn of 1823, Adams was therefore the central figure in the presidential campaign. Clay, Calhoun, and Crawford were all concentrating on undermining him, and he was battling their efforts to tar him as a lukewarm friend of liberty, an Anglophile, a Federalist, and a candidate with a hopelessly narrow electoral base. In view of the small numbers of legislators and voters whose shifts in opinion could transform the prospects for 1824, the contest was carried on relentlessly by all parties.

Knowing the stakes and strategies of the candidates, a detached observer aware of the pressing foreign policy issues might well have made the following predictions:

- That Adams would oppose acceptance of the proffered informal alliance with England. Likely to get most of the credit or blame for anything the administration did in foreign affairs, he would be held to have been its author. Those voters disposed to worry about his possible Federalist or Anglophile proclivities might feel that their fears had been confirmed. Furthermore, Adams would be open to fresh attack from Clay for failing to maintain America's independence. The result would be to cost him important marginal votes in the West, erode his support in the Middle States, and perhaps even lose him influential backers in Vermont, New Hampshire, and Maine. Adams's political interests would be best served if the British offer were spurned.
- That Adams would also oppose actual recognition of Greece. In the first place, he was likely to fear trouble with the continental powers, producing the domestic effects that he had tried to avert by counseling Monroe to be forceful in language but cautious in deed. In the second place, he had to anticipate embarrassment from the fact that the logical person to be envoy or commissioner to Greece was Edward Everett of Harvard, who had composed the pro-Greek manifesto in the *North American Review*, made no secret of his desire to have the job, and expected Adams's help in getting it. Since Everett was a Federalist, Adams had reason to expect that the appointment would fuel Republican prejudices. On the other hand, to deny Everett the post would be to offend Federalists in

New England and elsewhere who might otherwise go to the polls for Adams and who seemed almost certain to do so if Calhoun fell out of the race. It was in Adams's interest as a candidate that any change in American posture toward Greece be postponed until after the election.

- That Crawford and Calhoun and their adherents would favor both alliance with England and recognition of Greece if Adams could be made to seem the sponsor of these acts because of the harm they might work on his election prospects.
- That Calhoun would advocate these steps with special vehemence because they promised him the added benefit of arousing public concern about a possible war and hence turning public attention to his department and to the preparedness measures which he had all along been advocating.

The test of what was and what was not in the personal political interest of the various candidates would have yielded much more specific predictions than any test based on suppositions about their ideological positions or about conditions in the politics of other countries. Moreover, most of these predictions would have been right on the nose. . . .

⁂

Implications

In the instance of the Monroe Doctrine, the positions adopted by American policymakers seem to me to be best explained as functions of their domestic ambitions—Monroe's, to leave the presidency without being followed by recrimination and to be succeeded by someone who would not repudiate his policies; Adams's, Calhoun's, and Clay's, to become President; Jefferson's, Gallatin's, and perhaps Madison's, to see Crawford succeed. Consistently with their fundamental beliefs, any of these men could have taken different positions. Adams, for example, could have reasoned just as easily as Jefferson that concert with England would guarantee America's independence, security, and peace. He actually said as much not long before the specific issues materialized. The processes producing the actual foreign policy decisions are better understood as bargaining encounters among men with differing perspectives and ambitions than as debates about the merits of different policies. And the outcomes are most explicable as ones that equilibrated the competing or conflicting interests of men with differing political assets.

This conclusion may seem cynical. It is not meant to be. For it is in fact an affirmation that foreign policy can be determined less by the cleverness or wisdom of a few policymakers than by the political structure which determines their incentives. . . .

POSTSCRIPT

Was the Monroe Doctrine of 1823 Designed to Protect the Latin American Countries from European Intervention?

The Monroe Doctrine, as it was later called, was really three paragraphs of President Monroe's annual message of December 2, 1823 to Congress. In *The Creation of a Republican Empire 1776–1865,* Volume I of *The Cambridge History of American Foreign Relations* (Cambridge University Press, 1993), Professor Bradford Perkins describes the message as "either a dreadful summary of events over the preceding year—he was perhaps the worst stylist among our early presidents—or a series of recommendations on domestic policy. But one paragraph announced the non-Colonization doctrine, and another section devoted a paragraph each to nonintervention and to isolation."

Professor Dexter Perkins was the leading expert on the Monroe Doctrine. The first of his three volumes on the subject was printed in 1927 and remains the classic work. Though other historians have differed with some of Professor Perkins interpretations, scholars still respect his multi-archival research.

Perkins argues that John Quincy Adams was the architect of the non-colonization principle. This stemmed from his negotiations with the Russians concerning the trade boundaries dominated by Russia in the Pacific Northwest. While Adams was willing to negotiate allowing Russia to extend its trade monopoly from the 55th to the 51st parallel, he convinced President Monroe to include the non-colonization principle in his annual message.

Adams was also responsible for Monroe's assertion of the principle of nonintervention into his annual message. He was afraid that the Holy Alliance of Russia, Prussia, and Austria was committed to putting down revolutions in Europe. Russia and France had already helped restore the powers of Spain's reactionary king, Ferdinand VII. Did they intend to help Spain recover her empire in Latin America?

British diplomats approached the United States with offers to issue a joint statement condemning the intervention of any European powers in Latin America to restore Spain's empire. But Adams felt that the crisis had passed by 1823 and convinced Monroe to issue a unilateral pronouncement rather than a joint one with Congress.

Finally Adams convinced Monroe to restate the principles of isolationism and the two Americas when the president eliminated from his message condemnation of French intervention in Spain and support for the Greek struggle for independence from the Ottoman Empire. The secretary of state believed it was too risky and also illogical for the United States to intervene in European affairs if we expected the European nations to stay out of Latin America.

Some historians think that Perkins' interpretation of the events is incomplete. His discussion of the economic interests of the United States is nonexistent. In the late 1950s William Appleman Williams reoriented the framework for writing diplomatic history. *The Tragedy of American History,* revised and enlarged (Delta Books, 1962) and *The Contours of American History* (World Publishing Co., 1961) emphasized the themes of "Open Door Imperialism" in the "Creation of an American Empire." William Earl Weeks has pursued these themes in his books on John Quincy Adams and American Global Empire (University of Kentucky Press, 1992) and *Building the Continental Empire: American Expansion from the Revolution to the Civil War* (Ivan R. Dee, 1996).

Perkins also neglected to study how the Latin American republics responded to the Monroe Doctrine. In 1824 Columbia suggested an alliance based on the principle of non-intervention but it was turned down. A similar request by Brazil the next year was also rejected. In 1826 when President John Quincy Adams proposed sending delegates to an inter-American Conference at Panama, it created a furor in Congress, and our delegates arrived too late to participate. Research on U.S. relations with Latin America is sketchy and outdated. Some of the best books were written in the 1930s: Gaston Nerval, *Autopsy of the Monroe Doctrine* (Macmillan Co., 1934) and Lius Quintanilla, *A Latin Speaks* (The Macmillan Co., 1934).

Professor Ernest May emphasizes the political considerations surrounding *The Making of the Monroe Doctrine* (The Belknap Press, 1985). Neither Dexter Perkins nor the writers with economic viewpoints talk about the foreign policy views of the major candidates who hope to succeed Monroe as president in 1825. By looking at the campaign for president in 1824, according to Professor May, John Quincy Adams trashes England in his speeches and convinces President Monroe to issue a unilateral rather than a joint pronouncement. This makes the future president appear to be much less pro-British than his father, President John Adams, had been in the 1790s.

May's interpretation of the electioneering politics surrounding the Monroe Doctrine has been questioned in an earlier biography of *John Quincy Adams and the Foundations of American Foreign Policy* (Harcourt, Brace, & Co., 1949) and Harry Ammon, *James Monroe* (McGraw Hill, 1971). Both authors believe that Adams and Monroe were motivated by considerations of national interest. International rather than domestic political considerations motivated Adams who believed that the Holy Alliance was not a threat to Latin America, that England had economic reasons for keeping Latin America independent, and that Monroe should assert his non-colonization and non-intervention policies unilaterally.

For a sustained critique of May's book, see Harry Ammon, "Monroe Doctrine: Domestic Politics or National Decision?" *Diplomatic History,* v (Winter, 1981). The best collection of essays on *The Monroe Doctrine,* though old, remains edited by Armon Rappaport (D.C. Health and Co., 1964). Two recent biographies deserve notice: Noble E. Cunningham, Jr., *The Presidency of James Monroe* (University Press of Kansas, 1996) and Paul C. Nagel, *John Quincy Adams: A Public Life, A Private Life* (Knopf, 1998).

ISSUE 10

Was Andrew Jackson's Indian Removal Policy Motivated by Humanitarian Impulses?

YES: Robert V. Remini, from *Andrew Jackson and the Course of American Freedom, 1822–1832, vol. 2* (Harper & Row, 1981)

NO: Anthony F. C. Wallace, from *The Long, Bitter Trail: Andrew Jackson and the Indians* (Hill & Wang, 1993)

ISSUE SUMMARY

YES: Historical biographer Robert V. Remini argues that Andrew Jackson did not seek to destroy Native American life and culture. He portrays Jackson as a national leader who sincerely believed that the Indian Removal Act of 1830 was the only way to protect Native Americans from annihilation at the hands of white settlers.

NO: Historian and anthropologist Anthony F. C. Wallace contends that Andrew Jackson oversaw a harsh policy with regard to Native Americans. This policy resulted in the usurpation of land, attempts to destroy tribal culture, and the forcible removal of Native Americans from the southeastern United States to a designated territory west of the Mississippi River.

Andrew Jackson's election to the presidency in 1828 ushered in an era marked by a growing demand for political and economic opportunities for the "common man." As the "people's president," Jackson embodied the democratic ideal in the United States. In his role as chief executive, Jackson symbolized a strong philosophical attachment to the elimination of impediments to voting (at least for adult white males), the creation of opportunities for the common man to participate directly in government through officeholding, and the destruction of vestiges of economic elitism that served only the rich, well-born, and able. In addition, Jackson was a nationalist who defended states' rights as long as those rights did not threaten the sanctity of the Union.

The rise of Jacksonian democracy occurred during a dramatic territorial growth increase in the years immediately following the War of 1812. A new state joined the Union each year between 1816 and 1821. As the populations of these states increased, white citizens demanded that their governments, at both the state and national levels, do something about the Native American tribes in their midst who held claims to land in these regions by virtue of previous treaties. (Jackson had negotiated several of these treaties. Some included provisions for the members of the southern tribes to remain on their lands in preparation for obtaining citizenship.) Most white settlers preferred the removal of Native Americans to western territories where, presumably, they could live unencumbered forever. The result was the "Trail of Tears," the brutal forced migration of Native Americans in the 1830s that resulted in the loss of thousands of lives.

According to historian Wilcomb Washburn, "No individual is more closely identified with . . . the policy of removal of the Indians east of the Mississippi to lands west of the river—than President Andrew Jackson." While most historians are in agreement with the details of Jackson's Indian removal policy, there is significant debate with respect to his motivation. Did Jackson's racist antipathy to the Indians pave the way for the "Trail of Tears"? Or did he support this policy out of a humanitarian desire to protect Native Americans from the impending wrath of white settlers and their state governments who refused to negotiate with the southern tribes as sovereign nations?

In the following selection, Robert V. Remini, Jackson's foremost biographer, states that the criticism of Jackson's Indian Removal Act is unfair. He argues that Jackson firmly believed that removal was the only policy that would prevent the decimation of Native Americans. Remini concludes that Jackson attempted to deal as fairly as possible with the representatives of the Choctaws, Cherokees, Chickasaws, Creeks, and Seminoles, known then as the "Five Civilized Tribes."

In the second selection, Anthony F. C. Wallace maintains that Jackson viewed Native Americans as savages and, although he did not propose their extermination, he supported a policy of coercion to force their removal from the southeastern states. This approach, according to Wallace, was consistent with several powerful forces in Democratic politics, including the exaltation of the common white man, expansionism, and open acceptance of racism.

YES

Robert V. Remini

"Brothers, Listen . . . You Must Submit"

It is an awesome contradiction that at the moment the United States was entering a new age of economic and social betterment for its citizens—the industrial revolution underway, democracy expanding, social and political reforms in progress—the Indians were driven from their homes and forced to seek refuge in remote areas west of the Mississippi River. [Andrew] Jackson, the supreme exponent of liberty in terms of preventing government intervention and intrusion, took it upon himself to expel the Indians from their ancient haunts and decree that they must reside outside the company of civilized white men. It was a depressing and terrible commentary on American life and institutions in the 1830s.

The policy of white Americans toward Indians was a shambles, right from the beginning. Sometimes the policy was benign—such as sharing educational advantages—but more often than not it was malevolent. Colonists drove the Indians from their midst, stole their lands and, when necessary, murdered them. To the colonists, Indians were inferior and their culture a throwback to a darker age.

When independence was declared and a new government established committed to liberty and justice for all, the situation of the Indians within the continental limits of the United States contradicted the ennobling ideas of both the Declaration and the Constitution. Nevertheless, the Founding Fathers convinced themselves that men of reason, intelligence and good will could resolve the Indian problem. In their view the Indians were "noble savages," arrested in cultural development, but they would one day take their rightful place beside white society. Once they were "civilized" they would be absorbed.

President George Washington formulated a policy to encourage the "civilizing" process, and Jefferson continued it. They presumed that once the Indians adopted the practice of private property, built homes, farmed, educated their children, and embraced Christianity these Native Americans would win acceptance from white Americans. Both Presidents wished the Indians to become cultural white men. If they did not, said Jefferson, then they must be driven to the Rocky Mountains.

The policy of removal was first suggested by Jefferson as the alternative to the "civilizing" process, and as far as many Americans were concerned removal

From Robert V. Remini, *Andrew Jackson and the Course of American Freedom, 1822–1832, vol. 2* (Harper & Row, 1981). Copyright © 1981 by Robert V. Remini. Notes omitted.

made more sense than any other proposal. Henry Clay, for example, insisted that it was impossible to civilize these "savages." They were, he argued, inferior to white men and "their disappearance from the human family would be no great loss to the world."

Despite Clay's racist notions—shared by many Americans—the government's efforts to convert the Indians into cultural white men made considerable progress in the 1820s. The Cherokees, in particular, showed notable technological and material advances as a result of increased contact with traders, government agents, and missionaries, along with the growth of a considerable population of mixed-bloods.

As the Indians continued to resist the efforts to get rid of them—the thought of abandoning the land on which their ancestors lived and died was especially painful for them—the states insisted on exercising jurisdiction over Indian lands within their boundaries. It soon became apparent that unless the federal government instituted a policy of removal it would have to do something about protecting the Indians against the incursions of the states. But the federal government was feckless. It did neither. Men like President John Quincy Adams felt that removal was probably the only policy to follow but he could not bring himself to implement it. Nor could he face down a state like Georgia. So he did nothing. Many men of good will simply turned their faces away. They, too, did nothing.

Not Jackson. He had no hesitation about taking action. And he believed that removal was indeed the only policy available if the Indians were to be protected from certain annihilation. His ideas about the Indians developed from his life on the frontier, his expansionist dreams, his commitment to states' rights, and his intense nationalism. He saw the nation as an indivisible unit whose strength and future were dependent on its ability to repel outside foes. He wanted all Americans from every state and territory to participate in his dream of empire, but they must acknowledge allegiance to a permanent and indissoluble bond under a federal system. Although devoted to states' rights and limited government in Washington, Jackson rejected any notion that jeopardized the safety of the United States. That included nullification and secession. That also included the Indians. . . .

The Indian Removal Act of 1830 authorized Jackson to carry out the policy outlined in his first message to Congress. He could exchange unorganized public land in the trans-Mississippi west for Indian land in the east. Those Indians who moved would be given perpetual title to their new land as well as compensation for improvements on their old. The cost of their removal would be absorbed by the federal government. They would also be given assistance for their "support and subsistence" for the first year after removal. An appropriation of $500,000 was authorized to carry out these provisions.

This monumental piece of legislation spelled the doom of the American Indian. It was harsh, arrogant, racist—and inevitable. It was too late to acknowledge any rights for the Indians. As [Senator Theodore] Frelinghuysen [of New Jersey] remarked, all the white man had ever said to the Indian from the moment they first came into contact was "give!" Once stripped of his possessions the Indian was virtually abandoned.

Of the many significant predictions and warnings voiced during the debates in Congress that eventually came true, two deserve particular attention. One of them made a mockery of Jackson's concern for freedom. The President insisted that the Indians would not be forced to remove. If they wished to reside within the state they might do so but only on condition that they understood they would be subject to state law. He would never force them to remove, never compel them to surrender their lands. That high and noble sentiment as interpreted by land-greedy state officials meant absolutely nothing. Fraud and deception also accompanied the exchange of land. Jackson himself tried desperately to discourage corruption among the government agents chosen to arrange the removal, but the events as they actually transpired ran totally opposite to what he expected and promised.

The other prediction that mocked Jackson's commitment to economy was the cost of the operation. In the completed legislation the Congress had appropriated $500,000 but the actual cost of removal is incalculable. For one thing the process extended over many years and involved many tribes. Naturally some Indians resisted Jackson's will and the government was required to apply force. The resulting bloodshed and killing and the cost of these Indian wars cannot be quantified. For a political party that prized economy above almost everything else the policy of Indian removal was a radial departure from principle. Still many Democrats argued that the actual cost was a small price to pay for the enormous expanse of land that was added to the American empire. In Jackson's eight years in office seventy-odd treaties were signed and ratified, which added 100 million acres of Indian land to the public domain at a cost of roughly $68 million and 32 million acres of land west of the Mississippi River. The expense was enormous, but so was the land-grab.

Andrew Jackson has been saddled with a considerable portion of the blame for this monstrous deed. He makes an easy mark. But the criticism is unfair if it distorts the role he actually played. His objective was not the destruction of Indian life and culture. Quite the contrary. He believed that removal was the Indian's only salvation against certain extinction. Nor did he despoil Indians. He struggled to prevent fraud and corruption, and he promised there would be no coercion in winning Indian approval of his plan for removal. Yet he himself practiced a subtle kind of coercion. He told the tribes he would abandon them to the mercy of the states if they did not agree to migrate west.

The Indian problem posed a terrible dilemma and Jackson had little to gain by attempting to resolve it. He could have imitated his predecessors and done nothing. But that was not Andrew Jackson. He felt he had a duty. And when removal was accomplished he felt he had done the American people a great service. He felt he had followed the "dictates of humanity" and saved the Indians from certain death.

Not that the President was motivated by concern for the Indians—their language or customs, their culture, or anything else. Andrew Jackson was motivated principally by two considerations: first, his concern for the military safety of the United States, which dictated that Indians must not occupy areas that might jeopardize the defense of this nation; and second, his commitment to the principle that all persons residing within states are subject to the jurisdiction and laws of those states. Under no circumstances did Indian tribes constitute sovereign entities when they occupied territory within existing state boundaries. The quickest way to undermine the security of the Union, he argued, was to jeopardize the sovereignty of the states by recognizing Indian tribes as a third sovereignty.

But there was a clear inconsistency—if not a contradiction—in this argument. If the tribes were not sovereign why bother to sign treaties (requiring Senate approval) for their land? Actually Jackson appreciated the inconsistency, and it bothered him. He never really approved of bargaining or negotiating with tribes. He felt that Congress should simply determine what needed to be done and then instruct the Indians to conform to it. Congress can "occupy and possess" any part of Indian territory, he once said, "whenever the safety, interest or defence of the country" dictated. But as President, Jackson could not simply set aside the practice and tradition of generations because of a presumed contradiction. So he negotiated and signed treaties with dozens of tribes, at the same time denying that they enjoyed sovereign rights.

The reaction of the American people to Jackson's removal policy was predictable. Some were outraged, particularly the Quakers and other religious groups. Many seemed uncomfortable about it but agreed that it had to be done. Probably a larger number of Americans favored removal and applauded the President's action in settling the Indian problem once and for all. In short, there was no public outcry against it. In fact it was hardly noticed. The horror of removal with its "Trail of Tears" came much later and after Jackson had left office.

Apart from everything else, the Indian Removal Act served an important political purpose. For one thing it forced Jackson to exercise leadership as the head of the Democratic party within Congress. It prepared him for even bigger battles later on. For another it gave "greater ideological and structural coherence" to the party. It separated loyal and obedient friends of the administration from all others. It became a "distinguishing feature" of Jacksonian Democrats. . . .

According to the Treaty of Dancing Rabbit Creek, the Choctaws agreed to evacuate all their land in Mississippi and emigrate to an area west of the Arkansas Territory to what is now Oklahoma. In addition the Indians would receive money, household and farm equipment, subsistence for one year, and reimbursement for improvements on their vacated property. In effect the Choctaws ceded to the United States 10.5 million acres of land east of the Mississippi River. They promised to emigrate in stages: the first group in the fall of 1831, the second in 1832, and the last in 1833.

Jackson immediately submitted the treaty to Congress when it reconvened in December, 1830, and [Secretary of War John] Eaton, in his annual report, assured the members that agreement was reached through persuasion only. No secret agreements, no bribes, no promises. Everything had been open and aboveboard! The Senate swallowed the lie whole and ratified the treaty on February 25, 1831, by a vote of 35 to 12. Said one Choctaw chief: "Our doom is sealed."

Since the Treaty of Dancing Rabbit Creek was the first to win Senate approval the President was very anxious to make it a model of removal. He wanted everything to go smoothly so that the American people would understand that removal was humane and beneficial to both the Indians and the

American nation at large. Furthermore, he hoped its success would encourage other tribes to capitulate to his policy and thereby send a veritable human tide streaming across the Mississippi into the plains beyond.

The actual removal of the Choctaw Nation violated every principle for which Jackson stood. From start to finish the operation was a fraud. Corruption, theft, mismanagement, inefficiency—all contributed to the destruction of a once-great people. The Choctaws asked to be guided to their new country by General George Gibson, a man they trusted and with whom they had scouted their new home. Even this was denied them. The bureaucracy dictated another choice. So they left the "land of their fathers" filled with fear and anxiety. To make matters worse the winter of 1831–1832 was "living hell." The elements conspired to add to their misery. The suffering was stupefying. Those who watched the horror never forgot it. Many wept. The Indians themselves showed not a single sign of their agony.

Jackson tried to prevent this calamity but he was too far away to exercise any real control, and the temptations and opportunities for graft and corruption were too great for some agents to resist. When he learned of the Choctaw experience and the suffering involved, Jackson was deeply offended. He did what he could to prevent its recurrence. He proposed a new set of guidelines for future removals. He hoped they would reform the system and erase mismanagement and the opportunity for theft.

To begin with, the entire operation of Indian removal was transferred from civilian hands to the military. Then the office of commissioner of Indian affairs was established under the war department to coordinate and direct all matters pertaining to the Indians. In large part these changes reflected Jackson's anguish over what had happened to the Choctaws, but they also resulted from his concern over public opinion. Popular outrage could kill the whole program of removal. . . .

The experience of removal is one of the horror stories of the modern era. Beginning with the Choctaws it decimated whole tribes. An entire race of people suffered. What it did to their lives, their culture, their language, their customs is a tragedy of truly staggering proportions. The irony is that removal was intended to prevent this calamity.

Would it have been worse had the Indians remained in the East? Jackson thought so. He said they would "disappear and be forgotten." One thing does seem certain: the Indians would have been forced to yield to state laws and white society. Indian Nations *per se* would have been obliterated and possibly Indian civilization with them.

In October, 1832, a year and a half after the Choctaw treaty was ratified, General [John] Coffee signed a treaty with the Chickasaws that met Jackson's complete approval. "Surely the religious enthusiasts," wrote the President in conveying his delight to Coffee, "or those who have been weeping over the oppression of the Indians will not find fault with it for want of liberality or justice to the Indians." By this time Jackson had grown callous. His promise to economize got the better of him. "The stipulation that they remove at their own expence and on their own means, is an excellent feature in it. The whole treaty is just. We want them in a state of safety removed from the states and free from colision with the whites; and if the land does this it is well disposed of and freed from being a corrupting source to our Legislature."

Coffee's success with the Chickasaws followed those with the Creeks and Seminoles. On March 24, 1832, the destruction of the Creek Nation begun with the Treaty of Fort Jackson in 1814 was completed when the chiefs signed an agreement to remove rather than fight it out in the courts. The Seminoles accepted a provisional treaty on May 9, 1832, pending approval of the site for relocation. Thus, by the close of Jackson's first administration the Choctaws, Creeks, Chickasaws, and Seminoles had capitulated. Of the so-called Five Civilized Tribes only the Cherokees held out.

Not for long. They found small consolation from the courts. The Cherokees' lawyer, William Wirt, sued in the Supreme Court for an injunction that would permit the Indians to remain in Georgia unmolested by state law. He argued that the Cherokees had a right to self-government as a foreign nation and that this right had long been recognized by the United States in its treaties with the Indians. He hoped to make it appear that Jackson himself was the nullifier of federal law. In effect he challenged the entire removal policy by asking for a restraining order against Georgia.

Chief Justice John Marshall in the case *Cherokee Nation* v. *Georgia* handed down his opinion on March 18, 1831. He rejected Wirt's contention that the Cherokees were a sovereign nation. He also rejected Jackson's insistence that they were subject to state law. The Indians, he said, were "domestic dependent nations," subject to the United States as a ward to a guardian. They were not subject to individual states, he declared. Indian territory was in fact part of the United States.

The Indians chose to regard the opinion as essentially favorable in that it commanded the United States to protect their rights and property. So they refused to submit—either to Georgia or to Jackson. Meanwhile, Georgia passed legislation in late December, 1830, prohibiting white men from entering Indian country after March 1, 1831, without a license from the state. This was clearly aimed at troublesome missionaries who encouraged Indians in their "disobedience." Samuel A. Worcester and Dr. Elizur Butler, two missionaries, defied the law; they were arrested and sentenced to four years imprisonment in a state penitentiary. They sued, and in the case *Worcester* v. *Georgia* the Supreme Court decided on March 3, 1832, that the Georgia law was unconstitutional. Speaking for the majority in a feeble voice, John Marshall croaked out the court's decision. All the laws of Georgia dealing with the Cherokees were unconstitutional, he declared. He issued a formal mandate two days later ordering the Georgia Superior Court to reverse its decision.

Georgia, of course, had refused to acknowledge the court's right to direct its actions and had boycotted the judicial proceedings. The state had no intention of obeying the court's order. Since the court adjourned almost immediately after rendering its decision nothing further could be done. According to the Judiciary Act of 1789 the Supreme Court could issue its order of compliance only when a case had already been remanded without response. Since the court would not reconvene until January, 1833, no further action by the government could take place. Thus, until the court either summoned state officials before it for contempt or issued a writ of habeas corpus for the release of the two missionaries there was nothing further to be done. The President was under no obligation to act. In fact there is some question as to whether the court itself could act since the existing habeas corpus law did not apply in this case because the missionaries were not being detained by federal authorities. And since the Superior Court of Georgia did not acknowledge in writing its refusal to obey, Marshall's decision could not be enforced. Jackson understood this. He knew there was nothing for him to do. "The decision of the supreme court has fell still born," he wrote John Coffee, "and they find that it cannot coerce Georgia to yield to its mandate."

It was later reported by Horace Greeley that Jackson's response to the Marshall decision was total defiance. "Well: John Marshall has made his decision: *now let him enforce it!*" Greeley cited George N. Briggs, a Representative from Massachusetts, as his source for the statement. The quotation certainly sounds like Jackson and many historians have chosen to believe that he said it. The fact is that Jackson did not say it because there was no reason to do so. There was nothing for him to enforce. Why, then, would he refuse an action that no one asked him to take? As he said, the decision was stillborn. The court rendered an opinion which abandoned the Indians to their inevitable fate. "It cannot coerce Georgia to yield to its mandate," said Jackson, "and I believe [Major John] Ridge has expressed despair, and that it is better for them [the Cherokees] to treat and move."

Even if Jackson did not use the exact words Greeley put into his mouth, even if no direct action was required at the moment, some historians have argued that the quotation represents in fact Jackson's true attitude. There is evidence that Jackson "sportively said in private conversation" that if summoned "to support the decree of the Court he will call on those who have brought about the decision to enforce it." Actually nobody expected Jackson to enforce the decision, including the two missionaries, and therefore a lot of people simply assumed that the President would defy the court if pressured. In the rush to show Jackson as bombastic and blustery, however, an important point is missed. What should be remembered is that Jackson reacted with extreme caution to this crisis because a precipitous act could have triggered a confrontation with Georgia. Prudence, not defiance, characterized his reaction to both the challenge of Georgia and later the threat of nullification by South Carolina. As one historian has said, Jackson deserves praise for his caution in dealing with potentially explosive issues and should not be condemned for his so-called inaction.

Still the President had encouraged Georgia in its intransigence. He shares responsibility in producing this near-confrontation. He was so desperate to achieve Indian removal that he almost produced a crisis between federal and state authorities. Nor can it be denied, as one North Carolina Congressman observed, that "Gen Jackson could by a nod of the head or a crook of the finger induce Georgia to submit to the law. It is by the promise or belief of his countenance and support that Georgia is stimulated to her disorderly and rebellious conduct."

Jackson chose not to nod his head or crook his finger for several reasons, the most important of which was his determination to remove the Cherokees. But he had other concerns. As the time neared for the Supreme Court to reconvene and deliberate on Georgia's defiance, a controversy with South Carolina over nullification developed. Jackson had to be extremely careful that no action of his induced Georgia to join South Carolina in the dispute. Nullification might lead to secession and civil war. He therefore maneuvered to isolate South Carolina and force Georgia to back away from its position of confrontation. He needed to nudge Georgia into obeying the court order and free the two missionaries. Consequently he moved swiftly to win removal of the Indians. His secretary of war worked quietly to convince the legal counsel for the missionaries and the friends of the Cherokees in Congress, such as Theodore Frelinghuysen, that the President would not budge from his position nor interfere in the operation of Georgia laws and that the best solution for everyone was for the Indians to remove. Meanwhile the Creeks capitulated, and a treaty of removal was ratified by the Senate in April, 1832.

Although Senator Frelinghuysen "prayed to God" that Georgia would peacefully acquiesce in the decision of the Supreme Court he soon concluded that the Cherokees must yield. Even Justice John McLean, who wrote a concurring opinion in the *Worcester* case, counseled the Cherokee delegation in Washington to sign a removal treaty. Van Buren's Albany Regency actively intervened because of their concern over a possible southern backlash against their leader. Van Buren himself encouraged his friend Senator John Forsyth to intercede with the newly elected governor of Georgia, Wilson Lumpkin, keeping Jackson carefully informed of his actions. More significant, however, were the letters written by the secretary of war to Lumpkin. These letters pleaded for a pardon for the two missionaries and stated that the President himself gave his unconditional endorsement of the request. Finally Forsyth conferred with William Wirt who in turn conferred with a representative of the two missionaries, and they all agreed to make no further motion before the Supreme Court. That done, Governor Lumpkin ordered the "keeper" of the penitentiary on January 14, 1833 to release Worcester and Butler under an arrangement devised by Forsyth. Thus, while the President held steady to his course and directed the activities of the men in contact with Lumpkin, both the problem of Georgia's defiance and the fate of the two missionaries were quietly resolved without injurious consequences to the rest of the nation. It was one of Jackson's finest actions as a statesman.

Ultimately, the Cherokees also yielded to the President. On December 29, 1835, at New Echota a treaty was signed arranging an exchange of land. A protracted legal argument had gained the Indians a little time but nothing else. Removal now applied to all eastern Indians, not simply the southern tribes. After the Black Hawk War of 1832 Jackson responded to the demands of Americans in the northwest to send all Indians beyond the Mississippi. A hungry band of Sac and Fox Indians under the leadership of Black Hawk had recrossed the Mississippi in the spring of 1832 to find food. People on the frontier panicked and Governor John Reynolds of Illinois called out the militia and appealed to Jackson for assistance. Federal troops were immediately dispatched under Generals Winfield Scott and Henry Atkinson. A short and bloody war resulted, largely instigated by drunken militia troops, and when it ended the northwestern tribes were so demoralized that they offered little resistance to Jackson's steady pressure for their removal west of the Mississippi.

The result of the Black Hawk War, said the President in his fourth message to Congress, had been very "creditable to the troops" engaged in the action. "Severe as is the lesson to the Indians," he lectured, "it was rendered necessary by their unprovoked aggressions, and it is to be hoped that its impression will be permanent and salutary."

It was useless for the Indians to resist Jackson's demands. Nearly 46,000 of them went west. Thousands died in transit. Even those under no treaty obligation to emigrate were eventually forced to remove. And the removal experiences were all pretty much like that of the Choctaws—all horrible, all rife with corruption and fraud, all disgraceful to the American nation.

The policy of removal formed an important part of Jackson's overall program of limiting federal authority and supporting states' rights. Despite the accusation of increased executive authority, Jackson successfully buttressed state sovereignty and jurisdiction over all inhabitants within state boundaries. This is a government of the people, Jackson argued, and the President is the agent of the people. The President and the Congress exercise their jurisdiction over "*the people of the union.* [W]ho are the people of the union?" he asked. Then, answering his own question, he said: "all those subject to the jurisdiction of the sovereign states, none else." Indians are also subject to the states, he went on. They are subject "to the sovereign power of the state within whose sovereign limits they reside." An "absolute independence of the Indian tribes from state authority can never bear an intelligent investigation, and a quasi independence of state authority when located within its Territorial limits is *absurd.*"

In addition to establishing the removal policy Jackson also restructured the bureaucracy handling Indian problems. Since 1824 a Bureau of Indian Affairs headed by Thomas L. McKenney had supervised the government's relations with the Indians. By the time Jackson assumed the presidency the Bureau had become an "enormous quagmire" from an administrative point of view. McKenney was retained in office to take advantage of his reputation to win passage of the Removal bill. Once Removal passed, McKenney was dismissed. (For one thing he had supported Adams in 1828). Then the Bureau was reorganized. On June 30, 1834, Congress passed the necessary legislation establishing the Office of Indian Affairs under an Indian commissioner, and this administrative machinery remained in place well into the twentieth century. The Indian service was restructured into a more cohesive operation than had previously been the case. It regularized procedures that had been practiced as a matter of custom rather than law.

Ultimately Jackson's policy of removal and reorganization of the Indian service won acceptance by most Americans. The President was seen as a forceful executive who addressed one of the nation's most bedeviling problems and solved it. Even Americans who fretted over the fate of the Indians eventually went along with removal. The policy seemed enlightened and humane. It seemed rational and logical. It constituted, Americans thought, the only possible solution to the Indian problem.

The Long, Bitter Trail: Andrew Jackson and the Indians

Georgia in the late 1820s was a prosperous and rapidly developing common-wealth. The state government encouraged the growth of an extensive system of private banks that lent money to aspiring farmers and entrepreneurs. Family farms were the norm; there were few cotton plantations larger than 500 acres. Railroads and shallow-draft steamboats were opening up the agricultural interior and connecting the cotton country with seaports at Savannah and Brunswick, through which passed the trade not only with Great Britain but also with the industrial Northern states. Georgia was less inclined than her neighbor South Carolina to espouse the doctrine of nullification, so hateful to President Jackson, propounded by that state's legislature and advocated by her native son Vice President John C. Calhoun. Increasingly, too, the Georgia electorate was turning away from the faction headed by Jackson's old political rival, William H. Crawford, and was favoring the party more friendly to the President. Jackson had motives for rewarding Georgia that went beyond his commitment to Indian removal.

Thus Georgians felt that they had the right to claim the President's sympathetic attention in time of need. And now was that time. The Cherokee constitution in effect nullified Georgia law and made the Indian nation a "state within a state." Left to themselves, the Cherokees would become a prosperous, independent commonwealth, and they would never sell their land (indeed, by Cherokee law, the further sale of land to the United States was a crime). On December 20, 1828, immediately after the election of Andrew Jackson as President of the United States, the Georgia legislature passed a law extending the state's jurisdiction—i.e., its laws, its police powers, and its courts—over the Cherokees living within the state. Enforcement was to be deferred until June 1, 1830, to give the President and Congress time to act in support of Georgia.

Georgia's action forced the President's hand. He must see to it that a removal policy long covertly pursued by the White House would now be enacted into law by the Congress. The new President quickly took steps to implement a removal program that would, among other things, resolve the Georgia crisis. As his Secretary of War he appointed his old friend and political supporter from Tennessee, Senator John Eaton. No doubt with the advice of Superintendent McKenney, who had convinced himself of the need for removal, Eaton included in his first (1829) Report to the President a recommendation for wholesale removal of the Eastern Indians to a self-governing "Indian territory" in the West, where the U.S. Army would protect them from intruding whites and keep the peace among the tribes.

The Twenty-first Congress convened for its first session in December 1829, and as was (and still is) the custom, the President delivered to it a message reporting on the State of the Union and making recommendations for new legislation. Not unexpectedly, he paid considerable attention to the Indian question. . . . About half the discussion of Indian affairs was devoted to the constitutional issue raised by the Cherokee claim to independence and political sovereignty within the state of Georgia. Jackson stated that in his view the Native Americans residing within the boundaries of old or new states were subject to the laws of those states. He recognized the efforts of some tribes to become "civilized" but saw the only hope for their survival to be removal to a Western territory. The rhetoric was candid but compassionate in tone, no doubt intended to disarm criticism, suggesting that removal was not merely legally justified but morally necessary, and that he was responding not to the greed of land speculators and would-be settlers but to a moral imperative to save the Indians from extinction. Emigration, of course, should be strictly voluntary with individuals. Those who chose to leave would be provided with an "ample district West of the Mississippi," to be guaranteed to them as long as they occupied it. Each tribe would have its own territory and its own government and would be free to receive "benevolent" instructors in the "arts of civilization." In the future, there might arise "an interesting commonwealth, destined to perpetuate the race, and to attest the humanity and justice of this Government." For those who chose to remain, he gave assurance that they would "without doubt" be allowed to keep possession of their houses and gardens. But he warned them that they must obey the laws of the states in which they lived, and must be prepared to give up all claims to "tracts of country on which they have neither dwelt nor made improvements, merely because they have seen them from the mountain, or passed them in the chace." Eventually, those who stayed behind could expect to "become merged in the mass of our population."

On February 24, 1830, a removal bill was reported out from the House Committee on Indian Affairs (John Bell of Tennessee, chairman). The same bill was also introduced into the Senate by its Indian Committee (also chaired by a Jackson man from Tennessee). The text of the bill . . . was briefer than the President's message recommending it. In eight sections, it authorized the President to set aside an Indian territory on public lands west of the Mississippi; to exchange districts there for land now occupied by Indians in the East; to grant the tribes absolute ownership of their new homes "forever"; to treat with tribes for the rearrangement of boundaries in order to effect the removal; to ensure that property left behind by emigrating Indians be properly appraised and fair compensation be paid; to give the emigrants "aid and assistance" on their journey and for the first year after their arrival in their new country; to protect the emigrants from hostile Indians in the West and from any other intruders; to continue the "superintendence" now exercised over the Indians by the Trade and Intercourse Laws. And to carry out these responsibilities, the Congress appropriated the sum (soon to prove woefully inadequate) of $500,000.

The debate on the bill was long and bitter, for the subject of Indian removal touched upon a number of very emotional issues: the constitutional question of states' rights versus federal prerogatives, Christian charity, national honor, racial and cultural prejudices, manifest destiny, and of course just plain greed. The opening salvo was the Report of the Indian Committee of the House. The report defended the constitutional right of the states to exercise sovereignty over residents, including Indians, within their borders. It discussed the nature of Indian title, naïvely asserting that in pre-Columbian times "the whole country was a common hunting ground"; they claimed as private or tribal property only their "moveable wigwams" and in some parts of the continent "their small corn patches." The committee declared that the Indians were incapable of "civiliza-tion," despite their recent "extravagant pretensions," so loudly touted by mis-guided zealots opposed to emigration. Among the Cherokees, the report asserted, only a small oligarchy of twenty-five or thirty families controlled the govern-ment and only these, and about two hundred mixed-blood families who made up what the report referred to as a "middle class," could claim to have made any progress toward what the committee regarded as "civilization." These favored few opposed emigration. But the remainder, allegedly living in indolence, poverty, and vice, were generally in favor of removal as the only way to escape destitution and eventual annihilation. Obviously, in the committee's view, it was not merely justifiable but morally imperative to save the Southern tribes from extinction by helping them to emigrate to the West.

Both Houses of Congress were deluged by hundreds of petitions and memorials, solicited by religious groups and benevolent societies opposed to Indian removal. Town meetings were held, particularly in the Northern states, demanding justice for the Native Americans. Joseph Hemphill, congressman from Pennsylvania, published a review of Cass's article "Indian Reform," excoriat-ing him for recommending an oppressive policy toward the Indians; and he included in his condemnation the Reverend Isaac McCoy, who had written a book, *The Practicability of Indian Reform*, urging removal as the only means of civilizing the natives. The American Board of Commissioners exerted wide influ-ence on Protestant denominations in the cause of Indian rights. Not to be out-done, friends of Jackson organized their own pro-removal missionary society, its masthead adorned with the names of prominent officials and clergymen who favored the bill. Its efforts were eclipsed by the older American Board, however, whose leader, Jeremiah Evarts, under the *nom de plume* William Penn, had already published his *Essays on the Present Crisis in the Condition of the American Indians*.

In the spring of 1830, active debate began in the chambers of Congress. The attack on the bill was launched in the Senate by Theodore Frelinghuysen of New Jersey, a distinguished lawyer whose deep religious convictions had already earned him the respect of colleagues in both parties. Frelinghuysen, a Whig, was an example of the "Christian party in politics," for at one time or another he was president of the American Board of Commissioners for Foreign Missions (sixteen years), president of the American Bible Society (sixteen years), president of the American Tract Society (six years), vice president of the American Sunday School Union (fifty years), and for many years an officer of the American Temperance Union and the American Colonization Society. His stand on the Indian question was to earn him a national reputation as "the Christian states-man" and in 1844 a place on the Whig ticket as (unsuccessful) candidate for Vice President of the United States, along with Henry Clay for President. Senator Frelinghuysen's speech, which took three days to deliver, pointed out that the Indian policy of the United States, from the time of Washington on, had been based on the principle that the United States was obligated to protect peaceful natives living in unceded territory from intrusion by whites under any pretext, by force if necessary. Treaties with the Native Americans, according to the Constitution, were, like other treaties, the law of the land. The Jackson Adminis-tration, by refusing to enforce existing treaties, was violating the Constitution.

Why was more Indian land needed now, when annual sales of public lands amounted to no more than 1 million acres? The Indian occupants of the continent had already peacefully sold more than 214 million acres, and much of that remained vacant. To be sure, hunters would eventually sell to agricul-turists, but willingly and in response to reasonable argument, not by coercion, as this bill, in the hands of this administration, promised. Furthermore, many of the Native Americans, in response to the official reform policy of the United States government, were adopting white customs and could be expected to amalgamate with the whites, if left alone where they were. Frelinghuysen con-cluded with an essentially moral appeal:

> Sir, if we abandon these aboriginal proprietors of our soil, these early allies and adopted children of our forefathers, how shall we justify it to our country? . . . How shall we justify this trespass to ourselves? . . . Let us beware how, by oppressive encroachments upon the sacred privileges of our Indian neighbors, we minister to the agonies of future remorse.

The pro-removal reply to Frelinghuysen was delivered by Senator John Forsyth of Georgia. Like his opponent, Forsyth was a lawyer and a former attorney general of his state. He had served as a representative in Congress, as minister to Spain (he secured the King's ratification of the 1819 treaty ceding Florida to the United States), and, most recently, he had served as governor of Georgia (1827–29). He was a loyal Jackson follower, would later support Jackson and oppose Calhoun over nullification, and in 1834 he was rewarded by appointment as Secretary of State. He was a skilled orator and had the reputation of being the best debater of his time.

Forsyth dismissed Frelinghuysen's words as a mere self-interested plea by the "Christian party in politics" to create unwarranted sympathy for the Indians, among whom their missionaries lived so prosperously. He pointed to the deplorable conditions under which the Native Americans now lived and to the long history of the removal policy. Forsyth, as a true friend of the Indians, had long had doubts that removal would promote their civilization, but he would vote for this bill because it would relieve the states "from a population useless and bothersome" and would place these wild hunters in a country better supplied with game. But most of Forsyth's time was spent on legal arguments about states' rights (particularly Georgia's) to exercise sovereignty over Indians, about old treaties and proclamations, and about natural law. He concluded that Georgia had a right to expect the United States to remove the Indians (without coercion, of course) to a happier hunting ground west of the Mississippi.

The debate raged for weeks in both the Senate and the House. Amendments were proposed in the Senate that would have weakened the bill by protecting the Indians' interests; three times these amendments were defeated by a single vote. In general, delegates from the Northern and Eastern states, many of them National Republicans, anti-Masons, and moral reformers, stood against the bill, and Southern and Western delegates—many, like Jackson, with little interest in evangelical Christianity—favored it. Eventually, on April 23, 1830, the Senate voted 28 to 19 to pass the measure. On May 24, the House passed the bill by a narrower margin, 102 to 97.

President Jackson signed the Removal Act on the same day. It was, some maintained, the "leading measure" of his administration; indeed, "the greatest question that ever came before Congress, short of the question of peace and war." Jackson himself said that Indian removal was the "most arduous part of my duty" as President.

⋄◈⋄

A fairly clear federal policy with regard to the transfer to white owners of title to newly purchased Indian lands, based on a generation of experience, was already in place when the Removal Act was passed and signed. In some cessions, individual Indians were allowed to retain small tracts, called "allotments" (in distinction to tribally owned "reservations"), generally small parcels of land around their residences. These allotments could be sold by their Indian owners to settlers or land companies by government-approved contract. The remainder of the ceded territory became part of the public lands of the United States (except for Georgia, where, by special agreement, lands purchased by the United States were turned over to the state). The usual practice of the federal government was to dispose of the public lands as quickly as possible. The lands were first surveyed and then sold, a large proportion initially at public auction at a minimum price of $1.25 an acre, and the remainder at subsequent privately arranged sales.

Meanwhile, "actual settlers" would be entering these public lands, staking out claims, building cabins, making improvements. Along with the squatters, "land lookers" sent by land companies were prowling about, identifying the best locations for speculative investment. The government did not try to stop the squatters, who often were tacitly accorded a "preemption right" to 80 or 160 acres around their improvements at the minimum price of $1.25 an acre. "Speculator" land companies, while they were condemned in political rhetoric as unfair monopolistic competitors of the "actual settler," at least sometimes supported the settlers' interests. Government did not really want to discourage the speculators any more than the settlers. After all, many politicians and officials (as we have seen, including Jackson and his friends) were speculators in Indian lands themselves, and anyway, there were rarely enough settlers on hand to buy up all the land offered for sale. Besides, some tracts like town sites required expensive development before resale to "actual settlers."

The government did not expect to realize much if any profit from the sale of the public lands. Some of the less desirable tracts, slow to move, eventually went for as little as 12½ cents an acre after languishing for up to five years. Some of the more attractive sites, on the other hand, might bring prices at auction well above the $1.25-an-acre minimum. But even though the Indians would be given only a few cents an acre for their land, the government was likely to agree to pay for the expense of their relocation out of the proceeds from the sale of their former domain. And there were costs associated with preparing the public lands for sale: surveys, the opening of roads, and the operations of the Land Office itself, both in Washington and in the field. Public policy was to get the public lands into private hands, for economic development, as quickly as possible.

Thus the Jackson administration was ready to do its "land-office business" as soon as the Indians could be persuaded to sell and agree to remove. In fact, efforts to that end were already under way.

The Trail of Tears

Responsibility for arranging the actual removal of the Indians was now in the hands of the administration. Jackson had in place a removal team: his protégé John Eaton, the Secretary of War; Thomas McKenney, Superintendent of the Indian Office, a declared supporter of removal; General Coffee, his old comrade-in-arms, always ready to serve as the situation demanded—as Indian fighter, treaty negotiator, or surveyor of purchased lands. He also had available the staff of Indian agents who served under McKenney. But McKenney, despite his support for the principle of voluntary removal, soon balked at the harassment tactics of the administration. He was removed from office in August 1830. In 1831, after another official had served for a year, the position was filled by a loyal Jacksonite, Elbert Herring, who supported the removal policy until he left in 1836. Along with McKenney, about half the experienced Indian agents in the field were replaced by Jackson men. They could be counted on to execute administration policy more readily than those whose long acquaintance with Native Americans had made them too sympathetic. In 1831, Eaton, mired in an embarrassing domestic scandal, was replaced as Secretary of War by Lewis Cass, who . . . was not only a loyal Democrat but also a leading advocate of removal. Not incidentally, his political leadership in the Michigan Territory, which was about to become a state, would come in handy at election time in 1832.

It was the team of Jackson, Cass, and Herring that supervised the removal of most of the Southern Indians from 1830 through 1836. By the end of 1836, the Choctaws and Creeks had emigrated, and by the close of 1837 the Chickasaws had followed. Cherokee resistance was not broken, however, until 1839, and the Seminoles were not removed until 1842, after a long and bloody war.

In principle, emigration was to be voluntary; the Removal Act did not require Native Americans to emigrate, and those who wished to remain could do so. But the actual policy of the administration was to encourage removal by all possible means, fair or foul.

Jackson as usual spoke publicly in a tone of friendship and concern for Indian welfare. In a letter of instruction to an agent who was to visit the Choctaws in October 1829 (even before the Removal Act was passed) he outlined the message from "their father," the President, urging them to emigrate. The threats were veiled. "They and my white children are too near each other to live in harmony and peace." The state of Mississippi had the right to extend a burdensome jurisdiction over them, and "the general government will be obliged to sustain the States in the exercise of their right." He, as President, could be their friend only if they removed beyond the Mississippi, where they should have a "land of their own, which they shall possess as long as Grass grows or water runs . . . and I never speak with forked tongue."

A harsh policy was nevertheless quickly put in place. To weaken the power of the chiefs, many of whom opposed removal, the traditional practice of paying annuities in a lump sum, to be used by the chiefs on behalf of the tribe for capital improvements and education, was terminated and annuities were doled out piecemeal to individual Indians. The amounts were pitifully small—each Cherokee was to receive forty-four cents per year, for example, and even that was to be withheld until he reached the West. Some annuities were not paid at all, being diverted by local agents to pay spurious damage claims allowed by state courts against Indians.

The principal acts of harassment, however, were carried out by the governments and citizens of the Southern states. The extension of state sovereignty over the tribes within their borders led quickly to the passage of destructive legislation. The tribal governments, so carefully organized in imitation of white institutions, were simply abolished; it became illegal for tribes to establish their own laws and to convict and punish lawbreakers. The chiefs were to have no power. Tribal assemblies were banned. Indians were subject to state taxes, militia duty, and suits for debt. Indians were denied the right to vote, to bring suit, even to testify in court (as heathens all—despite the evidence of conversion for many—they could not swear a Christian oath). Intruders were encouraged to settle on Indian territory; lands were sold even before they had been ceded. In Georgia, after gold was discovered on Cherokee property, the Indians were prohibited from digging or mining gold on their own land, while hundreds of white prospectors were allowed to trespass and steal the gold with impunity.

And all the while, the federal government stood idly by, refusing to intervene in the application of state laws. The result was chaos. Thousands of intruders swarmed over the Indian country in a frenzied quest for land and gold, destroying Indian farms and crops. The missionaries tried to persuade their Indian friends to stand firm against removal. But Georgia passed a law requiring missionaries to take an oath of loyalty to the state or leave the Indian country, and when a number refused, they were seized, imprisoned, tried, convicted, and sentenced to long prison terms. All but two were pardoned after they signed a pledge to obey the laws of Georgia. The recalcitrant ones, the famous Samuel

Worcester, former head of the American Board's school at Brainerd, publisher of *The Cherokee Phoenix,* and an ardent anti-removal advocate, and an assistant missionary, Elizur Butler, chose to appeal their convictions. While they languished in prison, the case wound its way up to the Supreme Court, where the issue was interpreted in the context of Georgia's claim of state sovereignty. The Supreme Court found against Georgia's right to supersede federal authority over Indian tribes and thus set aside Georgia's assertion of state sovereignty over the Cherokees and their missionaries. Jackson was not impressed, however, and is reputed to have said, "Justice Marshall has made his decision, now let him enforce it." Whether he actually used these words has been questioned; but they represent his sentiments, for the administration did nothing to aid the missionaries or effectively to deter intruders. Worcester was not released from prison until the following year (1833).

The other major legal challenge to the state's sovereignty was an earlier suit pressed by the Cherokee nation that directly challenged the constitutionality of Georgia's attempt to execute state law within the Indian country. Former Attorney General William Wirt (who also represented Samuel Worcester) applied to the Supreme Court for an injunction. But this case was dismissed on the technical ground that an Indian nation was not a foreign state but a "domestic dependent nation," a "ward" of its "guardian," the United States, and therefore could not bring suit before the Supreme Court.

It is abundantly clear that Jackson and his administration were determined to permit the extension of state sovereignty because it would result in the harassment of Indians, powerless to resist, by speculators and intruders hungry for Indian land. Jackson, of course, was not always so indulgent of states' rights, as is shown by his famous threat later on to use military force against South Carolina if that state acted on John Calhoun's doctrine of nullification.

POSTSCRIPT

Was Andrew Jackson's Indian Removal Policy Motivated by Humanitarian Impulses?

One of the interesting sidelights of the federal government's efforts to develop a policy with regard to Native American tribes residing in individual states revolved around the questions of tribal sovereignty versus states' rights. The Cherokee, in particular, proved troublesome in this regard. Since 1791 the United States had recognized the Cherokee as a nation in a number of treaties, and in 1827 delegates of this tribe initiated action to draft a constitution that would more formally recognize this status. In doing so, Native Americans confronted a barrier in the U.S. Constitution that prohibited the establishment of a new state in a preexisting state without the latter's approval. In response, Georgia, where most of the Cherokee lived, opposed the plan and called for the removal of all Native Americans. At this juncture, Cherokee leaders sought an injunction to prevent the state of Georgia from enforcing its laws within Native American territory. The case reached the U.S. Supreme Court, which, in *Cherokee Nation v. Georgia* (1831), expressed sympathy for the Native Americans' position but denied that the Cherokee held the status of a foreign nation. The following year, in the midst of efforts to remove all Native Americans from the southeastern United States, Chief Justice John Marshall, in *Worcester v. Georgia* (1832), ruled that the state had no right to extend sovereignty over the Cherokee within its borders.

Major studies of the Indian removal policy in Jacksonian America include Angie Debo's classic *And Still the Waters Run: The Betrayal of the Five Civilized Tribes* (University of Oklahoma Press, 1940); Allen Guttman, *States Rights and Indian Removal: The Cherokee Nation vs. the State of Georgia* (D. C. Heath, 1965); John Ehle, *Trail of Tears: The Rise and Fall of the Cherokee Nation* (Doubleday, 1988); Mary E. Young, *Redskins, Ruffleshirts, and Rednecks: Indian Allotments in Alabama and Mississippi, 1830–1860* (University of Oklahoma Press, 1961); and Arthur H. DeRosier, Jr., *The Removal of the Choctaw Indians* (University of Tennessee Press, 1970). Perhaps the best analysis of Jackson's sometimes ambiguous attitude toward Native Americans is Michael Paul Rogin, *Fathers and Children: Andrew Jackson and the Subjugation of the American Indian* (Alfred A. Knopf, 1975).

For general studies of Native American history that include discussions of Jackson's attitudes and policies with regard to Native Americans, see Wilcomb E. Washburn, *The Indian in America* (Harper & Row, 1975); Robert F. Berkhofer, Jr., *The White Man's Indian: Images of the American Indian From Columbus to the Present* (Alfred A. Knopf, 1978); and Francis Paul Prucha's edited collection of readings *The Indian in American History* (Holt, Rinehart & Winston, 1971).

The historical literature on Jacksonian philosophy and policies is extensive. Remini is Jackson's definitive, generally sympathetic biographer. His three-volume study, *Andrew Jackson and the Course of American Empire, 1767–1821* (Harper & Row, 1977); *Andrew Jackson and the Course of American Freedom, 1822–1832* (Harper & Row, 1981); and *Andrew Jackson and the Course of American Democracy, 1833–1845* (Harper & Row, 1984), is the culmination of a long career of study and writing. Older though equally excellent studies include Arthur Schlesinger, Jr., *The Age of Jackson* (Little, Brown, 1946); John William Ward, *Andrew Jackson: Symbol for an Age* (Oxford University Press, 1955); and Marvin Meyers, *The Jacksonian Persuasion: Politics and Belief* (Stanford University Press, 1957). Useful primary sources on the "age of Jackson" are collected in Edward Pessen, ed., *Jacksonian Panorama* (Bobbs-Merrill, 1976). The period is also explored in Glyndon G. Van Deusen, *The Jacksonian Era, 1828–1848* (Harper & Row, 1959); Edward Pessen, *Jacksonian America: Society, Personality, and Politics* (Dorsey Press, 1969); and Henry L. Watson, *Liberty and Power: The Politics of Jacksonian America* (Hill & Wang, 1990). Finally, Alexis de Tocqueville's classic *Democracy in America* (HarperCollins, 1988) sheds a great deal of light on the still-young nation of Jackson's time from the perspective of a foreign observer.

On the Internet . . .

Birth of a Nation & Antebellum America

This site, maintained by Mike Madin, provides links to a wide assortment of topics from the early national and antebellum eras.

`http://www.academicinfo.net/usindnew.html`

The Descendants of Mexican War Veterans

An excellent source for the history of the Mexican-American War (1846–1848), which includes images, primary documents, and maps.

`http://www.dmwv.org/mexwar/mexwar1.htm`

The Atlantic Slave Trade and Slave Life in the Americas: A Visual Record

This site, maintained by Jerome S. Handler and Michael L. Tuite, Jr., is a project of the Virginia Foundation for the Humanities and the Digital Media Lab at the University of Virginia Library. The site includes information and images on various aspects of slave life, including family organization.

`http://hitchcock.itc.virginia.edu/Slavery/`

Abolitionism, 1830–1850

Another outstanding site from the collections housed at the University of Virginia, which highlights the antislavery protest and includes a number of important abolitionist tracks.

`http://www.iath.virginia.edu/utc/abolitn/abhp.html`

Antebellum America

*P*ressures and trends that began building in the early years of the American nation continued to gather momentum until conflict was almost inevitable. Slavery remained a blight on the nation. Population growth and territorial expansion brought the United States into conflict with other countries. The United States had to respond to challenges from Americans who felt alienated because the ideals of human rights and democratic participation that guided the founding of the nation had been applied only to selected segments of the population.

- Did Slavery Destroy the Black Family?

- Was the Mexican War an Exercise in American Imperialism?

- Were the Abolitionists "Unrestrained Fanatics"?

ISSUE 11

Did Slavery Destroy the Black Family?

YES: Wilma A. Dunaway, from *The African-American Family in Slavery and Emancipation* (Cambridge University Press, 2003)

NO: Eugene D. Genovese, from *Roll Jordan Roll: The World the Slaves Made* (Random House, 1974)

ISSUE SUMMARY

YES: Professor Wilma A. Dunaway believes that modern historians have exaggerated the amount of control slaves exercised over their lives and underplayed the cruelty of the slave experience—family separations, nutritional deficiencies, sexual exploitation and physical abuse—that occurred on the majority of small plantations.

NO: Professor Genovese argues that slaves developed their own system of family and cultural values within the southern paternalistic and pre-capitalistic slave society.

All the North American colonies had some slaves in the seventeenth century. But by the 1670s, slaves became the most important workforce in the southern colonies because of the intensive labor needed to cultivate tobacco fields and rice paddies. The enlightment philosophy that permeated the American Revolution-aries belief that "all men were created equal" might have caused slavery's eventual demise. But the invention of the cotton gin and the development of a "market revolution" of textile factories in Old and New England gave slavery a rebirth as millions of slaves were sold from the traditional tobacco-growing areas of the upper South to cotton-producing regions in Alabama and Mississippi and the sugar fields of Louisiana.

Until recently, historians debated the slavery issue with the same arguments used over a century ago by the abolitionists and plantation owners. Slavery had been viewed as a paternalistic institution that civilized and Christianized the heathen African who, though bought and sold by his masters, was better off than many free northern workers; he was, at least, cared for in his non-working hours and old age by his masters. The prodigious research of Georgia-born professor

Ulrich B. Phillips and his followers, who mined the records of the large plantation owners, gave a picture of slavery that reflected the views of those slave masters. Because Phillips considered blacks intellectually inferior to whites, his books seem woefully outdated to the American student. But Phillips' book such as *American Negro Slavery* (New York, 1918; reprint, Louisiana State University Press, 1966) and those of his students dominated the field for over thirty years.

The climate of opinion changed after World War II. Hitler made the concept of "race" a dirty word that no respected biologist or social scientist would use. Assuming that "the slaves were merely ordinary human beings and that innately Negroes were, after all, only white men with black skins," Professor Kenneth Stampp wrote a history of slavery from a northern white liberal, or abolitionist, point of view. *The Peculiar Institution* (Vintage, 1956) utilized many of the same sources as Phillips's books but came to radically different conclusions; slavery was now considered an inhuman institution.

In 1959 Stanley Elkins synthesized these seemingly contradictory interpretations in his controversial but path-breaking study *Slavery: A Problem in American Institutional and Intellectual Life,* 3rd edition (University of Chicago Press, 1976). Elkins clearly accepted Stampp's emphasis on the harshness of the slave system by hypothesizing that slavery was a "closed" system in which masters dominated their slaves in the same way that Nazi concentration camp guards in World War II had controlled the lives of their prisoners. Such an environment, he insisted, generated severe psychological dysfunctions that produced the personality traits of Phillips's "Sambo" character type. Elkins book provoked an intense debate in the 1960s and 1970s. Although his image of the slave as "Sambo" was rejected by scholars, *Slavery* was an important work because it forced historians to reconceptualize and tell slavery from the point of view of the slave themselves.

In the second selection, Professor Eugene Genovese agreed with Elkins that it was important to view slavery through the eyes of the slave owners. But like many writers in the 1970s, Genovese disagreed with Elkins about the use of traditional sources to uncover slave culture. In his many books and articles, Genovese combined a search through the plantation records with a careful reading of slave autobiographies and the controversial records of the former slave interviews recorded in the 1930s by writers working for the federal Works Progress Administration (WPA). As a Marxist who defended Ulrich Phillips's conception of the plantation as a pre-capitalist feudal institution, Genovese's later writings reflected less concern for the economic aspects and more for the cultural interactions of blacks and whites in the antebellum South. He argues that southern slavery existed in a pre-capitalistic society dominated by a paternalistic ruling class of white slaveholders who ruled over their white and slave families. Under this system of paternalism, cultural bonds were forged between master and slave which recognized the slaves' humanity and enabled them to develop their own system of family and cultural values.

Have modern historians romanticized the ability of the slaves to maintain strong family ties? In the first selection, professor Wilma A. Dunaway argues that modern historians have exaggerated the amount of control slaves exercised over their lives and underplayed the cruelty of the slave experience–family separations, nutritional deficiencies, sexual exploitation, and physical abuse, which occurred on the majority of small plantations.

 **YES**

Introduction

. . . The conventional wisdom is that owners rarely broke up slave families; that slaves were adequately fed, clothed, and sheltered; and that slave health or death risks were no greater than those experienced by white adults. Why have so many investigations come to these optimistic conclusions? U.S. slavery studies have been handicapped by four fundamental weaknesses:

- a flawed view of the slave family,
- scholarly neglect of small plantations,
- limited analysis of Upper South enslavement,
- academic exaggeration of slave agency.

The Flawed View of the Slave Family

U.S. slavery studies have been dominated by the view that it was not economically rational for masters to break up black families. According to Fogel and Engerman, households were the units through which work was organized and through which the rations of basic survival needs were distributed. By discouraging runaways, families also rooted slaves to owners. Gutman's work established the view that slave families were organized as stable, nuclear, single-residence households grounded in long-term marriages. After thirty years of research, Fogel is still convinced that two-thirds of all U.S. slaves lived in two-parent households. Recent studies, like those of Berlin and Rowland, are grounded in and celebrate these optimistic generalizations about the African-American slave family.

None of these writers believes that U.S. slave owners interfered in the construction or continuation of black families. Fogel argues that such intervention would have worked against the economic interests of the owners, while Gutman focuses on the abilities of slaves to engage in day-to-day resistance to keep their households intact. Fogel and most scholars argue that sexual exploitation of slave women did not happen very often. Moreover, the conventional wisdom has been that slaveholders discouraged high fertility because female laborers were used in the fields to a greater extent than male workers. Consequently, the predominant view is that most slave women did not have their first child until about age twenty-one and that teenage pregnancies were rare.

To permit women to return to work as quickly as possible, owners protected children by providing collectivized child care.

Scholarly Neglect of Small Plantations

Those who have supported the dominant paradigm neglected small slaveholdings, the second methodological blunder of U.S. slave studies. Gutman acknowledged this inadequacy of his own work when he commented in passing that "little is yet known about the domestic arrangements and kin networks as well as the communities that developed among slaves living on farms and in towns and cities." Fogel stressed that "failure to take adequate account of the differences between slave experiences and culture on large and small plantations" has been a fundamental blunder by slavery specialists. Because findings have been derived from analysis of plantations that owned more than fifty slaves, generalizations about family stability have been derived from institutional arrangements that represented the life experiences of a small minority of the enslaved population. In reality, more than 88 percent of U.S. slaves resided at locations where there were fewer than fifty slaves.

Revisionist researchers provide ample evidence that slave family stability varied with size of the slaveholding. Analyzing sixty-six slave societies around the world in several historical eras, Patterson found that slavery was most brutal and most exploitative in those societies characterized by smallholdings. Contrary to the dominant paradigm, Patterson found that family separations, slave trading, sexual exploitation, and physical abuse occurred much more often in societies where the masters owned small numbers of slaves. There were several factors that were more likely to destabilize family life on small plantations than on large ones. According to Patterson, small slaveholdings allowed "far more contact with (and manipulation of) the owner" and "greater exposure to sexual exploitation." Compared to large plantations, slave families on small plantations were more often disrupted by masters, and black households on small plantations were much more frequently headed by one parent. Stephen Crawford showed that slave women on small plantations had their first child at an earlier age and were pregnant more frequently than black females on large plantations. Steckel argued that hunger and malnutrition were worse on small plantations, causing higher mortality among the infants, children, and pregnant women held there.

Scholarly Neglect of the Upper South

In addition to their neglect of small plantations, scholars who support the dominant paradigm have directed inadequate attention to enslavement in the Upper South. Instead, much of what is accepted as conventional wisdom is grounded in the political economy and the culture of the Lower South. Why is it so important to study the Upper South? In the United States, world demand for cotton triggered the largest domestic slave trade in the history of the world. Between 1790 and 1860, the Lower South slave population nearly quadrupled because the Upper South exported nearly one million black laborers. In a fifty-year period, two-fifths of the African-Americans who were enslaved in the Upper South were forced to migrate to the cotton economy; the vast majority were sold through interstate transactions, and about 15 percent were removed in relocations with owners.

Because of that vast interregional forced migration, Upper South slaves experienced family histories that contradict the accepted wisdom in U.S. slave studies. Though their arguments still have not altered the dominant paradigm, revisionist researchers offer evidence that slave family stability varied with southern subregion. Tadman contends that, after the international slave trade closed in 1808, the Upper South operated like a "stock-raising system" where "a proportion of the natural increase of its slaves was regularly sold off." As a result, the chances of an Upper South slave falling into the hands of interstate traders were quite high. Between 1820 and 1860, one-tenth of all Upper South slaves were relocated to the Lower South each decade. Nearly one of every three slave children living in the Upper South in 1820 was gone by 1860. Among Mississippi slaves who had been removed from the Upper South, nearly half the males and two-fifths of the females had been separated from spouses with whom they had lived at least five years. Stevenson contends that Virginia slave families were disproportionately matrifocal because of the slave trading and labor strategies of Upper South masters. Clearly, the fifty-year forced labor migration of slaves must be taken into account in scholarly assessments of family stability and of household living conditions.

Scholarly Preoccupation with Slave Agency

The fourth weakness in U.S. slavery studies has been a preoccupation with slave agency. As Kolchin has observed, most scholars "have abandoned the victimization model in favor of an emphasis on the slaves' resiliency and autonomy." Like a number of other scholars, I have grown increasingly concerned that too many recent studies have the effect of whitewashing from slavery the worst structural constraints. Because so much priority has been placed on these research directions, there has been inadequate attention directed toward threats to slave family maintenance. Notions like "windows of autonomy within slavery" or an "independent slave economy" seriously overstate the degree to which slaves had control over their own lives, and they trivialize the brutalities and the inequities of enslavement. Patterson is scathing in his criticism of the excesses of studies that assign too much autonomy to slaves.

> During the 1970s, a revisionist literature emerged in reaction to the earlier scholarship on slavery that had emphasized the destructive impact of the institution on Afro-American life. In their laudable attempts to demonstrate that slaves, in spite of their condition, did exercise some agency and did develop their own unique patterns of culture and social organization, the revisionists went to the opposite extreme, creating what Peter Parish calls a "historiographical hornet's nest," which came "dangerously close to writing the slaveholder out of the story completely."

In their haste to celebrate the resilience and the dignity of slaves, scholars have underestimated the degree to which slaveholders placed families at risk. Taken to its extreme, the search for individual agency shifts to the oppressed the blame for the horrors and inequalities of the institutions that enslaved them. If, for example, we push to its rhetorical endpoint the claim of Berlin and Rowland that slaves "manipulated to their own benefit the slaveowners' belief that regular family relations made for good business," then we would arrive at the inaccurate conclusion (as some have) that the half of the U.S. slave population who resided in single-parent households did so as an expression of their African-derived cultural preferences, not because of any structural interference by owners. If we push to its rhetorical endpoint the claim that there was an independent slave economy, then we must ultimately believe that a hungry household was just not exerting enough personal agency at "independent" food cultivation opportunities. Such views are simply not supported by the narratives of those who experienced enslavement. Nowhere in the 600 slave narratives that I have analyzed (within and outside the Mountain South) have I found a single slave who celebrated moments of independence or autonomy in the manner that many academics do. Some slaves did resist, but ex-slaves voiced comprehension that their dangerous, often costly acts of civil disobedience resulted in no long-term systemic change.

The Target Area for This Study

In sharp contrast to previous studies, I will test the dominant paradigm of the slave family against findings about a slaveholding region that was *typical* of the circumstances in which a majority of U.S. slaves were held. That is, I will examine enslavement in a region that was *not* characterized by large plantations and that did *not* specialize in cotton production. Even though more than half of all U.S. slaves lived where there were fewer than four slave families, there is very little research about family life in areas with low black population densities. Despite Crawford's groundbreaking finding that plantation size was the most significant determinant of quality of slave life, this is the first study of a multistate region of the United States that was characterized by small plantations.

This study breaks new ground by investigating the slave family in a slaveholding region that has been ignored by scholars. I will explore the complexities of the Mountain South where slavery flourished amidst a nonslaveholding majority and a large surplus of poor white landless laborers. In geographic and geological terms, the Mountain South (also known as Southern Appalachia) makes up that part of the U.S. Southeast that rose from the floor of the ocean to form the Appalachian Mountain chain 10,000 years ago. In a previous book, I documented the historical integration of this region into the capitalist world system. The incorporation of Southern Appalachia entailed nearly one hundred fifty years of ecological, politico-economic, and cultural changes. . . . Fundamentally, the Mountain South was a *provisioning zone,* which supplied raw materials to other agricultural or industrial regions of the world economy.

On the one hand, this inland region exported foodstuffs to other peripheries and semiperipheries of the western hemisphere, those areas that specialized in cash crops for export. The demand for flour, meal, and grain liquors was high in plantation economies (like the North American South and most of Latin America), where labor was budgeted toward the production of staple crops. So it was not accidental that the region's surplus producers concentrated their land and labor resources into the generation of wheat and corn, often in terrain where such production was ecologically unsound. Nor was it a chance occurrence that the Southern Appalachians specialized in the production of livestock, as did inland mountainous sections of other zones of the New World. There was high demand for work animals, meat, animal by-products, and leather in those peripheries and semiperipheries that did not allocate land to less-profitable livestock production.

On the other hand, the Mountain South supplied raw materials to emergent industrial centers in the American Northeast and western Europe. The appetite for Appalachian minerals, timber, cotton, and wool was great in those industrial arenas. In addition, regional exports of manufactured tobacco, grain liquors, and foodstuffs provisioned those sectors of the world economy where industry and towns had displaced farms. By the 1840s, the northeastern United States was specializing in manufacturing and international shipping, and that region's growing trade/production centers were experiencing food deficits. Consequently, much of the Appalachian surplus received in Southern ports was reexported to the urban-industrial centers of the American Northeast and to foreign plantation zones of the world economy. In return for raw ores and agricultural products, Southern markets—including the mountain counties—consumed nearly one-quarter of the transportable manufacturing output of the North and received a sizeable segment of the redistributed international imports (e.g., coffee, tea) handled by Northeastern capitalists.

Beginning in the 1820s, Great Britain lowered tariffs and eliminated trade barriers to foreign grains. Subsequently, European and colonial markets were opened to North American commodities. Little wonder, then, that flour and processed meats were the country's major nineteenth-century exports, or that more than two-thirds of those exports went to England and France. Outside the country, then, Appalachian commodities flowed to the manufacturing centers of Europe, to the West Indies, to the Caribbean, and to South America. Through far-reaching commodity flows, Appalachian raw materials—in the form of agricultural, livestock, or extractive resources—were exchanged for core manufactures and tropical imports.

Slavery in the American Mountain South

Peripheral capitalism unfolded in Southern Appalachia as a mode of production that combined several forms of land tenure and labor. Because control over land—the primary factor of production—was denied to them, the unpropertied majority of the free population was transformed into an impoverished *semiproletariat*. However, articulation with the world economy did not trigger only the appearance of free wage labor or white tenancy. Capitalist dynamics in the Mountain South also generated a variety of unfree labor mechanisms. To use the words of Phillips, "the process of incorporation . . . involved the subordination of the labor force to the dictates of export-oriented commodity production, and thus occasioned increased coercion of the labor force as commodity production became generalized." As a result, the region's landholders combined *free* laborers from the ranks of the landless tenants, croppers, waged workers, and poor women with *unfree* laborers from four sources. Legally restricted from free movement in the marketplace, the region's free blacks, Cherokee households, and indentured paupers contributed coerced labor to the region's farms. However, Southern Appalachia's largest group of unfree laborers were nearly three hundred thousand slaves who made up about 15 percent of the region's 1860 population. About three of every ten adults in the region's labor force were enslaved. In the Appalachian zones of Alabama, Georgia, South Carolina, and Virginia, enslaved and free blacks made up one-fifth to one-quarter of the population. In the Appalachian zones of Maryland, North Carolina, and Tennessee, blacks accounted for only slightly more than one-tenth of the population. West Virginia and eastern Kentucky had the smallest percentage of blacks in their communities. The lowest incidence of slavery occurred in the *mountainous* Appalachian counties where 1 of every 6.4 laborers was enslaved. At the other end of the spectrum, the *ridge-valley* counties utilized unfree laborers more than twice as often as they were used in the zones with the most rugged terrain.

Consisting of 215 mountainous and hilly counties in nine states, this large land area was characterized in the antebellum period by nonslaveholding farms and enterprises, a large landless white labor force, small plantations, mixed farming, and extractive industry. Berlin's conceptualization of a *slave society* caused us to predict that slavery did not dominate the Mountain South because there were not large numbers of plantations or slaves. I contested that assumption in a previous book. A region was not buffered from the political, economic, and social impacts of enslavement simply because it was characterized by low black population density and small slaveholdings. On the one hand, a Lower South farm owner was twelve times more likely to run a large plantation than his Appalachian counterpart. On the other hand, Mountain slaveholders monopolized a much higher proportion of their communities' land and wealth than did Lower South planters. This region was linked by rivers and roads to the coastal trade centers of the Tidewater and the Lower South, and it lay at the geographical heart of antebellum trade routes that connected the South to the North and the Upper South to the Lower South. Consequently, two major slave-trading networks cut directly through the region and became major conduits for overland and river transport of slave coffles. No wonder, then that the political economies of all Mountain South counties were in the grip of slavery. Even in counties with the smallest slave populations (including those in Kentucky and West Virginia), slaveholders owned a disproportionate share of wealth and land, held a majority of important state and county offices, and championed proslavery agendas rather than the social and economic interests of the nonslaveholders in their own communities. Moreover, public policies were enacted by state legislatures controlled and manipulated by slaveholders. In addition, every Appalachian county and every white citizen benefited in certain ways and/or was damaged by enslavement, even when there were few black laborers in the county and even when the individual citizen owned no slaves. For example, slaves were disproportionately represented among hired laborers in the public services and transportation systems that benefited whites of all

Appalachian counties, including those with small slave populations. Furthermore, the lives of poor white Appalachians were made more miserable because slaveholders restricted economic diversification, fostered ideological demeaning of the poor, expanded tenancy and sharecropping, and prevented emergence of free public education. Moreover, this region was more politically divided over slavery than any other section of the South. Black and poor white Appalachians were disproportionately represented among the soldiers and military laborers for the Union Army. The Civil War tore apart Appalachian communities, so that the Mountain South was probably more damaged by army and guerilla activity than any other part of the country.

In an earlier work, I identified six indicators that distinguish the Mountain South from the Lower South.

- One of every 7.5 enslaved Appalachians was either a Native American or descended from a Native American. Thus, black Appalachians were 4.5 times more likely than other U.S. slaves to be Native American or to have Indian heritage, reflecting the presence of eight indigenous peoples in this land area.
- Mountain slaves were employed outside agriculture much more frequently than Lower South slaves. At least one-quarter of all mountain slaves were employed full time in nonagricultural occupations. Thus, slaves were disproportionately represented in the region's town commerce, travel capitalism, transportation networks, manufactories, and extractive industries.
- In comparison to areas of high black population density, mountain plantations were much more likely to employ ethnically mixed labor forces and to combine tenancy with slavery.
- Compared to the Lower South, mountain plantations relied much more heavily on women and children for field labor.
- Fogel argued that "the task system was never used as extensively in the South as the gang system." Except for the few large slaveholders, Mountain South plantations primarily managed laborers by assigning daily or weekly tasks and by rotating workers to a variety of occupations. Moreover, small plantations relied on community pooling strategies, like corn huskings, when they needed a larger labor force. Since a majority of U.S. slaves resided on holdings smaller than fifty, like those of the Mountain South, it is likely that gang labor did not characterize Southern plantations to the extent that Fogel claimed.
- Mountain slaves almost always combined field work with nonfield skills, and they were much more likely to be artisans than other U.S. slaves.

Several findings about the Mountain South cry out for scholarly rethinking of assumptions about areas with low black population densities and small plantations.

- On small plantations, slave women worked in the fields, engaged in resistance, and were whipped just about as often as men.
- Mountain masters meted out the most severe forms of punishment to slaves much more frequently than their counterparts in other Southern regions. Appalachian ex-slaves reported frequent or obsessive physical

punishment nearly twice as often as other WPA interviewees. There was greater brutality and repression on small plantations than on large plantations. Moreover, areas with low black population densities were disproportionately represented in court convictions of slaves for capital crimes against whites. As on large plantations, small plantations punished slaves primarily for social infractions, not to motivate higher work productivity.

- As Berlin observed, "the Africanization of plantation society was not a matter of numbers." Thus, slaves on small plantations engaged in much more day-to-day resistance and counter-hegemonic cultural formation than had been previously thought. . . .

Methods, Sources, and Definitions

To research this complex topic, I have triangulated quantitative, archival, primary, and secondary documents. I derived my statistical analysis from a database of nearly twenty-six thousand households drawn from nineteenth-century county tax lists and census manuscripts. In addition to those samples, I relied on archived records from farms, plantations, commercial sites, and industries. A majority of the slaveholder collections utilized for this research derived from *small* and *middling* plantations. However, I did not ignore rich Appalachian planters, like Thomas Jefferson or John Calhoun. Never to quote or cite an Appalachian planter is to deny that they existed and to ignore that they were the richest, most politically powerful families in Appalachian counties. Indeed, I present information about them to demonstrate that they are similar to their Lower South counterparts and, therefore, very different from the typical farmers in their communities. It is also necessary to draw upon planter documents to show that larger plantations implemented different crop choices, surveillance strategies, and labor management practices than did small-holdings. Still, those rich planters account for less than 1 percent of all the citations and details provided in this study.

. . . I have used the term *plantation* consistently to refer to a slaveholding enterprise. I have purposefully done this to distinguish such economic operations from the nonslaveholding farms that characterized the Mountain South. Far too many scholars confront me at meetings with the mythological construct that the typical Appalachian slaveholder was a benign small farmer who only kept a couple of slaves to help his wife out in the kitchen. By using *plantation* to distinguish all slaveholding farms, I seek to erode the stereotype that small plantations might be the social, political, and economic equivalent of small non-slaveholding farms in their communities. On the one hand, small plantations could not have owned black laborers if those families had not accumulated surplus wealth far in excess of the household assets averaged by the majority of nonslaveholding Appalachians. On the other hand, planters and smallholders alike controlled far more than their equitable share of the political power and economic resources in their communities. Because small slaveholders aspired to be planters, they did not often align themselves with the political and economic interests of nonslaveholders. According to Berlin, "what distinguished the slave plantation from other forms of production was neither the particularities of the crop that was cultivated nor the scale of its cultivation. . . . The plantation's distinguishing mark was its peculiar social order, which conceded nearly everything to the slaveowner and nothing to the slave." That social order was grounded in a racial ideology in which chattel bondage and white supremacy became entwined. For that reason, it is crucial to distinguish a nonslaveholding farm from a slaveholding farm. In the Mountain South, a slaveholder did not have to reach planter status to be set apart from neighbors whose antagonism to enslavement would cause them to align themselves with the Union in greater numbers than in any other region of the American South. To distinguish plantations by size, I utilize the definitions that are typically applied by U.S. slavery specialists. A *planter* or *large plantation* held fifty or more slaves, while a *middling plantation* or slaveholder owned twenty to forty-nine slaves. Thus, a *small plantation* was one on which there were nineteen or fewer slaves. . . .

Slave Narratives from the Mountain South

I grounded this study in analysis of narratives of nearly three hundred slaves and more than four hundred white Civil War veterans. I spent many months locating Appalachian slave narratives within the Federal Writers Project, at regional archives, and among published personal histories. Beginning with Rawick's forty-one published volumes of the WPA slave narratives, I scrutinized every page for county of origin, for interregional sales or relocations that shifted slaves into or out of the Mountain South, and for occurrences during the Civil War that displaced slaves. After that process, I identified other archival and published accounts, finding several narratives in unusual locations, including archives at Fisk University and the University of Kentucky. In this way, I did not ignore the life histories of slaves who were born outside the Mountain South and migrated there or those who were removed to other regions. Ultimately, I aggregated the first comprehensive list of Mountain South slave narratives.

How representative of the region are these narratives? In comparison to the entire WPA collection, Appalachian slave narratives are exceptional in the degree to which they depict small plantations. By checking the slave narratives against census manuscripts and slave schedules, I established that the vast majority of the Appalachian narratives were collected from individuals who had been enslaved on plantations that held fewer than twenty slaves. Consequently, Blue Ridge Virginia is underrepresented while the Appalachian counties of Kentucky, North Carolina, and West Virginia are overrepresented. Thus, those areas that held the fewest slaves in this region are more than adequately covered. Appalachian slave narratives are not handicapped by the kinds of shortcomings that plague the national WPA collection. Large plantations, males, and house servants are overrepresented among the entire universe of respondents. In addition, two-fifths of the ex-slaves had experienced fewer than ten years of enslavement. The most serious distortions derived from the class and racial biases of whites who conducted the vast majority of the interviews. Most of the mountain respondents had been field hands, and very few were employed full time as artisans or domestic servants. In terms of gender differentiation, the Appalachian sample is almost evenly divided. In contrast to the entire WPA collection, three-quarters of the mountain ex-slaves were older than ten when freed. Indeed, when emancipated, one-third of the respondents were sixteen or older, and 12 percent were twenty-five or older. Thus, nearly half the Appalachian ex-slaves had endured fifteen years or more of enslavement, and they were old enough to form and to retain oral histories. Perhaps the greatest strength of this regional collection has to do with the ethnicity of interviewers. More than two-fifths of the narratives were written by the ex-slaves themselves or collected by black field workers, including many Tennessee and Georgia interviews that were conducted under the auspices of Fisk University and the Atlanta Urban League. Because the mountain narratives were collected over a vast land area in nine states, this collection offers another advantage. The geographical distances between respondents offer opportunities for testing the widespread transmission of African-American culture.

I have come away from this effort with a deep respect for the quality and the reliability of these indigenous narratives. When I tested ex-slave claims against public records, I found them to be more accurate than most of the slaveholder manuscripts that I scrutinized, and quite often much less ideologically blinded than many of the scholarly works I have consulted. Therefore, I made the conscious intellectual decision to engage in "the making of *history* in the final instance" by respecting the indigenous knowledge of the ex-slaves whose transcripts I analyzed. That means that I did not dismiss and refuse to explore every slave voice that challenged conventional academic rhetoric. In most instances, I triangulated the indigenous view against public records and found the slave's knowledge to be more reliable than some recent scholarly representations. In other instances, I perceived that Appalachian slaves are a *people without written history* and that it is important to document the oral myths in which they grounded their community building. Because mountain slave narratives present a view of enslavement that attacks the conventional wisdom, I recognized that they and I were engaging in a process that Trouillot calls "the production of alternative narratives." When contacted by a Fisk University researcher in 1937, one Chattanooga ex-slave comprehended that he possessed a knowledge about slavery that was different from the social constructions of the African-American interviewer. "I don't care about telling about it [slavery] sometime," he commented cynically, "because there is always somebody on the outside that knows more about it than I do, and I was right in it." Clearly, this poorly educated man understood that historical facts are not created equal and that knowledge construction is biased by differential control of the means of historical production. On the one hand, I set myself the difficult goal of avoiding the kind of intellectual elitism the ex-slave feared while at the same time trying to avoid the pitfall of informant misrepresentation. On the other hand, I heeded the advice of C. Vann Woodward and did not view the use of slave narratives as any more treacherous or unreliable than other sources or research methods. . . .

≈◈≈

Toward a New Paradigm of the U.S. Slave Family

In his 1989 capstone study, Fogel argued that enslavement was morally repre-
hensible because owners denied to African-Americans freedom from domination, economic opportunity, citizenship, and cultural self-determination. It is
disturbing that Fogel excluded from his moral indictment the forcible removal
of kin and masters' disruptions of black households. While I strongly endorse
his call for an "effort to construct a new paradigm on the slave family," I would
hope to see writers assign greater priority to the human pain of family separations than has occurred over the last three decades. Celebration of resistance
and cultural persistence to the exclusion of investigations of those forces that
broke families will not advance a new school of thought in directions that are
any more accurate and reliable than previous generalizations. As we move
toward a new paradigm, we need to follow nine lines of new inquiry.

- We need new research that documents slave family life in institutional
  arrangements that represent the residential and work circumstances of a
  majority of African-Americans. That requires directing greater attention
  to plantations smaller than fifty, to the Upper South and slaveselling
  areas, and to nonagricultural laborers.
- We need to make realistic assessments of all labor migrations. Adherents
  to the dominant paradigm have been preoccupied with slave selling
  and have presumed that permanent separations were not caused by
  hireouts, migrations with owners, slave inheritance within the owner's
  family, and assignment to distant work sites. However, it is clear in the
  slave narratives that all these forced migrations severed kinship ties,
  threatened marriages, generated great numbers of female-headed households, and weakened bonds between children and fathers.
- New research needs to reevaluate the strengths and weaknesses of *abroad
  marriages* because scholars have tended to presume that such relationships were more stable than they actually were. Such arrangements left
  women to generate the survival needs of their households and to protect
  children without the daily support of husbands or other adult males.
  Moreover, masters withdrew family visits so routinely that households could not count on regular reunions of spouses or of parents and
  children.
- In future approaches, we need to define family disruption more broadly.
  Marriage breakups are only one indicator. Loss of children occurred
  much more frequently, breaking ties between parents and offspring and
  between siblings. Moreover, few African-Americans maintained long-
  term connections with extended kin.
- Taking into account variations by size of slaveholding, by subregion,
  and by type of production, we need to reexamine threats to family persistence caused by inadequate nutrition, shortfalls in basic survival needs,
  and ecological conditions.
- Scholars need to abandon the myth that family stability is measured in
  terms of the presence of a *nuclear family*. First, such a family construct did
  not characterize antebellum white households, and it is doubtful that
  this ideal type has ever typified Americans. Second, stability characterizes

nonnuclear family constructions in many nonwestern societies. Third, the absence of adult males was not a cultural choice because enslaved women were never in a structural position to control household composition without owners' intervention. Fourth, many enslaved women pooled survival resources by relying on support from other females.

- We need to learn from contemporary demographic trends in many poor countries where high infant mortality rates fuel population growth. On a different conceptual plane than has typified earlier discussions, we need to rethink the connection between high slave child mortality and fertility patterns of enslaved women.

- We need to investigate threats to slave families that occurred during the Civil War and the emancipation process. Families were separated, often permanently, by military labor impressments, enlistment of black soldiers, and the removal of kin to contraband camps. There was an increased incidence of Upper South slave selling and owner migrations throughout the war, magnifying the chances that a slave would be permanently separated from kin. Emancipation came slower in the Upper South, particularly in those counties with large numbers of pro-Union slaveholders or low black population densities. After liberation, most ex-slaves remained with former owners two years or longer, continuing to reside in the same cabins they had occupied during enslavement. Reconstruction labor policies worked against family rebuilding and increased the likelihood of new family disruptions (e.g., indenturement of children to former owners).

- Finally, scholars need to take a fresh look at the historical overlap between African and indigenous enslavement. First, the import of Africans did not trigger so abrupt an end to Native American enslavement as historians have claimed. Second, researchers have ignored hardships for ethnically mixed slave families caused by forced removals of indigenous peoples from the U.S. Southeast. Third, there was a higher incidence of Native American heritage among southwestern African-Americans who were more often owned by or interacted frequently with Indians.

While Fogel stresses "the critical importance of quantitative consideration," I argue that integrating the perspective of the affected slaves is even more crucial. Even though the existing paradigm is heavily grounded in cliometrics, demography, and sophisticated economic projections, it has still failed to capture the diversity of slave family life on different sized plantations and in different sections of the American South. What we need in the future are approaches that triangulate quantitative analyses with slave accounts to draw comparisons between subregions of the American South, between different parts of the world, and between large and small plantations. The best rationale for a new paradigm can be heard in the painful voices of African-Americans. Elderly ex-slaves mourned the loss of parents, spouses, children, siblings, and grandparents. Even when they had been separated from kin at very early ages, they sensed that a significant element of their souls had been wrenched from them. A mountain slave says it best: "We never met again. . . . That parting I can never forget." In the minds of black Appalachians, poverty, illiteracy, and racial inequality were not the worst legacies of enslavement. Bad as those structural factors were, it was the forced removals of family that broke their hearts and generated a community wound that was not healed by liberation. Moreover, half the Appalachian ex-slaves carried into the twentieth century the structural impacts of past diasporas, exacerbated by new family separations borne of a chaotic war and an inhumane emancipation process.

Eugene D. Genovese

The World of the Slaves

According to the slaveholders, slave men had little sense of responsibility toward their families and abused them so mercilessly that Ole Massa constantly had to intervene to protect the women and children. Skeptics might wonder how these allegedly emasculated men so easily dominated the strong-willed and physically powerful women of the matriarchal legend, but the slaveholders never troubled themselves about such inconsistencies.

"Negroes are by nature tyrannical in their dispositions," Robert Collins of Macon, Ga., announced, "and, if allowed, the stronger will abuse the weaker; husbands will often abuse their wives and mothers their children." Thus, he concluded, masters and overseers must protect the pace of the quarters and punish aggressors.

Life in the quarters, like lower-class life generally, sometimes exploded in violence. Court records, plantation papers and ex-slave accounts reveal evidence of wife-beating but do not remotely sustain the pretension that without white interference the quarters would have rung with the groans of abused womanhood. Too many black men did not believe in beating their wives, and too many black women, made physically strong by hard field work, were not about to be beaten. So, why should slaveholders, who thought nothing of stripping a woman naked and whipping her till she bled, express so much concern? The pontificating of the ideologues might be dismissed as politically serviceable rubbish, but the concern of the slaveholders who wrote in agricultural journals primarily for each other's eyes and who penned private instructions for overseers demands explanation.

The slaveholders needed order and feared that domestic abuse would undermine the morale of the labor force. By asserting himself as the protector of black women and domestic peace, the slaveholder asserted himself as *paterfamilias* and reinforced his claims to being sole father of a "family, black and white." In this light, the efforts of the drivers or plantation preachers or other prestigious slaves to restrain abusive husbands represented an attempt by the quarters to rule themselves.

The slaveholders intuitively grasped something else. A black man whose authority in the house rested on his use of force may have picked the worst way to assert himself, but in a world in which so much conspired to reduce men to

From Eugene D. Genovese, *Roll, Jordan, Roll: The World the Slaves Made* (Random House, 1974). Copyright © 1972, 1974 by Eugene D. Genovese. Reprinted by permission of Pantheon Books, a division of Random House, Inc.

"guests in the house" and to emasculate them, even this kind of assertion, however unmanly by external standards, held some positive meaning.

Defending Their Own

The slave women did not often welcome Ole Massa's protection. They preferred to take care of themselves or, when they needed help, to turn to their fathers, brothers or friend. As any policeman in a lower-class neighborhood, white or black, knows, a woman who is getting the worst of a street fight with her man and who is screaming for help usually wants relief from the blows; she does not want her man subjected to an outsider's righteous indignation and may well join him in repelling an attack.

When Ellen Botts' mother—the much respected Mammy of a sugar plantation—showed up with a lump on her head inflicted by her hot-tempered husband, she told her master that she had had an accident. She would deal with her husband herself and certainly did not want to see him whipped. When James Redpath asked a slave woman in South Carolina if slave women expected to leave their husbands when they fell out, he got the contemptuous answer meddlers in other people's love lives ought to expect. "Oh, no, not all us; we sometimes quarrel in de daytime and make all up at night."

The slaveholders, in their tender concern for black women who suffered abuse from their husbands, remained curiously silent about those who fell back on their husbands' protection. Laura Bell's father won her mother's hand by volunteering to take a whipping in her place. Most slaveholders had the sense to prohibit such gallantry, but no few black men braved their wrath by interposing themselves between their wives or daughters and the white man who sought to harm them. Not only husbands but male friends killed, beat or drove off overseers for whipping their women.

Black women fell victims to white lust, but many escaped because the whites knew they had black men who would rather die than stand idly by. In some cases black men protected their women and got off with a whipping or no punishment at all; in other cases they sacrificed their lives.

Even short of death, the pride of assertive manliness could reach fearful proportions. An overseer tried to rape Josiah Henson's mother but was overpowered by his father. Yielding to his wife's pleas and their overseer's promise of no reprisal, the enraged slave desisted from killing him. The overseer broke his promise. Henson's father suffered 100 lashes and had an ear nailed to the whipping post and then severed.

"Previous to this affair my father, from all I can learn, had been a good-humored and light-hearted man, the ringleader in all fun at corn-huskings and Christmas buffoonery. His banjo was the life of the farm, and all night long at a merry-making would he play on it while the other Negroes danced. But from this hour he became utterly changed. Sullen, morose, and dogged, nothing could be done with him."

Threats of being sold south had no effect on him. The thoughts running through his mind as he came to prefer separation from the wife he loved to enduring life there must remain a matter of speculation. His master sold him to Alabama, and he was never heard from again.

Resisting Oppression

The slaveholders deprived black men of the role of provider; refused to dignify their marriages or legitimize their issue; compelled them to submit to physical abuse in the presence of their women and children; made them choose between remaining silent while their wives and daughters were raped or seduced and risking death; and threatened them with separation from their family at any moment.

Many men caved in under the onslaught and became irresponsible husbands and indifferent fathers. The women who had to contend with such men sometimes showed stubborn cheerfulness and sometimes raging bitterness; they raised the children, maintained order at home, and rotated men in and out of bed. Enough men and women fell into this pattern to give rise to the legends of the matriarchy, the emasculated but brutal male, and the fatherless children.

Many men and women resisted the "infantilization," "emasculation" and "dehumanization" inherent in the system's aggression against the slave family. How many? No one will ever know. At issue is the quality of human relationships, which cannot be measured. But there exists as much evidence of resistance and of a struggle for a decent family life as of demoralization. A brutal social system broke the spirit of many and rendered others less responsible than human beings ought to be. But enough men came out of this test of fire whole, if necessarily scarred, to demonstrate that the slaves had powerful inner resources. A terrible system of human oppression took a heavy toll of its victims, but their collective accomplishment in resisting the system constitutes a heroic story. That resistance provided black people with solid norms of family life and role differentiation, even if circumstances caused a dangerously high lapse from those norms. The slaves from their own experience had come to value a two-parent, male-centered household, no matter how much difficulty they had in realizing the ideal.

The role of the male slave as husband and father therefore requires a fresh look. If many men lived up to their assigned irresponsibility, others, probably a majority, overcame all obstacles and provided a positive male image for their wives and children. An ex-slave recalled his boyhood:

"I loved my father. He was such a good man. He was a good carpenter and could do anything. My mother just rejoiced in him. Whenever he sat down to talk she just sat and looked and listened. She would never cross him for anything. If they went to church together she always waited for him to interpret what the preacher had said or what he taught was the will of God. I was small but I noticed all of these things. I sometimes think I learned more in my early childhood about how to live than I have learned since."

Protective fathers appeared in the lullabies slave mothers sang to their children:

> Kink head, wherefore you skeered?
> Old snake crawled off, 'cause he's afeared.
> Pappy will smite him on de back
> With a great big club—Ker whack! Ker whack!

Many ex-slaves recalled their fathers as stern disciplinarians, and the slaveholders' complaints about fathers' abusing their children may be read as supporting evidence. Other slave men left their children a memory of kindness and affection that remained through life. Will Adams' father, a foreman on a Texas plantation, came in exhausted after a long day's work but never failed to take his son out of bed and to play with him for hours. The spirituals and other slave songs reflected the importance of the father in the lives of the children; many of them sang of the reunification of the family in heaven and of the father's return.

Middle-Class Norms

Men knew that they might have to part from their wives and children, but that knowledge did not engender indifference so much as a certain stoical submission to that which had to be endured. Under painful conditions, many did their best even while others succumbed. Mingo White's father, upon being sold, did nothing unusual when he charged a male friend with responsibility for looking after his son. A principle of stewardship had arisen in the quarters. Even in the absence of a father, some male would likely step in to help raise a boy to manhood. When the war ended, men crisscrossed the South to reclaim their families and to assert authority over their children.

Slave children usually did have an image of a strong black man before them. Critical scholars have made the mistake of measuring the slave family by middle-class norms; naturally, they have found it wanting.

Even when a slave boy was growing up without a father in the house, he had as a model a tough, resourceful driver, a skilled mechanic or two, and older field hands with some time for the children of the quarters. Some of those men devoted themselves to playing surrogate father to all the children. They told them stories, taught them to fish and trap animals, and instructed them in the ways of survival in a hostile white world.

The norm in the quarters called for adults to look after children, whether blood relatives or not. Every plantation had some men who played this role. Under the worst of circumstances, one or two would have been enough; usually, however, there were a number. And there were the preachers. To the extent that the slaves heard their preachers, the children saw before them influential black men whose eloquence and moral force commanded the respect of the adults.

The slave children, like the ghetto children of later decades, saw a pattern of behavior that implied clear sexual differentiation and a notion of masculinity with its own strengths and weaknesses.

Don't Mess With Mammy

The daughters of the Confederacy suggested in 1923 that Congress set aside a site in Washington for a suitable memorial to the antebellum plantation Mammy. The good ladies had picked their symbol carefully, for no figure stands out so prominently in the moonlight-and-magnolias legend of the Old South. The hostile reaction of so many blacks confirmed the judgment. As the old regime has come under increasingly critical scrutiny, Mammy has had a steadily worsening press. She remains the most elusive and important black presence in the Big House. To understand her is to move toward understanding the tragedy of plantation paternalism.

First, the white legend, Lewis H. Blair, attacking racial segregation in 1889, wrote:

"Most of us above 30 years of age had our mammy, and generally she was the first to receive us from the doctor's hands, and was the first to proclaim, with heart bursting with pride, the arrival of a fine baby. Up to the age of 10 we saw as much of the mammy as of the mother, perhaps more, and we loved her quite as well. The mammy first taught us to lisp and to walk, played with us and told us wonderful stories, taught us who made us and who redeemed us, dried our tears and soothed our bursting hearts, and saved us many a well-deserved whipping. . . ."

Word Had Force of Law

Mammy comes through the black sources in much the same way, but only so far. Lindey Faucette of North Carolina remembered her grandmother, Mammie Beckie, who "toted de keys," whose word had the force of law with Marse John and Mis' Annie, and who slept in the bed with her mistress when the master's law practice kept him in town all night. Alice Sewell of Alabama especially recalled the plantation Mammy's comforting the relatives of deceased slaves, arranging for the burial, and leading the funeral services. Ellen Botts of Louisiana noted: "All de niggers have to stoop to Aunt Rachel like they curtsy to Missy." And Adeline Johnson, who had served as a Mammy in South Carolina, spoke in her old age in accents that would have warmed the hearts of those Daughters of the Confederacy.

"I hope and prays to git to hebben. Whether I's white or black when I git dere, I'll be satisfied to see my Savior dat my old marster worshipped and my husband preached 'bout. I wants to be in hebben wid all my white folks, just to wait on them and love them and serve them, sorta lak I did in slavery time. Dat will be 'nough hebben for Adeline."

Who were these Mammies? What did they actually do? Primarily, the Mammy raised the white children and ran the Big House either as the mistress' executive officer or her de facto superior. Her power extended over black and white so long as she exercised restraint, and she was not to be crossed.

She carried herself like a surrogate mistress—neatly attired, barking orders, conscious of her dignity, full of self-respect. She played the diplomat and settled the interminable disputes that arose among the house servants; when diplomacy failed, she resorted to her whip and restored order. She served as confidante to the children, the mistress, and even the master. She expected to be consulted on the love affairs and marriages of the white children and might even be consulted on the business affairs of the plantation. She presided over the dignity of the whole plantation and taught the courtesies to the white children as well as to those black children destined to work in the Big House. On the small and medium-sized plantations she had to carry much of the house work herself, and her relationship to the field slaves drew closer.

In general, she gave the whites the perfect slave—a loyal, faithful, contented, efficient, conscientious member of the family who always knew her place; and she gave the slaves a white-approved standard of black behavior. She also had to be a tough, worldly-wise, enormously resourceful woman; that is, she had to develop all the strength of character not usually attributed to an Aunt Jane.

Mammy supposedly paid more attention to the white children than to her own. Even W. E. B. Du Bois, who was rarely taken in by appearances and legends, thought so. He described the Mammy as "one of the most pitiful of the world's Christs. . . . She was an embodied Sorrow, an anomaly crucified on the cross of her own neglected children for the sake of the children of masters who bought and sold her as they bought and sold cattle."

The Mammy typically took her responsibilities to the white family as a matter of high personal honor and in so doing undoubtedly could not give her own children as much love and attention as they deserved. House nannies, white and black, free and slave, have often fallen into this trap. But the idea that the Mammies actually loved the white children more than their own rests on nothing more than wishful white perceptions. That they loved the white children they themselves raised—hardly astonishing for warm, sensitive, generous women—in no way proves that they loved their own children the less. Rather, their position in the Big House, including their close attention to the white children sometimes at the expense of their own, constituted the firmest protection they could have acquired for themselves and their immediate families. Mammies did not often have to worry about being sold or about having their husbands or children sold. The sacrifices they made for the whites earned them genuine affection in return, which provided a guarantee of protection, safety, and privilege for their own children.

Barrier Against Abuse

The relationship between the Mammies and their white folks exhibited that reciprocity so characteristic of paternalism. "Of course," a planter in Virginia told a northern reporter in 1865, "if a servant has the charge of one of my little ones, and I see the child grow fond of her, and that she loves the child, I cannot but feel kindly towards her." Of course, Mom Genia Woodbury, who had been a slave in South Carolina, acknowledged that when white folks treat you kindly, you develop kind feelings toward their children.

The devotion of the white children, who regularly sought her as their protector, confidante, and substitute mother, established a considerable barrier against the abuse of Mammy or her family. "We would not hesitate about coming to see you," Laura S. Tibbets of Louisiana wrote her sister-in-law, "if I could bring my servants, but I could not bring my baby without assistance. She is a great deal fonder of her Mammy than she is of me. She nurses her and it would be a great trial to go without her."

The immunity that Mammy secured for herself did not fully cover husband and children, but it went far enough to shield them from the worst. Mammy distraught, hurt, or angry was not to be borne. More than one overseer learned to his cost to walk gingerly around her and hers. Ma Eppes of Alabama said that an overseer had whipped the plantation Mammy when the mistress was away:

"When Miss Sarah comed back and found it out she was the maddest white lady I ever seed. She sent for the overseer and she say, 'Allen, what you mean by whipping Mammy? You know I don't allow you to touch my house servants . . . I'd rather see them marks on my old shoulders than to see'em on Mammy's. They wouldn't hurt me no worse.' Then she say, 'Allen, take your family and git offen my place. Don't you let sundown catch you here.' So he left. He wasn't nothing but white trash nohow."

Another overseer made the incredible mistake of asking his employer for permission to punish Mammy. The reply: "What! What! Why I would as soon think of punishing my own mother! Why man you'd have four of the biggest men in Mississippi down on you if you even dare suggest such a thing, and she knows it! All you can do is to knuckle down to Mammy."

The plantation Mammy was not, as is so easily assumed, some "white man's nigger," some pathetic appendage to the powerful whites of the Big House. Her strength of character, iron will and impressive self-discipline belie any glib generalizations.

She did not reject her people in order to identify with stronger whites, but she did place herself in a relationship to her own people that reinforced the paternalist social order. Thus, she carried herself with courage, compassion, dignity and self-respect and might have provided a black model for these qualities among people who needed one, had not the constricting circumstances of her own development cut her off, in essential respects, from playing that role. Her tragedy lay not in her abandonment of her own people but in her inability to offer her individual power and beauty to black people on terms they could not accept without themselves sliding further into a system of paternalistic dependency.

Some Chose Freedom

The boldest slaves struck the hardest blow an individual could against the regime: they escaped to freedom. During the 1850s about a thousand slaves a year ran away to the North, Canada, and Mexico. Increased vigilance by the slaveholders and their police apparatus may have reduced the number from 1,011 in 1850 to 803 in 1860 as the census reports insist, but even so, the economic drain and political irritation remained serious.

The slaves in the border states, especially the extreme northern tier, had a much better chance to escape than did those in Mississippi or Alabama. But even in Texas, Arkansas and Louisiana, slaveholders had to exercise vigilance, for many slaves went over the Mexican border or escaped to friendly Indians.

Who ran away? Any slave might slip into the woods for a few days, but those whose departure rated an advertisement and organized chase—those who headed for freedom in the North, the Southern cities, or the swamps—fell into a pattern. At least 80 per cent were men between the ages of 16 and 35. At least one-third of the runaways belonged to the ranks of the skilled and privileged slaves—those with some education and with some knowledge of the outside world—and women occupied these ranks only as house servants.

The whip provided the single biggest provocation to running away. Many slaves ran in anticipation of a whipping or other severe punishment, and others in anger after having suffered it. In some cases—too many—slaves ran not simply from a particular whipping but from the torments regularly inflicted by cruel or sadistic masters or overseers.

A large if underdetermined number of slaves ran away to rejoin loved ones from whom they had been forcibly parted. Newspaper advertisements frequently contained such words as "He is no doubt trying to reach his wife." Slaveholders had great trouble with newly purchased slaves who immediately left to try to find parents or children as well as wives. In some instances the slaves had unexpected success when their masters, touched by the evidence of devotion and courage, reunited the family by resale.

In many more cases family ties prevented slaves from running away or kept them close to home when they did run. Frederick Law Olmsted reported from the lower Mississippi Valley that planters kept a sharp eye on mothers, for few slaves would leave permanently if they had to leave their mothers behind to face the master's wrath.

"The Thousand Obstacles"

Among the deterrents to making the long run to free states none loomed larger than the fear of the unknown. Most knew only the immediate area and often only a narrow strip of that. Even many skilled and relatively sophisticated slaves lacked an elementary knowledge of geography and had no means of transportation.

If most slaves feared to think about flight to the North, many feared even to think of short-term flight to the nearby woods or swamps. The slaves faced particularly difficult conditions in the swampy areas alongside the great plantation districts of Louisiana and the eastern low country. Solomon Northrup, a slave on a Louisiana cotton plantation in the 1840s, wrote:

"No man who has never been placed in such a situation can comprehend the thousand obstacles thrown in the way of the fleeing slave. Every white-man's hand is raised against him—the patrollers are watching for him—the hounds are ready to follow on his track, and the nature of the country is such as renders it impossible to pass through it with any safety."

And yet, large numbers of slaves did brave the elements, the dogs, and the patrols; did swallow their fears; and did take to the woods. No plantation of any size totally avoided the runaway problem. Everywhere, the slavesholders had to build a certain loss of labor-time and a certain amount of irritation into their yearly calculations.

Slaves from one plantation assisted runaways from other plantations under certain circumstances. The slaves from neighboring plantations often knew each other well. They met for prayer meetings, corn shuckings, Christmas, and other holiday barbecues; often formed close attachments; and sometimes extended their idea of a plantation family to at least some of these friends and acquaintances. Within this wider circle, the slaves would readily help each other if they shunned those they regarded as strangers. But even strangers might find succor if they were fleeing the plantations of slaveholders known to be cruel.

Those who fled to freedom made an inestimable contribution to the people they left behind, which must be weighed against their participation in a safety-valve effect. These were slaves who, short of taking the path of insurrection, most clearly repudiated the regime; who dramatically chose freedom at the highest risk; who never let others forget that there was an alternative to their condition.

POSTSCRIPT

Did Slavery Destroy the Black Family?

Major reinterpretations of slavery occurred in the 1970s. Professor John Blassingame was one of the first African American historians to challenge the Elkins thesis of the slave as "Sambo" and write a history of slavery from the point of view of the slaves themselves.

Blassingame centers his view of *The Slave Community: Plantation Life in the Antebellum South* revised and enlarged edition (Oxford University Press, 1972, 1979) around the slave family. Unlike other slave societies, Blassingame believes the even sex ration between males and females in the antebellum South contributed to the solidarity and generally monogamous relationships between husbands and wives. The author is no romantic, however, because he argues elsewhere that almost one-third of all slave marriages were broken up because of the sale of one partner to another plantation.

Blassingame was the first historian to make use of slave testimonies. A good example of Blassingame's use of sources—speakers, interviews, letters, and autobiographies—are collected in his *Slave Testimony: Two Centuries of Letters, Speeches, Interviews and Autobiographies* (Oxford University Press, 1979).

Several white historians such as Herbert Gutman and Eugene Genovese believed that careful usage of oral interviews greatly enhanced our view of nineteenth-century slavery. In his iconoclastic sprawling view of *The Black Family in Slavery and Freedom, 1750–1925* (Pantheon, 1976), Gutman argues that slaves were more monogamous, were less promiscuous, and did not marry kin as did the white slaveholding families. Furthermore Gutman argues somewhat controversially that the master had no influence on the slave family.

Professor Eugene Genovese has written dozens of journal articles, review essays, and books about the antebellum South. He views the antebellum South as a pre-capitalist agrarian society in which master and slave were bound together in a set of mutual duties and responsibilities similar to the arrangements of lords and serfs under the feudal system of middle ages Europe. Most of Genovese's contentions are rejected by modern historians of slavery. Robert W. Fogel and Stanley L. Engerman, in their controversial study of *Time on the Cross: The Economics of American Slavery*, 2 vols. (Hougton Mifflin, 1974), argued that planters were capitalists, ran plantations that were "35 percent more efficient than the northern system of family farms," and developed a system of rewards for the hardworking slaves who internalized the values of their masters.

In the *Taking Sides* selection from his major synthesis *Roll Jordan Roll* (Pantheon, 1974), Professor Genovese describes the important role men played on the plantation in defending women from advances by the owners at the risk of being beaten, killed, or sold to another plantation. When families were split, children would receive guidance from other males in the quarters. Genovese also explains how important "mammy" was to the "plantation mistress." At the same time, he notes that "mammy" made sure that her own family was treated well and remained intact because of her importance to the owner's family. Finally Genovese sketches the unhappiness that slaves felt about the institution in discussing the thousands of runaways—primarily single males—who attempted to escape under insurmountable odds to free states and Canada.

In the first selection, Professor Wilma Dunaway challenges the dominant paradigm that has celebrated the autonomy of the slave family in the histories of Professors Blassingame, Genovese, Gutman, Rawick, and others. Most of Professor Dunaway's generalizations come from an earlier study on *Slavery in the American Mountain South* (Cambridge University Press, 2003). Her research is rooted in a database of antebellum census returns and tax records from 215 Appalachian countries and almost 400 manuscript collections that range over nine states from Maryland and West Virginia to the deep South states of Georgia and Alabama. She also uses the oral history interviews of former slaves in the 1920s and 1930s by professional historians and New Deal government workers.

Her books demonstrated the strengths and weaknesses of local history. Dunaway argues that the Appalachian region with its medium and small plantations was more typical than the deep South regions with their large cotton-dominated plantations. According to Dunaway, Appalachian slaves were treated harshly by their masters. Whippings were standard practice, slaves sales to the plantations of the deep South were common without regard for family attachments, and fewer than 12 percent of mountain slaves grew market-based gardens because of exhaustion from 14-hour work days. Many slaves were engaged in industrial rather than agricultural jobs. Most grew corn and wheat for the "new global markets" rather than cotton. Slaves worked side by side with "landless tenants, croppers, wage workers, and unfree laborers." Interestingly there were a number of Cherokee Indian slave owners, but also Cherokee Indian slaves who worked with Afro-American slaves and slaves with mixed blood.

But local history has its limitations. Dunaway may also overgeneralize about the Appalachian experience as establishing a new or really pre-1970s paradigm for slavery. Perhaps, as Professor Berlin points out, the slave experience is too varied in terms of time, region, and size to lend itself to easy generalizations.

The two most important historiographical works on slavery are Mark Smith, *Debating Slavery: Economy and Society in the Antebellum American South* (Cambridge University Press, 1998) and Peter J. Parish, *Slavery: History and Historians* (Harper and Row, 1989). The best anthology of primary sources and secondary readings is *Slavery and Emancipation,* edited by Rick Halpern and Enrico Dal Lago (Blackwell Publishing, 2002). Two other useful anthologies of secondary readings are William Dudley, ed., *American Slavery* (Greenhaven Press, 2000), and Lawrence B. Goodhart, et. al., eds., *Slavery in American Society,* 3rd ed. (D.C. Heath and Company, 1993).

Finally, in addition to the works of Professor Berlin, *American Slavery 1619–1877* (Hill and Wang, 1993) by Peter Kolchin is an indispensable summary as well as the special issue on the "Genovese Forum" in the *Radical History Review* 88 (Winter 2004), 3–83, an analysis of the work of the "Marxian Conservative" scholar by several of his peers.

ISSUE 12

Was the Mexican War an Exercise in American Imperialism?

YES: Rodolfo Acuña, from *Occupied America: A History of Chicanos,* 3rd ed. (Harper & Row, 1988)

NO: Norman A. Graebner, from "The Mexican War: A Study in Causation," *Pacific Historical Review* (August 1980)

ISSUE SUMMARY

YES: Professor of history Rodolfo Acuña argues that Euroamericans took advantage of the young, independent, and unstable government of Mexico and waged unjust and aggressive wars against the Mexican government in the 1830s and 1840s in order to take away half of Mexico's original soil.

NO: Professor of diplomatic history Norman A. Graebner argues that President James Polk pursued an aggressive policy that he believed would force Mexico to sell New Mexico and California to the United States and to recognize the annexation of Texas without starting a war.

As David M. Plecher points out in his balanced but critical discussion of *The Diplomacy of Annexation: Texas, Oregon and the Mexican War* (University of Missouri Press, 1973), the long-range effects on American foreign policy of the Mexican War were immense. Between 1845 and 1848, the United States acquired more than 1,200 square miles of territory and increased its size by over a third of its present area. This included the annexation of Texas and the subsequent states of the southwest that stretched to the Pacific coast incorporating California and the Oregon territory up to the 49th parallel. European efforts to gain a foothold in North America virtually ceased. By the 1860s, the British gradually abandoned their political aspirations in Central America, "content to compete for economic gains with the potent but unmilitary weapon of their factory system and their merchant marine." Meanwhile, the United States flexed her muscles at the end of the Civil War and used the Monroe Doctrine for the first time to force the French puppet ruler out of Mexico.

The origins of the Mexican War began with the controversy over Texas, a Spanish possession for three centuries. In 1821, Texas became the northern-most province of the newly established country of Mexico. Sparsely populated with a mixture of Hispanics and Indians, the Mexican government encouraged immigration from the United States. By 1835, the Anglo population had swelled to 30,000 plus over 2,000 slaves, while the Mexican population was only 5,000.

Fearful of losing control over Texas, the Mexican government prohibited further immigration from the United States in 1830. But it was too late. The Mexican government was divided and had changed hands several times. The centers of power were thousands of miles from Texas. In 1829, the Mexican government abolished slavery, an edict that was difficult to enforce. Finally General Santa Anna attempted to abolish the federation and impose military rule over the entire country. Whether it was due to Mexican intransigence or the Anglos assertiveness, the settlers rebelled in September 1835. The war was short-lived. Santa Anna was captured at the battle of San Jacinto in April 1836, and Texas was granted her independence.

For nine years, Texas remained an independent Republic. Politicians were afraid that if Texas were annexed it would be carved into four or five states, thereby upsetting the balance of power between the evenly divided free states and slave states that had been created in 1819 by the Missouri Compromise. But the pro-slavery President John Tyler pushed through Congress a resolution annexing Texas in the three days of his presidency in 1845.

The Mexican government was incensed and broke diplomatic relations with the United States. President James K. Polk sent John Slidell as the American emissary to Mexico to negotiate monetary claims of American citizens in Mexico, to purchase California, and to settle the southwestern boundary of Texas at the Rio Grande River and not farther north at the Nueces River, which Mexico recognized as the boundary. Upon Slidell's arrival, news leaked out about his proposals. The Mexican government, fearful of losing power but realizing war might happen, rejected Slidell's offer. In March 1846, President Polk stationed General Zachary Taylor in the disputed territory along the Rio Grande with an army of 4,000 troops. On May 9, Slidell returned to Washington and informed Polk he was rebuffed. Polk met with his cabinet to consider war. By chance that same evening, Polk received a dispatch from General Taylor informing him that on April 25 the Mexican army crossed the Rio Grande and killed or wounded 16 of his men. On May 11, Polk submitted his war message claiming "American blood was shed on American soil." Congress voted overwhelmingly for war 174 to 14 in the House and 40 to 2 in the Senate despite the vocal minority of Whig protesters and intellectuals who opposed the war.

Was the Mexican War an exercise in American Imperialism? In the first selection, Rodolfo Acuña argues that Euroamericans took advantage of the young, independent, and unstable government of Mexico by waging an unjust and aggressive war against Mexico in the 1830s and 1840s for the purpose of taking away more than half of its original lands. In the second selection, Norman A. Graebner contends that President Polk pursued the aggressive policy of a stronger nation in order to force Mexico to sell New Mexico and California to the United States and to recognize America's annexation of Texas without causing a war.

Rodolfo Acuña

 **YES**

Legacy of Hate: The Conquest of Mexico's Northwest

An Overview

The United States invaded Mexico in the mid-nineteenth century during a period of dramatic change. Rapid technological breakthroughs transformed the North American nation, from a farm society into an industrial competitor. The process converted North America into a principal in the world market-place. The wars with Mexico, symptoms of this transformation, stemmed from the need to accumulate more land, to celebrate heroes, and to prove the nation's power by military superiority.

This [selection] examines the link between the Texas (1836) and the Mexican (1845–1848) Wars. It analyzes North American aggression, showing how European peoples known as "Americans" acquired what is today the Southwest. The words "expansion" and "invasion" are used interchangeably. The North American invasions of Mexico are equated with the forging of European empires in Asia, Africa, and Latin America. The urge to expand, in the case of the United States, was not based on the need for land—the Louisiana Purchase, central Illinois, southern Georgia, and West Virginia lay vacant. Rather, the motive was profit—and the wars proved profitable, with the Euroamerican nation seizing over half of Mexico.

North Americans fought the Texas War—that is, U.S. dollars financed it, U.S. arms were used on Mexican soil, and Euroamericans almost exclusively profited from it. President Andrew Jackson approved of the war and ignored North American neutrality laws. The so-called Republic held Texas in trustee-ship until 1844, when the United States annexed it. This act amounted to a declaration of war on Mexico. When Mexico responded by breaking diplo-matic relations, the North Americans used this excuse to manufacture the war. Many North Americans questioned the morality of the war but supported their government because it was their country, right or wrong.

This [selection] does not focus on the wars' battles or heroes, but on how North Americans rationalized these invasions and have developed historical amnesia about its causes and results. War is neither romantic nor just, and the United States did not act benevolently toward Mexico. North Americans com-mitted atrocities, and, when they could, Mexicans responded. Eventually, the

Treaty of Guadalupe Hidalgo ended the Mexican-American War, and northern Mexico became part of the North American empire. The treaty, however, did not stop the bitterness or the violence between the two peoples. In fact, it gave birth to a legacy of hate.

Background to the Invasion of Texas

Anglo justifications for the conquest have ignored or distorted events that led up to the initial clash in 1836. To Anglo-Americans, the Texas War was caused by a tyrannical or, at best, an incompetent Mexican government that was anti-thetical to the ideals of democracy and justice. The roots of the conflict actually extended back to as early as 1767, when Benjamin Franklin marked Mexico and Cuba for future expansion. Anglo-American filibusters* planned expeditions into Texas in the 1790s. The Louisiana Purchase, in 1803, stimulated U.S. ambitions in the Southwest, and six years later Thomas Jefferson predicted that the Spanish borderlands "are ours the first moment war is forced upon us." The war with Great Britain in 1812 intensified Anglo-American designs on the Spanish territory.

Florida set the pattern for expansionist activities in Texas. In 1818 several posts in east Florida were seized in unauthorized, but never officially condemned, U.S. military expeditions. Negotiations then in progress with Spain finally terminated in the Adams-Onis, or Transcontinental, Treaty (1819), in which Spain ceded Florida to the United States and the United States, in turn, renounced its claim to Texas. Texas itself was part of Coahuila. Many North Americans still claimed that Texas belonged to the United States, repeating Jefferson's claim that Texas's boundary extended to the Río Grande and that it was part of the Louisiana Purchase. They condemned the Adams-Onis Treaty.

Anglo-Americans continued pretensions to Texas and made forays into Texas similar to those they had made into Florida. In 1819 James Long led an abortive invasion to establish the "Republic of Texas." Long, like many Anglos, believed that Texas belonged to the United States and that "Congress had no right or power to sell, exchange, or relinquish an 'American possession.'"

In spite of the hostility, the Mexican government opened Texas, provided that settlers agreed to certain conditions. Moses Austin was given permission to settle in Texas, but he died shortly afterwards, and his son continued his venture. In December 1821 Stephen Austin founded the settlement of San Félipe de Austin. Large numbers of Anglo-Americans entered Texas in the 1820s as refugees from the depression of 1819. In the 1830s entrepreneurs sought to profit from the availability of cheap land. By 1830 there were about 20,000 settlers, along with some 2,000 slaves.

Settlers agreed to obey the conditions set by the Mexican government—that all immigrants be Catholics and that they take an oath of allegiance to Mexico. However, Anglo-Americans became resentful when Mexico tried to enforce the agreements. Mexico, in turn, became increasingly alarmed at the flood of immigrants from the U.S.

---

*[A *filibuster* is an adventurer who engages in insurrectionist or revolutionary activity in a foreign country.]

Many settlers considered the native Mexicans to be the intruders. In a dispute with Mexicans and Indians, as well as with Anglo-American settlers, Hayden Edwards arbitrarily attempted to evict settlers from the land before the conflicting claims could be sorted out by the Mexican authorities. As a result Mexican authorities nullified his settlement contract and ordered him to leave the territory. Edwards and his followers seized the town of Nacogdoches and on December 21, 1826, proclaimed the Republic of Fredonia. Mexican officials, supported by some Anglo-Americans (such as Stephen Austin), suffocated the Edwards revolt. However, many U.S. newspapers played up the rebellion as "200 Men Against a Nation!" and described Edwards and his followers as "apostles of democracy crushed by an alien civilization."

In 1824 President John Quincy Adams "began putting pressure on Mexico in the hope of persuading her to rectify the frontier. Any of the Texan rivers west of the Sabine—the Brazos, the Colorado, the Nueces—was preferable to the Sabine, though the Río Grande was the one desired." In 1826 Adams offered to buy Texas for the sum of $1 million. When Mexican authorities refused the offer, the United States launched an aggressive foreign policy, attempting to coerce Mexico into selling Texas.

Mexico could not consolidate its control over Texas: the number of Anglo-American settlers and the vastness of the territory made it an almost impossible task. Anglo-Americans had already created a privileged caste, which depended in great part on the economic advantage given to them by their slaves. When Mexico abolished slavery, on September 15, 1829, Euroamericans circumvented the law by "freeing" their slaves and then signing them to lifelong contracts as indentured servants. Anglos resented the Mexican order and considered it an infringement on their personal liberties. In 1830 Mexico prohibited further Anglo-American immigration. Meanwhile, Andrew Jackson increased tensions by attempting to purchase Texas for as much as $5 million.

Mexican authorities resented the Anglo-Americans' refusal to submit to Mexican laws. Mexico moved reinforcements into Coahuila, and readied them in case of trouble. Anglos viewed this move as an act of hostility.

Anglo colonists refused to pay customs and actively supported smuggling activities. When the "war party" rioted at Anahuac in December 1831, it had the popular support of Anglos. One of its leaders was Sam Houston, who "was a known protégé of Andrew Jackson, now president of the United States. . . . Houston's motivation was to bring Texas into the United States." . . .

The Invasion of Texas

Not all the Anglo-Americans favored the conflict. Austin, at first, belonged to the peace party. Ultimately, this faction joined the "hawks." Eugene C. Barker states that the immediate cause of the war was "the overthrow of the nominal republic [by Santa Anna] and the substitution of centralized oligarchy," which allegedly would have centralized Mexican control. Barker admits that "earnest patriots like Benjamin Lundy, William Ellery Channing, and John Quincy Adams saw in the Texas revolution a disgraceful affair promoted by the sordid slaveholders and land speculators."

Barker parallels the Texas filibuster and the American Revolution, stating: "In each, the general cause of revolt was the same—a sudden effort to extend imperial authority at the expense of local privilege." According to Barker, in both instances the central governments attempted to enforce existing laws that conflicted with the illegal activities of some very articulate people. Barker further justified the Anglo-Americans' actions by observing: "At the close of summer in 1835 the Texans saw themselves in danger of becoming the alien subjects of a people to whom they deliberately believed themselves morally, intellectually, and politically superior. The racial feeling, indeed, underlay and colored Texan-Mexican relations from the establishment of the first Anglo-American colony in 1821." The conflict, according to Barker, was inevitable and, consequently, justified.

Texas history is a mixture of selected fact and generalized myth. Many historians admit that smugglers were upset with Mexico's enforcement of her import laws, that Euroamericans were angry about emancipation laws, and that an increasing number of the new arrivals from the United States actively agitated for independence. But despite these admissions, many historians like Barker refuse to blame the United States.

Austin gave the call to arms on September 19, 1835, stating, "War is our only recourse. There is no other remedy." Anglo-Americans enjoyed very real advantages in 1835. They were "defending" terrain with which they were familiar. The 5,000 Mexicans living in the territory did not join them, but the Anglo population had swelled to almost 30,000. The Mexican nation was divided, and the centers of power were thousands of miles from Texas. From the interior of Mexico, Santa Anna led an army of about 6,000 conscripts, many of whom had been forced into the army and then marched hundreds of miles over hot, arid desert land. Many were Mayan and did not speak Spanish. In February 1836 the majority arrived in Texas, sick and ill-prepared to fight.

In San Antonio the dissidents took refuge in a former mission, the Alamo. The siege began in the first week of March. In the days that followed, the defenders inflicted heavy casualties on the Mexican forces, but eventually the Mexicans won out. A score of popular books have been written about Mexican cruelty in relation to the Alamo and about the heroics of the doomed men. The result was the creation of the Alamo myth. Within the broad framework of what actually happened—187 filibusters barricading themselves in the Alamo in defiance of Santa Anna's force, which, according to Mexican sources, numbered 1,400, and the eventual triumph of the Mexicans—there has been major distortion.

Walter Lord, in an article entitled "Myths and Realities of the Alamo," sets the record straight. Texas mythology portrays the Alamo heroes as freedom-loving defenders of their homes; supposedly they were all good Texans. Actually, two-thirds of the defenders had recently arrived from the United States, and only a half dozen had been in Texas for more than six years. The men in the Alamo were adventurers. William Barret Travis had fled to Texas after killing a man, abandoning his wife and two children. James Bowie, an infamous brawler, made a fortune running slaves and had wandered into Texas searching for lost mines and more money. The fading Davey Crockett, a legend in his own time, fought for the sake of fighting. Many in the Alamo had come to Texas for riches and glory. These defenders were hardly the sort of men who could be classified as peaceful settlers fighting for their homes.

The folklore of the Alamo goes beyond the legendary names of the defenders. According to Lord, it is riddled with dramatic half-truths that have been accepted as history. Defenders are portrayed as selfless heroes who sacrificed their lives to buy more time for their comrades-in-arms. As the story goes, William Barret Travis told his men that they were doomed; he drew a line in the sand with his sword, saying that all who crossed it would elect to remain and fight to the last. Supposedly all the men there valiantly stepped across the line, with a man in a cot begging to be carried across it. Countless Hollywood movies have dramatized the bravery of the defenders.

In reality the Alamo had little strategic value, it was the best protected fort west of the Mississippi, and the men fully expected help. The defenders had 21 cannons to the Mexicans' 8 or 10. They were expert shooters equipped with rifles with a range of 200 yards, while the Mexicans were inadequately trained and armed with smooth-bore muskets with a range of only 70 yards. The Anglos were protected by the walls and had clear shots, while the Mexicans advanced in the open and fired at concealed targets. In short, ill-prepared, ill-equipped, and ill-fed Mexicans attacked well-armed and professional soldiers. In addition, from all reliable sources, it is doubtful whether Travis ever drew a line in the sand. San Antonio survivors, females and noncombatants, did not tell the story until many years later, when the tale had gained currency and the myth was legend. Probably the most widely circulated story was that of the last stand of the aging Davey Crockett, who fell "fighting like a tiger," killing Mexicans with his bare hands. This is a myth; seven of the defenders surrendered, and Crockett was among them. They were executed. And, finally, one man, Louis Rose, did escape.

Travis's stand delayed Santa Anna's timetable by only four days, as the Mexicans took San Antonio on March 6, 1836. At first, the stand at the Alamo did not even have propaganda value. Afterwards, Houston's army dwindled, with many volunteers rushing home to help their families flee from the advancing Mexican army. Most Anglo-Americans realized that they had been badly beaten. It did, nevertheless, result in massive aid from the United States in the form of volunteers, weapons and money. The cry of "Remember the Alamo" became a call to arms for Anglo-Americans in both Texas and the United States.

After the Alamo and the defeat of another garrison at Goliad, southeast of San Antonio, Santa Anna was in full control. He ran Sam Houston out of the territory northwest of the San Jacinto River and then camped an army of about 1,100 men near San Jacinto. There, he skirmished with Houston on April 20, 1836, but did not follow up his advantage. Predicting that Houston would attack on April 22, Santa Anna and his troops settled down and rested for the anticipated battle. The filibusters, however, attacked during the *siesta* hour on April 21. Santa Anna knew that Houston had an army of 1,000, yet he was lax in his precautionary defenses. The surprise attack caught him totally off guard. Shouts of "Remember the Alamo! Remember Goliad!" filled the air. Houston's successful surprise attack ended the war. He captured Santa Anna, who signed the territory away. Although the Mexican Congress repudiated the treaty, Houston was elected president of the Republic of Texas.

Few Mexican prisoners were taken at the battle of San Jacinto. Those who surrendered "were clubbed and stabbed, some on their knees. The slaughter . . . became methodical: the Texan riflemen knelt and poured a steady fire into the packed, jostling ranks." They shot the "Meskins" down as they fled. The final count showed 630 Mexicans dead versus 2 Texans.

Even Santa Anna was not let off lightly; according to Dr. Castañeda, Santa Anna "was mercilessly dragged from the ship he had boarded, subjected to more than six months' mental torture and indignities in Texas prison camps."

The Euroamerican victory paved the way for the Mexican-American War. Officially the United States had not taken sides, but men, money, and supplies poured in to aid fellow Anglo-Americans. U.S. citizens participated in the invasion of Texas with the open support of their government. Mexico's minister to the United States, Manuel Eduardo Gorostiza, protested the "arming and shipment of troops and supplies to territory which was part of Mexico, and the dispatch of United States troops into territory clearly defined by treaty as Mexican territory." General Edmund P. Gaines, Southwest commander, was sent into western Louisiana on January 23, 1836; shortly thereafter, he crossed into Texas in an action that was interpreted to be in support of the Anglo-American filibusters in Texas: "The Jackson Administration made it plain to the Mexican minister that it mattered little whether Mexico approved, that the important thing was to protect the border against Indians and Mexicans." U.S. citizens in and out of Texas loudly applauded Jackson's actions. The Mexican minister resigned his post in protest. "The success of the Texas Revolution thrust the Anglo-American frontier up against the Far Southwest, and the region came at once into the scope of Anglo ambition."

The Invasion of Mexico

In the mid-1840s, Mexico was again the target. Expansion and capitalist development moved together. The two Mexican wars gave U.S. commerce, industry, mining, agriculture, and stockraising a tremendous stimulus. "The truth is that [by the 1840s] the Pacific Coast belonged to the commercial empire that the United States was already building in that ocean."

The U.S. population of 17 million people of European extraction and 3 million slaves was considerably larger than Mexico's 7 million, of which 4 million were Indian and 3 million *mestizo* and European. The United States acted arrogantly in foreign affairs, partly because its citizens believed in their own cultural and racial superiority. Mexico was plagued with financial problems, internal ethnic conflicts, and poor leadership. General anarchy within the nation conspired against its cohesive development.

By 1844 war with Mexico over Texas and the Southwest was only a matter of time. James K. Polk, who strongly advocated the annexation of Texas and expansionism in general, won the presidency by only a small margin, but his election was interpreted as a mandate for national expansion. Outgoing

President Tyler acted by calling upon Congress to annex Texas by joint resolution; the measure was passed a few days before the inauguration of Polk, who accepted the arrangement. In December 1845, Texas became a state.

Mexico promptly broke off diplomatic relations with the United States, and Polk ordered General Zachary Taylor into Texas to "protect" the border. The location of the border was in doubt. The North Americans claimed it was at the Río Grande, but based on historical precedent, Mexico insisted it was 150 miles farther north, at the Nueces River. Taylor marched his forces across the Nueces into the disputed territory, wanting to provoke an attack.

In November 1845, Polk sent John Slidell on a secret mission to Mexico to negotiate for the disputed area. The presence of Anglo-American troops between the Nueces and the Río Grande and the annexation of Texas made negotiations an absurdity. They refused to accept Polk's minister's credentials, although they did offer to give him an ad hoc status. Slidell declined anything less than full recognition and returned to Washington in March 1846, convinced that Mexico would have to be "chastised" before it would negotiate. By March 28, Taylor had advanced to the Río Grande with an army of 4,000.

Polk, incensed at Mexico's refusal to meet with Slidell on his terms and at General Mairano Paredes's reaffirmation of his country's claims to all of Texas, began to draft his declaration of war when he learned of the Mexican attack on U.S. troops in the disputed territory. Polk immediately declared that the United States had been provoked into war, that Mexico had "shed American blood upon the American soil." On May 13, 1846, Congress declared war and authorized the recruitment and supplying of 50,000 troops.

Years later, Ulysses S. Grant wrote that he believed that Polk provoked the war and that the annexation of Texas was, in fact, an act of aggression. He added: "I had a horror of the Mexican War . . . only I had not moral courage enough to resign. . . . I considered my supreme duty was to my flag."

The poorly equipped and poorly led Mexican army stood little chance against the expansion-minded Anglos. Even before the war Polk planned the campaign in stages: (1) Mexicans would be cleared out of Texas; (2) Anglos would occupy California and New Mexico; and (3) U.S. forces would march to Mexico City to force the beaten government to make peace on Polk's terms. And that was the way the campaign basically went. In the end, at a relatively small cost in men and money, the war netted the United States huge territorial gains. In all, the United States took over 1 million square miles from Mexico.

The Rationale for Conquest

In his *Origins of the War with Mexico: The Polk-Stockton Intrigue,* Glenn W. Price states: "Americans have found it rather more difficult than other peoples to deal rationally with their wars. We have thought of ourselves as unique, and of this society as specially planned and created to avoid the errors of all other nations." Many Anglo-American historians have attempted to dismiss it simply as a "bad war," which took place during the era of Manifest Destiny.

Manifest Destiny had its roots in Puritan ideas, which continue to influence Anglo-American thought to this day. According to the Puritan ethic, salvation is determined by God. The establishment of the City of God on earth is not only the duty of those chosen people predestined for salvation but is also the proof of their state of grace. Anglo-Americans believed that God had made them custodians of democracy and that they had a mission—that is, that they were predestined to spread its principles. As the young nation survived its infancy, established its power in the defeat of the British in the War of 1812, expanded westward, and enjoyed both commercial and industrial success, its sense of mission heightened. Many citizens believed that God had destined them to own and occupy all of the land from ocean to ocean and pole to pole. Their mission, their destiny made manifest, was to spread the principles of democracy and Christianity to the unfortunates of the hemisphere. By dismissing the war simply as part of the era of Manifest Destiny the apologists for the war ignore the consequences of the doctrine.

The Monroe Doctrine of the 1820s told the world that the Americas were no longer open for colonization or conquest; however, it did not say anything about that limitation applying to the United States. Uppermost in the minds of the U.S. government, the military, and much of the public was the acquisition of territory. No one ever intended to leave Mexico without extracting territory. Land was the main motive for the war.

This aggression was justified by a rhetoric of peace. Consider, for example, Polk's war message of May 11, 1846, in which he gave his reasons for going to war:

> The strong desire to establish peace with Mexico on liberal and honorable terms, and the readiness of this Government to regulate and adjust our boundary and other causes of difference with that power on such fair and equitable principles as would lead to permanent relations of the most friendly nature, induced me in September last to seek reopening of diplomatic relations between the two countries.

The United States, he continued, had made every effort not to provoke Mexico, but the Mexican government had refused to receive an Anglo-American minister. Polk reviewed the events leading to the war and concluded:

> As war exists, and notwithstanding all our efforts to avoid it, exists by the act of Mexico herself, we are called upon by every consideration of duty and patriotism to vindicate with decision the honor, the rights, and the interests of our country.

Historical distance from the war has not lessened the need to justify U.S. aggression. In 1920 Justin H. Smith received a Pulitzer prize in history for a work that blamed the war on Mexico. What is amazing is that Smith allegedly examined over 100,000 manuscripts, 120,000 books and pamphlets, and 200 or more periodicals to come to this conclusion. He was rewarded for relieving the Anglo-American conscience. His two-volume "study," entitled *The War with*

Mexico, used analyses such as the following to support its thesis that the Mexicans were at fault for the war:

> At the beginning of her independent existence, our people felt earnestly and enthusiastically anxious to maintain cordial relations with our sister republic, and many crossed the line of absurd sentimentality in the cause. Friction was inevitable, however. The Americans were direct, positive, brusque, angular and pushing; and they would not understand their neighbors in the south. The Mexicans were equally unable to fathom our goodwill, sincerity, patriotism, resoluteness and courage; and certain features of their character and national condition made it far from easy to get on with them.

This attitude of self-righteousness on the part of government officials and historians toward U.S. aggressions spills over to the relationships between the majority society and minority groups. Anglo-Americans believe that the war was advantageous to the Southwest and to the Mexicans who remained or later migrated there. They now had the benefits of democracy and were liberated from their tyrannical past. In other words, Mexicans should be grateful to the Anglo-Americans. If Mexicans and the Anglo-Americans clash, the rationale runs, naturally it is because Mexicans cannot understand or appreciate the merits of a free society, which must be defended against ingrates. Therefore, domestic war, or repression, is justified by the same kind of rhetoric that justifies international aggression.

Professor Gene M. Brack questions historians who base their research on Justin Smith's outdated work: "American historians have consistently praised Justin Smith's influential and outrageously ethnocentric account."

The Myth of a Nonviolent Nation

Most studies on the Mexican-American War dwell on the causes and results of the war, sometimes dealing with war strategy. One must go beyond this point, since the war left bitterness, and since Anglo-American actions in Mexico are vividly remembered. Mexicans' attitude toward Anglo-Americans has been influenced by the war just as the easy victory of the United States conditioned Anglo-American behavior toward Mexicans. Fortunately, some Anglo-Americans condemned this aggression and flatly accused their leaders of being insolent and land-hungry, and of having manufactured the war. Abiel Abbott Livermore in *The War with Mexico Reviewed,* accused his country, writing:

> Again, the pride of race has swollen to still greater insolence the pride of country, always quite active enough for the due observance of the claims of universal brotherhood. The Anglo-Saxons have been apparently persuaded to think themselves the chosen people, annointed race of the Lord, commissioned to drive out the heathen, and plant their religion and institutions in every Canaan they could subjugate. . . . Our treatment both of the red man and the black man has habituated us to feel our power and forget right. . . . The passion for land, also, is a leading characteristic of the American people. . . . The god Terminus is an unknown deity in America. Like the hunger of the pauper boy of fiction, the cry had been, 'more, more, give us more.'

Livermore's work, published in 1850, was awarded the American Peace Society prize for "the best review of the Mexican War and the principles of Christianity, and an enlightened statesmanship."

In truth, the United States conducted a violent and brutal war. Zachary Taylor's artillery leveled the Mexican city of Matamoros, killing hundreds of innocent civilians with *la bomba* (the bomb). Many Mexicans jumped into the Río Grande, relieved of their pain by a watery grave. The occupation that followed was even more terrorizing. Taylor was unable to control his volunteers:

> The regulars regarded the volunteers, of whom about two thousand had reached Matamoros by the end of May, with impatience and contempt. . . . They robbed Mexicans of their cattle and corn, stole their fences for firewood, got drunk, and killed several inoffensive inhabitants of the town in the streets. . . .

The Treaty of Guadalupe Hidalgo

By late August 1847 the war was almost at an end. Scott's defeat of Santa Anna in a hard-fought battle at Churubusco put Anglo-Americans at the gates of Mexico City. Santa Anna made overtures for an armistice that broke down after two weeks, and the war resumed. On September 13, 1847, Scott drove into the city. Although Mexicans fought valiantly, the battle left 4,000 dead, with another 3,000 prisoners. On September 13, before the occupation of Mexico City began, *Los Niños Héroes* (The Boy Heroes) leapt to their deaths rather than surrender. These teenage cadets were Francisco Márquez, Agustín Melgar, Juan Escutia, Fernando Montes de Oca, Vicente Suárez, and Juan de la Barrera. They became "a symbol and image of this unrighteous war."

The Mexicans continued fighting. The presiding justice of the Supreme Court, Manuel de la Peña, assumed the presidency. He knew that Mexico had lost and that he had to salvage as much as possible. Pressure increased, with U.S. troops in control of much of Mexico.

Nicholas Trist, sent to Mexico to act as peace commissioner, had arrived in Vera Cruz on May 6, 1847, but controversy with Scott over Trist's authority and illness delayed an armistice, and hostilities continued. After the fall of Mexico City, Secretary of State James Buchanan wanted to revise Trist's instructions. He ordered Trist to break off negotiations and return home. Polk wanted more land from Mexico. Trist, however, with the support of Winfield Scott, decided to ignore Polk's order, and began negotiations on January 2, 1848, on the original terms. Mexico, badly beaten, her government in a state of turmoil, had no choice but to agree to the Anglo-Americans' proposals.

On February 2, 1848, the Mexicans ratified the Treaty of Guadalupe Hidalgo, with Mexico accepting the Río Grande as the Texas border and ceding the Southwest (which incorporated the present-day states of California, New Mexico, Nevada, and parts of Colorado, Arizona, and Utah) to the United States in return for $15 million.

Polk, furious about the treaty, considered Trist "contemptibly base" for having ignored his orders. Yet he had no choice but to submit the treaty to the Senate. With the exception of Article X, which concerned the rights of Mexicans in the ceded territory, the Senate ratified the treaty on March 10, 1848, by a vote of 28 to 14. To insist on more territory would have meant more fighting, and both Polk and the Senate realized that the war was already unpopular in many circles. The treaty was sent to the Mexican Congress for ratification; although the Congress had difficulty forming a quorum, the treaty was ratified on May 19 by a 52 to 35 vote. Hostilities between the two nations officially ended. Trist, however, was branded as a "scoundrel," because Polk was disappointed in the settlement. There was considerable support in the United States for acquisition of all Mexico.

During the treaty talks Mexican negotiators, concerned about Mexicans left behind, expressed great reservations about these people being forced to "merge or blend" into Anglo-American culture. They protested the exclusion of provisions that protected Mexican citizens' rights, land titles, and religion. They wanted to protect their rights by treaty.

Articles VIII, IX, and X specifically referred to the rights of Mexicans. Under the treaty, Mexicans left behind had one year to choose whether to return to Mexico or remain in "occupied Mexico." About 2,000 elected to leave; most remained in what they considered *their* land.

Article IX of the treaty guaranteed Mexicans "the enjoyment of all the rights of citizens of the United States according to the principles of the Constitution; and in the meantime shall be maintained and protected in the free enjoyment of their liberty and property, and secured in the free exercise of their religion without restriction." Lynn I. Perrigo, in *The American Southwest*, summarizes the guarantees of Articles VIII and IX: "In other words, besides the rights and duties of American citizenship, they [the Mexicans] would have some special privileges derived from their previous customs in language, law, and religion."

The omitted Article X had comprehensive guarantees protecting "all prior and pending titles to property of every description." When Article X was deleted by the U.S. Senate, Mexican officials protested. Anglo-American emissaries reassured them by drafting a Statement of Protocol on May 26, 1848:

> The American government by suppressing the Xth article of the Treaty of Guadalupe Hidalgo did not in any way intend to annul the grants of lands made by Mexico in the ceded territories. These grants . . . preserve the legal value which they may possess, and the grantees may cause their legitimate (titles) to be acknowledged before the American tribunals.
>
> Conformable to the law of the United States, legitimate titles to every description of property, personal and real, existing in the ceded territories, are those which were legitimate titles under the Mexican law of California and New Mexico up to the 13th of May, 1846, and in Texas up to the 2nd of March, 1836.

Considering the Mexican opposition to the treaty, it is doubtful whether the Mexican Congress would have ratified the treaty without this clarification. The vote was close.

The Statement of Protocol was strengthened by Articles VIII and IX, which guaranteed Mexicans rights of property and protection under the law. In addition, court decisions have generally interpreted the treaty as protecting land titles and water rights. In practice, however, the treaty was ignored and during the nineteenth century most Mexicans in the United States were considered as a class apart from the dominant race. Nearly every one of the obligations discussed above was violated, confirming the prophecy of Mexican diplomat Manuel Crescion Rejón, who, at the time the treaty was signed, commented:

> Our race, our unfortunate people will have to wander in search of hospitality in a strange land, only to be ejected later. Descendants of the Indians that we are, the North Americans hate us, their spokesmen depreciate us, even if they recognize the justice of our cause, and they consider us unworthy to form with them one nation and one society, they clearly manifest that their future expansion begins with the territory that they take from us and pushing [sic] aside our citizens who inhabit the land.

As a result of the Texas War and the Anglo-American aggressions of 1845–1848, the occupation of conquered territory began. In material terms, in exchange for 12,000 lives and more than $100 million, the United States acquired a colony two and a half times as large as France, containing rich farmlands and natural resources such as gold, silver, zinc, copper, oil, and uranium, which would make possible its unprecedented industrial boom. It acquired ports on the Pacific that generated further economic expansion across that ocean. Mexico was left with its shrunken resources to face the continued advances of the United States.

Summary

The colonial experience of the United States differs from that of Third World nations. Its history resembles that of Australia and/or South Africa, where colonizers relegated indigenous populations to fourth-class citizenship or noncitizenship. North American independence came at the right time, slightly predating the industrialization of nineteenth-century Europe. Its merchants took over a lucrative trade network from the British; the new Republic established a government that supported trade, industry, and commercial agriculture. A North American ideology which presumed that Latin Americans had stolen the name "America" and that God, the realtor, had given them the land, encouraged colonial expansion.

Mexico, like most Third World nations after independence, needed a period of stability. North American penetration into Texas in the 1820s and 1830s threatened Mexico. The U.S. economic system encouraged expansion, and many of the first wave of migrants to Texas had lost their farms due to the depression of 1819. Land in Texas, generously cheap, provided room for the spread of slavery. Although many North Americans in all probability intended to obey Mexican laws and meet conditions for obtaining land grants, North American ethnocentrism and self-interest soon eroded those intentions. Clearly land values would zoom if Texas were part of the United States.

North American historians have frequently portrayed the Texas invasion as a second encounter in the "American War of Independence." Myths such as that of a tyrannical Mexican government have justified the war. In truth, the cause of the war was profit. Mexico did not invade Texas; it belonged to Mexico. Few if any of the North Americans in Texas had been born there or had lived in Texas for more than five years. Most had just recently arrived. Some rich Mexicans supported the North Americans for obvious reasons—it was in their economic self-interest. A stalemate resulted, with Euroamericans establishing the Texas Republic. In 1844, the United States broke the standoff and annexed Texas.

President James K. Polk manufactured the war with Mexico. Some North Americans opposed the war—not on grounds that it violated Mexico's territorial integrity, but because of the probability of the extension of slavery. Many North American military leaders admitted that the war was unjust, and that the United States had committed an act of aggression. However, patriotism and support for the war overwhelmed reason in the march "To the Halls of the Montezumas [sic]." North Americans, buoyant in their prosperity, wanted to prove that the United States was a world-class power.

The war became a Protestant Crusade. Texans made emotional pleas to avenge the Alamo. Both appeals were instrumental in arousing North Americans to the call to arms, to prove their valor and power of the young "American" democracy. North American soldiers committed atrocities against Mexican civilians; few were punished.

The Treaty of Guadalupe Hidalgo ended the war, and the United States grabbed over half of Mexico's soil. The war proved costly to Mexico and to Mexicans left behind. According to the treaty, Mexicans who elected to stay in the conquered territory would become U.S. citizens with all the rights of citizenship. However, the Treaty of Guadalupe Hidalgo, like those signed with the indigenous people of North American, depended on the good faith of the United States and its ability to keep its word.

NO

Norman A. Graebner

The Mexican War:
A Study in Causation

On May 11, 1846, President James K. Polk presented his war message to Congress. After reviewing the skirmish between General Zachary Taylor's dragoons and a body of Mexican soldiers along the Rio Grande, the president asserted that Mexico "has passed the boundary of the United States, has invaded our territory and shed American blood upon the American soil. . . . War exists, and, notwithstanding all our efforts to avoid it, exists by act of Mexico." No country could have had a superior case for war. Democrats in large numbers (for it was largely a partisan matter) responded with the patriotic fervor which Polk expected of them. "Our government has permitted itself to be insulted long enough," wrote one Georgian. "The blood of her citizens has been spilt on her own soil. It appeals to us for vengeance." Still, some members of Congress, recalling more accurately than the president the circumstances of the conflict, soon rendered the Mexican War the most reviled in American history—at least until the Vietnam War of the 1960s. One outraged Whig termed the war "illegal, unrighteous, and damnable," and Whigs questioned both Polk's honesty and his sense of geography. Congressman Joshua R. Giddings of Ohio accused the president of "planting the standard of the United States on foreign soil, and using the military forces of the United States to violate every principle of international law and moral justice." To vote for the war, admitted Senator John C. Calhoun, was "to plunge a dagger into his own heart, and more so." Indeed, some critics in Congress openly wished the Mexicans well.

For over a century such profound differences in perception have pervaded American writings on the Mexican War. Even in the past decade, historians have reached conclusions on the question of war guilt as disparate as those which separated Polk from his wartime conservative and abolitionist critics. . . .

In some measure the diversity of judgment on the Mexican War, as on other wars, is understandable. By basing their analyses on official rationalizations, historians often ignore the more universal causes of war which transcend individual conflicts and which can establish the bases for greater consensus. Neither the officials in Washington nor those in Mexico City ever acknowledged any alternatives to the actions which they took. But governments generally have more choices in any controversy than they are prepared to admit.

From Norman A. Graebner, "The Mexican War: A Study in Causation," *Pacific Historical Review,* vol. 49, no. 3 (August 1980), pp. 405–426. Copyright © 1980 by The American Historical Association, Pacific Coast Branch. Reprinted by permission of University of California Press Journals. Notes omitted.

Circumstances determine their extent. The more powerful a nation, the more remote its dangers, the greater its options between action and inaction. Often for the weak, unfortunately, the alternative is capitulation or war. . . . Polk and his advisers developed their Mexican policies on the dual assumption that Mexico was weak and that the acquisition of certain Mexican territories would satisfy admirably the long-range interests of the United States. Within that context, Polk's policies were direct, timely, and successful. But the president had choices. Mexico, whatever its internal condition, was no direct threat to the United States. Polk, had he so desired, could have avoided war; indeed, he could have ignored Mexico in 1845 with absolute impunity.

⋘◉⋙

In explaining the Mexican War historians have dwelled on the causes of friction in American-Mexican relations. In part these lay in the disparate qualities of the two populations, in part in the vast discrepancies between the two countries in energy, efficiency, power, and national wealth. Through two decades of independence Mexico had experienced a continuous rise and fall of governments; by the 1840s survival had become the primary concern of every regime. Conscious of their weakness, the successive governments in Mexico City resented the superior power and effectiveness of the United States and feared American notions of destiny that anticipated the annexation of Mexico's northern provinces. Having failed to prevent the formation of the Texas Republic, Mexico reacted to Andrew Jackson's recognition of Texan independence in March 1837 with deep indignation. Thereafter the Mexican raids into Texas, such as the one on San Antonio in 1842, aggravated the bitterness of Texans toward Mexico, for such forays had no purpose beyond terrorizing the frontier settlements.

Such mutual animosities, extensive as they were, do not account for the Mexican War. Governments as divided and chaotic as the Mexican regimes of the 1840s usually have difficulty in maintaining positive and profitable relations with their neighbors; their behavior often produces annoyance, but seldom armed conflict. Belligerence toward other countries had flowed through U.S. history like a torrent without, in itself, setting off a war. Nations do not fight over cultural differences or verbal recriminations; they fight over perceived threats to their interests created by the ambitions or demands of others.

What increased the animosity between Mexico City and Washington was a series of specific issues over which the two countries perennially quarreled—claims, boundaries, and the future of Texas. Nations have made claims a pretext for intervention, but never a pretext for war. Every nineteenth-century effort to collect debts through force assumed the absence of effective resistance, for no debt was worth the price of war. To collect its debt from Mexico in 1838, for example, France blockaded Mexico's gulf ports and bombarded Vera Cruz. The U.S. claims against Mexico created special problems which discounted their seriousness as a rationale for war. True, the Mexican government failed to protect the possessions and the safety of Americans in Mexico from robbery, theft, and other illegal actions, but U.S. citizens were under no obligation to do business in Mexico and should have understood the risk of transporting goods and money in that country. Minister Waddy Thompson wrote from Mexico City in 1842 that it would be "with somewhat of bad grace that we should war upon a country because it could not pay its debts when so many of our own states are in the same situation." Even as the United States after 1842 attempted futilely to collect the $2 million awarded its citizens by a claims commission, it was far more deeply in debt to Britain over speculative losses. Minister Wilson Shannon reported in the summer of 1844 that the claims issue defied settlement in Mexico City and recommended that Washington take the needed action to compel Mexico to pay. If Polk would take up the challenge and sacrifice American human and material resources in a war against Mexico, he would do so for reasons other than the enforcement of claims. The president knew well that Mexico could not pay, yet as late as May 9, 1846, he was ready to ask Congress for a declaration of war on the question of unpaid claims alone.

Congress's joint resolution for Texas annexation in February 1845 raised the specter of war among editors and politicians alike. As early as 1843 the Mexican government had warned the American minister in Mexico City that annexation would render war inevitable; Mexican officials in Washington repeated that warning. To Mexico, therefore, the move to annex Texas was an unbearable affront. Within one month after Polk's inauguration on March 4, General Juan Almonte, the Mexican minister in Washington, boarded a packet in New York and sailed for Vera Cruz to sever his country's diplomatic relations with the United States. Even before the Texas Convention could meet on July 4 to vote annexation, rumors of a possible Mexican invasion of Texas prompted Polk to advance Taylor's forces from Fort Jesup in Louisiana down the Texas coast. Polk instructed Taylor to extend his protection to the Rio Grande but to avoid any areas to the north of that river occupied by Mexican troops. Simultaneously the president reinforced the American squadron in the Gulf of Mexico. "The threatened invasion of Texas by a large Mexican army," Polk informed Andrew J. Donelson, the American chargé in Texas, on June 15, "is well calculated to excite great interest here and increases our solicitude concerning the final action by the Congress and the Convention of Texas." Polk assured Donelson that he intended to defend Texas to the limit of his constitutional power. Donelson resisted the pressure of those Texans who wanted Taylor to advance to the Rio Grande; instead, he placed the general at Corpus Christi on the Nueces River. Taylor agreed that the line from the mouth of the Nueces to San Antonio covered the Texas settlements and afforded a favorable base from which to defend the frontier.

Those who took the rumors of Mexican aggressiveness seriously lauded the president's action. With Texas virtually a part of the United States, argued the *Washington Union,* "We owe it to ourselves, to the proud and elevated character which America maintains among the nations of the earth, to guard our own territory from the invasion of the ruthless Mexicans." The *New York Morning News* observed that Polk's policy would, on the whole, "command a general concurrence of the public opinion of his country." Some Democratic leaders, fearful of a Mexican attack, urged the president to strengthen Taylor's forces and order them to take the offensive should Mexican soldiers cross the Rio Grande. Others believed the reports from Mexico exaggerated, for there was no apparent relationship between the country's expressions of belligerence and its capacity to act. Secretary of War William L. Marcy admitted that his information was no better than that of other commentators. "I have at no time," he wrote in July, "felt that war with Mexico was probable—and do not now believe it is, yet it is in the range of possible occurrences. I have officially acted on the hypothesis that our peace may be temporarily disturbed without however believing it will be." Still convinced that the administration had no grounds for alarm, Marcy wrote on August 12: "The presence of a considerable force in Texas will do no hurt and possibly may be of great use." In September William S. Parrott, Polk's special agent in Mexico, assured the president that there would be neither a Mexican declaration of war nor an invasion of Texas.

Polk insisted that the administration's show of force in Texas would prevent rather than provoke war. "I do not anticipate that Mexico will be mad enough to declare war," he wrote in July, but "I think she would have done so but for the appearance of a strong naval force in the Gulf and our army moving in the direction of her frontier on land." Polk restated this judgment on July 28 in a letter to General Robert Armstrong, the U.S. consul at Liverpool: "I think there need be but little apprehension of war with Mexico. If however she shall be mad enough to make war we are prepared to meet her." The president assured Senator William H. Haywood of North Carolina that the American forces in Texas would never aggress against Mexico; however, they would prevent any Mexican forces from crossing the Rio Grande. In conversation with Senator William S. Archer of Virginia on September 1, the president added confidently that "the appearance of our land and naval forces on the borders of Mexico & in the Gulf would probably deter and prevent Mexico from either declaring war or invading Texas." Polk's continuing conviction that Mexico would not attack suggests that his deployment of U.S. land and naval forces along Mexico's periphery was designed less to protect Texas than to support an aggressive diplomacy which might extract a satisfactory treaty from Mexico without war. For Anson Jones, the last president of the Texas Republic, Polk's deployments had precisely that purpose:

> Texas never actually needed the protection of the United States after I came into office. . . . There was no necessity for it after the 'preliminary Treaty,' as we were at peace with Mexico, and knew perfectly well that that Government, though she might bluster a little, had not the slightest idea of invading Texas either by land or water; and that nothing would provoke her to (active) hostilities, but the presence of troops in the immediate neighborhood of the Rio Grande, threatening her towns and settlements on the southwest side of that river. . . . But Donelson appeared so intent upon 'encumbering us with help,' that finally, to get rid of his annoyance, he was told he might give us as much protection as he pleased. . . . The protection asked for was only *prospective* and contingent; the *protection* he had in view was *immediate* and *aggressive*.

For Polk the exertion of military and diplomatic pressure on a disorganized Mexico was not a prelude to war. Whig critics of annexation had predicted war; this alone compelled the administration to avoid a conflict over Texas. In his memoirs Jones recalled that in 1845 Commodore Robert F. Stockton, with either the approval or the connivance of Polk, attempted to convince him that he should place Texas "in an attitude of active hostility toward Mexico, so that, when Texas was finally brought into the Union, *she might bring war with her.*" If Stockton engaged in such an intrigue, he apparently did so on his own initiative, for no evidence exists to implicate the administration. Polk not only preferred to achieve his purposes by means other than war but also assumed that his military measures in Texas, limited as they were, would convince the Mexican government that it could not escape the necessity of coming to terms with the United States. Washington's policy toward Mexico during 1845 achieved the broad national purpose of Texas annexation. Beyond that it brought U.S. power to bear on Mexico in a manner calculated to further the processes of negotiation. Whether the burgeoning tension would lead to a negotiated boundary settlement or to war hinged on two factors: the nature of Polk's demands and Mexico's response to them. The president announced his objectives to Mexico's troubled officialdom through his instructions to John Slidell, his special emissary who departed for Mexico in November 1845 with the assurance that the government there was prepared to reestablish formal diplomatic relations with the United States and negotiate a territorial settlement. . . .

≈⟨◉⟩≈

Actually, Slidell's presence in Mexico inaugurated a diplomatic crisis not unlike those which precede most wars. Fundamentally the Polk administration, in dispatching Slidell, gave the Mexicans the same two choices that the dominant power in any confrontation gives to the weaker: the acceptance of a body of concrete diplomatic demands or eventual war. Slidell's instructions described U.S. territorial objectives with considerable clarity. If Mexico knew little of Polk's growing acquisitiveness toward California during the autumn of 1845, Slidell proclaimed the president's intentions with his proposals to purchase varying portions of California for as much as $25 million. Other countries such as England and Spain had consigned important areas of the New World through peaceful negotiations, but the United States, except in its Mexican relations, had never asked any country to part with a portion of its own territory. Yet Polk could not understand why Mexico should reveal any special reluctance to part with Texas, the Rio Grande, New Mexico, or California. What made the terms of Slidell's instructions appear fair to him was Mexico's military and financial helplessness. Polk's defenders noted that California was not a sine qua non of any settlement and that the president offered to settle the immediate controversy over the acquisition of the Rio Grande boundary alone in exchange for the cancellation of claims. Unfortunately, amid the passions of December 1845, such distinctions were lost. Furthermore, a settlement of the Texas boundary would not have resolved the California question at all.

Throughout the crisis months of 1845 and 1846, spokesmen of the Polk administration repeatedly warned the Mexican government that its choices were limited. In June 1845, Polk's mouthpiece, the *Washington Union,* had observed characteristically that, if Mexico resisted Washington's demands, "a corps of properly organized volunteers . . . would invade, overrun, and occupy Mexico. They would enable us not only to take California, but to keep it."

American officials, in their contempt for Mexico, spoke privately of the need to chastize that country for its annoyances and insults. Parrott wrote to Secretary of State James Buchanan in October that he wished "to see this people well flogged by Uncle Sam's boys, ere we enter upon negotiations. . . . I know [the Mexicans] better, perhaps, than any other American citizen and I am fully persuaded, they can never love or respect us, as we should be loved and respected by them, until we shall have given them a positive proof of our superiority." Mexico's pretensions would continue, wrote Slidell in late December, "until the Mexican people shall be convinced by hostile demonstrations, that our differences must be settled promptly, either by negotiation or the sword." In January 1846 the *Union* publicly threatened Mexico with war if it rejected the just demands of the United States: "The result of such a course on her part may compel us to resort to more decisive measures. . . . to obtain the settlement of our legitimate claims." As Slidell prepared to leave Mexico in March 1846, he again reminded the administration: "Depend upon it, we can never get along well with them, until we have given them a good drubbing." In Washington on May 8, Slidell advised the president "to take the redress of the wrongs and injuries which we had so long borne from Mexico into our own hands, and to act with promptness and energy."

Mexico responded to Polk's challenge with an outward display of belligerence and an inward dread of war. Mexicans feared above all that the United States intended to overrun their country and seize much of their territory. Polk and his advisers assumed that Mexico, to avoid an American invasion, would give up its provinces peacefully. Obviously Mexico faced growing diplomatic and military pressures to negotiate away its territories; it faced no moral obligation to do so. Herrera and Paredes had the sovereign right to protect their regimes by avoiding any formal recognition of Slidell and by rejecting any of the boundary proposals embodied in his instructions, provided that in the process they did not endanger any legitimate interests of the American people. At least to some Mexicans, Slidell's terms demanded nothing less than Mexico's capitulation. By what standard was $2 million a proper payment for the Rio Grande boundary, or $25 million a fair price for California? No government would have accepted such terms. Having rejected negotiation in the face of superior force, Mexico would meet the challenge with a final gesture of defiance. In either case it was destined to lose, but historically nations have preferred to fight than to give away territory under diplomatic pressure alone. Gene M. Brack, in his long study of Mexico's deep-seated fear and resentment of the United States, explained Mexico's ultimate behavior in such terms:

> President Polk knew that Mexico could offer but feeble resistance militarily, and he knew that Mexico needed money. No proper American would exchange territory and the national honor for cash, but President Polk mistakenly believed that the application of military pressure would convince Mexicans to do so. They did not respond logically, but patriotically. Left with the choice of war or territorial concessions, the former course, however dim the prospects of success, could be the only one.

Mexico, in its resistance, gave Polk the three choices which every nation gives another in an uncompromisable confrontation: to withdraw his demands and permit the issues to drift, unresolved; to reduce his goals in the interest of an immediate settlement; or to escalate the pressures in the hope of securing an eventual settlement on his own terms. Normally when the internal conditions of a country undermine its relations with others, a diplomatic corps simply removes itself from the hostile environment and awaits a better day. Mexico, despite its animosity, did not endanger the security interests of the United States; it had not invaded Texas and did not contemplate doing so. Mexico had refused to pay the claims, but those claims were not equal to the price of a one-week war. Whether Mexico negotiated a boundary for Texas in 1846 mattered little; the United States had lived with unsettled boundaries for decades without considering war. Settlers, in time, would have forced a decision, but in 1846 the region between the Nueces and the Rio Grande was a vast, generally unoccupied wilderness. Thus there was nothing, other than Polk's ambitions, to prevent the United States from withdrawing its diplomats from Mexico City and permitting its relations to drift. But Polk, whatever the language of his instructions, did not send Slidell to Mexico to normalize relations with that government. He expected Slidell to negotiate an immediate boundary settlement favorable to the United States, and nothing less.

Recognizing no need to reduce his demands on Mexico, Polk, without hesitation, took the third course which Mexico offered. Congress bound the president to the annexation of Texas; thereafter the Polk administration was free to formulate its own policies toward Mexico. With the Slidell mission Polk embarked upon a program of gradual coercion to achieve a settlement, preferably without war. That program led logically from his dispatching an army to Texas and his denunciation of Mexico in his annual message of December 1845 to his new instructions of January 1846, which ordered General Taylor to the Rio Grande. Colonel Atocha, spokesman for the deposed Mexican leader, Antonio López de Santa Anna, encouraged Polk to pursue his policy of escalation. The president recorded Atocha's advice:

> He said our army should be marched at once from Corpus Christi to the Del Norte, and a strong naval force assembled at Vera Cruz, that Mr. Slidell, the U.S. Minister, should withdraw from Jalappa, and go on board one of our ships of War at Vera Cruz, and in that position should demand the payment of [the] amount due our citizens; that it was well known the Mexican Government was unable to pay in money, and that when they saw a strong force ready to strike on their coasts and border, they would, he had no doubt, feel their danger and agree to the boundary suggested. He said that Paredes, Almonte, & Gen'l Santa Anna were all willing for such an arrangement, but that they dare not make it until it was made apparent to the Archbishop of Mexico & the people generally that it was necessary to save their country from a war with the U. States.

Thereafter Polk never questioned the efficacy of coercion. He asserted at a cabinet meeting on February 17 that "it would be necessary to take strong measures towards Mexico before our difficulties with that Government could be settled." Similarly on April 18 Polk told Calhoun that "our relations with Mexico had reached a point where we could not stand still but must treat all nations whether weak or strong alike, and that I saw no alternative but strong measures towards Mexico." A week later the president again brought the Mexican question before the cabinet. "I expressed my opinion," he noted in his diary, "that we must take redress for the injuries done us into our own hands, that we had attempted to conciliate Mexico in vain, and had forborne until forbearance was no longer either a virtue or patriotic." Convinced that Paredes needed money, Polk suggested to leading senators that Congress appropriate $1 million both to encourage Paredes to negotiate and to sustain him in power until the United States could ratify the treaty. The president failed to secure Calhoun's required support.

Polk's persistence led him and the country to war. Like all escalations in the exertion of force, his decision responded less to unwanted and unanticipated resistance than to the requirements of the clearly perceived and inflexible purposes which guided the administration. What perpetuated the president's escalation to the point of war was his determination to pursue goals to the end whose achievement lay outside the possibilities of successful negotiations. Senator Thomas Hart Benton of Missouri saw this situation when he wrote: "It is impossible to conceive of an administration less warlike, or more intriguing, than that of Mr. Polk. They were *men of peace, with objects to be accomplished by means of war*; so that war was a necessity and an indispensability to their purpose."

Polk understood fully the state of Mexican opinion. In placing General Taylor on the Rio Grande he revealed again his contempt for Mexico. Under no national obligation to expose the country's armed forces, he would not have advanced Taylor in the face of a superior military force. Mexico had been undiplomatic; its denunciations of the United States were insulting and provocative. But if Mexico's behavior antagonized Polk, it did not antagonize the Whigs, the abolitionists, or even much of the Democratic party. Such groups did not regard Mexico as a threat; they warned the administration repeatedly that Taylor's presence on the Rio Grande would provoke war. But in the balance against peace was the pressure of American expansionism. Much of the Democratic and expansionist press, having accepted without restraint both the purposes of the Polk administration and its charges of Mexican perfidy, urged the president on to more vigorous action. . . .

Confronted with the prospect of further decline which they could neither accept nor prevent, [the Mexicans] lashed out with the intention of protecting their self-esteem and compelling the United States, if it was determined to have the Rio Grande, New Mexico, and California, to pay for its prizes with something other than money. On April 23, Paredes issued a proclamation declaring a defensive war against the United States. Predictably, one day later the Mexicans fired on a detachment of U.S. dragoons. Taylor's report of the attack reached Polk on Saturday evening, May 9. On Sunday the president drafted his war message and delivered it to Congress on the following day. Had Polk avoided the crisis, he might have gained the time required to permit the emigrants of 1845 and 1846 to settle the California issue without war.

What clouds the issue of the Mexican War's justification was the acquisition of New Mexico and California, for contemporaries and historians could not logically condemn the war and laud the Polk administration for its territorial achievements. Perhaps it is true that time would have permitted American pioneers to transform California into another Texas. But even then California's acquisition by the United States would have emanated from the use of force, for the elimination of Mexican sovereignty, whether through revolution or war, demanded the successful use of power. If the power employed in revolution would have been less obtrusive than that exerted in war, its role would have been no less essential. There simply was no way that the United States could acquire California peacefully. If the distraught Mexico of 1845 would not sell the distant province, no regime thereafter would have done so. Without forceful destruction of Mexico's sovereign power, California would have entered the twentieth century as an increasingly important region of another country.

Thus the Mexican War poses the dilemma of all international relations. Nations whose geographic and political status fails to coincide with their ambition and power can balance the two sets of factors in only one manner: through the employment of force. They succeed or fail according to circumstances; and for the United States, the conditions for achieving its empire in the Southwest and its desired frontage on the Pacific were so ideal that later generations could refer to the process as the mere fulfillment of destiny. "The Mexican Republic," lamented a Mexican writer in 1848, " . . . had among other misfortunes of less account, the great one of being in the vicinity of a strong and energetic people." What the Mexican War revealed in equal measure is the simple fact that only those countries which have achieved their destiny, whatever that may be, can afford to extol the virtues of peaceful change.

POSTSCRIPT

Was the Mexican War an Exercise in American Imperialism?

According to Graebner, President James Polk assumed that Mexico was weak and that acquiring certain Mexican territories would satisfy "the long-range interests" of the United States. But when Mexico refused Polk's attempts to purchase New Mexico and California, he was left with three options: withdraw his demands, modify and soften his proposals, or aggressively pursue his original goals. According to Graebner, the president chose the third option.

Graebner is one of the most prominent members of the "realist" school of diplomatic historians. His writings were influenced by the cold war realists, political scientists, diplomats, and journalists of the 1950s who believed that American foreign policy oscillated between heedless isolationism and crusading wars without developing coherent policies that suited the national interests of the United States.

Graebner's views on the Mexican War have not gone unchallenged. For example, both David M. Pletcher's *The Diplomacy of Annexation* (University of Missouri Press, 1973), which remains the definitive study of the Polk administration, and Charles Seller's biography *James K. Polk*, 2 vols. (Princeton University Press, 1957–1966) are critical of Polk's actions in pushing the Mexican government to assert its authority in the disputed territory.

Acuña offers a Mexican perspective on the war in the first chapter of his book *Occupied America: A History of Chicanos*, 3rd ed. (Harper & Row, 1988), from which his selection is taken. He rejects the cool, detached, realistic analysis of Graebner and argues in very passionate terms that the North Americans waged an unjust, aggressive war against their weaker neighbor to the south for the purpose of profit.

Acuña disagrees with older historians like Justin Smith and Eugene Barker, who justified the war as an inevitable conflict between a unique, nonviolent, capitalist, Protestant, democratic nation whose economic, religious, and political values were superior to a backward, feudal, Catholic, and authoritarian country.

Acuña also takes issue with Graebner, who considers Manifest Destiny to be mere political rhetoric with very limited goals. In Acuña's analysis, Manifest Destiny "had its roots in Puritan ideas, which continue to influence Anglo-American thought to this day. . . . Many citizens believed that God had destined them to own and occupy all of the land from ocean to ocean and pole to pole. Their mission, their destiny made manifest, was to spread the principles of democracy and Christianity to the unfortunates of the hemisphere."

Acuña receives support for his views from American historians like William Appleman Williams, who influenced an entire generation of diplomatic historians with his thesis on economic expansion, *The Tragedy of American*

Diplomacy (Delta, 1962). Mexican historian Ramón Eduardo Ruiz, in his book *Triumphs and Tragedy: A History of the Mexican People* (W. W. Norton, 1992), is more balanced and nuanced than Acuña but is just as critical of the racist ideology behind the rhetoric of Manifest Destiny that justified taking land away from not only Mexican Americans but also the North American Indians. In his article "Manifest Destiny and the Mexican War," in Howard H. Quint et al., eds., *Main Problems in American History, vol. 1*, 5th ed. (Dorsey Press, 1988), Ruiz maintains that Mexico never recovered economically from the loss of its territories to the United States 150 years ago. In an interesting twist, Ruiz also contends that the United States did not absorb all of Mexico into the United States after the Mexican War because it did not want any further increase to its nonwhite population base.

Both Graebner and Acuña appear ethnocentric in their analysis of the origins of the war. Graebner neglects the emotionalism and instability of Mexican politics at the time, which may have precluded the rational analysis a realistic historian might have expected in the decision-making process. Acuña also oversimplifies the motives of the Euroamericans, and he appears blinded to the political divisions between slaveholders and nonslaveholders and between Whig and Democratic politicians over the wisdom of going to war with Mexico.

The best two collections of readings from the major writers on the Mexican War are old but essential: see Archie McDonald, ed., *The Mexican War: Crisis for American Democracy* (D. C. Heath, 1969) and Ramón Eduardo Ruiz, ed., *The Mexican War: Was It Manifest Destiny?* (Holt, Rinehart & Winston, 1963).

There are several nontraditional books that cover the Mexican War, including John H. Schroeder, *Mr. Polk's War: American Opposition and Dissent, 1846–1848* (University of Wisconsin Press, 1973). Robert W. Johannsen summarizes the ways in which contemporaries viewed the war in *To the Halls of the Montezumas: The Mexican War in the American Imagination* (Oxford University Press, 1985).

ISSUE 13

Were the Abolitionists "Unrestrained Fanatics"?

YES: C. Vann Woodward, from *The Burden of Southern History*, 3d ed. (Louisiana State University Press, 1993)

NO: Donald G. Mathews, from "The Abolitionists on Slavery: The Critique Behind the Social Movement," *Journal of Southern History* (May 1967)

ISSUE SUMMARY

YES: C. Vann Woodward depicts John Brown as a fanatic who committed wholesale murder in Kansas in 1856 and whose ill-fated assault on Harpers Ferry, Virginia, in 1859, while admired by his fellow abolitionists and many northern intellectuals, was an irrational act of treason against the United States.

NO: Donald G. Mathews describes abolitionists as uncompromising agitators, not unprincipled fanatics, who employed flamboyant rhetoric but who crafted a balanced and thoughtful critique of the institution of slavery as a social evil that violated the nation's basic values.

Opposition to slavery in the area that became the United States dates back to the seventeenth and eighteenth centuries, when Puritan leaders, such as Samuel Sewall, and Quakers, such as John Woolman and Anthony Benezet, published a number of pamphlets condemning the existence of the slave system. This religious link to antislavery sentiment is also evident in the writings of John Wesley as well as in the decision of the Society of Friends in 1688 to prohibit their members from owning bondservants. Slavery was said to be contrary to Christian principles. These attacks, however, did little to diminish the institution. Complaints that the English government had instituted a series of measures that "enslaved" the colonies in British North America raised thorny questions about the presence of *real* slavery in those colonies. How could American colonists demand their freedom from King George III, who was cast in the role of oppressive master, while denying freedom and liberty to African American bondsmen?

Such a contradiction inspired a gradual emancipation movement in the North, which often was accompanied by compensation for the former slave owners.

In addition, antislavery societies sprang up throughout the nation to continue the crusade against bondage. Interestingly, the majority of these organizations were located in the South. Prior to the 1830s, the most prominent antislavery organization was the American Colonization Society, which offered a two-fold program: (1) gradual, compensated emancipation of slaves and (2) exportation of the freed men to colonies outside the boundaries of the United States, mostly to Africa.

In the 1830s, antislavery activity underwent an important transformation. A new strain of antislavery sentiment expressed itself in the abolitionist movement. Drawing momentum both from the revivalism of the Second Great Awakening and the example set by England (which prohibited slavery in its imperial holdings in 1833), abolitionists called for the immediate end to slavery without compensation to masters for the loss of their property. Abolitionists viewed slavery not so much as a practical problem to be resolved, but rather as a moral offense incapable of resolution through traditional channels of political compromise. In January 1831, William Lloyd Garrison, who for many came to symbolize the abolitionist crusade, published the first issue of *The Liberator*, a newspaper dedicated to the immediate end to slavery. In his first editorial, Garrison expressed the self-righteous indignation of many in the abolitionist movement when he warned slaveholders and their supporters to "urge me not to use moderation in a cause like the present. I am in earnest—I will not equivocate—I will not excuse—I will not retreat a single inch—AND I WILL BE HEARD. . . ."

Unfortunately for Garrison, relatively few Americans were inclined to respond positively to his call. His newspaper generated little interest outside Boston, New York, Philadelphia, and other major urban centers of the North. This situation, however, changed within a matter of months. In August 1831, a slave preacher named Nat Turner led a rebellion of slaves in Southampton County, Virginia, that resulted in the death of fifty-eight whites. Although the revolt was quickly suppressed and Turner and his supporters were executed, the incident spread fear throughout the South. Governor John B. Floyd of Virginia turned an accusatory finger toward the abolitionists when he concluded that the Turner uprising was "undoubtedly designed and matured by unrestrained fanatics in some of the neighboring states." Moreover, it would be charged, these abolitionists contributed to a crisis environment that degenerated over the next generation and ultimately produced civil war.

One such abolitionist was John Brown who became a martyr in the antislavery pantheon when he was executed following his unsuccessful raid on the federal arsenal in Harpers Ferry, Virginia in 1859. The late noted historian of the American South, C. Vann Woodward, explains that Brown had no qualms about using violence to conduct his fanatical war on slavery.

In the second selection, Donald Mathews insists that, although abolitionists often employed heated rhetoric in their condemnation of the slave system, they were neither irrational nor illogical. Instead, he concludes, the abolitionists were intelligent reformers whose opposition to slavery was presented in a thoughtful, balanced critique of slavery.

C. Vann Woodward  **YES**

John Brown's Private War

The figure of John Brown is still wrapped in obscurity and myth. . . . His fifty-nine years were divided sharply into two periods. The obscurity of his first fifty-five years was of the sort natural to a humble life unassociated with events of importance. The obscurity of his last four years, filled with conspiratorial activities, was in large part the deliberate work of Brown, his fellow conspirators, and their admirers. . . .

After 1855 John Brown abandoned his unprofitable business career when he was almost penniless and for the rest of his life was without remunerative employment. He depended for support upon donations from people whom he convinced of his integrity and reliability. Here and elsewhere there is strong evidence that Brown was somehow able to inspire confidence and intense personal loyalty.

The Kansas phase of Brown's guerrilla warfare has given rise to the "Legend of Fifty-six," a fabric of myth that has been subjected to a more rigorous examination than any other phase of Brown's life has ever received. [James C.] Malin establishes beyond question that "John Brown did not appear to have had much influence either in making or marring Kansas history," that his exploits "brought tragedy to innocent settlers," but that "in no place did he appear as a major factor." He also establishes a close correlation between the struggle over freedom and slavery and local clashes over conflicting land titles on the Kansas frontier, and he points out that "the business of stealing horses under the cloak of fighting for freedom and running them off to the Nebraska-Iowa border for sale" is a neglected aspect of the struggle for "Bleeding Kansas." John Brown and his men engaged freely and profitably in this business and justified their plunder as the spoils of war. Two covenants that Brown drew up for his followers contained a clause specifically providing for the division of captured property among the members of his guerrilla band.

It would be a gross distortion, however, to dismiss John Brown as a frontier horse thief. He was much too passionately and fanatically in earnest about his war on slavery to permit of any such oversimplification. His utter fearlessness, courage, and devotion to the cause were greatly admired by respectable anti-slavery men who saw in the old Puritan an ideal revolutionary leader.

One exploit of Brown in Kansas, however, would seem to have put him forever beyond the pale of association with intelligent opponents of slavery. This

Reprinted by permission of Louisiana State University Press from the BURDEN OF SOUTHERN HISTORY by C. Vann Woodward. Copyright © 1968 by C. Vann Woodward.

was the famous Pottawatomie massacre of May 24, 1856. John Brown, leading four of his sons, a son-in-law, and two other men, descended by night upon an unsuspecting settlement of four proslavery families. Proceeding from one home to another the raiders took five men out, murdered them, and left their bodies horribly mutilated. None of the victims was a slaveholder, and two of them were born in Germany and had no contact with the South. By way of explanation Brown said the murders had been "decreed by Almighty God, ordained from Eternity." He later denied responsibility for the act, and some of the Eastern capitalists and intellectuals who supported him refused to believe him guilty. In view of the report of the murders that was laid before the country on July 11, 1856, in the form of a committee report in the House of Representatives, it is somewhat difficult to excuse such ignorance among intelligent men. . . .

In the spring of 1858 plans for a raid on Virginia began to take definite shape. To a convention of fellow conspirators in Chatham, Canada, in May, John Brown presented his remarkable "Provisional Constitution and Ordinances for the People of the United States." It represented the form of government he proposed to establish by force of arms with a handful of conspirators and an armed insurrection of slaves. Complete with legislative, executive, and judicial branches, Brown's revolutionary government was in effect a military dictatorship, since all acts of his congress had to be approved by the commander-in-chief of the army in order to become valid. Needless to say, John Brown was elected commander-in-chief.

By July, 1859, Commander-in-Chief Brown had established himself at a farm on the Maryland side of the Potomac River, four miles north of Harpers Ferry. There he assembled twenty-one followers and accumulated ammunition and other supplies, including 200 revolvers, 200 rifles, and 950 pikes specially manufactured for the slaves he expected to rise up in insurrection. On Sunday night, October 16, after posting a guard of three men at the farm, he set forth with eighteen followers, five of them Negroes, and all of them young men, to start his war of liberation and found his abolitionist republic. Brown's first objective, to capture the United States arsenal at Harpers Ferry, was easily accomplished since it was without military guard. In the Federal armory and the rifle works, also captured, were sufficient arms to start the bloodiest slave insurrection in history.

The commander-in-chief appears to have launched his invasion without any definite plan of campaign and then proceeded to violate every military principle in the book. He cut himself off from his base of supplies, failed to keep open his only avenues of retreat, dispersed his small force, and bottled the bulk of them up in a trap where defeat was inevitable. "In fact, it was so absurd," remarked Abraham Lincoln, "that the slaves, with all their ignorance, saw plainly enough it could not succeed." Not one of them joined Brown voluntarily, and those he impressed quickly departed. The insurrectionists killed one United States Marine and four inhabitants of Harpers Ferry, including the mayor and a Negro freeman. Ten of their own number, including two of Brown's sons, were killed, five were taken prisoner by a small force of Marines commanded by Robert E. Lee, and seven escaped, though two of them were later arrested. John Brown's insurrection ended in a tragic and dismal failure.

When news of the invasion was first flashed across the country, the most common reaction was that this was obviously the act of a madman, that John Brown was insane. This explanation was particularly attractive to Republican politicians and editors, whose party suffered the keenest embarrassment from the incident. Fall elections were on, and the new Congress was about to convene. Democrats immediately charged that John Brown's raid was the inevitable consequence of the "irresistible-conflict" and "higher-law" abolitionism preached by Republican leaders William H. Seward and Salmon P. Chase. "Brown's invasion," wrote Senator Henry Wilson of Massachusetts, "has thrown us, who were in a splendid position, into a defensive position. . . . If we are defeated next year we shall owe it to that foolish and insane movement of Brown's." The emphasis on insanity was taken up widely by Wilson's contemporaries and later adopted by historians.

It seems best to deal with the insanity question promptly, for it is likely to confuse the issue and cause us to miss the meaning of Harpers Ferry. In dealing with the problem it is important not to blink, as many of his biographers have done, at the evidence of John Brown's close association with insanity in both his heredity and his environment. In the Brown Papers at the Library of Congress are nineteen affidavits signed by relatives and friends attesting the record of insanity in the Brown family. John Brown's maternal grandmother and his mother both died insane. His three aunts and two uncles, sisters and brothers of his mother, were intermittently insane, and so was his only sister, her daughter, and one of his brothers. Of six first cousins, all more or less mad, two were deranged from time to time, two had been repeatedly committed to the state insane asylum, and two were still confined at the time. Of John Brown's immediate family, his first wife and one of his sons died insane, and a second son was insane at intervals. On these matters the affidavits, signers of which include Brown's uncle, a half brother, a brother-in-law, and three first cousins, are in substantial agreement. On the sanity of John Brown himself, however, opinion varied. Several believed that he was a "monomaniac," one that he was insane on subjects of religion and slavery, and an uncle thought his nephew had been "subject to periods of insanity" for twenty years. . . .

"John Brown may be a lunatic," observed the Boston *Post,* but if so, "then one-fourth of the people of Massachusetts are madmen," and perhaps three-fourths of the ministers of religion. Begging that Brown's life be spared, Amos A. Lawrence wrote Governor Wise: "Brown is a Puritan whose mind has become disordered by hardship and illness. He has the qualities wh. endear him to our people." The association of ideas was doubtless unintentional, but to the Virginian it must have seemed that Lawrence was saying that in New England a disordered mind was an endearing quality. The Reverend J. M. Manning of Old South Church, Boston, pronounced Harpers Ferry "an unlawful, a foolhardy, a suicidal act" and declared, "I stand before it wondering and admiring." Horace Greeley called it "the work of a madman" for which he had not "one reproachful word," and for the "grandeur and nobility" of which he was "reverently grateful." And the New York *Independent* declared that while "Harpers Ferry was insane, the controlling motive of this demonstration was sublime." It was both foolhardy and godly, insane and sublime, treasonous and admirable.

The prestige and character of the men who lent John Brown active, if sometimes secret, support likewise suggest caution in dismissing Harpers Ferry as merely the work of a madman. Among Brown's fellow conspirators the most notable were the so-called Secret Six. Far from being horse thieves and petty traders, the Secret Six came from the cream of Northern society. Capitalist, philanthropist, philosopher, surgeon, professor, minister—they were men of reputability and learning, four of them with Harvard degrees.

With a Harvard Divinity School degree, a knowledge of twenty languages, and a library of sixteen thousand volumes, Theodore Parker was perhaps the most prodigiously learned American of his time. In constant correspondence with the leading Republican politicians, he has been called "the Conscience of a Party." What Gerrit Smith, the very wealthy philanthropist and one-time congressman of Peterboro, New York, lacked in mental endowments he made up in good works—earnest efforts to improve the habits of his fellow men. These included not only crusades against alcohol and tobacco in all forms, but also coffee, tea, meat, and spices—"almost everything which gave pleasure," according to his biographer. Generous with donations to dietary reform, dress reform, woman's rights, educational and "non-resistance" movements, Smith took no interest whatever in factory and labor reform, but he was passionately absorbed in the antislavery movement and a liberal contributor to John Brown. Dr. Samuel G. Howe of Boston, husband of the famous Julia Ward Howe, was justly renowned for his humanitarian work for the blind and mentally defective. In his youth he had gone on a Byronic crusade in Greece against the Turk. These experiences contributed greatly to his moral prestige, if little to his political sophistication. The most generous man of wealth among the conspirators was George L. Stearns of Boston, a prosperous manufacturer of lead pipe. In the opinion of this revolutionary capitalist, John Brown was "the representative man of this century, as Washington was of the last." Finally there were two younger men, fledgling conspirators. The son of a prosperous Boston merchant who was bursar of Harvard, Thomas Wentworth Higginson became pastor of a church in Worcester after taking his divinity degree at Harvard. Young Franklin B. Sanborn was an apostle of Parker and a protégé of Emerson, who persuaded Sanborn to take charge of a school in Concord.

The most tangible service the Secret Six rendered the conspiracy lay in secretly diverting to John Brown, for use at Harpers Ferry, money and arms that had been contributed to the Massachusetts-Kansas Aid Committee for use in "Bleeding Kansas." . . . By this means the Kansas Committee was converted into a respectable front for subversive purposes, and thousands of innocent contributors to what appeared to be a patriotic organization discovered later that they had furnished rifles for a treasonous attack on a Federal arsenal. . . .

The Secret Six appear to have been fascinated by the drama of conspiratorial activity. There were assumed names, coded messages, furtive committee meetings, dissembling of motives, and secret caches of arms. And over all the romance and glamor of a noble cause—the liberation of man. Although they knew perfectly well the general purpose of Brown, the Secret Six were careful to request him not to tell them the precise time and place of the invasion. The wily old revolutionist could have told them much that they did not know about the psychology of fellow travelers. Brown had earlier laid down this strategy for conspirators who were hard pressed: "Go into the houses of your most prominent and influential white friends with your wives; and that will effectually fasten upon them the suspicion of being connected with you, and will compel them to make a common cause with you, whether they would otherwise live up to their professions or not." The same strategy is suggested by Brown's leaving behind, in the Maryland farmhouse where they would inevitably be captured, all his private papers, hundreds of letters of himself and followers, implicating nobody knew how many respectable fellow travelers. . . .

The assistance that the Secret Six conspirators were able to give John Brown and his Legend was as nothing compared with that rendered by other Northern intellectuals. Among them was the cultural and moral aristocracy of America in the period that has been called a "Renaissance." Some of these men, Ralph Waldo Emerson and Henry Thoreau among them, had met and admired Brown and even made small contributions to his cause. But they were safely beyond reproach of the law and were never taken into his confidence in the way that the Secret Six were. Their service was rendered after the event in justifying and glorifying Brown and his invasion.

In this work the intellectuals were ably assisted by a genius, a genius at self-justification—John Brown himself. From his prison cell he poured out a stream of letters, serene and restrained, filled with Biblical language and fired with overpowering conviction that his will and God's were one and the same. These letters and his famous speech at the trial constructed for the hero a new set of motives and plans and a new role. For Brown had changed roles. In October he invaded Virginia as a conqueror armed for conquest, carrying with him guns and pikes for the army he expected to rally to his standard and a new constitution to replace the one he overthrew. In that role he was a miserable failure. Then in November he declared at his trial: "I never did intend murder, or treason, or the destruction of property, or to excite or incite slaves to rebellion, or to make an insurrection." He only intended to liberate slaves without bloodshed, as he falsely declared he had done in Missouri the year before. How these statements can be reconciled with the hundreds of pikes, revolvers, and rifles, the capture of an armory, the taking of hostages, the killing of unarmed civilians, the destruction of government property, and the arming of slaves is difficult to see. Nor is it possible to believe that Brown thought he could seize a Federal arsenal, shoot down United States Marines, and overthrow a government without committing treason. . . .

Emerson seemed hesitant in his first private reactions to Harpers Ferry. Thoreau, on the other hand, never hesitated a moment. On the day after Brown's capture he compared the hero's inevitable execution with the crucifixion of Christ. Harpers Ferry was "the best news that America ever had"; Brown, "the bravest and humanest man in all the country," "a Transcendentalist above all," and he declared: "I rejoice that I live in this age, that I was his contemporary." Emerson quickly fell into line with Thoreau, and in his November 8 lecture on "Courage" described Brown as "the saint, whose fate yet hangs in suspense, but whose martyrdom, if it shall be perfected, will make the gallows as glorious as the cross." Within a few weeks Emerson gave three important lectures, in all of which he glorified John Brown.

With the Sage of Concord and his major prophet in accord on the martyr, the majority of the transcendental hierarchy sooner or later joined in—William E. Channing, Bronson and Louisa May Alcott, Longfellow, Bryant, and Lowell, and of course Wendell Phillips and Theodore Parker. Parker pronounced Brown "not only a martyr . . . but also a SAINT." Thoreau and Henry Ward Beecher frankly admitted they hoped Brown would hang. To spare a life would be to spoil a martyr. They were interested in him not as a man but as a symbol, a moral ideal, and a saint for a crusade. In the rituals of canonization the gallows replaced the cross as a symbol. . . .

The task to which the intellectuals of the cult dedicated themselves was the idealizing of John Brown as a symbol of the moral order and the social purpose of the Northern cause. Wendell Phillips expressed this best when he declared in the Boston Music Hall: "'Law' and 'order' are only means for the halting ignorance of the last generation. John Brown is the impersonation of God's order and God's law, moulding a better future, and setting for it an example." In substituting the new revolutionary law and order for traditional law and order, the intellectuals encountered some tough problems in morals and values. It was essential for them to justify a code of political methods and morals that was at odds with the Anglo-American tradition.

John Brown's own solution to this problem was quite simple. It is set forth in the preamble of his Provisional Constitution of the United States, which declares that in reality slavery is an "unjustifiable War of one portion of its citizens upon another." War, in which all is fair, amounted to a suspension of ethical restraints. This type of reasoning is identical with that of the revolutionaries who hold that class struggle is in reality a class war. The assumption naturally facilitates the justification of deeds otherwise indefensible. These might include the dissembling of motives, systematic deception, theft, murder, or the liquidation of an enemy class. . . .

The crisis of Harpers Ferry was a crisis of means, not of ends. John Brown did not raise the question of whether slavery should be abolished or tolerated. That question had been raised in scores of ways and debated for a generation. Millions held strong convictions on the subject. Upon abolition, as an *end,* there was no difference between John Brown and the American and Foreign Anti-Slavery Society. But as to the *means* of attaining abolition, there was as much difference between them, so far as the record goes, as there is between the modern British Labour Party and the government of Soviet Russia on the means of abolishing capitalism. The Anti-Slavery Society was solemnly committed to the position of nonviolent means. In the very petition that Lewis Tappan, secretary of the society, addressed to Governor Wise in behalf of Brown he repeated the rubric about "the use of all carnal weapons for deliverance from bondage." But in their rapture over Brown as martyr and saint the abolitionists lost sight of their differences with him over the point of means and ended by totally compromising their creed of nonviolence.

But what of those who clung to the democratic principle that differences should be settled by ballots and that the will of the majority should prevail? Phillips pointed out: "In God's world there are no majorities, no minorities; one, on God's side, is a majority." And Thoreau asked, "When were the good and the brave ever in a majority?" So much for majority rule. What of the issue of treason? The Reverend Fales H. Newhall of Roxbury declared that the word "treason" had been "made holy in the American language"; and the Reverend Edwin M. Wheelock of Boston blessed "the sacred, and the radiant 'treason' of John Brown."

No aversion to bloodshed seemed to impede the spread of the Brown cult. William Lloyd Garrison thought that "every slaveholder has forfeited his right to live" if he impeded emancipation. The Reverend Theodore Parker predicted a slave insurrection in which "The Fire of Vengeance" would run "from man to man, from town to town" through the South. "What shall put it out?" he asked. "The White Man's blood." The Reverend Mr. Wheelock thought Brown's "mission was to inaugurate slave insurrection as the divine weapon of the antislavery cause." He asked: "Do we shrink from the bloodshed that would follow?" and answered, "No such wrong [as slavery] was ever cleansed by rose-water." Rather than see slavery continued the Reverend George B. Cheever of New York declared: "It were infinitely better that three hundred thousand slave-holders were abolished, struck out of existence." In these pronouncements the doctrine that the end justifies the means had arrived pretty close to justifying the liquidation of an enemy class.

The reactions of the extremists have been stressed in part because it was the extremist view that eventually prevailed in the apotheosis of John Brown and, in part, because by this stage of the crisis each section tended to judge the other by the excesses of a few. "Republicans were all John Browns to the Southerners," as Professor Dwight L. Dumond has observed, "and slaveholders were all Simon Legrees to the Northerners." As a matter of fact Northern conservatives and unionists staged huge anti-Brown demonstrations that equaled or outdid those staged by the Brown partisans. Nathan Appleton wrote a Virginian: "I have never in my long life seen a fuller or more enthusiastic demonstration" than the anti-Brown meeting in Faneuil Hall in Boston. The Republican press described a similar meeting in New York as "the largest and most enthusiastic" ever held in that city. Northern politicians of high rank, including Lincoln, Douglas, Seward, Edward Everett, and Henry Wilson, spoke out against John Brown and his methods. The Republican party registered its official position by a plank in the 1860 platform denouncing the Harpers Ferry raid. Lincoln approved of Brown's execution, "even though he agreed with us in thinking slavery wrong." Agreement on ends did not mean agreement on means. "That cannot excuse violence, bloodshed, and treason," said Lincoln. . . .

Among the Brown partisans not one has been found but who believed that Harpers Ferry had resulted in great gain for the extremist cause. So profoundly were they convinced of this that they worried little over the conservative dissent. "How vast the change in men's hearts!" exclaimed Phillips. "Insurrection was a harsh, horrid word to millions a month ago." Now it was "the lesson of the hour." Garrison rejoiced that thousands who could not listen to his gentlest rebuke ten years before "now easily swallow John Brown whole, and his rifle in the bargain." "They all called him crazy then," wrote Thoreau; "Who calls him crazy now?" To the poet it seemed that "the North is suddenly all Transcendentalist." On the day John Brown was hanged church bells were tolled in commemoration in New England towns, out along the Mohawk Valley, in Cleveland and the Western Reserve, in Chicago and northern Illinois. In Albany one hundred rounds were fired from a cannon. Writing to his daughter the following day, Joshua Giddings of Ohio said, "I find the hatred of slavery greatly intensified by the fate of Brown and men are ready to march to Virginia and dispose of her despotism at once." It was not long before they *were* marching to Virginia, and marching to the tune of "John Brown's Body." . . .

Donald G. Mathews

 **NO**

The Abolitionists on Slavery:
The Critique Behind the
Social Movement

The abolitionists as agitators and moralists tried to change the mind of the American democrat. They appealed to his better nature and thundered against his fallen condition in pulpit, press, and petition in order to obtain for Negroes the same opportunity that white men had to participate in the nation's destiny. The goal was noble indeed, but the movement which tried to change American society was, as all human enterprises, compromised by the diverse motives, ideologies, and activities of its adherents. . . . Part of the ambiguity that supposedly shrouds antislavery history involves the assumption of many scholars that, since abolitionists were trying to destroy slavery, they could not have understood it. Careful investigation, however, will show that this assumption is untrue. . . .

[I]n reading what abolitionists said about slavery and slaveholders, one gets the distinct impression of exaggerated rhetoric and elaborate condemnation on the one hand combined with astute insight, humane sympathy, and wide knowledge on the other. In fact, if one takes Herbert Butterfield's advice to practice "imaginative sympathy" in dealing with the past, he may almost conclude that abolitionists were right when they claimed to be able to understand slavery better than anyone else since they were "uncorrupted by a bribe." In any event, behind the flamboyant rhetoric and beyond the vicious allusions of popular oratory there was a legitimate critique of slavery. In order to discuss this critique it will not do to make distinctions between rational and irrational, sensible and nonsensical, sober and emotional abolitionists, since these categories are too vague and invidious for serious discussion. But it might be useful for the historian to make a distinction between the various functions of abolitionism, between its functions as a social movement, as a large-scale agitation, and finally as a legitimate and thoughtful critique of the institution of slavery. Once these distinctions are made, it may be easier to see that abolitionists held a balanced view of slavery even as they attempted to change prevalent attitudes towards it. . . .

[T]housands of people joined the abolition movement in some capacity. They were encouraged to do so by itinerant organizers who built up a network

From the *Journal of Social History* by Donald G. Mathews, vol. XXXIII, no. 2, May 1967, pp. 163–177, 180–182. Copyright © 1967. Reproduced with permission of Journal of Social History via Copyright Clearance Center.

of local and state agencies and saw to it that the ideas of the movement were broadcast and perpetuated by subscription to one of the many antislavery periodicals. Slogans such as "immediate emancipation without expatriation" emerged from the endless discussions and articles which poured forth from the publicists who shaped the ideas of the movement. Along with the slogans often came the same lack of humor and viciousness of language which characterized the Great Revival's attack upon sin, the Democrat's attack upon Whig, and the rhetoric of many social movements which aimed at conversion either in religion or politics. Thus, when reading abolition literature, one is not called upon to explain away its exaggerations, but to understand them as a function of a movement which existed to perpetuate itself regardless of the value of its goals. As revivalists had been taught to be specific and harsh and to allow no "false comforts for sinners," so abolitionists acted in relation to slaveholders and slavery as they labored to build a movement. When they addressed those whom they hoped to convert they were as uncompromising as William Lloyd Garrison promised to be in the first edition of his *Liberator*. Unconditional attack was simply the approved method of the temperance reformation and the revivals; abolitionist crusaders saw no reason to discard weapons that had been so successful in previous sallies against evil. . . .

Nevertheless, when one takes into account how much abolitionist rhetoric had to accomplish and goes behind the functionally angry words to investigate what the historical evidence reveals, he finds a balanced, intelligent, and sometimes sophisticated understanding of the world which the antislavery radicals were trying to change. Historians divide abolitionists into Garrisonians, New Yorkers, denominationalists, and many more subgroups beloved of the specialist. But whether one does this or simply takes them straight as noncolonizationist, antislavery moralists (not politicians or nonextensionists), he will see that abolitionists (1) thought of slaveholders not merely as sinners but also as good men; (2) thought slavery a complex institution; but (3) understood it primarily as arbitrary and absolute power.

One of the basic charges leveled against abolitionists has been that they were morally simplistic in their condemnation of slaveholders. Repudiating social complexity as a legitimate vindication of slaveholding, they demanded that the abolition of slavery be begun at once. Years of waiting for conscientious Southerners to find a way to ease slavery out of existence had produced nothing to convince radical antislavery men that Negro servitude would die without purposeful action. The matter was made urgent for the revivalistically oriented abolitionists by their conviction that slavery was a sin: it was not a moral evil which everyone could regret and for which no one was responsible; it was not a political evil to be left to compromising politicians; it was not an economic evil to be left to self-interested slaveholders to manage—it was a sin. It broke the laws of God. It made man into merchantable property and deprived him of his humanity—his freedom to make of himself what he would. Thus, anyone involved in slavery as a master was culpably responsible to God. This conclusion put abolitionists in the position of calling decent, churchgoing Southerners sinners. Even though they worshiped three times a day, attended prayer meeting on Wednesday night, took their slaves with them to camp meeting, paid their debts, and gave money to foreign missions, slave-holders were sinners. This view became for many contemporaries as well as for historians the hallmark of abolitionist attitudes towards the South: abolitionists thought of slaveholders and their advocates as evil people.

In reaction to what they supposed was moralistic simplicity, antiaboli-tionists and later-day historians committed what could be called "the fallacy of misplaced righteousness." That is, by implication they attributed the personal moral respectability of individual Southerners to the institution of slavery. They pointed out that abolitionists were disastrously overstating their case by neglecting the complexities of the historical process, human motivation, and institutional entrenchment. Actually, the South was peopled, not by sinners as abolitionists so self-righteously assumed, but rather by good men caught in a difficult situation. Many Southern slaveholders were decent people, it was said, who secretly regretted the deep injustices of slavery, who treated their slaves well, and sent them to church on Sunday. Some Negroes even attained some status within the system. One ought not to curse good masters who were unfortunately involved in slavery, but praise them for responsibility in the midst of unjust institutions. These good men—reluctant and kindly slaveholders trying to make slavery as easy as possible for the slaves—were the tragic victims of a cruel and unjust fate. Furthermore, those people who believed the aboli-tionists irresponsible pointed out that slavery was not so bad as Theodore Dwight Weld claimed it to be in his pamphlet of 1839, *American Slavery as It Is*. As all sections, the South had its evil men (such as slave traders) who gave its peculiar institutions a bad name. The good, however, should not be confused with them and called sinners.

The "fallacy of misplaced righteousness" obscures what reformers are talk-ing about in times of social change. Good men, abolitionists pointed out, were the chief vindicators of American Negro slavery. Had the antislavery vanguard been totally unaware of the moral character of slavery and its relationships, they could justly be accused of being irrelevant fanatics. But the abolitionists were not content with middle-class morality as some historians have been. The simple assumption that abolitionists thought of Southern slaveholders only as unre-generate sinners needs to be challenged to reveal what they did in fact say and simply to set the story straight.

The Missouri controversies had educated thoughtful Southerners to believe that Northern interest in slavery was primarily political. Therefore, they were in no mood to appreciate the care with which some abolitionists attempted to explain that slavery was a national problem and that sectional power or virtue was not really at issue. Abolitionists did maintain, however, that their not being from the South was an aid in gaining perspective. Mrs. Lydia Maria Child wrote in her pamphlet on slavery in 1833:

> It would be very absurd to imagine that the inhabitants of one State are worse than the inhabitants of another, unless some peculiar circumstances, of universal influence, tend to make them so. Human nature is everywhere the same; but developed differently, by different incitements and temptations. . . . If we were educated at the South, we should no doubt vindicate slavery, and inherit as a birthright all the evils it engrafts upon the character. If they

lived on our rocky soil, and under our inclement skies, their shrewdness would sometimes border on knavery, and their frugality sometimes degenerate into parsimony. We both have our virtues and our faults, induced by the influences under which we live. . . .

Abolitionists were willing to admit the obvious: that people accustomed to slavery would be inclined to vindicate it.

In spite of this fact, there were Southerners to whom antislavery men thought they might effectively appeal—the responsible, churchgoing, humane slaveholders who would be sensitive to an honest discussion of slavery. Wrote a Methodist: "I sincerely sympathize with the slave, and as truly with many masters. I believe that northern men would be southern men in their circumstances; and that southern men would be northern men in ours, where moral principle was equally felt." The operative words were "where moral principle was equally felt." Abolitionists believed (or at least a great many of them did) that the moral regeneration of America institutionalized by steady increases in church membership would be the energizing force of abolition. They had seen this moral regeneration become moral action in the creation of new benevolent societies, and they saw no reason why slaves could not be helped just as much as drunkards, prostitutes, and the heathen. Thus they preached a new gospel because, as Orange Scott, the Methodist antislavery leader, wrote, it was "by preaching against great and destructive evils, *particularly, pointedly,* and *perseveringly,* that the world [was] to be reformed."

Preaching even to "good men" did not work. James G. Birney's special pilgrimage demonstrates what it did not take abolitionists everywhere long to find out: that the so-called good people of the South would not listen. As a colonization agent in the South in 1833, Birney, the owner of several slaves and heir to many others, found that the more he condemned slavery the less enthusiasm he engendered among his listeners. Nevertheless, he persisted in his efforts to convince the respectable portion of the community that it ought to think about abolishing slavery as soon as humanly possible. After his own conversion to abolitionism, Birney tried to convince the Kentucky Presbyterian clergy to urge abolition—but the result was a mild and evasive answer. He then tried to reach the community by reasonable discussion in an antislavery paper—but he was driven from Kentucky as a traitor. Even in the North, Birney's appeal to the churches as America's great moral institutions was repudiated by those whom he had hoped to convert. Not surprisingly, Birney and most of his abolitionist confreres were convinced that the good people were the bulwarks of slavery.

The morality ascribed to responsible people in the South did not impress abolitionists. Some conservative antislavery men tried to develop theories of moral responsibility which allowed for "moral men in immoral society," but most insisted that all slaveholders would have to be held responsible for their status. In this conclusion they denied the relevance of explanations deriving from the "fallacy of misplaced righteousness." Abolitionists admitted that slaveholders might be humanely motivated, that they might treat slaves well, that they might preach the Gospel (however mutilated) to them; but, in all cases, the Negroes were still slaves. This fact alone ran contrary to any concept of freedom, human dignity, and Christian love. Slavery was too evil in principle to be vindicated by the heroic sadness of a conscience-stricken master or by the sympathy of the most gentle mistress. "In the hand of a good man or a bad man . . . *this principle is the same;*" wrote one abolitionist, "it [slavery] possesses not one redeeming quality." In other words, the fact that Southern slaveholders were good men was not relevant in the discussion of slavery. . . .

When abolitionists turned from the slaveholder to the system he represented they were no more simplistic behind their bombastic rhetoric than when they were dealing with the Pollyanna propriety of the "fallacy of misplaced righteousness." They could all agree that slavery was a complex, well-developed social and economic institution which could not be destroyed in one day. In fact, it would take so long to extinguish the psychological, moral, and cultural scars of slavery that its abolition should be begun immediately. Whether the abolitionist wanted "immediate emancipation gradually accomplished" or "immediate unconditional emancipation," he had no intention of irresponsibly turning the slaves loose without some guidance. From the beginning of their agitation abolitionists could agree with William Lloyd Garrison's plea that Negro slaves be emancipated according to carefully worked out and equitably executed legal procedures which would in the end guarantee Negroes the equality they had been so long denied. The immediacy in immediate emancipation referred to the revivalist-agitator's desire to begin at once in order that something might be done eventually; but the formula in no way contradicted the abolitionist's belief that slavery was not a simple institution. . . .

They maintained that their agitation and ethical importunity was justified because of slavery's effect upon the Negro and its ultimate character as absolute power. It was understood as absolute power because the slave had no legal claim upon the white man with which he could protect himself and because that most precious of American possessions, the right to one's own labor, was denied him. Slaves worked not because they would be better off if they did, but because they would be worse off if they did not. Force, fear, and fraud made slavery operate, abolitionists charged, and what they meant was that men's labor was extracted from them by an inherited system of bondage which ultimately relied upon brute force. They meant that men faced the future not with the hope and courage of the American Hercules but only with despair. And by fraud they meant that the church's Gospel had been used to enslave not free men's minds, that the law and planned ignorance which perpetuated slavery deprived Negroes of the same kind of advancement enjoyed by other Americans. They meant that the Negro was, for all intents and purposes, completely in the hands of the white man.

The best evidence of this fact, abolitionists thought, was the cruelties inflicted by whites on Negroes. Every discussion of the abolitionist attack on slavery includes an appropriate section for atrocities; and this was certainly a major aspect of antislavery propaganda. Everyone who has read this material is well acquainted with the vivid portrayal of all the infamies men can inflict upon their fellows, a striking method by which antislavery publicists could "clank the chains" of slavery in the ears of indifferent Americans. The atrocity stories, while possibly interesting in themselves to some abolitionists and historians, were printed not merely to arouse hatred of the kindly old slaveholder but also to demonstrate that slavery ultimately meant absolute and unchecked power. Abolitionists knew that some slaves were better treated than others—house servants and artisans were assumed to be safer than slaves less visible to the public—and they admitted that some slaveholders could be kind to their servants. But the significant aspect of slavery was not kind treatment. And cruelty was considered not as an exception to kind treatment, but as the natural result of the power to give or withhold kind treatment. With no effective way to defend themselves against the masters, Negroes bore mutilations, brands, and scars as identification not only of runaways in advertisements but also of the entire slave system. Men owned slaves not for altruistic purposes but to exploit their labor; and since the incentive to work was the thoroughly negative one of force not wages, since Negroes as men would intentionally frustrate the masters, and since men with absolute power used it, the natural result of slavery was cruelty. This was of course an abstract argument, but mutilated runaways seemed convincing empirical proof of its truth. Halos there were over the heads of some slaveowners; but scars on the backs of runaways were more significant. . . .

Corruption of people was a primary concern in the abolitionists' scheme of values, but slavery also corrupted the nation and the South. It became abstracted as diabolical power which stripped Americans of the security of their persons. It deprived them of their rights to petition Congress, to assemble peaceably, to publish freely, to dissent from majority opinion. And when the fugitive slave law was passed in 1850, the South's peculiar institution was interpreted as undermining the security of Northern legal processes. Southerners' fear of slaves, of new ideas, and of other white men was weakening the entire nation. Not only was this insecurity affecting freedom, but also the national defense. For if Americans were ever called to fight a strong foreign enemy, their efforts would be endangered by limiting available manpower to white men and limiting those whites' effectiveness by the necessity of policing slaves.

Slavery had corrupted the American economy even as it had its politics and security. It endangered all property by using arguments based upon property rights to defend holding men as slaves. The repugnancy men had for slavery could conceivably be transferred to property, thus devaluing the foundation of American wealth and stability. This consideration was overshadowed by the much more important concern for the economic disadvantages of slavery. Although an economic argument was never emphasized to the exclusion of others, it was usually present in abolitionist literature. Richard Hildreth was particularly eloquent in his *Despotism in America,* where he argued that slavery was a bad labor system which crippled American economic growth. Labor (the principal source of value) was not free to produce and consume at full capacity in a slave society. Slave laborers were presumed to be less productive than free because the former had no positive incentive. Only force and authority kept them at their tasks whereas wages and the hope of advancement would increase productivity if they were free.

Not only were the South and nation deprived of the full labor of the Negroes, but also of the whites. The low status of labor as being proper only to slaves supposedly paralyzed the poor whites as well as enervated the masters, whose disdain for work precluded the full utilization of labor resources. Slavery not only penalized the poor white man by devaluing labor, but also by requiring greater capitalization for expansion in the South than in the North. Since Southerners bought their laborers instead of hiring them, only the rich could increase their power appreciably. These supposed limitations on economic expansion were linked also with the fact that slaves did not consume as much as free laborers since their desires were so curtailed. With consumption at a low point, there was consequently less prosperity. This theory that slavery hindered optimum economic growth was complemented by other economic arguments. Most posited the superiority of industrial over agrarian society or accepted slavery as a single explanation of even those economic problems which derived from a one-crop economy. But in the economic and political sphere as in the personal, abolitionists understood slavery to be an unwarranted delimitation of freedom—arbitrary power.

There are many deficiencies in the arguments that abolitionists directed against slavery. Their data may have been faulty, but not the direction in which their understanding was taking them—towards an emphasis on social justice. Their objectivity was of course compromised by their partisan activity; but with all of the scientific knowledge of the twentieth century they would have come essentially to the same conclusions they reached a hundred years earlier. They would have admitted all the findings of historical investigation because they had a great appreciation for facts. But they would also have insisted that slavery, for all of its variety and complexity, still meant the white man's absolute power over the Negro.

Reflecting upon this view, one is struck by the contrast between the abolitionists' understanding of complexity and social determinism as opposed to their much-emphasized voluntarism. They were impressed by the effects of man's social situation in determining his values, goals, and general understanding, and yet they expected some men somehow to transcend their social context and by a sheer act of will break the chains binding their minds as well as their slaves. Frustrated in this, abolitionists retreated either to politics or to the mental and moral utopia of being "right" in a world that was wrong. Their "realism" in doing this is not so important as their pioneering attempt to understand social determinism and at the same time to thwart it. . . .

This kind of thinking about slavery, linked as it was with social agitation, personal frustration, civil war, and incomplete understanding was never fulfilled by a purposive and just transition from slavery to freedom. . . . But unlike most Americans, the abolitionists had at least tried to understand slavery in a new perspective even if with old formulae. And their attempt made them a vanguard in the fight to abridge the complexity of slavery by willful destruction of its absolute power.

POSTSCRIPT

Were the Abolitionists "Unrestrained Fanatics"?

One of the weaknesses of most studies of abolitionism, which is reflected in both of the preceding essays, is that they are generally written from a monochromatic perspective. In other words, historians typically discuss whites within the abolitionist crusade and give little, if any, attention to the roles African Americans played in the movement. Whites are portrayed as the active agents of reform, while blacks are the passive recipients of humanitarian efforts to eliminate the scourge of slavery. Students should be aware that African Americans, slave and free, also rebelled against the institution of slavery both directly and indirectly.

Benjamin Quarles in *Black Abolitionists* (Oxford University Press, 1969) describes a wide range of roles played by blacks in the abolitionist movement. The African American challenge to the slave system is also evident in the network known as the "underground railroad." Larry Gara, in *The Liberty Line: The Legend of the Underground Railroad* (University of Kentucky Press, 1961), concludes that the real heroes of the underground railroad were not white abolitionists but the slaves themselves who depended primarily upon their own resources or assistance they received from other African Americans, slave and free.

Other studies treating the role of black abolitionists in the antislavery movement include James M. McPherson, *The Struggle for Equality: Abolitionists and the Negro in the Civil War and Reconstruction* (Princeton University Press, 1964), Jane H. and William H. Pease, *They Who Would Be Free: Blacks' Search for Freedom, 1830–1861* (Atheneum, 1974), Benjamin Quarles, *Allies for Freedom: Blacks and John Brown* (Oxford University Press, 1974), R. J. M. Blackett, *Building an Antislavery Wall: Black Americans in the Atlantic Abolitionist Movement, 1830–1860* (Louisiana State University Press, 1983) and *Beating Against the Barriers: The Lives of Six Nineteenth-Century Afro-Americans* (Louisiana State University Press, 1986), Ronald K. Burke, *Samuel Ringgold Ward: Christian Abolitionist* (Garland, 1995), Nell Irvin Painter, *Sojourner Truth: A Life, A Symbol* (W. W. Norton, 1997), and Catherine Clinton, *Harriet Tubman: The Road to Freedom* (2004). Frederick Douglass' contributions are evaluated in Benjamin Quarles, *Frederick Douglass* (Atheneum, 1968; originally published 1948), Nathan Irvin Huggins, *Slave and Citizen: The Life of Frederick Douglass* (Little, Brown, 1980), Waldo E. Martin, Jr., *The Mind of Frederick Douglass* (University of North Carolina Press, 1984), and William S. McFeely, *Frederick Douglass* (W. W. Norton, 1991).

Conflicting views of the abolitionists are presented in Richard O. Curry, ed., *The Abolitionists: Reformers or Fanatics?* (Holt, Rinehart and Winston, 1965). For general discussions of the abolitionist movement, see Gerald Sorin, *Abolitionism: A New Perspective* (Praeger, 1972), Lewis Perry, *Radical Abolitionism: Anarchy and the*

Government of God in Antislavery Thought (Cornell University Press, 1973), James Brewer Stewart, *Holy Warriors: The Abolitionists and American Slavery* (Hill and Wang, 1976), Lawrence J. Friedman, *Gregarious Saints: Self and Community in American Abolitionism, 1830–1870* (Cambridge University Press, 1982), Stanley Harrold, *The Abolitionists in the South, 1831–1861* (University Press of Kentucky, 1995), Richard S. Newman, *The Transformation of American Abolitionism: Fighting Slavery in the Early Republic* (University of North Carolina Press, 2002), and John Stauffer, *The Black Hearts of Men: Radical Abolitionists and the Transformation of Race* (Harvard University Press, 2002). The lives of individual participants in the abolitionist movement are discussed in Henry Mayer, *All on Fire: William Lloyd Garrison and the Abolition of Slavery* (St. Martin's, 1998), Gerda Lerner, *The Grimké Sisters from South Carolina: Pioneers for Woman's Rights and Abolition* (Schocken Books, 1967), and Irving H. Bartlett, *Wendell and Ann Phillips: The Community of Reform, 1840–1880* (Harvard University Press, 1979). John Brown's controversial role in the movement is evaluated in Stephen B. Oates, *To Purge This Land With Blood: A Biography of John Brown* (Harper and Row, 1970), Louis A. DeCaro, Jr., *"Fire From the Midst of You": A Religious Life of John Brown* (New York University Press, 2002), and Merrill D. Peterson, *John Brown: The Legend Revisited* (University of Virginia Press, 2002).

On the Internet . . .

AmericanCivilWar.com

The goal of this site is to provide a comprehensive source of Civil War information from the public domain or works published with the authors' permission. The sources are directed at students and Civil War buffs of all ages.

```
http://americancivilwar.com/index.html
```

The Valley of the Shadow Project

Developed under the direction of Edward Ayers and his graduate students at the University of Virginia, this site includes digital archives of thousands of primary source materials related to life in the Civil War–era communities in Augusta County, Virginia, and Franklin County, Pennsylvania.

```
http://valley.vcdh.virginia.edu/
```

Abraham Lincoln Online

Dedicated to the sixteenth president of the United States, this site offers educational links, Lincoln's speeches and writings, information on historic places, and much more.

```
http://www.netins.net/showcase/creative/
                lincoln.html
```

Reconstruction Era Documents

This page includes links to various Reconstruction Era documents by such authors as Frederick Douglass, Booker T. Washington, and W. E. B. Du Bois.

```
http://www.libraries.rutgers.edu/rul/rr_gateway/
       research_guides/history/civwar.shtml
```

PART 4

Conflict and Resolution

*T*he changing nature of the United States and the demands of its own principles finally erupted into violent conflict. Perhaps it was an inevitable step in the process of building a coherent nation from a number of distinct and diverse groups. The leaders, attitudes, and resources that were available to the North and the South were to determine the course of the war itself, as well as the difficult national healing process that followed.

- Have Historians Overemphasized the Slavery Issue as a Cause of the Civil War?

- Is Robert E. Lee Overrated as a General?

- Did Abraham Lincoln Free the Slaves?

- Did William M. Tweed Corrupt Post–Civil War New York?

- Was Reconstruction a "Splendid Failure"?

ISSUE 14

Have Historians Overemphasized the Slavery Issue as a Cause of the Civil War?

YES: Joel H. Silbey, from *The Partisan Imperative: The Dynamics of American Politics Before the Civil War* (Oxford University Press, 1985)

NO: Michael F. Holt, from *The Political Crisis of the 1850s* (John Wiley & Sons, 1978)

ISSUE SUMMARY

YES: Professor of history Joel H. Silbey argues that historians have overemphasized the sectional conflict over slavery and have neglected to analyze local ethnocultural issues among the events leading to the Civil War.

NO: Professor of history Michael F. Holt maintains that both Northern Republicans and Southern Democrats seized the slavery issue to sharply distinguish party differences and thus reinvigorate the loyalty of party voters.

In the 85 years between the start of the American Revolution and the coming of the Civil War, Americans made the necessary political compromises on the slavery issue in order not to split the nation apart. The Northwest Ordinance of 1787 forbade slavery from spreading into those designated territories under its control, and the new Constitution written in the same year prohibited the slave trade from Africa after 1808.

There was some hope in the early nineteenth century that slavery might die from natural causes. The Revolutionary generation was well aware of the contradiction between the values of an egalitarian society and the practices of a slave-holding aristocracy. Philosophically, slavery was viewed as a necessary evil, not a positive good. Several Northern states abolished slavery after 1800, and the erosion of the tobacco lands in Virginia and Maryland contributed to the lessening importance of a slave labor system.

Unfortunately, two factors—territorial expansion and the market economy— made slavery the key to the South's wealth in the 35 years before the Civil War.

First, new slave states were created out of a population expanding into lands ceded to the United States as a result of the Treaty of Paris of 1783 and the Louisiana Purchase of 1803. Second, slaves were sold from the upper to the lower regions of the South because the cotton gin (invented by Eli Whitney in 1793) made it possible to harvest large quantities of cotton, ship it to the textile mills of New England and the British Isles, and turn it into cloth and finished clothing as part of the new, specialized market economy.

The slavery issue came to the forefront in 1819 when some Northern congressmen proposed that slavery be banned from the states being carved out of the Louisiana Purchase. A heated debate ensued, but the Missouri Compromise of 1821 drew a line that preserved the balance between free and slave states and that (with the exception of Missouri) prohibited slavery north of the $36°\ 30'$ latitude.

The annexation of Texas in 1845 and the acquisition of New Mexico, Utah, and California three years later reopened the slavery question. The question of whether or not to annex Texas to the Union, after she gained her independence from Mexico in 1836, scared politicians from all sections because they were afraid of upsetting the political balance between free and slave states. Attempts at compromises in 1850 and 1854 only accelerated the situation. The Kansas-Nebraska Act of 1854, which repealed the Missouri Compromise, allowed the citizens of those territories to decide whether or not they wanted slavery. Abolitionists were furious because Illinois senator Stephen A. Douglas's doctrine of "popular sovereignty" had the potential to allow slavery to spread to territories where it was previously forbidden by the Missouri Compromise. For the next three years, Kansas became a battleground between pro-slavery forces and "Free-soilers" who voted to keep slavery out of the territory.

The Kansas-Nebraska Act had major political implications. The second party system of Whigs versus Democrats fell apart, and a new realignment took place. The Whig Party disappeared. In the South the need to defend slavery caused pro-business and yeoman-farmer Whigs from the back country to join the Southern Democrats in a unified alliance against the North. Major and minor parties in the North joined to form the new Republican Party, whose unifying principle was to confine slavery to states where it already existed but not to allow it to spread to any new territories. Quickly the Republicans mounted a successful challenge against the Democrats.

The 1860 presidential election was won by the Republican Abraham Lincoln. However, the Southern states refused to accept the election of Lincoln. Seven states seceded from the Union before he was inaugurated on March 4, 1861. When Lincoln refused to abandon the federal forts off the coast of Charleston in April 1861, the governor of South Carolina fired on Fort Sumter. The Civil War had begun. Four more states then joined the Confederacy.

Have historians overemphasized the sectional conflict over the slavery question as a cause of the Civil War? In the following selection, Joel H. Silbey argues that historians have overemphasized the conflict over slavery and have neglected to analyze local ethnocultural issues among the events leading to the Civil War. In the second selection, Michael F. Holt contends that politicians in the 1850s used the slavery issue to sharply distinguish party differences.

Joel H. Silbey  **YES**

The Civil War Synthesis in American Political History

The Civil War has dominated our studies of the period between the Age of Jackson and 1861. Most historians of the era have devoted their principal attention to investigating and analyzing the reasons for differences between the North and South, the resulting sectional conflict, and the degeneration of this strife into a complete breakdown of our political system in war. Because of this focus, most scholars have accepted, without question, that differences between the North and the South were the major political influences at work among the American people in the years between the mid-1840s and the war. Despite occasional warnings about the dangers of overemphasizing sectional influences, the sectional interpretation holds an honored and secure place in the historiography of the antebellum years. We now possess a formidable number of works which, in one way or another, center attention on the politics of sectionalism and clearly demonstrate how much the Civil War dominates our study of American political history before 1861.

Obviously nothing is wrong in such emphasis if sectionalism was indeed the dominant political influence in the antebellum era. However, there is the danger in such emphasis of claiming too much, that in centering attention on the war and its causes we may ignore or play down other contemporary political influences and fail to weigh adequately the importance of nonsectional forces in antebellum politics. And, in fact, several recent studies of American political behavior have raised serious doubts about the importance of sectional differences as far as most Americans were concerned. These have even suggested that the sectional emphasis has created a false synthesis in our study of history which increases the importance of one factor, ignores the significance of other factors, and ultimately distorts the reality of American political life between 1844 and 1861.

⚜

Scholars long have used the presidential election of 1844 as one of their major starting points for the sectional analysis of American political history. In a

From Joel H. Silbey, *The Partisan Imperative: The Dynamics of American Politics Before the Civil War* (Oxford University Press, 1985). Adapted from Joel H. Silbey, "The Civil War Synthesis in American Political History," *Civil War History*, vol. 10, no. 2 (June 1964). Copyright © 1964 by Kent State University Press. Reprinted by permission of Kent State University Press. Notes omitted.

general sense they have considered American expansion into Texas to be the most important issue of that campaign. The issue stemmed from the fact that Texas was a slave area and many articulate Northerners attacked the movement to annex Texas as a slave plot designed to enhance Southern influence within the Union. Allegedly because of these attacks, and the Southerners' defending themselves, many people in both North and South found themselves caught up in such sectional bitterness that the United States took a major step toward civil war. Part of this bitterness can be seen, it is pointed out, in the popular vote in New York State where the Whig candidate for the presidency, Henry Clay, lost votes to the abolitionist Liberty party because he was a slaveholder. The loss of these votes cost him New York and ultimately the election. As a result of Clay's defeat, historians have concluded that as early as 1844 the problem of slavery extension was important enough to arouse people to act primarily in sectional terms and thus for this episode to be a milestone on the road to war.

Recently Professor Lee Benson published a study of New York State politics in the Jacksonian era. Although Benson mainly concerned himself with other problems, some of his findings directly challenge the conception that slavery and sectional matters were of major importance in New York in 1844. In his analysis Benson utilized a more systematic statistical compilation of data than have previous workers in the field of political history. Observing that scholars traditionally have looked at what people said they did rather than at what they actually did, Benson compiled a great number of election returns for New York State in this period. His purpose was to see who actually voted for whom and to place the election in historical perspective by pinpointing changes in voting over time and thus identifying the basic trends of political behavior. Through such analysis Benson arrived at a major revision of the nature of New York State voting in 1844.

Benson pointed out, first of all, that the abolitionist, anti-Texas Liberty party whose vote total should have increased if the New York population wanted to strike against a slave plot in Texas, actually lost votes over what it had received in the most immediate previous election, that of 1843. Further analysis indicated that there was no widespread reaction to the Texas issue in New York State on the part of any large group of voters, although a high degree of anti-Texas feeling indeed existed among certain limited groups in the population. Such sentiment, however, did not affect voting margins in New York State. Finally, Benson concluded that mass voting in New York in 1844 pivoted not on the sectional issue but rather on more traditional divisions between ethnic and religious groups whose voting was a reaction to matters closer to home. These proved of a more personal and psychological nature than that of Texas and its related issue of slavery extension. Sectional bitterness, contrary to previous historical conceptions, neither dominated nor seriously influenced the 1844 vote in New York. Although Benson confined his study to one state, his conclusions introduce doubts about the influence of sectionalism in other supposedly less pivotal states.

Another aspect of the sectional interpretation of American politics in the pre-Civil War era involves Congress. Political historians have considered that body to be both a forum wherein leaders personally expressed attitudes that intensified sectional bitterness, as well as an arena which reflected the general pattern of influences operative in the country at large. Therefore, writers on the period have considered the behavior of congressmen to have been more and more dominated by sectionalism, particularly after David Wilmot introduced his antislavery extension proviso into the House of Representatives in 1846. Although there may have been other issues and influences present, it is accepted that these were almost completely overborne in the late 1840s and 1850s in favor of a widespread reaction to sectional differences.

In a recently completed study, I have analyzed congressional voting in the allegedly crucial pivotal decade 1841–52, the period which historians identify as embodying the transition from nationalism to sectionalism in congressional behavior. This examination indicates that a picture of the decade as one in which sectional influences steadily grew stronger, overwhelmed all other bases of divisions, and became a permanent feature of the voting behavior of a majority of congressmen, is grossly oversimplified and a distortion of reality. In brief, although sectional influences, issues, and voting did exist, particularly between 1846 and 1850, sectional matters were not the only problems confronting congressmen. In the period before the introduction of the Wilmot Proviso in 1846, national issues such as the tariff, financial policy, foreign affairs, and land policy divided congressmen along political, not sectional, lines. Furthermore, in this earlier period issues which many believed to have shown a high degree of sectional content, such as admittance of Texas and Oregon, reveal highly partisan national divisions and little sectional voting.

Even after the rise of the slavery-extension issue, other questions of a national character remained important. Slavery was but one of several issues before Congress and it was quite possible for congressmen to vote against one another as Northern and Southern sectionalists on an issue and then to join together, regardless of section, against other Northerners and Southerners on another matter. Certainly some men from both geographic areas were primarily influenced by sectional considerations at all times on all issues, but they were a minority of all congressmen in the period. The majority of congressmen were not so overwhelmingly influenced by their being Northerners or Southerners, but continued to think and act in national terms, and even resisted attempts by several sectionally minded congressmen to forge coalitions, regardless of party, against the other section.

A careful study of congressional voting in these years also demonstrates that another assumption of historians about the nature of politics is oversimplified: the period around 1846 did *not* begin the steady forward movement of congressional politics toward sectionalism and war. Rather, it was quite possible in the period between 1846 and 1852 for congressmen to assail one another bitterly in sectional terms, physically attack one another, and even threaten secession, and still for the majority of them to return in the following session to a different approach—that of nonsectional political differences with a concomitant restoration of nonsectional coalitions. For example, it was possible

in 1850, after several years of sectional fighting, for a national coalition of
Senators and Representatives to join together and settle in compromise terms
the differences between North and South over expansion. And they were
able to do this despite the simultaneous existence of a great deal of sectional
maneuvering by some congressmen in an attempt to prevent any such compromise. Furthermore, during this same session Congress also dealt with matters of
railroad land grants in a way that eschewed sectional biases. Obviously the
usual picture of an inexorable growth of sectional partisanship after 1846 is
quite overdone. And lest these examples appeared to be isolated phenomena,
preliminary research both by Gerald Wolff and by myself demonstrates that as
late as 1854 there was still no complete or overwhelming sectional voting even
on such an issue as the Kansas-Nebraska Act.

Such analyses of congressional behavior in an alleged transition period
reinforce what Lee Benson's work on New York politics demonstrated: many
varieties and many complexities existed with respect to political behavior in
the antebellum period, so that even slavery failed to be a dominating influence
among all people at all times—or even among most people at most times—
during the 1840s and early 1850s. Again, our previous image of American politics in this period must be reconsidered in light of this fact and despite the
emergence of a Civil War in 1861.

Perhaps no aspect of antebellum politics should demonstrate more fully the
overpowering importance of sectional influences than the presidential election
of 1860. In the preliminaries to that contest the Democratic party split on the
rock of slavery, the Republican party emerged as a power in the Northern states
with a good chance of winning the presidency, and loud voices in the Southern
states called for secession because of Northern attacks on their institutions. In
dealing with these events, historians, as in their treatment of other aspects of
antebellum politics, have devoted their primary attention to sectional bickering
and maneuvering among party leaders, because they considered this activity to
be the most important facet of the campaign and the key to explaining the
election. Although such a focus obviously has merit if one is thinking in terms
of the armed conflict which broke out only five months after the election, once
again, as in the earlier cases considered here, recent research has raised perti-
nent questions about the political realities of the situation. We may indeed ask
what were the issues of the campaign as seen by the majority of voters.

Earlier studies of the 1860 election, in concerning themselves primarily
with the responses and activities of political leaders, have taken popular voting
behavior for granted. This aspect has either been ignored or else characterized
as reflecting the same influences and attitudes as that of the leadership. Therefore, the mass of men, it is alleged, voted in response to sectional influences in
1860. For instance, several scholars concerned with the Germans in the Middle
West in this period have characterized the attitudes of that group as overwhelmingly antislavery. Thus the Republican party attracted the mass of the German
vote because the liberal "Forty-Eighters" saw casting a Lincoln vote as a way to

strike a blow against slavery in the United States. Going beyond this, some historians have reached similar conclusions about other Middle Western immigrant groups. As a result, according to most historians, although narrowly divided, the area went for Lincoln thanks in large part to its newest citizens, who were Northern sectionalists in their political behavior. Such conclusions obviously reinforce the apparent importance of geographic partisanship in 1860.

Testing this hypothesis, two recent scholars systematically studied and analyzed election returns in Iowa during 1860. Such examinations are important because they should reveal, if the sectional theory is correct, preoccupation among Iowa voters—especially immigrants—with the slavery question and the increasingly bitter differences between North and South. Only one of these studies, that of Professor George H. Daniels of Northwestern University, has appeared in print. But Daniels's findings shatter earlier interpretations which pinpointed sectional concerns as the central theme of the 1860 election.

Briefly stated, Daniels isolated the predominantly German townships in Iowa and, following Lee Benson's methodological lead, analyzed their vote. He found that, far from being solidly Republican voters, or moved primarily by the slavery question, the Germans of Iowa voted overwhelmingly in favor of the Democratic party. And Daniels discovered that the primary issue motivating the Germans in 1860 was an ethnic one. They were conscious of the anti-alien Know-Nothing movement which had been so strong in the United States during the 1850s and they identified the Republican party as the heir and last refuge of Know-Nothingism. If the Germans of Iowa were attracted to the Republicans by the latter's antislavery attitudes, such attraction was more than overcome by the Republicans' aura of antiforeignism. Furthermore, the Republicans were also identified in the minds of the Iowa Germans as the party of prohibitionism, a social view strongly opposed by most Germans. Thus, as Daniels concludes, ". . . The rank and file Germans who did the bulk of the voting considered their own liberty to be of paramount importance. Apparently ignoring the advice of their leaders, they cast their ballots for the party which consistently promised them liberty from prohibition and native-American legislation." As a result, the Germans of Iowa voted Democratic, not Republican, in 1860.

Lest this appear to be an isolated case, the research of Robert Swierenga on Dutch voting behavior in Iowa in 1860 confirms Daniels's findings. Swierenga demonstrated that the Dutch also voted Democratic despite their vaunted antislavery attitudes; again, revulsion from certain Republican ideals overpowered any attraction toward that party on the slavery issue.

Such research into the election of 1860, as in the earlier cases of the election of 1844 and congressional voting behavior in the 1840s and early 1850s, suggests how far the sectional and slavery preconceptions of American historians have distorted reality. Many nonsectional issues were apparently more immediately important to the groups involved than any imminent concern with Northern-Southern differences. Once again, the Civil War synthesis appears to be historically inaccurate and in need of serious revision.

Several other provocative studies recently have appeared which, while dealing with nonpolitical subjects, support the conclusion that sectional problems, the slavery issue, and increasing bitterness between North and South were not always uppermost concerns to most Americans in the fifteen years before the outbreak of the war. Building upon the work of Leon Litwack, which emphasizes the general Northern antagonism toward the Negro before 1860, and that of Larry Gara demonstrating the fallacy of the idea that a well-organized and widespread underground railroad existed in the North, Professor C. Vann Woodward has cautioned students against an easy acceptance of a "North-Star" image—a picture of a universally militant Northern population determined to ease the burden of the slave in America. Rather, as Woodward points out, a great many Northerners remained indifferent to the plight of the slave and hostile to the would-be antislavery reformer in their midst.

In this same tenor, Milton Powell of Michigan State University has challenged long-held assumptions that the Northern Methodist church was a bulwark of antislavery sentiment after splitting with its Southern branch in 1844. As Powell makes clear, Northern Methodists were concerned about many other problems in which slavery played no part, as well as being beset by conditions which served to tone down any antislavery attitudes they may have held. More importantly, this led many of them to ignore slavery as an issue because of its latent tendency to divide the organization to which they belonged. Thus, even in areas outside of the political realm, the actual conditions of antebellum society challenge the validity of the sectional concept in its most general and far-reaching form.

This review of recent research indicates that much of our previous work on the prewar period should be reexamined free from the bias caused by looking first at the fact of the Civil War and then turning back to view the events of the previous decade in relation only to that fact. Although it is true that the studies discussed here are few in number and by no means include the entire realm of American politics in the antebellum era, their diversity in time and their revisionist conclusions do strongly suggest the fallacy of many previous assumptions. No longer should any historian blithely accept the traditional concept of a universal preoccupation with the sectional issue.

But a larger matter is also pointed up by this recent research and the destruction of this particular myth about political sectionalism. For a question immediately arises as to how historians generally could have accepted so readily and for so long such oversimplifications and inaccuracies. Fortunately for future research, answers to this question have been implicitly given by the scholars under review, and involve methodological problems concerning evidence and a certain naïveté about the political process.

Historians generally have utilized as evidence the writings and commentaries of contemporary observers of, and participants in, the events being examined. But, as both Benson and Daniels emphasize, this can endanger our understanding of reality. For instance, not enough attention has been paid to who actually said what, or of the motives of a given reporter or the position he was in to know and understand what was going on around him. Most particularly, scholars have not always been properly skeptical about whether the observer's comments truly reflected actuality. As Daniels pointed out in his article on German voting behavior, "contemporary opinion, including that of newspapers, is a poor guide."

If such is true, and the evidence presented by these studies indicates that it is, a question is raised as to how a historian is to discover contemporary opinion if newspapers are not always reliable as sources. The work of Benson, Daniels, and myself suggests an answer: the wider use of statistics. When we talk of public opinion (that is, how the mass of men acted or thought) we are talking in terms of aggregate numbers, of majorities. One way of determining what the public thought is by measuring majority opinion in certain circumstances—elections, for example, or the voting of congressmen—and then analyzing the content and breakdown of the figures derived. If, for example, 80 percent of the Germans in Iowa voted Democratic in 1860, this tells us more about German public opinion in 1860 than does a sprightly quote from one of the Germans in the other 20 percent who voted Republican "to uphold freedom." Historians are making much more use of statistics than formerly and are utilizing more sophisticated techniques of quantitative analysis. And such usage seems to be prelude to, judging by the works discussed here, a fuller and more accurate understanding of our past.

There are also other ways of approaching the problems posed by the 1850s. Not enough attention has been paid, it seems to me, to the fact that there are many different levels of political behavior—mass voting, legislative activity, leadership manipulation, for example—and that what is influential and important on one level of politics may not be on another. Certainly the Germans and Dutch of Iowa in 1860 were not paying much attention to the desires of their leaders. They were responding to influences deemed more important than those influences shaping the responses of their leaders. As Swierenga pointed out in his analysis of Dutch voting:

> While Scholte [a leader of the Dutch community] fulminated against Democrats as slave mongers, as opponents of the Pacific Railroad and Homestead Bills, and as destroyers of the Constitution, the Dutch citizens blithely ignored him and the national issues he propounded and voted their personal prejudices against Republican nativists and prohibitionists.

Obviously, when historians generalize about the nature of political behavior they must also be sure which group and level of political activity they mean, and so identify it, and not confuse different levels or assume positive correlations between the actions of people on one level with those on another level. Such precision will contribute greatly to accuracy and overcome tendencies toward distortion.

Finally, based on the work under discussion here, it is clear that historians must become more aware of the complexities of human behavior. All people, even of the same stratum of society or living in the same geographic area, do not respond with the same intensity to the same social or political stimuli.

Not everyone perceives his best interests in the same way, or considers the same things to be the most important problems confronting him. Depending upon time and circumstances, one man may respond primarily to economic influences; another one, at the same time and place, to religious influences; and so on. Sometimes most people in a given community will respond to the same influences equally, but we must be careful to observe *when* this is true and not generalize from it that this is *always* true. Single-factor explanations for human behavior do not seem to work, and we must remain aware of that fact.

With improved methodological tools and concepts historians may begin to engage in more systematic and complete analyses of popular voting, legislative voting, and the motivations and actions of political leaders. They will be able to weigh the relative influence of sectional problems against other items of interest and concern on all levels of political behavior. Until this is done, however, we do know on the basis of what already has been suggested that we cannot really accept glib explanations about the antebellum period. The Civil War has had a pernicious influence on the study of American political development that preceded it—pernicious because it has distorted the reality of political behavior in the era and has caused an overemphasis on sectionalism. It has led us to look not for what was occurring in American politics in those years, but rather for what was occurring in American politics that tended toward sectional breakdown and civil war—a quite different matter.

The Political Crisis of the 1850s

Historians have long looked to politics for the origins of the Civil War, and they have offered two major interpretations of political developments between 1845 and 1860. Both are primarily concerned with the breakdown of the old party system and the rise of the Republicans and not with the second aspect of the crisis—the loss of faith in politicians, the desire for reform, and their relationship to republican ideology. By spelling out my reservations about and disagreements with these interpretations, the assumptions behind and, I hope, the logic of my own approach to the political crisis of the 1850s will become clearer.

The standard interpretation maintains that intensifying sectional disagreements over slavery inevitably burst into the political arena, smashed the old national parties, and forced the formation of new, sectionally oriented ones. The Second Party System was artificial, some historians contend, since it could survive only by avoiding divisive sectional issues and by confining political debate to sectionally neutral economic questions on which the national parties had coherent stands. Once sectional pressure was reaggravated by the events of the late 1840s and early 1850s, those fragile structures shattered and were replaced. "On the level of politics," writes Eric Foner, "the coming of the Civil War is the intrusion of sectional ideology into the political system, despite the efforts of political leaders of both parties [Whigs and Democrats] to keep it out. Once this happened, political competition worked to exacerbate, rather than to solve, social and sectional conflicts."

There is much to be said for this interpretation. The Republican party did rise to dominance in the North largely because of an increase of Northern hostility toward the South, and its ascendance worsened relations between the sections. Attributing the political developments prior to its rise to the same sectional force that caused the rise has the virtue of simplicity. But that argument distorts a rapidly changing and very complex political situation between 1845 and 1860. There were three discrete, sequential political developments in those years that shaped the political crisis that led to war—the disappearance of the Whig party and with it of the old framework of two-party competition, a realignment of voters as they switched party affiliation, and a shift from a nationally balanced party system where both major parties competed on fairly even terms in all parts of the nation to a sectionally polarized one with Republicans dominant in the North and Democrats in the South. Although related, these were distinct phases, occurring with some exceptions in that order, and they were caused by different things. Although the inflammation of sectional antagonism between 1855 and 1860 helped to account for the new sectional alignment of parties, sectional conflict by itself caused neither the voter realignment of middecade nor the most crucial event of the period—the death of the Whig party, especially its death at the state level. It bears repeating that the demise of the Whig party, and with it of the traditional framework of two-party competition at the local, state, and national levels, was the most critical development in this sequence. Its disappearance helped foster popular doubts about the legitimacy of politics as usual, raised fears that powerful conspiracies were undermining republicanism, allowed the rise of the Republican party in the North, and created the situation in the lower South that produced secession there and not elsewhere.

The theory that the Second Party System was artificial and was shattered once the slavery issue arose, like the larger theory of the war's causation it reflects, founders on the problem of timing. There is considerable evidence that sectional conflict over slavery characterized the Second Party System throughout its history. Slavery was not swept under the rug; it was often the stuff of political debate. Proponents of the traditional interpretation, indeed, have often confused internal divisions within the national parties with their demise. Although they point to different dates when the rupture was fatal, they have assumed that once the national parties were split into Northern and Southern wings over slavery, the parties were finished. Yet the Whig and Jacksonian parties, like almost all political organizations at any time, had frequently been divided—over slavery as well as other issues. They functioned for years in that condition. To establish the existence of sectional splits within the national parties is not to answer the vexed question of why those divisions were fatal in the 1850s and not in the 1830s and 1840s. If it was the sectional conflict that destroyed the old party system, the crucial question is why the parties were able to manage that conflict at some times and not at others. For a number of reasons, the easy reply that the volatile slavery issue simply became more explosive in the 1850s than earlier is not an adequate answer to this question.

The second major interpretation of the politics of the 1850s also has its merits and liabilities. Arguing that traditional historians have viewed events in the 1850s with the hindsight knowledge that the Civil War occurred, a new group of political historians insist that the extent to which sectionalism affected political behavior, especially popular voting behavior at the grass-roots level, has been exaggerated. Local social tensions, especially ethnic and religious tensions, motivated voters in the 1850s, they contend, not national issues like slavery, which was of so much concern to national political elites. What applies to Congress and national leaders, these new political historians say in effect, does not apply to the local level of politics. Prohibitionism, nativism, and anti-Catholicism produced the voter realignment in which the Whigs disappeared and new parties emerged in the North.

By focusing on voting behavior, this ethnocultural interpretation presents a compelling analysis of why an anti-Democratic majority was created in many parts of the North. Explaining why Northern voters realigned between 1853 and 1856, however, does not answer why the Republican party appeared or why party politics were sectionally polarized at the end of the decade. Prophets of the ethnocultural thesis, moreover, have done little to explain Southern politics, yet developments in Dixie where Catholics and immigrants were few were just as important as events in the North in leading to war. Nor do voting studies really explain the crucial first phase—the death of the Whig party. Party reorganization accompanied voter realignment in the 1850s, and ethnocultural tensions alone do not explain why new parties were necessary. Why didn't anti-Democratic voters simply become Whigs? This question has a particular urgency when one realizes that in the 1840s ethnocultural issues had also been present and that the Whigs and Democrats had aligned on opposite sides of them. The problem with stressing ethnocultural issues, as with stressing sectionalism, is why those issues could be contained within, indeed could invigorate, old party lines at one time yet could help to destroy them at another.

The fundamental weakness of previous interpretations of why the old two-party system broke down is their misunderstanding of how and why it worked. They have not adequately explored either the relationship between political parties and issues or the impact of the federal system with its divided responsibilities among local, state, and national governments on the parties and the party system. Whether historians stress sectionalism or ethnocultural issues, their central assumption seems to be that issues arising from the society at large caused political events. The Second Party System functioned because it dealt with "safe" economic questions, but once those issues were replaced or displaced by new disruptive matters the parties broke down and realignment followed. Yet what made the Second Party System work in the end was not issues *per se* or the presence of safe issues and absence of dangerous ones. In the end what made the two-party system operate was its ability to allow political competition on a broad range of issues that varied from time to time and place to place. If the genius of the American political system has been the peaceful resolution of conflict, what has supported two-party systems has been the conflict itself, not its resolution. As long as parties fought with each other over issues or took opposing stands even when they failed to promote opposing programs, as long as they defined alternative ways to secure republican ideals, voters perceived them as different and maintained their loyalty to them. Party health and popular faith in the political process depended on the perception of party difference, which in turn depended on the reality—or at least the appearance—of interparty conflict. As long as parties seemed different from each other, voters viewed them as viable vehicles through which to influence government.

Politicians had long recognized that group conflict was endemic to American society and that the vitality of individual parties depended on the intensity of their competition with opposing parties. Thomas Jefferson had perceived in 1798 that "in every free and deliberating society, there must, from the nature of man, be opposite parties, and violent dissensions and discords." "Seeing that we must have somebody to quarrel with," he wrote John Taylor, "I had rather keep our New England associates for that purpose, than to see our bickerings transferred to others." Even more explicit in their recognition of what made parties work were the founders of New York's Albany Regency in the 1820s. They deplored the lack of internal discipline and cohesion in the

Jeffersonian Republican party once the Federalists disappeared, and they moved quickly to remedy it. Although any party might suffer defeats, they realized, "it is certain to acquire additional strength . . . by the attacks of adverse parties." A political party, indeed, was "most in jeopardy when an opposition is not sufficiently defined." During "the contest between the great rival parties [Federalists and Jeffersonians] each found in the strength of the other a powerful motive of union and vigor." Significantly, those like Daniel Webster who deplored the emergence of mass parties in the 1820s and 1830s also recognized that strife was necessary to perpetuate party organization and that the best way to break it down was to cease opposition and work for consensus. Politicians in the 1840s and 1850s continued to believe that interparty conflict was needed to unify their own party and maintain their voting support. Thus an Alabama Democrat confessed that his party pushed a certain measure at the beginning of the 1840 legislative session explicitly as "the best means for drawing the party lines as soon as possible" while by 1852, when opposition to that state's Democracy appeared to disintegrate, another warned perceptively, "I think the only danger to the Democratic party is that it will become too much an omnibus in this State. We have nothing to fear from either the Union, or Whig party or both combined. From their friendship and adherence much." Many of the important decisions in the 1840s and 1850s reflected the search by political leaders for issues that would sharply define the lines between parties and thus reinvigorate the loyalty of party voters.

If conflict sustained the old two-party system, what destroyed it was the loss of the ability to provide interparty competition on *any* important issue at *any* level of the federal system. Because the political system's vitality and legitimacy with the voters depended on the clarity of the definition of the parties as opponents, the blurring of that definition undid the system. What destroyed the Second Party System was consensus, not conflict. The growing congruence between the parties on almost all issues by the early 1850s dulled the sense of party difference and thereby eroded voters' loyalty to the old parties. Once competing groups in society decided that the party system no longer provided them viable alternatives in which they could carry on conflict with each other, they repudiated the old system by dropping out, seeking third parties that would meet their needs, or turning to nonpartisan or extrapolitical action to achieve their goals. Because the collapse of the Second Party System was such a vital link in the war's causation, therefore, one arrives at a paradox. While the Civil War is normally viewed as the one time when conflict prevailed over consensus in American politics, the prevalence of consensus over conflict in crucial parts of the political system contributed in a very real way to the outbreak of war in the first place. . . .

The sectionalization of American politics was emphatically *not* simply a reflection or product of basic popular disagreements over black slavery. Those had long existed without such a complete polarization developing. Even though a series of events beginning with the Kansas-Nebraska Act greatly increased sectional consciousness, it is a mistake to think of sectional antagonism as a spontaneous and self-perpetuating force that imposed itself on the political arena against the will of politicians and coerced parties to conform to the lines of sectional conflict. Popular grievances, no matter how intense, do not dictate party strategies. Political leaders do. Some one has to politicize events, to define their political relevance in terms of a choice between or among parties, before popular grievances can have political impact. It was not events alone that caused Northerners and Southerners to view each other as enemies of the basic rights they both cherished. Politicians who pursued very traditional partisan strategies were largely responsible for the ultimate break-down of the political process. Much of the story of the coming of the Civil War is the story of the successful efforts of Democratic politicians in the South and Republican politicians in the North to keep the sectional conflict at the center of political debate and to defeat political rivals who hoped to exploit other issues to achieve election.

For at least thirty years political leaders had recognized that the way to build political parties, to create voter loyalty and mobilize support, and to win elections was to find issues or positions on issues that distinguished them from their opponents and that therefore could appeal to various groups who disliked their opponents by offering them an alternative for political action—in sociological terms, to make their party a vehicle for negative reference group behavior. Because of the American ethos, the most successful tactic had been to pose as a champion of republican values and to portray the opponent as antirepublican, as unlawful, tyrannical, or aristocratic. Jackson, Van Buren, and Polk, Antimasons and Whigs, had all followed this dynamic of the political system. Stephen A. Douglas and William H. Seward had pursued the same strategy in their unsuccessful attempt to rebuild the disintegrating Second Party System with the Kansas-Nebraska Act in 1854. After faith in the old parties had collapsed irreparably, when the shape of future political alignments was uncertain, Republican politicians quite consciously seized on the slavery and sectional issue in order to build a new party. Claiming to be the exclusive Northern Party that was necessary to halt slavery extension and defeat the Slave Power conspiracy was the way they chose to distinguish themselves from Democrats, whom they denounced as pro-Southern, and from the Know Nothings, who had chosen a different organizing principle—anti-Catholicism and nativism—to construct their new party.

To say that Republican politicians agitated and exploited sectional grievances in order to build a winning party is a simple description of fact. It is not meant to imply that winning was their only objective or to be a value judgment about the sincerity or insincerity of their personal hatred of black slavery. Some undoubtedly found slavery morally intolerable and hoped to use the national government to weaken it by preventing its expansion, abolishing it in federal enclaves like the District of Columbia, and undermining it within Southern states by whatever means were constitutionally possible, such as opening the mails to abolitionist literature and prohibiting the interstate slave trade. The antislavery pedigree of Republican leaders, however, was in a sense irrelevant to the triumph of the Republican party. The leaders were divided over the policies they might pursue if they won control of the national government, and leadership views were often far in advance of those held by their electorate. Much more important was the campaign they ran to obtain power, their skill in politicizing the issues at hand in such a way as to convince

Northern voters that control of the national government by an exclusive Northern party was necessary to resist Slave Power aggressions. The Republicans won more because of what they were against than because of what they were for, because of what they wanted to stop, not what they hoped to do. . . .

The key to unraveling the paradoxes in Republican rhetoric, the juxtaposition of egalitarianism and racism, of pledges not to interfere with slavery in the South alongside calls to end slavery and join a great crusade for freedom, is to remember that the word "slavery" had long had a definite meaning aside from the institution of black slavery in the South. It was in this sense that many Republicans used the word. Slavery implied subordination to tyranny, the loss of liberty and equality, the absence of republicanism. Slavery resulted when republican government was overthrown or usurped, and that, charged Republicans, was exactly what the Slave Power was trying to do. Hence the slavery that many Republicans objected to most was not the bondage of blacks in the South but the subjugation of Northern whites to the despotism of a tiny oligarchy of slaveholders bent on destroying their rights, a minority who controlled the Democratic party and through it the machinery of the federal government. Thus one Republican complained privately in 1857, "The Slave power will not submit. The tyrants of the lash will not withhold until they have put padlocks on the lives of freemen. The Union which our fathers formed seventy years ago is not the Union today . . . the sons of the Revolutionary fathers are becoming *slaves* or *masters*." Thus a Chicago Republican congressman, after reciting a litany of supposed Slave Power aggressions against the North, later recalled, "All these things followed the taking possession of the Government and lands by the slave power, until we [in the North] were the slaves of slaves, being chained to the car of this Slave Juggernaut." Thus the black abolitionist Frederick Douglass perceptively observed, "The cry of Free Men was raised, not for the extension of liberty to the black man, but for the protection of the liberty of the white."

The basic objective of Republican campaigns from 1856 to 1860, therefore, was to persuade Northerners that slaveholders meant to enslave them through their control of the national government and to enlist Northern voters behind the Republican party in a defensive phalanx to ward off *that* slavery, and not in an offensive crusade to end black slavery, by driving the Slave Power from its control of the national government. For such a tactic to succeed, the Republicans required two things. First, to make an asset and not a liability of their existence as an exclusive Northern party, they needed events to increase Northern antagonism toward the South so that men believed the South, and not foreigners and Catholics or the Republicans themselves, posed the chief threat to the republic. More important, they had successfully to identify the Democratic party as an agent or lackey of the South. Because the Republicans campaigned only in the North, because Northern voters chose among Northern candidates instead of between Northerners and Southerners, only by making Northern Democrats surrogates for the Slave Power could they make their case that Republicans alone, and not simply any Northern politicians, were needed to resist and overthrow the slavocracy. Because they dared not promise overt action against slaveholders except for stopping slavery expansion, in other words, Republicans could not exploit Northern anger, no matter how intense it was, unless they could convince Northern voters that supporting the Republicans and defeating Northern Democrats was an efficacious and constitutional way to defeat the Slave Power itself.

By the summer of 1856 it was much easier to identify the Democracy with the South than it had been earlier. For one thing, the results of the congressional elections of 1854 and 1855 had dramatically shifted the balance of sectional power within the Democratic party, a result that was plainly evident when the 34th Congress met during 1856. From 1834 to 1854 the Democratic congressional delegation had usually been reasonably balanced between North and South. In the 33rd Congress, Northern Democrats had even outnumbered Southern Democrats in the House by a margin of 91 to 67. But in 1856 there were only 25 Northerners as compared to 63 Southerners, and even though Northern Democratic representation would increase after the 1856 elections, the sectional balance would never be restored before the Civil War. The South seemed to dominate the Democracy, and that fact was especially difficult to hide during a presidential election year. Because the Democrats, unlike the Republicans, met in a common national convention with Southerners and campaigned in both sections, Democrats could not deny their Southern connection. The democratic platform endorsing the Kansas-Nebraska Act strengthened that identification, thereby flushing out regular Northern Democrats who had tried to evade the Nebraska issue in 1854 and 1855 and infuriating anti-Nebraska Democrats who had clung to the party in hopes of reversing its policy but who now bolted to the Republicans. . . .

The Democratic party within the Deep South had, in fact, changed in significant ways. During the 1830s and 1840s, it had normally been controlled by and represented the interests of nonslaveholders from the hill country and piney woods regions. Even at that time slaveholders and their lawyer allies from the normally Whig black belt areas had contested for leadership of the Democracy. Sharing the same economic concerns as their Whig neighbors in those plantation regions, concerns that nonslaveholding Democrats generally opposed, Democrats from the black belt had bid for control of the party by trying to shift attention to national issues and asserting that the threat to Southern equality posed the greatest menace to the liberties of all Southern voters. During the 1850s, for a variety of reasons, those slaveholding elements took over the Democracy, and in state after state it became much less receptive at the state level to the wishes of the nonslaveholding majority who nonetheless remained Democrats because of traditional Jacksonian loyalties. For one thing, Franklin Pierce favored Southern Rights Democrats in the distribution of federal patronage. Second, as the Whig party dissolved, Democratic politicians from the slaveholding regions won over some of its former adherents by stressing the menace to slaveholders' interests, thereby increasing their own power within the Democratic party. Finally, during the 1850s, the cotton culture spread away from the old black belt to staunchly Democratic regions, thus enlarging the constituency that would respond to politicians riding the slavery issue.

As a result of this transformation, the economic priorities of the Democratic party changed. Democratic newspapers openly advised Democratic legislators not to offend their new Whig allies, and the new Democratic leaders wanted positive economic programs in any case. Occasionally the nonslaveholders found individual champions of the old Jacksonian orthodoxy like Governor George Winston of Alabama and Governor Joe Brown of Georgia who vetoed probusiness legislation, but Democratic legislatures invariably overrode those vetoes. To nonslaveholders, the Democratic party, as a party, and the political process as a whole no longer seemed as responsive as they once had been.

The shift of power within the dominant Democracy hastened the almost exclusive concentration of political rhetoric on the slavery and sectional issues. For one thing, slaveholders were more genuinely concerned about potential threats to black slavery than nonslaveholders. For another, the Democrats attributed their rise to dominance by 1852 to their ability to appear more pro-Southern than the Whigs, and they saw no reason to change a winning strategy. Third, the new leaders of the party continued to feel the need of holding the loyalty of the nonslaveholding backbone of the Democratic electorate. That support had always been won by identifying and crusading against antirepublican monsters. Because the new leaders did not want to attack the economic programs they were themselves promoting and because internal opposition was so weak from former Whigs who approved of those programs, they more and more portrayed the external Republican party as the chief danger to the liberty, equality, and self-esteem of all Southerners, slaveholders and nonslaveholders alike. Like the Republicans in the North, they translated the sectional conflict into the republican idiom in order to win the votes of men who were not primarily concerned with black slavery.

POSTSCRIPT

Have Historians Overemphasized the Slavery Issue as a Cause of the Civil War?

Silbey's selection represents the first sustained attack on the sectional interpretation of the events leading to the Civil War. Historians, he contends, have created a false "Civil War synthesis" that positions slavery as the major issue that divided America, thereby distorting "the reality of American political life between 1844 and 1861."

Silbey is one of the "new political historians" who have applied the techniques of modern-day political scientists in analyzing the election returns and voting patterns of Americans' nineteenth- and early-twentieth-century predecessors. These historians use computers and regression analysis of voting patterns, they favor a quantitative analysis of past behavior, and they reject the traditional sources of quotes from partisan newspapers and major politicians because these sources provide anecdotal and often misleading portraits of our past. Silbey and other new political historians maintain that all politics are local. Therefore, the primary issues in the 1860 election for voters and their politicians were ethnic and cultural, and party loyalty was more important than sectional considerations.

Holt is also interested in analyzing the struggles for power at the state and local levels by the major political parties, but he is critical of the ethnocultural school that Silbey represents. In Holt's view, Silbey's emphasis on voter analysis explains why an anti-Democratic bloc of voters developed in the North. But it does not explain why the Whig Party disappeared nor why the Republican Party became the majority party in the northern and western states by 1850. More important, since Silbey and other ethnoculturalists have little to say about Southern politics, reasons why secession and the subsequent Civil War took place are left unanswered.

Holt also rejects the more traditional view that the Civil War resulted from the "intensifying sectional disagreements over slavery." Instead, he promotes a more complicated picture of the events leading to the Civil War. Between 1845 and 1860, he maintains, three important things happened: the breakdown of the Whig Party; the realignment of voters; and "a shift from a nationally balanced party system where both major parties competed on fairly even terms in all parts of the nation to a sectionally polarized one with Republicans dominant in the North and Democrats in the South."

Holt builds his argument on the assumption that two-party competition at the state and local levels is healthy in resolving conflicts. With the demise of the Whig Party in the middle 1850s, the two-party system of competition broke down at the state and local levels. A national realignment was completed by 1860: Republicans controlled Northern states, while Democrats dominated the Southern ones. Holt maintains that the Whig and Democratic parties had argued over the slavery issue in the 1830s and 1840s but that they did not fragment into state and local parties. He implies that if the second-party system continued through the 1850s, the slavery issue might have been resolved in a more peaceful manner.

One criticism of both Silbey and Holt is that neither author interprets the political events leading up to the Civil War within the context of the socioeconomic changes taking place in the country. Both authors explain how many Americans manifested their hostility to the Irish Catholics who came here in the 1840s and 1850s by joining the Know-Nothing Party, which in turn caused a realignment of the political parties. But they make no mention of the reasons why the Irish and other immigrants came here: the market revolution and the need for workers to build and staff the canals, railroads, and factories.

The list of books about the Civil War is extensive. Two good starting points are John Niven, *The Coming of the Civil War, 1837–1861* (Harlan Davidson, 1990) and Bruce Levine, *Half Slave and Half Free* (Hill & Wang, 1992). An older, extensive work with a compelling narrative and sound interpretations is David Potter, *The Impending Crisis, 1848–1861* (Harper & Row, 1976). Michael Perman has updated the well-worn problems of American civilization in *The Coming of the American Civil War*, 3rd ed. (D. C. Heath, 1993).

Both Silbey and Holt have published numerous articles in scholarly journals. Silbey, who has extensive knowledge of the nineteenth-century Democratic Party, has collected his articles in *The American Political Nation 1838–1893* (Stanford University Press, 1991). A collection of Holt's articles can be found in *Political Parties and American Political Development From the Age of Jackson to the Age of Lincoln* (Louisiana State University Press, 1992).

Historians who reject the ethnocultural school, which minimizes the slavery issue as the cause of the Civil War, include Eric Foner and Kenneth M. Stampp. Foner's *Free Soil, Free Labor, Free Men* (Oxford University Press, 1970) is an excellent study of the bourgeois capitalism and conservative idealism that formed the ideological basis of the Republican Party before the Civil War. In *America in 1857: A Nation on the Brink* (Oxford University Press, 1990), Stampp argues that conflict became inevitable after the election of James Buchanan to the presidency, the firestorm in Kansas, and the Supreme Court's decision in *Dred Scott v. Sandford*. A summary of the traditional view is found in Richard H. Sewell's *House Divided: Sectionalism and Civil War, 1848–1865* (Johns Hopkins University Press, 1988).

ISSUE 15

Is Robert E. Lee Overrated as a General?

YES: Alan T. Nolan, from *"Rally, Once Again!" Selected Civil War Writings of Alan T. Nolan* (Madison House, 2000)

NO: Gary W. Gallagher, from "Another Look at the Generalship of R. E. Lee," in Gary W. Gallagher, ed., *Lee the Soldier* (University of Nebraska Press, 1996)

ISSUE SUMMARY

YES: Attorney Alan T. Nolan argues that General Robert E. Lee was a flawed grand strategist whose offensive operations produced heavy casualties in an unnecessarily prolonged war that the South could not win.

NO: According to professor of American history Gary W. Gallagher, General Lee was the most revered and unifying figure in the Confederacy, and he "formulated a national strategy predicated on the probability of success in Virginia and the value of battlefield victories."

Over the past 125 years contemporaries and historians have advanced dozens of explanations for the defeat of the Confederacy in the Civil War. Most of these can be divided into two categories: internal and external.

According to a number of historians, internal divisions doomed the Confederacy. In his book *State Rights in the Confederacy* (Peter Smith, 1961), Frank Owsley maintains that the centrifugal forces of state rights killed the Confederacy. Owsley contends that governors in North Carolina and Georgia withheld men and equipment from the Confederate armies in order to build up their own state militias. On the Confederate tombstone, he said, should be inscribed: "Died of State Rights."

A second version of the internal conflict argument appeared in a 1960 essay in a symposium entitled *Why the North Won the Civil War* (Louisiana State University Press, 1960). In it, the editor, Pulitzer Prize–winning historian David Donald, argued that the resistance of Southerners to conscription, taxes, and limitations on speeches that were critical of the war effort fatally crippled the Confederacy's war effort. Instead of state rights, said Donald, the Confederate tombstone should read: "Died of Democracy."

A third variant of the internal conflict argument has recently been promoted by four Southern scholars: Richard E. Beringer, Herman Hattaway, Archer Jones, and William N. Still, Jr. Their main thesis is that the Confederacy lacked the will to win because of its inability to fashion a viable Southern nationalism, increasing religious doubts that God was on the Confederacy's side, and guilt over slavery.

Historians who emphasize external reasons for the Confederacy's failure stress two factors: The Union's overwhelming numbers and resources and the uneven quality of leadership between the two sides. The North possessed two-and-one-half times the South's population, three times its railroad capacity, and nine times its industrial production. The Unionists also appear to have had better leadership. Abraham Lincoln is ranked as America's greatest president because he united his political objectives of saving the Union and freeing the slaves with a military strategy designed to defeat the Confederacy. Lincoln's generals—Ulysses S. Grant, William T. Sherman, and Philip H. Sheridan—outsmarted the Confederate leadership. In 1864, for example, massive frontal attacks were made against the Confederates in the eastern and western theaters. At the same time, Sherman destroyed much of the agricultural base of the Southerners as he marched his troops through South Carolina and Georgia.

But what if the South had won the Civil War? Could the same external explanations that are attributed to the Union victory also be used to explain a Confederate win? Would one Confederate soldier be considered equal to four Union soldiers? Would a triumvirate of yeoman farmers, slaveholding planters, and small industrialists have proven the superiority of agrarian values over industrial ones? Would Jefferson Davis's leadership emerge as superior to Lincoln's? Would the great military leaders be Robert E. Lee, Thomas "Stonewall" Jackson, and Braxton Bragg instead of Grant, Sherman, and Sheridan?

No Civil War figure is more difficult to comprehend than General Lee. A product of the Virginia aristocracy, Lee ranked second in his class at West Point and distinguished himself as an army engineer, bridge builder, and scout during the Mexican War. While home in Virginia on an extended furlough to care for his invalid wife in October 1859, he took command of a detachment of marines to capture John Brown and his men inside the roundhouse during a raid on Harpers Ferry. Offered the command of all federal forces when the Civil War broke out, Lee made the fateful decision to resign his army commission and fight for the Confederacy.

In the first of the following selections, Alan T. Nolan challenges what he believes to be one of the biggest myths of the Civil War—the genius of Robert E. Lee. Written in the style of a lawyer's brief, Nolan portrays the "marble man" as a flawed grand strategist whose offensive operations produced heavy casualties in a war that was unnecessarily prolonged and that the South could not win.

In the second selection, Gary W. Gallagher contends that Lee was a truly revered and unifying figure in the Confederacy. According to Gallagher, most Southerners approved of Lee's offensive tactics, were appreciative of his battlefield victories, and believed that the Northern troops could not win the war unless they captured his army.

Alan T. Nolan

 **YES**

"Rally, Once Again!"

General Lee—A Different View

I believe that Lee's generalship hurt the Confederates' chances for victory. I do not fault his tactics or operational strategy. I do fault his sense of the South's *grand strategy*. Tactics, of course, refers to *how* a battle is fought. Operational strategy concerns the plan of a campaign or battle. *Grand strategy* pertains to the use of military forces in order to win the war.

I concede that Lee was an effective and sometimes brilliant field commander, but his towering reputation results from viewing his leadership a campaign or a battle at a time and disregarding considerations of grand strategy. I argue that in grand strategic terms Lee did not understand the war, an ultimate failure that his sometimes brilliant operational strategy and tactics simply do not overcome.

In order to evaluate my thesis, one has to identify his or her own opinion as to how the South could have won: with an offensive grand strategy that risked the depletion of its inferior numbers in an effort to defeat the North militarily, or the defensive, that is, fighting the war so as to prolong it and punish the North so that it would have decided that coercion was impossible or not worth the cost. Because of its relatively limited manpower and manufacturing base, the Confederacy was never in a position to defeat the North militarily. Its only chance was to make the war so costly to the North that the North would give it up. To do this, it was essential for Lee to observe a conserving, defensive grand strategy, the counterpart of Washington's grand strategy in the Revolution. The Americans could not and did not militarily defeat the British regulars, but within a grand defensive context they kept armies in the field and harassed the enemy until it gave up the contest.

In arguing for the defensive grand strategy, I am not advocating a perimeter war, a war of position or the exclusively defensive operational strategy and tactics of General Joseph E. Johnston in the Atlanta campaign. Nor do I believe that Lee could simply have remained idle. Within a defensive context he could have maneuvered and raided, as did Washington, and still avoided the expensive battles that his offensives induced. Occasional reasoned operationally strategic

"General Lee—A Different View" is from Alan T. Nolan, *"Rally, Once Again!" Selected Civil War Writings of Alan T. Nolan* (Madison House, 2000). Copyright © 2000 by Alan T. Nolan. Reprinted by permission of Madison House Books. "The Price of Honor" is from Alan T. Nolan, *Lee Considered: General Robert E. Lee and Civil War History* (University of North Carolina Press, 1991). Copyright © 1991 by University of North Carolina Press. Reprinted by permission.

offensives and tactics could have been undertaken within the framework of the grand strategic defensive. Washington's leadership is again the model.

Lee's grand strategic view was set forth in a letter of July 6, 1864, to President Davis:

> If we can defeat or drive the armies of the enemy from the field, we shall have peace. All of our efforts and energies should be devoted to that object.

This is a statement of offensive grand strategy. Lee believed that to win the war the South had to overpower the North militarily, to decimate and disperse its armies. A reference to 1862–63 is appropriate. Having taken command of the Army of Northern Virginia on June 1, 1862, for two years Lee vigorously pursued the strategic offensive in an effort to defeat the North militarily: the Peninsula, the Second Bull Run Campaign, the Maryland Campaign, Chancellorsville, and the Pennsylvania Campaign. He either attacked or, in the case of Second Bull Run and the Maryland Campaign, maneuvered offensively so as to precipitate large and costly battles. He did this although he had predicted that a siege in the Richmond defenses would be fatal to his army. In order to avoid being fixed, to avoid a siege, an army must be mobile. And mobility, the capacity to maneuver, requires numbers in some reasonable relationship to the enemy's numbers. In the course of his offensives, Lee took disproportionate, irreplaceable and unaffordable losses that undermined the viability of his army, deprived it of mobility, and ultimately committed it to a siege. A comparison of Lee's and the Federals' losses is instructive [see Table 1].

Fredericksburg, Lee's only 1862–3 genuinely defensive battle, provides a significant contrast: Burnside lost almost 11,000 killed and wounded (10.9%) as compared to Lee's 4,656 (6.4%).

Table 1

	Federals	Confederates
The Seven Days	9,796	19,739
	10.7%	20.7%
Second Bull Run	10,096	9,108
	13.3%	18.8%
Antietam	11,657	11,724
	15.5%	22.6%
Chancellorsville	11,116	10,746
	11.4%	18.7%
Gettysburg	17,684	22,638
	21.2%	30.2%

Classic examples of Lee's mistaken offensive grand strategy are provided by his decisions that led to the battles at Antietam and Gettysburg. Having been victorious at Second Bull Run, Lee was in an ideal position in September 1862 to desist from a prompt offensive move. In spite of statements by some writers that he had no alternative to moving into Maryland, even Freeman concedes that after Second Bull Run he could have moved a "slight distance southward" from Manassas, "to Warrenton, for instance. . . . That would put the Army of Northern Virginia on the flank of any force advancing to Richmond, and would give it the advantage of direct rail communications with the capitaL" In spite of this alternative, Lee moved into Maryland, which forseeably drew the Federal army after him and resulted in the costly battle at Antietam. Lee knew that substantial casualties were inevitable in that battle whether he won or lost. The situation immediately after Chancellorsville is also illuminating. In that battle, Lee had demonstrated his offensive tactical brilliance—and he had taken heavy losses in the process. According to his aide, Col. Charles Marshall, and Lee's own comments, Lee then had three options: to attack Hooker across the Rappahannock, to position himself to defend against another Federal effort to attack him across the Rappahannock, and to raid into Maryland and Pennsylvania. Having wisely rejected attempting to attack Hooker across the river, Lee chose the Northern raid option. This choice ended at Gettysburg where, to quote Freeman, Lee's army was "wrecked." Surely Gettysburg, requiring a crossing and recrossing of the Potomac and with extended lines of communication, was the most risky of the options. As in the case of the 1862 move into Maryland, win, lose or draw, the Maryland-Pennsylvania move of 1863 was bound to result in substantial casualties.

Lee's offensive view of the war also appears in his dispatches after Gettysburg. On August 31, 1863, in a letter to Longstreet he said that "I can see nothing better to be done than to endeavor to bring General Meade out and use our efforts to crush his army." On October 11, 1863, he wrote the Secretary of War from near Madison Courthouse that, "Yesterday I moved the army to this position with the hope of getting an opportunity to strike a blow at the enemy." Less than a week later he informed President Davis from Bristoe Station as follows: "I have the honor to inform you that with the view of bringing on an engagement with the army of Gen. Meade . . . this army . . . arrived near Culpeper on the 11th." Later in 1863, he spoke of "preparations made to attack (Meade)," which were frustrated by Meade's retreat. In February of 1864 he wrote Davis of his desire to "drive him (the enemy) to the Potomac." Even after the Wilderness and Spotsylvania, Lee wrote Davis that "it seems to me our best policy to unite upon it (Grant's army) and endeavor to crush it." Also in 1864 he told General Jubal A. Early that "we must destroy this army of Grant's before he gets to the James River." Already reduced by his 1862–63 offensives, it was simply not possible for Lee to "crush" or "destroy" Grant's overwhelming force. He could injure or slow it down, but not destroy it. The point is that, as had been true from the beginning of his army command, even at this late date Lee thought strategically in Armageddon terms. Early's Shenandoah Valley campaign in 1864 is significant in another respect. Early was sent to the valley to draw Federal forces away from Petersburg and Richmond. To draw Federals into the valley and *keep them there,* Early's force had only to be present in the valley. But Lee's offensive spirit caused him to tell Early to attack the Federals' valley forces. Early pursued the offensive. His outnumbered army took heavy losses and was ultimately decimated and resoundingly defeated. This permitted the Federals to be returned to Grant before Richmond. The offensive urged by Lee countered Lee's purpose in sending Early to the valley.

Lee's 1862–63 costly offensive warfare defied his own concern about relative manpower. His correspondence with Davis and the Secretary of War is replete with statements of that concern. During the 1862–63 period, he wrote regularly of the "superior numbers of the enemy," the necessity to "husband our strength," "the falling off in (his army's) aggregate shows that its ranks are growing weaker and that its losses are not supplied by recruits and that the enemy "can be easily reinforced, while no addition can be made to our numbers." Some may contend that Lee's grand strategy was defensive, an offensive defensive. To make this claim, they must somehow exorcise Lee's own words, his consistent advocacy of the attack, and the way he used his army for two years, until its losses deprived him of mobility and the offensive option.

Forced to the strategic defensive by 1864, Lee demonstrated the value of that posture, exacting such a price from the North that it came close to abandoning the war. I contend that had he carried out his leadership in this way during the two costly offensive years, as he did only at Fredericksburg, he would have slowed the enemy's increase in numerical superiority to the extent that it arose from Lee's heavy, disproportionate, and irreplaceable losses. He would have saved a substantial portion of the approximately 100,000 soldiers that he lost on the offensive. With these additional numbers, he could have maintained mobility and avoided a siege. Maneuvers like Early's 1864 movement in the valley could have been undertaken with sufficient numbers to be effective. The Federals, on the offensive, could have suffered for an earlier or longer period the ceaseless Federal losses that began in May of 1864. The Northern people could have politically abandoned their support of the war.

Some who disagree with me argue that the defensive would not have punished the North more than the 1862–63 offensives did. That may be so, but, as indicated by Fredericksburg, the defensive would not have wasted Lee's own force, which was the principal defect with his offensives. My detractors further contend that traditional military doctrine advocates the offensive because it permits selection of the time and place of the battle. But the endemically outnumbered Lee was not in a traditional situation that afforded him a chance of winning the war militarily. It is also said that the Southern people would not have accepted the defensive. There is no evidence that Lee or the Confederate Administration relied on this factor in pursuing the 1862–3 offensives. Further, if Lee had believed that the offensive was destructive to his chances, his obligation, and that of the Administration, was to bring the public along with them. Time, the duration of the war, was a problem for both sides, the South because of its relatively limited supply base and the North because of the risk that the public would abandon the contest as hopeless.

In short, I believe that Lee's offensive grand strategy was destructive to the South's chances. Lee's task was not to win great battles, to be spectacular, but to win the war The military historian Lt. Col. George A. Bruce states that "the art of war consists in using the forces of a nation to secure the end for which it is waged, and not in a succession of great battles that tend to defeat it." In 1862–63 Lee sought out the great battles. He went on the defensive in 1864 against his own strategic sense, only because his prior losses forced this posture. Maj. Gen. J. F. C. Fuller, the English military historian, seems to me to have fairly characterized Lee's leadership during the first two years of his command: Lee "rushed forth to find a battlefield, to challenge a contest between himself and the North." In this process, he unilaterally accomplished the attrition of his army that led to its being besieged and ultimately surrendered. His losses ultimately prevented his sustaining his army and punishing the North sufficiently to induce it to abandon the war—the only chance the South had to win. . . .

The Price of Honor: R. E. Lee and the Question of Confederate Surrender

. . . Robert E. Lee's belief in the inevitability of his final defeat, and the contrast between that belief and his combative persistence, together raise the question of his motivation. There are several worthwhile lines of inquiry regarding his motives, but before examining them it is necessary to consider briefly the question of his authority to surrender: did he have the authority to surrender his army and, if so, what circumstances permitted him to exercise that authority?

It is plain that Lee did have the right to surrender and was aware that he did. Between 7 April and 9 April 1865, as his correspondence with U.S. Grant proceeded, Lee consulted certain trusted aides and debated with himself the issue of surrender. But he insisted that, "if it is right, then *I* will take *all* the responsibility." On 9 April, the deed was done at Appomattox. On 12 April, Lee reported the surrender to Jefferson Davis, explaining that maintaining the battle "one day longer . . . would have been at a great sacrifice of life, and at its end I did not see how a surrender could have been avoided." In short, on 9 April 1865, believing that ultimate surrender was inevitable, he could not justify the sacrifice of life that further prolonging the combat would entail.

The situation at Appomattox was surely grim, but as has been noted, Lee had viewed the South's situation in the same grim terms for anywhere from twenty to five months prior to 9 April 1865. He had the same authority then to surrender as he had on 9 April. As the casualties and other losses—physical, financial, and emotional—mounted, what interest did Lee believe he was serving in continuing the hopeless struggle? His own statements suggest four possible answers to this question: he believed that the North was such a monstrous tyrant that defeat and death were the only moral responses; God willed his continuing to fight in spite of the inevitability of defeat; he was bound to persist because he was subject to Confederate civilian control, which did not want him to surrender; or his personal sense of duty demanded it.

The first answer suggests the philosophical proposition that there are worse fates than defeat and death. Americans in Lee's day, as well as today, were the heirs of a liberty-or-death tradition. Lee identified with this tradition. Despite his personal opposition to secession, he is quoted as having said, "We had, I was satisfied, sacred principles to maintain and rights to defend, for which we were in duty bound to do our best, even if we perished in the endeavor." On 7 April or 8 April, sometime within two days of the surrender, General William N. Pendleton, representing a group of officers, suggested surrender to Lee. Lee rejected the idea, stating that rather than surrender "we must all determine to die at our posts." But the liberty-or-death motive does not adequately explain Lee's prolonging the war after he adopted a belief in its futility, bearing in mind that he did in fact surrender, despite his prior rhetorical flourishes. Furthermore, he flatly rejected General Edward Porter Alexander's suggestion of guerrilla warfare as an alternative means of continuing the war because of its deleterious effect on the country as a whole. His 20 April 1865 letter to President Davis also discouraged Alexander's guerrilla warfare suggestion and urged Davis to seek a general peace. And on 13 June 1865, Lee applied for amnesty and the "benefits and full restoration of all rights and privileges" as a citizen of the United States. Each of these facts contradicts the notion that Lee was motivated by the belief that ultimate resistance to the Federals was the appropriate moral position.

Untroubled by any questions concerning the correctness of Lee's conduct, his biographer Douglas Southall Freeman comes close to suggesting that Lee persisted in the war because he believed that, regardless of the odds and the inevitability of defeat, God wanted him to keep fighting. Thus, Freeman stated that "nothing of his serenity during the war or of his silent labor in defeat can be understood unless one realizes that he submitted himself in all things faithfully to the will of a Divinity which, in his simple faith, was directing wisely the fate of nations and the daily life of His children." It is certainly true that Lee had a strong personal sense of the presence of God and God's responsibility for human events. But given the general's Herculean efforts, and his reliance on God to give him victories, it seems unreasonable to suggest that he persisted in futile combat because of some sense that God intended him to do so. Had this been his conviction, he presumably would not have surrendered on 9 April 1865.

Freeman was at pains to point out that Lee accepted wholeheartedly the American constitutional premise of military subordination to the civil government: "Lee . . . applied literally and loyally his conviction that the President was the commander-in-chief." This constitutional principle was consistent with one of the general's life principles described by Freeman as "respect for constituted authority" and "his creed of obedience to constituted authority." Biographer Clifford Dowdey's description of certain events in February and March 1865 provides an interesting insight into the question of Lee's deference to authority. Referring to the period following the Hampton Roads meeting of 3 February 1865, between Confederate representatives and Abraham Lincoln and his aides, Dowdey wrote:

> Lee had held a private conversation with Virginia's Senator R. M. T. Hunter. . . . Lee urged him to offer a resolution in the Senate that would obtain better terms than, as Hunter reported Lee as saying, "were likely to be given after a surrender." Hunter claimed that Davis had already impugned his motives for seeking peace terms, and told Lee, "if he thought the chances of success desperate, thought he ought to say so to the President."

Though Lee held frequent conversations with Davis during February, it is unlikely that he ever brought himself to introduce a subject which would be so distasteful to the President.

Dowdey then recounted the views of Secretary of War James A. Seddon, his successor in that office, John C. Breckenridge, and James Longstreet, all of whom shared Lee's recognition of the fact the war was lost and peace was needed. Dowdey concluded by observing, "The crux of the matter was that men in a position to know recognized that the South was defeated, *but no one was willing to assume the responsibility of trying to convince Davis of this*"! (emphasis added). Lee had by this time become general-in-chief of the Confederate armies. Considering Dowdey's unflinching admiration for Lee, his attributing Lee's position and that of the others mentioned to an unwillingness to take responsibility is surely an unintended indictment. In any event, although it is evident that Lee accepted subordination to civilian authority, he ultimately took responsibility for the surrender and simply announced it to Davis. It cannot, therefore, be said that civilian control was the reason for Lee's persistence.

Finally, can Lee's resolve to fight on in the face of certain defeat be explained by his sense of duty and honor? Historian Gaines M. Foster has described the South as "a culture based on honor," and Bertram Wyatt-Brown has detailed the entire complex white culture of the South in terms of a code called "Honor." The authors of *Why the South Lost the Civil War* have attempted to give a short definition of the concept: "When Confederates talked of honor they did not mean pride so much as moral integrity, personal bravery, Christian graciousness, deference to and respect for others, and self-worth, recognized by their peers."

In Lee, honor and its companion, duty, were, to be sure, highly and self-consciously developed; so too was their consequence, the self-regard that Wyatt-Brown describes. All biographies of Lee quote at length his many aphorisms about these values. He said, for example, that the Confederates were "duty bound to do our best, even if we perished." On 22 February 1865, in a letter to his wife, he stated, "I shall . . . endeavour to do my duty & fight to the last." In a March 1865 interview with General John B. Gordon, he spoke of "what duty to the army and our people required of us." Preparing to evacuate the Petersburg-Richmond line and move west toward Appomattox, "he acted," Lieutenant Colonel Walter H. Taylor noted, "as one who was conscious of having accomplished all that was possible in the line of duty, and who was undisturbed by the adverse conditions in which he found himself."

In regard to the effort to escape the pursuing Federals between Richmond and Appomattox, Freeman observed: "So long as this chance was open to him, his sense of duty did not permit him to consider any alternative" and "as long as there was a prospect of escape Lee felt it was his duty to fight on. He would not yield one hour before he must." Freeman also noted approvingly Lee's memorandum to himself: "There is a true glory and a true honor: the glory of duty done—the honor of the integrity of principle." Commenting on "the dominance of a sense of duty in [Lee's] actions," Dowdey stated that "this is not so much a sense of duty in the abstract as a duty to do the best he could.

The point can clearly be seen when duty, *as a sense of the pride of a professional in his craft,* caused him to practice meticulously the techniques of command *long after any military purpose could be achieved"* (emphasis added).

Such a narrow definition of Lee's sense of honor and duty seems to be another unintended indictment by Dowdey. However defined, this sense of honor appears, after all, to have been an essentially personal emotional commitment that compelled Lee to fight on, regardless of the cost and long after he believed that it was futile to continue the contest. Referring to the Confederacy's hopeless situation during the winter of 1864–1865 and sympathetic to his personal commitment, Dowdey recognized "the moral obligation that required [Lee] to act as though defeat could be held off."

In a chapter entitled "The Sword of Robert E. Lee," Freeman set forth "an accounting of his service to the state." Having noted Lee's mobilization of Virginia, the Seven Days, the repulse of Federal offensives against Richmond, and his victories in six of ten major battles from Gaines's Mill through Spotsylvania, Freeman proceeded,

> During the twenty-four months when he had been free to employ open manoeuvre, a period that had ended with Cold Harbor, he had sustained approximately 103,000 casualties and had inflicted 145,000. Holding, as he usually had, to the offensive, his combat losses had been greater in proportion to his numbers than those of the Federals, but he had demonstrated how strategy may increase an opponent's casualties, for his losses included only 16,000 prisoners, whereas he had taken 38,000. Chained at length to the Richmond defenses, he had saved the capital from capture for ten months. All this he had done in the face of repeated defeats for the Southern troops in nearly every other part of the Confederacy. . . . These difficulties of the South would have been even worse had not the Army of Northern Virginia occupied so much of the thought and armed strength of the North. Lee is to be judged, in fact, not merely by what he accomplished with his own troops but by what he prevented the hosts of the Union from doing sooner elsewhere.

In reciting what Lee had accomplished, Freeman did not allude to the fact that for perhaps the last twenty months of these efforts, and surely for a substantial lesser period, Lee was proceeding in a cause that he personally believed was lost.

James M. McPherson has summarized the ultimate consequences of the prolonging of the war, to which Lee's accomplishments made a significant contribution:

> the South was not only invaded and conquered, it was utterly destroyed. By 1865 the Union forces had . . . destroyed two-thirds of the assessed value of Southern wealth, two-fifths of the South's livestock, and one-quarter of her white men between the ages of twenty and forty. More than half the farm machinery was ruined, and the damage to railroads and industries was incalculable. . . . Southern wealth decreased by 60 percent (or 30 percent if the slaves are not counted as wealth). These figures provide eloquent testimony to the tragic irony of the South's counterrevolution of 1861 to preserve its way of life.

In conjunction, the statements of Freeman and McPherson raise reasonable questions regarding Lee and history and Lee's role as an American idol. On the one hand, the Lee tradition projects a tragic hero, a man who courageously pursued a cause that he believed to be doomed. On the other hand, this heroic tradition must be balanced against the consequences of Lee's heroism. There is, of course, a nobility and poignancy, a romance, in the tragic and relentless pursuit of a hopeless cause. But in practical terms such pursuit is subject to a very different interpretation.

In reality, military leadership is not just a private or personal activity. Nor is a military leader's sense of honor and duty simply a private and personal impulse. Military leadership and the leader's sense of duty are of concern not only to the leader, but also to the followers and to the enemy, ordinary people, many of whom die, are maimed, or otherwise suffer. In short, military leadership involves responsibility for what happens to other persons. There is, therefore, no matter how sincerely a leader may believe in the justice of a cause, a difference between undertaking or continuing military leadership in a cause that the leader feels can succeed and undertaking or continuing such leadership in a cause that the leader feels is hopeless. In the latter circumstance, the leader knows that his order "once more into the breach" will kill or injure many of his soldiers as well as the enemy's and also realizes that his order and these deaths and injuries are without, in Dowdey's phrase, "any military purpose." Lacking a military purpose, they also have no political purpose. Thus they are without any rational purpose.

The absence of any rational purpose behind Lee's persistence is suggested by his sense of the meaning of the deaths of his men as revealed by his early advocate, the Reverend J. William Jones. Among the general's wartime papers that Jones found after his death were "maxims, proverbs, quotations from the Psalms, selections from standard authors, and reflections of his own." One of these, in Lee's own hand, read, "The warmest instincts of every man's soul declare the glory of the soldier's death. It is more appropriate to the Christian than to the Greek to sing: 'Glorious his fate, and envied is his lot, Who for his country fights and for it dies.'"

As suggested earlier by McPherson's description of the war's impact on the South, the conflict involved catastrophic consequences for the people of the United States both North and South. During the war as a whole more than half a million soldiers died. Untold thousands were maimed. The families of all of these men also suffered grievously. Whatever portion of the catastrophe occurred after the time when Lee had become convinced that the war was lost—whether Lee came to believe this twenty, fifteen, ten, or only five months before the end—significant harm took place, in the West as well as the East, before Lee finally called a halt to the fighting. For the plain people who suffered, Lincoln's "him who shall have borne the battle, and . . . his widow, and his orphan," the consequences of the war were dire in the extreme.

Freeman wrote bitterly about Southerners who were fearful or doubtful or who wished for peace, comparing them unfavorably to the dauntless Lee and to President Davis. But the authors of *Why the South Lost the Civil War* made a different observation: "By late 1864, very likely earlier, those Confederates who argued for an end of war, even if that meant returning to the Union, did not include only the war-weary defeatists. Many among those who took that statesman-like position may have lost their will, but they weigh more on the scales of humanity than those who would have fought to the last man."

The Lee orthodoxy insists that the Confederate officers and soldiers at Appomattox were tearful and heartbroken at their surrender—they wanted to keep fighting. But even purveyors of the orthodoxy occasionally, perhaps unwittingly, contradict the tradition. Thus, quoting Lieutenant Colonel Charles Venable, Dowdey wrote that soldiers who learned of Lee's intent to surrender were "convulsed with passionate grief." But Dowdey also reported that "Lee was aware that many of his soldiers, officers and men, were ready to end 'the long agony'. . . . He could sense the attitude." He also described enlisted men who, en route to Appomattox, "overcome by exhaustion . . . were lying stretched out flat or sitting with their heads on their knees, waiting to be gathered up by the enemy." A suggestive Federal account by an eyewitness agreed with Dowdey's report. "Billy," an enlisted man in the 1st Michigan Volunteers, wrote to his family from Appomattox on the day of the surrender. He described the pursuit to Appomattox and then added, "The best of it is the Rebs are as pleased over the surrender as we are, and when the surrender was made known to them cheer after cheer went up along their whole line." . . .

On 9 April 1865, Lee apparently felt that he had fully and finally served his personal sense of duty. He had fulfilled, at last, what Dowdey described as his personal sense of "duty to do the best he could, . . . a sense of the pride of a professional in his craft." He was prepared, at last, again quoting Dowdey, "to assume the responsibility" for introducing a subject "distasteful" to Jefferson Davis. The awful human cost of his persistence had, of course, been paid by countless other people, including his own soldiers.

Giving Lee full credit for good faith and high personal character, the historian must nonetheless—as a practitioner of a discipline regarded as one of the humanities—take into account the human and social consequences of his continuing to lead others in a war that he believed was lost. It is fair to observe that Virginia, reputedly the focus of Lee's primary interest, suffered especially devastating losses of life and property because it was the scene of almost constant warfare. The facts cast serious doubt on the traditional assumption that Lee's persistence was wholly admirable.

Gary W. Gallagher  **NO**

Another Look at the
Generalship of R. E. Lee

Americans have embraced Abraham Lincoln and R. E. Lee as the two great figures of the Civil War. In one of the many ironies associated with the conflict, the principal rebel chieftain overshadows Ulysses S. Grant, William Tecumseh Sherman, and all other Federal generals who helped to save the Union. Although Lee's transcendent reputation as a great captain remains firmly ensconced in the popular mind and virtually no one challenges his brilliance as a field commander, scholars increasingly have questioned his larger contribution to the Confederate war effort. Did he fail to see beyond his beloved Virginia, crippling Confederate strategic planning through a stubborn refusal to release troops badly needed elsewhere? Did his strategic and tactical choices lengthen the conflict, thereby increasing the odds that Northern civilian morale would falter? Or did his penchant for the offensive unnecessarily bleed Confederate manpower when a defensive strategy punctuated by limited counteroffensives would have conserved Southern resources? Did his celebrated victories improve the odds for Confederate nationhood, or were they nothing but gaudy sideshows that diverted attention from more significant military events elsewhere? In short, what was Lee's impact on the outcome of the war?

One of the most common criticisms of Lee alleges a lack of appreciation for the problems and importance of the trans-Appalachian Confederacy. J. F. C. Fuller frequently alluded to Lee's inability to see the war as a whole. The British author stated in one characteristic passage that Lee "was so obsessed by Virginia that he considered it the most important area of the Confederacy. . . . To him the Confederacy was but the base of Virginia." A number of subsequent historians expanded upon the idea that Lee failed to take in the entire strategic situation. Especially strident in this regard was Thomas L. Connelly, who wondered "whether Lee possessed a sufficiently broad military mind to deal with over-all Confederate matters." Connelly saw Lee as intensely parochial, blinded by a desire to protect Richmond and unwilling, or unable, to look beyond each immediate threat to his native state and its capital. When Lee did turn his attention to the West, averred Connelly, he invariably made suggestions "in the context of his strategy for Virginia." Connelly and Archer Jones reiterated many of these points in their study of Confederate command and strategy. They

From Gary W. Gallagher, "Another Look at the Generalship of R. E. Lee," in Gary W. Gallagher, ed., *Lee the Soldier* (University of Nebraska Press, 1996). Originally published in Gary W. Gallagher, ed., *The Second Day at Gettysburg: Essays on Confederate and Union Leadership* (Kent State University Press, 1993). Copyright © 1993 by Kent State University Press. Reprinted by permission. Notes omitted.

questioned Lee's knowledge about the geography of the West and deplored his habit of requesting reinforcements for the Army of Northern Virginia at the expense of other Confederate armies. Even Lee's grudging deployment of two-thirds of James Longstreet's First Corps to Georgia in September 1863 had a Virginia twist—he hoped that the movement might save Knoxville and shield Virginia's western flank.

Connelly and Jones admitted that all theater commanders tended to see their own region as most important but asserted that Lee's viewing Virginia in this way proved especially harmful. He had been Jefferson Davis's military adviser in the early days of the war and remained close to the president throughout the conflict; moreover, his reputation exceeded that of any other Confederate army commander. The result was as predictable as it was pernicious for the Confederacy: "His prestige as a winner and his unusual opportunity to advise undoubtedly to some degree influenced the government to take a narrower view on strategy and to go for the short gain in Virginia where victory seemed more possible." In the opinion of Connelly and Jones, Lee's influence was such that a powerful "Western Concentration Bloc," the roster of which included Joseph E. Johnston, P. G. T. Beauregard, James Longstreet, and John C. Breckinridge, could not counter his lone voice. The consequent failure to shift forces to threatened areas west of Virginia hindered the Southern cause.

Lee's aggressive style of generalship, with its attendant high casualties, also has generated much criticism. Grady McWhiney and Perry D. Jamieson propounded the thesis that a reckless devotion to offensive tactics bled the South "nearly to death in the first three years of the war" and sealed the fate of the Confederacy. Lee fit this pattern perfectly, they observed, sustaining losses approaching 20 percent in his first half-dozen battles compared to fewer than 15 percent for the Federals. A controversial aspect of McWhiney and Jamieson's book ascribed the South's love of direct assaults to a common Celtic ancestry. Whether or not readers accept the proposition that a cultural imperative prompted Lee to order attacks, McWhiney and Jamieson succeeded in accentuating his heavy losses throughout the war. Elsewhere, McWhiney bluntly claimed that the "aggressiveness of Robert E. Lee, the greatest Yankee killer of all time, cost the Confederacy dearly."

A number of other historians agreed with McWhiney. The Army of Northern Virginia suffered more than fifty thousand casualties in the three months after Lee assumed command, claimed Thomas L. Connelly, and overall "the South's largest field army, contained in the smallest war theater, was bled to death by Lee's offensive tactics." Russell F. Weigley asserted that Lee shared Napoleon's "passion for the strategy of annihilation and the climactic, decisive battle" and "destroyed in the end not the enemy armies) but his own." J. F. C. Fuller believed that Lee's only hope for success lay in emulating "the great Fabius," who often retreated to avoid costly battles. Instead, time and again Lee "rushed forth to find a battlefield" and "by his restless audacity, he mined such strategy as his government created." Alan T. Nolan's reasoned analysis of Lee explored the question of "whether the general's actions related positively or negatively to the war objectives and national policy of his government." Nolan thought that Lee came up far short when measured against this standard. His strategy and tactics won specific contests and made headlines but traded irreplaceable manpower for only fleeting advantage. "If one covets the haunting romance of the Lost Cause," wrote Nolan, "then the inflicting of casualties on the enemy, tactical victory in great battles, and audacity are enough." But such accomplishments did not bring the Confederacy closer to independence. Lee's relentless pursuit of the offensive contravened the strategy best calculated to win Southern independence and thus "contributed to the loss of the Lost Cause."

One last piece of testimony on this point typifies a common tension between admiration for Lee's generalship and a sense that his aggressive actions might have hurt the Confederacy. In a lecture delivered at a symposium on Lee in 1984, Frank E. Vandiver commented that his subject "lost a lot of men by attacking and attacking and attacking" and "may have been too addicted to the offensive, even against outstanding firepower." Vandiver then quickly hedged his conclusion: "I think that you have to balance the fact that he lost a lot of men and stuck to the offensive against what he considered to be the strategic necessities of attack. So I would level the charge that he might have been too addicted to the offensive with some trepidation."

These historians raise serious questions about the relationship between Lee's generalship and Confederate chances for independence. A different reading of the evidence, however, suggests that Lee pursued a strategy attuned to the expectations of most Confederate citizens and calculated to exert maximum influence on those who made policy in the North and in Europe. Far from being innocent of the importance of the West and the psychological dimension of his operations, he might have seen more clearly than any of his peers the best road to Confederate independence. His victories buoyed Southern hopes when defeat lay in all other directions, dampened spirits in the North, and impressed European political leaders. They also propelled him to a position where, long before the end of the war, he stood unchallenged as a military hero and his Army of Northern Virginia had become synonymous with the Confederacy in the minds of many Southern whites. While his army remained in the field there was hope for victory; his capitulation extinguished such hope and in effect ended the war. Lee had selected a strategy that paradoxically enabled the Confederacy to resist for four years *and* guaranteed that it would not survive the surrender of his army at Appomattox.

Modern historians usually attribute Confederate military defeat to failure in the West, where vast chunks of territory and crucial cities fell to the Federals. They often add that Lee's unwillingness to send part of his own army to bolster forces beyond the Appalachians may have hastened Confederate defeat. Is this belief in the primacy of western campaigns a modern misreading of the actual situation? Certainly it was the Virginia theater that captivated foreign observers. For example, Lee's victories at the Seven Days and Second Manassas in the summer of 1862 conveyed to London and Paris a sense of impending Confederate success. Apparently unimpressed by the string of Union triumphs in the West that extended from Fort Henry through the fall of New Orleans, Prime Minister Viscount Palmerston and Emperor Napoleon III leaned toward some type of intervention by the first week in September. Northern public opinion also seemed to give greater weight to the Seven Days than to events in Tennessee, prompting Lincoln's famous complaint to French Count Agénor-Etienne de Gasparin in early August: "Yet it seems unreasonable that a series of successes, extending through half-a-year, and clearing more than a hundred thousand square miles of country, should help us so little, while a single half-defeat should hurt us so much."

Other evidence of a Northern preoccupation with the East abounds. Albert Castel has noted that Lincoln himself, who beyond doubt believed the West to be more important, visited the Army of the Potomac several times but never favored a western army with his presence. (Jefferson Davis joined his western armies on three occasions.) Senator Charles Sumner revealed a good deal about attitudes among powerful Northern politicians when he wrote during the winter of 1865 that Secretary of War Edwin M. Stanton thought "peace can be had only when Lee's army is beaten, captured or dispersed." Sumner had "for a long time been sanguine that, when Lee's army is out of the way, the whole rebellion will disappear." So long as Lee remained active, "there is still hope for the rebels, & the unionists of the South are afraid to show themselves." Among the most telling indications of the public mood was a demand that Grant go east when he became general-in-chief of the Union armies in March 1864. He could have run the war as efficiently from Tennessee or Georgia, but the North wanted its best general to bring his talents to bear on the frustrating Virginia theater.

If anything, the South exhibited a more pronounced interest in the East. Following reverses in Tennessee and along the Mississippi River during the winter and spring of 1862, Confederates looked increasingly to Virginia for good news from the battlefield. Stonewall Jackson supplied it in the spring of 1862 with his Shenandoah Valley campaign—after that, Lee and the Army of Northern Virginia provided the only reliable counterpoint to Northern gains in other theaters and consequently earned a special position in the minds of their fellow Confederates. William M. Blackford of Lynchburg, an antislavery man who nonetheless supported the Confederacy and sent five sons into Southern service, applauded the cumulative effect of Lee's 1862 campaigns: "The defeats of the enemy in the Valley, in the Peninsular, in the Piedmont, the invasion of Maryland, the capture of Harper's Ferry and lastly the victory at Fredericksburg," he remarked. "taken all together, are achievements which do not often crown one year." Lamenting the fall of Vicksburg in late July 1863, Kate Stone, a young refugee in Texas, added that "[o]ur only hope is in Lee the Invincible." Ten months and the reverse at Gettysburg did not alter Stone's thinking about Lee. "A great battle is rumored in Virginia," she wrote in May 1864. "Grant's first fight in his 'On to Richmond.' He is opposed by the Invincible Lee and so we are satisfied we won the victory." A Louisiana officer serving in the West echoed Stone's opinion on 27 May 1864, dismissing talk of a setback in Virginia with an expression of "complete faith in General Lee, who has never been known to suffer defeat, and probably never will."

No one better illustrated the tendency to focus on Lee than Catherine Ann Devereux Edmondston of North Carolina. "What a position does he occupy," she recorded in her diary on 11 June 1864, "the idol, the point of trust, of confidence & repose of thousands! How nobly has he won the confidence, the admiration of the nation." Shifting to a comparison between Lee and officers who had failed in other theaters, Edmondston remarked: "God grant that he may long be spared to us. He nullifies Bragg, Ransom. & a host of other incapables." The *Charleston Daily Courier* implicitly contrasted Lee with Confederate generals in the West when it noted that "Grant is now opposed to a General who stands in the foremost rank of Captains, and his army is confronted with men accustomed to victory." More explicit was a Georgian who after the fall of Atlanta gazed long-ingly at the commander in Virginia: "Oh, for a General Lee at the head of every *corps d'armee!*"

Well before the close of the war, Lee's position in the Confederacy ap-proximated that held by Washington during the American Revolution. "It is impossible for me to describe the emotions of my heart. . . . I felt proud that the Southern Confederacy could boast of such a man," a North Carolina lieu-tenant wrote after Lee had reviewed his unit in May 1863. "In fact, I was almost too proud for the occasion for I could not open my mouth to give vent to the emotions that were struggling within." The *Lynchburg Virginian* affirmed after Chancellorsville that the "central figure of this war is, beyond all question, that of Robert E. Lee." Alluding to the phenomenon of Lee's offsetting Confederate reverses in the West, the Virginian admired his "calm, broad military intellect that reduced the chaos after Donelson to form and order." "He should certainly have entire control of all military operations through-out the Confederate States," stated one of the generals artillerists in mid-1864. "In fact I should like to see him as King or Dictator. He is one of the few great men who ever lived, who could be trusted." Lee's belated elevation to general-in-chief of the Con-federate armies in February 1865 prompted Edward O. Guerrant, an officer serving in southwest Virginia, to observe that "[this] has inspired our country with more hope, courage, & confidence than it has had for a year or two. . . . It puts us all in good humor, & good spirits, and for myself—I feel more confi-dent of our final triumph than for several months past." Gen. Henry A. Wise told Lee on 6 April 1865 that there "has been no country, general, for a year or more. You are the country to these men. They have fought for you."

Testimony from soldiers lends powerful support to Wise's statements. A Georgian in the Army of Northern Virginia wrote shortly after Gettysburg that "[i]t looks like it does not do any good to whip them here in this state, and out West they are tearing everything to pieces. . . . But I am willing to fight them as long as General Lee says fight." When Lee reviewed the First Corps after its return to Virginia from East Tennessee in April 1864, a South Carolinian described an emotional scene: "[T]he men caught sight of his well known figure, [and] a wild and prolonged cheer . . . ran along the lines and rose to the heavens. Hats were thrown high, and many persons became almost frantic with emotion. . . . One heard on all sides such expressions as: 'What a splendid figure!' 'What a noble face and head!' 'Our destiny is in his hands!' 'He is the best and greatest man on this continent!'" A perceptive foreign observer picked up on this attitude when he described Lee in March 1865 as the "idol of his soldiers & the Hope of His country" and spoke of "the prestige which surrounds his person & the almost fanatical belief in his judgment & capacity wh[ich] is the one idea of an entire people."

Many Confederates tied Lee directly to the sainted Washington. During the fall of 1862, the *Columbus* (Georgia) *Times* spoke of his winning everybody's confidence and noted that he "has much of the Washingtonian dignity about him, and is much respected by all with whom he is thrown." Peter W. Alexander, perhaps the most widely read Confederate war correspondent, assessed Lee just before the battle of Fredericksburg in December 1862: "Like Washington, he is a wise man, and a good man, and possesses in an eminent degree those qualities which are indispensable in the great leader and champion upon whom the country rests its hope." Alexander added that the Confederacy "should feel grateful that Heaven has raised up one in our midst so worthy of our confidence and so capable to lead"—the "grand-son of Washington, so to speak . . . the wise and modest chief who commands the Army of Northern Virginia." In the wake of Lee's triumph at Fredericksburg in December 1862, Georgian Mary Jones expressed thanks "that in this great struggle the head of our army is a noble son of Virginia, and worthy of the intimate relation in which he stands connected with our immortal Washington. What confidence his wisdom, integrity, and valor and undoubted piety inspire!" Eliza Frances Andrews, another resident of Georgia, called Lee simply "that star of light before which even Washington's glory pales."

In line with such sentiment inside and outside his army, Lee's surrender understandably signaled the end of the war to most Confederates (as it did to most Northerners). President Davis might speak bravely of the war's simply moving into a new phase after Appomattox, but a trio of women voiced far more common sentiments. "How can I write it?" asked Catherine Edmondston. "How find words to tell what has befallen us? *Gen Lee has surrendered!* . . . We stand appalled at our disaster! . . . [That] *Lee,* Lee upon whom hung the hopes of the whole country, should be a prisoner seems almost too dreadful to be realized!" The first report of Lee's capitulation reached Eliza Andrews on 18 April 1865: "No one seems to doubt it," she wrote sadly, "and everybody feels ready to give up hope. 'It is useless to struggle longer,' seems to be the common cry, and the poor wounded men go hobbling about the streets with despair on their faces." From Florida, a young woman reacted with the "wish we were all dead. It is as if the very earth had crumbled beneath our feet." A North Carolinian in the Army of Northern Virginia spoke for many soldiers and civilians in a single succinct sentence written the day Lee agreed to Grant's terms: "The life of the 'C.S.' is gon' when Gen Lee and his army surrendered."

The foregoing testimony indicates a widespread tendency *during the war* to concentrate attention on Lee and Virginia. Lee himself discerned the centrality of his military operations to Confederate morale (after Gettysburg he commented on the "unreasonable expectations of the public" concerning the Army of Northern Virginia), as well as to perceptions in the North and Europe. A man of far more than ordinary intelligence, he read Northern and Southern newspapers assiduously, corresponded widely, and discussed the political and civilian dimensions of the conflict with a broad range of persons. He appreciated the incalculable industrial and emotional value of Richmond as well as the profound concern for Washington among Northern leaders. He knew the records and personalities of officers who led Confederate armies in the West.

He watched the dreary procession of defeats from Fort Donelson and Pea Ridge through Shiloh, Perryville, Stones River, Vicksburg, and Chattanooga. Robustly aware of his own ability and the superior quality of his army, he faced successive opponents with high expectations of success. A combination of these factors likely persuaded him that victories in Virginia were both more probable and calculated to yield larger results than whatever might transpire in the West.

Within this context, it followed that the Confederacy should augment his army to the greatest degree possible. Lee's official restraint prevented his questioning overtly the competence of fellow army commanders; however, in opposing the transfer of George E. Pickett's division to the West in May 1863, he mentioned the "uncertainty of its application" under John C. Pemberton. That guarded phrase came from the pen of a man who quite simply believed he was the best the Confederacy had and thus should be given adequate resources to do his job. Braxton Bragg's sheer waste of two divisions under James Longstreet in the fall of 1863 demonstrated the soundness of Lee's reluctance to reinforce western armies at the expense of the Army of Northern Virginia. As Richard M. McMurry has suggested, the "Rebels' dilemma was that they did not have either the leadership or the manpower and materiel" to hang on to both Virginia and the West. That being the case, perhaps they should have sent available resources to Virginia: "Such a strategy would have employed their best army under their best general at the point where conditions were most favorable to them. If the Confederates could not have won their independence under such circumstances, they could not have won it anywhere under any possible circumstances." To put it another way, the Confederacy could lose the war in either the West or the East, but it could win the war only in the East.

What about Lee's supposed overreliance on the offensive? His periodic use of highly questionable and costly assaults is beyond debate. Natural audacity overcame the dictates of reason when he ordered frontal attacks at Malvern Hill, on the third day at Gettysburg, and elsewhere, and when he elected to give battle north of the Potomac after 15 September 1862. But these unfortunate decisions should not unduly influence interpretations of his larger military record. After all, Grant and Sherman also resorted to unimaginative direct attacks at various times in their careers. Many critics fail to give Lee credit for what he accomplished through aggressive generalship. At the Seven Days he blunted a Federal offensive that seemed destined to pin defending Confederates in Richmond; his counterpunch in the campaign of Second Manassas pushed the eastern military frontier back to the Potomac and confronted Lincoln with a major crisis at home and abroad. The tactical masterpiece at Chancellorsville, coming as it did on the heels of a defensive win at Fredericksburg, again sent tremors through the North. Lee failed to follow up either pair of victories with a third win at Antietam or Gettysburg; however, in September 1862 and June 1863 it was not at all clear that the Army of Northern Virginia would suffer defeat in Maryland and Pennsylvania. A victory in either circumstance might have altered the course of the conflict.

Too many critics of Lee's offensive movements neglect to place them within the context of what the Confederate people would tolerate. It is easy from a late-twentieth-century perspective to study maps, point to the defensive power of the rifle-musket, speculate about the potential of wide-scale guerrilla warfare, and reach a conclusion that Lee's aggressive strategic and tactical decisions shortened the life of the Confederacy. From the opening of the war, however, Southern civilians, newspaper editors, and political leaders clamored for decisive action on the battlefield and berated generals who shunned confrontations with the Federals.

As early as the winter of 1861–62, the Richmond Dispatch described a "public mind . . . restless and anxious to be relieved by some decisive action that shall have a positive influence in the progress of the war." In mid-June 1862, shortly after Lee assumed command of the Army of Northern Virginia, the *Richmond Enquirer* conceded the value of entrenchments but stressed the need for offensive moves. "To attack the enemy at every opportunity. To harass him, cut him up, and draw him into general engagements," insisted the *Enquirer*, "is the policy of every commander who has confidence in the strength and spirit of his army. . . . [L]et activity, aggression. Attack, stand recorded and declared as our line of policy." Three months later the Macon (Georgia) *Journal & Messenger* greeted news of Lee's raid into Maryland in typically bellicose fashion: "Having in this war exercised Christian forbearance to its utmost extent, by acting on the defensive, it will now be gratifying to all to see . . . the war carried upon the soil of those barbarians who have so long been robbing and murdering our quiet and unoffending citizens." Confederate writings, both public and private, bristle with innumerable sentiments of this type.

Although Confederates often linked Lee and George Washington, they really craved a type of generalship different from that of their Revolutionary hero. Joseph E. Johnston retreated often, fought only when absolutely necessary, and otherwise fit Washington's military mold quite closely. Such behavior created an impression in the Confederacy that he gave up too much territory far too easily. A young lieutenant in Savannah complained to his father on 12 May 1862 about the Peninsula campaign: "General Joseph Johnston, from whom we were led to expect so much, has done little else than *evacuate*, until the very mention of the word sickens one *usque ad nauseam*." Twelve days later Virginia planter William Bulware excoriated Johnston in a conversation with Edmund Ruffin. The general had avoided battle for days and given up twenty miles of ground, facts that demonstrated his "incompetency and mismanagement." Bulware predicted that Johnston would continue to withdraw, causing the "surrender of Richmond, & evacuation of all lower Virginia." Criticism intensified during Johnston's retreat toward Atlanta in 1864. "I don't think he will suit the emergency," complained Josiah Gorgas long before Johnston reached Atlanta. "He is falling back just as fast as his legs can carry him. . . . Where he will stop Heaven only knows." Long since disenchanted with Johnston's tendency to retreat (together with many other facets of his behavior), Jefferson Davis finally replaced him with John Bell Hood, an officer who understood Southern expectations and immediately went on the offensive.

Lee's style of generalship suited the temperament of his people—though many fellow Confederates initially harbored doubts about his competency to succeed Joseph Johnston in field command. Known as "Granny Lee" or the "King of Spades" early in the war, he seemed more devoted to fortifications than to smiting the enemy. Edward Porter Alexander recalled that John M. Daniel, editor of the Richmond Examiner, bitterly attacked Lee in June 1862 as one who would misuse the army: "It would only be allowed to dig, that being the West Point idea of war, & West Point now being in command; that guns & ammunition would now only be in the way, spades & shovels being the only implements Gen. Lee knew anything about, &c., &c." The correspondent for the Enquirer remarked at this same time that "you have only to go into the army, amongst the men in the ranks, to hear curses heaped upon West Point and the spade."

Questions about Lee's aggressiveness disappeared rapidly after his victory in the Seven Days. His admittedly bloody battles in 1862–63 created an aura of invincibility that offset gloomy events in the West, and that aura clung to him and his army through the defensive struggles of 1864–65. Lee's initial eighteen months as commander of the Army of Northern Virginia built credibility on which he drew for the rest of the war to sustain civilian morale. Confidence in his army as it lay pinned in the trenches at Petersburg during the summer of 1864 remained high, while Northerners experienced their darkest period of doubt. Far from hastening the demise of the Confederacy, Lee's generalship provided hope that probably carried the South beyond the point at which its citizens otherwise would have abandoned their quest for nationhood.

Nor was Lee's generalship hopelessly "old-fashioned." The simplistic notion that Grant was among the first modern generals and Lee one of the last of the old school withers under the slightest scrutiny. Lee differed in many respects from Grant and Sherman—most notably in his rejection of war against civilians—but had come to terms with many facets of a modern struggle between societies. He predicted from the beginning a long war that would demand tremendous sacrifice in the Confederacy. A member of the Virginia secession convention recounted how Lee warned the delegates shortly after Fort Sumter fell that "they were just on the threshold of a long and bloody war." He knew the Northern people well and believed "they never would yield . . . except at the conclusion of a long and desperate struggle." "The war may last 10 years," he predicted to his wife on 30 April 1861, and no part of Virginia would offer safe refuge from the armies. Clear eyed about the chances for European intervention at the time of the *Trent* affair, Lee insisted that Confederates "must make up our minds to fight our battles & win our independence alone. No one will help us." He believed in the subordination of "every other consideration . . . to the great end of the public safety," testified Colonel Charles Marshall of his staff, "and that since the whole duty of the nation would be war until independence should be secured, the whole nation should for the time be converted into an army, the producers to feed and the soldiers to fight."

Lee's actions underscored this attitude. Although wearing the uniform of a republic fond of rhetoric praising state and individual rights, he demanded that the national interest come first. He issued an order in March 1862, for example, calling for more unified control of Southern railroad traffic to better satisfy the "exigencies of the service." As early as December 1861, he urged extending the terms of service for soldiers then under arms who originally had signed on for just twelve months: "The troops, in my opinion, should be organized for the war," he wrote. "We cannot stop short of its termination, be it long or short." A staunch supporter of national conscription, Lee played a key role in the process that resulted in the Confederate conscription law of April 1862. Beyond coercing military service, Lee supported the concentration of manpower in the principal Southern field armies, the central government's right to procure needed war material through impressment, and other measures strikingly at odds with the doctrine of state rights.

Late in the war Lee publicly endorsed arming black men and granting them freedom in return for Confederate service. He thus undercut the institution of slavery (with state rights one of the twin pillars on which the Confederacy had been founded), proclaiming openly what he long had urged confidentially. Loath to disagree with his government or intrude in the political sphere during the conflict, Lee had waited to express himself officially on this question until too late to affect Confederate fortunes. He later spoke privately of telling Jefferson Davis "often and early in the war that the slaves should be emancipated, that it was the only way to remove a weakness at home and to get sympathy abroad." A presidential "proclamation of gradual emancipation and the use of the negroes as soldiers" would have furthered the Confederate cause, but Davis resisted taking this step because of the political firestorm it would ignite.

Contrary to what critics such as John Keegan say, Lee was not a man of "limited imagination" whose "essentially conventional outlook" helped undo the Confederacy. He formulated a national strategy predicated on the probability of success in Virginia and the value of battlefield victories. The ultimate failure of his strategy neither proves that it was wrongheaded nor diminishes Lee's pivotal part in keeping Confederate resistance alive through four brutally destructive years. That continued resistance held the key to potential victory— Southern armies almost certainly lacked the capacity to defeat decisively their Northern counterparts, but a protracted conflict marked by periodic Confederate successes on the battlefield more than once threatened to destroy the North's will to continue the war. Indeed, the greatest single obstacle to Northern victory after June 1862 was R. E. Lee and his Army of Northern Virginia. Without Lee and that famous field command, the Confederate experiment in rebellion almost certainly would have ended much sooner.

POSTSCRIPT

Is Robert E. Lee Overrated as a General?

Most of the biographers and military historians who write about Robert E. Lee treat him with awe and reverence. Lost-cause ex-Confederate warriors created Lee's image as a noble warrior and as a soldier of unparalleled skill. He died in 1870 while still president of Washington College in Lexington, Virginia (later renamed Washington and Lee College). After his death, monuments to the general appeared across the South, and in the twentieth century his birthday came to be celebrated as a holiday in many states below the Mason-Dixon line.

Typical were the remarks of a Virginia congressman who, in the House of Representatives on Lee's 123rd birthday, commented on the "beautiful and perfect symmetry of character" of "the matchless soldier . . . [whose] genius for war at once placed him in the front ranks of the soldier of all ages." The hagiographical treatment of Lee culminated in 1935, when Virginia newsman Douglas Southall Freeman won the Pulitzer Prize for his massively detailed and worshipful *R. E. Lee: A Biography,* 4 vols. (Scribner's, 1937–1940), a work that is still in print today and that has influenced most writings about the general.

Only a handful of books have dared to criticize this idolatrous portrait of Lee. In 1933 J. F. C. Fuller's *Grant and Lee: A Study in Personality and Generalship* (Indiana University Press, 1957) foreshadowed later criticisms of Lee's strategic vision and offensive tactics. It took almost 50 years for a second critical work to appear: Thomas L. Connelly's *The Marble Man: Robert E. Lee and His Image in American Society* (Louisiana State University Press, 1978). In it, Connelly attacked Lee's obsession with Virginia, psychoanalyzed the man probably beyond the historical evidence, and argued that the Lee image was the creation primarily of the lost-cause, post–Civil War South.

Nolan's selection is a summary of his book *Lee Considered: General Robert E. Lee and Civil War History* (University of North Carolina Press, 1991), a frank reevaluation of the traditional uncritical image of Lee. Nolan charges that Lee sustained an excessive number of casualties because his grand strategy was flawed. Although he was a brilliant tactician, says Nolan, Lee might have won the war had he resorted primarily to a defensive war and not an offensive grand strategy, which Nolan maintains caused Lee to sustain heavy casualties of irreplaceable troops to an enemy that easily outnumbered the Confederacy three to one in potential manpower.

Nolan also argues that Lee unnecessarily prolonged the war even though he knew it was lost a year before he surrendered. Nolan states that Lee's "sense of honor appears . . . to have been an essentially personal emotional commitment that compelled Lee to fight on, regardless of the cost and long after he believed that it was futile to continue the contest." Finally, Nolan denies that Lee fought on because he was subject to civilian control over the military.

Gallagher is the leader of the younger generation of historians who have been reevaluating the events of the Civil War in the 1990s. While not as worshipful as Douglas Southall Freeman about the general, Gallagher feels that critics like Nolan have gone too far. He defends Lee for his brilliance as both a tactician and a grand strategist. He defends Lee's Virginia strategy, arguing that many Western confederate generals wasted the troops that were sent them in flawed campaigns. Although he lost the war, Gallagher asserts that Lee's "style of generalship suited the temperament of his people" and that Lee was beloved during the war by both his troops and the Confederate population as a whole. Gallagher argues that Lee's only hope was to take to the offensive yet hold onto Virginia. He maintains that Lincoln, Grant, and other Northern politicians knew that if they wanted to win the war they would have to defeat Lee's army.

The starting point for this issue is Gallagher's edited book *Lee the Soldier* (University of Nebraska Press, 1996), which contains a sample of almost every important book and article written about Lee's military career. Anything written by Gallagher is worth reading. See his collection of articles on Civil War battlefields, Ken Burns's prize-winning 11-hour PBS television series *The Civil War,* and other related topics in *Lee and His Generals in War and Memory* (Louisiana State University Press, 1998). For Gallagher's assessment of the dozen books and articles on Lee that have come out since 1995, see "An Old-Fashioned Soldier in a Modern War? Robert E. Lee as Confederate General," *Civil War History* (December 1999).

A peripheral but important question pertaining to this issue is addressed in "Why the South Lost the Civil War: Ten Experts Explain the Fall of Dixie," *American History* (October 1995). The Spring 1993 issue of the *Maryland Historical Magazine* contains a collection of articles written in the late 1980s as well as a review essay by David Osher and Peter Wallenstein of *Why the Confederacy Lost* edited by Gabor S. Boritt (Oxford University Press, 1992). These articles should be compared with those written by the historians of the previous generation who met at Gettysburg College in 1958 to discuss the reasons for the Confederate loss, which can be found in David Donald, ed., *Why the North Won the Civil War* (Louisiana State University Press, 1960). The controversial view that the South "lost its will" to win the Civil War is argued in Richard E. Beringer et al., *Why the South Lost the Civil War* (University of Georgia Press, 1986).

Two articles that reconcile the military history of the battles with the new social history are Joseph T. Glatthar, "The 'New' Civil War History: An Overview," *The Pennsylvania Magazine of History and Biography* (July 1991) and Marvin R. Cain, "A 'Face of Battle' Needed: An Assessment of Motives and Men in Civil War Historiography," *Civil War History* (March 1982). Of the many military books, start with the following three: James M. McPherson's Pulitzer Prize–winning *Battle Cry of Freedom: The Civil War Era* (Oxford University Press, 1988), which reconciles political and military events; Thomas L. Connelly and Archer Jones, *The Politics of Command: Factions and Ideas in Confederate Strategy* (Louisiana State University Press, 1973); and Russell F. Weigley's *A Great Civil War: A Military and Political History, 1861–1865* (Indiana University Press, 2000).

ISSUE 16

Did Abraham Lincoln
Free the Slaves?

YES: Allen C. Guelzo, from *Lincoln's Emancipation Proclamation: The End of Slavery in America* (Simon & Schuster, 2004)

NO: Vincent Harding, from *There Is a River: The Black Struggle for Freedom in America* (Vintage Books, 1981)

ISSUE SUMMARY

YES: Allen Guelzo insists that Abraham Lincoln was committed to freeing the nation's slaves from the day of his inauguration and that, by laying the foundation for liberating some four million African Americans held in bondage, the Emancipation Proclamation represents the most epochal of Lincoln's writings.

NO: Vincent Harding credits slaves themselves for engaging in a dramatic movement of self-liberation while Abraham Lincoln initially refused to declare the destruction of slavery as a war aim and then issued the Emancipation Proclamation, which failed to free any slaves in areas over which he had any authority.

In April 1861, less than a month after his inauguration, President Abraham Lincoln attempted to send provisions to Fort Sumter, a federal military installation nestled in the harbor of Charleston, South Carolina, part of the newly formed Confederate States of America. Southern troops under the command of General P. G. T. Beauregard opened fire on the fort, forcing its surrender on April 14. The American Civil War had begun.

Numerous explanations have been offered for the cause of this "war between the states." Many contemporaries and some historians saw the conflict as the product of a conspiracy housed either in the North or South, depending upon one's regional perspective. For many in the northern states, the chief culprits were the planters and their political allies who were willing to defend southern institutions at all costs. South of the Mason-Dixon line, blame was laid at the feet of the fanatical abolitionists (see Issue 13) and the free-soil architects of the Republican party. Some viewed secession and war as the consequence of a constitutional struggle between states' rights advocates and defenders of the federal government, while others focused upon the economic rivalries or the cultural differences between North and South. Embedded in each of these interpretations, however, is the powerful influence of the institution of slavery.

Abraham Lincoln fully understood the role slavery had played in the outbreak of the Civil War. In March 1865, as the war was nearing its end, he presented the following analysis: "One eighth of the whole population [in 1861] was colored slaves, not distributed generally over the Union, but localized in the southern part of it. These slaves constituted a peculiar and powerful interest. All knew that this interest was somehow the cause of the war. To strengthen, perpetuate, and extend this interest was the object [of the South] . . . , while the [North] . . . claimed no right to do more than to restrict the territorial enlargement of it."

In light of Lincoln's recognition of the role slavery played in the clash between North and South, none should find it surprising that the Emancipation Proclamation, which the President issued, established a policy to end slavery. Hence, the demise of slavery became a war aim, and Lincoln seemed to have earned his place in history as "the Great Emancipator." Upon learning of the president's announcement, the fugitive slave and abolitionist Frederick Douglass was ecstatic. "We shout for joy," he declared, "that we live to record this righteous decree."

But Douglass had not always been so encouraged by Lincoln's commitment to freedom. Lincoln was not an abolitionist by any stretch of the imagination, but Douglass was convinced that the Republican victory in the presidential election of 1860 had brought to the White House a leader with a deserved reputation as an antislavery man. That confidence declined, however, in the early months of Lincoln's presidency as Douglass and other abolitionists lobbied for emancipation during the secession crisis and, when the war began, as a military necessity only to have their demands fall on deaf ears. Lincoln consistently avoided any public pronouncements that would suggest his desire to end slavery as a war aim. The priority was preserving the Union, and Lincoln did not view emancipation as essential to that goal.

Until the president changed his course, it appeared that the slaves would have to free themselves. This is precisely what some scholars insist happened. Southern slaves, they argue, became the key agents for liberation by abandoning their masters, undermining the plantation routine, serving as spies for Union troops, and taking up arms against the Confederacy. Black northerners pitched in as well by enlisting in the United States Army to defeat the Confederacy and end slavery.

The question "Who freed the slaves?" is the focus of the following essays. Allen Guelzo portrays Lincoln as a president deeply committed to ending slavery. The Emancipation Proclamation was drafted as an emergency measure to substitute for the slower process of a long-term legislative solution in the midst of the Civil War. Coupled with the Thirteenth Amendment, which had Lincoln's support prior to his assassination, this action laid a firm foundation for sounding the death knell to the slave system in the South.

For Vincent Harding, credit for the end of slavery belongs to the masses of slaves who sought self-liberation by running away from their masters, undermining plantation operations, engaging in local insurrections, and offering their services to the Union army and navy.

Allen C. Guelzo

 **YES**

Introduction

T he Emancipation Proclamation is surely the unhappiest of all of Abraham Lincoln's great presidential papers. Taken at face value, the Emancipation Proclamation was the most revolutionary pronouncement ever signed by an American president, striking the legal shackles from four million black slaves and setting the nation's face toward the total abolition of slavery within three more years. Today, however, the Proclamation is probably best known for what it did *not* do, beginning with its apparent failure to rise to the level of eloquence Lincoln achieved in the Gettysburg Address or the Second Inaugural. Even in the 1860s, Karl Marx, the author of a few proclamations of his own, found that the language of the Proclamation, with its ponderous *whereas*es and *therefore*s, reminded him of "ordinary summonses sent by one lawyer to another on the opposing side." When the Lincoln Memorial was dedicated in 1922, quotations from the Second Inaugural and the Gettysburg Address flanked the great Daniel Chester French statue of the seated Lincoln, but there was no matching quotation from the Proclamation, only a vague, elliptical representation in Jules Guerin's mural, *Emancipation of a Race,* which was mostly lost to sight near the ceiling of one of the memorial's side chambers.

But the unkindest cut at the Proclamation came from the hands of Columbia University historian Richard Hofstadter, in his essay on Lincoln in *The American Political Tradition and the Men Who Made It* (1948). A onetime member of the circle of American Marxist intellectuals around *Partisan Review,* Hofstadter repudiated the traditional Progressive view of American political history as a struggle between the legacies of the liberal Thomas Jefferson and the conservative Alexander Hamilton. Instead, Hofstadter viewed American politics as a single, consistent, and deeply cynical story of how capitalism had corrupted Jeffersonians and Hamiltonians alike and turned the United States into "a democracy of cupidity rather than a democracy of fraternity." But he reserved his angriest words for Lincoln and for the Emancipation Proclamation. Lincoln's opposition to slavery, in Hofstadter's reckoning, was kindled only by the threat it posed to free white labor and the development of industrial capitalism. Lincoln "was, as always, thinking primarily of the free white worker" and was "never much troubled about the Negro." No one, then, should be fooled by the Proclamation. Its motives were entirely other than had been advertised, and that fact explained its stylistic flaccidity. "Had the political strategy of the moment called for a momentous human document

From LINCOLN'S EMANCIPATION PROCLAMATION: THE END OF SLAVERY IN AMERICA by Allen C. Guelzo. Copyright © 2004 by Simon & Schuster. Reprinted by permission.

of the stature of the Declaration of Independence, Lincoln could have risen to the occasion." Instead, what he composed on New Year's Day, 1863, "had all the moral grandeur of a bill of lading." It accomplished nothing because it was intended to accomplish nothing "beyond its propaganda value."

The influence of Hofstadter's easily repeatable quip about "the moral grandeur of a bill of lading" has had long innings, and even the most favorably disposed of modern Lincoln biographers have found themselves forced to concede that the Proclamation "lacked the memorable rhetoric of his most notable utterances." And perhaps for that reason, no serious study of the Proclamation has appeared since John Hope Franklin's brief *The Emancipation Proclamation* in 1963, written for its centennial. (That centennial itself was a disappointing affair, capped by President John F. Kennedy's refusal to give the principal address at ceremonies at the Lincoln Memorial on September 22, 1963, for fear of suffering deeper losses of Southern Democrats in his reelection bid the next year.) As the Proclamation's negative symbolic power has risen, efforts to interpret the text have diminished, and examination of the Proclamation's contents has subsided into offhand guesswork and angry prejudice. The Proclamation has become a document (as Garry Wills once described the Declaration of Independence) "dark with unexamined lights." As with Jefferson's Declaration, we have lost in the cultural eddies of the last hundred and forty years the assumptions that would make the Emancipation Proclamation readable.

Recapturing at least some of those assumptions will begin, I think, with recognizing in Abraham Lincoln our last Enlightenment politician. The contours of Lincoln's mind—his allegiance to "reason, cold, calculating, unimpassioned reason"; his aversion to the politics of passion; the distance he maintained from organized religion; his affection for Shakespeare, Paine, and Robert Burns; and his unquestioning belief in universal natural rights—were all shaped by the hand of the Enlightenment. But the most important among the Enlightenment's political virtues for Lincoln, and for his Proclamation, was prudence.

Prudence carries with it today the connotation of "prude"—a person of exaggerated caution, bland temperance, hesitation, a lack of imagination and will, fearfulness, and a bad case of mincing steps. This view would have surprised the classical philosophers, who thought of prudence as one of the four cardinal virtues and who linked it to shrewdness, exceptionally good judgment, and the gift of *coup d'oeil*—the "coup of the eye"—which could take in the whole of a situation at once and know almost automatically how to proceed. Among political scientists, it has more specific meanings, but those meanings are usually just as repellent—of cunning, *realpolitik,* and in some quarters, an unhealthy preoccupation with the neo-classicism of Leo Strauss. (So let me say, for the benefit of the hunters of subtexts, that I can cheerfully confess to never having read Leo Strauss, nor, for that matter, to possessing much aptitude for the peculiar dialect spoken by my political science friends.) It is an ironic rather than a tragic attitude, in which the calculus of costs is critical rather than crucial or incidental. It prefers incremental progress to categorical solutions and fosters that progress through the offering of motives rather than expecting to change dispositions. Yet, unlike mere moderation, it has a sense of purposeful motion and declines to be paralyzed by a preoccupation with process, even while it remains aware that there is no goal so easily attained or so fully attained that it rationalizes dispensing with process altogether. Montesquieu found the origins of political greatness in "prudence, wisdom, perseverance," since prudence would "guard the passions of individuals for the sake of order and guard the guardians for the sake of freedom." In the new American republic, James Madison argued (in the forty-third of the *Federalist Papers*) for ratification of the 1787 Constitution on the grounds of "the rights of humanity," the "considerations of a common interest," and on "prudence." So also for Lincoln: The practice of politics involved the rule of prudence, and "obeying the dictates of prudence" was as important for Lincoln as obeying "the obligations of law." He hoped, as president, that "it will appear that we have practiced prudence," and in 1861, he promised that the management of the Civil War would be "done consistently with the prudence . . . which ought always to regulate the public service" and without allowing the war to degenerate "into a violent and remorseless revolutionary struggle."

It is this politics of prudence which opens up for us a way to understand Lincoln's strategy in "the mighty experiment" of emancipation. The most salient feature to emerge from the sixteen months between his inauguration and the first presentation of the Proclamation to his cabinet on July 22, 1862, is the consistency with which Lincoln's face was set toward the goal of emancipation from the day he first took the presidential oath. Lincoln was not exaggerating when he claimed in 1858 that he "hated" slavery:

> I hate it because of the monstrous injustice of slavery itself. I hate it because it deprives our republican example of its just influence in the world—enables the enemies of free institutions, with plausibility, to taunt us as hypocrites—causes the real friends of freedom to doubt our sincerity, and especially because it forces so many really good men amongst ourselves into an open war with the very fundamental principles of civil liberty—criticising the Declaration of Independence, and insisting that there is no right principle of action but self-interest.

But in Lincoln's case, prudence demanded that he balance the integrity of *ends* (the elimination of slavery) with the integrity of *means* (his oath to uphold the Constitution and his near-religious reverence for the rule of law). Lincoln understood emancipation not as the satisfaction of a "spirit" overriding the law, nor as the moment of fusion between the Constitution and absolute moral theory, but as a goal to be achieved through prudential means, so that worthwhile consequences might result. He could not be persuaded that emancipation required the headlong abandonment of everything save the single absolute of abolition, or that purity of intention was all that mattered, or that the exercise of the will rather than the reason was the best ethical foot forward.

Far too often, Lincoln's apologists hope to give the lie to Hofstadter's scalding attack by pulling apart means and ends, either apologizing for the former or explaining away the latter, a sure sign that they have no better grasp on the politics of prudence than Hofstadter. Most often, this pulling apart happens whenever we are tempted to plead that Lincoln was either a man in *progress* or a man of *patience*. That is, Lincoln was (as Horace Greeley put it) "a growing man," growing in this case from a stance of moral indifference and ignorance about emancipation at the time of his election in 1860, toward deep conviction about African-American freedom by the time of the Emancipation Proclamation less than two years later. Or else that Lincoln already had all the racial goodwill necessary for emancipation but had to wait until the right moment in the war or the right moment in the growth of Northern acceptance of the idea of emancipation. These are both generous sentiments, but I am not sure that generosity is quite what is needed for understanding Lincoln's proclamation. Rather than needing to develop *progress,* I believe that Abraham Lincoln understood from the first that his administration was the beginning of the end of slavery and that he would not leave office without some form of legislative emancipation policy in place. By his design, the burden would have to rest mainly on the state legislatures, largely because Lincoln mistrusted the federal judiciary and expected that any emancipation initiatives which came directly from his hand would be struck down in the courts. This mistrust is also what lies behind another curiosity: Lincoln's rebuffs to the covert emancipations that Congress constructed under the cover of the two Confiscation Acts (of August 1861 and July 1862), the "contraband" theory confected by the ingenious Benjamin Butler, and the two martial-law emancipation proclamations attempted by John Charles Frémont and David Hunter. Lincoln ignored the Confiscation Acts, showed no interest in Butler's "contraband" theory, and actually revoked the martial-law proclamations—not because he was indifferent to emancipation, but because he was convinced (and with good reason) that none of these methods would survive challenges in federal court.

But why, if he was attuned so scrupulously to the use of the right legal means for emancipation, did Lincoln turn in the summer of 1862 and issue an Emancipation Proclamation—which was, for all practical purposes, the very sort of martial-law dictum he had twice before canceled? The answer can be summed up in one word: time. It seems clear to me that Lincoln recognized by July 1862 that he could not wait for the legislative option—and not because he had patiently waited to discern public opinion and found the North readier than the state legislatures to move ahead. If anything, Northern public opinion remained loudly and frantically hostile to the prospect of emancipation, much less emancipation by presidential decree. Instead of exhibiting *patience,* Lincoln felt stymied by the unanticipated stubbornness with which even Unionist slaveholders refused to cooperate with the mildest legislative emancipation policy he could devise, and threatened by generals who were politically committed to a negotiated peace. (We usually underrate the menace posed by the generals, largely because, in the end, it did not materialize, but on at least some level, Lincoln feared that emancipation risked triggering a military coup d'etat by General George McClellan and the Army of the Potomac.) Thus Lincoln's Proclamation was one of the biggest political gambles in American history.

But gambles are not necessarily inconsistent with prudence, and Lincoln's gamble may be considered a prudent one for the role that providence came to play in it. For a man with such a vague religious profile, Lincoln nevertheless understood that a significant part of the politics of prudence involved a deference to providence—whether one defined *providence* as the work of an active and interventionist God or merely the forces of history, economics, or ideas.

Lincoln was raised in an environment saturated with notions of providential determinism, beginning with his upbringing among the "hard-shell" Separate Baptists. As he did with so much else in his upbringing, Lincoln lost what little faith he might have had, and he acquired more notoriety than was good for an ambitious young politico in Illinois as an "infidel." It was an Enlightenment infidelity, a rationalistic deism stoked in equal parts by the smile of Voltaire and the arguments of Tom Paine. But even then, Lincoln's unbelief had this much still in common with the Calvinism he had forsaken—both subscribed alike to the notion that all events were determined by forces beyond human power.

This is not the most optimistic way of looking at the world, but it can lend a certain confidence to one's plans if the direction in which determinism is pointing also happens to be the upward path you are following. Lincoln, like so many other secular determinists shaped by the Enlightenment's delight with the idea of a mechanically predictable universe—Thomas Henry Buckle, Karl Marx, Adolphe Quetelet, Pierre Laplace—thought that progress, improvement, and invention were written into the script of human affairs beyond the power of human effacement. And that meant, from Lincoln's vantage point, that an institution as hateful and retrograde as slavery had to be as inalterably doomed as superstition and tyranny. Whatever the occasional wrong moves—the economic surge of the cotton South, the overthrow of the safeguards against slavery's expansion by the Kansas-Nebraska Act, even the Civil War itself—the fundamental direction of events was inevitable and required only a certain amount of machinery-tending to put things back on the rails.

The carnage, the stalemate, and the incomprehensible rebel victories of the War's first year conspired to strip Lincoln of his optimism in the natural, pleasant ascent of progress, but not of his fundamental belief in providence. Instead, the war saw him veer away from a providence defined by indifference and the iron law of cause and effect, and back toward the providence of a mysterious and self-concealing God whose will for the human future did not necessarily move according to the sweet and logical processes of progress. And in the case of emancipation, Lincoln came to see the Proclamation as the only alternative God had left to emancipation being swept off the table entirely.

All the same, Lincoln never intended the Proclamation to be a substitute for a long-term legislative solution, and in fact, that hope for a legislative solution eventually bore fruit as the Thirteenth Amendment. The Proclamation was an emergency measure, a substitute for the permanent plan that would really rid the country of slavery, but a substitute as sincere and profound as the timbers that shore up an endangered mine shaft and prevent it from collapsing entirely.

Understanding prudence as the key to Lincoln's political behavior gives us the "big picture" behind the Emancipation Proclamation. It does not speak automatically to four very specific questions about the Emancipation Proclamation that I am asked nearly everywhere I go. First and most frequent is the Hofstadter question: *Why is the language of the Proclamation so bland and legalistic?* The answer, I think, really should be obvious, and it was not because Lincoln wrote the Proclamation grudgingly and of necessity. Very simply: The Proclamation is a legal document, and legal documents cannot afford very much in the way of flourishes. They have work to do. In this instance, we are dealing with a document with a very great deal of it to do, and one which had to be composed with the understanding that every syllable was liable to the most concentrated legal parsing by the federal court system. If it falls short of the eloquence of the Gettysburg Address, I only have to point out that the Gettysburg Address was not a document anyone could take into court, and at least in legal terms, it was not intended to accomplish anything. In other words, Lincoln could afford eloquence at Gettysburg; he could not in the Proclamation.

The second question is linked to the Hofstadter question, if only because Hofstadter believed, wrongly, that a linkage between the two existed: *Did the Proclamation actually do anything?* Because the Proclamation limited emancipation only to the states or parts of states still in rebellion and did not include the slaves in the four loyal slave states—Delaware, Maryland, Kentucky, and Missouri—it has been easy to lampoon the Proclamation as a puff of political air. But laws are not the less laws merely because circumstances render them inoperative at a given time or place. I should be ashamed to offer myself as an example, but I do so only because it will force Lincoln's critics to examine their own terms: Every day that I traveled between Paoli and Princeton, I took liberties with the speed limit which the Commonwealth of Pennsylvania and the State of New Jersey forbid. (Judging from the abandon with which other drivers flew past me, most of my readers, it is safe to say, are doubtless implicated in similar offenses.) The guardians of the turnpike might have lacked the energy, the technology, or even the power to enforce the legislated speed limits, but they certainly possessed the perfect and unimpaired authority to do so, as I would have discovered if ever once they had gotten me to stop. The same is true with Lincoln and the Proclamation. Lincoln may not have had the *power* available to him to free every slave in the Confederacy, but he certainly had the *authority,* and in law, the authority is as good as the power. The proof is in the pudding: No slave declared free by the Proclamation was ever returned to slavery once he or she had made it to the safety of Union-held territory.

This raises a related question: *Did the slaves free themselves?* In 1979, Leon Litwack laid the foundations for an alternative view of emancipation when he urged historians to regard emancipation not as an event beginning and ending with Lincoln but as a process in which pressure was exerted on Lincoln and Congress by the slaves themselves. By running away, by labor sabotage, and by volunteering to serve the Union armies, the slaves forced Lincoln's hand toward emancipation. But looked at in the larger context of nineteenth-century American race relations, the "self-emancipation" thesis asks for too great a suspension of disbelief. Without the legal freedom conferred first by the Emancipation Proclamation, no runaway would have remained "self-emancipated" for very long. The files on the first year and a half of the war bulge with accounts of thwarted slaveowners with court papers in their hands and sheriffs at their sides, stalking through the camps of Union regiments in pursuit of slave runaways as though a barbecue rather than a war was in progress. Without the Proclamation, the Confederacy even in defeat would have retained legal title to its slaves, and there is little in the oppressive patterns of coercion Southerners employed before the Civil War or afterward in Reconstruction to suggest that they would not have been willing to reclaim as many of their self-emancipated runaways as they could; and if the record of the federal courts in the post—Civil War decades is any proof, the courts would probably have helped them.

In the same skeptical spirit, a fourth question is frequently aimed at the intentions behind the Proclamation: *Did Lincoln issue the Proclamation only to ward off European intervention or inflate Union morale?* To this, I can only say that if intervention and morale were Lincoln's primary concerns, then an Emancipation Proclamation was probably the worst method, and at the worst time, with which to have met them. Abroad, there was as much danger that an Emancipation Proclamation would trigger foreign intervention as there was that the Proclamation would discourage it. At home, Pennsylvania politician Alexander McClure warned Lincoln that "political defeat would be inevitable in the great States of the Union in the elections soon to follow if he issued the Emancipation Proclamation." Significantly, Lincoln agreed "as to the political effect of the proclamation." He knew that the Proclamation, for all that he hoped it would forestall the generals and put the Union cause unreservedly on the side of the angels, might just as easily convince them to accelerate plans for an intervention or put Lincoln's administration on the side of the losers. To his surprise, McClure found that this made no dent in Lincoln's determination. Those who have sung in Richard Hofstadter's choir need, as McClure needed, to take a new measure of that determination.

But it is not simply the complexities of Lincoln's mental habits or the difficulty involved in piecing together the circumstances and chronology of Lincoln's decision to emancipate which make the Proclamation so difficult for us to grasp. A good deal of our befuddlement is wrapped up in the way that our notions of political ethics have changed since Lincoln's day. Even as Lincoln emerged onto the national political scene in the 1850s, the politics of prudence that had guided Enlightenment political theory was being devalued in favor of a Romantic politics of ethical absolutism. One source of that absolutism lay close to home for Americans in the radical perfectionism of evangelical Protestant revivalism; another was the influence of Immanuel Kant, mediated through English and American Romantics such as Emerson, Samuel Taylor Coleridge, Frederick Augustus Rauch, and James Marsh, the "Vermont Transcendentalist." What the American Romantics particularly admired in Kant was his attempt to locate a source for ethical judgments within men (instead of imposed externally, through divine revelation or natural law), in a "categorical imperative" that yields absolute and universal answers to ethical dilemmas. "We do not need science and philosophy to know what we should do to be honest and good, yea, even wise and virtuous," argued Kant in his *Fundamental Principles of the Metaphysic of Morals.* What we need to do is obey the imperative. Kant's hope was to be able to isolate moral decisions from the flux of circumstance, culture, and individual experience, and thus escape the threat of moral relativism. He was, in other words, looking for a way out of the mechanistic universe, where ethics is simply a pretty name we give to justify whatever decisions circumstances force upon us. Kant sought to base the right or wrong of things solely on the principle that moved the will to choose one thing over another. Purifying the will trumps the claims of all other values, and willing purely is all that is necessary to overcome injustice. As much as Kant believed in universal rational criteria for ethical behavior, those criteria spoke in (as Isaiah Berlin put it) "the language of inner voices."

It is the convergence of American evangelical absolutism and the ethic of the imperative that, more than anything else, erects a translucent shield between our habits of mind and Lincoln's, passing enough light to make us think we see but not enough to allow us to understand. This is not to say that Lincoln, as a man of the Enlightenment, possessed a superior morality or always did well and right. Nor does it mean that Lincoln was untinged by certain elements of Romanticism himself or that he conforms in precise anticipation to all our American anxieties about race and reconciliation at the beginning of the twenty-first century. It would be special pleading to claim that Lincoln was in the end the most perfect friend black Americans have ever had. But it would also be the cheapest and most ignorant of skepticisms to deny that he was the most significant. And if the Emancipation Proclamation was not, as Richard Hofstadter so mordantly complained half a century ago, the most eloquent of Lincoln's writings, it was unquestionably the most epochal. It may have had little more "moral grandeur" than a "bill of lading," but Lincoln's Emancipation Proclamation was still a bill that itemized the destinies of four millions of human beings, bound in the way of danger for the port of American freedom.

The Blood-Red Ironies of God

Although the destruction of the oppressors God may not effect by the oppressed, yet the Lord our God will surely bring other destructions upon them—for not infrequently will he cause them to rise up against one another, to be split and divided, and to oppress each other, and sometimes to open hostilities with sword in hand.

— David Walker, 1829

On certain stark and bloody levels, a terrible irony seemed to be at work. For those who interpreted the events of their own times through the wisdom and anguish of the past, the guns of Charleston certainly sounded like the signal for the fulfillment of David Walker's radical prophecies. Here at last was the coming of the righteous God in judgment, preparing to bring "destructions" upon America. Here was the divine culmination of the struggle toward freedom and justice long waged by the oppressed black people. From such a vantage point, the conflict now bursting out was the ultimate justification of the costly freedom movement, a welcome vindication of the trust in Providence. And yet the war was not simply an ally. Like all wars, it brought with it a train of demoralizing, destructive elements, deeply affecting even those persons and causes which seemed to be its chief beneficiaries. In the case of black people, the guns broke in upon their freedom struggle at many levels, diverted and diffused certain of its significant radical elements, and became a source of profound confusion and disarray among its most committed forces. This was especially the case where independent radical black struggle for justice and self-determination was concerned. . . .

When the war broke out, black men and women were convinced that it had to destroy slavery. Especially in the North, this inner certainty flooded their consciousness, buoyed up their hopes. Now it appeared that God was providing a way out of the darkness of slavery and degradation, a way which would release some of the frightening tension of the previous decade. Because they wanted a way out so desperately, because it was hard to be driven by a fierce urgency, fearsome to experience the personal honing in spite of one's own softer and blunter ways, the children of Africa in America clutched at a solution which would not cause them to be driven into the depths of radicalism. For they must have realized that the chances were good that they might not survive without being seriously, unpredictably transformed. Therefore, when the guns began, black people shunted aside the knowledge of certain fierce realities.

In that mood their men surged forward to volunteer for service in the Union cause, repressing bitter memories. In spite of their misgivings, disregarding the fact that it was not the North which had initiated this righteous war, they offered their bodies for the Northern cause, believing that it was—or would be—the cause of black freedom. If the excited, forgetful young volunteers sought justification, they could find it in the *Anglo-African:* "Talk as we may, we are concerned in this fight and our fate hangs upon its issues. The South must be subjugated, or we shall be enslaved. In aiding the Federal government in whatever way we can, we are aiding to secure our own liberty; for this war can end only in the subjugation of the North or the South." When hard pressed, the journal, like the young men it encouraged, knew very well the nature of the "liberty" they had found so far in the unsubjugated North, and the writer admitted that the North was not consciously fighting for black rights. However, the *Anglo-African* chose to see a power beyond the councils of the North: "Circumstances have been so arranged by the decrees of Providence, that in struggling for their own nationality they are forced to defend our rights." . . .

And what of the South? What of those sometimes God-obsessed black believers who had long lifted their cries for deliverance in songs and shouts, in poetry filled with rich and vibrant images? Did they sense the coming of Moses now? Was this finally the day of the delivering God, when he would set his people free? Did they hear Nat Turner's spirit speaking in the guns? Did they believe he was calling them to freedom through all the lines of skirmishers who left their blood upon the leaves? Did they have any difficulty knowing which of the white armies was Pharaoh's?

The answers were as complex as life itself. In many parts of the nation and the world there had been predictions that secession, disunion, and war would lead to a massive black insurrection which would finally vindicate Turner and Walker, and drown the South in blood. Such predictions were made without knowledge of the profound racism and fear which pervaded the white North, and certainly without awareness of the keen perceptions of black people in the South. For most of the enslaved people knew their oppressors, and certainly realized that such a black uprising would expose the presence of Pharaoh's armies everywhere. To choose that path to freedom would surely unite the white North and South more quickly than any other single development, making black men, women, and children the enemy—the isolated, unprepared enemy. For anyone who needed concrete evidence, Gen. George B. McClellan, the commander of the Union's Army of the Ohio, had supplied it in his "Proclamation to the people of Western Virginia" on May 26, 1861: "Not only will we abstain from all interferences with your slaves, but we will, with an iron hand, crush any attempt at insurrection on their part."

So, heeding their own intuitive political wisdom, the black masses confirmed in their actions certain words which had recently appeared in the *Anglo-African.* Thomas Hamilton, the editor, had heard of Lincoln's decision to countermand an emancipation order issued by one of his most fervent Republican generals, John C. Fremont, in Missouri. Hamilton predicted: "The forlorn hope of insurrection among the slaves may as well be abandoned. They are too well informed and too *wise* to court destruction at the hands of the combined

Northern and Southern armies—for the man who had reduced back to slavery the slaves of rebels in Missouri would order the army of the United States to put down a slave insurrection in Virginia or Georgia." He was right, of course, and the enslaved population was also right. Therefore, instead of mass insurrection, the Civil War created the context for a vast broadening and intensifying of the self-liberating black movement which had developed prior to the war. Central to this black freedom action, as always, was the continuing series of breaks with the system of slavery, the denials of the system's power, the self-emancipation of steadily increasing thousands of fugitives. Thus, wherever possible, black people avoided the deadly prospects of massive, sustained confrontation, for their ultimate objective was freedom, not martyrdom.

As the guns resounded across the Southern lands, the movement of black folk out of slavery began to build. Quickly it approached and surpassed every level of force previously known. Eventually the flood of fugitives amazed all observers and dismayed not a few, as it sent waves of men, women, and children rushing into the camps of the Northern armies. In this overwhelming human movement, black people of the South offered their own responses to the war, to its conundrums and mysteries. Their action testified to their belief that deliverance was indeed coming through the war, but for thousands of them it was not a deliverance to be bestowed by others. Rather it was to be independently seized and transformed through all the courage, wisdom, and strength of their waiting black lives.

This rapidly increasing movement of black runaways had been noted as soon as the reality of Southern secession had been clearly established. Shortly after the guns of April began to sound in Charleston harbor, large companies of fugitives broke loose from Virginia and the Carolinas and moved toward Richmond. Again, one day in Virginia in the spring of 1861, a black fugitive appeared at the Union-held Fortress Monroe. Two days later eight more arrived, the next day more than fifty, soon hundreds. The word spread throughout the area: there was a "freedom fort," as the fugitives called it, and within a short time thousands were flooding toward it. Similarly, in Louisiana two families waded six miles across a swamp, "spending two days and nights in mud and water to their waists, their children clinging to their backs, and with nothing to eat." In Georgia, a woman with her twenty-two children and grandchildren floated down the river on "a dilapidated flatboat" until she made contact with the Union armies. In South Carolina, black folk floated to freedom on "basket boats made out of reeds," thus reviving an ancient African craft. A contemporary source said of the black surge toward freedom in those first two years of the war: "Many thousands of blacks of all ages, ragged, with no possessions, except the bundles which they carried, had assembled at Norfolk, Hampton, Alexandria and Washington. Others . . . in multitudes . . . flocked north from Tennessee, Kentucky, Arkansas, and Missouri."

This was black struggle in the South as the guns roared, coming out of loyal and disloyal states, creating their own liberty. This was the black movement toward a new history, a new life, a new beginning. W. E. B. Du Bois later said, "The whole move was not dramatic or hysterical, rather it was like the great unbroken swell of the ocean before it dashes on the reefs." Yet there was great drama as that flowing movement of courageous black men and women and children sensed the movement of history, heard the voice of God, created and signed their own emancipation proclamations, and seized the time. Their God was moving and they moved with him.

And wherever this moving army of self-free men and women and children went, wherever they stopped to wait and rest and eat and work, and watch the movement of the armies in the fields and forests—in all these unlikely sanctuaries, they sent up their poetry of freedom. Some of them were old songs, taking on new meaning:

> Thus said the Lord, Bold Moses said
> Let my people go
> If not I'll smite your first-born dead
> Let my people go.
> No more shall they in bondage toil
> Let my people go.

But now there was no need to hide behind the stories of thousands of years gone by, now it was clearly a song of black struggle, of deliverance for their own time of need. Now the singers themselves understood more fully what they meant when they sang again:

> One of dese mornings, five o'clock
> Dis ole world gonna reel and rock,
> Pharaoh's Army got drownded
> Oh, Mary, don't you weep.

They were part of the drowning river. Out there, overlooking the battlefields of the South, they were the witnesses to the terrible truth of their own sons, to the this-worldliness of their prayers and aspirations. Remembering that morning in Charleston harbor, who could say they were wrong? "Dis ole world gonna reel and rock . . ."

Every day they came into the Northern lines, in every condition, in every season of the year, in every state of health. Children came wandering, set in the right direction by falling, dying parents who finally knew why they had lived until then. Women came, stumbling and screaming, their wombs bursting with the promise of new and free black life. Old folks who had lost all track of their age, who knew only that they had once heard of a war against "the Redcoats," also came, some blind, some deaf, yet no less eager to taste a bit of that long-anticipated freedom of their dreams. No more auction block, no more driver's lash, many thousands gone.

This was the river of black struggle in the South, waiting for no one to declare freedom for them, hearing only the declarations of God in the sound of the guns, and moving.

By land, by river, creating their own pilgrim armies and their own modes of travel, they moved south as well as north, heading down to the captured areas of the coast of South Carolina. *Frederick Douglass's Monthly* of February 1862 quoted the report of a *New York Times* correspondent in Port Royal: "Everywhere I find the same state of things existing; everywhere the blacks hurry in droves to our lines; they crowd in small boats around our ships; they swarm upon our decks; they hurry to our officers from the cotton houses of their masters, in an hour or two after our guns are fired. . . . I mean each statement I make to be taken literally; it is not garnished for rhetorical effect." As usual, black people were prepared to take advantage of every disruption in the life of the oppressing white community. When they heard the guns, they were ready, grasping freedom with their own hands, walking to it, swimming to it, sailing to it— determined that it should be theirs. By all these ways, defying masters, patrols, Confederate soldiers, slowly, surely, they pressed themselves into the central reality of the war.

. . . By the end of the spring of 1862, tens of thousands [of self-liberated fugitives] were camped out in whatever areas the Northern armies had occupied, thereby making themselves an unavoidable military and political issue. In Washington, D.C., the commander-in-chief of the Union armies had developed no serious plans for the channeling of the black river. Consequently, in the confusion which all war engenders, his generals in the field made and carried out their own plans. They were badly strapped for manpower, and the black fugitives provided some answers to whatever prayers generals pray. The blacks could relieve white fighting men from garrison duties. They could serve as spies, scouts, and couriers in the countryside they knew so well. They could work the familiar land, growing crops for the food and profit of the Union armies. But as the war dragged on and Northern whites lost some of their early enthusiasm, many Union commanders saw the black men among them primarily as potential soldiers. Many of the black men were eager to fight, but Lincoln was still not prepared to go that far.

Nevertheless, some Union commanders like Gen. David Hunter in South Carolina were again issuing their own emancipation proclamations and beginning to recruit black soldiers. In places like occupied New Orleans it was the unmanageable and threatening movement of the blacks themselves which placed additional pressures on the Union's leader. Reports were pouring into Washington which told not only of the flood of fugitives, but of black unrest everywhere. Black men were literally fighting their way past the local police forces to get themselves and their families into the Union encampments. There was word of agricultural workers killing or otherwise getting rid of their overseers, and taking over entire plantations. Commanders like Gen. Ben Butler warned that only Union bayonets prevented widespread black insurrection. (In August 1862, to preserve order and satisfy his need for manpower, Butler himself had begun to recruit black troups in New Orleans, beginning with the well-known Louisiana Native Guards.) The dark presence at the center of the national conflict could no longer be denied. Lincoln's armies were in the midst of a surging movement of black people who were in effect freeing themselves from slavery. His generals were at once desperate for the military resources represented by the so-called contrabands, and convinced that only through military discipline could this volatile, potentially revolutionary black element be contained. As a result, before 1862 was over, black troops were being enlisted to fight for their own freedom in both South Carolina and Louisiana.

NO / Vincent Harding   365

In Washington, Congress was discussing its own plans for emancipation, primarily as a weapon against the South, hoping to deprive the Confederacy of a major source of human power and transfer it into Union hands. Their debates and imminent action represented another critical focus of pressure on the President. While Lincoln continued to hesitate about the legal, constitutional, moral, and military aspects of the matter, he was also being constantly attacked in the North for his conduct of the war. The whites were weary and wanted far better news from the fronts. The blacks were angry about his continued refusal to speak clearly to the issue of their people's freedom and the black right to military service. In the summer of 1862 Frederick Douglass declared in his newspaper: "Abraham Lincoln is no more fit for the place he holds than was James Buchanan. . . . The country is destined to become sick of both [Gen. George B.] McClellan and Lincoln, and the sooner the better. The one plays lawyer for the benefit of the rebels, and the other handles the army for the benefit of the trai-tors. We should not be surprised if both should be hurled from their places before this rebellion is ended. . . . The signs of the times indicate that the people will have to take this war into their own hands." But Frederick Douglass was not one to dwell on such revolutionary options. (Besides, had he considered what would happen to the black cause, if the white "people" really did take the war into their own hands?) Fortunately, by the time Douglass's words were pub-lished, he had seen new and far more hopeful signs of the times.

In September 1862 Abraham Lincoln, in a double-minded attempt both to bargain with and weaken the South while replying to the pressures of the North, finally made public his proposed Emancipation Proclamation. Under its ambiguous terms, the states in rebellion would be given until the close of the year to end their rebellious action. If any did so, their captive black people would not be affected; otherwise, the Emancipation Proclamation would go into effect on January 1, 1863, theoretically freeing all the enslaved population of the Confederate states and promising federal power to maintain that freedom.

What actually was involved was quite another matter. Of great import was the fact that the proclamation excluded from its provisions the "loyal" slave states of Missouri, Kentucky, Delaware, and Maryland, the anti-Confederate West Virginia Territory, and loyal areas in certain other Confederate states. Legally, then, nearly one million black people whose masters were "loyal" to the Union had no part of the emancipation offered. In effect, Lincoln was announcing freedom to the captives over whom he had least control, while allowing those in states clearly under the rule of his government to remain in slavery. However, on another more legalistic level, Lincoln was justifying his armies' use of the Confederates' black "property," and preparing the way for an even more exten-sive use of black power by the military forces of the Union. Here, the logic of his move was clear, providing an executive confirmation and extension of Con-gress's Second Confiscation Act of 1862: once the Emancipation Proclamation went into effect, the tens of thousands of black people who were creating their own freedom, and making themselves available as workers in the Union camps, could be used by the North without legal qualms. Technically, they would no longer be private property, no longer cause problems for a President concerned about property rights.

It was indeed a strange vessel that the Lord had chosen, but black folk in the South were not waiting on such legal niceties. Not long after the preliminary proclamation, an insurrectionary plot was uncovered among a group of blacks in Culpepper County, Virginia. Some were slaves and some free, and the message of their action carried a special resonance for South and North alike, and perhaps for the President himself. For a copy of Lincoln's preliminary proclamation was reportedly found among the possessions of one of the conspirators. Though at least seventeen of the group were executed, their death could not expunge the fact that they had attempted to seize the time, to wrest their emancipation out of the hands of an uncertain President. On Nat's old "gaining ground" they had perhaps heard the voice of his God and, forming their own small army, were once again searching for Jerusalem.

Such action symbolized a major difference in the movement of the Southern and Northern branches of the struggle. In the South, though most of the self-liberating black people eventually entered the camps, or came otherwise under the aegis of the Northern armies, they were undoubtedly acting on significant, independent initiatives. During the first years of the war, the mainstream of the struggle in the South continued to bear this independent, self-authenticating character, refusing to wait for an official emancipation.

In such settings black hope blossomed, fed by its own activity. Even in the ambiguous context of the contraband communities the signs were there. In 1862–63, in Corinth, Mississippi, newly free blacks in one of the best of the contraband camps organized themselves under federal oversight, and created the beginnings of an impressive, cohesive community of work, education, family life, and worship. They built their own modest homes, planted and grew their crops (creating thousands of dollars of profit for the Union), supported their own schools, and eventually developed their own military company to fight with the Union armies. It was not surprising, then, that black fugitives flocked there from as far away as Georgia. Nor was it unexpected that, in 1863, federal military plans demanded the dismantling of the model facility. Nevertheless, the self-reliant black thrust toward the future had been initiated, and Corinth was only one among many hopeful contraband communities.

Such movement, and the vision which impelled it, were integral aspects of the freedom struggle in the South. Meanwhile, to aid that struggle, by 1863 Harriet Tubman had entered the South Carolina war zone. Working on behalf of the Union forces, she organized a corps of black contrabands and traveled with them through the countryside to collect information for army raids, and to urge the still-enslaved blacks to leave their masters. Apparently the intrepid leader and her scouts were successful at both tasks, though Tubman complained that her long dresses sometimes impeded her radical activities.

In the North the situation was somewhat different. Word of Lincoln's anticipated proclamation had an electrifying effect on the black community there, but at the same time further removed the focus from the black freedom-seizing movement in the South. The promised proclamation now gave the Northerners more reason than ever to look to others for release, to invest their hope in the Union cause. Now it seemed as if they would not need to be isolated opponents of an antagonistic federal government. Again, because they wanted to believe, needed to hope, yearned to prove themselves worthy, they thought they saw ever more clearly the glory of the coming; before long, in their eyes the proclamation was clothed in what appeared to be almost angelic light. As such, it became an essentially religious rallying point for the development of a new, confusing mainstream struggle: one which, nervous and excited, approached and embraced the central government and the Republican Party as agents of deliverance. Doubts from the past were now cast aside, for their struggle was unquestionably in the hands of Providence and the Grand Army of the Republic. The voice of God was joined to that of Abraham Lincoln.

. . . [F]rom a certain legal point of view it could be argued that the Emancipation Proclamation set free no enslaved black people at all. Since by December 31, 1862, no Confederate state had accepted Lincoln's invitation to return to the fold with their slaves unthreatened, and since Lincoln acknowledged that he had no real way of enforcing such a proclamation within the rebellious states, the proclamation's power to set anyone free was dubious at best. (Rather, it confirmed and gave ambiguous legal standing to the freedom which black people had already claimed through their own surging, living proclamations.)

Indeed, in his annual address to Congress on December 1, 1862, Lincoln had not seemed primarily concerned with the proclamation. Instead, he had taken that crucial opportunity to propose three constitutional amendments which reaffirmed his long-standing approach to national slavery. The proposed amendments included provisions for gradual emancipation (with a deadline as late as 1900), financial compensation to the owners, and colonization for the freed people. In other words, given the opportunity to place his impending proclamation of limited, immediate emancipation into the firmer context of a constitutional amendment demanding freedom for all enslaved blacks, Lincoln chose another path, one far more in keeping with his own history.

But none of this could dampen the joy of the black North. Within that community, it was the Emancipation Proclamation of January 1, 1863, which especially symbolized all that the people so deeply longed to experience, and its formal announcement sent a storm of long-pent-up emotion surging through the churches and meeting halls. It was almost as if the Northern and Southern struggles had again been joined, this time not through wilderness flights, armed resistance, and civil disobedience, but by a nationwide, centuries-long cord of boundless ecstasy. In spite of its limitations, the proclamation was taken as the greatest sign yet provided by the hand of Providence. The river had burst its boundaries, had shattered slavery's dam. It appeared as if the theodicy of the Northern black experience was finally prevailing. For the freedom struggle, especially in the South, had begun to overwhelm the white man's war, and had forced the President and the nation officially to turn their faces toward the moving black masses. Wherever black people could assemble, by themselves or with whites, they came together to lift joyful voices of thanksgiving, to sing songs of faith, to proclaim, "Jehovah hath triumphed, his people are free." For them, a new year and a new era had been joined in one.

On the evening of December 31, 1862, Frederick Douglass was in Boston attending one of the hundreds of freedom-watch-night services being held across the North in anticipation of the proclamation. That night, a line of messengers had been set up between the telegraph office and the platform of the Tremont Temple, where the Boston meeting was being held. After waiting more than two hours in agonized hope, the crowd was finally rewarded as word of the official proclamation reached them. Douglass said: "The effect of this announcement was startling beyond description, and the scene was wild and grand. Joy and gladness exhausted all forms of expression, from shouts of praise to sobs and tears . . . a Negro preacher, a man of wonderful vocal power, expressed the heart-felt emotion of the hour, when he led all voice in the anthem, 'Sound the loud timbrel o'er Egypt's dark sea, Jehovah hath triumphed, his people are free.'"

Such rapture was understandable, but like all ecstatic experiences, it carried its own enigmatic penalties. Out of it was born the mythology of Abraham Lincoln as Emancipator, a myth less important in its detail than in its larger meaning and consequences for black struggle. The heart of the matter was this: while the concrete historical realities of the time testified to the costly, daring, courageous activities of hundreds of thousands of black people breaking loose from slavery and setting themselves free, the myth gave the credit for this freedom to a white Republican president. In those same times when black men and women saw visions of a new society of equals, and heard voices pressing them against the American Union of white supremacy, Abraham Lincoln was unable to see beyond the limits of his own race, class, and time, and dreamed of a Haitian island and of Central American colonies to rid the country of the constantly accusing, constantly challenging black presence. Yet in the mythology of blacks and whites alike, it was the independent, radical action of the black movement toward freedom which was diminished, and the coerced, ambiguous role of a white deliverer which gained pre-eminence.

POSTSCRIPT

Did Abraham Lincoln
Free the Slaves?

Abraham Lincoln's reputation as "the Great Emancipator" traditionally has been based upon his decision in 1862 to issue the Emancipation Proclamation. While Harding stresses that Lincoln was forced to act by the large number of slaves who already had engaged in a process of self-liberation, he and other scholars point out the limited impact of Lincoln's emancipation policy. Announced in September 1862, the measure would not go into effect until January 1, 1863, and it would apply only to those slave states still in rebellion against the Union. In other words, emancipation would become law in states where the federal government was in no position to enforce the measure. Also, the status of slaves residing in states that had not seceded (Missouri, Kentucky, Maryland, and Delaware) would not be altered by this fiat. Theoretically, then, the Proclamation would have few benefits for those held in bondage in the Confederacy.

Critics of Lincoln's uncertain approach to ending slavery in particular and to the rights of African Americans, slave and free, in general also cite a number of other examples that draw Lincoln's commitment to freedom into question. During the presidential campaign of 1860, candidate Lincoln had insisted that he had no desire to abolish slavery where the institution already existed. There was, of course, the President's statement that he would be willing to keep slavery intact if that was the best means of preserving the Union. His alternative claim that he would be willing to free all the slaves to maintain the sanctity of the Union appeared as just so much rhetoric when compared to his policies as president. For example, Lincoln initially opposed arming black citizens for military service, he countermanded several of his field generals' emancipation orders, and he consistently expressed doubts that blacks and whites would be able to live in the United States as equal citizens. Then, in December 1862, between his announcement of the preliminary emancipation proclamation and the time that the order was to go into effect, the President proposed a constitutional amendment that would provide for gradual emancipation, with compensation to the slave owners followed by colonization of the liberated blacks to a site outside the boundaries of the United States.

In assessing Lincoln's racial attitudes and policies, care should be taken not to read this historical record solely from a twenty-first century perspective. Lincoln may not have been the embodiment of the unblemished racial egalitarian that some might hope for, but few whites were, including most of the abolitionists. Still, as historian Benjamin Quarles has written, Lincoln "treated Negroes as they wanted to be treated—as human beings." Unlike most white Americans of his day, Lincoln opposed slavery, developed a policy that held out hope for emancipation, and supported the Thirteenth Amendment.

Lincoln is the most written-about president. Students should consult Carl Sandburg, *Abraham Lincoln*, 6 vols. (Harcourt, Brace & World, 1926–1939), a poetic panorama that focuses upon the mythic Lincoln. Benjamin Thomas, *Abraham Lincoln: A Biography* (Alfred A. Knopf, 1952), Stephen B. Oates, *With Malice Toward None: The Life of Abraham Lincoln* (Harper & Row, 1977), Philip Shaw Paludan, *The Presidency of Abraham Lincoln* (University Press of Kansas, 1994), and David Donald, *Lincoln* (Simon & Schuster, 1995) are excellent one-volume biographies. David Donald, *Lincoln Reconsidered: Essays on the Civil War Era* (Alfred A. Knopf, 1956) and Richard N. Current, *The Lincoln Nobody Knows* (McGraw-Hill, 1958) offer incisive interpretations of many aspects of Lincoln's political career and philosophy. George B. Forgie, in *Patricide in the House Divided: A Psychological Interpretation* (W. W. Norton, 1979), and Dwight G. Anderson, in *Abraham Lincoln: The Quest for Immortality* (Alfred A. Knopf, 1982), offer psychoanalytical approaches to Lincoln. Lincoln's responsibility for the precipitating event of the Civil War is explored in Richard N. Current, *Lincoln and the First Shot* (Lippincott, 1963). T. Harry Williams, *Lincoln and His Generals* (Alfred A. Knopf, 1952), looks at Lincoln as commander in chief and remains one of the best Lincoln studies. Gabor S. Boritt, ed., *The Historian's Lincoln: Pseudohistory, Psychohistory, and History* (University of Illinois Press, 1988) is a valuable collection. For Lincoln's role as "the Great Emancipator" and his attitudes toward race and slavery, see Benjamin Quarles, *Lincoln and the Negro* (Oxford University Press, 1962), James M. McPherson, *Abraham Lincoln and the Second American Revolution* (Oxford University Press, 1990), and Mark E. Neely. Jr., *The Fate of Liberty: Abraham Lincoln and Civil Liberties* (Oxford University Press, 1991). John Hope Franklin's *The Emancipation Proclamation* (Anchor, 1965) was the key study of this presidential policy prior to the publication of Guelzo's recent analysis.

In addition to the work of Vincent Harding, the self-emancipation thesis is developed in Ira Berlin, Barbara J. Fields, Thavolia Glymph, Joseph P. Reidy, and Leslie S. Rowland, eds., *Freedom: A Documentary History of Emancipation, 1861–1867*, 4 vols. (Cambridge University Press, 1982–1993). Lerone Bennett's *Forced Into Glory: Abraham Lincoln's White Dream* (Johnson Publishing Company, 2000) is highly critical of Lincoln's racial attitudes and commitment to emancipation. The role of African Americans in the Civil War is the subject of James McPherson, ed., *The Negro's Civil War* (Pantheon, 1965). Black military experience is treated in Benjamin Quarles, *The Negro in the Civil War* (Little, Brown, 1969), Dudley Cornish, *The Sable Arm: Black Troops in the Union Army, 1861–1865* (Longmans, 1956), Joseph Glatthaar, *Forged in Battle: The Civil War Alliance of Black Soldiers and White Officers* (Free Press, 1990), Ervin L. Jordan, Jr., *Black Confederates and Afro-Yankees in Civil War Virginia* (University Press of Virginia, 1995), and James G. Hollandsworth, Jr., *The Louisiana Native Guards: The Black Military Experience During the Civil War* (Louisiana State University Press, 1995).

ISSUE 17

Did William M. Tweed Corrupt Post–Civil War New York?

YES: Alexander B. Callow, Jr., from *The Tweed Ring* (Oxford University Press, 1966)

NO: Leo Hershkowitz, from *Tweed's New York: Another Look* (Anchor Press, 1977)

ISSUE SUMMARY

YES: Professor emeritus of history Alexander B. Callow, Jr., asserts that by exercising a corrupting influence over the city and state governments as well as over key elements within the business community, William M. "Boss" Tweed and his infamous "ring" extracted enormous sums of ill-gotten money for their own benefit in post–Civil War New York.

NO: Professor of history Leo Hershkowitz portrays Tweed as a devoted public servant who championed New York City's interests during his 20-year career and whose reputation as the symbol for urban political corruption is grossly undeserved.

On the eve of the Civil War, the United States remained primarily a rural, agrarian nation. Of the country's 31 million inhabitants, 80 percent were characterized as "rural" dwellers by the United States Bureau of the Census; only 392 "urban" places (incorporated towns with 2,500 or more residents, or unincorporated areas with at least 2,500 people per square mile) dotted the national landscape; a mere nine U.S. cities contained populations in excess of 100,000.

After 1865 the growth of urban America was directly linked to the economic and technological changes that produced the country's Industrial Revolution, as well as to rapid immigration, which filled the nation's cities with what seemed to native-born Americans to be a multitude of foreigners from around the globe. Reflecting many of the characteristics of modern America, these industrial cities produced a number of problems for the people who lived in them—problems associated with fire and police protection, sanitation, utilities, and a wide range of social services. These coincided with increased concerns over employment opportunities and demands for transportation and housing improvements. Typically, municipal governments became the clearinghouses for such demands. They also became the targets for charges of corruption.

Political corruption is virtually synonymous with the post–Civil War era. From the scandals of the Grant administration at the beginning of the so-called Gilded Age to the almost universal condemnation of the activities of alleged political opportunists (carpetbaggers and scalawags) involved in reconstructing the former states of the Confederacy, these years have traditionally been portrayed as being saturated by intrigue, malfeasance, and betrayal of the public trust. Whether at the local, state, or national levels of government, and regardless of party affiliation, charges of corruption seemed commonplace. Nowhere did this appear to be more the case than in the realm of New York politics dominated by the Tammany Hall Democratic "machine" and its notorious "boss," William M. Tweed.

Born in New York City in 1823 to Irish immigrant parents, Tweed rose to political prominence by serving as alderman, congressman, and state senator. He developed a power base in local and state politics both during and immediately after the Civil War, and he controlled that base until reform initiatives by the *New York Times* and Samuel J. Tilden brought him down. He died in jail, serving a sentence for failing to audit claims against the city, in 1878.

Undoubtedly, James Lord Bryce had Tweed and the infamous "Tweed Ring" in mind when he depicted city government in the United States as a "conspicuous failure." But does Tweed deserve the charges of wrongdoing that have been heaped upon him? Did his activities run counter to the best interests of his constituents? Is it conceivable that this long-standing symbol of corruption in urban America has been unduly maligned? These questions are addressed in the selections that follow.

According to Alexander B. Callow, Jr., William Tweed's malefic reputation is well deserved. "Boss" Tweed, he says, perfected the art of political corruption by controlling three vital sources of graft: the city, the state, and the business community. Under Tweed's direction, the Tweed Ring extracted wealth from New York's city and state governments by controlling the key legislative and financial agencies that awarded charters and franchises and were responsible for city improvements. The record of bribery and excessive charges for construction, says Callow, are incontrovertible, and Tweed used his political power to benefit personally from the graft collected.

Leo Hershkowitz, on the other hand, defends Tweed's reputation and insists that the "Boss's" image was fabricated by journalists, such as cartoonist Thomas Nast, to sell newspapers in New York. New York's diversity of peoples and interests, says Hershkowitz, made it impossible for one person to control the political realm to the extent that is attributed to Tweed. Hershkowitz points out that Tweed was never convicted on charges of graft or theft and concludes that, in fact, the Tammany leader effectively represented the interests of New York residents by opening schools, building hospitals, paving streets, and providing a wide variety of other necessary services.

YES

Alexander B. Callow, Jr.

"Honest" Graft

Post-Civil-War New York has been described as being encircled by a host of political rings, rings within rings, each depending on the other. There was the Gravel Ring, the Detective Ring, the Supervisors' Ring, the Courthouse Ring, the Albany Ring, the Street Commissioners' Ring, the Manure Ring, the Market Ring, and, consolidating and hovering above all, the Tweed Ring. And what was a political ring? It was the source of "magic wisdom" that made Tammany Hall a political power, said a big chief of the Tammany braves. Samuel Tilden, who almost became President of the United States on the claim he had smashed a "ring," said:

> The very definition of a "Ring" is that it encircles enough influential men in
> the organization of each party to control the action of both party machines;
> men who in public push to extremes the abstract ideas of their respective
> parties, while they secretly join their hands in schemes for personal power
> and profit.

Scholars and public alike have generally accepted Tilden's definition of the Tweed Ring. Why was it that later city bosses like [Richard] Croker had a "machine," while Tweed had a "Ring"—a word, as it were, with a more ominous ring, a political synonym for conspiracy, venality, and corruption? If the Tweed Ring's skills at organization have never been rightfully emphasized, its achievements in corruption certainly have, although large-scale graft existed before the emergence of the Tweed Ring, and continued after its downfall.

We shall probably never know exactly how much the Ring stole. Calculations have run as high as $300 million, which was probably too high, even for the Tweed Ring. The *New York Evening Post* estimated it at $59 million; the *Times* thought it was more like $75 million to $80 million. . . .

Years after the fall of the Ring, Matthew J. O'Rourke, who had made a study of the Ring's plunders, estimated that if fraudulent bonds were included, the Ring probably stole about $200 million. Henry J. Taintor made the closest study. For six years he had been employed by the City to determine the amount of the Ring's graft. It cost the City over $73,000 to maintain Taintor's investigation, and for a moment during the Tweed Ring investigation in 1877 there was the suspicion, later dispelled, that a dreadful irony had occurred: that Taintor, in investigating graft, had been tempted himself, and had padded his bills. At any rate, he testified his research showed that the Ring had stolen at least $60 million, but even this was not an accurate figure, he said, because he

From Alexander B. Callow, Jr., *The Tweed Ring* (Oxford University Press, 1966). Copyright © 1966 by Alexander Callow. Notes omitted.

did not possess all the records. Whatever the figure, in order to maintain a political machine as well as to increase their personal fortune, the Tweed Ring's operation was on a gigantic scale.

There [were] three primary sources of graft: the city, the state, and the business community. In the city, the Ring's control of the key legislative and financial agencies, from the Supervisors and Aldermen to the Comptroller and Mayor, gave it command of New York's financial machinery and bountiful opportunity for graft. Every warrant, then, charged against the city treasury passed the Ring's scrutiny and was subject to its manipulation. Every scheme for city improvement, be they new streets, new buildings, new city parks, had to be financed from the city treasury, controlled by the Ring. The results were often graft, reflected in excessive charges and needless waste. Every charter and franchise for new businesses had to meet the approval of the city legislature and the Mayor, and many companies, therefore, had to pay the tribute of the bribe to get them passed. All the city's financial affairs, such as bond issues, tax-collecting, rentals on city properties, were vulnerable as sources of graft. In effect, there was a direct relationship between power and graft. The Ring's political influence was so extensive that one roadblock to graft, the check and balance system—pitting the upper house of the City legislature against the lower house, and the Mayor as a check to the combined houses of the legislature—was simply nullified. When this happened, the city's financial operations became an open target.

This was largely true for the State legislature as well. Any check and balance between state and city, governor and legislature, was nullified. The Ring controlled the governor, John Hoffman; it controlled the powerful block of city Democrats in the State legislature. When he was elected State Senator in 1867 (and assumed office in 1868, when the Senate convened), Boss Tweed, as Chairman of the influential State Finance Committee, and as a member of the important Internal Affairs of Towns and Counties, Charitable and Religious, and Municipal Affairs committees, was in a commanding position to influence tax-levies, bond issues, and special projects for the city—all sources of graft. As the leader of the Black Horse Cavalry, a corrupt band of State legislators, he could control legislation leading to graft.

Not all the money came from the City and State treasury. The business community was an important source of profit, both as allies and victims. The Tweed Ring operated as lobby brokers for businessmen seeking to pass or kill legislation vital to their interests. Services rendered for the Erie Railroad, for example, brought in thousands of dollars. Businessmen provided large "kickbacks" in payment for receiving profitable contracts. The "cinch" bill, legislative extortion threatening business firms and individuals, was used extensively by the Ring through both the City and State legislatures.

Unlike the sly, sophisticated tactics of modern-day graft—the highly complicated dummy corporation, the undercover payoff via the "respectable" attorney—the Ring operated in a remarkably open and straightforward fashion. In effect, the shortest distance to the city treasury was a straight line. While the Ring used several methods for plunder, the largest share of the booty was gained by a method simple, direct, brazen, daring—and often sloppy. Every person who received a contract from the city, whether for supplies or for work on the city buildings and public works was instructed to alter his bills before submitting them for payment. At first the tribute was levied somewhat irregularly at 10 percent, then it was raised to 55 percent; in July 1869 it jumped to 60 percent; and from November 1869 on, the tradesmen received 35 percent and the Ring 65 percent on all bills and warrants. When bills from contractors and tradesmen did not come in fast enough, Tweed ordered vouchers to be made out to imaginary firms and individuals. On large contracts, Tweed acted directly and got immediately to the point. When he was told that electric fire alarms would cost the city $60,000, he asked the contractor, "If we get you a contract for $450,000 will you give us $225,000?" No time was wasted. The contractor answered with a simple yes and got the contract. Nor did the Boss quibble over small sums. Once a merchant told Tweed that Comptroller [Richard B.] Connolly had refused to pay his bill. Only by "kicking-back" 20 percent of the bill, would the merchant ever get paid. Tweed wrote Connolly: "For God's sake pay—'s bill. He tells me you people ask 20 percent. The whole d—d thing isn't but $1100. If you don't pay it, I will. Thine."

The division of the spoils varied: Tweed received from 10 to 25 percent; Connolly from 10 to 20 percent; [Peter B.] Sweeny 10 percent; [A. Oakey] Hall 5 to 10 percent. There was a percentage for the "sinking fund," and James Watson and W. E. Woodward shared 5 percent. These last two, clerks of the gang, did the paper work and forging. "You must do just as Jimmy tells you, and you will get your money," was a well-known saying among Tweed Ring contractors.

James Watson, the Ring's bookkeeper, was City Auditor in Connolly's office. He first demonstrated his talents while a convict. In 1850 Watson was an agent for a prosperous firm which suddenly began to experience severe losses that Watson found inconvenient to explain. He fled to California. He was brought back to New York in irons and clapped in Ludlow Street jail. An active fellow with pleasant manners, he soon won the friendship of the warden. He took charge of the prison records and performed with such admirable efficiency, especially in calculations, that he was released, with the warden's help, and was appointed a collector in the Sheriff's office. He held that position under three Sheriffs. When the Tweed Ring was formed in 1866, he was made City Auditor, a position that paid a small salary. Four years later, he was worth anywhere from two to three million dollars. It was said that he was a simple man and lived in a curious state of "ostentatious modesty." He had only one luxury—fast trotting horses, a passion that later helped to ruin the Tweed Ring.

W. E. Woodward occupied a key post as clerk to the Supervisors; he helped to rig the percentages of the business that came through that office. At the time of the Aldermen's investigation of the Ring in 1877, the Aldermen were curious how a mere clerk could own a $150,000 home, the best home, in fact, in Norwalk, Connecticut. Asked how he could do this on a salary that never exceeded $5000, Woodward gave a straightforward answer. "I used to take all I could get, and the Board of Supervisors were very liberal to me."

In the Comptroller's Office, Slippery Dick Connolly performed feats that justified his name, as his successor in 1871, the reformer, Andrew Green, confirmed when he found the treasury thoroughly sacked. As Comptroller, Connolly served the Ring three ways. He spent the money collected through the city's regular channels of revenue—taxes, rents from such city properties as markets, docks armories, etc. While some of the money was spent legitimately, a good deal of it was either embezzled or found its way into fraudulent contracts, excessive rents, or padded payrolls, a percentage of which was "kicked-back" into the Ring's coffers. However, only about a third of the city's money came from taxes or rents; the rest came from securities. Thus when a tax-levy of some $30 or more million was spent, usually at a brisk pace, Connolly's next job was to realize $30 to $50 millions more by issuing stocks and bonds.

Connolly performed this task like a financial conjuror. He created a litter of stocks and bonds raised for every conceivable project, ingenious in wording and intent. There were Accumulated Debt Bonds, Assessment Fund bonds, Croton Aqueduct Bonds, Croton Reservoir Bonds, Central Park Improvement Fund Stocks, City Improvement Stocks, Street Improvement Bonds, Fire Department Stocks, Tax Relief Bonds, Bridge Revenue Bonds, New Court House Stock. Repairs to the County Offices and Building Stocks, Dock Bonds, and bonds for the Soldiers' Relief Fund. The war chest to provide funds for padded payrolls, for example, was raised by the sale of appropriately named Riot Damages Indemnity Bonds. As a result of Connolly's various enterprises, the city groaned under a debt which increased by nearly $70 million from 1869 to 1871.

Finally, it was Connolly's responsibility to mask the Ring's fraudulent expenditures by slippery accounting techniques. In this, he was helped by the extensive power of the Ring which nullified an elaborate series of regulations established to prevent fraud. By state law, every warrant and claim drawn against the City must be itemized and accompanied by a signed affidavit certifying its authenticity. Before it could be cashed it must be thoroughly examined and signed by the Comptroller, City Auditor, the Board of Supervisors, and the Mayor. But since the Ring "owned" all these offices, it was relatively simple to rig a phony warrant and get the required signatures. Indeed, the Ring became so powerful that it owned its own bank, the Tenth National, to ensure the safe deposit of its booty. (Tweed, Connolly, Hall, James Ingersoll, and James Fisk, Jr., were the Tenth National's distinguished directors.) . . .

Added to all this was another lush source for graft. Connolly and his lieutenant James Watson were in a position to audit and pay off fictitious claims against the city. With logic, the New York City Council of Political Reform said: "In a sound fiscal system one officer *adjusts* claims and another *pays* them. From the weakness of human nature it is not deemed wise or prudent for the government of any great city or county to allow the *same* officer to adjust a claim *who* is to *pay* it; lest he may be tempted by a share of the money to conspire with the claimant and allow an unjust claim. But in our city, in 1868 and 1870, a *single* officer, the Comptroller, *adjusted* and *paid*, by adding so much to the permanent debt, $12,500,000 of claims!"

The Comptroller's office was also a point of frustration for those with legitimate claims against the city. They were kept waiting sometimes for years, before they could get their money. Subsequently, they often sold their claim to one of the Ring's agents for 50 or 60 cents on the dollar. Immediately after the transaction took place, the new owner was promptly paid. A clerk in Connolly's office, named Mike Moloney, was in charge of this branch of business.

Moloney sits opposite the door by which his victims enter and watches for them with all the avidity that a spider might watch the approach of a fly. The moment an unlucky claimant makes his appearance Moloney jumps on his feet and steps forward to the counter to meet him. Bending forward he listens to the application of the victim, and then by a series of ominous shakes of his head, and "the oft-told tale" repeated in half-smothered whispers, he tries to convince the applicant that there is no prospect of him receiving his money for some time to come, and that, if he really needs it, he had better go over to City Hall and see Mr. Thomas Colligan. (The victim sees Mr. Colligan) . . . and comes out feeling much the same as if he had lost his pocketbook, while the genial Mr. Colligan pockets the "little difference," invites Moloney to dinner, and quietly divides the spoils while sipping Champagne or smoking a Havana.

It is difficult to know where to begin in dealing with the many specific schemes of the Tweed Ring. Perhaps it is best to begin with what E. L. Godkin once called "one of those neat and profitable little curiosities of fraud which the memory holds after graver things are forgotten."

In 1841, a man named Valentine, a clerk in the Common Council, persuaded the city to finance the publication of a city almanac which he would edit. Initially, it was a small volume of not quite 200 pages, which had a map of the city and a list of all persons associated with the government of New York City and their business and home addresses. Although the City Directory contained the same information, for some obscure reason the almanac seemed valuable. Down through the years, the almanac increased in bulkiness, and, more important, in cost to the taxpayers, until it became "a manual of folly, extravagance, and dishonesty." By 1865, *Valentine's Manual*, as it was called, had become a 879-page monument of costliness and superficiality. Among 141 pictures was a large, folding four-page lithograph, illustrating—"O precious gift to posterity!"—a facsimile of each Alderman's autograph. Expensive lithographs covered a number of vital subjects: a fur store built in 1820; a house that Valentine had once lived in; a grocery and tea store of ancient vintage; Tammany Hall as it looked in 1830; a Fifth Avenue billiard saloon; and a host of "portraits of undistinguished persons." Well over 400 pages were cluttered with extracts from old government documents, newspapers, and "memories." The cost of printing was $57,172.30; the number of copies printed, 10,000. A few copies found their way into second-hand bookstores, which paid two dollars apiece for them, $3.36 less than a copy cost the city. An outraged public opinion forced Mayor Hoffman to veto the resolution authorizing a similar expenditure for 1866. He found that Appleton's or Harper's would have published the same number of copies for $30,000 instead of $53,672. The Aldermen, however, overrode his veto. . . .

The Tweed Ring created several companies which moved in to monopolize every phase of city printing as well as city advertising. One such firm was the New York Printing Company. Its expansion reflected all the gusto of American business enterprises. It began in a shabby little office on Centre Street, but almost at once business became so good that it absorbed three of the largest printing establishments in the city. The New York Printing Company was growing, said a newspaper, "but like other mushrooms it grows in the dark. It is spreading under the cover of night, and running its roots into the Treasury by deep underground passages." On a capital stock of $10,000 it paid a dividend of $50,000 to $75,000 to each of its stockholders. The city apparently liked its work, for during 1870–71 the firm obtained $260,283.81 of its business. All these amounts incorporated a 25 percent tribute to the Ring. The company became so versatile in printing all kinds of material that the city paid it another $300,000 for printing in book form the records of New York City from 1675 to 1776. Nor did the firm confine its customers to the City and County. Insurance companies and steamboat and ferry companies were extremely vulnerable to a legislative bill which, in the public interest, could hurt them by regulating their activities and profits. Hence, they all received a notice that the New York Printing Company would be happy to do their printing.

The Tweed Ring composed the major stockholders of the Manufacturing Stationers' Company, which sold stationery supplies to city offices and schools. In 1870 the City and County paid it over $3 million. Among its many bills, there was this interesting one: for six reams of note paper, two dozen penholders, four ink bottles, one dozen sponges, and three dozen boxes of rubber bands, the city paid $10,000. James Parton singled out the Manufacturing Stationers' Company for its treachery.

> We have before us a successful bid for supplying the city offices with stationery, in which we find the bidder offering to supply "blue folio post" at one cent per ream; "magnum bonum pens," at one cent per gross; "lead pencils," at one cent per dozen; "English sealing-wax," at one cent per pound; and eighty-three other articles of stationery, at the uniform price of one cent for the usual parcel. This was the "lowest bid," and it was, of course, the one accepted. It appeared, however, when the bill was presented for payment, that the particular kind of paper styled "blue folio post" had never been called for, nor any considerable quantity of the other articles proposed to be supplied for one cent. No one, strange to say, had ever wanted "magnum bonum" pens at one cent a gross, but in all the offices the cry had been for "Perry's extra fine," at three dollars. Scarcely any one had used "envelopes letter-size" at one cent per hundred but there had been countless calls for "envelopes note-size" at one cent each. Between the paper called "blue folio post," at one cent per ream, and paper called "foolscap extra ruled," at *five dollars and a half*, the difference was too slight to be perceived; but every one had used the foolscap. Of what avail are contracts, when the officials who award them, and the other officials who pay the bill, are in league with the contractor to steal the public money?

As the fictional Boss Blossom Brick said, "Official advertising is the Pain Killer of Politics." During the Civil War three men started an insignificant newspaper titled *The Transcript*. They were George Stout, "a journalist unknown to fame," Charles E. Wilbour, a court stenographer and "literary man, somewhat less unknown," and Cornelius Corson, "an employee in the City Hall, and not devoid of influence in that quarter." When Tweed, Connolly, and Sweeny became their partners, business, but not circulation, picked up. The Common Council (the Aldermen and Assistant Aldermen) ordered that a full list of all persons liable to serve in the army, amounting to some 50,000 names, should be printed in the *Transcript*. Later, thirty-five copies of the list were published in book-form, "though the bill was rendered for a large edition." From then on the *Transcript* enjoyed days of high prosperity. It published the major share of all "city advertising," which meant official records of the courts, and official statements and declarations, statistical reports, new ordinances, in effect, the facts and figures of city business. The rates were exorbitant enough to ensure a heady profit; for example, messages from the Mayor cost a dollar a line. A great deal of the advertisements came from Tweed's Department of Public Works, and from the Bureau of Assessments, where Richard Tweed was in control. Although the newspaper never sold more than a hundred copies, the city paid it $801,874 from 1869 to 1871 for publishing its official business and advertisements. The December 3, 1870, issue, for example, consisted of 504 pages. Advertisements were charged at a rate of 25 cents a line, higher than prevailing newspaper rates. It was estimated that the Ring received $68,000 in profits for that issue alone. The Christmas number for that year was a special: a double extra of 1000 pages, all advertisements, for which double rates were charged. It appeared to one newspaper that the Ring paid for its Christmas presents out of the public till. The profits, then, made by the three companies of the Ring which corralled city printing reached a grand total over a three-year period of $2,641,828.30, of which nine-tenths was pure profit.

As Boss Blossom Brick said, "Give the people plenty of taffy and the newspapers plenty of advertising—then help yourself to anything that's lying around loose." Funneling the taxpayers' dollars through the *Transcript* was a way to finance Tweed's mansion on Fifth Avenue and his palatial estate in Greenwich, Connecticut; but there was another method of using city advertising which ensured, for a few years at least, that gracious living could be enjoyed. The Tweed Ring found that the best way to protect itself against newspaper criticism was to distribute city advertising as a token of peace. It became a kind of hush money which bound the press to silence. Until the storm broke, in 1871, probably no New York political regime ever enjoyed less newspaper criticism than the Tweed Ring, and only when the evidence became painfully obvious and practically overwhelming did the press join the crusade against evil begun by the *New York Times* and *Harper's Weekly*. Before the storm, there had been some criticism, but it was spotty and half-hearted. The *Tribune* might thunder for a while, the *Sun* became nasty—as was its style—but a general grant of advertising had the same effect as placing alum on the tongue.

By law, the city corporation was limited to nine daily and eight weekly papers in which to advertise. But the Tweed Ring, with its usual disregard for procedure, extended delicious morsels of city advertising to twenty-six daily and forty-four weekly newspapers in the city alone, and seventeen weekly journals outside the city, making a total of eighty-seven organs. Probably no political regime in the history of New York City had exerted so much influence on the press. . . .

Not content with the method of using advertising, the Ring also won the hearts of City Hall reporters by giving them $200 gifts at Christmas. This practice had started as early as 1862, under the administration of Mayor George Opdyke (who disapproved), but the Ring elaborated on the scheme. It also subsidized six to eight reporters on nearly all the city papers with fees of $2000 to $2500 to exercise the proper discretion when it came to writing about politics. There was the reward of patronage for the especially deserving: Stephen Hayes, on the *Herald* staff during the high days of the Ring, was rewarded with a sinecure in the Marine Court ($2500 a year), and Michael Kelly, also of the *Herald*, received positions in both the Fire Department and the Department of Public Works. Moreover, reporters from various newspapers of the country, from a Cleveland newspaper to the *Mobile Register*, were hired to write favorable notices of the Democratic administration in New York. And if a firm went too far and tried to print a pamphlet exposing the Ring, it might find its offices broken into by the Ring's men and the type altered to present a glowing account of the Ring's activities—as did the printing company of Stone, Jordan and Thomson.

At the time the Ring was breaking up, the City found itself confronted with claims amounting to over a million and a half dollars negotiated between newspapers and the Ring, some fraudulent and some not, for not all journals which received city advertising did so on the basis of a conspiracy with the Ring. But enough of them did to ensure the complacency and the apathy which seemed to grip many during the Ring's rule.

The Ring needed complacency and apathy when it came to operations behind the opening, widening, and improving of the city streets. With the city's enormous growth came a legitimate demand for new streets and the improvement of old ones. It became one of the Ring's most lucrative forms of graft. It was, indeed, a democratic form of graft—laborers got work; City Hall clerks were able to supplement their incomes; political debts were paid off in commissionerships, judges no longer had to rely entirely on their salaries; Ring members and friends prospered from the assessments involved and the excitement of "gambling" in real estate. As in the case of Recorder and Street Commissioner [John] Hackett, the key factor was the appointment of reliable Commissioners by the Ring judges, upon the suggestion of Corporation Counsel [John] O'Gorman. From then on a pattern emerged: Tammany favorites and members of the Ring's families constantly appeared as Commissioners; awards for damages were exorbitantly high; Commissioners charged "from ten to one hundred times as much as the law allowed" for their services and expenses, despite the fact that the Commissioners as employees of the city were disqualified by law from receiving any pay.

To "open" a new street did not mean to begin construction work. It was a legal term signifying that the land had been bought and was now officially "opened." Announcements of the transaction were published, and those property owners involved were invited to declare any objections to the Commissioners. The clerk drew up a report and the thing was done. Actually it usually amounted to a mere formality.

The cost for this activity under the Tweed Ring, however, would seem to indicate that an enormous amount of work went into it. What usually happened was that the surveyor reproduced a map of the street from maps made in 1811, when Manhattan island, except for a small area at its northern end, was surveyed so well that the maps were still adequate in post-Civil War New York. On the borders of the copy made by the surveyor, the clerk wrote the names of the owners of the lots on both sides of the street, copying his information from the tax books. Then the fun began. "The surveyor charges as though he had made original surveys and drawn original maps. The clerk charges as though his reports were the result of original searchers and researchers. The commissioners charge as though the opening had been the tardy fruit of actual negotiations." For the year ending in June 1866, it was estimated that the cost for "opening" twenty-five streets was $257,192.12. Of this cost, $4433 was charged for rent of an office, which ordinarily rented for $300 a year; "disbursements and postagestamps" cost $950; and one surveyor's bill alone accounted for an astounding $54,000.

The Broadway widening "job" was a good example of the Ring in action. On May 17, 1869, the State legislature passed an act providing for the widening of Broadway between Thirty-fourth and Fifty-ninth streets, whereupon the Ring seized control of the legal machinery that decided assessments and damages to the property involved. With the friendly judge Albert Cardozo presiding, and two of the three Commissioners good Ring men, the Ring and a selected few began to buy property. Two of them paid $24,500 for a lot for which the Commissioners generously awarded them damages of $25,100. The new front was worth $10,000 more. Another lot sold for $27,500, but this payment was absorbed by a $30,355 award in damages. It was the resale value of the property, however, where the profit was made, and lots on Broadway were worth thousands. With tactics of this sort, the Ring managed to purchase some of the most valuable property in New York City.

With minor variations, the Broadway widening scheme was repeated in the Madison Avenue extension, the Church Street extension, the opening of Lexington Avenue through Stuyvesant Park, the Park Place widening, and the so-called "Fifth Avenue raid," where the Ring profited from the widening, extending, and "improvement" of that street. To one writer, who greatly exaggerated, it seemed that streets were opened "which no mortal had seen, no foot had trod; and they appeared only on the city map as spaces between imaginary lines leading from No-where to No-place." To a New York citizen in 1871 who examined the New York State *Senate Journal* of 1869, it might have seemed that the State legislature had gone No-where. On page 61 was an act entitled, "An act to afford relief against frauds and irregularities in assessments for local improvements in the city of New York."

Whether the source of graft was street openings, real estate speculation, city advertising, padded contractor's bills, juggled city records and bond issues fat with graft, a simple but imaginative profit on the City Directory, or a straightforward attack on the city treasury by supplying printing and stationery goods, the Tweed Ring explored the various paths to civic dishonesty. The roads to graft, however, were paved by the very interests the Ring exploited. The financial community, consumed in its own self-interests, stood to gain from the massive pump-priming in city improvements. The "open door" policy of state and city welfare deadened the voice of religious and philanthropic organizations; the newspapers, split by political partisanship and competitive self-interest, were softened by the morsels of political handouts; and the "people" were indifferent. The Tweed Ring thrived on the lack of civic conscience, and the result was graft.

Tweed's New York: Another Look

Myth

William M. Tweed, the notorious "Boss" Tweed, is one of the great myths of American history. His ugly features, small beady eyes, huge banana-like nose, vulturish expression and bloated body are the personification of big-city corruption. Thomas Nast, political propagandist and executioner of *Harper's Weekly*, has made them a triumph of the caricaturist art. Tweed's deeds, or rather misdeeds, as fashioned by historians and the like, are perhaps even better known. They have been told and retold in countless textbooks, monographs, biographies, articles, reminiscences, and have become an American epic whose proportions with each recounting become more fantastic, more shocking. Here are fables of monumental robberies of the New York City treasury, of fraud, deceit, treachery, of monstrous villainies, of carpets, furniture and of courthouses. Like fables, they are largely untrue, but like most legends, they perpetuate themselves and are renewed and enlarged with each telling.

The myth has become so much a part of history and Tweed such a convenient reference for the after-dinner speaker, pulp writer, or simply something to frighten little children with, that if there wasn't a Tweed, he would have to be invented, and he was.

Tweed is a fat, urban Jesse James without any saving graces. James is a western Robin Hood, a sort of criminal St. Francis. Tweed's patron saint is an eastern St. Tammany, refuge for the greedy, vulgar, corrupt—in short, consummate—politician. Tweed is the essence of urban rot, malodorous, the embodiment of all that is evil and cancerous in American municipal and political life. The monster lives. In a recent tax-evasion case, the prosecution charged a defendant with failure to report income allegedly obtained illegally. During the course of the trial, an enlarged Nast cartoon of "Boss Tweed" was produced to illustrate the similarity of crimes. The jury voted for conviction. Interestingly, the United States Court of Appeals reversed the verdict partly because the court felt use of the cartoon had prejudiced the jury. Eternally threatened plans to destroy the "Tweed Courthouse" (the name itself is an example of the myth) still standing behind New York's City Hall caused many New Yorkers to ask that the building be spared as a monument to graft and a reminder of the necessity of rooting out piggish politicians who take their slops at the public trough.

From Leo Hershkowitz, *Tweed's New York: Another Look* (Anchor Press, 1977). Copyright © 1977 by Leo Hershkowitz. Reprinted by permission of Doubleday, a division of Bantam Doubleday Dell Publishing Group, Inc.

Almost miraculously, the building, though supposedly built by corrupt politicians and contractors, is one of the finest examples of Italian Renaissance design in the country. It has not collapsed into a pile of plaster and sawdust, as critics predicted it would.

A popular cast-iron bank depicts an oily-faced tuxedoed figure, supposedly a banker, greedily swallowing the pennies of innocent children. What really "sells" the bank is calling it "Boss Tweed," even if one has nothing to do with the other. The myth is so salable and so deeply rooted that it is as American as "apple pie" or "Mother." A noted TV station produced a "documentary" on Tweed. When told that a mass of evidence exists that questions the "facts," representatives of the station offered an opinion, without pausing even to look at the material, that they wished all such records were destroyed. What price integrity as long as the legend lives, and it does so with abandon.

When political leaders think of New York, the vile image of Tweed taught them with their earliest history lessons returns to mind and appeals on behalf of the city fall on deaf ears. When Congress or the state legislature meet to debate New York's future, Tweed like some ghoulish specter rises up and beckons an end to discussion.

The myth is outrageously simple. Tweed was born in New York. Big, strong, ambitious and ruthless, he climbed out of the streets, and leaped like a snarling "Tammany Tiger" on unsuspecting citizens. Through fraud, deceit and intimidation, he was elected to various city and state offices, and even served a term in Congress. Tweed yearned for bigger and better things. He met kindred souls whom he placed in strategic places as members of "The Ring" to pillage the city treasury, conquer the state and finally the nation. By using the simple device of padded or fictitious bills for items not delivered or not needed, millions were stolen. The county courthouse, the "Tweed Courthouse," became the symbol and center of the operation. Subservient members of "The Ring" were Peter B. ("Brains") Sweeny, city chamberlain; Richard B. ("Slippery Dick") Connolly, city comptroller; A. Oakey Hall ("The Elegant One"), mayor; and John T. ("Toots") Hoffman, mayor and governor. Hoffman would hopefully become President to serve Tweed better. An army of poor, unwashed and ignorant were also recruited. These were recent Irish and German immigrants, whose largely illegal votes were cheaply bought in return for jobs given away at City Hall or a turkey at Christmas. Judges were necessary to stay the hands of the law, so added to the conspiracy were George G. Barnard, John H. McCunn and Albert Cardozo. Misguided though willing contractors like Andrew Garvey, "Prince of Plasterers"; James H. Ingersoll, the "Chairmaker"; John Keyser, the "Plumber"; and numerous others were awarded contracts, but kicked back up to 75 per cent to Tweed and "The Ring." Tweed received the lion's or rather "Tiger's" share of perhaps 50 to 200 million dollars at a time when an average workman received two to three dollars a day.

The fable continues that this monumental looting was halted by courageous, honest men. There were Democrats like Samuel J. Tilden, who on the strength of his attacks against "The Ring" became governor and presidential candidate. Honest Republicans like George Jones, editor of the *Times*, combined to disgrace "The Ring" with the help of Nast and *Harper's Weekly*. Indictments were handed down against Tweed, who was found guilty and sentenced to the penitentiary. Finally, like most of the others of "The Ring," he fled the country. Recognized in Spain by a sailor, or someone or other who just happened to be an avid reader of *Harper's Weekly*—the myth is never clear on details—and was quite familiar with the Boss's features, he was returned to prison to die a lonely but deserved death, a lesson to evildoers.

With great delight, happy historians, political activists, popularizers, drooled over juicy tidbits like carpets and plumbing and people named Dummy and Cash, never bothering to look at dust-gathering records, or even those quite dust-free. It would seem that research would interfere with exorcising the devil or prevent the development of some interesting theories. One theory concerned the failure of adequate communication in an evolving, increasingly complicated metropolis. It was a lack of such communication as seen in a decentralized and chaotic government which explains the emergence of Tweed and the "Big Pay-off." Others see Tweed emerging from the schismatic web of Tammany politics to seize and consolidate power by "pulling wires," hiring professional toughs and modernizing control within Tammany.

Lord James Bryce, a hostile critic of American urban government, in his classic *American Commonwealth* found Tweed the end product of "rancid dangerous Democracy." The scornful Englishman felt that "The time was ripe, for the lowest class of voters, foreign and native, had now been thoroughly organized and knew themselves able to control the city."

This voting mob was ready to follow Tammany Hall, which he concluded "had become the Acropolis of the city; and he who could capture it might rule as tyrant." Bryce found Tweed's unscrupulousness matched by the crafty talents of others, creating a perfect blend of flagrant corruption. But the essential ingredient was democracy and failure to follow traditional leadership. It was such democracy which allowed a Falstaff-like Tweed to emerge as a hero; a "Portuguese Jew" like Albert Cardozo who was born in New York to "prostitute" his legal talents for party purposes; or a Fernando Wood, Tweed's predecessor in Tammany, to become a major figure from such small beginnings that he was "reported to have entered New York as the leg of an artificial elephant in a travelling show." Bryce thus denounced Tweed and a form of government that had little if any respect for birth or breeding, but rewarded the mean, the base-born for their audacity and treachery.

It all sounds so plausible, but does it help Tweed emerge from behind Thomas Nast's leering cartoons? The problem with Tweed and the myth is that it is all so much vapor and so little substance, and what has been written has not dispelled shadows; only deepened them. So little has been done to obtain even basic information about the man, and what is known is generally wrong. Perhaps never has so much nonsense been written about an individual.

A few questions to start. Was it possible for one man or even a group of men to plan such a vast swindle involving hundreds if not thousands of officials, clerks, laborers, contractors, and hope to succeed? If Tweed plotted such an operation which supposedly involved bribing the state legislature, coercing judges, muzzling the press, aborting the gossip of bank officers and city auditors, he must have been a genius, a Houdini, Machiavelli, Napoleon rolled into one. Such a mind surely would have withstood the trivial intrusion of a hundred brash reformers. Yet he was shaken from his lofty perch, tumbled into prison and hounded to death. All this was done without organized resistance and in literally the twinkling of an eye. Tweed had such "power" that he was thrown out of his party without a word spoken in his behalf, even before he was found guilty of anything. There was, except for counsel, no one to defend him, no congressman, senator, assemblyman, no one in authority. "The Ring" was so strongly forged that it shattered at the slightest pressure, its component parts flying about with no other thought than every man for himself. If "The Ring" was supposed to be a strong political or financial alliance well led and directed, then it like "Boss" Tweed was simply a figment of historical imagination, a pretty bit of caricature.

At no time did such a "Ring" dominate New York City politics, let alone the state or national scene. Supposed "Ring" members rarely had much to do with one another, socially or otherwise. Sweeny was a friend of Victor Hugo's, Hall aspired to make a mark in the theater, Tweed aspired to office, Connolly had Connolly. There was little to bind the so-called "Ring." Except by an accident of history that they served in various city posts at the same time, there is little to relate one with the other.

Even the dreaded "Tammany Tiger" was a paper one. Certainly in Tweed's day Tammany did not dominate New York politics. Perhaps it never did. The city was and is a complex, competitive system of diverse interest. It was then and is now too heterogeneous, too much made up of various groups, classes, outlooks, beliefs for any part or let alone one person to control. New Yorkers' cosmopolitanism and tolerance have a tragic price.

The city cannot send representatives to Washington or to Albany who can express the single-minded view of smaller, simpler communities. Its large immigrant population creates suspicion: is New York an American city? A rural backwater has more political clout than all of the city when it comes to power on national or state levels.

Partly this is in consequence of an age-old struggle between the city and the farm, and eternal tug of war between the city in its search for greater self-government and rural conservative interests who find New York a threat to themselves and their entrenched power. There were some deeply rooted animosities. Cities are not natural. God made the earth, trees, animals and man. Cities are man-made. Natural things are pure, innocent and obedient to order, while man is sinful, evil, disobedient, whose works like cities are suspect. There may be a Garden of Eden, but there is no City of Eden, only Sodom and Gomorrah. This kind of morality underlines economic and political selection. It is served by the Tweed myth, since the horrors of municipal corruption and Tammany bossism plainly demonstrate the impossibility of the city even governing itself. It is in a deeper sense an implied failure of man governing himself apart from some external power. As New York cannot be given greater home rule, it must even be more closely regulated and watched by the state; so too man must observe a higher authority.

To make matters worse, New York also destroys its political talent, its best lost in the heat of murderous combat. It was a rare aspirant indeed who could emerge from his trials to become a national figure of any permanence.

Alexander Hamilton and Aaron Burr were testimony to this. De Witt Clinton and Edward Livingston were further examples of early casualties. By mid-nineteenth century, no New York City politician had any voice in national or state affairs. Fernando Wood, potentially a great politician and a champion of the city's interest against the state rural lobby, was destroyed by bitter intra-party fighting. William Tweed might have provided the city with a voice and he too was destroyed, but in such a way that the city too suffered in countless ways—not the least of which forever identified the metropolis as a spawning ground for corruption and filth. Why then pay it any attention? Why spend money on the sewers? Tweed was and is a convenient stick with which to beat the city over the head, preferably at regular intervals. In many ways, the tragedy of New York is that Tweed did not succeed, that a strong unified political force was not created, that the paper tiger was not real.

As for Tweed, there remain the stories. There is no evidence that he created the "Tammany Tiger" or ordered it to be used as his personal symbol. The clawing, snarling, toothed tiger was Nast's idea, part of the image he wished to create. It was plastered on Tweed and Tammany and sold. What politician would use such a symbol to win votes or influence people, except a madman or a cartoonist like Nast?

One of the universally accepted myths is that of Tweed's reactions to the July 1871 disclosures exposing "The Ring." He is supposed to have snarled like his tiger to a group of cowering reporters, reformers and the public at large, "What are you going to do about it?" Again, what politician, especially in this country, would make such an asinine statement, no matter how sure he was of his position? It was certainly not Tweed's style, and if he made "The Ring," he was not that stupid. In truth, the phrase was never used by Tweed, but invented by Nast as a caption for a June 10, 1871, cartoon a month before Tweed and "The Ring" made headlines. Reporters asked Tweed that question after the deluge and his troubles with the law. It was never Tweed's question. It was all "Boss," all Nast and all nonsense.

Tweed was no saint, but he was not the Nast creature. He was more a victim than a scoundrel or thief. Characteristically, Tweed was intensely loyal, warmhearted, outgoing, given to aiding the underdog and the underprivileged. But he was also gullible, naïve and easily fooled. If he were a real "boss," he should have been able, like Sweeny and others, to avoid inundating calamity. He was a good family man, and there simply is no scandal to report so far as his personal habits are concerned. Even his bitterest enemies could find nothing. He was not an intellectual, he was not at home with a Sweeny or an Oakey Hall, but found a close friendship with Jubilee Jim Fisk, the brilliant short-lived Roman candle and bon vivant.

Why then Tweed? First, he was what he was. In his prime, he reportedly weighed close to three hundred pounds. A "slim" Tweed would not be as inviting a target. Point one, for dieters. His features could be easily exaggerated by someone like Nast, and he was enough in the public eye for the *Times* and *Harper's*. He was ambitious, but not ruthless. He had money, but not enough to throw a scare into or buy off his opponents. He had power, but not enough to withstand attacks by newspapers, law, rivals and supposed friends.

Further, and much more importantly, he represented the interests of New York. He had established legislative programs which opened schools, hospitals, museums, programs tailored to meet the needs of a rapidly expanding constituency. His identification with the interests of the city was enough for the traditional rural-suburban leadership to seek his destruction. He provided a means for Republicans from President U.S. Grant on down to those in the local level to make people forget the corruptions in Republican circles, like the Whisky Ring, Indian Ring or Crédit Mobilier—all schemes to defraud millions from the government—but see instead the balloon-like figure of Tweed, Tammany and the defeat of Democratic opposition. National Democrats like Horatio Seymour and the inept "Sammy" Tilden could point to Tweed and gain cheers and votes for their efforts to "delouse" the party. If there ever was a scapegoat, its name was Tweed.

The Tweed story does not need exaggeration, lies, half-truths, rumors to make it interesting. It is in itself an incredible story. Debunking the myth is part of it, but there is much more. There are bigots like Nast, George T. Strong and others who saw in Tweed an outsider threatening their position by his supposedly championing the "drunken-ignorant Irish," the overly ambitious German-Jewish immigrants and those seeking to change the status quo. That he sought to provide answers to the increasing complications of urban life did not help. Tweed never traveled in upper-class society. With all his apparent success, he was never able to wash away the tarnish of the Lower East Side. Moreover, there are some of the most incredible trials and abuses of the judicial process on record. There are hand-picked judges and juries, not as might be expected by Tweed, but by the prosecution. The misuse of grand jury indictments should become legendary.

Tweed was never tried for or found guilty of graft or theft, the crime Tweed stands accused of by history. He was convicted after some strange, improper, even illegal judicial proceedings, which were in many ways worse than anything Tweed supposedly committed, of a misdemeanor—failing to audit claims against the city. Hall was tried three times on the same charge and was not convicted. Connolly and Sweeny were never tried.

Tweed died in prison after having spent some four years there, and he would have remained longer but for his death—only one of these years was he in a penitentiary, on the misdemeanor conviction. The remaining years he spent in the county jail because he could not raise an exorbitant bail in a civil suit. The manipulation of the law by those sworn to uphold the law was a real crime. Then add the threatening, tampering with, and intimidation of witnesses, as well as the use of informers and agent provocateurs. Under these conditions, Snow White would have been hanged for loitering to commit prostitution.

The threat to individual liberty by an unbridled omnipresent legal system is rarely as clear as in the Tweed case. The innocent and guilty are too often given the same even-handed justice.

Couple this with yellow journalism and abuse of power by the press and Nast. Horace Greeley in his bid for the presidency in 1871 complained that he did not know whether he was running for that office or the penitentiary. Tweed was as much a victim of irresponsible journalism. Tweed, too, was "hot copy." He was also tried and convicted by newspapers in a too often repeated process in which rabid reporters and editors became judge and jury and head-lines substitute for trial and district attorneys, while editors scratch each other's backs for the sake of publicity—where an indictment is often all that is neces-sary to make a point, sell papers and win votes. . . .

Epilogue

And so Tweed passed into history to become the fabled legend. It was an unde-served fate. Except for Tweed's own very questionable "confession," there was really no evidence of a "Tweed Ring," no direct evidence of Tweed's thievery, no evidence, excepting the testimony of the informer contractors, of "whole-sale" plunder by Tweed. What preceded is a story of political profiteering at the expense of Tweed, of vaulting personal ambitions fed on Tweed's carcass, of a conspiracy of self-justification of the corruption of law by the upholders of that law, of a venal irresponsible press and a citizenry delighting in the exorcism of witchery. If Tweed was involved then all those about him were equally guilty. He was never tried for theft. The only criminal trial that was held was for a mis-demeanor of failing to audit, and this trial was held before a hand-picked judge and jury at a time when Tweed-hunting was at its height.

Probably the "truth" about Tweed, "The Ring" and the "stolen" millions will never be known. It is possible to measure the difference between graft and profit? If Keyser charged so much for plastering, perhaps another could do the work for less, but would it be the same work, could it be done on time? How do you compare the cost of one carpet with that of another? Price is only one con-sideration. At one point, a decision has to be reached on any contract, no mat-ter who is selected; there will always be someone who could have done it cheaper. Surely there were overcharges, but by how much? The throwing about of figures, 10, 30, 50, 200 million, is of no help. Is it possible to decide at what point profit becomes graft? It is difficult to answer these questions or work out an almost insoluble puzzle. In the end, the easiest solution is of course to blame Tweed, rather than examine financial records, vouchers, warrants. These were allowed to lie dormant silently collecting the dust of a century, in the end hopefully to disappear. How much easier to nail the "Elephant" to a wall or listen to the romanticism of history and the excesses of rhetoric created by Godkin, Bryce, Wingate, Lynch and so many others.

Tweed emerges as anything but a master thief. It was the contractors who willingly padded bills, never calling attention to any undue pressure upon them to do so; it was those lower-echelon agents in the city, especially Woodward and Watson, who were in direct liaison with the contractors, not Tweed. And lastly blame should be placed on the city and state. The former because it did not regulate expenditures properly and failed to pay its bills on time, a point brought up time and again by the contractors, and the latter because it inter-fered in city business; the city's welfare was subverted by state political inter-ests. The Tweed story, or better the contractors' story, is about as good a reason for New York City home rule as can be offered.

Where did the legendary millions go? None of the contractors, with the possible exception of Garvey, had sizable sums of money, and even he wasn't to be compared to the "robber barons" like Morgan or Whitney or Rockefeller. These could sneeze out in a moment what purported to be the total Tweed plunder. What of Hall, Connolly, Sweeny, Hoffman? There is nothing to show they received any princely sums. No one connected with the so-called "Ring" set up a dynasty or retired to luxurious seclusion. Certainly not Tweed. If money was stolen, it held a Pharaoh's curse. Those who touched it did not enjoy it. So many died suddenly, so many died in dishonor and loneliness. None suffered as much as did William Magear Tweed and the City of New York.

Tweed spent some twenty years in public service. In the Fire Department, as alderman, member of the Board of Supervisors and Board of Education, member of Congress, state senator, commissioner of public works—it was a long list and resulted in a great deal of public good. He was instrumental in modernizing governmental and educational institutions, in developing needed reforms in public welfare programs, in incorporating schools, hospitals, establishing public baths, in preserving a site in Central Park for the Metropolitan Museum of Art, in widening Broadway, extending Prospect Park and removing fences from around public parks, establishing Riverside Park and Drive, annexing the Bronx as a forerunner of the incorporation of Greater New York, in building the Brooklyn Bridge, in founding the Lenox Library. He was of considerable service during the Civil War. Tweed moved the city forward in so many ways and could have been, if he had not been destroyed, a progressive force in shaping the interests and destiny of a great city and its people.

Tweed's concepts about urbanization and accommodation while not philosophically formalized were years beyond their time. Twenty or thirty years later such programs were adopted by reformers and urban planners. Tweed was a pioneer spokesman for an emerging New York, one of the few that spoke for its interests, one of the very few that could have had his voice heard in Albany. Tweed grew with the city, his death was a tragedy for the future metropolis.

His life in the end was wasted, not so much by what he did, but by what was done to him, his work and the city being relegated to the garbage heap, both branded by the same indelible iron. He became a club with which to beat New York, really the ultimate goal of the blessed reformers.

It is time to seek a re-evaluation of Tweed and his time. If Tweed was not so bad, neither was the city. Old legends die hard, old ideas have deep roots, but hopefully some of the old legends will die and the deep roots wither away.

What was learned from the episode? Practically nothing. Politics, politicians, jurists and venal journalists certainly continued to ply their trade, spurred by their success, as in the past, with hardly a glance or hesitation, comforted in the downfall of the "Boss." The devil had been killed; would anyone bother to look at the judges or ask anyone else to do the Lord's work? Every once in a while, a bill is introduced in the Massachusetts legislature to have the Salem witches exonerated and declared non-witches. Some are. It might be time to have the New York state legislature and history provide a similar service for Tweed. Surely, there are other devils around to take his place. And a statue for Tweed? Yes, it would be his city alive and well.

POSTSCRIPT

Did William M. Tweed Corrupt Post–Civil War New York?

The opposing viewpoints of Callow and Hershkowitz regarding "Boss" Tweed's place in history is representative of a long-standing scholarly debate about the consequences of machine politics in the United States. James Bryce, *The American Commonwealth*, 2 vols. (Macmillan, 1888); Moisei Ostrogorski, *Democracy and the Organization of Political Parties* (1902; reprint, Anchor Books, 1964); Lincoln Steffens, *The Shame of the Cities* (McClure, Phillips, 1904); and Ernest S. Griffith, *A History of American City Government: The Conspicuous Failure, 1870–1900* (National Civic League Press, 1974) present a litany of misdeeds associated with those who controlled municipal government.

Efforts to rehabilitate the sullied reputations of the machine politicians can be dated to the comments of Tammany Hall ward healer George Washington Plunkitt, whose turn-of-the-century observations included a subtle distinction between "honest" and "dishonest" graft. A more scholarly explanation was presented by Robert K. Merton, a political scientist, who identified numerous "latent functions" of the political machine. A generally positive description of the operations of urban government can also be found in Jon C. Teaford, *The Unheralded Triumph: City Government in America, 1860–1900* (Johns Hopkins University Press, 1984).

There are several excellent urban history texts that devote space to the development of municipal government, including discussions of political machines, in the nineteenth century. Among these are Howard P. Chudacoff and Judith E. Smith, *The Evolution of American Urban Society*, 3d ed. (Prentice Hall, 1981) and Charles N. Glaab and A. Theodore Brown, *A History of Urban America*, 3d ed. (Macmillan, 1983). Various developments in the post–Civil War period are discussed in Raymond A. Mohl, *The New City: Urban America in the Industrial Age, 1860–1920* (Harlan Davidson, 1985). Boss politics is analyzed in Robert K. Merton, *Social Theory and Social Structure* (Free Press, 1957) and John M. Allswang, *Bosses, Machines, and Urban Voters: An American Symbiosis* (Kennikat Press, 1977). In addition to the studies by Callow and Hershkowitz excerpted here, the most famous of the nineteenth-century urban bosses is evaluated in Seymour Mandelbaum, *Boss Tweed's New York* (John Wiley, 1965). For a study of New York City in the early years of Tweed's career, see Edward K. Spann, *The New Metropolis: New York City, 1840–1857* (Columbia University Press, 1981).

ISSUE 18

Was Reconstruction a "Splendid Failure"?

YES: Eric Foner, from "The New View of Reconstruction," *American Heritage* (October/November 1983)

NO: LaWanda Cox, from *Lincoln and Black Freedom: A Study in Presidential Leadership* (University of South Carolina Press, 1981)

ISSUE SUMMARY

YES: Eric Foner asserts that although Reconstruction did not achieve radical goals, it was a "splendid failure" because it offered African Americans in the South a temporary vision of a free society.

NO: LaWanda Cox explores the hypothetical question of whether Reconstruction would have succeeded had Lincoln lived and concludes that, despite his many talents, not even Lincoln could have guaranteed the success of the full range of reform, for African Americans.

Given the complex issues of the post–Civil War years, it is not surprising that the era of Reconstruction (1865–1877) is shrouded in controversy. For the better part of a century following the war, historians typically characterized Reconstruction as a total failure that had proved detrimental to all Americans—northerners and southerners, whites and blacks. According to this traditional interpretation, a vengeful Congress, dominated by radical Republicans, imposed military rule upon the southern states. Carpetbaggers from the North, along with traitorous white scalawags and their black accomplices in the South, established coalition governments that rewrote state constitutions, raised taxes, looted state treasuries, and disenfranchised former Confederates while extending the ballot to the freedmen. This era finally ended in 1877 when courageous southern white Democrats successfully "redeemed" their region from "Negro rule" by toppling the Republican state governments.

This portrait of Reconstruction dominated the historical profession until the 1960s. One reason for this is that white historians (both northerners and southerners) who wrote about this period operated from two basic assumptions: (1) The South was capable of solving its own problems without federal government interference, and (2) the former slaves were intellectually inferior to whites and incapable of running a government (much less one in which some whites would be their subordinates). African American historians, such as W. E. B. Du Bois, wrote several essays and books that challenged this negative portrayal of Reconstruction, but their works seldom were taken seriously in the academic world and rarely were read by the general public. Still, these black historians foreshadowed the acceptance of revisionist interpretations of Reconstruction, which coincided with the successes of the civil rights movement (or "Second Reconstruction") in the 1960s.

Without ignoring obvious problems and limitations connected with this period, revisionist historians identified a number of accomplishments of the Republican state governments in the South and their supporters in Washington, D.C. For example, revisionists argued that the state constitutions that were written during Reconstruction were the most democratic documents that the South had seen up to that time. Also, while taxes increased in the southern states, the revenues generated by these levies financed the rebuilding and expansion of the South's railroad network, the creation of a number of social service institutions, and the establishment of a public school system that benefited African Americans as well as whites. At the federal level, Reconstruction achieved the ratification of the Fourteenth and Fifteenth Amendments, which extended significant privileges of citizenship (including the right to vote) to African Americans, both North and South. Revisionists also placed the charges of corruption leveled by traditionalists against the Republican regimes in the South in a more appropriate context by insisting that political corruption was a *national* malady. Although the leaders of the Republican state governments in the South engaged in a number of corrupt activities, they were no more guilty than several federal officeholders in the Grant administration, or the members of New York City's notorious Tweed Ring (a Democratic urban political machine), or even the southern white Democrats (the Redeemers) who replaced the radical Republicans in positions of power in the former Confederate states. Finally, revisionist historians sharply attacked the notion that African Americans dominated the reconstructed governments of the South. They pointed out that there were no black governors, only two black senators, and fifteen black congressmen during this period.

In the essays that follow, Eric Foner and LaWanda Cox present thought-provoking analyses of the Reconstruction period. In the first selection, Foner concedes that Reconstruction was not very radical, much less revolutionary. Nevertheless, he argues, it was a "splendid failure" (a phrase coined by Du Bois) because it offered African Americans a vision of how a free society could look.

LaWanda Cox approaches this question from the counterfactual premise that Abraham Lincoln lived to oversee the political, economic, and social experiment that was Reconstruction. If anyone could have met the challenges of the post–Civil War era, she states, it was Lincoln. On the other hand, however, even had Lincoln gained broad consent from the white South during his second presidential term, Republican lawmakers' commitment to state responsibility for the rights of citizens, coupled with deeply entrenched racism in the South, would have derailed the more progressive aspects of Reconstruction legislation.

YES

Eric Foner

The New View of Reconstruction

In the past twenty years, no period of American history has been the subject of a more thoroughgoing reevaluation than Reconstruction—the violent, dramatic, and still controversial era following the Civil War. Race relations, politics, social life, and economic change during Reconstruction have all been reinterpreted in the light of changed attitudes toward the place of blacks within American society. If historians have not yet forged a fully satisfying portrait of Reconstruction as a whole, the traditional interpretation that dominated historical writing for much of this century has irrevocably been laid to rest.

Anyone who attended high school before 1960 learned that Reconstruction was an era of unrelieved sordidness in American political and social life. The martyred Lincoln, according to this view, had planned a quick and painless readmission of the Southern states as equal members of the national family. President Andrew Johnson, his successor, attempted to carry out Lincoln's policies but was foiled by the Radical Republicans (also known as Vindictives or Jacobins). Motivated by an irrational hatred of Rebels or by ties with Northern capitalists out to plunder the South, the Radicals swept aside Johnson's lenient program and fastened black supremacy upon the defeated Confederacy. An orgy of corruption followed, presided over by unscrupulous carpet-baggers (Northerners who ventured south to reap the spoils of office), traitorous scalawags (Southern whites who cooperated with the new governments for personal gain), and the ignorant and childlike freedmen, who were incapable of properly exercising the political power that had been thrust upon them. After much needless suffering, the white community of the South banded together to overthrow these "black" governments and restore home rule (their euphemism for white supremacy). All told, Reconstruction was just about the darkest page in the American saga.

Originating in anti-Reconstruction propaganda of Southern Democrats during the 1870s, this traditional interpretation achieved scholarly legitimacy around the turn of the century through the work of William Dunning and his students at Columbia University. It reached the larger public through films like *Birth of a Nation* and *Gone With the Wind* and that best-selling work of myth-making masquerading as history, *The Tragic Era* by Claude G. Bowers. In language as exaggerated as it was colorful, Bowers told how Andrew Johnson "fought the bravest battle for constitutional liberty and for the preservation of our institutions ever waged by an Executive" but was overwhelmed by the "poisonous propaganda" of the Radicals. Southern whites, as a result, "literally

From Eric Foner, "The New View of Reconstruction," *American Heritage*, vol. 34, no. 6 (October/November 1983). Copyright © 1983 by *American Heritage*. Reprinted by permission.

were put to the torture" by "emissaries of hate" who manipulated the "simple-minded" freedmen, "inflaming the negroes' egotism" and even inspiring "lustful assaults" by blacks upon white womanhood.

In a discipline that sometimes seems to pride itself on the rapid rise and fall of historical interpretations, this traditional portrait of Reconstruction enjoyed remarkable staying power. The long reign of the old interpretation is not difficult to explain. It presented a set of easily identifiable heroes and villains. It enjoyed the imprimatur of the nation's leading scholars. And it accorded with the political and social realities of the first half of this century. This image of Reconstruction helped freeze the mind of the white South in unalterable opposition to any movement for breaching the ascendancy of the Democratic party, eliminating segregation, or readmitting disfranchised blacks to the vote.

❧❦❧

Nevertheless, the demise of the traditional interpretation was inevitable, for it ignored the testimony of the central participant in the drama of Reconstruction—the black freedman. Furthermore, it was grounded in the conviction that blacks were unfit to share in political power. As Dunning's Columbia colleague John W. Burgess put it, "A black skin means membership in a race of men which has never of itself succeeded in subjecting passion to reason, has never, therefore, created any civilization of any kind." Once objective scholarship and modern experience rendered that assumption untenable, the entire edifice was bound to fall.

The work of "revising" the history of Reconstruction began with the writings of a handful of survivors of the era, such as John R. Lynch, who had served as a black congressman from Mississippi after the Civil War. In the 1930s white scholars like Francis Simkins and Robert Woody carried the task forward. Then, in 1935, the black historian and activist W. E. B. Du Bois produced *Black Reconstruction in America,* a monumental reevaluation that closed with an irrefutable indictment of a historical profession that had sacrificed scholarly objectivity on the altar of racial bias. "One fact and one alone," he wrote, "explains the attitude of most recent writers toward Reconstruction; they cannot conceive of Negroes as men." Du Bois's work, however, was ignored by most historians.

It was not until the 1960s that the full force of the revisionist wave broke over the field. Then, in rapid succession, virtually every assumption of the traditional viewpoint was systematically dismantled. A drastically different portrait emerged to take its place. President Lincoln did not have a coherent "plan" for Reconstruction, but at the time of his assassination he had been cautiously contemplating black suffrage. Andrew Johnson was a stubborn, racist politician who lacked the ability to compromise. By isolating himself from the broad currents of public opinion that had nourished Lincoln's career, Johnson created an impasse with Congress that Lincoln would certainly have avoided, thus throwing away his political power and destroying his own plans for reconstructing the South.

The Radicals in Congress were acquitted of both vindictive motives and the charge of serving as the stalking-horses of Northern capitalism. They emerged instead as idealists in the best nineteenth-century reform tradition. Radical leaders like Charles Sumner and Thaddeus Stevens had worked for the rights of blacks long before any conceivable political advantage flowed from such a commitment. Stevens refused to sign the Pennsylvania Constitution of 1838 because it disfranchised the state's black citizens; Sumner led a fight in the 1850s to integrate Boston's public schools. Their Reconstruction policies were based on principle, not petty political advantage, for the central issue dividing Johnson and these Radical Republicans was the civil rights of freedmen. Studies of congressional policy-making such as Eric L. McKitrick's *Andrew Johnson and Reconstruction,* also revealed that Reconstruction legislation, ranging from the Civil Rights Act of 1866 to the Fourteenth and Fifteenth Amendments, enjoyed broad support from moderate and conservative Republicans. It was not simply the work of a narrow radical faction.

⚓

Even more startling was the revised portrait of Reconstruction in the South itself. Imbued with the spirit of the civil rights movement and rejecting entirely the racial assumptions that had underpinned the traditional interpretation, these historians evaluated Reconstruction from the black point of view. Works like Joel Williamson's *After Slavery* portrayed the period as a time of extraordinary political, social, and economic progress for blacks. The establishment of public school systems, the granting of equal citizenship to blacks, the effort to restore the devastated Southern economy, the attempt to construct an interracial political democracy from the ashes of slavery, all these were commendable achievements, not the elements of Bowers's "tragic era."

Unlike earlier writers, the revisionists stressed the active role of the freedmen in shaping Reconstruction. Black initiative established as many schools as did Northern religious societies and the Freedmen's Bureau. The right to vote was not simply thrust upon them by meddling outsiders, since blacks began agitating for the suffrage as soon as they were freed. In 1865 black conventions throughout the South issued eloquent, though unheeded, appeals for equal civil and political rights.

With the advent of Radical Reconstruction in 1867, the freedmen did enjoy a real measure of political power. But black supremacy never existed. In most states blacks held only a small fraction of political offices, and even in South Carolina, where they comprised a majority of the state legislature's lower house, effective power remained in white hands. As for corruption, moral standards in both government and private enterprise were at low ebb throughout the nation in the postwar years—the era of Boss Tweed, the Credit Mobilier scandal, and the Whiskey Ring. Southern corruption could hardly be blamed on former slaves.

Other actors in the Reconstruction drama also came in for reevaluation. Most carpetbaggers were former Union soldiers seeking economic opportunity in the postwar South, not unscrupulous adventurers. Their motives, a typically American amalgam of humanitarianism and the pursuit of profit, were no more insidious than those of Western pioneers. Scalawags, previously seen as traitors to the white race, now emerged as "Old Line" Whig Unionists who had opposed secession in the first place or as poor whites who had long resented planters' domination of Southern life and who saw in Reconstruction a chance to recast Southern society along more democratic lines. Strongholds of Southern white Republicanism like east Tennessee and western North Carolina had been the scene of resistance to Confederate rule throughout the Civil War; now, as one scalawag newspaper put it, the choice was "between salvation at the hand of the Negro or destruction at the hand of the rebels."

At the same time, the Ku Klux Klan and kindred groups, whose campaign of violence against black and white Republicans had been minimized or excused in older writings, were portrayed as they really were. Earlier scholars had conveyed the impression that the Klan intimidated blacks mainly by dressing as ghosts and playing on the freedmen's superstitions. In fact, black fears were all too real: the Klan was a terrorist organization that beat and killed its political opponents to deprive blacks of their newly won rights. The complicity of the Democratic party and the silence of prominent whites in the face of such outrages stood as an indictment of the moral code the South had inherited from the days of slavery.

By the end of the 1960s, then, the old interpretation had been completely reversed. Southern freedmen were the heroes, the "Redeemers" who overthrew Reconstruction were the villains, and if the era was "tragic," it was because change did not go far enough. Reconstruction had been a time of real progress and its failure a lost opportunity for the South and the nation. But the legacy of Reconstruction—the Fourteenth and Fifteenth Amendments—endured to inspire future efforts for civil rights. As Kenneth Stampp wrote in *The Era of Reconstruction,* a superb summary of revisionist findings published in 1965, "If it was worth four years of civil war to save the Union, it was worth a few years of radical reconstruction to give the American Negro the ultimate promise of equal civil and political rights."

As Stampp's statement suggests, the reevaluation of the first Reconstruction was inspired in large measure by the impact of the second—the modern civil rights movement. And with the waning of that movement in recent years, writing on Reconstruction has undergone still another transformation. Instead of seeing the Civil War and its aftermath as a second American Revolution (as Charles Beard had), a regression into barbarism (as Bowers argued), or a golden opportunity squandered (as the revisionists saw it), recent writers argue that Radical Reconstruction was not really very radical. Since land was not distributed to the former slaves, they remained economically dependent upon their former owners. The planter class survived both the war and Reconstruction with its property (apart from slaves) and prestige more or less intact.

Not only changing times but also the changing concerns of historians have contributed to this latest reassessment of Reconstruction. The hallmark of the past decade's historical writing has been an emphasis upon "social history"—the evocation of the past lives of ordinary Americans—and the downplaying of strictly political events. When applied to Reconstruction, this concern with the "social" suggested that black suffrage and officeholding, once seen as the most radical departures of the Reconstruction era, were relatively insignificant.

Recent historians have focused their investigations not upon the politics of Reconstruction but upon the social and economic aspects of the transition from slavery to freedom. Herbert Gutman's influential study of the black family during and after slavery found little change in family structure or relations between men and women resulting from emancipation. Under slavery most blacks had lived in nuclear family units, although they faced the constant threat of separation from loved ones by sale. Reconstruction provided the opportunity for blacks to solidify their preexisting family ties. Conflicts over whether black women should work in the cotton fields (planters said yes, many black families said no) and over white attempts to "apprentice" black children revealed that the autonomy of family life was a major preoccupation of the freedmen. Indeed, whether manifested in their withdrawal from churches controlled by whites, in the blossoming of black fraternal, benevolent, and self-improvement organizations, or in the demise of the slave quarters and their replacement by small tenant farms occupied by individual families, the quest for independence from white authority and control over their own day-to-day lives shaped the black response to emancipation.

In the post–Civil War South the surest guarantee of economic autonomy, blacks believed, was land. To the freedmen the justice of a claim to land based on their years of unrequited labor appeared self-evident. As an Alabama black convention put it, "The property which they [the planters] hold was nearly all earned by the sweat of *our* brows." As Leon Litwack showed in *Been in the Storm So Long,* a Pulitzer Prize–winning account of the black response to emancipation, many freedmen in 1865 and 1866 refused to sign labor contracts, expecting the federal government to give them land. In some localities, as one Alabama overseer reported, they "set up claims to the plantation and all on it."

In the end, of course, the vast majority of Southern blacks remained propertyless and poor. But exactly why the South, and especially its black population, suffered from dire poverty and economic retardation in the decades following the Civil War is a matter of much dispute. In *One Kind of Freedom,* economists Roger Ransom and Richard Sutch indicted country merchants for monopolizing credit and charging usurious interest rates, forcing black tenants into debt and locking the South into a dependence on cotton production that impoverished the entire region. But Jonathan Wiener, in his study of postwar Alabama, argued that planters used their political power to compel blacks to remain on the plantations. Planters succeeded in stabilizing the plantation system, but only by blocking the growth of alternative enterprises, like factories, that might draw off black laborers, thus locking the region into a pattern of economic backwardness.

꒰◉꒱

If the thrust of recent writing has emphasized the social and economic aspects of Reconstruction, politics has not been entirely neglected. But political studies have also reflected the postrevisionist mood summarized by C. Vann Woodward when he observed "how essentially nonrevolutionary and conservative Reconstruction really was." Recent writers, unlike their revisionist predecessors, have found little to praise in federal policy toward the emancipated blacks.

A new sensitivity to the strength of prejudice and laissez-faire ideas in the nineteenth-century North has led many historians to doubt whether the Republican party ever made a genuine commitment to racial justice in the South. The granting of black suffrage was an alternative to a long-term federal responsibility for protecting the rights of the former slaves. Once enfranchised, blacks could be left to fend for themselves. With the exception of a few Radicals like Thaddeus Stevens, nearly all Northern policy-makers and educators are criticized today for assuming that, so long as the unfettered operations of the marketplace afforded blacks the opportunity to advance through diligent labor, federal efforts to assist them in acquiring land were unnecessary.

Probably the most innovative recent writing on Reconstruction politics has centered on a broad reassessment of black Republicanism, largely undertaken by a new generation of black historians. Scholars like Thomas Holt and Nell Painter insist that Reconstruction was not simply a matter of black and white. Conflicts within the black community, no less than divisions among whites, shaped Reconstruction politics. Where revisionist scholars, both black and white, had celebrated the accomplishments of black political leaders, Holt, Painter, and others charge that they failed to address the economic plight of the black masses. Painter criticized "representative colored men," as national black leaders were called, for failing to provide ordinary freedmen with effective political leadership. Holt found that black officeholders in South Carolina mostly emerged from the old free mulatto class of Charleston, which shared many assumptions with prominent whites. "Basically bourgeois in their origins and orientation," he wrote, they "failed to act in the interest of black peasants."

In emphasizing the persistence from slavery of divisions between free blacks and slaves, these writers reflect the increasing concern with continuity and conservatism in Reconstruction. Their work reflects a startling extension of revisionist premises. If, as has been argued for the past twenty years, blacks were active agents rather than mere victims of manipulation, then they could not be absolved of blame for the ultimate failure of Reconstruction.

Despite the excellence of recent writing and the continual expansion of our knowledge of the period, historians of Reconstruction today face a unique dilemma. An old interpretation has been overthrown, but a coherent new synthesis has yet to take its place. The revisionists of the 1960s effectively established a series of negative points: the Reconstruction governments were not as bad as had been portrayed, black supremacy was a myth, the Radicals were not cynical manipulators of the freedmen. Yet no convincing overall portrait of the quality of political and social life emerged from their writings. More recent historians have rightly pointed to elements of continuity that spanned the nineteenth-century Southern experience, especially the survival, in modified form, of the plantation system. Nevertheless, by denying the real changes that did occur, they have failed to provide a convincing portrait of an era characterized above all by drama, turmoil, and social change.

Building upon the findings of the past twenty years of scholarship, a new portrait of Reconstruction ought to begin by viewing it not as a specific time period, bounded by the years 1865 and 1877, but as an episode in a prolonged historical process—American society's adjustment to the consequences of the

Civil War and emancipation. The Civil War, of course, raised the decisive questions of America's national existence: the relations between local and national authority, the definition of citizenship, the balance between force and consent in generating obedience to authority. The war and Reconstruction, as Allan Nevins observed over fifty years ago, marked the "emergence of modern America." This was the era of the completion of the national railroad network, the creation of the modern steel industry, the conquest of the West and final subduing of the Indians, and the expansion of the mining frontier. Lincoln's America—the world of the small farm and artisan shop—gave way to a rapidly industrializing economy. The issues that galvanized postwar Northern politics—from the question of the greenback currency to the mode of paying holders of the national debt—arose from the economic changes unleashed by the Civil War.

Above all, the war irrevocably abolished slavery. Since 1619, when "twenty negars" disembarked from a Dutch ship in Virginia, racial injustice had haunted American life, mocking its professed ideals even as tobacco and cotton, the products of slave labor, helped finance the nation's economic development. Now the implications of the black presence could no longer be ignored. The Civil War resolved the problem of slavery but, as the Philadelphia diarist Sydney George Fisher observed in June 1865, it opened an even more intractable problem: "What shall we do with the Negro?" Indeed, he went on, this was a problem *"incapable* of any solution that will satisfy both North and South."

As Fisher realized, the focal point of Reconstruction was the social revolution known as emancipation. Plantation slavery was simultaneously a system of labor, a form of racial domination, and the foundation upon which arose a distinctive ruling class within the South. Its demise threw open the most fundamental questions of economy, society, and politics. A new system of labor, social, racial, and political relations had to be created to replace slavery.

The United States was not the only nation to experience emancipation in the nineteenth century. Neither plantation slavery nor abolition were unique to the United States. But Reconstruction was. In a comparative perspective Radical Reconstruction stands as a remarkable experiment, the only effort of a society experiencing abolition to bring the former slaves within the umbrella of equal citizenship. Because the Radicals did not achieve everything they wanted, historians have lately tended to play down the stunning departure represented by black suffrage and officeholding. Former slaves, most fewer than two years removed from bondage, debated the fundamental questions of the polity: What is a republican form of government? Should the state provide equal education for all? How could political equality be reconciled with a society in which property was so unequally distributed? There was something inspiring in the way such men met the challenge of Reconstruction. "I knew nothing more than to obey my master," James K. Greene, an Alabama black politician later recalled. "But the tocsin of freedom sounded and knocked at the door and we walked out like free men and we met the exigencies as they grew up, and shouldered the responsibilities."

You never saw a people more excited on the subject of politics than are the negroes of the south," one planter observed in 1867. And there were more than a few Southern whites as well who in these years shook off the prejudices of the past to embrace the vision of a new South dedicated to the principles of equal citizenship and social justice. One ordinary South Carolinian expressed the new sense of possibility in 1868 to the Republican governor of the state: "I am sorry that I cannot write an elegant stiled letter to your excellency. But I rejoice to think that God almighty has given to the poor of S. C. a Gov. to hear to feel to protect the humble poor without distinction to race or color. . . . I am a native borned S. C. a poor man never owned a Negro in my life nor my father before me. . . . Remember the true and loyal are the poor of the whites and blacks, outside of these you can find none loyal."

Few modern scholars believe the Reconstruction governments established in the South in 1867 and 1868 fulfilled the aspirations of their humble constituents. While their achievements in such realms as education, civil rights, and the economic rebuilding of the South are now widely appreciated, historians today believe they failed to affect either the economic plight of the emancipated slave or the ongoing transformation of independent white farmers into cotton tenants. Yet their opponents did perceive the Reconstruction governments in precisely this way—as representatives of a revolution that had put the bottom rail, both racial and economic, on top. This perception helps explain the ferocity of the attacks leveled against them and the pervasiveness of violence in the postmancipation South.

The spectacle of black men voting and holding office was anathema to large numbers of Southern whites. Even more disturbing, at least in the view of those who still controlled the plantation regions of the South, was the emergence of local officials, black and white, who sympathized with the plight of the black laborer. Alabama's vagrancy law was a "dead letter" in 1870, "because those who are charged with its enforcement are indebted to the vagrant vote for their offices and emoluments." Political debates over the level and incidence of taxation, the control of crops, and the resolution of contract disputes revealed that a primary issue of Reconstruction was the role of government in a plantation society. During presidential Reconstruction, and after "Redemption," with planters and their allies in control of politics, the law emerged as a means of stabilizing and promoting the plantation system. If Radical Reconstruction failed to redistribute the land of the South, the ouster of the planter class from control of politics at least ensured that the sanctions of the criminal law would not be employed to discipline the black labor force.

⋅⟨☉⟩⋅

An understanding of this fundamental conflict over the relation between government and society helps explain the pervasive complaints concerning corruption and "extravagance" during Radical Reconstruction. Corruption there was aplenty; tax rates did rise sharply. More significant than the rate of taxation, however, was the change in its incidence. For the first time, planters and white farmers had to pay a significant portion of their income to the government, while propertyless blacks often escaped scot-free. Several states, moreover, enacted heavy taxes on uncultivated land to discourage land speculation and force land onto the market, benefiting, it was hoped, the freedmen.

As time passed, complaints about the "extravagance" and corruption of Southern governments found a sympathetic audience among influential Northerners. The Democratic charge that universal suffrage in the South was responsible for high taxes and governmental extravagance coincided with a rising conviction among the urban middle classes of the North that city government had to be taken out of the hands of the immigrant poor and returned to the "best men"—the educated, professional, financially independent citizens unable to exert much political influence at a time of mass parties and machine politics. Increasingly the "respectable" middle classes began to retreat from the very notion of universal suffrage. The poor were no longer perceived as honest producers, the backbone of the social order; now they became the "dangerous classes," the "mob." As the historian Francis Parkman put it, too much power rested with "masses of imported ignorance and hereditary ineptitude." To Parkman the Irish of the Northern cities and the blacks of the South were equally incapable of utilizing the ballot: "Witness the municipal corruptions of New York, and the monstrosities of negro rule in South Carolina." Such attitudes helped to justify Northern inaction as, one by one, the Reconstruction regimes of the South were overthrown by political violence.

•❧•

In the end, then, neither the abolition of slavery nor Reconstruction succeeded in resolving the debate over the meaning of freedom in American life. Twenty years before the American Civil War, writing about the prospect of abolition in France's colonies, Alexis de Tocqueville had written, "If the Negroes have the right to become free, the [planters] have the incontestable right not to be ruined by the Negroes' freedom." And in the United States, as in nearly every plantation society that experienced the end of slavery, a rigid social and political dichotomy between former master and former slave, an ideology of racism, and a dependent labor force with limited economic opportunities all survived abolition. Unless one means by freedom the simple fact of not being a slave, emancipation thrust blacks into a kind of no-man's land, a partial freedom that made a mockery of the American ideal of equal citizenship.

Yet by the same token the ultimate outcome underscores the uniqueness of Reconstruction itself. Alone among the societies that abolished slavery in the nineteenth century, the United States, for a moment, offered the freedmen a measure of political control over their own destinies. However brief its sway, Reconstruction allowed scope for a remarkable political and social mobilization of the black community. It opened doors of opportunity that could never be completely closed. Reconstruction transformed the lives of Southern blacks in ways unmeasurable by statistics and unreachable by law. It raised their expectations and aspirations, redefined their status in relation to the larger society, and allowed space for the creation of institutions that enabled them to survive the repression that followed. And it established constitutional principles of civil and political equality that, while flagrantly violated after Reconstruction, planted the seeds of future struggle.

Certainly, in terms of the sense of possibility with which it opened, Reconstruction failed. But as Du Bois observed, it was a "splendid failure." For its animating vision—a society in which social advancement would be open to all on the basis of individual merit, not inherited caste distinctions—is as old as America itself and remains relevant to a nation still grappling with the unresolved legacy of emancipation.

NO

Reflections on the Limits
of the Possible

... Lincoln's presidential style, at odds with that forthrightness which stands high in twentieth-century criteria for presidential leadership, was not inappropriate to the situation he faced. The manner in which he unveiled the crucial, controversial element of his Reconstruction policy—some measure of suffrage for blacks—was designed to crystallize support and minimize opposition. At the time only the most minimal suffrage proposal could command an intraparty consensus; this was all that he asked, actually less than his supporters had sought in Louisiana. Yet he managed to open the door to future enfranchisement for more blacks than the relatively few, Union soldiers and the "very intelligent," whose qualifications he commended. In phrasing that avoided a definite formulation of either means or goal he suggested the desirability of a fuller franchise, one that would meet what "the colored man" "desires." In the same address he stated that "the sole object of the government" was to get the secession states back into "their proper practical relation with the Union" and asked that "all join in doing the acts necessary" to restore them. He refrained from defining the "acts necessary." To counter criticism that he had set up the reconstructed state government, Lincoln minimized his role in Louisiana, but he did not disavow his authority as commander in chief to shape the Reconstruction process. By virtue of that power he had just sent General Banks back to New Orleans with military authority to perform an essentially civil mission—to promote the kind of Unionist government and racial policy the administration desired.

Although his statements could be otherwise interpreted, Lincoln's purpose, like that of his party, went beyond the readmission of the secession states. In early 1865 he was in an excellent position to implement a larger purpose by combining a minimum of direct force with a maximum use of other means of asserting the power and influence of the presidency. Lincoln's election victory the previous November had greatly strengthened his hand with Congress and with the northern public. Final military victory could only have increased the public esteem and congressional respect he had won. In the summer and fall that followed, Lincoln would have found additional support in a mounting sense of indignation in the North as reports from the South confirmed warnings that the freedom of blacks would be in peril if left in the hands of southern

From LINCOLN AND BLACK FREEDOM: A STUDY IN PRESIDENTIAL LEADERSHIP by LaWanda Cox, pp. 172–183. Copyright © 1981 by University of South Carolina Press. Reprinted by permission.

whites. A widespread perception of injustice can be a powerful political force, as indeed it became in 1866.

It would have been uncharacteristic of Lincoln not to have recognized the opportunity. In his pragmatic fashion, advancing step by step as events permitted, with caution but when necessary with great boldness, it is just possible that Lincoln might have succeeded in making a policy of basic citizenship rights for blacks "acceptable to those who must support it, tolerable to those who must put up with it." The challenge to presidential leadership was formidable. If any man could have met the challenge, that man was Lincoln.

❧❦❧

Had Lincoln in the course of a second term succeeded in obtaining a far broader consent from the white South to terms that would satisfy northern Republican opinion than did Congress in 1867–1869, ultimate victory in the battle over the ex-slave's status as free man would not necessarily have followed. There would still have been the need to build institutions that could safeguard and expand what had been won—laws that the courts would uphold, an economy offering escape from poverty and dependency, a Union-Republican party in the South recognized by its opponents as a legitimate contestant for political power. The opportunities open to Lincoln for institutionalizing gains made toward equal citizenship irrespective of color were limited.

A fatal weakness of Reconstruction, constitutional historians have argued, arose from the constitutional conservatism of Republican lawmakers, particularly their deference to the traditional federal structure embodied in the Constitution. This led them to preserve the primacy of state responsibility for the rights of citizens, thereby denying to the national government effective power to protect the rights of blacks. It has been contended that Reconstruction required "a major constitutional upheaval," that it "could have been effected only by a revolutionary destruction of the states and the substitution of a unitary constitutional system." Part of the argument is unassailable. The new scholarship has demolished the old stereotype of Republican leaders as constitutional revolutionaries. They had, indeed, been waging a war for constitution as well as for nation with every intent of maintaining both. And the concern of Republicans for state and local government was no superficial adulation of the constitution; it was deeply rooted in their commitment to self-government. Yet unlike Democrats who denounced as unconstitutional any amendment to the constitution that enlarged federal authority at the expense of the states, Republicans did not uphold state rights federalism without qualification. They believed that they had found a way to protect freedmen in their new citizenship status by modifying, rather than destroying, the traditional federal structure.

What is questionable in the case against "respect for federalism" as fatally compromising Reconstruction is the assumption that the state rights federalist approach to the problem made a solution impossible. Not all scholars would agree. Some believe that the Reconstruction amendments needed only to have been more carefully framed. Others hold that as written they were adequate to the task. The Supreme Court, of course, seemed to disagree, overturning much of the legislation Congress passed under the amendments. Beginning with the Slaughterhouse decision of 1873, which did not directly affect blacks but carried ominous implications for them, a Republican Court handed down a series of constrictive decisions described in retrospect as "vacuous" and as "a major triumph for the South." Concern to preserve the functions of the states strongly influenced those decisions. Some authorities hold that without destroying federalism the Court could have devised a workable new division of authority between state and nation which would have enabled the latter to protect the rights of blacks against violation by either states or individuals. The Court did not foreclose all avenues of congressional action to protect black rights. However, by 1875 when it rendered the first adverse decision directly relating to the national enforcement effort, further legislation to meet the Court's criteria of adequacy was politically impossible because of the strength in Congress of the Democratic political opposition.

The Supreme Court seemed to have denied to congressional Reconstruction much needed legitimacy and legal sanctions. Without them, it is questionable that the Reconstruction effort could have been successfully defended during the postemancipation decades. The Court's narrow interpretation of which civil rights pertained to national as distinct from state citizenship added to the difficulties the Court had raised for the exercise of power to protect rights recognized as subject to the nation's authority. The decisions presented monumental obstacles to the enforcement of black rights. Better drafted amendments, laws, and indictments, more resourceful judicial reasoning, or less concern in the early decisions for technicalities might have avoided or remedied them. Lincoln's presence was unlikely to have increased those possibilities directly. Yet had he been president in the immediate post-Appomattox period he might have succeeded in dissipating southern resistance, in unifying Republicans on the preconditions for restoration, and in inducing reconstructed state governments to accept those conditions—a tall order. The resulting climate of opinion could have led the Court to play a positive role in the nineteenth-century Reconstruction effort. A possibility, but a very tenuous possibility.

Similarly circumscribed was any potential role for Lincoln in helping shape economic developments to assure freedmen an escape from poverty and dependence. No explanation for the tragic outcome of the postwar decades for black America has been more generally accepted in modern scholarship than that Reconstruction failed because the national government did not provide land for the freedman. The thesis has been sharply challenged, and the challenge has not been met. The work of historians and economists in exploring afresh the roots of poverty, particularly of black poverty, in the postbellum South afford some relevant perspectives. Between 1974 and 1979 six book-length studies appeared with significant bearing on the problem of black poverty, and others were in progress; conference papers and published articles also reflected the vigor of scholarly interest in the question.

No consensus has developed either as explanation for the continuing dependence and poverty of southern blacks or as an analysis of the potential economic effect of land distribution. However, four of five econometricians who addressed the latter question concluded that grants of land, while desirable and beneficial, would not have solved the predicament of the freedmen and their children. Robert Higgs has written that "historians have no doubt exaggerated the economic impact of such a grant." Gavin Wright holds that "the tenancy systems of the South cannot be assigned primary blame for Southern poverty," that a more equitable distribution of land "would not have produced dramatic improvements in living standards" or "generated sustained progress." In their book, *One Kind of Freedom,* Roger Ransom and Richard Sutch appear to accept what Heman Belz has characterized as the "new orthodoxy" of the historians, but they dramatically qualified that position in a subsequent paper. They argued that confiscation and redistribution would have resulted in little improvement in the postbellum situation, which they characterize as one of economic stagnation and exploitation, unless accompanied by federally funded compensation for landowners thereby providing liquid capital for reinvigorating agriculture and possibly developing manufactures. This retrospective prescription is restrained as compared to the requirements outlined by twentieth-century experts who seek land distribution as an avenue out of rural poverty. They see successful land reform as requiring supplementary government programs providing credit, seed and fertilizer distribution, marketing facilities, rural and feeder transportation, pricing mechanisms affecting both what the farmer buys and what he sells, technical research, and agricultural education.

More than a land program was needed to insure the freedman's economic future. Although areas of land with high fertility prospered, it seems doubtful that income from cotton between the close of the war and the turn of the century, even if equitably distributed, could have sustained much beyond a marginal level of existence for those who worked the cotton fields whether as wage earner, cropper, tenant, or small owner. And the lower South because of its soils and climate, as Julius Rubin has convincingly shown, had no viable alternative to cotton as a commercial crop until the scientific and technological advances of the twentieth century. Nor could nonmarket subsistence farming offer much by way of material reward. The "more" that was needed can be envisaged in retrospect, and was glimpsed by contemporaries, but it is not clear how it could have been achieved. Gavin Wright has concluded that the postbellum South "required either a massive migration away from the region or a massive Southern industrial revolution." Both in the North and the South there was enthusiasm for promoting southern industry, but only the future could reveal how elusive would be that "New South" of ever-renewed expectations. Despite scholarship, new and old, there is no certain explanation of why the South failed to catch up with the North. If historians and economists should agree upon a diagnosis, it is unlikely that they will uncover a remedy that could have been recognized and implemented a century ago. The heritage of slavery most certainly will be part of the diagnosis. It left behind an underdeveloped, overwhelmingly rural economy tied to the world market and bereft of adequate foundations for rapid economic growth. Recovery and growth had to be attempted in a period of initial crop disasters, of disadvantage for primary products in terms of world trade, and by the mid-1870s of prolonged and recurrent economic crises. There were high hopes for southern industrialization in the 1880s, but the effort substantially failed. With opportunity drastically limited in the South and industry expanding in the North, there was yet no great out-migration of blacks until the twentieth century. The reasons for this also are not altogether clear. Neither the restraints placed on southern agricultural labor by law and custom nor the discrimination blacks faced in the North is sufficient explanation. The ways in which European immigrants blocked black advance deserve further study, as does the attitude of blacks themselves both toward leaving the South and toward the unskilled, menial labor which alone might have afforded them large-scale entry into the northern labor market.

Lincoln was a man of his age. The concepts and perceptions then dominant, although not unreasonable on the basis of past experience, were inadequate to meet the challenge of transforming the South. Postwar expectations were buoyant. King Cotton was expected to regain his throne with beneficent results for all. Freed from the incubus of slavery, the South would be reshaped after the image of the bustling North, with large landholdings disintegrated by natural forces, village and school house replacing plantation quarters, internal improvements and local industry transforming the economy. The former slave would share the bright future through diligence and thrift, and the forces of the marketplace. There were, of course, dissenters, both radicals like George W. Julian and Thaddeus Stevens who would confiscate the great estates and conservatives such as those cotton manufacturers, by no means all, who would perpetuate the plantation in some form. Neither had sufficient influence at war's end to shape national policy. Republican leaders who did make postwar policy would have reached beyond prevailing concepts of self-help, the law of supply and demand, and the danger of "class legislation" to enact a modest land program had not President Johnson vetoed it with an appeal to all the economic verities of the day.

In the interest of the emancipated, Lincoln could have been expected to approve and encourage such deviations from the doctrinaire. And it would have been completely out of character for Lincoln to have exercised his power of pardon, as did President Johnson, with ruthless disregard for the former slave's interest and justifiable expectations. Indeed, there are intimations that Lincoln considered using that power to obtain from former masters grants of land for former slaves. Whatever support the national government might have given to the freedman's quest for land would have been a psychological boon, more symbol than substance of equal citizenship and independence, but not without some economic advantage. A land program more effective than the southern homestead act was a real possibility, lost due to President Johnson's opposition. With Lincoln, a Whiggish heritage, as well as humanity and a sense of responsibility for the emancipated, reinforced a pragmatic approach to the relationship between government and the future of the freedmen. Nor was he inhibited by the anxiety felt by many, including Thaddeus Stevens, over the unprecedented debt incurred in fighting the war. In early 1865 he calmly contemplated adding to the war's cost by indemnifying southerners for property seized and not restored. Whatever sums Congress might have appropriated to finance land purchase for freedmen could only have helped alleviate the South's postwar paucity of capital and credit. Its economic recovery would also have benefited from the lesser turbulence of the immediate postwar years had there been no war between president and Congress. Limited gains would have been possible and probable, but there existed neither the power nor the perception necessary to forestall the poverty that engulfed so many southerners, black and white, during the last decades of the nineteenth century.

There were limits to the possible. Yet the dismal outcome for southern blacks as the nation entered the twentieth century need not have been as unrelieved as it was in fact. More than a land program, the civil and political rights Republicans established in law, had they been secured in practice, could have mitigated the discrimination that worsened their condition and constricted whatever opportunities might otherwise have existed for escape from poverty. Moreover, the extraordinary effort black men made to vote—and to vote independently in the face of white cajolery, intimidation, and economic pressure—strongly suggests that for the emancipated to cast a ballot was to affirm the reality of freedom and the dignity of black manhood.

The priority Republicans gave to civil and political rights in their fight to establish a meaningful new status for ex-slaves has been too readily discounted by historians. Small landholdings could not have protected blacks from intimidation, or even from many forms of economic coercion. They would not have brought economic power. In the face of overwhelming white opposition, they could not have safeguarded the new equality of civil and political status. Where blacks voted freely, on the other hand, there was always the potential for sharing political power and using it as a means to protect and advance their interests. There is considerable evidence that this did happen. Local officials elected by black votes during the years of Republican control upheld blacks against planters, state legislators repealed Black Codes, shifted the burden of taxation from the poor, granted agricultural laborers a first lien on crops, increased expenditures for education. Eric Foner has concluded that at least in some areas Republican Reconstruction resulted in subtle but significant changes that protected black labor and prevented planters from using the state to bolster their position. Harold D. Woodman's study of state laws affecting agriculture confirms the generalization that a legislative priority of the Redeemer governments was passage of measures to give landowners greater control over the labor force. By the end of the century legal bonds had been so tightened that as prosperity returned to cotton culture neither cropper nor renter but only their employer was in a position to profit. In a study of rural Edgefield County, South Carolina, Vernon Burton has found that black voting made possible real gains in economic position and social status between 1867 and 1877. Howard Rabinowitz's examination of the urban South discloses that Republican city governments brought blacks a greater share of elected and appointed offices, more jobs in construction work, in fire and police departments. And beyond immediate gains, black votes meant support for educational facilities through which blacks could acquire the literacy and skills essential for advancement.

Security for black civil and political rights required acceptance by white southerners. An acquiescence induced by a judicious combination of force and consent needed for its perpetuation reinforcement by self-interest. The most effective vehicle of self-interest would have been a Union-Republican party able to command substantial continuing support from native whites. The

Republican party that gained temporary dominance through the congressional legislation of 1867 enfranchising blacks failed to meet the test of substantial white support. Despite a strong white following in a few states, its scalawag component from the start was too limited to offset the opposition's attack on it as the party of the black man and the Yankee. And white participation diminished as appeals to race prejudice and sectional animosity intensified.

The potential for a major second party among southern whites existed in the aftermath of Confederate defeat. The Democratic party was in disarray, discredited for having led the South out of the Union and having lost the war. Old Whig loyalties subsumed by the slavery issue had nonetheless endured; southern unionism had survivied in varying degrees from wartime adherence to the Union to reluctant support of the Confederacy. Opposition to Jefferson Davis' leadership and willingness to accept northern peace terms had grown as the hope for southern victory diminished. Such sources of Democratic opposition overlapped with the potential for ready recruits to Union-Republicanism from urban dwellers, from men whose origins had been abroad or in the North, from those whose class or intrasectional interests created hostility to the dominant planter leadership of the Democracy. A "New South" of enterprise and industry presented an attractive vision to many a native son. And there were always those who looked to the loaves and the fishes dispensed from Washington.

Had party recruitment and organization, with full presidential support, begun at the end of hostilities and escaped the period of confusion and bitterness that thinned the ranks of the willing during the conflict between Johnson and Congress, the result could have been promising. Greater white support and the accession of black voters by increments might have eased racial tension and lessened deadly factionalism within the party. Lincoln's political skill and Whig background would certainly have served party-building well, as would the perception of presidential policy as one of moderation and reconciliation. The extent to which southern whites did in fact support the Republican party after 1867 despite its image as Radical, alien, and black-dominated, an image that stigmatized and often ostracized them, suggests the potency of a common goal, or a common enmity, in bridging the chasm between the races.

Even under the guidance of a Lincoln, the building of a permanent biracial major party in the South was by no means assured. A broad enduring coalition of disparate elements would face the necessity of reconciling sharply divergent economic interests. Agricultural workers sought maximum autonomy, more than bare necessities, and an opportunity for land ownership while planter-merchants strove to control labor and maximize profit. The burden of increased taxation to meet essential but unaccustomed social services, particularly for blacks, meant an inescapable clash of class and racial interests. Concessions by the more privileged were especially difficult in a South of limited available resources and credit, impoverished by war and enmeshed in inflated costs, crop disasters, and falling cotton prices. By the mid-1870s a nationwide depression intensified regional problems. Efforts to promote a more varied and vigorous economy by state favor, credit, and appropriation became a political liability as the primary effect appeared to be the proliferation of civic corruption and entrepreneurial plunder.

Outside the South a vigorous Republican party and two-party system managed to endure despite the clash of intraparty economic interests. A similar development in the South faced the additional and more intractable conflict inherent in the new black-white relationship. Within the Republican party that took shape after 1867, factionalism often cut between blacks and carpet-baggers, on the one hand, and scalawags on the other; but there was also a considerable amount of accommodation, not all of it from blacks. A study of the voting record of 87 Republicans, 52 of them native whites, who served in the North Carolina House of Representatives in the 1868 to 1870 session shows scalawags trailing carpetbaggers and blacks in voting on issues of Negro rights and support for public schools, yet compiling a positive overall record, a score of 61.2 and 55.9 respectively. On the few desegregation questions that came to a roll call, however, only a small minority of native whites voted favorably. In Mississippi when the black-carpetbagger faction gained control, they quietly ignored the platform calling for school integration even though black legislators were sufficiently numerous and powerful to have pressed the issue. Black officeholding was a similar matter where fair treatment held danger, and black leaders often showed restraint. Such issues were explosive. They not only threatened the unity of the party but undermined its ability to attract white votes or minimize opposition demagoguery and violence. A Lincolnian approach to building an interracial party would have diminished the racial hazard, but could hardly have eliminated it.

The years of political Reconstruction, to borrow an apt phrase from Thomas B. Alexander's study of Tennessee, offered no "narrowly missed opportunities to leap a century forward in reform." Not even a Lincoln could have wrought such a miracle. To have secured something less, yet something substantially more than blacks had gained by the end of the nineteenth century, did not lie beyond the limits of the possible given a president who at war's end would have joined party in an effort to realize "as nearly as we can" the fullness of freedom for blacks.

Possible is not probable. To the major obstacles must be added the hazards disclosed by the Louisiana story. Lincoln's Louisiana policy had been compromised by Banks' blunders of execution and attacked by Durant and fellow Radicals in part because they distrusted Lincoln's intent. The effective implementation of a president's policy by his surrogates is a problem to plague any administration. Distrust by those otherwise allied in a common goal pertained more distinctively to the man and his style of leadership. Yet Radical distrust of Lincoln may also have reflected dilemmas inherent in presidential leadership—the need for candor and for persuasion, for vision and for practicality, for courage and for flexibility, for heeding while leading a national consensus. Obscured by his characteristic self-effacement, after his own fashion Lincoln as president was both lion and fox. . . .

POSTSCRIPT

Was Reconstruction a "Splendid Failure"?

In *Nothing But Freedom: Emancipation and Its Legacy* (Louisiana State University Press, 1984), Eric Foner advances his interpretation by comparing the treatment of ex-slaves in the United States with that of newly emancipated slaves in Haiti and the British West Indies. Only in the United States, he contends, were the freedslaves given voting and economic rights. Although these rights had been stripped away from the majority of black southerners by 1900, Reconstruction had, nevertheless, created a legacy of freedom that inspired succeeding generations of African Americans.

C. Vann Woodward, in "Reconstruction: A Counterfactual Playback," an essay in his thought-provoking *The Future of the Past* (Oxford University Press, 1988), shares Cox's pessimism about the outcome of Reconstruction. For all the successes listed by the revisionists, he argues that the experiment failed. He challenges Foner's conclusions by insisting that former slaves were as poorly treated in the United States as they were in other countries. He also maintains that the confiscation of former plantations and the redistribution of land to the former slaves would have failed in the same way that the Homestead Act of 1862 failed to generate equal distribution of government lands to poor white settlers. Finally, Woodward contends that reformers who worked with African Americans during Reconstruction and native Americans a decade or two later were often the same people and that they failed in both instances because their goals were out of touch with the realities of the late nineteenth century.

Thomas Holt's *Black Over White: Negro Political Leadership in South Carolina During Reconstruction* (University of Illinois Press, 1977) is representative of state and local studies that employ modern social science methodology to yield new perspectives. While critical of white Republican leaders, Holt (who is African American) also blames the failure of Reconstruction in South Carolina on freeborn mulatto politicians, whose background distanced them economically, socially, and culturally from the masses of freedmen. Consequently, these political leaders failed to develop a clear and unifying ideology to challenge white South Carolinians who wanted to restore white supremacy.

The study of the Reconstruction period benefits from an extensive bibliography. Traditional accounts of Reconstruction include William Archibald Dunning's *Reconstruction, Political and Economic, 1865–1877* (Harper & Brothers, 1907); Claude Bowers' *The Tragic Era: The Revolution after Lincoln* (Riverside Press, 1929); and E. Merton Coulter's, *The South During Reconstruction, 1865–1877* (Louisiana State University Press, 1947), the last major work written from the Dunning (or traditional) point of view. Early revisionist views are presented in W. E. B. Du Bois, *Black Reconstruction in America: An Essay Toward a History of the*

Part Which Black Folk Played in the Attempt to Reconstruct Democracy in America, 1860–1880 (Harcourt, Brace, 1935), a Marxist analysis; John Hope Franklin, *Reconstruction: After the Civil War* (University of Chicago Press, 1961); and Kenneth M. Stampp, *The Era of Reconstruction, 1865–1877* (Alfred A. Knopf, 1965). Foner's *Reconstruction: America's Unfinished Revolution, 1863–1877* (Harper & Row, 1988) includes the most complete bibliographies on the subject. Brief overviews are available in Forrest G. Wood, *The Era of Reconstruction, 1863–1877* (Harlan Davidson, 1975) and Michael Perman, *Emancipation and Reconstruction, 1862–1879* (Harlan Davidson, 1987). One of the best-written studies of a specific episode during the Reconstruction years is Willie Lee Rose's *Rehearsal for Reconstruction: The Port Royal Experiment* (Bobbs-Merrill, 1964), which describes the failed effort at land reform in the sea islands of South Carolina. Richard Nelson Current's *Those Terrible Carpetbaggers: A Reinterpretation* (Oxford University Press, 1988) is a superb challenge to the traditional view of these much-maligned Reconstruction participants. Heather Cox Richardson, *The Death of Reconstruction: Race, Labor, and Politics in the Post–Civil War North, 1865–1901* (Harvard University Press, 2001) is a significant post-revisionist analysis of the failure of Reconstruction. Finally, for collections of interpretive essays on various aspects of the Reconstruction experience, see Staughton Lynd, ed., *Reconstruction* (Harper & Row, 1967); Seth M. Scheiner, ed., *Reconstruction: A Tragic Era?* (Holt, Rinehart and Winston, 1968); and Edwin C. Rozwenc, ed., *Reconstruction in the South*, 2d ed. (Heath, 1972).

Contributors to This Volume

EDITORS

LARRY MADARAS is a professor of history and political science at Howard Community College in Columbia, Maryland. He received a B.A. from the College of the Holy Cross in 1959 and an M.A. and a Ph.D. from New York University in 1961 and 1964, respectively. He has also taught at Spring Hill College, the University of South Alabama, and the University of Maryland at College Park. He has been a Fulbright Fellow and has held two fellowships from the National Endowment for the Humanities. He is the author of dozens of journal articles and book reviews.

JAMES M. SoRELLE is a professor of history and former chair of the Department of History at Baylor University in Waco, Texas. He received a B.A. and M.A. from the University of Houston in 1972 and 1974, respectively, and a Ph.D. from Kent State University in 1980. In addition to introductory courses in United States and world history, he teaches upper-level sections in African American, urban, and late nineteenth- and twentieth-century U.S. history and a graduate seminar on the civil rights movement. His scholarly articles have appeared in *Houston Review, Southwestern Historical Quarterly,* and *Black Dixie: Essays in Afro-Texan History and Culture in Houston* (Texas A&M University Press, 1992), edited by Howard Beeth and Cary D. Wintz. He also has contributed entries to *The Oxford Companion to Politics of the World, Encyclopedia of African American Culture and History,* and *Encyclopedia of the Confederacy.*

STAFF

Larry Loeppke	Managing Editor
Jill Peter	Senior Developmental Editor
Nichole Altman	Developmental Editor
Beth Kundert	Production Manager
Jane Mohr	Project Manager
Tara McDermott	Design Coordinator
Bonnie Coakley	Editorial Assistant
Lori Church	Permissions Coordinator

AUTHORS

RODOLFO ACUÑA is a professor of Chicano studies at California State University, Northridge. He is credited with being active in the efforts to establish Chicano studies curricula at several universities. He is the author of *Anything but Mexican: Chicanos in Contemporary Los Angeles* (Verso, 1996).

PATRICIA U. BONOMI is professor emeritus of history at New York University. She is the author of *Colonial Dutch Studies: An Interdisciplinary Approach* (New York University Press, 1988) and *The Lord Cornbury Scandal: The Politics of Reputation in British America* (University of North Carolina Press, 1998).

MORTON BORDEN is professor emeritus of history at the University of California, Santa Barbara. He is also the author of *Parties and Politics in the Early Republic, 1789–1815* (Routledge & K. Pal, 1968).

JON BUTLER is the William Robertson Coe Professor of American History and chair of the history department at Yale University. He is the author of *Awash in a Sea of Faith: Christianizing the American People* (Harvard University Press, 1990), *Becoming America: The Revolution Before 1776* (Harvard University Press, 2000), and *Religion in Colonial America* (Oxford University Press, 2000).

ALEXANDER B. CALLOW, JR., is a lecturer emeritus in American urban history at the University of California, Santa Barbara. He is the editor of *American Urban History: An Interpretive Reader With Commentaries,* 3rd ed. (Oxford University Press, 1982).

LaWANDA COX is professor emeritus of history at Hunter College. She is the author, with John H. Cox, of *Politics, Principle, and Prejudice, 1865–1866: Dilemma of Reconstruction America* (Macmillan, 1963). Her most important scholarly writings can be found in Donald E. Nieman, ed., *Freedom, Racism, and Reconstruction: Collected Writings of LaWanda Cox* (University of Georgia Press, 1997).

CARL N. DEGLER is the Margaret Byrne Professor Emeritus of American History at Stanford University. He is a member of the editorial board for the Plantation Society as well as a member and former president of the American History Society and the Organization of American Historians. His book *Neither Black Nor White: Slavery and Race Relations in Brazil and the United States* (University of Wisconsin Press, 1971) won the Pulitzer Prize for history. He is also the author of *In Search of Human Nature: The Decline and Revival of Darwinism in American Social Thought* (Oxford University Press, 1992), and *At Odds: Women and the Family in America from the Revolution to the Present* (Oxford University Press, 1997).

WILMA A. DUNAWAY is associate professor of sociology at Virginia Polytechnic Institute and State University. Her first book, *The First American Frontier: Transition to Capitalism in Southern Appalachia, 1700–1860* (University of North Carolina Press, 1996) won the 1996 Weatherford Award for the best book about Southern Appalachia.

ERIC FONER is the DeWitt Clinton Professor of History at Columbia University in New York City. He earned his B.A. and his Ph.D. from Columbia in 1963 and 1969, respectively, and he was elected president of the American Historical Association in 2000. His many publications include *A Short History of Reconstruction, 1863–1877* (Harper & Row, 1990) and *America's Reconstruction: People and Politics After the Civil War,* coauthored with Olivia Mahoney (HarperPerennial, 1995).

GARY W. GALLAGHER is a professor of American history at Pennsylvania State University in University Park, Pennsylvania. He earned his Ph.D. from the University of Texas at Austin in 1982, and he specializes in the U.S. Civil War and Reconstruction. He is the author of *Fighting for the Confederacy: The Personal Recollections of General Edward Porter Alexander* (University of North Carolina Press, 1989), which won the 1990 Douglas Southall Freeman Award, and the editor of *The Antietam Campaign* (University of North Carolina Press, 1999).

EUGENE D. GENOVESE, a prominent Marxist historian and Civil War scholar, is president of the Historical Society, a professional organization of historians, and a former president of the Organization of American Historians. His many publications include *A Consuming Fire: The Fall of the Confederacy in the Mind of the White Christian South* (University of Georgia Press, 1998) and *The Southern Front: History and Politics in the Cultural War* (University of Missouri Press, 1995).

NORMAN A. GRAEBNER is the Randolph P. Compton Professor Emeritus of History at the University of Virginia in Charlottesville, Virginia. He has held a number of other academic appointments and has received distinguished teacher awards at every campus at which he has taught. He has edited and written numerous books, articles, and texts on American history, including *Foundations of American Foreign Policy: A Realist Appraisal From Franklin to McKinley* (Scholarly Resources Press, 1985) and *Empire on the Pacific: A Study in American Continental Expansion,* 2d ed. (Regina Books, 1983).

ALLEN C. GUELZO is Henry R. Luce Professor of the Civil War Era at Gettysburg College. His book *Abraham Lincoln: Redeemer President* (Eerdmans, 1999) won the Lincoln Prize for best book in the field of Civil War history. He is also the author of *Edwards on the Will: A Century of American Theological Debate* (Wesleyan University Press, 1989) and *For the Union of Evangelical Christianity: The Irony of the Reformed Episcopalians* (Pennsylvania State University Press, 1994).

OSCAR HANDLIN is professor emeritus of history at Harvard University. He is the author of numerous books, including *The Uprooted: The Epic Story of the Great Migrations That Made the American People* (Little, Brown, 1951), *Boston's Immigrants, 1790–1880: A Study in Acculturation* (rev. and enl. ed., Belknap Press, 1991), and with Lilian Handlin, *Liberty in America,* 4 vols. (Harper & Row, 1986–1994).

VINCENT HARDING is a professor of religion and social transformation at the Iliff School of Theology in Denver, Colorado, and has long been involved in domestic and international movements for peace and justice.

He is the author of *Hope and History: Why We Must Share the Story of the Movement* (Orbis Books, 1990) and coauthor, with Robin D. G. Kelley and Earl Lewis, of *We Changed the World: African Americans, 1945–1970* (Oxford University Press, 1997).

LEO HERSHKOWITZ is a professor of history at Queens College, City University of New York. His publications include *Courts and Law in Early New York: Selected Essays,* coedited with Milton M. Klein (Kennikat Press, 1978).

MICHAEL F. HOLT is the Langbourne M. Williams Professor of American History at the University of Virginia in Charlottesville, Virginia. He has published a collection of his many journal articles in *Political Parties and American Political Development From the Age of Jackson to the Age of Lincoln* (Louisiana State University Press, 1992), and he is the author of *The Rise and Fall of the American Whig Party: Jacksonian Politics and the Onset of the Civil War* (Oxford University Press, 1999).

LYLE KOEHLER was an instructor of history at the University of Cincinnati where he held several other administrative positions. He is the author of numerous scholarly articles in the fields of colonial American history and ethnic studies.

GLORIA L. MAIN is professor of history at the University of Colorado, Boulder. She is also the author of *Tobacco Colony: Life in Early Maryland, 1650–1720* (Princeton University Press, 1983) and *Peoples of a Spacious Land: Families and Cultures in Colonial New England* (Harvard University Press, 2001).

DONALD G. MATHEWS is professor of history at the University of North Carolina, Chapel Hill. He is the author of *Slavery and Methodism: A Chapter in American Morality, 1780–1845* (Princeton University Press, 1965) and *Religion in the Old South* (University of Chicago, 1977).

ERNEST R. MAY is professor of history at Harvard University. He is the author of numerous distinguished studies in diplomatic history, including *The World War and American Isolation, 1914–1917* (Harvard University Press, 1959), *Imperial Democracy: The Emergence of the United States as a Great Power* (Harcourt, Brace & World, 1961), and *Lessons of the Past: The Use and Misuse of History in American Foreign Policy* (Oxford University Press, 1973).

FORREST McDONALD, Distinguished University Research Professor of History Emeritus at the University of Alabama, was the 1980 recipient of the George Washington medal from Freedom's Foundation in Valley Forge, Pennsylvania. He is also the author of *Alexander Hamilton: A Biography* (W. W. Norton, 1982) and *Novus Ordo Seclorum: The Intellectual Origins of the Constitution* (University Press of Kansas, 1985).

WILLIAM H. McNEILL is professor emeritus of history at the University of Chicago where he was the Robert A. Milliken Distinguished Service Professor prior to his retirement. He is the author of *The Rise of the West: A History of the Human Community* (University of Chicago, 1970), which received the National Book Award, *Plagues and Peoples* (Anchor Press, 1976), and *A World History* (4th ed., Oxford University Press, 1998).

RUSSELL R. MENARD is professor of history at the University of Minnesota. He is the author of dozens of articles on the colonial Chesapeake as well as

Economy and Society in Colonial Maryland (Garland, 1985) and *Migrants, Servants and Slaves: Unfree Labor in Colonial British America* (Ashgate, 2001).

EDMUND S. MORGAN is the Sterling Professor Emeritus of history at Yale University and the author of sixteen books on the colonial period. These works include *The Puritan Family: Religion and Domestic Relations in Seventeenth-Century New England* (Harper & Row, 1966), *The Puritan Dilemma: The Story of John Winthrop* (2d ed., Longman, 1998), and *Benjamin Franklin* (Yale University Press, 2002). His most recent book, *The Genuine Article: A Historian Looks at Early America* (W. W. Norton, 2004), is a collection of his review essays that appeared in *The New York Review of Books*. In 2000, he received the National Humanities Medal.

ALAN T. NOLAN has been with the law firm of Ice Miller Donadio & Ryan in Indianapolis, Indiana, since 1948. He has also been chairman of the board of trustees of the Indiana Historical Society since 1986. He has written extensively on Civil War history, including the book *The Iron Brigade: A Military History,* 2d ed. (State Historical Society of Wisconsin, 1975), and he is coeditor, with Gary W. Gallagher, of *The Myth of the Lost Cause and Civil War History* (Indiana University Press, 2000).

DEXTER PERKINS (1889–1984) was professor emeritus of history at the University of Rochester and University Professor Emeritus at Cornell University. The author of many books on American diplomatic history, his *Hands Off: History of the Monroe Doctrine* (Little Brown, 1941) remains the standard on this subject.

ROBERT V. REMINI is a professor emeritus of history at the University of Illinois at Chicago. He won the D. B. Hardeman Prize for *Daniel Webster: The Man and His Time* (W. W. Norton, 1997), and he has written biographies on Andrew Jackson, Henry Clay, and Martin Van Buren.

JOHN P. ROCHE (1923–1993) was the Olin Distinguished Professor of American Civilization and Foreign Affairs at the Fletcher School of Law and Diplomacy in Medford, Massachusetts, and director of the Fletcher Media Institute. His many publications include *Shadow and Substance: Essays on the Theory and Structure of Politics* (Macmillan, 1964).

ROBERT ROYAL is vice president and the Olin Fellow in Religion and Society at the Ethics and Public Policy Center in Washington, D.C. He is the author of *The Catholic Martyrs of the Twentieth Century: A Comprehensive World History* (Crossroad, 2000) and *The Virgin and the Dynamo: Use and Abuse of Religion in Environmental Debates* (W. B. Eerdmans, 1999).

KIRKPATRICK SALE is a contributing editor to *The Nation* and the author of *Rebels Against the Future: The Luddites and Their War on the Industrial Revolution: Lessons for the Computer Age* (Perseus Press, 1996).

JOEL H. SILBEY is the President White Professor of History Emeritus at Cornell University. He has written several books and many important articles on the political parties during the Civil War. Among his publications are *Respectable Minority: The Democratic Party in the Civil War Era, 1860–1868* (W. W. Norton, 1977), *The Partisan Imperative: The Dynamics of American Politics*

Before the Civil War (Oxford University Press, 1985), *The American Political Nation, 1838–1893* (Stanford University Press, 1991), and *Martin Van Buren and the Emergence of American Popular Politics* (Rowman & Littlefield, 2002).

ANTHONY F. C. WALLACE is an anthropologist whose published works include *King of the Delawares: Teedyuscung, 1700–1763* (Syracuse University Press, 1990) and *St. Clair: A Nineteenth-Century Coal Town's Experience With a Disaster-Prone Industry* (Cornell University Press, 1988).

GORDON S. WOOD is the Alva O. Way University Professor of history at Brown University, where he has taught since 1969. He has also taught at Harvard University, the University of Michigan, and Cambridge University. He is a member of the National Council of History Education's board of trustees. He is also the author of *The Creation of the American Republic, 1776–1787* (University of North Carolina, 1969) and *The American Revolution: A History* (Modern Library, 2002).

C. VANN WOODWARD (1908–1999), considered the dean of historians of the South prior to his death, was Sterling Professor of History at Yale University. He won the Pulitzer Prize in 1982 for *Mary Chesnut's Civil War* (Yale University Press, 1981). His other most distinguished books include *Origins of the New South, 1877–1913* (Louisiana University Press, 1951), *The Future of the Past* (Oxford University Press, 1989), *Reunion and Reaction: The Compromise of 1877 and the End of Reconstruction* (rev. ed., Oxford University Press, 1991), and *The Strange Career of Jim Crow* (3d rev. ed., Oxford University Press, 1979).

ALFRED F. YOUNG was a professor at Northern Illinois University in De Kalb, Illinois, before retiring. He is the author of *Dissent: Explorations in the History of American Radicalism* (Northern Illinois University Press, 1992) and coeditor, with Lawrence W. Towner and Robert W. Karrow, of *Past Imperfect: Essays on History, Libraries, and the Humanities* (University of Chicago Press, 1993).

Index